Reserved Words

and	array	begin	case
const	div	do	downto
else	end	file	for
forward	function	goto	if
in	label	mod	nil
not	or	of	packed
procedure	program	record	repeat
set	then	to	type
until	var	while	with

Program Outline

program *heading*
Definition part
  label
  const
  type
Declaration part
  var
  procedure *or* **function**
begin
  Statement part
end.

Actions

procedure call;	{*DrawArc* (5, 3.2, *Radius*);}
simple statement;	{*A*:=*B*+1;}
compound statement;	{**begin** *action* **end**;}
structured statement;	{**if** *Playing* **then** *Continue*;}
empty statement;	{ ; }

Control Structures

case *expression* **of**
  value: *action*;
  value: *action*   {constant list}
end;

for *variable* := *value* **to** {or **downto**} *value*
  do *action*;

if *boolean value*
  then *action*
  else *action*;   {optional}

while *boolean value*
  do *action*;

repeat
  action;
until *boolean value*;

with *record identifier*
  do *action*;

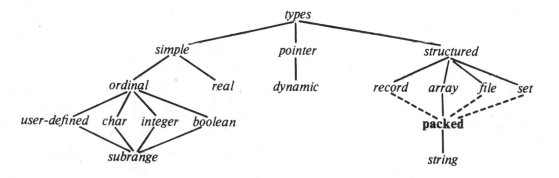

(continued inside back cover)

Oh! Pascal!

by Doug Cooper and Michael Clancy

University of California, Berkeley

W·W·NORTON & COMPANY

New York and London

Acknowledgments

Permission to use copyrighted materials from the following sources is hereby acknowledged.

"A Fine Romance" by Dorothy Fields and Jerome Kern. Copyright © 1936 T. B. Harms
Company (c/o The Welk Music Group, Santa Monica CA 90401). Copyright renewed.
International copyright secured. All rights reserved.

"To Think That Two and Two Are Four," from *The Collected Poems of A. E. Housman* © 1940
by Henry Holt and Company. Henry Holt and Company, Jonathan Cape Ltd., and the Society of
Authors, as literary representative of the Trustees of the Estate of the late A. E. Housman.

"Essential to a computer...," from *Pascal-User Manual and Report*, Second Edition by
K. Jensen and N. Wirth. Copyright © 1974 by Springer-Verlag, Berlin, Heidelberg, New York.

W. W. Norton & Company, Inc. 500 Fifth Avenue, New York, N.Y. 10110
W. W. Norton & Company Ltd., 37 Great Russell Street, London WC1B 3NU

ISBN 0 393 95205 3

4 5 6 7 8 9 0

Oh! Pascal! was designed and typeset by Doug Cooper.

Contents

CONTENTS

CONTENTS

We wrote *Oh! Pascal!* to provide a clear, non-mathematically oriented introduction to programing and Pascal. We take it for granted that Pascal is a superior instructional language, that the way to learn programing is to write programs, and that problem solving should be taught in the first programing course. Our book is aimed at students who, although otherwise sober and upright, seem to lack an intuitive feel for computer science. We try to anticipate and answer questions, as well as to explain the facts in a friendly, refreshing manner.

Most of all, we've tried to make *Oh! Pascal!* a self-teaching book (as opposed to a reference manual that sticks to very small words). We've attempted a presentation that's detailed enough for people studying on their own, yet lucid, readable, and enjoyable enough for more traditional students to read before lecture. Most of *Oh! Pascal!'s* innovations, as described below, are motivated by this goal.

1) We emphasize general problem-solving techniques.

Most books begin and end their discussion of problem solving with stepwise refinement. However, many other methods that good problem-solvers (and programers) take for granted have never been formalized in the student's mind, and need to be presented explicitly. A host of techniques for dealing with problems—massaging them, lateral thinking, examining solution spaces, etc.—are employed frequently throughout the book. We've been greatly influenced by people like James Adams (*Conceptual Blockbusting*, W.W. Norton), and Richard Skemp (*Psychology of Learning Mathematics*, Penguin), and we know that solving programing problems, per se, is often the least of a novice's woes.

2) An early discussion of procedures.

Pascal has to be taught in a way that encourages good programing. Thus, procedures are introduced when a conceptual need for them arises—during the first discussion of top-down design—even before the basic control structures have been defined. Our experience has been that this approach encourages modular program design, well-defined algorithms, and makes large-scale programs much easier to tackle later on.

3) Interactive programs are shown in action—the reader isn't forced to infer their differences from batch.

Like many other teachers, we struggled for years with texts that were designed for batch-oriented Pascal systems. These texts really penalize interactive programers, because some techniques that are easily motivated in batch programs (especially the use of *eof*) greatly confuse interactive programs.

In *Oh! Pascal!*, we started by writing all examples for interactive use, then modified and added until a sufficient set was suited for batch systems.* Throughout the book we point out features (or lack of

---

* We use 'lazy I/O', as widely implemented, and allowed by the current draft standard.

features) that make specific programs more suited to batch or interactive use. As a result, we think that both groups of programers get the impression that the book was aimed at them, rather than at the others. All programs show typical input and output.

4) Antibugging and debugging sections follow each chapter.

Every chapter is followed by a discussion of the potential hazards it has introduced. Especially difficult points are reiterated, typical error messages are deciphered, and general programing advice is dispensed. A special advantage of these sections is the opportunity to present *incorrect* examples, while carefully isolating them from the main text.

5) The **for** and **case** structures are introduced before the others.

This lets the student practice developing algorithms, and writing programs, before dealing with the brand-new notion of *boolean* expressions. Students gain experience with some of Pascal's bug-prone, but crucial, syntax details (like compound and empty statements) before they get to have fun writing infinite loops.

6) Every chapter includes self-check questions, and a self-test.

Numerous self-check questions, complete with answers, are scattered throughout the text. Each chapter is followed by 10-20 exercises and brief programing problems that are answered at the end of the book, as well as harder exercises for assignment. All in all, there are about 500 exercises in *Oh! Pascal!*

A number of other features were suggested by shortcomings we've found in other Pascal texts. Since long programs seem to be fundamentally different from short ones, we've included several lengthy examples; the longest (and last) runs five pages. At the same time, we emphasize the pseudocode development of all example programs, long or short.

We try to demystify and humanize Pascal and programing. Many students are intimidated by computers, and have little confidence in their own ability. We try to point out limitations of Pascal, and the reasons for them. We motivate the language through the requirements of programing and problem solving, instead of presenting it as a limited, but nonetheless arbitrary, set of commands.

We're proud of the visual appearance of the book. Programing textbooks usually suffer terribly at the hands of compositors who force the reader to lose her place while she finds a program 'figure', or make programs break arbitrarily from one page to the next to keep each page's length the same.* By producing camera copy ourselves, we were able to show every example in-line with the text. Example programs longer than one page are almost invariably on facing pages, and are always broken at procedure boundaries.

---

* Incidentally, all personal pronouns in *Oh! Pascal!* are feminine. After hundreds of years of 'he' and 'his', a few decades of 'she' and 'her' shouldn't bother anyone.

A second advantage of doing our own typesetting is the accuracy it allows. Every program, and most subprograms, have been run without error or warning messages using the -s option (Standard Pascal only) of the Berkeley Pascal compiler (pc) and interpreter (pi). All program output displayed was produced by the actual source program shown in the text as it was being typeset. All examples and definitions conform to the Draft ANSI/IEEE Pascal Standard (X3J9/81-093).

We've included a glossary, chapter reviews, and reference matter inside the front and back covers. Space has been left for noting local system characteristics. We've also provided greatly simplified syntax charts. Although they don't constitute a formal definition of Pascal, they're a good reference for beginning programers.

Finally, the title. It seems that bookstores shelve Pascal books inconsistently; some list by title, and others by subject. Lest a Pascal book escape notice, publishing wisdom requires that its title begin with the letter 'p'. As a result, the world has acquired *Pascal, Pascal Programing, Programing Standard Pascal, Programing For Poets (Using Pascal), Pascal Programing Structures, Practical Introduction To Pascal, Problem Solving and Programing in Pascal,* etc.

Wishing to dissent, but unwilling to make too radical a departure from the established norm, we decided that our title should start with one of two alternative letters—either 'o' or 'q'. To make a long story short, *Oh! Pascal!* was finally chosen. The alternatives (*O.K. Pascal, Quest For Pascal,* etc.) were too ridiculous to merit serious consideration.

Grateful thanks for early encouragement must go to Michael Spivak. We would also like to acknowledge the help, inspiration, and current or former existence of (carefully randomized using the 52 card pickup algorithm) Patti Hansen, Rachel M. Silverman, Michael Powell, Bruce Char, Phyllis Stern, Diane McNichol, David Lichtenstein, the Who, Neil Patterson, Dave Presotto, Andy Warhol, Barry Smith, John Foderaro, the Computer Science Division of U.C. Berkeley, Joanna Boudreaux, Dick Fateman's Sufferance, Gia Carangi, Joseph Ossanna, the MIT/SAIL jargon file, W.P.O.D., Bill Karjane, Thomas McGuane, Peter Kessler and Kirk McKusick (the Kompiler Kids), Unsung Contributors and Reviewers, and, naturally, Ernie K.

For my grandparents Molly and Sam Brecher.

d.b.c.

There's an old story about an untutored bumpkin who listened to some students as they talked about the stars. Although the concepts they discussed were strange and new, he felt he could understand how astronomers used telescopes to measure the distance from the earth to the celestial bodies. It even seemed reasonable that they could predict the stars' relative positions and motion. What totally puzzled him, though, was how the devil they were able to find out the stars' names!

Some people approach computers in the same way, as if their languages were complicated mathematical codes that the first computer scientists managed to break. It usually comes as a great surprise to find that most computer programs are written in plain English, and that learning the language is the easiest part of learning to *program.* Programing is quite independent of any language, and for us, it's only a means to an end. *Oh! Pascal!* is about using computers for *problem solving.*

When computers are involved, problem solving means developing *algorithms.** An algorithm is an outline of the steps required to solve a problem. Is a recipe an algorithm? If it were, a Pascal textbook would consist of chapter after chapter of programs. Recipes, like programs, are highly restricted algorithms at best, because they're sets of exact rules that have to be followed to achieve one specific end. Why should *we* spend our time following instructions—that's the computer's job. A good cook can't always make up new recipes, or remember old ones, but a programer can devise new algorithms at any time.

An algorithm is a sequence of actions that's organized and detailed enough to be the basis of a program. Algorithms aren't written in any particular computer language, because they're not given to a computer. We can implement (put into effect) most algorithms in any language we like. To develop algorithms, we'll try to understand the process people go through in solving a problem, then take advantage of a computer's capabilities to improve our method of solution.

Now, most people take their skill at solving problems (or bemoan their lack thereof) for granted. Can your problem-solving ability be improved? Well, people engaged in other activities spend plenty of time trying to maximize their natural talent. Take athletes, for instance. They practice for hours, and employ coaches to watch for flaws in form. They read about their sports, talk to other participants, watch films of themselves in action, and mentally rehearse their moves. Nowadays, some athletes even use computers to analyze their performance, and suggest improvements. It all seems to help.

How can we go about improving our ability to think? Well, as James Adams pointed out in his *Conceptual Blockbusting—A Guide to Better Ideas,* most people view 'improving the mind' as acquiring more knowledge. Since our aim is to produce algorithms, though, we'll concentrate on practice, and on learning new ways of solving problems.

* As new terms are introduced, they'll be written in *bold italic*. These terms are usually included in the Glossary.

Build-up	*Display*	*Simulate*
Eliminate	*Organize*	*Test*
Work Forward	*List*	*Play*
Work Backward	*Check*	*Manipulate*
Associate	*Diagram*	*Copy*
Classify	*Chart*	*Interpret*
Generalize	*Verbalize*	*Transform*
Exemplify	*Visualize*	*Translate*
Compare	*Memorize*	*Expand*
Relate	*Recall*	*Reduce*
Commit	*Record*	*Exaggerate*
Defer	*Retrieve*	*Understate*
Leap In	*Search*	*Adapt*
Hold Back	*Select*	*Substitute*
Focus	*Plan*	*Combine*
Release	*Predict*	*Separate*
Force	*Assume*	*Change*
Relax	*Question*	*Vary*
Dream	*Hypothesize*	*Cycle*
Imagine	*Guess*	*Repeat*
Purge	*Define*	*Systemize*
Incubate	*Symbolize*	*Randomize*

Some Problem-Solving Strategies

The first step in solving a problem is always the hardest. The table of strategies above is a list of suggestions to help you get unstuck. As we start to work on algorithms, we'll introduce some other general problem-solving methods. There are different thinking approaches— *visual* and *lateral* thinking are two that we'll discuss. There are also techniques (like *massage*) that aim at making problems more manageable.

Some other procedures are particularly well-suited for the development of program algorithms. Throughout the text we'll be discussing ideas of *top-down* and *bottom-up* algorithm design. We'll see how an algorithm's *elegance* effects a program, and debate the merits of *efficiency*. We'll also find out about some solution methods that were impractical before the advent of computers— *exhaustive search* and *brute force* approaches.

Once we have an algorithm, how do we turn it into a program? Well, every computer, regardless of make or model, understands a basic instruction set known as a **machine language**. Machine language is a low-level, nuts and bolts code that isn't much more sophisticated than the instructions we can punch into a programable hand calculator. It's hard to write programs in a machine language because we have to tell the computer exactly what to do (put this number here, store that number there), each step of the way. In addition, separate programs have to be written for every make of computer, because there's no universal machine language.

Since nobody enjoys memorizing and writing dozens of eight and sixteen digit binary numbers (the machine language commands), more powerful *high-level languages*, like FORTRAN, COBOL, BASIC, and Pascal have been designed. Now, creating a programing language isn't all that difficult. First, the commands the language will contain are chosen. Then, a program called a *compiler* or *interpreter* is written. It translates the new language into a machine-language form the computer understands.* When a high-level language is popular, compiler programs are written for practically every make of computer. This makes programs that use the new language portable. They can be written and run just about everywhere.

What makes a language popular, and why do people keep designing new ones? One reason is the ease of using the language. When computers first came around, a lot of effort was put into making up languages that helped them run faster. Nowadays, languages are designed to be easily employed and understood—for the convenience of programers instead of machines.

Programing languages are also designed in response to different problem-solving requirements. Just as there are several types of hand calculators (statistical, business, etc.), there are job-specific computer languages. You can turn most algorithms into programs using *any* language, in the same way that you *could* use a business calculator to figure out statistics, or vice versa. However, it makes better sense to use the most appropriate tool. We can discover the particular purpose of some languages (but not Pascal) from their names:

FORTRAN: FORmula TRANslator is one of the earliest and most widespread languages. It's intended mainly for scientific applications.

COBOL: COmmon Business Oriented Language was developed as a standard for business computing. Many COBOL instructions are designed specifically for payroll or accounting applications.

BASIC: Beginner's All-purpose Symbolic Instruction Code is a simple language that's used to teach basic computer applications. Although it's easy to learn, BASIC doesn't go very far. It's a poor basis for understanding programing.

Pascal was named after the 17th century mathematician and religious fanatic Blaise Pascal. Since it's not an acronym (it doesn't stand for anything) only the first letter is capitalized. Pascal was created with two main goals:

1. To provide a teaching language that would bring out concepts common to all languages, while avoiding inconsistencies and unnecessary detail.

---

* For the rest of the text we'll ignore interpreters, and just refer to compilers.

2. To define a truly standard language that would be cheap and easy to implement on any computer.

In a sense, Pascal is a *lingua franca*, or common tongue, of programing. It's easy to learn, and provides an excellent foundation for learning other languages. We've found that people who know Pascal can master BASIC in an afternoon, and pick up FORTRAN in a week or two.

But what does Pascal *look* like? Niklaus Wirth, who designed the language, intended that Pascal be as clear, readable, and unambiguous as possible. The displays inside the front cover (particularly the table of control structures) show all the *reserved words* of Pascal. Clearly, Pascal isn't written in binary code. We're reminded of this famous ad:

If u cn rd ths ad, u cn gt a gd jb—Learn Speedwriting!

One of Pascal's big advantages over the other languages is that we can write a program in almost exactly the same terms we used to develop its algorithm. Some day soon we expect to be seeing this sign in the subways:

```
if YouCanReadThis
then begin
    StartWork;
    Earn (BigBucks)
end;
```

As we make up algorithms, and get to know the Pascal language, we'll also be learning how to program. Now, the notion that programing is a set of skills that's separate from any particular computer language is a fairly recent idea. In the early days, people generally wrote programs as they saw fit. Programs were judged by whether or not they ran—not by how well they were written.

As programing projects became larger, concern about the quality of programs grew as well. The cost of computer hardware dropped (and continues to drop) rapidly, and became relatively small in comparison to human programing costs. In many instances, more time was spent in maintaining existing programs (by rewriting and updating them), than in creating new ones. As a result, interest focused on methods of writing programs that not only worked, but could be understood by people other than the author.

Can good programing be taught? Way back when, there was a notion that the ability to program was a mystical talent that couldn't be analyzed. But programing, like thinking, can be practiced and improved. Building an awareness of the differences between good and bad programs is the first step, since programing problems are usually *divergent*. This means that they can be solved in many different ways.

How can one program be good, and another program bad, when they both solve the same problem? Well, a lot depends on program *style*. A well-written program doesn't just outwit the computer. It's put together in a way that someone who may have to read it two or ten years hence can understand. It implements the literal set of instructions that a computer requires, without losing or confusing a human reader who deals in concepts.

Stylish programs also solve a little bit more than the problem. Programs that are too narrowly defined might work in a world of machines, but they're not flexible enough for the demands of real life. People and computers both make mistakes, and a program should be *robust* enough to take them in stride.

Good luck in your study of programing, problem solving, and Pascal. If, while you're reading *Oh! Pascal!*, you think of anything that might improve the next edition, please write the authors, care of W.W. Norton & Co. As is the current rage, bounties will be paid for spotting errors in the text.

The poorly designed Pruitt-Igoe housing project. Built, 1955–demolished, 1975. *St. Louis Post-Dispatch*.

1

Getting Acquainted with Programs

What makes computers tick? Well, they need a little electricity, a lot of patience, plenty of air conditioning, and (finally) a program. In this chapter we'll see what Pascal programs look like, and start to understand how they're put together.

The simplest job a program can do is *output*—printing some kind of information. The output programs we'll write in section 1-1 won't compute anything, but they'll demonstrate computer operation in an uncomplicated way. Section 1-2 introduces program data. First, we'll see how *variables* for storing data are created. Then, we'll write a program that accepts *input*—it gets its data from a program user. Finally, in section 1-3, we'll revisit output and learn how to program some simple calculations.

Out of necessity, this chapter contains a lot of information—probably more than any other chapter. It's important to avoid being overwhelmed. A couple of tricks may help make things easier. First, read the chapter twice. Don't try to learn or memorize everything at once because there's simply too much. Skimming the chapter first will give you an idea of what's really important, and what's just a complicated (but small) detail.

Second, try to understand Pascal as it fits together, rather than as an arbitrary collection of separate facts. Don't be afraid to question the language designer's wisdom ('Why'd he do it that way?'), or our method of explanation. Pascal was largely designed as a teaching language, and as students you're the final arbiters of its success or failure.

The last section of this chapter is the first in a series of special sections on *antibugging* and *debugging*—avoiding programing mistakes, and fixing the ones that slip by. We recommend that you read these sections before tackling the problems.

*(Sometimes) it's best to start
over from the beginning.*

1-1
Programing
for Output

BEHOLD A COMPLETE Pascal program.

> **program** *FirstRun* (*output*) ;   {This is our first program.}
> **begin**
> > *writeln* ('Hello. I love you.')
> **end.**

FirstRun is a short program whose effect and output you can probably figure out already. We'll begin our study of Pascal by seeing how *First-Run* was constructed.

The first step in writing a program is to indicate that what we're writing *is* a program. The first word of every Pascal program is the ***reserved word***:*

program

(Throughout the text, reserved words—actual Pascal words—are printed in **bold face type**. Only one typeface will appear on your terminal or punched cards.) Next, we need to name our program. In computer science, names are called ***identifiers***.

> An identifier, or name, *must* begin with a letter, and then may contain any series of digits or letters.

We can agree that:

R2D2   *PattiHansen*   *SpotOnTop40*

are all perfectly legal names. But since an identifier cannot contain punctuation or spaces, or begin with a digit, these are all *illegal* names:

2Bor02B   *First*Run*   *Farrah Fawcett-Majors*

Not all Pascal compilers remember all the characters in an identifier, even though the definition of ***Standard Pascal*** requires them to. If a compiler's limit is eight characters (like the first Pascal compiler) then these two identifiers will seem identical within a program:

NapoleonBonaparte
NapoleonJones

Some other compilers may slightly extend Pascal by letting non-letters appear within an identifier to improve readability (*TIME_TO_LEAVE*). You should note your compiler's deviations from Standard Pascal inside the front cover. This will help you write programs that can be run on any Pascal system.

When we give our program a name, its first line becomes:

program *FirstRun*

(All identifiers will be shown in *italic*.) By the way, reserved words can't be used as identifiers; we couldn't call a program **program if**, or **program program**. When in doubt, check the complete list of reserved words inside the cover.

---

* New words are written in ***bold italic*** and are usually included in the glossary.

:··:

Q. Which of the following are valid Standard Pascal identifiers?

birthday	*case*	*CaseNumber*
TooHot?	*First_Initial*	*3rdValue*
−Number	*OldName*	*downto.what*
'grade'	*1Program*	*Beginning*

A. Not too many of these are valid—only *birthday, CaseNumber, OldName,* and *Beginning* may be used correctly.

:··:

Explanations about a program's operation are called **comments**. They go between **curly brackets** (like these: { }):

> **program** *FirstRun*   {This is our first program.}

because the computer ignores anything written between curly brackets. Some keyboards may not include curly brackets (also called *braces*), so Pascal allows alternate symbols as synonyms—'(*' is the same as '{', and '*)' has the same meaning as '}'. For example:

> **program** *FirstRun*   (*This is also a comment.*)

Comments and Syntax Charts

:···:
: As far as program operation is concerned, comments are unneces- :
: sary. In practice, they're used in *every* program as explanatory :
: notes to ourselves, or to other people reading the program.   :
:···:

It's quite all right to have comments extend over several lines, as long as a left curly bracket appears at the beginning, and a right curly bracket turns up at the end. A separate pair of brackets need not *delimit* (mark) each comment line. For example:

> {   Program *FirstRun*
>   by
>   Rachel Jetaime   }
>
> **program** *FirstRun*   {This is our first program.}

We finish a program's first line by adding special instructions to the computer about the information it will use or produce. The computer must know in advance if it will get data *from* us— **input**—or deliver results *to* us— **output**.* Since this particular program only has output, the first line is completed with:

> **program** *FirstRun* (*output*) ;   {This is our first program.}

If it had input as well, we would write:

> **program** *SecondRun* (*input, output*) ;   {We'll use a heading like this in section 1-2.}

* Actually, this explanation is to the truth as the stork is to the facts of life—not very accurate, but a good enough explanation for the time being. *Input* and *output* are discussed further in section 7-2.

> The first line of a program is called the ***program heading***. A semi-colon separates it from the next line of the program.

Now, the wary reader will anticipate having to remember a number of rules for putting Pascal programs together. If you have a good memory, you can memorize the format of a program heading. You could also mark a particularly good example to use as a permanent pattern. A third method involves drawing up a little diagram known as a *syntax chart*. A simplified syntax chart of a program heading is:

program heading

program $\longrightarrow$ *identifier* $\longrightarrow$ ($\longrightarrow$ *output* $\longrightarrow$) $\longrightarrow$;

The program heading chart shows the exact position of each word and punctuation mark in the heading of a program that has output, but no input. The chart says that the heading must begin with the reserved word **program**, followed by an *identifier* (the name of the program). Next comes a left parenthesis, the *output* information, and a right parenthesis. The heading is closed with a semicolon.

We can also make a syntax chart for an identifier, but it's a little more complicated.

identifier

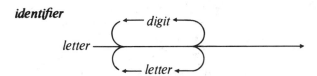

As long as we start on the left and follow the arrows, we'll have an identifier that satisfies our rules: It must start with a letter and can be followed by as many letters or digits as we wish. If we follow the shortest possible path, we'll have a perfectly legal one-letter identifier.

As you can see, the chart of an identifier almost seems to be more trouble than it's worth. Still, some people like to use syntax charts to clarify complicated syntax. Others won't find charts useful at all, and can ignore them and remember the rules some other way. We've simplified our syntax charts (in comparison to the charts that used to accompany the definition of Standard Pascal) to make them easier to follow.

Let's get back to *FirstRun.* Since it won't make any decisions or computations, we need not arrange for variables (introduced in the next section). We can get right to work on the *statement part*, where the program's business will take place. This part always begins with the reserved word **begin**. (This is all pretty reasonable, no?)

```
program FirstRun (output) ;     {This is our first program.}

begin
```

The statement part contains a series of instructions, called *statements*, for the computer to *execute*, or carry out. Printing (output) in Pascal is taken care of by special statements called *standard procedures*. A procedure is roughly akin to a built-in command, except that we can write our own procedures to supplement the standard ones. Like most Pascal identifiers, procedure names give some indication of their purpose.

> To write a line of output, use the standard output procedure *writeln* (pronounced 'write line'). The *text* (words) in an output line may *not* contain a carriage return.

It works like this:

    writeln ('Everything between the quote marks will get printed.')

(The procedure's name is in italics because it's an identifier.) Notice the parentheses and single quotes around the text we want printed. The quote marks tell the computer to print the text within the parentheses *literally*, or exactly as it is written. To get us off to a friendly start, our program will print 'Hello. I love you.'

    program FirstRun (output) ;   {This is our first program.}
    begin
        writeln ('Hello. I love you.')

Only one thing is missing from *FirstRun*—the reserved word **end**, which tells the computer that no more statements remain to be executed, or carried out, and that the program is ended.

    program FirstRun (output) ;   {This is our first program.}
    begin
        writeln ('Hello. I love you.')
    end.

> This **end**, the last Pascal word in the program, is always followed by a period.

Program *FirstRun* is complete. The next step is to have the computer *compile* the program—check it for errors and translate it into machine language. The exact procedure you'll have to follow to compile a program depends on your computer, since it's not specified by the definition of Pascal. In any case, when the program is run something like this will appear as output:

    Hello. I love you.

(We'll always use this funny typeface for printing program output.)

The output above isn't too exciting, but the idea of what we've just done is. We've written a program, and made a computer follow our commands. A language that last week was barely conceivable (and totally incomprehensible), is suddenly starting to mean something. A certain amount of mystery, and a little magic as well, have left our lives forever.

Let's complicate matters by writing a program with two *writeln* statements.

> In Pascal, the semicolon (;) is used as a statement separator. It belongs between any two statements or parts of a program.

When a program has more than one statement, each one is executed in order, as it appears. Our new program looks like this:

```
program SecondRun (output);
      {Demonstrates the statement separator.}

begin
      writeln ('Hello.  I love you.');
      writeln ('How about lunch?')
end.
      ↓      ↓      ↓      ↓      ↓
      Hello.  I love you.
      How about lunch?
```

(The downward arrows (↓ ↓) mean 'The program's output would look like this'.) The *writeln* procedure puts each line of output on a different line. Another standard procedure, called **write**, collects output that belongs on a *single* line. Printing is forced with a *writeln.* For example:

```
program TwoLines (output);
      {Demonstrates procedure write.}

begin
      write ('A fine ');               {These lines are stored...}
      write ('romance, ');
      writeln ('with no kisses.');     {...until a writeln forces printing.}
      write ('A fine romance, ');
      writeln ('my friend, this is!')
end.
             ↓      ↓      ↓      ↓      ↓
      A fine romance, with no kisses.
      A fine romance, my friend, this is!
```

> When a *writeln* is used by itself (see below), it causes the computer to print any pending *writes.* If no text is waiting to be printed, *writeln* prints a blank line.

write ('Little Miss Muffet sat ');
writeln ('on a tuffet,');
write ('Eating her curds and whey.');
writeln;   {This *writeln* forces the *write* to print its text.}
writeln;   {These two *writelns* put blank lines}
writeln;   {in the program output. }
write ('Along came a spider, ');
write ('who sat down ');
write ('beside her,');
writeln;
writeln ('And frightened Miss Muffet away.');

↓   ↓   ↓   ↓   ↓

```
Little Miss Muffet sat on a tuffet,
Eating her curds and whey.



Along came a spider, who sat down beside her,
And frightened Miss Muffet away.
```

Although the output of a *write* is usually held until a *writeln* is encountered, some Pascal systems will print any *writes* when input is expected, or at the end of the program. There's no hard and fast rule.

Another programing detail involves printing an apostrophe—the same character as the single quote mark. We neatly quote the quote by entering the apostrophe twice.

writeln ('You wouldn''t, I couldn''t, and she won''t!');

↓   ↓   ↓   ↓   ↓

```
You wouldn't, I couldn't, and she won't!
```

This coding trick is used in a number of programing languages.

Q. There are errors on each line of this program. Find them.

Self-Check
Questions

    program *Print.Paper* (*output*;)   {line 1}

    begin;   {line 2

      write ('To think that two and two are four,);   {line 3}

      writln (and neither five or three, ');   {line 4}

      write ('The heart of man has long been sore ';   (line 5)

      write ('and long 'tis like to be.')   {line 6}

    end   {line 7.}

A. Written correctly, the program would be:

    program *PrintPaper* (*output*);   {line 1}

    begin   {line 2}

      write ('To think that two and two are four, ');   {line 3}

      writeln ('and neither five or three, ');   {line 4}

      write ('The heart of man has long been sore ');   {line 5}

      writeln ('and long ''tis like to be.')   {line 6}

    end.   {line 7}

1-2
Variables
and Input

TRY READING A PROGRAM THAT USES a *variable*, and has *input* as well as output.

program *FeedBack* (*input, output*) ;

    {Inputs and outputs the value of a variable.}

var *QuakeYear*: *integer*;

    {This declares a variable called *QuakeYear*.}

begin

    writeln ('What was the year of the San Francisco earthquake?') ;

        {After printing this message, the computer waits for the program
        user to enter a value, or reads it from a punched card.}

    readln (*QuakeYear*) ;

    write ('The San Francisco earthquake occurred in') ;

    writeln (*QuakeYear*)

end.

      ↓   ↓   ↓   ↓   ↓

```
What was the year of the San Francisco earthquake?
1906
The San Francisco earthquake occurred in        1906
```

You can probably figure out everything that *FeedBack* does already. We'll begin our discussion of variables by learning about the values they can hold.

The Simple Value Types

The variables that computers use are like the memory keys of hand calculators—they store values. Naturally, they're much more powerful and convenient. First of all, we can create as many variables as a job calls for. We're not limited by the handful of storage spaces most calculators have. Second, we're not stuck with unenlightening names like *STO1* and *MEM9*. Variables can have any names that meet the rules for identifiers.

    Finally, we aren't restricted to storing numbers. Variables can hold different *types* of values, including integers (whole numbers), characters (like letters, punctuation marks, and single digits), real numbers (with decimals or exponents), or even logical values (the *true-false* or *boolean* values). We can even make up entirely new categories.* However, we always have to specify the type of values a variable is going to hold.

> Four commonly used types of values are predefined as the *standard simple types.* Their official names, used in writing programs, are *integer, char, boolean,* and *real.*

* We'll talk about this possibility in Chapter 9, when we discuss user-defined types.

In the text, type names are printed in italic to distinguish Pascal types from the integers and reals of mathematics.

integer: **integer** variables store integers—the positive and negative counting numbers $(-2, -1, 0, 1, 2)$.

char: **char** variables can hold any of the characters—letters, punctuation marks, or numerals—that appear on the keyboard.

boolean: **boolean** (boo'-lee-an) variables, sometimes called logical variables, have one of two values—*true* or *false*. They're used with the control structures shown inside the cover.

....
> Types *integer, char,* and *boolean* are called **ordinal** types.
....

This distinction isn't crucial right now. We'll use the term 'ordinal type' when we want to exclude type *real* from the other simple types.

real: Positive and negative numbers that include decimal points, or are expressed as powers of 10, must be stored in **real** variables $(-3.55, 0.0, 187E-02, 35.997E+11)$.

When they appear as part of the input or output of Pascal programs, *real* values are written in an unusual manner. For one thing, commas aren't allowed in either *reals* or *integers.* This gives a millionaire 1000000 dollars, rather than 1,000,000. Fortunately, very large or small numbers can be expressed as *reals* by using a shorthand called *floating-point notation.** In this notation, the number is expressed as a power of 10—the letter 'E' stands for 'times 10 to the power of'. For example:

$9E+14$ *equals* 9 times 10 to the 14th power *equals* 900000000000000.0

$6.5E-04$ *equals* 6.5 times 10 to the negative 4th power *equals* 0.00065

$-0.5E+02$ *equals* -0.5 times 10 squared *equals* -50.0

$0.00125E+04$ *equals* .00125 times 10 to the 4th power *equals* 12.500

A Pascal *real* given as a power of 10 need not contain a decimal point, but if it has one, there must always be a digit—even a zero—to the left of the decimal. Thus, the fraction ½ is thought of as 0.5, and not an unadorned .5, and a negative fourth is -0.25, instead of $-.25.**$ A syntax chart for *reals* looks like this:

real

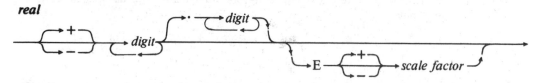

* This method is also called *scientific notation* and is often used on hand calculators.
** And what *is* .5, or $-.25$? In Pascal, we close our eyes and pretend they don't exist.

The smallest and largest *real* and *integer* values are allowed to vary from system to system—they are **system-defined**. When you find the limits of your system, note them inside the front cover.

Why are values grouped into different types in Pascal? Type separation helps the computer make some useful error inspections. When a program is compiled (translated into machine language), an automatic type-checking mechanism looks out for some kinds of potentially nonsensical activity. For example, if the compiler concludes that we're going to add an integer to a character, or subtract *true* from 45.378, it prints an error message that points out the imminent **type clash**. We can fix the mistake before trying to run the program.

Type checking also goes on while the program is running. This leads to an important restriction on Pascal variables.

> ### The Golden Rule of Types
>
> Give unto variables only values *of the same type.*
> Values *must* be of the same type as the variables they go to.

The most common type clash occurs when the programer forgets that *integer* variables must receive positive or negative integer values *without any decimals or exponents.* This is even true for *real* values that are whole numbers, but don't have the form of Pascal *integers* (like 5.0 or 13E+05).

There is only one exception to the rule: *integer* values may be given to *real* variables. However, the values are stored in floating-point notation, and appear to be *reals* when they're retrieved. If '4' is stored in a *real* variable, we'll get it back as 4.000000000000000E+00.

Aside from this exception, the type rule is inviolable. When it's broken, the program ignominiously **crashes**—stops running. While this is no great shame (it happens to everybody once in a while), it's no great honor, either.

Self-Check Questions

Q. Write these numbers as Pascal *reals.*

a) 341,234	*b)* .234	*c)* 234.73456
d) 88	*e)* .008562	*f)* −9427.003

A. Note that there's generally only one digit before the decimal in floating-point notation.

a) 3.41234E+05	*b)* 2.34E−01	*c)* 2.3473456E+02
d) 8.8E+01	*e)* 8.562E−03	*f)* −9.427003E+03

A **_variable declaration_** gives a variable's identifier and type. The declaration begins with the reserved word **var** (rhymes with 'car', or 'air'), which is a shorthand for *variable.* Then, each identifier is listed along with its type—the kind of value the variable will hold. There's a semicolon (as a statement separator) after each declaration. Notice the position of the colon (:) in these declarations:

var *AptNumber: integer*;
ShoeSize: real;
FirstInitial: char;
OutToLunch: boolean;

The Variable Declaration

The syntax chart of a variable declaration looks like this:

variable declaration

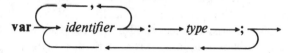

We needn't declare variables of every type, nor is the order of declaration important. To create more than one variable of a given type, separate the variable identifiers with commas, just like a list in a regular sentence. Make sure to include the colon right before the type.

var *TVchannel: integer*;   {One *integer* variable.}
GPA, BattingAverage: real;
Pagenumber, age: integer;   {More *integer* variables.}

You may wish to refer to section 1-1 to refresh your memory of the rules that govern identifiers. Something we didn't mention then is that two identifiers are considered to be the same if they only differ because of capitalization. These three identifiers are identical in Standard Pascal.

highnumber   *HIGHNUMBER*   *HighNumber*

This rule lets a program written on a computer with upper- and lower-case characters work equally well on a machine with only upper-case. However, it's a rule that's ignored in many implementations of Pascal.

Let's pause to make an important point about the way programs are typed in.

> Pascal programs are considered to be *free format.* The position of words in a program ('on the page,' so to speak) is generally unimportant, *as long as they are in the right order,* and no words, or words and numbers, are run together (like **program**_FirstRun_).

We can make a declaration that uses only one space (after **var**):

var *GPA,BattingAverage:real;Pagenumber,age,TVchannel:integer*;

Or, we can put in a zillion unnecessary spaces:

var *GPA* , *BattingAverage*
: *real* ; *Pagenumber*
,*age* ,*TVchannel*: *integer* ;

We can even write entire programs as single, awfully long lines, or place just one word or symbol on each page or card. We won't, though, because such programs are awkward to read and modify. The form our examples use—indentation, with only one thought per line, etc.—makes programs easier to correct and understand.

> When you write programs, try to approximate the format of programs in this book.

Where does the variable declaration belong? The first part of a program is the heading—the program's first line. Next comes the *declaration part*, which we just discussed. Finally comes the **statement part**, where the program's action takes place. In outline form, a program looks like this:

> *program heading*
> *declaration part*
> *statement part*

This order is just common sense. The program is named in the heading, its variables are defined in the declaration part, and finally they're used in the statement part.

Self-Check Questions

Q. Are these both valid variable declarations?

var *day, month*: *integer*; **var** *time*: *real*;
  time: *real*; *day*: *integer*;
    month: *integer*;

A. Yes. The syntax chart shows that the exact order of declarations is unimportant.

Q. Find at least two mistakes in each line.

variable: {line 1}
  trial; program: *integer*; {line 2}
  Middle Initial = *char*, {line 3}
end. {line 4}

A. Written correctly, the declaration looks like this:

var {line 1}
  trial: *integer*; {line 2—**program** is a reserved word.}
  MiddleInitial: *char*; {line 3}
    {line 4 is totally incorrect.}

A variable can be given a value in two ways—by having the value read in from an external source (like the keyboard or prepared punched cards), or by assigning it to the variable inside the program. In this section, we'll concentrate on the first method, which lets the program user supply a value while the program is running. To write a line of output, we used the standard procedure *writeln*. Reading a line of input requires the standard procedure *readln* (pronounced 'read line').

Input to Variables

> To use procedure **readln**, follow *readln* with the name of the variable whose value you want entered, between parentheses. Any extra values on the same input line will be discarded.

For example:

> *readln* (*VariableName*);

When a running program encounters a *readln*, it pauses to read a value. Whether or not the pause is apparent to the user depends on the program, and on the sort of equipment it's running on. In **interactive** programs the wait is obvious, because interactive programs communicate while they run. The program user waits at a keyboard for the program to **prompt** her to enter a value. This prompt is generated by a *writeln* within the program. For example:

```
program Interactive (input, output);

    {Demonstrates interactive program input and output.}

var Number: integer;

begin
    writeln ('This program interacts with its user.');
    writeln ('Please enter an integer value.');
    readln (Number);
    write ('The number you entered was:');
    writeln (Number)          {Print the value of Number.}
end.
```

```
          ↓       ↓       ↓       ↓       ↓
This program interacts with its user.
Please enter an integer value.
237
The number you entered was:          237
```

The program user had her computer compile *Interactive*, and begin execution. *Interactive* immediately printed its first two lines of output, then waited for the user to enter a value and hit the return key. This is the only value that the program user enters. We've shown it above in **bold**. Once a value (**237**) was entered, the computer was able to read it, then execute its final output statements.

Notice that the second statement, which prints 'Please enter an integer value.,' is essential to *Interactive's* successful operation. Without this prompt the program user would not have known that she was expected to supply any input. The program would hang, unable to carry out its *readln* statement, or any of its subsequent statements.

> The computer does *not* automatically cue the user to enter the values it is waiting for.

Batch programs, unlike interactive ones, do not communicate directly with their users. They may have input, of course, but all input must be prepared before the program is run. This makes more sense if you know that batch programs are often prepared on punched cards. Program data is put on another set of cards and given to the computer (or to a computer operator) along with the actual program. Since all its data is ready and waiting, the program can read in values as they're required. For example:

program *Batch* (*input, output*) ;
    {Demonstrates batch program input and output.}
var *Age, Elevation*: *integer*;
begin
    writeln ('About to read an age value.') ;
    readln (*Age*) ;
    write ('Your age is:') ;
    writeln (*Age*) ;
    writeln ('About to read an elevation value.') ;
    readln (*Elevation*) ;
    write ('The minimum elevation of Death Valley is:') ;
    writeln (*Elevation*)
end.   .

↓   ↓   ↓   ↓   ↓

16
−283

```
About to read an age value.
Your age is:          16
About to read an elevation value.
The minimum elevation of Death Valley is:          −283
```

In effect, the data of batch programs (again, in **bold face**) is entered before the program runs. The output statement that precedes each input statement isn't really a prompt. It's just there to provide a permanent record of what the program has done.

> Although program content or available equipment may force some programs to be either strictly batch or interactive, many programs can be written with either orientation.

We'll provide examples of both styles throughout the text.

There are a few variations on using *readln* for input.

Other Methods of Input

....
: More than one variable, separated by commas, can be listed in the :
: parentheses following a *readln.* :
....

readln (*Number, Age, Elevation*) ;

All the values must be entered by the program user *in the order listed,* on one or more lines or punched cards. As usual, extra values on the last line or card are discarded.

Now, when we read in *integer* or *real* values, spaces and carriage returns between values are ignored except as value separators. This means that input to a single *readln* statement can go on one line or card, or be spread out over several lines or cards. Given *integer* variables *a, b* and *c, real* variables *x, y,* and *z,* and the input statement shown below, input lines 1 and 2 are identical.

readln (*a, x, b, y, c, z*) ;

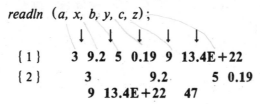

{1}   3 9.2 5 0.19 9 13.4E+22
{2}   3   9.2   5 0.19
          9 13.4E+22   47

The carriage return and extra spaces in input line 2 are ignored. The **47** at the end of the final line is also discarded, because the *readln* only expects to read six values. Another example clarifies this last point. Its last statement prints the values of the input variables.

readln (*a*) ;
readln (*b, c*) ;
writeln (*a, b, c*) ;

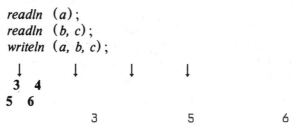

3 4
5 6

          3   5   6

As above, the extra value (in this case 4) is thrown out. Variable *b* takes the value 5, and *c* gets 6.

readln is usually given more than one variable when we don't have to prompt the program user for input, as in batch programs. Reading in more than one value at once is less common in interactive programs, because it tends to confuse program users.

....
: When *readln* appears on a line or punched card by itself: :
: :
:   readln;   {Nothing in parentheses.} :
: :
: the current line of input is discarded. :
....

This is a useful feature if we know that the data on an input line is faulty or unnecessary. However, it will be some time before we explore this application.

Values can also be input with the standard procedure *read,* which is quite similar to *readln.*

> When we use **read** the computer doesn't automatically jump ahead to the next line of input after finishing an input statement.

Among other benefits, this lets us input a word one character at a time. Suppose a program begins like this:

program *ReadCharacters* (*input, output*) ;

{A batch-oriented program that demonstrates *read*}

var *C1, C2, C3, C4, C5, C6: char;*

begin
    read (*C1*);
    read (*C2*);
    read (*C3*);
    read (*C4*);
    read (*C5*);
    read (*C6*);
    writeln (*C1, C2, C3, C4, C5, C6*)
        {This statement prints the variables' values.}
end.

Let's look at some different inputs, and their associated output. Assume that input is supplied on different lines (or punched cards) as given below. The output shown represents the values of variables *C1, C2, C3, C4,* C5, and *C6.* Any of these values may be a blank space, which we've printed as an underline (_).

input		output ↓ ↓ ↓
Hi there	⟶	H i _ t h e
Hi **there**	⟶	H i _ t h e _
57 4 **329**	⟶	5 7 _ 4 _ 3
A1 **B2 C3**	⟶	A 1 _ B 2 _

Note that a carriage return (or new card) is treated like a blank space.

Batch programs sometimes use *read* because it lets several input values, on a single punched card, be read in at different points of program execution. (*readln* is inappropriate because it discards any data that remains on a card after getting its input.) Interactive programs, on the other hand, may find that *readln* helps minimize problems with *char* input. We'll look at a typical problem in the antibugging section.

A special rule *must* be observed when using either *read* or *readln.*

> ### The Golden Rule of Input
>
> Always make sure that there's enough input.

If a batch program expects to read in eight characters or numbers, there had better be at least eight values ready to be read in. If there are too few, the program will crash. When an interactive program is given too few input values, it hangs without informing the program user that more input is required.

In chart form, *readln* and *read* look like this:

readln, read

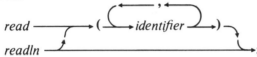

The differences between *readln* and *read* are reviewed in detail in section 7-2. More ambitious students will take a short detour to that section after learning about output in 1-3.

Q. Match the variables with the values they may represent. Which values may not be given to *any* variable? Assume we've made this declaration:

Self-Check Questions

    var *IntegerValue*: *integer*; *Letter*: *char*; *RealValue*: *real*;

a) 7	*b*) 0.0	*c*) T	*d*) .3519
e) −52	*f*) 0	*g*) 5.E+22	*h*) ;
i) .9E−3	*j*) 35.2E−17	*k*) −18E+6.0	*l*) dd
m) −667.3	*n*) 1,387	*o*) −7	*p*) −12E−7

A. *IntegerValue* may be 7, −52, 0, or −7.
    Letter may be '7', 'T', '0', or ';' .
    RealValue may be 7, 0.0, −52, 0, 35.2E−17, −667.3, −7, or −12E−7.
    The values .3519, 5.E+22, .9E−3, −18E+6.0, dd, and 1,387 may not be given to any variables.

1-3
Output of
Variable
Values

PROGRAM *ECHO*, BELOW, DEMONSTRATES THE way that the values of variables are printed.

> Variables can be given to ordinary *write* or *writeln* statements with, or in place of, text output. A comma separates each variable from other variables or text.

Variable identifiers are *not* put between single quote marks, because that would make them text output.

```
program Echo (input, output);
   {Demonstrates the output of variables.}
var Length, Width, Depth: integer;
begin
   writeln ('Please enter length, width, and depth.');
   readln (Length, Width, Depth);
   writeln ('Length is ', Length);
   write ('Depth is');
   writeln (Depth, '. Width and length are ', Width, Length);
   writeln (Length, Width, Depth)
end.
```

```
            ↓       ↓       ↓       ↓       ↓
Please enter length, width, and depth.
12 41 9
Length is       12
Depth is        9.  Width and length are    41 12
          12      41         9
```

It's common for both interactive and batch-oriented programs to *echo*, or immediately reprint, all values as they're entered. This can create a permanent record of program activity, and it helps prevent mistakes. Although the spacing of *integer* variable output looks a bit peculiar, we'll see why Pascal does it that way in a few pages.*

Mathematical operations like addition, subtraction, multiplication, and division may be performed within output statements.

> More precisely, an **expression** that consists of **operators** (the arithmetic signs) and **operands** (*real* or *integer* values) can be **evaluated** (figured out) in an output statement. The **result** of this evaluation (the answer) is printed.

Operands can be either variables or ordinary numbers. In formal terms, we'd say that numbers like 3 and 5.9 are **constant** (as opposed to *variable*) values of their respective types. For example, suppose that the values of *First* and *Second* are 3 and 4. Both these output statements are valid:

* Briefly, it's to facilitate the printing of numerical values in columns, rather than interspersed with text.

writeln ('The sum of 5 and the value First holds is', $5 + First$);
writeln (*First*, ' plus', *Second*, ' equals', $First + Second$);

```
      ↓       ↓       ↓       ↓       ↓       ↓
The sum of 5 and the value First holds is              8
         3 plus          4 equals              7
```

Let's look at arithmetic expressions a bit more closely. The symbols that represent some of the arithmetic operations are shown below.* Only the multiplication symbol ($*$) is unusual. An asterisk is used instead of a cross ($\times$) to avoid confusing it with a variable named X.

Symbol	Operation	Example
+	addition	*Salary + Graft*
−	subtraction	*Score − Penalty*
/	division	*Height / Weight*
*	multiplication	*Bet * Odds*

Program *EasyCalculations*, below, has statements that print the value, sum, difference, quotient, and product of two variables. Notice that there's always a single digit to the left of the decimal, since *reals* are printed in floating-point format. *EasyCalculations* is a batch-oriented program, because it doesn't prompt the program user to enter data.

program *EasyCalculations* (*input, output*);

   {Shows that expressions are evaluated before output.}

var *Cat, Rat*: *real*;

begin
    readln (*Cat, Rat*);
    writeln (*Cat, Rat*);
    writeln (*Cat+Rat, Cat−Rat*);
    writeln (*Cat   / Rat, Cat*
        *   *Rat*);
end.

```
          ↓       ↓       ↓       ↓
21.0  3.0
  2.100000000000000E+01  3.000000000000000E+00
  2.400000000000000E+01  1.800000000000000E+01
  7.000000000000000E+00  6.300000000000000E+01
```

The extra spaces in the program's final output statement have no untoward effect on execution, since Pascal programs are free-format. Carriage returns are only prohibited within text output.

---

* In Pascal (and most computer languages) a distinction is drawn between *integer* and *real* arithmetic. We won't let this trouble us until Chapter 2. Two more *integer* operations, **div** and **mod**, are explained there as well.

:·:··:

Self-Check
Questions

Q. Write output statements that:
   a) print two variable identifiers (say, *NoseLength* and *TruthIndex*);
   b) print their values;
   c) multiply them by each other;
   d) divide each of them by 5.3.
   e) Combine these operations in a coherent series of statements.

A. {*a*} *writeln* ('NoseLength, TruthIndex');
   {*b*} *writeln* (*NoseLength, TruthIndex*);
   {*c*} *writeln* (*NoseLength * TruthIndex*);
   {*d*} *writeln* (*NoseLength*/5.3, *TruthIndex*/5.3);

   {*e*} *write* ('The value of NoseLength is ', *NoseLength*, 'while ');
   writeln ('the TruthIndex is ', *TruthIndex*, '. Their product is ');
   write (*NoseLength* * *TruthIndex*, ', and divided by 5.3 they give us');
   writeln (*NoseLength*/5.3, 'and ', *TruthIndex*/5.3);

:··:

Output Format

Printing of numerical values is a little bit strange in Pascal. Program *Format*, below, shows their seemingly uneven line positioning.

program *Format* (*input, output*);

   {Shows Pascal's output printing format.}

var *Letter*: *char*;
   RealValue: *real*;
   IntegerValue: *integer*;

begin
   writeln ('Please enter a char, real, and integer value.');
   readln (*Letter, RealValue, IntegerValue*);
   writeln (*Letter*);
   writeln (*RealValue*);
   writeln (*IntegerValue*)
end.

```
         ↓         ↓         ↓         ↓         ↓
Please enter a char, real, and integer value.
B 281.5 66
B
  2.8150000000000000E+02
            66
```

Only the *char* variable *Letter* seems to be printed correctly. *Real-Value* and *IntegerValue* have been shifted more or less to the right, and *RealValue* has been printed in its full glory as a 16 digit *real*

:···:
: When they're printed as output by a Pascal program, *integer* and :
: *real* values are *right aligned*, or aligned with the right margin, of a :
: fixed space known as the number's **field width**. :
:···:

Thus, numbers are printed in a preset amount of space that's usually larger than the actual number. This is most obvious when printing out *integer* values.

This *integer* occupies 5 spaces...

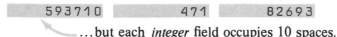

```
       593710              471            82693
```

...but each *integer* field occupies 10 spaces.

Fixed field width is a part of Pascal for a reason that anyone with the soul of an accountant will find obvious: it makes it easy to print columns of figures. For example, assume that the *integer* variables *a* through *i* have the values shown:

> *writeln* (*a*, *b*, *c*);
> *writeln* (*d*, *e*, *f*);
> *writeln* (*g*, *h*, *i*);

```
        ↓         ↓          ↓         ↓        ↓
      3141    6626175       855
  29979245          9     17321
        60       1414       728
```

It would be difficult to form such a table without the convenience of fixed field width.

As frequently happens in computer science, the solution to one problem can cause another. The **default** field width often appears inconveniently within an output line.*

> *writeln* ('The integer value entered was', *IntegerValue*);

```
        ↓         ↓         ↓         ↓         ↓
The integer value entered was          66
```

The printing of *real* values in floating-point notation is another of Pascal's default actions. *RealValue*, which we entered as 281.5, is output as 2.81500000000000E+02—a horrible-looking shorthand for '2.815 times 10 to the power 2'. There's a subtle danger inherent in this, as an impressive string of digits to the right of a decimal point implies an accuracy that doesn't necessarily exist.

Field widths, and the number of digits given in floating-point notation, are system-defined values. A typical *integer* field covers ten spaces, and *real* values are often printed in a twenty-two space field. A minor annoyance of Pascal is that positive *real* values are always preceded by at least one blank space when they're output, regardless of their field widths. *char* and text values, in contrast, are printed in the exact space they require. You should note your system-defined values inside the front cover.

Fortunately for the programer, the default field widths can be changed within a program. We can get rid of excess space by diminishing the field width, or provide extra room by increasing it.

---

* *Default* values and actions turn up frequently in computer systems. Such values or actions are considered to be some standard unless we explicitly specify otherwise.

> Follow the value being output with a colon, and the positive *integer*
> number of spaces in the desired field. You will never lose digits of
> an integer variable, or digits to the left of the decimal point of a
> real variable.

$$writeln\ (OutputValue:NewFieldWidth)\,;$$

If the new field width is greater than the number of characters in
the value, blanks are printed on the left. If we accidentally (or deliberately) specify a field width that is too *small* for an *integer* or text
value, the field automatically expands to accommodate the entire value.
As a result, programers often give a field width of one when they want
integer values printed in the smallest possible space. The final digit of
shortened *real* values is rounded.

In the examples below, note that field widths can be specified for
the output of text as well as variables. Assume that the value of *Year*
is 1492.

```
writeln ('WOW':10, 'MOM':10, 'WOW':10);
writeln ('In', Year:1, ', Columbus sailed the ocean blue.');
writeln ('In', Year:5, ', Columbus sailed the ocean blue.');
writeln ('In', Year, ', Columbus sailed the ocean blue.');
          ↓    ↓    ↓    ↓    ↓

        WOW        MOM        WOW
In1492, Columbus sailed the ocean blue.
In 1492, Columbus sailed the ocean blue.
In      1492, Columbus sailed the ocean blue.
```

Here's a syntax chart for *write* and *writeln* that shows the option
of setting output field width.

write and writeln

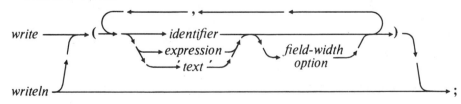

*Self-Check
Questions*

Q. Is this a valid Pascal statement? What is its effect?

$$writeln\ (Length + Width:1)\,;$$

A. The statement is perfectly legal, since field widths can be specified for
expressions. Its effect is to print the sum of *Length* and *Width* in the least
space required.

LOOKING FOR (AND FIXING) PROGRAM *bugs*, or mistakes, is called *debugging*. Most debugging should take place while a program is still on paper, well before it's entered, compiled, and run. Since it's always possible to introduce bugs (like misspellings) while typing in a program, even the best-planned programs may require a trial run or two before they're completely debugged. You should allow time for debugging as part of the normal programing process.

1-4
Antibugging and Debugging

Antibugging means programing in a way that helps avoid making bugs in the first place. Further along we'll see how some different programing techniques can help protect programs against bugs. For now, though, just reading these sections is probably antibugging enough.

Are bugs inevitable? We'd hate to think that they *have* to happen, but mistakes sometimes creep into computer programs because people don't think in the literal way that machines operate. Misplaced semicolons and spelling errors aren't very important to us, but they hopelessly confuse automatons. People have a remarkable, automatic, ability to fix problems that is miles beyond anything computers can do.

*What is wrong with
with this sentence?*

Bugs fall into two general categories. First, there are *syntax* bugs—mistakes made with the 'grammar' rules of Pascal. Second are *semantic* bugs—errors made in using Pascal. Syntax bugs can often be diagnosed by the computer as it compiles a program. Bugs caught like this are called *compile-time* errors. For example, the compiler spots certain mistakes by applying simple rules about correct Pascal. Some words invariably occur in pairs—every **begin** must be matched by an **end** later in the program. If a program is completely compiled and winds up short an **end**, you'll receive an error message that points out the omission.

```
"END" EXPECTED - - END OF PROGRAM NOT FOUND
```

This says that the computer expected the program to be longer, and to contain another **end.**

Syntax errors that involve punctuation are caught in a similar manner. For example, the semicolon is Pascal's statement separator, and the compiler expects to find a semicolon right before every statement. If two consecutive statements aren't separated by a semicolon (like *writeln writeln*), the compiler prints an error message. Some compilers are smarter than others, and will even temporarily patch the program. A compile-time message from the computer keeps the programer informed.

writeln
writeln

↑ I N S E R T E D   " ; "

This is just a temporary fix, because the original program isn't changed at all. It will work this time, but unless you fix the bug you'll get the same error message each time the program is compiled and run.

Incidentally, the error messages you see here probably won't be identical to the messages on your computer.

> *Oh! Pascal!* uses a set of error messages that are explicit enough to enlighten the most baffled programer.

The exact wording of error messages is implementation defined, just as the smartness of compilers varies from system to system. The error messages in our examples may be more detailed and exact than the ones you'll get, but they'll be a lot easier to understand.

Besides checking reserved words and punctuation, the compiler makes sure that all identifiers are legal. In effect, it checks names against a built-in syntax chart. It also examines each statement to make sure that all values involved are of the proper type. The example below errs by requesting a field width of 5.0 instead of 5.

writeln (23E-3:5.0);

↑ F I E L D   W I D T H   M U S T   B E   A N   I N T E G E R   V A L U E

Now, an unexpected side-effect of compile-time error-checking is that a real error early in the program may cause the computer to diagnose many apparent mistakes further on. This can be terribly intimidating, and make you feel like a total idiot. Suppose we've entered the following sequence of statements, with **begin** misspelled.

```
program ErrorProne (input, output);

var Data: integer;

begn
    writeln ('Please enter a number.');
    readln (Data);
    writeln (Data)
end.
```

The program only contains a minor bug, but it produces a sheaf of error messages.

```
PROGRAM ERRORPRONE (INPUT, OUTPUT);
VAR DATA:    INTEGER;
BEGN
     ↑ INSERTED ","
WRITELN  ( 'PLEASE ENTER A NUMBER. ');
        ↑ INSERTED ":"
            ↑ INVALID TYPE IDENTIFIER
READLN   (DATA);
        ↑ INSERTED ":"
WRITELN  (DATA);
          ↑ INSERTED ":"
  "DATA" IS DEFINED MORE THAN ONCE IN THIS BLOCK
 ↑ MALFORMED VARIABLE DECLARATION
END.
↑ UNEXPECTED "END" - - END OF PROGRAM NOT FOUND
```

If you can decipher this mess, you'll see that the misspelled **begn**
made the compiler treat the entire program as a long **var** declaration.
As far as the compiler was concerned, we were attempting to declare a
variable named *begn.* The bug threw the whole program out of kilter,
so we got a string of error messages a mile long.

....
:   :
:   The Golden Rule of Debugging   :
:   :
:   Don't fix what isn't broken. Don't make random changes.   :
:   :
....

When you're debugging a program, read the error messages first.
Then, get a *listing*, or hard-copy printout, of the program and try to
find the actual mistakes. When a short program produces a long series
of error messages, look for a simple reason—a misspelled word, or
misused feature. Don't despair. As you gain more experience, you'll
become adept at separating the real bugs from spurious ones.

A common mistake is to include a carriage return in the middle of
text output, like this:

> *writeln* ('This is illegal because a carriage return
>   can''t go between single quote marks.');

> {However, this is perfectly all right, because
> a comment can extend over several lines.   }

Another minor bug that has disastrous results is to forget one of the
single quote marks that surrounds text output.

Bugs serious enough to cause a program crash are called *run-time*
errors—they occur or manifest themselves while the program is running. They're not syntax bugs, because the programs they're in obey
the technical rules of Pascal. Instead, such bugs are either semantic
(due to a misuse of Pascal) or are initiated by the program user. What
do you think caused this run-time error message:

```
ABNORMAL TERMINATION - -
IMPROPER DATA FOUND AT INTEGER READ, LINE 32
```

Apparently, program line 32 was a *read* or *readln* statement that tried to get the value of an *integer* variable. The program user entered a value of the wrong type (perhaps it was *char* or *real*) and the program crashed.

> Be sure that interactive prompts ask for appropriate input.

Input data's ordering causes unexpected errors. When the computer reads *integer* or *real* values, it ignores spaces and carriage returns except as value separators. Thus:

readln (CharVariable, IntegerVariable, RealVariable) ;

will accept as input the sequence:

L 16 2.83

But if we re-order the input statement to be:

readln (IntegerVariable, CharVariable, RealVariable) ;

and then enter values like this:

16 L 2.83

we'll run into trouble. Although space characters are ignored when we're thinking arithmetically, they're legitimate *char* values. After 16 is correctly given in to *IntegerVariable*, the blank following it is stored in *CharVariable*. What value does *RealVariable* take on? The computer tries to give it the letter 'L'—a type clash—and the program crashes.

The best way to clarify confusing points of syntax or semantics (if thinking about it for a while doesn't work) is to experiment. The computer won't blow up or break down if you make a mistake, so don't worry about causing the entire system to crash. It's also a good idea to echo all input, to make sure that it's what you think it is.

> If you don't understand a bug or feature, write a four or five line program that tests only the point in question. If your original program turns out to be based on a mistaken premise, it's best to start over from the beginning.

The best tip of all is to ask somebody for help, and to be willing to help somebody yourself. Practice in spotting and explaining bugs is beneficial to everyone.

Summary

Programs are divided into several parts. First, the *program heading* names the program, and includes specifications about the program's *input* and *output*. Next comes the *declaration part*, where *variables* are declared. Finally, we have the *statement part*, which contains the program's actions. *Comments*, notes to a program reader that are ignored by the computer, can go anywhere in a program.

A program's actions are given as *statements*, separated by semicolons, and are executed in the order that they appear. In Chapter 1, we used a number of procedure statements for *input* and *output*. The standard output procedures are *write* and *writeln.* They can be used to print *text* (word) values given between single quote marks. Don't forget that *writeln* actually prints values, and moves on to the next line, whereas *write* only readies a value for printing. Although Pascal often prints numerical values in an unusual manner, its *default field widths* are easily modified by the programer.

Input statements also make use of standard procedures—*read* and *readln.* These differ in their handling of the remainder (if any) of a line of input. *Interactive* programs, which communicate with their users, should usually *prompt* for all input. *Batch* programs have their input supplied when the program is started, so prompts aren't necessary. However, both kinds of program often *echo*, or immediately reprint, input values.

When Pascal variables are declared, their specific *types* must be given. A number of types are predefined—*integer, char*, and *boolean* are the *ordinal types*, while *real* joins them as a standard *simple* type. Note that *real* values are stored in *floating−point notation*. An attempt to give a variable of one type a value of another causes a program *crash*.

Expressions consist of *operators* and *operands*; they are *evaluated*, and a *result* value is determined. The output procedures can be used to print expressions, as well as the *constant* values of each type.

Debugging and *antibugging* are attempts by the programer to find and prevent *bugs*, or mistakes. The compiler will usually spot *syntax* errors, and point them out with error messages. These are called *compile-time* errors, and should be fixed before running the program. *Run-time* errors that occur during the execution of a program are often caused by *semantic* bugs—misuses of Pascal that passed the compiler's inspection. A program *listing*, or printout, should always be obtained to help in debugging.

New Pascal

program	**begin**	(*input, output*)
var	**end**	*writeln*
write	*readln*	*read*
integer	*char*	*boolean*
real		

New Terms

reserved word	identifiers	Standard Pascal
comments	curly brackets	input
output	program heading	syntax chart
statement	statement part	execute
standard procedures	text	variable
input	ordinal types	standard simple types
floating-point notation	system-defined	type clash
crashes	variable declaration	declaration part
statement part	interactive	prompt
batch	echo	expression
operators	operands	evaluated
result	constant	field width
default	bugs	debugging
antibugging	syntax	semantic
compile-time	listing	run-time

Self-Test Exercises

1-1   When doesn't the identifier *input* have to appear in a program heading?

1-2   What would happen if the following line were inserted into a program?

{EXECUTION PROHIBITED WITHOUT OVERRIDE PERMISSION!!!}

1-3   Why are there blanks before some of the output words here? Did we make any mistakes?

writeln ('No', ',no,', ' you can''t', ' take that ', 'away', 'from me.');

1-4   Write a program that asks for a five-letter palindrome (a word that's spelled the same backward and forward), then prints the letters out in this pattern.

```
1 2 3 4 5
2 3 4 5 2
3 4 5 2 3
4 5 2 3 4
1 2 3 4 5
```

Try to figure out how many different ways you can spell the word according to this rule: start any place the first letter ('1' in the illustration) appears, then spell the word by moving to adjacent squares.

1-5   What are the four standard types? What is a type clash?

1-6   What is the value of an *integer* variable before we make any assignments to it? What about undefined *char* variables?

1-7   Explain the difference between a value or rule that is system defined, and one that's system dependent.

1-8   English sentences are supposed to obey syntactic and semantic rules, just like Pascal statements. Do these sentences contain syntax errors, or possible semantic errors?

a) What is this thing called, love?   *semantic*
b) To)be. or(not to be"   *syntactic*
c) I should say not?   *syntactic*
d) Green ideas sleep furiously.   *semantic*
e) I have to unequivocally say no.   *syntactic*
f) Woman without her man is nothing.   *syntactic*

1-9   The delicious recipe below is supposed to be supplied to a program. However, the program only has *integer* variables. How can the numerical data be read in?

> **32 onions**
> **12 heads of lettuce**
> **15 cloves garlic**
> **99 fish heads**

1-10   A program segment is shown below, along with its input. What will the segment's output be? Assume that *Number, Numeral,* and *Ignominious* are *integer* variables, and *Name* is a *char* variable.

> *readln* (*Number, Numeral*) ;
> *read* (*Name, Ignominious*) ;
> *writeln* (*Number, Numeral, Name, Ignominious*) ;
>
>   ↓   ↓   ↓
>
> 35
>   10   22 C 7
> X   007

1-11   What is the output of this statement?

> *writeln* ('A':1, 5:3+2, 6:4-1, 'D':2*2);

1-12   What kind of program errors can't be caught at compile time? Show an error that can't be found by the computer either at run-time or compile-time.

1-13   Suppose that these statements are going to be executed.

> *read* (*Number, Count*) ;
> *readln*;
> *readln* (*Letter, Fraction*) ;

Show input that will give *Count* the value 17, *Fraction* the value 0.618, *Letter* the value '=', and *Number* the value 0.

1-14   Get values for the *integer* variables *Month, Date,* and *Year* given the input **10/19/85**.

More Exercises

1-15   The price of stocks is commonly given to the nearest eighth; e.g. 77 3/8, or 23 1/2. Write a program that determines the value of a stock holding by reading in the number of shares held, and the whole portion, and numerator and denominator of the fractional portion, of the price per share.

1-16   Suppose that electricity costs 4.75 cents per kilowatt hour, and that a surcharge of 10% is added to the bill. A city utility tax of 3% is also levied; however, no tax is put on the surcharge, and no surcharge is placed on the tax. Write a program that computes an electric bill.

1-17   Write a program to print a standard business form. Find out how many usable lines a single sheet of output can contain (the printer will usually skip a few lines at the top and bottom of each page), and then print two or more forms on a single page. Use every available line, so that no paper will be wasted if the program is run twice.

1-18   One of the hardest, yet simplest, formulas in the world is Einstein's equation $E=mc^2$. Write a program that accepts as input a amount of mass in grams, and prints the amount of energy produced (in joules) when the matter is converted to energy. In the same program, find out how far light travels in a number of years the user enters.

1-19   When *integer* or *real* values are input, they don't have to be followed by blank spaces. The computer assumes that any input number ends when the first non-digit is encountered. Write a program that takes as input the month, day, and year in American form (e.g. 8/17/83 means August 17, 1983), and echoes the date in European form (e.g. 17,8,83 for the same date).

1-20   Ask a user to enter some digit that she particularly dislikes. Multiply it by 9, then multiply that by 12345679 (note that 8 is missing). What do you find? Modify the program to print out the entire multiplication as though you'd done it by hand.

1-21   Because a program user can't actually look inside the computer to see exactly what a program does, it's possible to make a program seem more intelligent than it really is. Write a program that appears to engage in small talk (by asking the user questions), but which in reality ignores her answers (because *everybody's* answers will be more or less the same). You can create a more convincing sense of interaction by periodically prompting for and echoing *integer* or single *char* data, like the user's street number or number of brothers and sisters.

1-22   How long can a single *write* or *writeln* be? How many words or characters can it contain? What happens if you type past the 'edge' of your screen, or past the end of a card? Will the line 'wrap-around' to the next line?

1-23   Can a *write* or *writeln* statement include a carriage return as part of its output? (This is aside from the normal advance caused by a *writeln*.) Are any other special characters, such as a backspace character, available?

1-24   What happens when you try to execute this statement?

> *writeln* ('') ;   {There's no space between the quotes.}

1-25   Write a program that prints the figures shown below one above the other. Modify your program to print them side-by-side. (If they're smart, batch users will just have to shuffle their punched cards, and interactive programmers only use their text editors to move lines around.) Does knowing about the modification you'll have to make change the way you might write the original program?

```
      *                        *  *  *  *  *
     * *                       *  *  *  *  *
    *  *  *                    *  *  *  *  *
   *  *  *  *                  *  *  *  *  *
  *  *  *  *  *  *             *  *  *  *  *
```

1-26   Write a program that writes your name in block letters. Is it easier to print the letters vertically or horizontally?

1-27   In *cryptarithmetic,* letters take the place of digits. However, all other mathematical symbols are used normally, e.g.:

$$SEND \ + \ MORE \ = \ MONEY$$

Write a program that prints cryptarithmetic problems horizontally (as above) and vertically (as in grade school arithmetic books—a horizontal line replaces the equals sign). Let the user enter two four-letter terms, a five-letter result, and the operation that is to be performed. You may want to modify your program to print special-case operations, like square roots or divisions.

1-28   A popular breakfast cereal's main ingredients are sugar, corn syrup, and sucrose. Write a program that reads in the amounts of each ingredient in a 50-gram serving (assume *integer* amounts), then prints out the amount of each, the average amount of the three ingredients, and the percentage of the entire serving that consists of sugar products.

1-29   The Rabbitski sequence of numbers is formed by following this rule: each number is the product of the two previous numbers. Write a program that accepts two numbers, and prints the first three members of the Rabbitski sequence they generate.

1-30   Here's a problem to test your powers of observation. Compute and print the fractions 1/7, 2/7, 3/7, 4/7, 5/7, and 6/7. What similarity do they have? (Hint: look at them with numerators in order 1, 3, 2, 6, 4, and 5.)

1-31   In a recent election for dog catcher, Mary won by 74 votes over Peter, 23 votes over Paul, and 86 votes over Joan. Unfortunately, the computer that tabulated the votes had a bug in it, and only printed out the total number of votes cast—9,485. How many votes did each candidate receive? (Hint: try using the *integer* division operator **div** instead of the *real* operator /. (2417, −74, −23, −86)

1-32   Monica Marin and her friend Nadine decided to have a pot-luck dinner, to which Monica brought three different dishes, and Nadine five. Just as they were about to begin dining, Claire showed up. Naturally, she was invited to join the meal. In thanks, Claire paid Monica $3 and Nadine $5—one dollar per dish. Monica protested, however, feeling that she had gotten too much. How should the $8 have been divided to pay for the eight plates of food?

1-33   A problem we'll continue throughout the text is that of defining a new programing language. Make up a new language, and name it after yourself. For Chapter 1, choose reserved words to replace **program, var, begin,** and **end**. Pre-define identifiers to replace the ones listed in the chapter summary. Draft rules of syntax that will make your new language's semantics equivalent to Pascal's.

WRITING—MACHINE

Of all the noble arts, that of writing is surely the most frequently pursued. Any person who lays claim to a certain education nowadays must be more or less proficient in the calligraphic art. The fact that this proficiency is not very easily acquired, is proved by the six-year training course followed by each of us to develop a clear and steady hand in the pursuit of which many still fail to achieve satisfactory results.

For that reason, and to increase the speed of writing, a few inventors held the view that the old method of drawing letters by hand should be abandoned in favour of mechanical reproduction of already existing letters. The first useful writing-machine was constructed in 1865 by an American named Sholes. In 1877 a typewriter which gave excellent service was devised by an American engineer called Remington, but it was not until the end of the 1880s that the usefulness of the typewriter was generally recognised, and only then did people cease to regard it as an aid solely for the myopic and sufferers from writer's cramp. It is no longer a rare occurrence for merchants or private persons to purchase a writing-machine to enable them to deal with their correspondence in a quicker and better way.

Turn-of-the century typewriter advertisement. Warder Collection.

2

Programing Calculations

It's time to stop using the computer as a glorified electric typewriter. In Chapter 1 we concentrated on moving values into and out of programs with the input and output procedures. In this chapter, we'll see how the *assignment* statement helps manipulate and store values within the computer.

Section 2-1 introduces the *assignment operator*, which is used to store values in variables. We'll compute values by using expressions, as we did before, but this time we'll look at expressions in detail, and perform different operations on different types of values.

Section 2-2 describes Pascal's *standard functions.* These are analogous to the function keys on a calculator (with some extras), and they compute values for assignment to variables. Although section 2-2 is long, it's mostly for reference and review. This is a good time to find out about any nonstandard functions your system may support.

Naturally, the programs we write will begin to get longer. Section 2-3 demonstrates some ways of ensuring that they don't get unnecessarily complicated as well. This section's main concern is with the style and *elegance* of programs. On the technical side, we'll see how to declare program *constants.*

As always, potential bugs and problems are described in the final section.

It's time to stop using the computer as a glorified typewriter.

**2-1
Assignments
and
Expressions**

ONCE AGAIN WE'LL BEGIN WITH AN example. Program *TailorSeries*, below, contains a sequence of **assignment statements**, as well as several expressions more complex than the ones we encountered in Chapter 1. It also formats its *real* output in a new way, by specifying *decimal accuracy.*

program *TailorSeries* (*input, output*) ;

{Demonstrates the assignment statement.}

var *NeckSize, HatSize, ShoeSize, ArmLength,
     Waistline, Weight*: *real*;

begin

   writeln ('This program computes sizes for a male customer.') ;
   writeln ('Please enter the customer''s waistline, in inches.') ;
   readln (*Waistline*) ;
   writeln ('Please enter the customer''s weight, in pounds.') ;
   readln (*Weight*) ;
   NeckSize := 3.0∗(*Weight*/*Waistline*) ;
   HatSize := *NeckSize*/2.125 ;
   ShoeSize := 50.0∗(*Waistline*/*Weight*) ;
   ArmLength := *Waistline*/2.0 ;
   writeln ('Neck size is', *NeckSize*:2:2) ;
   writeln ('Hat size is', *HatSize*:2:2) ;
   writeln ('Shoe size is', *ShoeSize*:2:2) ;
   writeln ('Arm length is', *ArmLength*:2:2)

end.   {*TailorSeries*}

↓   ↓   ↓   ↓   ↓

```
This program computes sizes for a male customer.
Please enter the customer's waistline, in inches.
32
Please enter the customer's weight, in pounds.
174
Neck size is 16.31
Hat size is 7.68
Shoe size is 9.20
Arm length is 16.00
```

TailorSeries is an indispensable tailor's aid. It determines all sorts of measurements from a male customer's waistline and weight. Values for *Waistline* and *Weight* are prompted and input by the program user. The other program variables get their values internally, in the shaded assignment statements.

> The **assignment operator** (:=) changes the value of a variable within a program—to assign it a starting value, or to alter its current value.

Although the assignment operator symbol is a colon followed by an equals sign, its meaning doesn't derive from its components. We're best off reading the assignment operator as 'gets'. For example:

$$age := 6;$$

says 'the variable *age* gets assigned the value 6,' or, more tersely, '*age* gets 6.' The colon distinguishes the assignment operator from an ordinary equals sign, which has a wholly different purpose in Pascal.

The assignment statement is the most frequently used statement in programing. It always takes the form:

variable identifier := *the value represented by an expression*;

The computer first performs a calculation by evaluating the expression on the right-hand side of the assignment. Then the result, or computed value, is given to the variable on the left. For example:

$$LuckyNumber := 7+5;$$

means that the variable *LuckyNumber* now represents the value 12—the sum of 7 and 5. Once it has a value, *LuckyNumber* can be used in an expression too:

$$Sum := LuckyNumber+9;$$

> A variable must be ***initialized***, or given a starting value, before it can appear in an expression. The variable is ***undefined*** until it is initialized.

Many Pascal systems will automatically initialize variables to zero, or an equivalent null value. However, no program that presumes to be written in Standard Pascal will use uninitialized, undefined variables.

The Golden Rule of types applies just as strongly to assignments as it did to input statements.

> Variables may only be assigned values of the same Pascal type.

If *Age* is an *integer* variable, and *Fraction* is of type *real*, then these are valid assignments:

$$Age := 16; \qquad Fraction := 16.5;$$

The assignments below are no good because there's a clash between the types of *Age*, 16.5, and *Fraction*:

$$Age := 16.5; \qquad Age := Fraction;$$

Assigning an *integer* value to a *real* variable is legal, but is syntactically flawed. In Chapter 1 we mentioned that an *integer* could be given to a *real* variable (using *readln* or *read*). Although assignments of this sort are also technically permitted, they can be confusing because the *integer* is stored as a *real*, and shown as output in floating-point notation. Such assignments should be avoided if possible.

Assignments to *char* variables pose a special problem. We need to avoid confusion between, say, the letter 'E' and a variable named *E*; or between the character '6' and the *integer* value 6.

> When a character is used as a value of type *char*, it must be enclosed within single quote marks.

Initial := 'E';   *SeventhDigitCharacter* := '6';

This is similar to our use of quote marks to distinguish text values in output statements. A *char* variable, however, can only represent a single character value. The assignment:

Monogram := 'RMS';

is in error, because it tries to give three different values ('R', 'M', and 'S') to the *char* variable *Monogram.*

It should go without saying that a variable can't materialize within an assignment statement unless it has been declared. Although some popular programing languages let variables be declared on the spot by being used, Pascal requires them to be declared in the program's declaration part.

Self-Check Questions

Q. Correct these assignment statements.

a) *2ndValue* := *1stValue* +*Correction*;   b) 5+7 = *Sum*;
c) *FirstLetter* := A;   d) *StartingCount* := *InitialSetting* := 0;
e) *Efficiency* := .35;   f) *Initial* := 'WS';
g) *Sum* := 9 **and** 13;   h) *TaxRate* := 5%;

A. The rewritten assignments:

a) *SecondValue* := *FirstValue* +*Correction*;
b) *Sum* := 5+7;
c) *FirstLetter* := 'A';
d) *StartingCount* := 0; *InitialSetting* := 0;
e) *Efficiency* := 0.35;
f) If *Initial* is a *char* variable, it can only represent one letter.
g) *Sum* := 9+13;
h) *TaxRate* := 0.05;

Representing Values as Expressions

Somewhere in the course of every program, each declared variable takes on a value. In Pascal, two important ideas are associated with values: their types, and their *representations.*

If you like, you can imagine a type as a group of values. The range of values in the group may be large (like the *reals* and *integers*), or small (like the 64-128 members of a typical character set, or the two *boolean* values). A type is further distinguished by the way its values are used. For example, we can add *integers* or subtract them; find their square roots or logarithms; or determine if an *integer* is odd or even. These activities are all nonsensical when applied to *char* values.

But no matter what its type is, a value must have some way of being shown. This brings us to the representation of values.

> The **representation** of a value is the collection of symbols that display it.

These are representations of the value we call 'seven' (but could just as well call 'hobgoblin', 'Brobdingnagian', or 'Rumplestiltskin'):

7   seven   VII

With a little imagination, we can come up with other, more horrible representations of 'seven'.

$$|-7| \qquad 9-2 \qquad 3+4 \qquad 49^{\frac{1}{2}}$$

In Pascal, the legal representations of values are more restrained. An *integer* value, for instance, may be shown with numerals (12), a variable identifier (*RollOfDice*), or a combination of numerals, identifiers, and operation signs (*RollOfDice*+2). A Pascal function call (we'll encounter these in a few pages) might also express an *integer* value—*sqr*(7) calls the squaring function, and calculates the square of 7. Thus, it is a valid representation of the value 'forty-nine'.

> In Pascal, any representation of a value is an expression, whether it's a numeral, variable identifier, function call, or sequence of operation signs and more basic expressions (called *operators* and *operands*).

Let's nail down some definitions that relate to expressions. To begin with, expressions are **stated**. Saying 'two plus two' is stating an arithmetic expression. The value the expression represents is computed by *evaluating* the expression. The answer obtained is the expression's *result.* Thus, in an assignment statement an expression is stated and evaluated. Its result value is assigned to a variable.

Self-Check
Questions

Q. Write each of these as a Pascal expression.

a) the sum of 5 and 9
c) the *real* representation of six
e) the *integer* value six

b) the character P
d) the character that represents six
f) negative 1 times *Value*

A. Here are some of the simplest expressions that do the job.

    a) 5+9
    c) 6.0, 6E+00, or 6.0E+00
    e) 6

    b) 'P'
    d) '6'
    f) −*Value*

Q. How is a *real* value indicated in an assignment statement?

A. *Reals* are written in the text of a program just as they're entered as input to a program (or, for that matter, just as they're printed as output *from* a program). Floating-point and ordinary decimal notation are both used.

    Tariff:= 0.065
    OneHairWeight:= 1.375E−21;
    OneGross:= 1.44E+02;
    SpeedOfLight:= 2.998E+08;

The Integer and Real Operators

The *integer* and *real* operators are rules for combining operand values into new expressions. This is just a formal way of saying that these operators perform addition, subtraction, multiplication, and division. We have to distinguish between *integer* and *real* operators because they have some differences in most computer languages. For example, we can take two *integers* and add them, subtract them, or multiply them, and the result, or answer, will always be an *integer*:

$$4+3 \text{ is } 7 \qquad 4-3 \text{ is } 1 \qquad 4*3 \text{ is } 12$$

But if we divide them, we can look at the result in two ways—as a *real*, or as two *integers*:

4 *divided by* 3 *is* 1.3333333333E+00   This is a *real* result
4 *divided by* 3 *is* 1, *and remainder* 1   This is an *integer* result

It turns out that the second form of division, which you probably haven't seen since grade school, is as useful as the first. Sometimes we don't care about a fractional remainder, and integer division lets us ignore it gracefully. Counting by dozens is a good example: 5.0833333333E+00 dozen doesn't mean much, but 5 dozen and 1 does. Conversely, on occasion the remainder is all we're interested in, and we should have a straightforward way of getting it.

Pascal's *real* operators were introduced in Chapter 1.

Real Operators

+	addition	Price + Surcharge
−	subtraction	Tuition − Scholarship
*	multiplication	32.87 * 6.5E−02
/	division	Spoils / 2.0

The *integer* operations are the same except that the slash has been replaced by two special operators for *integer* division—**div**, and **mod**. The first, **div**, gives us the quotient of a division *without any remainder*. In practice, it's as though the quotient had been rounded toward zero.

$$9 \textbf{ div } 5 \text{ is } 1 \cdot \qquad 24 \textbf{ div } 9 \text{ is } 2 \qquad -9 \textbf{ div } 5 \text{ is } -1$$

The second *integer* division operator, **mod**, does just the opposite. It ignores the 'whole' part of the quotient, and provides only the remainder.

$$9 \textbf{ mod } 5 \text{ is } 4 \qquad 24 \textbf{ mod } 9 \text{ is } 6 \qquad 9 \textbf{ mod } 24 \text{ is } 9$$

Although **div** and **mod** are reserved words in Pascal, they're thought of as symbols that represent operations, just like + and −.

Integer Operators

+	addition	FamilySize + 2
−	subtraction	ShoppingDays − 1
*	multiplication	Fine * DaysLate
div	'whole number' division	10 **div** 3 (is 3)
mod	'remainder' division	10 **mod** 3 (is 1)

Since they're *integer* operators, **div** and **mod** may only be used with *integer* valued operands, as in the examples above. We can't use *real* operands with **div** and **mod** even when it seems perfectly reasonable. The expressions shown below are both invalid, because 2.0 and 1E+02 are *real* values.

$$4 \textbf{ div } 2.0 \qquad 1E+02 \textbf{ mod } 50$$

> If an expression contains both *reals* and *integers* (or only *reals*), then the result of evaluating the expression will be of type *real* The result of any expression that uses the *real* division operator (/) is also of type *real*

3+1.0   *is*   4.0000000000E+00
2E+02−87   *is*   1.1300000000E+02
−0.1*5   *is*   −5.0000000000E−01
4/2   *is*   2.0000000000E+00
1/1   *is*   1.0000000000E+00

Q. Evaluate these expressions. Assume that the following assignments have been made: *Channel* := 6; and *Frequency* := 3.5. What is the type of each of the expressions?

Self-Check Questions

a) 102 **div** 25
b) *Channel* * *Frequency*
c) *Frequency* − *Channel*
d) 69 **mod** *Channel*
e) *Channel* **mod** 69
f) *Channel* **mod** *Frequency*
g) 12E+02 + *Frequency*
h) 12E+02 + *Channel*
i) *Channel*/1
j) *Channel* * 1.0

A. Note the mismatched types in *f.*

a) 4 *integer*
b) 21.0 *real*
c) −2.5 *real*
d) 3 *integer*
e) 6 *integer*
f) Type clash—invalid expression
g) 1203.5 *real*
h) 1206.0 *real*
i) 6.0 *real*
j) 6.0 *real*

Q. Which of the expressions above can be assigned to *integer* variables? To *real* variables?

A. Expressions *a, d,* and *e* represent *integer* values, and should be assigned to *integer* variables. Although *any* of the expressions shown here (with the exception of *f*) may be assigned to *real* variables, it's sloppy, potentially confusing type handling that should be avoided. Only *real*-valued expressions should be assigned to *real* variables.

Operator Precedence

In Pascal, as in ordinary arithmetic, we can combine several small expressions in a chain of operations. As long as the type rules are obeyed, we can make expressions as long and complicated as we desire.* However, a question arises: what part of an expression is evaluated first? How many different result values can you come up with for the following expression?

$$5 * 20 + 8 \text{ mod } 50 - 3 * 6 \text{ div } 4 + 9$$

Completing the operations as they appear—5 times 20, plus 8, **mod** 50, etc.—gives 16 as the result. But we might just as reasonably work from right to left, and get 140. We've arrived at the problem of *operator precedence*—which operations should take place first? Stop reading for a moment, and try to come up with a few plausible solutions to this problem.

Two options come to mind. We can say that some operations are more important than others, and proceed from the most important operations to the least important. On the other hand, we might want to continue a standard practice of arithmetic and algebra—use parentheses to indicate the sequence of operations. Pascal takes both of these ideas.

1. There is a *hierarchy*, or ordering, of precedence of operations. Expressions that contain more than one operator from a given level of the hierarchy are almost invariably evaluated from left to right.

2. We can use parentheses to change the order of evaluation, or to make it clearer.

The arithmetic operations exist on two levels. Addition and subtraction have less precedence than the other operations.

> The hierarchical rule of precedence is:
>
> *   /   **div   mod**   these operations are completed . . .
>   +   −   . . . before these operations.

Thus, we see that:

8.0/2.0 + 6.0	*evaluates to 10.0, not 1.0*
3−4*2	*is equal to −5, not −2*
5+25 **mod** 6	*equals 6, not 0*
3.5−1.25/0.5	*is 1.0, not 4.5*

When an expression contains more than a single operator from any one level, we do the multiplications and divisions first, then perform the lower level additions or subtractions.

---

* If you want people to think you know something about computer science, say 'We can state expressions of *arbitrary complexity*.'

$5.5-3.375/1.125$	is	$5.5-3.0$	is	2.5
$5*3+14 \textbf{ mod } 4$	is	$15+2$	is	17
$4.5/1.125-3.325*6.5$	is	$4.0-21.6125$	is	-17.6125
$7-6*2-33 \textbf{ div } 4-3$	is	$7-12-8-3$	is	-16

Parentheses change this order of evaluation, because a subexpression within parentheses gets evaluated before the rest of the expression.

$(5+3)*(8-2)$	*is equivalent to* $8*6$
$(6/3)*(2-4)$	*is the same as* $2.0*(-2)$
$2.5*(1.25+0.25)$	*is like* $2.5*1.5$

When we *nest* parentheses—use multiple levels of parentheses—calculations are done from the inside out, e.g.:

$$(8 \textbf{ mod } (2*(5-3*(4+6*(5 \textbf{ div } 2)) \textbf{ div } 10)))$$
$$(8 \textbf{ mod } (2*(5-3*(4+6*2) \textbf{ div } 10)))$$
$$(8 \textbf{ mod } (2*(5-3*(4+12) \textbf{ div } 10)))$$
$$(8 \textbf{ mod } (2*(5-3*16 \textbf{ div } 10)))$$
$$(8 \textbf{ mod } (2*(5-48 \textbf{ div } 10)))$$
$$(8 \textbf{ mod } (2*(5-4)))$$
$$(8 \textbf{ mod } (2*1))$$
$$(8 \textbf{ mod } 2)$$
$$0 \qquad \{as\ 8 \textbf{ div } 2\ equals\ 4\ exactly\}$$

You can appreciate that there is often more than one way of writing a particular expression. Sometimes we have to choose between using parentheses, and relying on the operator precedence rules. The main rule of thumb to follow is this:

> Figuring out what an expression means (to say nothing of evaluating it) should not bring great anguish to someone who is reading your program.

A string of operations can sometimes be confusing or ambiguous, even though it accomplishes exactly what you intend. Contrast:

PartialResult/ CompleteData − Correction

with:

(PartialResult/ CompleteData) − Correction

The first expression is correct, but unclear. The second is unambiguous. Write assignment statements and expressions that can be understood by human beings, as well as by computers.

Self-Check Questions

Q. In what order are these operations done: **div**, *, **mod**, / ?

A. Because these operators are all on the same level of the operator hierarchy, they have equal precedence. They are carried out as they appear, working from left to right.

Q. These expressions are evaluated in a certain sequence by the rules of Pascal. Insert parentheses to make it more explicit. Evaluate the expressions on a hand calculator.

   a) 5−9∗3+2
   b) 0.09/1.394∗8.6/5.004E+02
   c) 7∗8−9+12 **div** 5
   d) 1E+04/2.5E−01+350.0∗−0.10)
   e) 1+3∗9 **div** −6 **div** 7
   f) 5.9E+07+(−18E+03)−0.6/5.9E−02−8.1

A. These answers were calculated on a HP-29C pocket calculator.
   a) 5−(9∗3)+2 *is* −20
   b) ((0.09/1.394)∗8.6)/5.004E+02 *is* 1.732E−02 ~~?~~
   c) (7∗8)−9+(12 **div** 5) *is* 49
   d) (1E+04/2.5E−01) + (350.0∗(−0.10)) *is* 3.9965E+04 *? sign error* _−40035_
   e) 1+(((3∗9) **div** (−6)) **div** 7) *is* −3
   f) 5.9E+07+(−18E+03)−(0.6/5.9E−02)−8.1 *is* 5.89820E+07

:..:

2-2
The Standard Functions

TAKE A LOOK AT ANY POCKET CALCULATOR. Along with the keys that represent the arithmetic operators, we'll almost invariably find some buttons for more complex figuring tasks. A typical calculator has keys that find squares (x^2) or square roots $(x^{\frac{1}{2}})$, determine reciprocals $(1/x)$, or figure out percentages. More expensive scientific or business calculators may include many others. These buttons are usually called *function* keys. They make life much more pleasant, because a single keystroke completes an otherwise lengthy series of calculations.

   Now, it's reasonable to expect a written computer language to be at least as powerful as the 'touch' language of a hand calculator. Pascal contains functions that can be used with numerical values, and some for manipulating other ordinal values (like *char*) as well. We can even write new functions to deal with new situations. For now, though, we'll be content to study functions that are ***pre-defined*** as part of the language. They are called ***standard functions***, and are listed below.

Arithmetic Functions

sqr	*sqrt*		{Square and square root}
sin	*cos*	*arctan*	{Standard trigonometric functions}
exp	*ln*		{Exponential and natural log functions}
abs			{Absolute value}
round			{Rounding}
trunc			{Truncation}

Ordering Functions

succ	{Successor—the next ordinal value}
pred	{Predecessor—the previous ordinal value}
ord	{Position of an ordinal value}
chr	{*char* value in a given ordinal position}

Boolean Functions

odd	{Is an *integer* odd?}
eoln	{Are we at the end of an input line?}
eof	{Are we at the end of the input file?}

We use a Pascal function by making a *function call*. A function call usually has two parts—the name of the function, followed by the function's *argument* in parentheses.

We briefly mentioned earlier that $sqr(7)$ is a call of the squaring function. Its argument is '7', and the entire function call represents the value 49. Thus, a function call is an expression, just as a variable identifier is. It can appear as the argument of another function, or as part of an output statement.

$HypotenuseSquared := sqr(3) + sqr(4)$;
$writeln\ (sqr(7))$;   {Will print '   49'.}
$writeln\ (sqr(7) + 3)$;   {Will print '   52'.}
$NoChange := sqrt(sqr(7))$; {*NoChange* gets 7.}

Indeed, the argument of a function can be an expression of *any* length, as long as it is given between parentheses.

$writeln\ (sqr(7+3))$;   {Will print '   100'.}
$Root := sqrt(16-7)$;   {Root gets 3.}
$AnotherRoot := sqrt(16) - 7$; {AnotherRoot gets −3.}

The *result* of a function is the value it (and its argument) represents. It's found by evaluating the function call.

To spout all these new terms at once, we'll say that a function (call it 'f'), receives an argument (which we'll usually call 'x'). The value that the function call represents is the result of evaluating the expression $f(x)$.

Self-Check Questions

Q. What value will the following program segment print out?

$Side := 4$;
$sqr\ (Side)$;
$writeln\ ($'The square of the side is ', $Side)$;

A. The segment won't run at all, because the function call in the second line of the segment—$sqr\ (Side)$—is just a representation of the value 4 squared, or 16. It's as though we had written:

$Side := 4$;
16;   {The value $sqr(Side)$ represents.}
$writeln\ ($'The square of the side is ', $Side)$;

To get the desired effect, we should write:

$Side := 4$;
$SquaredSide := sqr(Side)$;
$writeln\ ($'The square of the side is ', $SquaredSide)$;

Arithmetic Functions

The first group of functions takes numerical values as arguments. Most are like the functions found on calculators, but Pascal includes a few extras. The square root and squaring functions are easy to understand.

$sqr(x)$ Squaring function. Represents the square of its argument (which we've called x). The argument may be either a *real* or *integer* value.

$sqrt(x)$ Square root function. It finds, and represents, the square root of its argument (which also may be *real* or *integer*).

Now, a question about the square root immediately surfaces. Does $sqr(x)$ represent an *integer* or *real* value? Reasonably enough, this depends on the type of its argument, x

> The **result type** of the call $sqr(x)$ is the same as the type of x

This means that $sqr(4)$ is 16, but $sqr(4.0)$ is 16.0. The square root function, on the other hand, always has a *real*-valued result, regardless of whether its argument is *integer* or *real*

$sqrt(4)$ *is* 2.0000000000E+00 $sqrt(4.0)$ *is* 2.0000000000E+00

The trigonometric functions also have *real* results. Their arguments may be either *real* or *integer*, but the argument is given in **radians**, rather than degrees.* In these examples, assume that the identifier *pi* represents the value 3.141592654.

Trig Function	*Pascal Name*	*Example*
sine	$sin(x)$	$sin(pi/2)$ is 1.0
		$sin(pi/4)$ is 7.07106781E−01
cosine	$cos(x)$	$cos(0)$ is 1.0
		$cos(pi/3)$ is 5.00000000E−01
arctangent (inverse tangent)	$arctan(x)$	$arctan(0)$ is 0
		$arctan(1)$ is 7.85398163E−01

You may wonder why the tangent function, or arcsine and arccosine functions aren't built into Pascal. The answer is economy. Any trigonometry or calculus text has a table that shows how to obtain all the trigonometric relationships from the *sin, cos,* and *arctan* functions. Predefining extra functions in Pascal would be redundant, and make the language less streamlined and compact.

* For reference, $180° = \pi$ radians (3.141592654 radians), $360° = 2\pi$ radians, $90° = \pi/2$ radians, etc.

Self-Check Questions

Q. Use a pocket calculator to evaluate the expressions in these assignments. Is there any difference between your results and the numbers we obtained with a PDP 11/70 computer? Why? Assume that *pi* = 3.141592654.

a) *RightAngle* := *sin*(2 * *pi*)/2;
b) *FourthRoot* := *sqrt*(*sqrt*(4.7458321E07));
c) *FifthPower* := 9 * *sqr*(*sqr*(9));
d) *CosineSquared* := *sqr*(*cos*(33.7));
e) *TangentSquaredPi* := *sqr*(*sin*(*pi*)/*cos*(*pi*));
f) *InverseSquared* := 1/*sqr*(97);

A. Since *real* calculations are only carried out to a certain number of decimal places ('digits of accuracy' would be a more precise term), there is invariably a small error due to rounding. The error made by a computer is (hopefully) smaller than the error found in a calculator's result.

a) *RightAngle* = 4.10206731706684E−10
b) *FourthRoot* = 8.30000000000000E+01
c) *FifthPower* = 59049
d) *CosineSquared* = 4.28128802782853E−01
e) *TangentSquaredPi* = 1.68269562737479E−19
f) *InverseSquared* = 1.06281220108407E−04

:..:

The next arithmetic functions we'll consider are the natural logarithm ('log' for short) functions.

ln(*x*) **Natural *log*** function. Represents the natural logarithm (log to the base *e*) of its *integer* or *real* argument *x* The argument must be greater than 0.

exp(*x*) **Exponential** function. The result of this function represents *e* (the base of the natural log system), raised to the *real* or *integer* power *x* (i.e. e^x).

The result type of both functions is *real,* which means that both function calls represent *real* values whether their arguments are *real* or *integer.* Note that we're working with natural logarithms (base *e*), and not *common* logs (base 10). There are no common log functions in Pascal because they, like the missing trig functions, can be derived using the natural logs.

We're not going to bore you (or confuse you, as the case may be) by explaining the purpose of logarithms. Still, logs *are* often found in formulas, and you should be able to plug in these function calls as necessary.

Math	Pascal
$\ln \dfrac{1+a}{1-a}$	*ln*((1 + *a*)/(1 − *a*))
$\dfrac{e^x}{2}$	*exp*(*x*)/2
$\ln(\dfrac{\pi}{2})$	*ln*(3.141592654/2)
$\dfrac{e^u - e^{-u}}{2}$	(*exp*(*u*) − *exp*(−*u*))/2

Log, Absolute Value, and Transfer Functions

[47]

The logarithm functions help overcome a shortcoming in Pascal that often annoys programers—the lack of a specific *exponentiation* operator. There's no predefined function for raising a number (call it *a*) to some power (call it *n*), as in a^n. Incidentally, the number *a* is known as the *mantissa*, while *n* is called the *exponent*.* Wirth decided not to define an exponentiation operator to make Pascal more compact, and to encourage programers to employ more efficient ways of finding powers. Some people think that he was penny wise, and pound foolish.

At any rate, an easy formula can be used to carry out exponentiation in Pascal:

$$a^n = exp\,(n*ln(a))$$

It is subject to the following restriction: the mantissa, *a*, must be a positive *real* or *integer* value. (We pointed this out in the definition of *ln(x)*.) Naturally, the formula may even be used by those who are ignorant of its reason for operation and who wish to remain so.

Math	Pascal
5^8	$exp(8*ln(5))$
$9.87^{-3.51}$	$exp(-3.51*ln(9.87))$
$4.3^{½}$	$exp(1/2*ln(4.3))$
$(-5)^{0.15}$	Negative mantissa; can't be done.

Let's move along to the other functions. On some occasions we have to be certain that an *integer* or *real* value is positive. The *abs* function does the job.

abs(x)   ***Absolute value.*** This function shows the absolute value $|x|$ of its *integer* or *real* argument *x* The result type of the function matches the type of its argument.

$abs(-10)$ is 10 $abs(-3.5)$ is 3.500000000000000E+00

Clever use of the absolute value function can prevent some inadvertent program bugs. For example, the following program segment is expected to update a user's savings account balance. Try to spot the bug it contains.

> *writeln* ('How much do you wish to withdraw?');
> *readln* (*AmountWithdrawn*);
> *Balance* := *Balance*−*AmountWithdrawn*;

Suppose the customer enters a negative number, like '−100', as the amount she wishes to withdraw. Instead of being subtracted from her balance, $100 will be *added* to *Balance*! This is clearly a profitable transaction for the customer. The bank, being a spoilsport, should rewrite the assignment statement like this:

> *Balance* := *Balance*−*abs*(*AmountWithdrawn*);

---

* Exponentiation is usually handled on calculators by the y^x key, and in many programing languages by a special exponentiation operator: '**'.

The change keeps a perfectly understandable mistake from ruining an otherwise working program.

The last two arithmetic functions do a job that's trivial on paper, but requires some specialization in the computer.

round(*x*) The rounding function represents its *real* argument, *x*, rounded to the nearest *integer* according to this rule:

> If *x* is positive, rounding is *up* for fractions including and greater than .5, and *down* for fractions that are less than .5.
>
> If *x* is negative, the result is rounded *down*—away from zero—when the fractional part is greater than or equal to .5, and *up*—toward zero—otherwise.*

> *round*(1.6) *is* 2   *round*(1.5) *is* 2
> *round*(−2.6) *is* −3   *round*(−1.5) *is* −2

trunc(*x*) The **truncating** function represents the 'whole' part of its *real* argument *x* as an *integer*. Any portion of the argument that is a fraction less than 1 is truncated—cut off. In effect, the argument is rounded to the nearest *integer* toward zero.

> *trunc*(4.8) *is* 4
> *trunc*(−3.9) *is* −3
> *trunc*(0.22573E+02) *is* 22

> Functions like *round* and *trunc* are called **transfer functions**, because they provide a temporary means of 'transferring' a value from one type to another.

---

round and *trunc* are transfer functions because they let us represent *real* values as *integers.*

Self-Check Questions

Q. Write these mathematical expressions as Pascal expressions. Assume that *pi* equals π.

  a) $8^{9.4}$ b) e^0 c) sine 45°   e) cosine $3.0672^{2\pi}$

A. Answers:

  a) *exp*(9.4∗*ln*(8))   b) 1 (any number to the zero power is 1.)
  c) *sin*(*pi*/4)   d) *cos*(*exp*(2∗*pi*∗*ln*(3.0672)))

Q. Can the *trunc* function be persuaded to round off a *real* value (call it *x*) according to the rules of the rounding function?

A. It can be done, but we have to know if *x* is greater or less than zero.

> *round*(*x*) is *trunc*(*x*+0.5)   if $x \geq 0$
> *round*(*x*) is *trunc*(*x*−0.5)   if $x < 0$

---

* This makes *round*(−*x*) equal to −*round*(*x*).

Ordering Functions

Lest you start to think that computing is all numbers, we hasten to introduce four functions—*pred, succ, ord,* and *char*—that are used to juggle other values. Although we'll find more applications of the ordering functions in Chapter 9 (when we discuss user-defined ordinal types) we'll just relate them to *char* values for now. A bit of background about computer character sets is needed to begin our discussion.

> All of the symbols—letters, numerals, punctuation—that the computer can input or output are considered to belong in a certain order, called the ***collating sequence*** of the computer's ***character set***. Every key on a terminal or keypunch keyboard has a specific place in this ordering.

The concept of character ordering is nothing unusual—kids memorize the alphabet in a certain order, and learn the digits in numerical order. But defining a collating sequence is necessary to clarify some relationships—Does lower-case come before upper-case? Do punctuation marks precede numerals?—we wouldn't normally worry about.

The most common character set-up is the ASCII* (ask'-ee) character set, of 95 printable characters, as well as many 'control', or special characters, that cannot be printed. Control characters are usually used internally by the computer, and we won't worry about them. The standard order of the printable characters is:

```
 ! " # $ % & ' ( ) * + - , . / 0 1 2 3 4 5 6 7 8 9 : ; < = > ? @
A B C D E F G H I J K L M N O P Q R S T U V W X Y Z [ \ ] ∧ — `
a b c d e f g h i j k l m n o p q r s t u v w x y z { | } ~
```

Note that the very first character is a space. Another character set, used on IBM computers, is the EBCDIC** (eb'-sih-dick') set. Although most of the characters are the same as those in the ASCII set, their ordering is considerably different. EBCDIC also begins with a space.

```
¢ . < ( + | & ! $ * ) ; ¬ - / ^ , % _ : # @ ' = "
a b c d e f g h i j k l m n o p q r s t u v w x y z \ { } [ ]
A B C D E F G H I J K L M N O P Q R S T U V W X Y Z 0 1 2 3 4 5 6 7 8 9
```

A shorter set of characters, with only 64 members, is common on the CDC 6000 series of computers.

```
: A B C D E F G H I J K L M N O P Q R S T U V W X Y Z 0 1 2 3 4 5 6 7 8 9
+ - * / ( ) $ =    , . ≡ [ ] % ≠ → ∨ ∧ ↑ ↓ < > ⩽ ⩾ ¬ ;
```

The lower-case characters are the most obvious omissions from the CDC 'scientific' set. Other missing characters include the curly brackets { }; this is why CDC Pascal users must enclose program comments in the alternative symbols (* and *). The space character falls between the equals sign and comma.

* That's the American Standard Code for Information Interchange.
** Extended Binary Coded Decimal Interchange Code.

Several other character sets exist, but they're essentially the same as those shown here. We must issue a caveat before we go on.

> Just because we show these character sets in a certain order does *not* mean that they're implemented in the same way on all systems. Check your computer before you rely on the ordering we've given.

We've used the ASCII character set in this text, because we've found that the combination of upper- and lower-case letters makes programs easier to read (*TaxTableRate* vs. *TAXTABLERATE*).

Although the ordering functions (except *chr*) may take arguments of any ordinal type, we'll confine our examples to arguments of type *char*. The first two functions, *pred* and *succ*, can be used to tell us something about the relative positioning of characters.

pred(x)   The **predecessor** function. If the argument (x) of this function is a value of type *char*, the expression *pred*(x) represents the character before x in the computer's character set.

$$pred(\text{'D'}) \text{ is 'C'} \qquad pred(\text{'6'}) \text{ is '5'}$$

succ(x)   The **successor** function represents the successor to its argument; in this case, the character immediately after the character x represents.

$$succ(\text{'Y'}) \text{ is 'Z'} \qquad succ(\text{'3'}) \text{ is '4'}$$

Naturally, the argument given to either function may be a variable, or any other expression that represents a *char* value. In the examples above, note the use of single quotes to distinguish the *char* constants 'D', '6', 'Y', and '3' from the *integers* 6 and 3, and variables named *D* and *Y*.

Those of you who are inclined to keep a lookout for trivia will recognize *pred* and *succ* as inverse functions—what one does, the other one undoes. What is the effect of this assignment?

$$SomeLetter := pred(succ(\text{'R'}));$$

First the computer finds the character after 'R', which is, of course, 'S'. The predecessor of 'S', naturally, is 'R'; and 'R' is assigned to *SomeLetter*. A slightly (but not much) trickier assignment is

$$SomeLetter := succ(succ(succ(succ(succ(succ(\text{'A'}))))));$$

If our parentheses match, the function call represents the successor to the successor to the successor to the successor to the successor to the successor to the letter 'A', and *SomeLetter* gets 'G'.

ord and *chr*, the other two ordering functions, can also be inverse functions. The examples below reflect the ordering of the ASCII set of characters. Don't forget that non-printing control characters precede the ordinary ones.

$ord(x)$ The **ordinal position** function represents the 'place number' of a value within its entire type. If its argument is a *char* value, $ord(x)$ represents x's position within the computer's collating sequence.*

$$ord('A') \; is \; 65 \qquad ord('0') \; is \; 48$$

$chr(x)$ The **character position** function represents the *char* value in a particular ordinal position. Its argument x must be an *integer* value.

$$chr(67) \; is \; 'C' \qquad chr(57) = '9'$$

It's apparent from inspection that *ord* and *chr* are transfer functions (just as *trunc* and *round* are), and may be inverse functions as well. This is useful, because sometimes we'll want to treat *integer* input as though it were a string of characters instead of a number.

Suppose we try a simple example. Assume that the value of a *char* variable *InputCharacter* is '0', '1', '2', '3', '4', '5', '6', '7', '8', or '9'. How can we convert *InputCharacter* to the *integer* it represents? The obvious assignment is tempting:

$$ConvertedToInteger := ord(InputCharacter);$$

But if you look at the ASCII, EBCDIC, and CDC character sets, the numeral '5' never occupies the fifth position. On the other hand, all three sequences show the digits in order from '0' through '9'. Thus, this assignment solves our problem:

$$ConvertedToInteger := ord(InputCharacter) - ord('0');$$

A test case or two (in particular, '0' and '9'), should convince you that the new assignment does just what we want it to. The trick of testing only the outside cases is called *boundary condition* testing. We assume that if an algorithm works for the highest and lowest numbers, it is well-behaved and will work for all the in-between numbers too.

· : · :

Self-Check Questions

Q. Can you write expressions that use the *ord* and *chr* functions to duplicate the effects of *pred* and *succ* with *char* arguments?

A. Assume that *Symbol* is a *char* variable.

$$pred(Symbol) \; is \; chr(ord(Symbol) - 1)$$
$$succ(Symbol) \; is \; chr(ord(Symbol) + 1)$$

: · . : · . : · . : · . : · . : · . : · . : · . : · . : · . : · . : · . : · . : · . : · . : · . : · . : · . . : · . : ·

* Computer scientists are a little peculiar for (among other reasons) invariably starting counts with zero, rather than one. The initial character in the ASCII set is the 'zeroth' character.

Let's take a brief look at the last group of standard functions. When one of the functions in the first two groups was evaluated, the result was usually *integer, real,* or *char.* The final three standard functions have *boolean* results. They indicate whether some situation is *true* or *false.*

For example, the function call *odd*(*Number*) represents the *boolean* value *true* or *false,* depending on whether the variable *Number* represents an odd or an even *integer.*

The other two functions are used when we're reading input into a program—*eoln* stands for 'end of line', and *eof* means 'end of file'. For example, if we weren't sure how much data a program was supposed to get, we could tell the computer to keep reading input until either *eoln* or *eof* was *true,* i.e. until it was at the end of an input line, or had exhausted the entire 'file' of input data. We'll start to use *boolean* values in Chapter 6, and learn about *eof* and *eoln* in Chapter 7.

THERE'S NO RECIPE FOR A PERFECT PROGRAM. A dollop of variables and a dash of comments are proper ingredients, but good programing (like good cooking) takes talent that doesn't come with the cookbook. The instructors at restaurant schools who realize this begin their courses by teaching prospective chefs the Zen of boiling water or breaking eggs. We, in turn, will introduce the finer points of programing by considering the many ways of naming a variable.

We'll begin with the programing equivalent of making ice cubes—we'll write a program that takes a circle's diameter and computes its circumference. Only one algorithm really makes sense—get the facts, use the circumference formula, and print the results.

> *Request information*
> *Perform calculations*
> *Print output*

A working program is barely longer than the algorithm:

program *C* (*input, output*) ; **var** *X,Y: real;*
begin *readln* (*X*) ;   *Y* := 3.14∗*X*; *writeln* (*Y*) **end.**

Simple as program *C* is, it's unacceptable because of poor style. The identifiers we've chosen, and the way the program is laid out, violate a basic precept of good programing.

> **The Golden Rule of Style**
>
> A program should be as easy for a human being to read and understand as it is for a computer to execute.

Now, William Shakespeare ("A rose, by any other name, would smell as sweet.") and Gertrude Stein ("A rose is a rose is a rose.") didn't think names were especially important. Computers agree with them entirely, because as long as an identifier is formed in accordance

Boolean Functions

**2-3
Focus on Programing: Constants, Style, and Elegance**

with Pascal's syntax rules, anything goes. However, Abbott and Costello knew better, as we've shown in a selection from their famous routine *Who's On First*? A name can carry a tremendous amount of information (or misinformation), and identifiers should be as meaningful as possible.

For example, suppose that a program does a series of geometry calculations. We *could* have a variable declaration like:

var *a, b, c, d, e, f, g*: *integer*;

But contrast that with:

var *area, base, circumference, depth, elevation, frustum, girth*: *integer*;

The second set of identifiers is **mnemonic** (nih-mahn'-ick). Every identifier is a memory aid that clarifies the purpose of each variable.

One might argue that it's easy to remember the meanings of shorthand variable names (like *a*, *b*, and *c*) in a brief program. Unfortunately, although computers never forget, people do. In time, you'll have occasion to dig up a program written weeks or months earlier, and try to rewrite it, or include it in a larger program. You may find to your dismay that convenient shorthands have turned into unbreakable codes.

Furthermore, although *you* may know what your shorthand means, nobody else does. If your program won't work, the person you ask for help *has to be able to figure out what's going on in the program.* Imagine yourself in the position of an instructor or manager inundated with hordes of buggy programs filled with variables named *x, y* and *z*!

> You're much more likely to get help if you use meaningful, self-explanatory variable names. Be sure that your identifiers mean something to *people* as well as to computers.

Mnemonic names can also be given to values, by defining them as **constants.** Constant definitions belong in a program's **definition part**, which comes right before the declaration part.

> *program heading*
> *definition part*
>   *constant definitions*
> *declaration part*
>   *variable declarations*
> *statement part*

> The constant definition part begins with the reserved word **const***. Then comes each constant's identifier, an equals sign, and its value. A semicolon separates successive definitions.

---

* This is Pascal's shorthand for *constant*, just as **var** is an abbreviation of *variable.*

(Lou Costello is considering becoming a ballplayer. Bud Abbott wants to make sure he knows what he's getting into).

Abbott: Strange as it may seem, they give ball players nowadays very peculiar names.

Costello: Funny names?

Abbott: Nicknames, nicknames. Now, on the St. Louis team we have Who's on first, What's on second, I Don't Know is on third—

Costello: That's what I want to find out. I want you to tell me the names of the fellows on the St. Louis team.

Abbott: I'm telling you. Who's on first, What's on second, I Don't Know is on third—

Costello: You know the fellows' names?

Abbott: Yes.

Costello: Well, then who's playing first?

Abbott: Yes.

Costello: I mean the fellow's name on first base.

Abbott: Who.

Costello: The fellow playin' first base.

Abbott: Who.

Costello: The guy on first base.

Abbott: Who is on first.

Costello: Well, what are you askin' me for?

Abbott: I'm not asking you—I'm telling you. Who is on first.

Costello: I'm asking you—who's on first?

Abbott: That's the man's name.

Costello: That's who's name?

Abbott: Yes.

~ ~ ~ ~ ~ ~

Costello: When you pay off the first baseman every month, who gets the money?

Abbott: Every dollar of it. And why not, the man's entitled to it.

Costello: Who is?

Abbott: Yes.

Costello: So who gets it?

Abbott: Why shouldn't he? Sometimes his wife comes down and collects it.

Costello: Who's wife?

Abbott: Yes. After all, the man earns it.

Costello: Who does?

Abbott: Absolutely.

Costello: Well, all I'm trying to find out is what's the guy's name on first base?

Abbott: Oh, no, no. What is on second base.

Costello: I'm not asking you who's on second.

Abbott: Who's on first!

~ ~ ~ ~ ~ ~

Costello: St. Louis has a good outfield?

Abbott: Oh, absolutely.

Costello: The left fielder's name?

Abbott: Why.

Costello: I don't know, I just thought I'd ask.

Abbott: Well, I just thought I'd tell you.

Costello: Then tell me who's playing left field?

Abbott: Who's playing first.

Costello: Stay out of the infield! The left fielder's name?

Abbott: Why.

Costello: Because.

Abbott: Oh, he's center field.

Costello: Wait a minute. You got a pitcher on the team?

Abbott: Wouldn't this be a fine team *without* a pitcher?

Costello: Tell me the pitcher's name.

Abbott: Tomorrow.

~ ~ ~ ~ ~ ~

Costello: Now, when the guy at bat bunts the ball—me being a good catcher—I want to throw the guy out at first base, so I pick up the ball and throw it to who?

Abbott: Now, that's the first thing you've said right.

Costello: I DON'T EVEN KNOW WHAT I'M TALKING ABOUT!

Abbott: Don't get excited. Take it easy.

Costello: I throw the ball to first base, whoever it is grabs the ball, so the guy runs to second. Who picks up the ball and throws it to what. What throws it to I don't know. I don't know throws it back to tomorrow—a triple play.

Abbott: Yeah, it could be. '

Costello: Another guy gets up and it's a long ball to center.

Abbott: Because.

Costello: Why? I don't know. And I don't care.

Abbott: What was that?

Costello: I said, I DON'T CARE!

Abbott: Oh, that's our shortstop!

The syntax chart of a constant definition looks like this:

constant definition

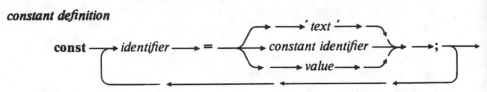

Once it has been defined, a constant's value *cannot* be changed during the course of a program. Note that an equals sign (=) is used in the constant declaration, and not the assignment operator (:=). The assignment operator is only used within an assignment statement.

> **const** *Planck* = 6.63E−34;   {The constant's type isn't given.}
>   *LastLetter* = 'Z';
>   *ThisYear* = 1981;

An important restriction of constant definitions is that they be specific values. A constant declaration can't contain variables, function calls, or arithmetic operations. This means that the value of a constant can't depend on program execution. These:

> **const** *Half* = 1/2;
>   *Root* = *sqrt*(4);   {Illegal constant definitions.}
>   *Rate* = *InputRate*;

are all illegal definitions. They require that a value be computed, or supplied by a variable identifier (like *InputRate*).

Once it has been defined, a constant identifier can be used in place of the value it represents. This is particularly convenient when the constant is a long mathematical or physical value that's used many times during the course of a program. There's no need to use an approximation (3.14) just to lessen the task of typing 3.141592654.

We can easily rewrite program *C* using mnemonic identifiers and defined constants. Although *FindCircumference* is longer than *C*, it can be understood more quickly.

program *FindCircumference* (*input, output*);

> {An interactive program that computes the circumference of a circle.}

const *pi* = 3.141592654;

var *Circumference, Diameter*: *real*;

begin
>   *writeln* ('What is the diameter of the circle?');
>   *readln* (*Diameter*);
>   *Circumference* := *pi**Diameter;
>   *writeln* ('The circle''s circumference is ', *Circumference*)

end.

```
            ↓     ↓     ↓     ↓     ↓
What is the diameter of the circle?
8.25
The circle's circumference is 2.59181393955000E+01
```

A special application of constants is the representation of a whole string of characters—what we've referred to as the text of output statements. The *text constant* must be enclosed by single quotes:

const *TrueLove* = 'Nicole';
      FiveBlanks = '   ';
      LicensePlate = '973 UBK';
      DottedLine = '..........';

Although none of these text constants can be assigned to variables of type *char* (because they all include two or more character values), we can print the values of text constants with output statements.

    writeln ('I wish ', *TrueLove*, ' would call me up!');

     ↓   ↓   ↓   ↓   ↓
  I wish Nicole would call me up!

A constant called *maxint* is predefined in every Pascal installation. It represents the maximum *integer* the compiler allows. You should note its value inside the front cover. *maxint* is the *only* predefined constant.

A common application of constants is to control the output representation of *real* values—the way that *reals* are printed. *Fixed-point* notation is the way that people (and not computers) usually show *reals.* The decimal point is fixed between the 'ones' and 'tenths' columns of the *real,* and there's no exponent. In contrast, floating-point notation puts the decimal to the right of the first digit, and an exponent must change to compensate for the floating decimal. For example:

Fixed-point	Floating-point
1.0	1.0E+00
10.0	1.00E+01
100.0	1.000E+02

Now, we've already seen that any value ready for output can be given a particular field width, or printing size, by the programer. When a *real* value has its output field width set, extra digits are rounded off. However, *real* values get one additional privilege.

When they're output, *real* values may be given a second field 'argument,' also preceded by a colon. It tells the computer to use fixed-point notation, and specifies the exact number of decimal places (the *real's* *decimal accuracy*) that should appear. Remaining decimals are rounded.

In the example below, the field width accorded each expression (100/8) is always ten spaces. However, the result values printed have progressively greater (and therefore better) decimal accuracy.

writeln (100/8:10:1, 100/8:10:2, 100/8:10:5)

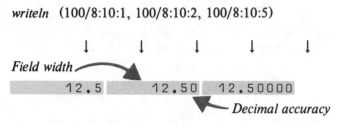

Field width

12.5   12.50   12.50000

Decimal accuracy

Programs that handle money are obvious candidates for fixed-point notation. A program like *SalesTax*, below, needs neither the sometime convenience of floating-point arithmetic (what would you make of a price tag that read $3.9899E+02?), nor the extreme accuracy of computer arithmetic ('With tax, that comes to one dollar and 5.86382547791 cents.').

program *SalesTax* (*input, output*);

{Asks for a price and amount tendered. Computes sales tax and change.}

const *TaxRate* = 0.065;   {The local tax rate—6.5%.}
     Field = 5;
     Decimals = 2;   {Output will be figured to two decimal places.}

var *Price, AmountTendered, Tax, SalesPrice, Change*: *real*;

begin
    writeln ('Please enter the price.');
    readln (*Price*);
    Tax := *TaxRate*∗*Price*;
    SalesPrice := *Price*+*Tax*;
    writeln ('The sales price is $', *SalesPrice:Field:Decimals*);
    writeln ('What do you need change for?');
    readln (*AmountTendered*);
    Change := *AmountTendered*−*SalesPrice*;
    writeln ('Your change is $', *Change:Field:Decimals*)
end. {*SalesTax*}

Please enter the price.
15.75
The sales price is $16.77
What do you need change for?
20.00
Your change is $3.23

Using constants is a matter of programing style. *FindCircumference* and *SalesTax* will both run without constants; in fact, no program needs defined constants in order to work. Yet, programs often need constants in order to be good programs. Suppose that a 2000-line program calculates property taxes like clockwork for a few years, and then—horrors! the tax rate changes. Must we search the entire program to update every instance of the old tax rate? Not if we had made the definition:

$$\textbf{const } TaxRate = 0.003$$

Changing the value of the constant *TaxRate* updates the whole program. Could *TaxRate* have been declared as a variable? Yes, but that would open the possibility of accidentally changing its value within the program. It's also misleading to call *TaxRate* a variable instead of a constant, because declaring something as a variable implies that its value will change frequently, or be obtained from the program's user.

Another motivation for using constants is less obvious. Writing a program is a little like writing an instruction booklet, since just including all the facts isn't enough. They have to be presented in a manner that even a casual reader can follow. Now, comments (between curly brackets) provide a running commentary, called **documentation**, that explains what's happening in a program. Defined constants, like mnemonic variable identifiers, help make a program **self-documenting**. For example, this statement doesn't say much:

$$a := b-5;$$

Better variable names, and a comment, help it out:

$Speed2 := Speed1 - 5;$
   {Find true speed by subtracting the fixed speedometer error.}

But mnemonic identifiers and a defined constant manage to do no-hands commenting—they document *without* additional comments. They're the best of all.

$CorrectedSpeed := IndicatedSpeed - SpeedometerError;$

: :

Q. What types do each of these constants represent?

a) *Width* = 5;
c) *number* = '5';
e) *Date* = '1981';
g) *Mass* = 1.79E−02;
i) *Weight* = *Mass*;

b) *Year* = 1981;
d) *Size* = 5E+02;
f) *Space* = ' ';
h) *TenSpaces* = '   ';
j) *Century* = *Year* **div** 100;

A. Note that text constants don't belong to any Pascal type.

a) integer
c) char
e) text constant
g) real
i) real

b) integer
d) real
f) char
h) text constant
j) invalid declaration

: :

Elegance in
Problem
Solving

An *elegant* solution is one you wish you'd thought of yourself. A program is elegant if its algorithm is simple and concise, yet solves a problem in a clear and complete manner. However, the idea of elegance isn't restricted to programing because it's an attribute of many kinds of solutions, and even some problems. A particularly elegant mathematical problem is the four-color theorem, which even first graders can understand (much to the dismay of the folks at Crayola). It states that any map can be colored with only four colors.

The *proof* of the four-color theorem, which evaded mathematicians for centuries, is another matter entirely. Recently, a team at the University of Illinois came up with a proof several hundred pages long through extensive computer research. Its validity, though, met with resistance from parts of the academic community who felt that the new proof was too long, too unwieldy, too complicated, *too inelegant.*

Now, exercises found in textbooks usually have elegant solutions. In some cases, the problems merely need to be restated in a more elegant manner to be solved. 'Word' problems (that algebra and calculus students universally hate) are a perfect example. The problem is deliberately stated in the most confusing, complicated, and *inelegant* manner possible. For example:

A cyclist is exactly one-third of a mile from home. She is riding toward her front door at precisely 10 miles per hour.

A fly has been traveling back and forth between the cyclist and the aforementioned door at the constant speed of thirty miles per hour, never stopping for rest. As our problem begins, the fly has just left the front wheel of the bicycle, and is heading toward the rider's door. When it reaches the house, the fly will turn back and fly to the bicycle again. It will continue this backward-and-forward motion between the onrushing cyclist and her door until it meets a horrifying death as they crash head on!

The question is this: How far will the fly travel before it dies?

Try to solve the problem before you read on.*

As you might expect, understanding the manic behavior of the fly (to say nothing of the suicidal tendencies of the cyclist) isn't a crucial part of the problem's solution. Furthermore, although the distance flown by the fly could be found by summing some ridiculous infinite geometric series, that isn't necessary either. Instead, we have to determine how long it takes the bicycle to reach the door—*Time.* Then, since we know the *Rate* at which the fly is flitting (30 *mph*), we can use everybody's favorite formula—*Distance* equals *Rate* times *Time*—to find out how far the fly goes.

---

* We grant that some readers, mindful of Zeno's paradox, will maintain that the fly never gets crushed at all.

Since the bike travels at 10 miles per hour, it will plow into the front door (and the fly) in two minutes, or 1/30 of an hour.

$$Distance = Rate * Time$$
$$1 \ mile = 30 \ mph * 1/30 \ hour$$

The fly travels exactly one mile. Had the problem been stated like this from the beginning—if a fly travels at 30 *mph*, how far will it go in 2 minutes?—there would have been no problem at all. It has an elegant solution—a simple, clear restatement.

A word that's used to describe the process of restating a problem is *massage*. Massaging a problem means rearranging its facts to get a better idea of what we're trying to find out, and to get rid of the clutter of irrelevant information. Indeed, learning how to massage problems is essentially the content of a high-school algebra course. A classic example of a problem that can be massaged into an elegant solution is:

Add together all the numbers from 1 through 100.

Again, try to solve this problem before you read on.

At this point, we see four possible solutions:

1. Write a program that contains an incredibly long assignment statement (or a hundred shorter ones).

2. Be adventurous! Look inside the cover for a control structure that looks appropriate, and learn how to use it.

3. Give up computer science, and go back to work on the novel. (Quitting is *always* a solution.)

4. Be clever.

It happens that this particular problem was given to the mathematician Carl Friedrich Gauss in 1786, when he was 9. His teacher, attempting to keep the class busy one morning, told them to add a long series of numbers. He had barely finished giving the assignment when Gauss stood up and handed in his slate, which contained a single number—the correct answer. How did he do it? Once more, try to figure it out if you haven't already.

What Gauss did involved looking *at* the *problem*, as well as *for* the *solution.* Were we to take the problem statement at face value, we'd be stuck trying to figure out a way to add a long sequence of numbers one at a time.

$$1 + 2 + 3 \cdots + 98 + 99 + 100$$

We might be able to think of a way of adding them quickly and painlessly—especially if we figured out how to use one of the control structures we'll meet a few chapters hence—but we'd still be adding them one by one.

But suppose that we massage the problem as Gauss did:

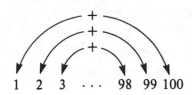

When numbers are added in this fashion, the sum is always 101. How many similar pairs are there? Well, every number from 1 to 50 has a matching number between 100 and 51, so there must be 50 pairs. Thus, the sum of all the numbers from 1 to 100 is:

$$50 * 101$$

or 5050.

Granted, this is the sort of trick—easy to understand, but not so easy to think up—that students dread. Nonetheless, taking the first step toward elegance by wondering 'Is there a formula that might solve this problem, *and others like it*?' isn't hard at all. Don't just follow the old problem-solving saw 'State the problem.' Instead, state the facts, and see if you can massage them into a problem that you *do* know how to solve.

Self-Check
Questions

Q. What *is* the formula for adding up a series of numbers?

A. The formula for an even number of positive numbers is easy—if the series starts with 1. It's

$$(first + last) * (last/2)$$

If the series starts at a number greater than 1, the formula is more complicated. The value of a single pair stays the same—*first + last*—but how many pairs will there be? And is it possible a single number will be stranded in the middle? Good luck in finding the answer.

2-4
Antibugging
and
Debugging

AT THIS POINT MOST PEOPLE START TO make hopeful (but illegal) additions to Pascal. A common bug is the self-initializing variable. (If constants are initialized when they're declared, why not variables?) For example:

```
var Trial:=7 : integer;
    Test: char;  Test:='A';
    BigNumber:=124E+63;
```

These are all nice tries, but none of them is legal Pascal, and none of them may be used in a program. Variables are only given identifiers and types when they're declared. Their values must be assigned with the program. Confusion probably arises because constants are just the reverse—they're given values when they're defined, and they *can't* be assigned to. Don't forget that constants are defined with an equals sign =, while variables are assigned values with the assignment operator :=.

Another popular (and unauthorized) extension to Pascal is the chain assignment. For example:

$$A:=B:=C:=D:=E:=0;$$

It seems like a good idea, and is certainly a fast way to initialize several variables to a single value. (In fact, it's even allowed in some other programing languages.) Unfortunately, the chain assignment *isn't* part of Pascal, and assignments must be made one at a time.

$$A:=0; \quad B:=0; \quad C:=0; \quad D:=0; \quad E:=0;$$

The notion of type can cause trouble. A variable may represent an *integer* value, or a *real* value, or a *char* value, or a *boolean* value, but it may never represent values of the wrong type. Similarly, operators and functions usually are restricted to operands or arguments of some particular type. Many type problems are picayune; for example, this expression:

$$4.0 \textbf{ div } 2$$

is illegal because both operands of **div** must be *integer*. Steer clear of these minor problems by remembering:

1. If **div** or **mod** are used in an expression, all of the values in the expression must be *integer*.

2. If /, or any *real* values are used in an expression, the result of the expression will be a *real* value.

3. The value a function call represents sometimes belongs to a different type than the function's argument.

4. The types of a variable, and a value being assigned to it, must be identical.

As we pointed out earlier, the fourth rule is a bit inconsistent. An *integer* value may be assigned to a *real* variable, but the opposite is not allowed. An ounce of prevention—using arithmetic values of the proper type rather than relying on Pascal's largesse—is worth a lot of program debugging.

Type checking may seem like an awful nuisance now, but it's an important built-in antibugging feature of Pascal. In languages that aren't strongly 'typed,' it's possible to accidentally read, say, a *char* value into an *integer* variable. Suppose, for instance, that a prompt reads *'Please enter a number'*, and the program user enters 'TEN' instead of '10'. Since characters are held as numbers within the computer, it's conceivable that 'TEN' would be read in as a very large number.

Pascal deals with this potential problem by performing run-time checks on data as it is entered, while the program is running. If data of the wrong type is encountered, a run-time error occurs, and the program halts—it crashes with an error message like:

```
ABNORMAL TERMINATION - -
IMPROPER DATA FOUND AT INTEGER READ, LINE 27
```

A crash, in this case, is the lesser of two evils. It's preferable to have the program stop running than to have it produce results that are absurd, but may not be caught. Cases where this did *not* happen— $200,000 auto license fees, and doghouses with million-dollar property tax evaluations—are well known.*

Another kind of run-time error is caused by improperly using the standard functions. The most obvious is an attempt to find the *real* square root of a negative number—it simply isn't defined. The program crashes with a message like:

```
ABNORMAL TERMINATION - -
ARGUMENT OF "SQRT" MUST BE POSITIVE
```

Certain other undefined values may or may not provoke run-time errors. For example, the character before the first character, *pred*(*chr*(0)), may turn out to be the *last* character in the computer's collating sequence. This means that we can't always rely on a run-time error to stop a program for us.

Using a function call as a statement, instead of as the representation of a value, is a common error. If we want to set *Side* equal to its own square root, this won't work:

> *readln* (*Side*);
> *sqrt*(*Side*);

Instead, we have to make a full assignment:

> *readln* (*Side*);
> *Side* := *sqrt*(*Side*);

Run-time errors are not restricted to problems of type. A shortage of program data can cause a crash as well, particularly in batch programs. An error message along the lines of:

```
ABNORMAL TERMINATION - -
ATTEMPT TO READ PAST END OF FILE
```

implies that the user did not provide enough data for her program— there are more *reads* and *readlns* than input values. Although we know that data comes from punched cards, tapes, or keyboards, the computer thinks that its input comes in a 'file.' If the program tries to read in information after its file of data is exhausted, the program crashes. Incidentally, a special control character is usually set aside to mark the end of an input file. As a result, hitting the wrong key on a keyboard will occasionally cause a crash.

---

* In Chapter 9 we'll see how to extend the idea of type checking even further. An *integer* variable, for example, can be declared in a way that limits its possible values—we might restrict it to representing integers between 0 and 100. Attempting to give it a value outside of these bounds (or a value of a different type) causes a run-time error.

Summary

The *assignment* statement, and the use of *expressions* to represent values, were the main topics of this chapter. By using the *assignment operator* (:=) we're able to assign a value to a variable. This value is obtained by *stating*, and having the computer evaluate, an expression. The variable on the left-hand side of the assignment statement 'gets' the result value.

There are some rules to follow in stating expressions. First is the rule of *operator precedence*. Expressions are evaluated according to an operator *hierarchy*. In this scheme, divisions and multiplications are carried out before additions and subtractions. However, parentheses can be used to change the order of evaluation. Good programing practice dictates that parentheses be used to clarify the order of evaluation of an expression, even if the parentheses don't change the order (and thus, are redundant).

Operators have types, just as values do, and an operator must have operands of the proper type. The programer must be sure that the *integer* division operators, **div** and **mod**, are given *integer* operands. *Fixed−point* notation is an alternative method of printing *real* values. The value's *decimal accuracy* is given as an additional argument to *write* or *writeln.*

Values can also be computed in Pascal programs by calling the *standard functions,* and giving them *arguments* of the proper type. The entire *function call* represents the result of evaluating the function. Certain functions are inverse functions—they negate each other—while others are called *transfer* functions, and represent the function's argument as a value of a different type.

The Pascal *constant* is defined in the program's *definition* part, right before the variable declarations. A constant can be used anywhere in a program or expression as the representation of a value. However, its value cannot be changed during the program, or computed at the start of the program. The use of constants and *mnemonic* variable identifiers is an important part of programing style. They help make programs *self-documenting*, or self-explanatory.

An effective problem-solving tool is the idea of *massaging* a problem, or restating it in a more easily solved manner. Another idea, called *elegance*, helps gauge the quality of a proposed solution.

:=	**div**	**mod**	**const**	New Pascal
sqr	*sqrt*			
sin	*cos*	*arctan*		
ln	*exp*			
abs	*round*	*trunc*		
pred	*succ*	*ord*	*chr*	

New Terms

assignment statement	*assignment operator*	*initialized*
undefined	*representation*	*stated*
operator precedence	*hierarchy*	*predefined*
standard function	*function call*	*argument*
result	*result type*	*radians*
natural log	*exponential*	*exponentiation*
mantissa	*exponent*	*absolute value*
truncating	*transfer functions*	*collating sequence*
character set	*predecessor*	*successor*
ordinal position	*character position*	*mnemonic*
constant	*definition part*	*text constant*
fixed-point	*decimal accuracy*	*documentation*
self-documenting	*elegant*	*massage*

Self-Test Exercises

2-1   Is this a valid assignment statement? Assume that *Bonzo* is an *integer* variable.

$$Bonzo \qquad : \qquad \qquad 74 \qquad ;$$
$$=$$

2-2   What are the types of these expressions when evaluated?   *a*)   5∗7; *b*)   10/2; *c*)   10.0 **div** 2.

2-3   How could you find the remainder of dividing 55.55 by 7?

2-4   Can variables be negative? Is this a valid assignment?

$$Whole := 77 ;$$
$$Opposite := -Whole;$$

What is the value of *Opposite*? What would it be if the starting value of *Whole* were −99?

2-5   How many levels of precedence are there for the arithmetic operators? Which operators have the lowest precedence? (Disregard unary negation.)

2-6   The square root function *sqrt* may be given either an *integer* or a *real* argument. What is the type of its result value in the calls *sqrt*(25) and *sqrt*(2.5E01)?

2-7   Does Pascal have a standard constant *pi*? What are its other standard constants?

2-8   What is Pascal's exponentiation operator? How can we raise *a* to the *b* power?

2-9   How can you find the cube root of a number in Pascal? The *n*th root?

2-10   Is −*abs*(*SomeNumber*) positive or negative?

2-11   How can you tell if the upper-case characters in your computer's character set are *contiguous* (which means they have no other characters interspersed with them)?

2-12   Pascal has only four standard types. However, we can define constants that are not *real, integer, char,* or *boolean.* What are these constants called?

2-13   In making numerical calculations, it's a good idea to remember that the result of a sequence of operations is no more accurate than its least accurate operand. Suppose that this assignment appears in a Pascal program. What should a statement to output the value of *Product* look like?

$$Product := 1.20775E-03 * 9.87 + 1.6666 / 9.0;$$

2-14 How many statements are required to initialize five different *integer* variables?

2-15 Suppose that *Letter* and *Number* are *char* and *integer* variables. Given an input statement:

$$read\ (Number,\ Letter)\ ;$$

show input that makes *Number* equal 73, and *Letter* equal 'T'.

2-16 In consideration of all the business programs that compute retail prices, write a consumer's program that figures out wholesale prices. Given a purchase price, it should deduct a 40% markup, and a 5.5% sales tax. Be sure to make the deductions in the right order.

More Exercises

2-17 Nowadays people often give credit card numbers over the phone. To stop people from making up numbers at random, credit card issuers embed codes within the number that depend on the number itself. A simple approach is to add the individual digits of the number, then tack on a 0 or 1, as required, to make the number odd. Thus, 49921 would be legitimate, but 52771 wouldn't.

Write a program that computes an add-on letter for an 8-digit number. The letter should be arrived at by adding the four pairs of digits in the number, finding the *integer* remainder of a division by 26, and then determining the character in that position in the computer's collating sequence.

2-18 Write a program that gauges inflation. It should take two prices as input, and print their cash difference, as well as the percentage increase to two decimal places. Then, modify the program so that, given the number of weeks between price quotes, it computes the yearly rate of inflation. Finally, upgrade the program to make it estimate a price a given number of weeks hence.

2-19 Three pairs of assignment statements are shown below. Write three individual assignments that take the place of the three pairs.

$$\{a\}\quad l := a+5;$$
$$l := b-2;$$
$$\{b\}\quad m := a+5;$$
$$m := m*2;$$
$$\{c\}\quad n := 2*n-2;$$
$$n := n\ \mathbf{div}\ 2 - 3;$$

2-20 Here's a little number-juggling program. Ask a user for the year of her birth, and her age. Then double the birth year, add five, multiply by fifty, add her age, subtract 250, and divide by 100. Write the answer out with two digits of decimal accuracy. What is it? Don't forget to use *constants* where possible.

2-21 Write a program to carry out the following chain of calculations: Begin by entering a number. Multiply it by 5, add 6 to the product, multiply by 4, add 9, multiply by 5. Now, cancel the last two digits of the final number, and subtract 1. What have you got?

2-22 The amount of illumination provided by a light source decreases by the inverse square of distance to it. Write a program that lets the user enter the brightness of a light at distance x, then computes the brightness at distance y.

2-23 The common field cricket chirps in direct proportion to the current temperature. Adding 40 to the number of times a cricket chirps in a minute, then dividing by 4, gives us the temperature. Write a program that outputs the current temperature (given a count of cricket chirps in fifteen seconds) to the nearest half degree.

2-24   As electronic stopwatches become cheaper and more accurate, we will no doubt be deluged with impossibly accurate measurements of time. Write a program that takes a time period given in seconds, and prints out the number of hours, minutes, and seconds it represents.

2-25   Since the planet Mercury always keeps one face toward the Sun, Mercurian clocks (called Mercurichrones) are not divided into periods of day and night. Instead, they break each rotation into 15 periods of 40 sub-periods each.

As we join this problem, Ziggy Stardust (just back from Mars) is about to land on Mercury. Suppose that he touches down at 19:56, Earth time. Write a program that finds out the current time on Mercury and the number of minutes in a Mercurian sub-period (you can define these as constants if you want), and then computes the time on Ziggy's 24-hour clock *and* on his new Mercurichrone after a given number of hours and minutes (entered as program data) have elapsed.

2-26   In the future, if there is one, there may be widespread use of electric cars. Naturally, this will render all programs that compute miles per gallon obsolete. Write a program that asks a user for the number of miles per watt (a basic unit of electricity consumption) her car gets, the distance she has traveled in miles, and the amount of time it took her in hours. Print out the distance traveled in kilometers, the amount of electricity consumed in kilowatts, her car's mileage in kilowatts per kilometer, and her average speed in kilometers per minute.

2-27   The field width specification given in a output statement can be an expression as well as a constant *integer* value. This is convenient because it lets us compute field widths when programs are run, as well as when they're written.

Write a program that prints the pattern shown below. Note that space is always evenly distributed between the symbols of any given line. The program user should enter the width of a piece of paper and the output symbol. The first and last symbols of the widest lines of the pattern should be against the edge of the page.

```
         *                    *                    *
                              *
                    *                   *
         *          *                   *            *
                    *          *                *
```

2-28   Write a program that accepts a number between 7 and 9 digits long, then echoes the same number written in a conventional way, i.e. with commas between every three digits from the right.

2-29   In many states, license plates contain three letters and three numbers, e.g. UBK 878. Naturally, license plates are manufactured in sequence, starting with AAA 000, AAA 001, and going to AAB 000, and eventually ZZZ 999. Write a program that takes as input a license plate's numbers and letters, and outputs the contents of the next plate to be manufactured.

2-30   Expressing a fraction as a decimal is easy—we just divide. But what about reversing the process? How can we express a decimal as a fraction? (We'll assume that the decimal is *rational* and *repeating*, like 0.333... or 0.646464..., and *can* be written as a fraction.) It can be done with the following formula:

Fraction = the repeating portion / 1 — the ratio between repeats

In the examples above, .3 and .64 are the 'repeating' portions, and the ratios between repeats are .1 and .01. We're really thinking about the numbers as sums—that is:

.3	.64
.03	.0064
.003	.000064
.333...	.646464...

Write a program that asks for the repeating portion of a decimal, and the ratio between repeats, and then tries to express the decimal as a fraction. Improve the program to *a*) show the fraction as a division of *Integers*; *b*) allow the decimal to have a 'whole' portion to the left of the decimal. What do we mean when we say that the computer's method of representing *real* values may make certain decimal fractions impossible to attain?

2-31   Extend your personal high-level computer language to include the definition of constants. Do you want to modify your rule for creating identifiers to allow alternative characters (that might help make them more mnemonic)? What functions and operators do you think your language should have?

3

Procedures for Problem Solving

Have you ever had a lot on your mind? Well, just how many things were you really thinking about? Two? Five? Ten? Some researchers went to work on precisely this question—how many distinct things can a person think about at once—and came up with an answer, given in the title of their paper— *The Magic Number Seven* (*Plus or Minus Two*).* On the average, people can keep 7 (plus or minus 2) facts in their active minds at any one time.

Does this cause problems in life? You bet it does! How long could you remember this sequence of numbers?

1 0 3 4 4 8 4 8 0 4 1 5 5 2 4 6 6 7 8

Fortunately, people automatically come up with a way around the '7' limit by dividing long sequences into shorter number units.

103-44-8480   (415) 524-6678

It's not hard to recognize these as Social Security and telephone numbers.

Procedures, the topic of this chapter, divide programs into action units. Most programing languages have some facility for creating procedures, but the concept is especially important in Pascal. A procedure is written to solve one part of a problem, and a program is a series of *calls* of different procedures. Each procedure call activates one segment of the complete program. Section 3-1 is devoted to a discussion of creating and using procedures.

Programers use procedures to make programs easier to write and understand. In section 3-2, we'll see how a problem-solving method called *stepwise refinement* tends to break a program into procedures almost automatically. We'll also find that procedures are an important part of *top-down design*.

This chapter isn't long, but it is important. It's the beginning of our study of *programing*, as opposed to mere coding. Dig in.

* G.A. Miller, Psych. Review 1963, No. 2, 3/56, pp. 81—97.

What's top-down design? If you've ever tried to 'stay on top' of a problem....

3-1
How to Program with Procedures

AS ALWAYS, AN EXAMPLE. Program *Reverse* contains three *procedures—GetTheNumbers*, *SwitchThem*, and *PrintTheResults*. Each one is similar in construction to a small Pascal program.

program *Reverse* (*input, output*);

　{Reverses two input *integers.*}

const *PrintSpace* = 1;　　　　{Provide the minimum output field.}

var *First, Second*: *integer*;

procedure *GetTheNumbers*;　　　{Orients the program user.}
　begin
　　writeln ('This program reverses two integers.');
　　writeln ('What is the first number?');
　　readln (*First*);
　　writeln ('What is the second number?');
　　readln (*Second*)
　end; {*GetTheNumbers*}

procedure *SwitchThem*;　　{Swaps the values of two global variables.}
　var *Temporary*: *integer*;
　begin
　　Temporary := *First*;
　　First := *Second*;
　　Second := *Temporary*
　end; {*SwitchThem*}

procedure *PrintTheResults*;　　　{Prints the reversed values.}
　begin
　　write ('In reversed order, the two numbers are ');
　　writeln (*First*:*PrintSpace*, ' and ', *Second*:*PrintSpace*, '.')
　end; {*PrintTheResults*}

begin {The main program, *Reverse*}
　GetTheNumbers;
　SwitchThem;　　　　{Three procedure calls}
　PrintTheResults
end. {*Reverse*}

```
      ↓      ↓      ↓      ↓      ↓
This program reverses two integers.
What is the first number?
27
What is the second number?
-935
In reversed order, the numbers are -935 and 27.
```

　　Procedures divide large programs into segments that are easier to read, write, and understand. They are **subprograms** that cannot be run on their own, but do part of the work of **main** programs. The actions of a procedure are given as a **procedure declaration**, in the last part of the main program's declaration part. We've shaded the procedure declarations in program *Reverse*, and show where they go in this all-purpose outline:

> *program heading*
> *definition part*
> > *constant definitions*
>
> *declaration part*
> > *variable declarations*
> > *procedure declarations*
>
> *statement part*

> The occurrence of a procedure name in the statement part of a program or subprogram is a ***call*** of that procedure. A procedure call is a statement that instructs the computer to execute (carry out) the statements contained in the procedure declaration.

A procedure can be called any number of times during a program. After the procedure's action is completed, the program moves on to the statement (if any) that follows the procedure call. Procedure calls generally appear in the main program's statement part (although one procedure may also call another).

As the statement part of *Reverse* shows, procedure calls make a program's action quite easy to follow. Thus, procedures are an important tool of programing style.

> **begin** {The main program, *Reverse.*}
> > *GetTheNumbers*;
> > *SwitchThem*;
> > *PrintTheResults*
>
> **end.** {*Reverse*}

The format of a procedure declaration is almost exactly like that of an ordinary program. We can define constants, and declare variables and more subprograms, within a procedure. (In a few pages we'll sort out some rules for telling main and subprogram identifiers apart.) Dissimilar features are:

1. The subprogram heading. Procedures begin with the reserved word **procedure**, instead of **program**.

2. The subprogram's end. Subprogram declarations are followed by semicolons, because a period is only used to mark the end of a main program.

No *input, output* information is required in the procedure heading—the main program handles all that. After the heading, the subprogram proceeds with its definitions, declarations, and statements, just as though it were a regular program. (After reading this chapter, you may want to consult Chapter 5, to learn about uses of the procedure heading.)

Since their syntactic differences are minimal, it's awfully easy to turn programs into procedures, and vice versa. *Chorus*, below, is an output procedure that's much like our first program.

```
procedure Chorus;

    begin
        writeln ('Oh, I don''t care too much for Army life!');
        writeln ('Gee Mom, I wanna go back where the roses grow');
        writeln ('But they won''t let me go home.')
    end; {Chorus}
```

It's not hard to picture *Chorus* being called several times in a larger program.

```
program Song (output);

    {Calls a single procedure more than once.}

procedure Chorus;

    begin
        writeln ('Oh, I don''t care too much for Army life!');
        writeln ('Gee Mom, I wanna go back where the roses grow');
        writeln ('But they won''t let me go home.')
    end; {Chorus}

begin {Song}
    writeln ('They say that in the Army, the coffee''s mighty fine.');
    writeln ('It''s good for cuts and bruises, and tastes like iodine.');
    Chorus;        {This is a call to procedure Chorus.}
    writeln;       {Skip a line}
    writeln ('They say that in the Army, the biscuits are real fine.');
    writeln ('One rolled off a table, and killed a pal of mine.');
    Chorus         {This calls Chorus again.}
end. {Song}
```

```
            ↓      ↓      ↓      ↓      ↓      ↓
They say that in the Army, the coffee's mighty fine.
It's good for cuts and bruises, and tastes like iodine.
Oh, I don't care too much for Army life!
Gee Mom, I wanna go back where the roses grow
But they won't let me go home.

They say that in the Army the biscuits are real fine.
One rolled off a table, and killed a pal of mine.
Oh, I don't care too much for Army life!
Gee Mom, I wanna go back where the roses grow
But they won't let me go home.
```

Q. Suppose that the statement part of program *Reverse* looked like this:

begin *GetTheNumbers*; *SwitchThem*; *PrintTheResults* **end**.

Would *Reverse* still be a valid program?

A. Yes. Remember that a procedure call is just a form of statement. Pascal's syntax is met as long as statements are separated by semicolons, even if several statements appear on a single line.

Local and Global Identifiers

Program *Song* was pleasantly uncomplicated because it contained no constants or variables. However, variables, constants, and procedures from the main program may be used in every subprogram.

> Identifiers that are defined or declared in the main program are *global* identifiers. They can be used everywhere: in the main program, in a procedure, or even in a procedure that's declared within a procedure.

Sometimes the term 'global identifier' isn't specific enough, so we'll refer to global variables or global constants instead. We also have to deal with the prospect of declaring variables, constants, and procedures *within* procedures.

> Identifiers given meaning within subprograms are *local* identifiers. A local identifier has no meaning in the main program, or in different subprograms. It can only be used in the subprogram it's declared in (or in subprograms declared within that subprogram).

A procedure can create temporary, strictly local use variables and constants that only exist while the procedure is being executed. If a procedure is called five times by the main program, its local variables, constants, and procedures (if any) are created and disposed of an equal number of times.

> The word *scope* describes the realm of a variable, constant, or procedure identifier. The scope of an identifier is the portion of a program—called a *block*—in which it can be used to represent a value or action.

A block consists of a definition part, declaration part, and statement part. When we think in terms of blocks, there's no real distinction between a program and a subprogram. Pascal is known as a *block-structured* language, because it is designed this way. Not all languages are block-structured; some have only local variables, some only globals, and some don't allow subprogram declarations at all.

In the illustration below, each block is shown as a box. The scope of a global variable or constant is the entire program—the largest block. A local identifier's scope is limited to the block it's declared in—'its' subprogram, and other subprograms declared within that subprogram. As far as the internal subprograms are concerned, an outer local identifier might as well be global.

program *A*
procedure *B*
  procedure *D*
    begin {D}
      :
    end; {D}
  begin {B}
    :
  end; {B}
procedure *C*
  procedure *E*
    begin {E}
      :
    end; {E}
  procedure *F*
    begin {F}
      :
    end; {F}
  begin {C}
    :
  end; {C}
begin {A}
  :
end. {A}

Identifiers—procedures, variables, constants—defined in :

Their scope is blocks:

Identifiers defined in	Their scope is blocks
program *A*	*A, B, C, D, E, F*
procedure *B*	*B, D*
procedure *C*	*C, E, F*
procedure *D*	*D*
procedure *E*	*E*
procedure *F*	*F*

Now, suppose that one name is used as an identifier more than once. As a result, a local variable, declared in a procedure, has the same name as a global variable declared in the main program. What happens when we use the identifier *a*) in the main program, and *b*) in the procedure?

We don't have to worry about problems in the main program, because local identifiers don't have meaning outside their blocks (the procedures they're declared in). All identifiers will have their global meanings. But stop and think for a minute about what might happen *inside* a procedure if a global and local variable have identical identifiers. Can you come up with a rule that avoids ambiguity between a global variable and a local variable bearing the same name?

One solution would be a prohibition against using an identifier more than once in a single program. However, subprograms are supposed to be portable—easy to transfer from one program to another—and it's impractical to make sure that every variable identifier is used only once. The solution is a rule that decides which identifier takes *precedence* in ambiguous situations.

> The most local identifier always takes precedence. This means that an assignment to a local variable won't change the value of a global variable with the same name.

Program *Music*, below, demonstrates the relative precedence of local and global variables and constants. Naturally, we could devise some horribly complicated examples of the identifier precedence rule. The classic case involves a program that contains many constants, variables, and procedures all named *x, y*, and *z* Our aim, though, is to write programs that make obvious sense, rather than the kind that are obscurely correct.

```
program Music (output);
    {Illustrates identifier precedence.}
const Scale = 'Bass clef ';    {This is a text constant.}
var JohnnyOneNote: char;

procedure Tune;    {Note the identically named local identifiers.}
    const Scale = 'Treble clef ';
    var JohnnyOneNote: char;
    begin
        JohnnyOneNote := 'A';
        writeln (Scale, JohnnyOneNote)
    end; {Tune}

begin {Music}
    JohnnyOneNote := 'D';
    writeln (Scale, JohnnyOneNote);
    Tune;
    writeln (Scale, JohnnyOneNote)
end. {Music}
            ↓   ↓   ↓   ↓   ↓
Bass Clef D
Treble Clef A
Bass Clef D
```

It's good programing practice, as well as common sense, to declare variables and constants locally whenever possible.

> If a variable or constant is only used in one procedure, it should be declared within that procedure.

This makes a procedure self-contained, and helps insulate it from the main program. Bugs in the procedure can be found more easily, and if the procedure works, it can be transferred to another program with minimal fuss.

Procedure identifiers—the names of procedures—also obey the rules of scope. In the scope illustration, procedures *D, E,* and *F* may *not* be called directly from the main program because they are, in effect, local procedures. However, procedure *B* can call procedure *D* because *D* is declared within *B.* Procedure *C* may call either *E* or *F* for the same reason. Furthermore:

> One procedure may call another procedure declared before it in the same block.

Procedure *C* might call *B,* or *F* might call *E* since each pair of procedures is declared in the same block, and in the proper order. However, they may *not* call each other in the reverse order—*B* can't call *C*—for a subtle reason.

Why not? Well, you have to know a little bit about how the compiler translates a Pascal program into machine language. The compiler learns about your program by reading it just as a person does. The translation from Pascal to machine language takes place while the program is being read. Consequently, the computer can't jump ahead to look for an identifier declaration. Identifiers must always be declared or defined before they are used, or alluded to by means of a 'forward reference' to the compiler. (We'll learn about these in Chapter 5.) To avoid problems for now, declare all procedures before other procedures call them.

Self-Check Questions

Q. Is this the start of a legitimate Pascal program?

program *HighlyConfidential* (*input, output*) ;

{Sorry, but we can't tell you what it does.}

var *CryptoXYZ*: *integer*;

procedure *CryptoXYZ*;

{This is even more secret than the program.}
:   *etc.*

A. No. *HighlyConfidential* is illegal because one identifier—*CryptoXYZ*—is used twice at the same level of a single block. It's no more valid than an attempt to declare two main program variables with the same name.

WHAT MAKES PROGRAMS COMPLICATED? Anything that makes books or movies hard to follow is also liable to complicate a program. The length, or the number of characters (or statements and variables) don't create confusion in and of themselves. Instead, the way they're put together causes trouble. Although few people will settle down and study a program as though it were *War and Peace,* programs *do* have plots. A program filled with devious twists and turns will never make the best seller list.*

Programers usually worry about the complexity of our product from the program readers' or writers' point of view, because human time is worth far more than computer time. In the minute it takes you to read this page, a relatively small computer can execute upwards of two hundred thousand statements. Consider this segment of code:

$Numerator := MeanTime + LastDataSequence;$
$Denominator := ln(PerformanceAverage) * HansensConstant;$
$Result := sqrt(Numerator/Denominator);$ etc.

It might be redundant in terms of computer operation (because of the space cost of an extra constant or variable, and the time cost of an extra statement), but it's desirable because it's far more **transparent** (easily understood) than:

$Result := sqrt((MeanTime + LastDataSequence)/(ln(PerformanceAverage)*9.3815));$

Procedures help make entire programs transparent. A program that is very long, or has complex code, may bog readers down with detail. A procedure name actively documents what the main program is doing. The interested reader (and computer) are referred to another section of the program, especially set aside for detailed code.

We usually find that even the simplest programs can be divided into procedures. Programs that figure something out (as opposed to doing bookkeeping) usually incorporate three basic steps: entry, manipulation, and display. First, data is entered by the program user. Second is the computational part of the program, where the data is manipulated, and results arrived at. Finally, the results obtained are displayed. This segment:

```
begin
    GetInput;
    ProcessTheData;
    PrintOutput
end.
```

could serve as the statement part of most of the programs we've written so far.

---

* But books and movies certainly do. The film **The Big Sleep** (from the Raymond Chandler novel) contains a murder even the director, Howard Hawks, never understood.

Stepwise Refinement

We can infer from the last paragraph that it's good to divide programs into procedures when we want to solve problems. This phrasing actually puts the cart before the horse. Dividing a *problem* into smaller parts is good because it makes it easier to develop procedures, and thus, programs.

> Breaking a problem down into more precisely stated subproblems is part of the ***top-down*** method of writing programs. It's called *stepwise refinement*.

What is stepwise refinement? First, a problem is stated as a collection of obvious subproblems in the hope that some of them will be easy enough to encode in Pascal. If none are, the problem statement is refined. Each subproblem is decomposed, and restated as a collection of even more elemental subproblems.

If a problem is particularly truculent, the refinement step may need to be repeated more than once. Eventually, however, the statement of a subproblem will begin to look like the code of a subprogram, and an abstract, English problem will be easy to turn into Pascal. 'Stepwise refinement' is a stilted and unnatural phrase,* but it accurately describes what we're doing—refining a problem, one step at a time, into its most basic description.

What's top-down design? If you've ever tried to 'stay on top' of a problem, you probably have an intuitive idea. Top-down design is a systematic plan of attack on all sorts of problems, rather than a blueprint for programing. The top-down approach calls for working from the general to the particular—from broad problem statements to smaller and more specific ones. Major decisions are made first, and lesser ones are delayed for as long as possible. In consequence:

> A program's algorithm is explored at all levels well before the details of its Pascal coding are dealt with.

The difference between stepwise refinement and top-down design is a little confusing since one encompasses the other. Stepwise refinement is a programing technique that aims at producing a detailed program outline. In essence, it's a protocol for repeatedly refining and tightening the specifications of a program.

Top-down design, on the other hand, keeps the big picture in the foreground. There's more to programing than writing assignment statements. Programs must be debugged and tested. Often they will have to be modified when new design specifications turn up. A program may interact with other programs, and must be put together in a way that allows coherent interprogram connections. Top-down design helps keep these concerns in the programer's mind while the program is being written. As an approach to programing, it *includes* stepwise refinement.

* *Relentless massage* might be better.

Let's look at an example of stepwise refinement. Suppose that a public library wishes to computerize its operations—a fairly ambitious programing project. The first step in cutting it down to size is a basic problem decomposition:

If we've left anything out, we can always backtrack to this step of the refinement. Let's go a stage further, and restate each of the first level's subproblems.

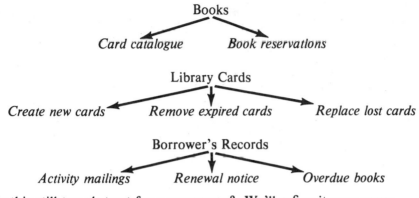

Is this still too abstract for a programer? We'll refine it once more.

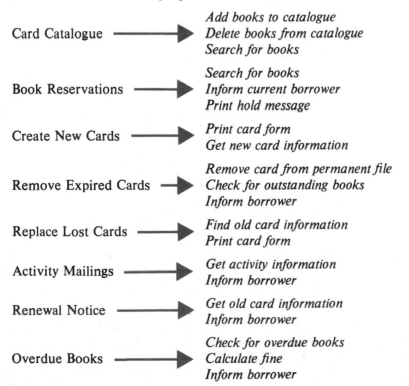

Our refinement starts to pay off as parts of the problem take shape as input and output procedures. As an extra bonus, we find that some of this level's refinements (like the *inform borrower* segments) are similar enough to be written as a single global procedure.

The entire program is still too complicated for us to encode with the Pascal we know now. In particular, we don't know how to store the vast amount of data held in a library's records. (We'll be studying *data structures* in Part Three, starting with Chapter 9.) Still, parts of the program *are* within reach:

procedure *CalculateFines*;

{This batch-oriented procedure reads today's date, and the
book's due date. Both days must be in the current month.}

const *FinePerDay* = 0.05;
var *TotalFine*: *real*;
　　　TodaysDate, DueDate, DaysLate: *integer*;
begin
　　writeln ('Reading today''s date, and the book''s due date.');
　　readln (*TodaysDate, DueDate*);
　　DaysLate := *TodaysDate−DueDate*;
　　TotalFine := *DaysLate∗FinePerDay*;
　　writeln ('The total fine is ', *TotalFine*:4:2)
end; {*CalculateFines*}

↓　　　↓　　　↓　　　↓　　　↓

23 9
```
Reading today's date, and the book's due date.
The total fine is  0.70
```

There are several reasons that stepwise refinement is an important programing method. Most obvious is the strategy's divide and conquer aspect. A formidable programing problem may turn out to be a combination of easily solved subproblems—in like a lion, and out like four or five lambs. Even if a crucial procedure is beyond our abilities at present, we can still work on the program because we've made *independent* subdivisions in the problem. As a result, the final program is *modular*. It's composed of separate pieces that can be written and tested by themselves, and then eventually merged together.

In real-life programing projects, the ability to find the seams of a problem is the earmark of a good programing manager. If several people are to work on a single program effectively, each must have a clearly delineated task. Each individual has to know exactly how 'her piece of the program interacts with the whole. Stepwise refinement slices a problem up in a natural, intuitive manner.

Stepwise refinement also lets a programer plan most of a program *without actually writing in Pascal.* It's easier to think in English than in any sort of computerese, and tackling a problem from the top puts off the nitty-gritty of encoding for as long as possible. Outlining a program in terms of its procedures (and its procedures *within* procedures) provides a transitional phase between words and code. We'll talk more about the concept of *pseudocode* later.

Here are two outlines: One demonstrates stepwise refinement as an approach to programing problems, and the other shows how procedures are part of top-down program design. Notice how smoothly they merge together—the plan for breaking down a problem goes hand-in-hand with the guide for building a program

Stepwise Refinement of a Problem

1. State the problem simply, decomposing it into its logical subproblems.

2. If you can immediately figure out how to encode any of the subproblems, do so. These will be the main procedures of your program. If the subproblems are too complex...

3. Refine the subproblems into smaller, more basic subproblems. Their solutions are written as procedures within procedures.

Top-Down Design and Procedures

1. Write the statement part of the main program first. In a program of any size, this will mainly consist of procedure calls. Each procedure should solve one part of the original problem.

2. The main program's statement part should be simple enough for a non-programer to read and understand, yet detailed enough to give a programer an idea of how the program works.

3. If a procedure is particularly complicated, or does more than one job, it should probably be broken down into sub-procedures.

> Remember that a procedure isn't a rug for sweeping code under! One page (or screenful) of code is enough for any human to try to read and understand. If the procedure is longer, *try to break it down.*

As programers get more experienced, the individual procedures they write tend to become more complex. This is because one's bag of programing tricks becomes more sophisticated—a program segment the novice perceived of as requiring several procedures suddenly seems easy. However, a procedure should never become a *deus ex machina,* or miraculous black box within a program.*

---

* The *deus ex machina* (literally 'god from a machine') ending was a popular dramatic device in early Greek theater. The plots were usually hopelessly entangled by the final act, so the playwright would have a car containing a narrator lowered onto the stage. The narrator, usually a minor deity, would resolve the sticky points, and wind up the play. *Deus ex machina* has come to symbolize a suspiciously providential, not quite fair, intervention.

3-3
Antibugging
and
Debugging

OF ALL THE PASCAL WE'VE PRESENTED SO FAR, only procedures may help prevent more trouble than they cause. The details of writing procedures are straightforward, because they closely follow the rules of writing main programs. Problems that arise from scope (where does a name have meaning?) and name precedence (to what procedure, variable, or constant does a particular name refer?) may be confusing at first, but they can be resolved by trial and error, or sidestepped by renaming identifiers. We've deliberately avoided complicated exercises in procedure writing.

The correct usage of procedures, though, lies at the heart of good programing. One common error is quite serious, even though the program it's found in may execute perfectly well. It is this:

> **begin** {main program}
> *RunProgram*   {procedure call}
> **end.** {main program}

Why bother using a procedure here at all? Does it make the program any easier to read? No, because it doesn't break down the program's action. Does it make the program any easier to write? Again, no, because we're just substituting a long, complicated procedure for a long, complicated program. The example above is merely a sham subprogram that doesn't take advantage of the procedure's benefits.

Procedures can be used as antibugging tools in a variety of ways. To make programs easier to read and understand, procedures should be commented extensively. Mark the start of each procedure declaration with a box that explains its purpose, as shown below.

```
( *     *     *     *     *     *     *     *     *     *     *     *     *
*                     PROCEDURE CLUMP                             *
*     THIS PROCEDURE IMPLEMENTS THE FRUMP, HAT                    *
*     ALGORITHM FOR PLANDATING.  GLOBAL VARIABLES                 *
*     AFFECTED ARE:                                               *
*          HATBAND, BAT:  INITIALIZED;                            *
*          KNEENUMBER:  UPDATED;                                  *
*     PROCEDURE DOUBLE (SEE ABOVE) IS ALSO CALLED.  *
*     *     *     *     *     *     *     *     *     *     *     *     * )
```

Professionally produced code is usually commented like this. In addition to clarifying the action of each procedure, comment boxes make individual procedures easy to locate in a long program listing. In fact, you'll probably find that merely putting a few blank lines between each procedure makes your code more understandable.

When a program is long and has many procedures it's a good idea to *precomment* them at the beginning of the program. Describe the program's action in terms of its procedure calls.

```
(*    *    *    *    *    *    *    *    *    *    *    *    *
*              PROGRAM SCRAMBLER                       *
*    THIS PROGRAM CAN BE USED TO ENCODE OR             *
*    DECODE DOCUMENTS OR COMMUNICATIONS.  IT           *
*    CALLS PROCEDURES:                                 *
*            INSTRUCTIONS                              *
*            CHOOSEOPTION                              *
*            ENTERCODEKEY                              *
*            ENCODE, DECODE  (ONE OPTION)              *
*            PRINTRESULTS                              *
*    ALL PROCEDURES ARE DESCRIBED IN DETAIL BELOW.     *
*    *    *    *    *    *    *    *    *    *    *    *    *)
```

In larger programs, the first page of comments may be as far as the reader gets. An outline like the one below contains all relevant information about the program and its history.

```
(*    *    *    *    *    *    *    *    *    *    *    *    *
*              PROGRAM NAME                            *
*              AUTHOR(S)                               *
*              DATES OF MODIFICATIONS                  *
*              PURPOSE OF PROGRAM                      *
*              DESCRIPTION OF ALGORITHM                *
*              LIST OF PROCEDURES                      *
*              IMPLEMENTATION NOTES                    *
*    *    *    *    *    *    *    *    *    *    *    *    *)
```

Procedures are useful when it comes to debugging. A particularly handy application is a *snapshot* procedure that prints the current value of all program variables. Why would anybody want such a procedure?

....
:   The Second Golden Rule of Debugging   :
: When you're sure that everything you're doing is right, and your :
: program *still* doesn't work, one of the things you're sure of is :
: wrong.   :
....

Frequently, a variable whose value you're certain of actually represents another value entirely—especially if your understanding of the scope and name precedence rules is weak. Snapshot procedures should be used at the first sign of trouble, and experienced programers often build them into programs as a matter of course. Calls for snapshots can be spread liberally around a program during testing, and then turned into comments or edited out (perhaps just by removing punch cards) when the program is operational. For example, this sequence of procedure calls:

GetInputValues;
PrintAllValues;
ProcessData;
PrintAllValues;
PrepareOutput;
PrintAllValues;   etc.

is quickly modified when the program works:

GetInputValues;
{*PrintAllValues*;}
ProcessData;
{*PrintAllValues*;}
PrepareOutput;
{*PrintAllValues*;}   etc.

> Programing in a manner that helps prevent errors is called *defensive programing*.

As we mentioned briefly, a procedure must be defined before it can be called. Thus, if procedure *A* calls procedure *B*, then *B* must be defined before *A*, or within *A*. This rule never causes trouble when procedures are defined in the order that they're used. However, situations can arise where procedures must be defined and called out of order. If you manage to run into this problem in the next chapter or two, congratulations, and please read the explanation of the **forward** procedure declaration in section 5-2. This notice is for your own edification only, as none of the problems or exercises will require this brand of declaration.

Summary

A *procedure* is a *subprogram* that does part of the work of a *main program*. Since a procedure can include variables, constants, and even procedures of its own, there are rules that specify the *scope* of identifiers, and the *precedence* of names. The scope rule gives Pascal a *block* structure—identifiers are known within their defining blocks, but not in surrounding blocks. A *local* identifier takes precedence over a relatively *global* one. This lets an identifier be used more than once in a single program.

Procedures are defined by *procedure declarations*, which come after constant definitions and variable declarations. Procedures are used by being *called*. Subject to the rules of scope, a procedure may be used anywhere, and any number of times, within its defining block.

Using procedures is an important part of the *top-down* approach to programing. They make programs modular, which makes them easier to design and encode. Procedures also make long programs more *transparent*—easier to read and understand. We'll begin to think of the statement part of a main program as consisting of a series of procedure calls, rather than ordinary single statements.

Stepwise refinement is a technique of problem solving that helps produce detailed program outlines. It dovetails nicely with top-down design by naturally dividing a problem into sub-problems. The programer can avoid Pascal coding for as long as possible, and work on small, manageable parts of the code—procedures—one at a time.

Defensive programing puts antibugging into action while a program is being written. Careful commenting usually makes procedures better defined, and easier to debug. *Snapshot* procedures, which print the current value of program variables, should be built into programs to help during debugging.

procedure

procedure	*subprogram*	*main program*
procedure declaration	*call*	*global scope*
local scope	*block*	*precedence*
transparent	*top-down design*	*stepwise refinement*
snapshot	*defensive programing*	

New Pascal

New Terms

Self-Test Exercises

3-1   What kind of definitions or declarations that appear in ordinary program can't show up in procedures?

3-2   Write a procedure that prints your name.

3-3   Suppose that a local and global variable have the same identifier. How does the computer tell them apart in your program?

3-4   What is a procedure call?

3-5   Suppose that *First, Second, Third,* and *Fourth* are *char* variables in ascending order. Write a procedure that reverses their order.

3-6   How could you reverse the digits of a three-digit number?

3-7   How can you tell the difference between constant, procedure, and variable identifiers?

3-8   What is a snapshot procedure? What is its purpose?

3-9   What's a good guideline for the length of a procedure?

3-10   Is top-down design a part of stepwise refinement?

More Exercises

3-11   Product expiration dates are often encoded to discourage consumers from complaining. A common technique is to use letters instead of numbers in dates. Suppose that the White Bread Mfg. Co. Inc. encodes the months as the letters 'A' through 'L', each digit of the day's date as the letters 'Q' through 'Z' and the year as the letters 'Z' through 'A' plus 1970, where 'Z' represents 1, and 'A' is 26. Days that would otherwise have only one digit are preceded by a zero. Write a program that decodes an expiration date.

3-12   Nadine Riverdale is going to get a job selling hot tubs. She can choose between three payment arrangements: *a)* a straight salary of $325 per week; *b)* a salary of $3.50 per hour for a 40-hour week, plus a 15% commission on sales, or, *c)* no salary at all, with a 20% commission, plus $1.00 for each item sold.

Write a program that Nadine can use to decide which plan is best for her, once she gets an idea of how many hot tubs she can expect to sell each week.

3-13   The Klutz Brothers were famous traveling thermometer-makers of the last century. Unfortunately, they had a rather pixyish sense of humor, and a poor understanding of physics. Joachim Klutz would often set the freezing point of his thermometers at, say, 50 degrees, and give a boiling point of 99, or 275. His brother Fred followed the same whimsical pattern.

Write a program that uses procedures to convert the temperature on one of Joachim's thermometers to an equivalent temperature in Fred's notation. Obtain the freezing and boiling points of each thermometer from the program user.

3-14   One difficulty people have with stepwise refinement is deciding exactly how much of a refinement to make at each level. Suppose that you have the problem of giving directions between two places in your town. Write directions for *a*) a lifelong resident; *b*) a newcomer to town; *c*) a foreigner; *d*) a small but intelligent child; *e*) your pet snail.

3-15   Monica Marin is going to go on the television game show Tic Tac Dough. Unfortunately, Monica isn't too familiar with even the rules of ordinary Tic Tac Toe. To help her, we'll write a program that prints completed games. Write a program that outputs a Tic Tac Toe board, asking for the contents of each square as it goes along.

3-16   Write procedures to produce block letters. Naturally, you'll have to do some analysis of the letter characters before you begin. To help out, we've divided the capital letters into the four groups below. Does this help you with your problem? How?

A M T U V W Y   B C D K   H I O X   F G J L N P Q R S Z

3-17   In the game of Hangman, a player tries to guess letters in a secret word. With each wrong guess, the stick figure of a hanging man is partially drawn. When six wrong guesses have been made, the figure is complete, and the player loses the game.

Write procedures to draw the hanging man as he looks after each guess. In other words, you should draw six pictures, with each picture incorporating the previous one. (Hint: Start with a *DrawHat* procedure, then let the *DrawHead* procedure call it, etc. Each procedure should call the procedure defined before it.)

3-18   Ask a user to enter a three digit number whose first digit is greater than its last. Now reverse the number, and subtract the reversal from the original number. Reverse this number, and add it to its unreversed form. What's the answer? Is it ever different? (There are two general exceptions, but you may have to find them by thinking, rather than by computer.)

3-19   If people can read minds, why can't computers? Our first trick lets the computer read a number from our minds. Here's how a human magician would perform the feat: Present a spectator with a large number, and have her circle any digit but 0. Have her read out the remaining digits, one at a time, in any order. When she's done, the magician names the circled digit.

How does the magician do it? She performs the operation *Number* **mod** 9, and subtracts the answer from 9. This is the value of the circled digit. Why does it work? Well, all depends on the original large number. When the calculation *OriginalNumber* **mod** 9 is performed, the result must be 0. We say that such a number has a *digital root* of 9. We can guarantee that a number's digital root is 9 by a variety of means:

a) Start with a number, rearrange its digits in any order, then subtract the smaller from the larger.

b) Start with a number, add its digits together, then subtract this sum from the original number.

c) Multiply any number by 9.

d) Start with any number, find the sum of its digits, multiply by 8, and add the result to the original number.

e) Start with a number, add two rearranged versions of the same number to it, then square the answer.

All of these operations result in a number whose digital root is 9. Thus, the spectator (or program user) can start with *any* number, and by following the magician's apparently meaningless directions turn it into a suitably magical number.

Revise this problem for the computer. Remember that half of any successful magic trick lies in patter, so be sure to write a talkative program.

3-20   Draft a syntax for declaring procedures in your new high-level language. How can you explain where in a program procedure declarations should be made? Should an extra **end** (or whatever *you* call it) mark the end of the procedure declaration?

4

Taking Control of Execution: **case** and **for**

Have you ever used an automatic bank teller machine? After inserting your bank card and punching in a secret code, you have a choice of transactions—deposit, withdraw, check balances, transfer funds, etc. When you hit the appropriate button, the machine asks for more details, and moves along with the transaction. If you're withdrawing money, it eventually counts out the correct number of bills.

If you've ever gone through this sequence you've run an interactive computer program. The bank card and code number let you 'log on' to the bank's computer, and the buttons you push belong to a highly specialized keyboard. And no matter what language the bank's computer is programed in, it uses control structures similar to Pascal's.

Pascal's **case** structure gives a program the power to choose between alternatives. An automatic teller program would use a **case** structure to decide which procedures—deposit, withdraw, balance, or transfer—to call. The **case** structure lets a single program do a variety of different jobs.

The **for** structure is used for *definite iteration.* It *loops,* which means that it repeats a single action a given number of times. The **for** structure is certainly appropriate for directing a device that counts out paper money.

Section 4-1 explains the usage of the **case** and **for** structures. Along the way, we'll learn about some Pascal details that are often confusing to beginning programers—the *compound, empty* and *structured* statements. In 4-2 we'll see how *pseudocode* helps stepwise refinement, deal with some longer examples, and discuss the problem-solving strategy called *brute force.* As usual, 4-3 covers potential bugs and how to avoid them.

Brute force implies that we repeat an unsophisticated solution step many, many times.

4-1
case
Structures,
for
Structures,
and Program
Actions

LET'S START WITH AN EXAMPLE. Program *ElectionDetection,* below, uses a **case** structure to take an action that depends on the value of *Year.* Although the program contains four potential output statements (shaded), only one is executed.

program *ElectionDetection* (*input, output*) ;

{Determines how close an election year is.}

var *Year*: *integer*;

begin

    writeln ('What year is this?') ;

    readln (*Year*) ;

    case (*Year* **mod** 4) **of**

        0 : *writeln* ('This is an election year.') ;

        1 : *writeln* ('Last year was an election year.') ;

        2 : *writeln* ('The election was two years ago.') ;

        3 : *writeln* ('The election will be next year.')

    end   {the **case** structure}

end.   {*ElectionDetection*}

```
               ↓        ↓        ↓        ↓        ↓
What year is this?
1983
The election will be next year.
```

> The first line of the **case** structure contains an ordinal-valued *case expression*.* Then comes a list of the **case** expression's potential values (called the *case constant* list) and the proper action to take for each one. The reserved word **end** always terminates the structure. It isn't preceded by a semicolon.

The general form of a **case** structure is:

    case *expression* **of**   {the case expression }

        Value1: *action*;

        Value2: *action*;   {the constant list}

        Value3, Value4, Value5: *action*;

        ValueN: *action*

    end;

Its syntax chart looks like this:

case *control structure*

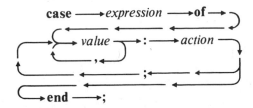

* To refresh your memory, an ordinal value is a value of any simple type except *real*

The **case** expression is frequently just a variable identifier. In *ElectionDetection*, though, *Year* **mod** 4 is the **case** expression. The values given in the constant list must be of the same Pascal type as the **case** expression. Incidentally, in this context the word *constant* means that actual values (like 4 or 'D') must be given. Expressions that represent values can't appear in the **case** constant list.

Sometimes, the same action may be initiated by two or more possible values of the **case** expression. In this situation, the constants are separated with commas:

```
case Score of
    10:  writeln ('Exceptionally Good');
    8, 9:  writeln ('Good');
    5, 6, 7:  writeln ('Barely Passing');
    3, 4:  writeln ('Flunking');
    0, 1, 2:  writeln ('Exceptionally Flunking')
end;
```

As long as no constant calls for two different actions (that would be illegal), the order in which values are specified is irrelevant. This **case** structure is semantically identical to the one above—it has the exact same effect:

```
case Score of
    7, 6:  writeln ('Barely Passing');
    3, 4:  writeln ('Flunking');
    10:  writeln ('Exceptionally Good');
    2, 0, 1:  writeln ('Exceptionally Flunking');
    8, 9:  writeln ('Good');
    5:  writeln ('Barely Passing')
end;
```

> The Golden Rule of Case Constant Lists
> Every potential value of the **case** expression must be specified in the case constant list. It's an error for the **case** expression to represent a value that is not given.

Consequently, it's important to be very precise when prompting for a value that serves as a **case** expression. (You may want to check the quick discussion of sets in 6-2 to find ways of avoiding this error. It's easy to follow.)

We feel compelled to apologize for the stilted reserved words Wirth used when he designed the **case** structure. A more natural effect might have been achieved with, say:

```
when expression equals        {This isn't legal Pascal.}
    value1 do action;
    value2 do action;    etc.
```

Wirth used the reserved words **case** and **of** because they're traditional in programing languages. When you become *PFC*'s (Programers First Class), and design your *own* programing languages....

. . . . :

Q. Which of these values could be used in a **case** structure's constant list?

a) *Time*	b) *Year* **div** 4	c) 5+2
d) ord('H')	e) 'B' *ok*	f) *B*
g) 9 *ok*	h) −4 *ok*	i) *true* *ok*

A. The *integer* values 9 and −4 are valid, as is the *char* value 'B'. Answer *i*,
true, is a *boolean* value, and may also be used. The remaining values— *Time*,
B, ord('H'), *Year* **div** 4, and 5+2—are identifiers or expressions, and may not
be used.

. . . . :

A Pascal Program's Actions

In their original definition and explanation of Pascal, Kathleen Jensen
and Niklaus Wirth pointed out that . . .

> Essential to a computer program is action . . . a program must do
> something with its data—even if that action is the choice of
> doing nothing!*

A Pascal program can take many kinds of *actions*. In this section
we'll look at the different categories actions fall into (listed below) and
see how control structures take advantage of them.

> *assignment statement*
> *procedure call*
> *compound statement*
> *empty statement*
> *structured statement*

An assignment statement is probably the most basic action. Procedure calls are also actions, and thus may be the alternatives of a **case**
structure. This structure:

```
case Character of
     'A', 'E', 'I', 'O', 'U', 'Y':  writeln ('Vowel');
     ',', '.':  Mark := Character;
     'D':  Character := Exception;
     '?':  readln (What);
     '(', ')':  writeln (Character);
     ' ':  BlankHandler
end;
```

controls the actions listed below. Note that since the **case** expression is
of type *char*, its constants are all given in single quote marks.

If *Character* is a vowel, print 'Vowel'.
If *Character* is a comma or period, assign it to a variable named *Mark.*
If *Character* is the letter 'D', assign it the value of a variable named *Exception.*

* Kathleen Jensen and Niklaus Wirth, *Pascal User Manual and Report*, Springer-Verlag
1974.

If *Character* is a '?', read in the value of a variable named *What*

If *Character* is a left or right parenthesis, echo *Character.*

If *Character* is a blank space, call a procedure named *BlankHandler.*

Now, all the actions in the last segment were solitary statements. However, a job that a programer thinks of as a single task (like prompting and reading in data) might require a sequence of assignment statements or procedure calls. As a consequence, carrying out one action may involve executing more than one statement.

Unfortunately, the syntax of the **case** structure specifies that a **case** constant can only be associated with one action. We need to assemble several actions into an indivisible unit.

> In Pascal, we can treat several statements or procedure calls as a single action by putting them between a **begin** and an **end.** This forms a *compound statement.*

In chart form, we have:

compound statement

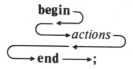

The **begin** and **end** play the role of statement parentheses, by marking the boundaries of an action.

```
writeln ('Enter A, B, or C for the recipe you desire.');
readln (Recipe);
case Recipe of
   'A':  begin
             writeln ('Preheat oven to 550.');
             PrintRoastRecipe
         end;   {Roast Recipe}
   'B':  begin
             writeln ('Ingredients for a Texas Banquet: 1 one-inch steak, ');
             writeln ('1 bottle whiskey, 1 large hound dog.');
             writeln ('Cook the steak for exactly 6 minutes, 45 seconds.');
             writeln ('Now, drink the bottle of whiskey,');
             writeln ('and feed the meat to the hound dog.')
         end;   {Texas Banquet}
   'C':  begin
             writeln ('How many servings?');
             readln (ServingNumber);
             GuestList := ServingNumber;
             PrintDinnerRecipe
         end   {DinnerParty}
end;   {Recipe case}
```

[95]

```
          ↓         ↓         ↓         ↓         ↓
Enter A, B, or C for the recipe you desire.
B
Ingredients for a Texas Banquet:   1 one-inch steak,
1 bottle whiskey, 1 large hound dog.
Cook the steak for exactly 6 minutes, 45 seconds.
Now, drink the bottle of whiskey,
and feed the meat to the hound dog.
```

Note that no semicolon immediately precedes the **end** of a compound statement. Actually, you should just remember that there *never* need be a semicolon right before any **end**, no matter where it appears.

Earlier we said that every possible value of the **case** expression should be represented in the case constant list. A result of this requirement is that some values of the **case** expression will appear in the constant list even if they don't call for an action. The *empty* statement lets these values invoke a harmless inaction.

> A semicolon can indicate an ***empty*** or null statement.

The semicolon itself isn't the empty statement—you should recall that it's Pascal's statement separator. However, the compiler (running rings around itself logically), assumes that every semicolon was preceded by a statement.* In effect, a semicolon creates an empty statement for fulfilling syntax requirements. It acts like a bandage on the Invisible Man by letting us (and the compiler) see a statement that isn't really there.

For example, procedure *ConsiderReadings*, below, delivers a message for most, but not all, of the possible values of *Reading*. If *Reading* has a value of 4, 5, 6, or 7, an empty statement is executed—nothing happens.

```
procedure ConsiderReadings;

  begin
    case Reading of
       0:  writeln ('Instrument test cancelled.');
       1, 2, 3:  writeln ('Check controls--reading too low.');
       4, 5, 6, 7:  ;
       8, 9, 10:  writeln ('Check gauge--reading too high.')
    end  {case}
  end;  {ConsiderReadings}
```

> Control structures and their actions are called ***structured*** statements.
> The compiler treats a structured statement as a single action.

---

* How many statements does **begin** ; **end** represent?

Imagining that an entire control structure is enclosed within a **begin** and **end** helps lead to correct syntax when using structured statements. It's also a good idea to label each **end** by naming the structure or compound statement that's being closed off. We've done this in previous examples.

Program *Scissors*, below, shows how to use a structured statement as one of the alternatives of a **case** structure. The program scores the children's game of *Scissors, Rock, Paper.* Two *char* inputs represent the two players. There are only three rules—Scissors cut Paper, Rock crushes Scissors, and Paper covers Rock. We've written *Scissors* in a way that demonstrates several methods of determining the score.

```
program Scissors (input, output);

    {Demonstrates use of structured statements.}

var FirstPlayer, SecondPlayer: char;

begin
    writeln ('Enter plays for two players--S, R, or P.');
    readln (FirstPlayer, SecondPlayer);
    case FirstPlayer of
      'S': case SecondPlayer of
             'S': writeln ('Scissor ties scissor.');
             'R': writeln ('Scissor is crushed by rock.');
             'P': writeln ('Scissor cuts paper.')
           end {inner case}
      'R': begin
             writeln ('Rock ties rock. ');
             case SecondPlayer of
               'S': writeln ('But rock crushes scissor.');
               'R': writeln ;
               'P': writeln ('But rock is wrapped by paper.')
             end {inner case}
           end; {compound statement}
      'P': begin
             write ('Paper ');
             case SecondPlayer of
               'S': write ('is cut by scissor.');
               'R': write ('wraps the rock.');
               'P': write ('ties paper.')
             end; {inner case}
             writeln
           end {compound statement}
    end {outer case}
end. {Scissors}
```

```
        ↓      ↓      ↓      ↓      ↓
Enter plays for two players--S, R, or P.
PR
Paper wraps the rock.
```

As a reference for the easily confused, here's a model case structure that includes one of everything.

```
case expression of
    value1: assignment statement;
    value2: procedure call;
    value3: ;   {empty statement}
    value4: begin
               statement;   {compound statement}
               statement
            end;
    value5: case
               case constant list   {structured statement}
            end
end;   {of the case structure}
```

Q. What outputs will this data produce from *Scissors*?

   a) **SS**   *b*) **RR**   *c*) **RS**   *d*) **R P**

A. *a*) Scissor ties scissor.
   b) Rock ties rock.
       {blank line}
   c) Rock ties rock.
       But rock crushes scissor.
   d) Note the space between **R** and **P**. Since the space is read as a *char* value, a run-time error occurs. The program has no output.

Looping with the **for** Structure

Why break a tradition? Here's an example of the **for** structure.

```
program ShowFor (output) ;
    {Demonstrates definite iteration.}
var LoopCount: integer;
begin
    writeln ('This program shows what a loop is.') ;
    for LoopCount := 1 to 5
        do begin
            write ('Hello again.') ;
            writeln ('This is loop number ', LoopCount:1)
        end; {for}
    writeln ('All done.')
end.
```

```
         ↓       ↓       ↓       ↓       ↓
This program shows what a loop is.
Hello again.  This is loop number 1
Hello again.  This is loop number 2
Hello again.  This is loop number 3
Hello again.  This is loop number 4
Hello again.  This is loop number 5
All done.
```

The **for** structure's action is shaded. The Pascal phrase

$$\textbf{for } \textit{LoopCount} := 1 \textbf{ to } 5$$

instructs the computer to repeat an action (in this instance, a compound statement) five times.

Pascal uses a rather clever mechanism to keep track of the number of times the action *loops*, or repeats. Instead of giving the exact number of times we want the action to occur, we state expressions that give the initial and final values of a regularly declared program variable.

....
The variable used to control a **for** structure is called the ***counter variable***. It can belong to any ordinal type.
....

> **for** *counter variable* := *initial value* **to** *final value*
> 　　**do** *action*;

When a **for** structure is entered, its counter variable is assigned the initial value. The counter variable is ***incremented***, or increased to the next higher value, each time the **for** structure's action is carried out. When the counter variable represents the final value, the loop iterates one last time, and the program moves on to the next statement.

Using the reserved word **downto** in place of **to** reverses the counting process. For this to work, of course, the initial value must be greater than the final value.

> **for** *counter variable* := *initial value* **downto** *final value*
> 　　**do** *action*;

In chart form, we can show the **for** structure as:

for *control structure*

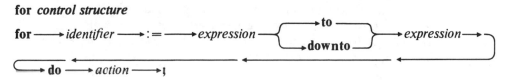

We can also make an auxiliary chart that defines an *action*, as described earlier.

action

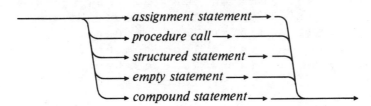

Why use such a round-about method to say how many times the loop should repeat? We do it out of necessity, since the counter variable can belong to any of Pascal's ordinal (counting) types. In *ShowFor*, the counter variable was an *integer*, and its value increased by 1 on each circuit of the **for** loop. The initial value is 1, the final value is 5, and the action is repeated

$$(\textit{final value} - \textit{initial value}) + 1$$

times—in other words, five times.

But suppose we wanted to 'count' by characters? Program *AlphabetSoup*, below, shows that we can use *char* values as easily as *integers*.

> **program** *AlphabetSoup* (*output*) ;
>
> {Prints the alphabet forward and backward.}
>
> **var** *CounterCharacter*: *char*;
>
> **begin**
>
>   **for** *CounterCharacter* := 'A' **to** 'Z'
>
>   **do** *write* (*CounterCharacter*) ;
>   *writeln*;
>   **for** *CounterCharacter* := 'z' **downto** 'a'
>
>   **do** *write* (*CounterCharacter*) ;
>   *writeln*
>
> **end.**

↓   ↓   ↓   ↓   ↓

ABCDEFGHIJKLMNOPQRSTUVWXYZ
zyxwvutsrqponmlkjihgfedcba

Note that compound statements aren't required in these examples, since each **for** structure's action is just a single statement.

Five Golden Rules govern possible values of the counter variable. You may wish to skim the rules now, and reread them more carefully after completing the entire chapter.

....
: 1. The counter variable, initial value, and final value must all :
: belong to the same ordinal type. :
....

They may not be of type *real*, because it makes no sense to talk of incrementing a *real* value—there is no next *real*. This structure:

> **for** *Counter* := 1.0 **to** 5.0 **do** *action*;

is illegal, because *Counter* may not be a *real* valued variable.

....
    2. The expressions that give the counter variable's initial and final values are evaluated when the structure is first entered.
....

Consequently, the number of times the loop iterates cannot be modified from within the loop's action. For example, this segment:

```
Lower := 1;
Upper := 3;
for Counter := Lower to Upper
   do begin
      Lower := 0;
      Upper := 1000;   {Has no effect on the counter variable.}
      writeln ('Hello.')
   end;   {for}
```

prints 'Hello' only three times, instead of one thousand and one times. The assignments made in the shaded segments are valid, but the initial and final values of the loop's counter variable have already been calculated and stored away. Consequently, the shaded statements serve no useful purpose.

....
              3. The counter variable must be locally declared.
....

This means that a global variable can't be used as a counter variable within a procedure. The counter variable must be declared in the procedure it's used in.

....
    4. It's an error to make an assignment to the counter variable from within the loop's action.
....

The counter variable, like any other variable, represents a value within the action of the **for** structure. But although it may be *used* within the **for** loop's action, it may not be *changed* there. An assignment to the counter variable, or an attempt to change its value by reading in a new value, is an error. The assignment in the program segment below is an error, because the counter variable can only be changed before or after the **for** structure.

```
for Counter := LowOdd to HighOdd
   do begin         {Print the odd numbers}
      writeln (Counter);
      Counter := Counter+ 1        {Invalid assignment}
   end;   {for}
```

The 'no assignments to the counter variable' rule is intended to keep programers (and programs) honest. The documentation implicit in the control structure's first line—that it will repeat for a certain number of times—cannot be undermined or invalidated by changing values from *within* the loop.

> 5. The value of the counter variable is undefined on exit from the **for** structure.

In effect, the variable is in the pristine condition it held when it was first declared. It should be reinitialized before being used in an expression.

Q. The first lines of some **for** structures are shown below. How many times do each of these structures call for an action to take place? Assume that these assignments have been made: *LastLetter* = 'F', *LowerBound* := −5, and *UpperBound* := 3.

    a) **for** *Index* := 0 **to** 5 **do**   *some action*;
    b) **for** *LetterID* := *LastLetter* **downto** 'B' **do**   *some action*;
    c) **for** *Pointer* := −5 **to** 3 **do**   *some action*;
    d) **for** *Count* := abs(*LowerBound*) **downto** trunc(4.92) **do**   *some action*;
    e) **for** *Index* := 5 **to** 5 **do**   *some action*;
    f) **for** *BadCount* := *UpperBound* **to** *LowerBound* **do**   *some action*;
    g) **for** *AnotherBadCount* := 3 **downto** 6 **do**   *some action*;

A. The actions of examples *f* and *g* will not take place at all. A 'repetition', by the way, is a single instance of an action.

    a) 6 repetitions.
    b) 5 repetitions.
    c) 9 repetitions.
    d) 2 repetitions.
    e) 1 repetition.
    f) 0 repetitions— *UpperBound* is greater than *LowerBound*
    g) 0 repetitions—3 is less than 6.

IN 4-1 WE SAW THAT A **CASE** STRUCTURE COULD INVOKE a variety of actions. The same actions may be regulated by a **for** structure. The action that immediately follows the opening line of the structure is repeated.

Program *FindAverage,* below, computes the average of a series of numbers. Procedure *GetValues* is called 50 times to read in a number, and update *SumOfNumbers.* Finally, *FindAverage* determines the average value, and prints it out. *FindAverage* is strictly a batch program that does not prompt for input, or echo input values.

```
program FindAverage (input, output);

    {Averages NumberOfValues input values.}

const NumberOfValues = 50;   {Amount of input expected.}

var Counter: integer;
    SumOfNumbers, Average: real;

procedure GetValues;

    var Number: real;

    begin
        read (Number);
        SumOfNumbers := SumOfNumbers + Number
    end;  {GetValues}

begin
    SumOfNumbers := 0;
    for Counter := 1 to NumberOfValues
        do GetValues;
    Average := SumOfNumbers / NumberOfValues;
    writeln ('The average of ', NumberOfValues:1, ' values is', Average)
end.  {FindAverage}
```

$$\downarrow \qquad \downarrow \qquad \downarrow \qquad \downarrow \qquad \downarrow$$

```
23 1E+02 −29.4 836 7.72 740 19 3 0.85 782 8.3 5 893 4 2 89 8.47 923.1
8934 −78.4 93 612 9.23 −9 0.07823 3 83 −21.9 4 1213 63 089 34.7 937
72.09 659 72 95.23 63 9 8.723 −943 912 30 6.75 832 8.312 3 754.3 −8
The average of 50 values is  3.79103064600000E+02
```

A structured statement that is part or all of a control structure's action is called a ***nested*** structure. Nesting is common in Pascal, and is responsible for the way programs sweep across the page from left to right and back again. But rather than being caused by the language, nesting tends to arise from writing programs by stepwise refinement. Such programs are nested because small partial solutions are contained within larger partial solutions.

In program *CountDigits,* below, a **case** structure is nested within a **for** loop. Like *FindAverage, CountDigits* is designed for batch operation. It takes a list of 25 single digits (between zero and nine), and determines how many odds, evens, and zeros it includes. Notice how labeling the **ends** helps clarify what's going on.

```
program CountDigits (input, output);
    {Count odd, even, and zero digits in input.}
const NumberInList = 25;
var ListCounter, Digit, Evens, Odds, Zeros: integer;
begin
    Evens := 0;
    Odds := 0;          {Initialize the 'total' variables}
    Zeros := 0;
    for ListCounter := 1 to NumberInList
        do begin
            read (Digit);
            case Digit of   {Increment the proper total.}
                0:  Zeros := Zeros+1;
                1, 3, 5, 7, 9:  Odds := Odds+1;
                2, 4, 6, 8:  Evens := Evens+1
            end {case}
        end; {for}
    writeln ('There are ', Zeros:1, ' zeros, ', Odds:1, ' odd');
    writeln ('numbers, and ', Evens:1, ' even numbers.')
end.  {CountDigits}
```

<pre>
       ↓   ↓   ↓   ↓   ↓
0 3 8 2 3 8 3 6 9 5 3 7 8 4 9 4 3 8 1 3 9 0 5 7 6
There are 2 zeros, 14 odd
numbers, and 9 even numbers.
</pre>

A more diabolical form of nesting involves nested **for** loops—loops within loops. We'll consider a simple example whose solution can help solve more complicated problems.

Write a program that prints a rectangular pattern of stars of any given width (or number of columns) and depth (or number of lines). For example, the pattern below is six columns wide, and four lines deep.

<pre>
                * * * * * *
                * * * * * *
                * * * * * *
                * * * * * *
</pre>

This kind of task cries out for a **for** structure. Let's try to solve it using stepwise refinement. As we go, we'll write our algorithm in *pseudocode.*

> *Pseudocode* is an intermediate language between English and Pascal. Proportions of each are prescribed by the programer, but the closer to completion the solution is, the more Pascal appears.

Pseudocode lets us describe an algorithm in Pascal-like terms, without being restricted by the rules of Pascal programs. It's far more natural and convenient than the flowcharts programers once employed for drafting programs.

The first step of the refinement is to recognize the pattern as a single line repeated the proper number of times.

> **for** *the correct number of lines*
> **do** *print a single line*

Each line, in turn, is generated by repeating one action—printing a star—as many times as there are columns.

> **for** *the correct number of columns*
> **do** *print a single star*

Joining these partial solutions leads to a nested **for** loop.

> **for** *the correct number of lines*
> **for** *the correct number of columns*
> **do** *print a single star*

Converting the pseudocode into real Pascal is a routine matter. First we'll write the code for a single line, spacing between each star:

> **for** *StarCount* := 1 **to** *ColumnNumber*
> **do** *write* ('* ');

Each line of stars must be followed by a *writeln* that forces output, and puts the printer in position for the beginning of the next line.

> **for** *LineCount* := 1 **to** *NumberOfLines*
> **do begin**
>   **for** *StarCount* := 1 **to** *ColumnNumber*
>   **do** *write* ('* ');   {This prints only a }
>   *writeln*   {single line of stars.}
> **end**;

The completed program is shown below.

```
program PrintPattern (input, output);
    {An interactive program that prints a grid of stars.}
var LineCount, StarCount,        {The for loop counter variables.}
    NumberOfLines, ColumnNumber: integer;
begin
    writeln ('This program will print a rectangular grid of stars.');
    writeln ('You supply the dimensions.  How wide should it be?');
    readln (ColumnNumber);
    writeln ('How deep should it be?');
    readln (NumberOfLines);
    for LineCount := 1 to NumberOfLines
        do begin {outer loop}
            for StarCount := 1 to ColumnNumber
                do write ('* ');  {This is the entire inner loop}
            writeln
        end {outer loop}
end.  {PrintPattern}
```

↓   ↓   ↓   ↓   ↓
```
This program will print a rectangular grid of stars.
You supply the dimensions.   How wide should it be?
10
How deep should it be?
3
*  *  *  *  *  *  *  *  *  *
*  *  *  *  *  *  *  *  *  *
*  *  *  *  *  *  *  *  *  *
```

If the concept of nested loops is hard for you to grasp, you can keep it at arm's length by using procedures. An outer loop can just call a procedure that implements the inner loop. For example, this procedure declaration:

> **procedure** *PrintOneLine*;
>
> > {Prints *ColumnNumber* stars.}
> >
> > **var** *StarCount*: *integer*;
> >
> > **begin**
> > > **for** *StarCount* := 1 **to** *ColumnNumber*
> > > > **do** *write* ('* ');
> > >
> > > *writeln*
> >
> > **end**;   {*PrintOneLine*}

gives us a procedure that could have been used like this in program *PrintPattern*:

> **for** *LineCount* := 1 **to** *NumberOfLines*
> > **do** *PrintOneLine*;   etc.

. . . .

Self-Check
Questions

Q. The two program segments below might have been written in place of the pattern-printing code of *PrintPattern* Unfortunately, each one contains a subtle error that causes incorrect output. What will each segment print?

> **for** *LineCount* := 1 **to** *NumberOfLines*   {First Segment}
> > **do for** *StarCount* := 1 **to** *ColumnNumber*
> > > **do** *write* ('* ');
> >
> > *writeln*;

> **for** *LineCount* := 1 **to** *NumberOfLines*   {Second Segment}
> > **do for** *StarCount* := 1 **to** *ColumnNumber*
> > > **do begin**
> > > > *write* ('* ');
> > > > *writeln*
> > >
> > > **end**;

A. Both segments suffer from improper nesting. The first segment prints the first row of stars correctly. However, the *writeln* is in the wrong position, and forces *every* row of stars to be printed on a single line of output. In other words, the *writeln* does not get executed until all the stars have already been printed out. Thus, the output will be one line of stars, (*NumberOfLines* ∗ *ColumnNumber*) long.

The second segment has the reverse ailment. The *writeln* takes effect after each individual star. This causes the output to be a tall stack of stars, one star wide, and (*NumberOfLines* ∗ *ColumnNumber*) stars high.

:..:..:...:..:..:..:...:...:..:..:..:..:

Let's try using the same techniques of refinement and nested loops to solve a more difficult problem.

> The word *therein* is interesting because at least eleven words can be 'cut' from it, without rearranging any letters. Find them.

A little bit of massage is in order here. Suppose that we start with the first letter, then print the first letter, then the first two, etc. We can easily pick out the real words— *the, there,* and *therein.*

> t   th   the   ther   there   therei   therein

Unfortunately, this is only a partial solution. We have to print the words that start with *h* (the second letter) as well.

> h   he   her   here   herei   herein

More words— *he, her,* etc.—spring to view. Obviously, if we repeat the process and print all the words that begin with the third letter, then the fourth letter, and so on, we'll have printed every possible word. In pseudocode, we have:

> **for** *each letter in 'therein'*
>   **do** *print the subwords that begin with that letter*;

Now, this is easy enough to write in English, but it needs more refinement before it turns into Pascal. The second step of our pseudocode must be broken into two stages—generate a subword, then print it.

> **for** *each letter in 'therein'*
>   **do for** *every subword that begins with that letter*
>   **do** *print that word*

An algorithm is beginning to take shape, and adding a refinement of *print that word* helps even more.

> **for** *each letter in 'therein'*
>   **do for** *every subword that begins with that letter*
>   **do for** *the subword's first through last letters*
>   **do** *print that letter*;

Continuing with Stepwise Refinement

The innermost step is practically written in Pascal. Let's imagine that the letters of *therein* are numbered 1 through 7. A **case** structure will serve to print the letter that corresponds to a particular number.

```
procedure Print;
    begin
        case Letter of
            1 : write ('t');
            2 : write ('h');
            3, 5 : write ('e');
            4 : write ('r');
            6 : write ('i');
            7 : write ('n')
        end
    end;  {Print}
```

We can imagine a paper demonstration of *Print* with *First* equal to 1, and *Last* set to 7:

```
for Letter := First to Last
    do Print;
writeln;
```

↓   ↓   ↓   ↓   ↓
therein

Now that we can print a word, we have to figure out a method of generating subwords. Let's look at the subwords of *therein*, and label each word's last letter:

1	2	3	4	5	6	7
t	*th*	*the*	*ther*	*there*	*therei*	*therein*

Instead of fixing *Last* at 7 (as we did in our paper demonstration) we should let it range from the word's first letter through its seventh. Trace through this code by hand to make sure it works.

```
{Print the subwords of therein.}
for Last := First to 7
    do begin
        for Letter := First to Last
            do Print;
        write ('   ')   {Space between words.}
    end;
writeln;
```

↓   ↓   ↓   ↓   ↓
t   th   the   ther   there   therei   therein

It works quite well, and implements the two inner loops of our early refinement.

do for *every subword that begins with a given*
    do for *the subword's first through last letters*
        do *print that letter;*

All that's left is to figure out a way of supplying this secondary loop with every 'first' letter in *therein.* But wait! We already know how to solve this problem with a **for** loop. Just let *First* represent the current first letter of *therein.*

> **for** *First* := 1 **to** 7
>> **do for** *every subword that begins with the first letter*
>>> **do for** *the subword's first through last letters*
>>>> **do** *print that letter;*

We've already verified our Pascal version of the shaded pseudocode. If you want, you should reread the code of the inner loops, and trace its output for different starting values of *First.* The completed program is shown below.

```
program SearchWord (output);
    {Prints all possible subwords of 'therein'.}
var First, Last, Letter: integer;
procedure Print;
    begin
        case Letter of
            1:  write ('t');
            2:  write ('h');
            3, 5:  write ('e');
            4:  write ('r');
            6:  write ('i');
            7:  write ('n')
        end
    end;  {Print}
begin  {SearchWord}
    for First := 1 to 7
        do begin
            for Last := First to 7
                do begin
                    for Letter := First to Last
                        do Print;
                    write ('   ')     {Space between words.}
                end;
            writeln
        end
end.   {SearchWord}
```

↓	↓	↓	↓	↓	↓	
t	th	the	ther	there	therei	therein
h	he	her	here	herei	herein	
e	er	ere	erei	erein		
r	re	rei	rein			
e	ei	ein				
i	in					
n						

The words we were able to find are:

the   there   he   her   here   herein   ere   re   rein   I   in

Do you think that we could have written program *SearchWord* without using stepwise refinement, or relying on pseudocode? Frankly, a triply-nested **for** loop is enough to frighten the most experienced progamer.

> The way we approached the solution—develop an algorithm, then encode it in an organized way—protected us from having to make massive leaps of faith in our code.

Brute Force and Efficiency

We can use the **for** structure to obtain a solution to Gauss' problem (adding the numbers from 1 through 100) from section 2-3. At the same time, we'll look at a time-honored method of solving problems called *brute force*.

Solving a problem by brute force is not exactly what it sounds like. We don't write the problem on a piece of paper, then stomp on it until an answer crawls out. Instead, brute force implies that we repeat an unsophisticated solution step many, many times. The classic brute force solution was the Count of Monte Cristo's plot for his escape from the dungeons of the Chateau d'If.* Did he have a carefully planned route, exact timing, and a diversion set up to distract the guards? No. Instead, he had a spoon, and fourteen years to spend digging himself out. *That's* brute force.

Now, brute force tends to sound like a nasty method of solution, to be eschewed in favor of clever, elegant algorithms whenever possible. Although this is true in an abstract sort of way, real-life considerations make brute force methods a natural part of everybody's problem-solving repertoire. Suppose, for example, that you have to find out the number of distinct two-letter combinations that can be made with the letters *a, b, c, d,* and *e* (e.g. *ab, ac, ad,* etc.). Stop for a moment and figure out the answer.

Of course there's a formula for figuring it out (there's always a formula), but what is it? 5 factorial divided by 2 factorial? 5 factorial over (5-2) factorial? 5 factorial minus 2 factorial? (Or does that have something to so with the formula for permutations?) In the time it takes to figure out the correct formula, we could write out every combination, count them up, and move on to bigger and better things.

Let's get back to the problem Gauss faced. Although he solved it in a rather elegant manner (not surprising, since his only tools were his

---

* As related in *The Count of Monte Cristo* by Alexandre Dumas.

head and his chalkboard), he might have come up with the following brute force solution had he access to a computer. *AddSeries* performs the computer equivalent of 'writing down all the combinations'.

```
program AddSeries (input, output);
var Sum, Counter: integer;
begin
    Sum := 0;
    for Counter := 1 to 100
        do Sum := Sum + Counter;
    writeln ('The grand total is ', Sum:1)
end.
```

↓   ↓   ↓   ↓   ↓

```
The grand total is 5050
```

Brute force is a touchy subject with some programers because of another consideration—*efficiency*. An algorithm is inefficient if it requires more computer time than a comparable, but more elegant, algorithm. Note that we're concerned with the efficiency of *algorithms*, by the way, rather than *coding* methods. Believe it or not, programers used to worry about such questions as which of these expressions:

$$a * (b + c) \quad vs. \quad (a * b) + (a * c)$$

would compile and execute more quickly. The answer varies from machine to machine, of course, and is practically irrelevant in any case. The few milliseconds saved by such coding improvements are insignificant in comparison to savings that could come from improving the underlying algorithm.

Program *AddSeries* is clearly inefficient in comparison to Gauss' single formula solution, in this case by a factor of 100 to 1.* Why bother fooling around with inefficient, brute-force algorithms? We see three reasons.

> Reason 1: Exploring a brute-force algorithm can lead to a better understanding of the problem.

There's a saying to the effect that you don't really understand a subject until you teach it. Why? Because teaching forces you to go through a thorough, step-by-step analysis of the subject matter.

Brute force is a thinking strategy, like any of the strategies we listed earlier. It's used to *expand* a problem, to *separate* it into its constituent parts, to *simulate* the process a machine might use in solving it, to *exaggerate* the amount of repetition that may go into an algorithm,

---

* Indeed, we can make this factor as awful as we desire, by adding numbers up to millions, or even billions!

to *focus* attention on details of the problem or solution that might otherwise go unnoticed . . . the list could go on forever. Sometimes the best way to a clever solution lies in formulating a deliberately unclever answer, and then looking at it, and improving it.

> Reason 2: The real costs of a programing project are not always what they seem. Efficiency is a relative term.

The cost of computer time is only one factor in the price of a programing effort. Human costs—the time, effort, and wages of programers—are usually greater than machine costs, and the gap is widening. This doesn't mean that grossly inefficient algorithms or quick and dirty programing methods should be tolerated. However, the savings that a more efficient method provides may be illusory. A brute-force algorithm is often the clearest and simplest way to do all or part of a job. A more efficient algorithm may exist, but it may not be cost-beneficial to discover it. Furthermore, an 'improved' algorithm might make the final program more complicated and difficult to understand.

> Reason 3: Brute-force algorithms tend to be adaptable. They are often easier to modify than more elegant, but more specialized, algorithms.

Consider Gauss' algorithm. The formula:

$$sum\ of\ numbers\ from\ first\ to\ last = (first + last) * last/2$$

is certainly efficient, but it's useless for solving other sum of the series problems. What about finding the sum of the squares of every number from 1 to 100? Or their cubes? Or their square roots? Our brute-force solution is a snap to adapt to solving these problems. Gauss' method is hopelessly narrow.

The real bottom-line of algorithms and programs, whether brute-force or elegant, is simple—*does it work?* In *The Psychology of Computer Programing,* Gerald Weinberg tells a story about a rescue programer who was brought in to design a program to schedule the production of automobiles. The original programer on the job was highly indignant over the rejection of his program, and complained that the new program was less than half as efficient as his discarded version. "However," retorted his relief, "my program works, and yours doesn't. If the program doesn't have to work, I can come up with an algorithm that runs twice as fast as yours!" Yes indeed.

4-3 Antibugging and Debugging

SUPPOSE THAT YOU'VE WRITTEN A PROGRAM that refuses to compile. Although you're sure the program ends with an **end**, you keep getting a compile-time error message like:

```
"END" EXPECTED - - END OF PROGRAM NOT FOUND
```

> Make sure your **case** structure ends with an **end**.

It's easy to leave out this **end**, and cause an error that's hard for the compiler to pinpoint. As far as the compiler is concerned, the last **end** in the program is merely the closing bracket of some compound statement or procedure.

Most programers use two methods to keep track of **end**s. First, *comment them*:

```
case Response of
    {body of the case structure}
end; {Response case}
```

The second technique is to indent, and make **begin**s and **end**s line up over each other (as we've been doing all along). Of course, this trick only works as well as you let it. If 70 or 80 lines of program come between a **begin** and an **end** (or a **case** and **end**), lining up matching pairs is more of a job for a surveyor than a programer.

> A procedure, control structure, or compound statement that extends over more than a single screenful of code, or page of program listing, should be broken down into procedures.

Compound statements can be confusing at first, but they're really not much trouble. The purpose of a compound statement is to make two or more statements (including procedure calls) appear to be a single statement. Is this a legal compound statement?

```
begin
    begin
        begin
            writeln ('Hi.')
        end
    end
end;
```

Yes, even though it's nested. It's no more or less improper than the expression $(((5))) + 3$. Even *this* is a legal compound statement, equivalent to the one above:

begin *write* ('H'); **begin begin** *write* ('i.') **end begin end**; *writeln* **end end**;

We can also try to clarify empty statements by taking them to excess.

```
begin
    begin ; ;
        begin ; ;
            writeln ('Hi again.') ; ;
        end ; ;
    end ; ;
end;
```

This is a perfectly legal compound statement, even though it's the most bizarre example of all. However, since the semicolon has a syntactic meaning in Pascal, accidentally misplacing it within a **case** structure can cause a calamity. We've used a semicolon instead of a colon on the third line below.

```
case Selector of
    1: DoFirstThing;
    2; DoSecondThing;
    3: DoThirdThing;    etc.
```

Can you predict the error messages the program segment might generate? They're rather subtle:

```
1 :   DOFIRSTTHING;
2 ;   DOSECONDTHING;
      MISSING "BEGIN"
↑  UNDECLARED PROCEDURE "2"
↑  "2" MAY NOT BE AN IDENTIFIER
```

Since '2' is preceded and followed by semicolons—statement separators—the compiler assumes that it is some kind of statement. However, 2 hasn't been defined as a procedure, and is an illegal identifier in any case.

The **case** structure can also be the cause of a run-time error. The message below appears when the **case** expression takes on a value that wasn't included, along with an appropriate action, in the constant list.

```
ABNORMAL TERMINATION - -
VALUE OF CASE EXPRESSION DOES NOT APPEAR IN CONSTANT LIST
```

Although this is an error in Standard Pascal, some implementations of Pascal don't deal so harshly with an unanticipated **case** expression value. In these versions of Pascal, the **case** expression 'falls through.' No value was specified, and no action is taken.

Why is a Pascal control structure implemented in different ways? Well, when he designed Pascal, Wirth felt that the constant list was part of the **case** structure's documentation. Letting a program continue operation when the **case** variable had a value *not* specified might be misleading to a program reader. Thus, an unanticipated value was supposed to generate a run-time error; a note that something unexpected was happening.

However, some Pascal implementors took a different view. They thought it was perfectly reasonable to expect the unexpected, and to provide a means of dealing with it less disastrous than a run-time crash.

A simple approach was to ignore the offending **case** variable, as described above. Another innovation was the exception clause—a specific 'else' or 'otherwise' action to be taken if the value of the **case** variable could not be found on the value list. These are nonstandard *extensions*, or additions, to Pascal.

Check your own Pascal system, and see which philosophy its implementors adhered to. You should note any extensions inside the front cover. Naturally, even if your system is nonstandard, you can usually write programs according to Standard Pascal. You will find that you must make a subjective decision: Is it better to write an absolutely standard program, sure to run on every system (even though it is very inflexible and prone to crashes), or to write your programs for a friendlier (although nonstandard) environment? Questions like this must usually be answered in every individual case—there are no hard and fast rules to apply.

Let's move on to the **for** structure. Difficulty with **for** is usually related to its Pascal syntax. As usual, the format used in typing the program has absolutely no effect on semantics. However, the general style of indenting we've used should be adhered to, because it simplifies the job of checking code. The two samples shown below are deliberately misleading. Their appearance says one thing, but their output tells a different story.

```
program ThreeCheers (input, output);
const HowMany = 3;
var Cheers: integer;
begin
    for Cheers := 1 to HowMany do           {This looks like a compound}
        writeln ('Hip hip, hooray!');       {statement, but it isn't.}
        writeln ('Congratulations.')
end.   {ThreeCheers}
```

          ↓   ↓   ↓   ↓   ↓
```
Hip hip, hooray!
Hip hip, hooray!
Hip hip, hooray!
Congratulations.
```

```
program Congratulations (input, output);
const HowMany = 3;
var Cheers: integer;
begin
    for Cheers := 1 to HowMany
        do begin
            writeln ('Hip hip, hooray!');   {This doesn't look like a}
    writeln ('Congratulations.')            {compound statement, but it is.}
    end
end.   {Congratulations}
```

```
      ↓         ↓         ↓         ↓         ↓
   Hip, hip, hooray!
   Congratulations.
   Hip, hip, hooray!
   Congratulations.
   Hip, hip, hooray!
   Congratulations.
```

Moral: Code is hard enough to read even *with* indenting. Don't make it unnecessarily difficult.

Another bug that's particularly difficult to spot is a misplaced semicolon. What's the matter with this **for** structure?

> **for** *Counter* := 1 **to** 5 **do** ;
>   **begin**
>   *DoSomething*;
>   *DoMore*
>   **end**;

The structure is supposed to call the procedures *DoSomething* and *DoMore* five times. Unfortunately, the semicolon right after the **do** forms an empty statement. This empty statement happens (for lack of a better word) five times, and the procedures are only called once.

As we pointed out in 4-1, certain restrictions are placed on the **for** loop's counter variable. In particular, assignments may not be made to it during the **for** loop's action. Within the loop it might be called a *read-only* variable; one may read its current value, but not assign it a new value.

Summary

The **case** and **for** structures are two of Pascal's control structures. The **case** structure brings decision-making into programs, because the value of a *case expression* determines which of several alternative actions will be executed. Possible values of the **case** expression, and the action to take for each one, are given in the structure's *constant list*. Each potential value must be specified there.

The **for** structure is a *loop* that repeats an action a certain number of times. A *counter variable* keeps track of the number of times the loop is to iterate. Although the value of the counter variable may be used within a **for** structure, the counter variable's value cannot be altered until the **for** structure has been left completely. Thus, the loop cannot be terminated early or late.

The counter variable can belong to any ordinal (non-*real*) type, and must be locally declared. Its value is *incremented* (increased or decreased by the smallest possible amount) each time the loop's action is executed. The counter variable cannot be assigned to within the loop, and its initial and final values can't be changed either. It is undefined on exit from the loop, and must be initialized before it can appear in an expression.

The *actions* that a **case** or **for** structure can control are varied. Assignment statements and procedure calls are actions, as are

compound statements—a series of actions bracketed by a **begin** and an
end; *empty statements*—non-actions designated with a semi-colon; and
structured statements—the action designated by any control structure.
A structured statement that contains another structured statement is
sometimes called a *nested* structure.

The ease with which computers repeat actions make them ideal
for executing *brute-force* algorithms, in which a simple step is carried
out many times. Although such algorithms may be *inefficient* in terms
of computer operation, they should be explored because they often help
clarify problems. Ultimately, the needs of the problem at hand, rather
than abstract notions of elegance or brute force, should define your
solution. No matter what kind of algorithm is chosen, *pseudo-code* is a
valuable aid in outlining programs.

Certain Pascal systems have changed the basic definition of the
language by allowing a general 'alternative' action for any value of the
case expression that aren't given in the value list. Although such
extensions are often convenient, the programs they appear in become
nonstandard.

case	**of**		New Pascal
for	**to**	**downto**	
begin	**end**	**:**	

case expression	*case constant*	*action*	New Terms
compound statement	*empty statement*	*structured statement*	
loop	*counter variable*	*incremented*	
nested	*pseudocode*	*brute force*	
efficiency	*extensions*		

Self-Test Exercises

4-1 What's the minimum number of reserved words that appear in a **case**
structure?

4-2 Suppose that the code below is the beginning of a **case** structure. What
values should appear in the structure's constant list?

> **case** $-(((ord(CapitalLetter) - ord('A'))$ **mod** 5) **of**   etc.

4-3 What is the purpose of this **case** structure?

> *write* (n);
> **case** *n* **of**
>   1: *writeln* ('st');
>   2: *writeln* ('nd');
>   3: *writeln* ('rd');
>   4, 5, 6, 7, 8, 9: *writeln* ('th')
> **end**;

4-4 Simplify this **case** structure as much as you can.

> **case** *ItemNumber* **of**
>   0: *writeln* ('Hats');
>   1: *writeln* ('Bats and Cats');
>   2: *writeln* ('Slats');
>   3: *writeln* ('Hats');
>   4: *writeln* ('Bats and Cats');
>   5: *writeln* ('Hats')
> **end**;

4-5 An angle is given as a positive *real* number of degrees. Angles from 0° to (but not including) 90° fall in the first quadrant, 90° to 180° are in the second, 180° to 270° are in the third, and 270° to 360° are in the fourth quadrant. The series of quadrants starts all over again at 360°. Write a procedure that reads the value of an angle, and prints out the angle, and the quadrant it falls in.

4-6 What are the possible outputs of this program segment? Assume that *First* and *Second* are *char* variables, and that the only possible inputs are **AB**, **BA**, **AA**, and **BB**.

```
read (First, Second) ;
case First of
  'A' : case Second of
          'A' : write ('It') ;
          'B' : write ('is')
        end ;
  'B' : begin
          write ('an') ;
          case Second of
            'A' : write ('Ancient') ;
            'B' : write ('Mariner')
          end
        end
end ;
writeln;
```

4-7 What's the output of this code?

```
Limit := 10 ;
for Counter := 1 to Limit
  do begin
       write (Counter + Limit:3 ) ;
       Limit := 5
     end ;
writeln;
```

4-8 Write a **for** loop that prints the even numbers between 1 and 25.

4-9 What Pascal type can't the counter variable of a **for** loop be?

4-10 What is the value of *Count* after this code is executed?

```
for Count := 10 downto 2
  do writeln (Count) ;
```

4-11 Write a procedure that counts the number of times the digits 4, 8, and 9 appear in forty characters worth of input.

4-12 What's the output of this procedure?

```
procedure Quiz;
  var Counter: integer;
  begin
    for Counter := 1 to 9
      do case Counter mod 5 of
           0 : write ('often ') ;
           1 : write ('What ') ;
           2,4 : write ('is ') ;
           3 : write ('not ')
         end;   {case}
    writeln
  end;   {Quiz}
```

4-13 Write code that prints the first letter of the first line of input, the second letter of the second line, etc. Stop on the *Last* character of line *Last*

4-14   How many 'Hubba's do each of these print?

```
for Rub := 1 to 3
    do for Dub := 1 to 3
        do for Tub := 1 to 3
            do writeln ('Hubba');

for Sub := 1 to 3
    do for Pub := 1 to 3
        do for Lub := Sub to Pub
            do writeln ('Hubba');
```

4-15   Write a procedure that reads ten numbers, and prints the difference between successive pairs. Thus, only nine numbers are printed.

More Exercises

4-16   What happens in your Pascal system if the value of the **case** expression is not contained in the **case** structure's constant list? Is any kind of **else** or **otherwise** clause allowed?

4-17   Write a markup/sale program. It should give the user the option of specifying a percentage markup or reduction, then compute a sales price.

4-18   Write a program that takes the values of a two-card blackjack hand as input, and prints out the point total of the hand. Note that input values may include the *char* values 'A', 'K', 'Q', and 'J', and that an ace's value is either 1 or 11. (Hint: an ace will always be 11 unless you have two aces. You may want to require that values be input in descending order.)

4-19   A simple conversion of letter grades to their equivalent grade points is easy. However, allowing the letter grade to be modified by a plus or minus complicates the matter. Write a program that shows the grade-point ranges of letter grades (including plus and minus grades). Use whatever conversion table applies at your school.

4-20   Before Great Britain went decimal, foreigners arriving at London's Heathrow Airport were usually rather confused about money. A traveller might know the exchange rate for one particular unit of English currency of money, as shown below, but have no idea about other sorts of conversion. Write a program which, after establishing the current exchange rate for *any* of the denominations shown, will convert any amount of U.S. currency into appropriate English amounts.

12 pence = 1 shilling
5 shillings = 1 crown
4 crowns = 1 pound
21 shillings = 1 guinea

4-21   Relative gravities of most planets in the solar system, the Sun, and the Moon, are shown below. They let us find what a given weight on Earth would weigh on each body.

Sun	27.94	Mercury	.37	Venus	.88
Moon	.17	Mars	.38	Jupiter	2.64
Saturn	1.15	Uranus	1.17	Neptune	1.18

Write a program that lets a user find her weight on any of these. It should ask her to enter the first letter of the planet or body she wants, and then, if there's an ambiguous situation (as we find for *S* or *M*) it should prompt her for the second letter. In other words, a nested **case** structure is required.

4-22   Write a program that, when given a television channel, will print out its call letters. (Why wouldn't this work with radio station frequencies?) Be sure the program works for any channel from 2 through 13, even if you have to print a message pointing out that a particular channel isn't assigned.

4-23   Write a program that extends felicitations on auspicious occasions like birthdays and anniversaries, as well as general greetings on holidays and special occasions. Have the user enter a single-letter code to specify the message required, along with any numerical information (age, which anniversary) required. Limit the numerical data to the range 1..10, and print the word (e.g. 'First', or '3rd') instead of the number.

4-24   Write a program that accepts as input a four-digit *integer*, then prints out the number in English. In a simple version, assume that the third digit is not 1. For example, the input **4713** is illegal. A harder program will allow all four-digit input.

4-25   Local necromancers have come up with the following method of finding a day. Begin by expressing the year, month, and date you're interested in as numbers. Add 10 to the month, and subtract 1 from the year. Let a variable C equal the year **div** 100, and another variable, named A, equal the year **mod** 100. Set a third variable called B equal to 13 times the number of the month, then subtract 1 and **div** by 5, then add A **div** 4, and C **div** 4. The number of the day of the week (where Sunday is 0) equals $B + A$ plus the number of the day of the month minus twice C, all **mod** 7.

Incidentally (because of a shortage of eye of newt), this algorithm won't work when the day of the month sought is the first or second. Write a program that prints out the day of the week Halloween falls on (or fell on) in 1066, 1492, 1776, and 2001.

4-26   Although telephone numbers currently consist only of digits, they used to begin with two letters followed by five digits. For example, what we now refer to as 548-0276 was once known as KI8-0276. The prefix 'KI' stood for 'Kingsbridge', and was the name of the local exchange.

A number of exchange names are shown below. Write a program that reads in a telephone number written in the form 'KI8-0276' (i.e. with the initials of one of the exchanges), then prints it with the exchange name fully spelled out, as in 'Kingsbridge 8-0276'. Be sure to provide test data.

Purdue	*Maltby*	*Rhinelander*
Roseland	*Elgin*	*Excelsior*
Cambridge	*Paradise*	*Central*

4-27   Write a program that, when given the call letters shown below, will print the broadcast frequency assigned to them. (Hint: first check the first letter—it may be unique. Then check the second letter, and if these match, the third.) Be sure to declare each procedure *before* you use it, even if it's used in another procedure.

ABC 94.4	NBC 102.4	CBS 102.9
CAB 88.9	NBA 93.4	NTR 104.4
BBC 97.4	AAA 101	TVA 106.9

4-28   Write a program to print every even number from 0 to 100. Every other letter from 'A' to 'Z'. Every fifth number from 0 to 100. Every sixth number from 2 to 110. Every third letter, starting with 'C'. Every fourth character in your computer's character set (better find out how many characters there are).

4-29   The cost of operating a small Beverly Hills bumper gold-plating company can be given by this formula:

$$Cost = Units^3 - 7\ Units^2 + \$432$$

where *Units* stands for the number of bumpers that are gold-plated each day. How many bumpers should be produced each day to minimize operating costs? The number is smaller than twenty.

4-30   Write a bank account program that keeps track of current balances, service charges, and interest. The program user should begin by telling the program the number of transactions that have to be recorded. Interest, at an annual rate of 6%, should be paid on the average balance in excess of $1,000, and a service charge of fifty cents should be levied on each withdrawal.

4-31   Write a program to print a temperature conversion table. Calculate and print the Fahrenheit equivalents of all Celsius temperatures *at 10 degree intervals* from 0° to 250°. The conversion formula is:

$$C = 5/9 \ (F-32)$$

4-32   List the integers from 1 to 20, their squares, square roots, cubes, and fourth roots, all in a five column table. There are a number of ways to write this program; implement one, and describe another.

4-33   Write a program to produce a table of factorials. Prompt the user for the upper limit of the table, i.e. how many numbers it should contain. Can you write the program to *a)* work from 1 factorial up, *b)* compute and print from the upper limit down, *c)* do only one additional multiplication for each additional factorial figured?

Write another program to produce a table of factorials. This time, however, ask the user for the upper *and* lower limits of the table. Only print the factorials of numbers within (and including) these limits.

4-34   The square of the sum of any series of numbers starting with 1 is equal to the sum of the cubes of each individual number. Prove that this is true for the sums of the series 1 . . . 10 through 1 . . . 20.

4-35   Here's the mechanism of a number-guessing game. Write it as a program. Begin by giving the computer a number between 2 and 9, and a number that contains that many digits. The longer number, however, may not contain any zeros, nor may any two of its digits be the same (e.g. 3, 927, and 7, 4729135 are valid pairs).

Now the fun begins. Take the leftmost digit of the large number, double it, add 1, and multiply by 5. Add the result to the next number to the right. Double this sum, add 1, and again multiply by 5. Continue this process until you reach the rightmost digit. From this final number subtract a number with the following properties: it is as many digits long as the original large number, and it consists only of fives. Divide the result by 10. Does it look familiar? Why does the process do what it does?

4-36   A series is called *geometric* if each value in it (called a *term*) is the product of a particular number (called the *common ratio*) and the preceding term. For example, the sequence: ¼, 1, 4 is geometric, with a common ratio of 4. The next number in the series will be 16—the last term times the common ratio. Naturally, the common ratio can be found by dividing any term by the term before it.

Write a program that will find the *n*th term of a geometric series. The program user should have the options of entering *a)* the first two terms; *b)* the first term and the common ratio; *c)* any two consecutive terms and one either term's position; *d)* any single term, its position, and the common ratio. Naturally, the user must also enter a value for *n* (Bonus: let the user ask for a term whose position is *less* than that of the given term or terms.)

4-37   It's time to compute final grades. Write a program that reads in 10 sets of 5 grades and computes *weighted* averages as follows: The first and second grades count for 10% each, the midterm for 25%, the next assignment for 20%, the next for only 5%, and the final exam for 30%. Print each grade, the weighted average for each student, and the average for the entire class.

4-38   How many one, two, three, four, and five letter combinations can you make from five different letters? Come up with a formula or a program that computes the answer.

4-39   Add structures for alternative choice, and definite iteration, to your personal computer language. Try requiring your equivalent of a **for** to have a matching **end** at the end of the structure. What bugs will this help prevent?

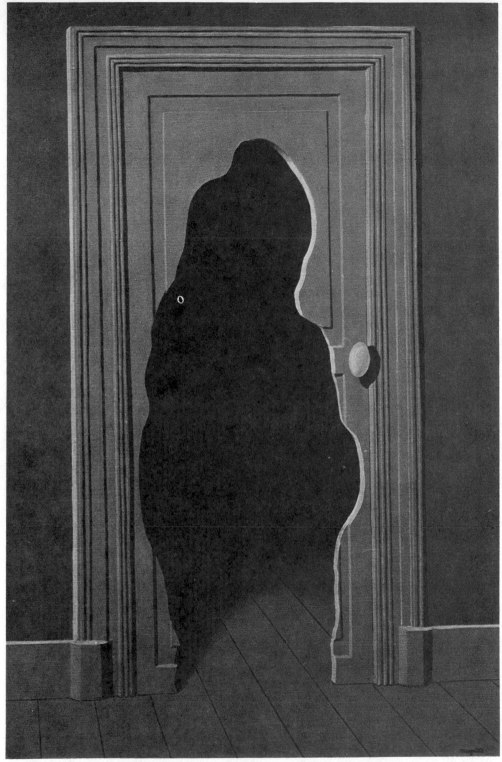

The Unexpected Answer/La réponse imprévue by René Magritte. 1933. Musées des Beaux-Arts de
Belgique, Brussels.

5

Procedures for Modularity

What's the difference between a village and a large city? Between a country road and an airport runway? Between the wind tunnel model of a bridge and the real bridge in place? The answer seems simple— one is larger than the other. Unfortunately, an increase in size usually entails much more than a rescaling of dimensions, because an underlying part of the design may change as well. A city (as compared to a village) has different patterns of transportation, communications, food distribution, housing, etc. Superficially, a city and a village are alike— both are population centers. However, the ways they're put together and lived in are quite dissimilar.

What does this have to do with programing? Well, it turns out that there are subtle differences, other than size, between small programs and big ones. There's no exact line of demarcation between a little program and a large one, just as there's no exact population limit that divides villages and cities. But when programs grow to a certain size they are large, and must be written in subtly different ways.

In this chapter we'll develop the idea of program *modules.* A module is a procedure that's written in a way that makes it independent of the rest of the program. We can make procedures modular by defining and using *parameters.* We'll learn about two sorts of parameters— *value-parameters,* and *variable-parameters.* In different ways these parameters are used to transmit information in and out of procedures. They let us write procedures without having to know the names of global variables.

The techniques presented in this chapter are tools that aren't necessary for every program. However, when your programs start to cross the fine line between small and large, you'll want to use parameters.

A global identifier buried inside a procedure is really as incongruous and unsettling as . . .

5-1
Programing
Procedures
with
Parameters

WHEN A PROCEDURE IS CALLED IT, LIKE a function, can be given arguments in parentheses. These are the *parameters* of the procedure.

> The word **parameter** describes a value or variable that is used by both a procedure and its calling program.

Don't get confused by the terms *argument* and *parameter*, which have similar meanings. The difference is that an argument is a particular instance of a particular parameter.*

There are several reasons for wanting to include arguments in a procedure call. Sometimes the effect of a procedure, like that of a function, depends on values provided when it's called. For example, imagine a procedure that draws a line of characters. The values that might differ from one call to the next are the length of the line, and the actual character the line consists of. Although we *could* implement such a procedure already, we'd have to make assignments to global *Length* and *Character* variables between each call. We'll see in a moment that *value-parameters* are a much better alternative.

Another motivation for allowing arguments comes when procedures modify global variables. The archetypical example is a procedure that exchanges the values of two global variables. A program that only switches *one* pair of variables could use a procedure without parameters. However, value-exchanging is usually a wholesale operation—a program must exchange the values of many different variables. *Passing* the variables to a procedure as *variable-parameters* solves the problem.

Conceptually, value-parameters provide a form of procedure input. A value-parameter is a new variable, complete with an identifier and its own storage space in the computer's memory. When a procedure is called, the computer assigns argument values to the appropriate value-parameters. When the procedure is left behind, the value-parameter storage spaces are taken back by the computer, and the value-parameters cease to exist.

Variable-parameters, on the other hand, provide procedure output. No new variables are created. Instead, for the duration of the procedure a memory space that had previously been known by just one identifier—the name of a global variable—is known by another name as well—the variable-parameter identifier. The two identifiers may even be identical. An assignment to the new identifier, like an assignment to the 'old', global identifier, changes the stored value.

Let's look at the different parameters in detail. The syntax chart of a procedure heading looks like this:

procedure heading

procedure ⟶ *identifier* ⟶ (⟶ *parameter list* ⟶) ⟶ ;

---

* In fact, an argument is sometimes known as an *actual* parameter.

Although we've always taken the straight and narrow path (and skipped the option of a *parameter list*), its chart expands to:

parameter list

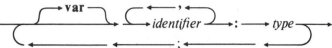

....

A *value-parameter* is a variable that is local to a subprogram. Its starting value is *passed* to it as an argument of the procedure call.

....

Since a value-parameter is a local variable, changing its value has no effect on the value of a like-named global variable. It's easy (and perfectly accurate) to think of value-parameters as self-initializing local variables, with the same exact scope and precedence as other local identifiers.

Procedure *DrawBar*, below, prints out a single line of a bar graph. Two of the values it uses—the length of the bar, and the character the bar is drawn with—are passed to *DrawBar* when it is called. In effect, these values are automatically assigned to the value-parameters *Length* and *BarCharacter*. An ordinary local variable is declared too, because the counter variable must be local.

```
program Bars (output);
    {Draws three rows of characters.}
const DollarSign = '$';
var Income: integer;
    Symbol: char;
procedure DrawBar (Length: integer;  BarCharacter: char);
    {Demonstrates value-parameters in drawing one bar of a graph.}
    var Counter: integer;
    begin
        for Counter := 1 to Length
            do write (BarCharacter);
        writeln
    end;  {DrawBar}
begin
    Income := 20;
    Symbol := '#';
    DrawBar (12, 'X');
    DrawBar (3*5, Symbol);
    DrawBar (Income, DollarSign)
end.  {Bars}
```

```
          ↓         ↓        ↓         ↓        ↓
XXXXXXXXXXXX
############
$$$$$$$$$$$$$$$$$$$$
```

When *DrawBar* is called, it's given two arguments—the values of *Length* and *BarCharacter*. Although (in the last two calls) *Symbol* and *Income* are variables, an assignment to *Length* or *BarCharacter* could not change their values. Only the *values* of the variables are passed to *DrawBar*. Changing these values globally requires another kind of parameter.

> A ***variable-parameter*** is a local identifier that can be used in place of a global variable identifier. It's a local synonym for (or renaming of) its argument.

An assignment to a variable-parameter is equivalent to a direct assignment to the global variable it's an alias or stand-in for. It lets us arrange to assign a value to a global variable whose name we didn't necessarily know when the procedure was written.

Procedure *Switch* exchanges the values of its parameters. Notice the reserved word **var** in the parameter list—it's a part of a variable-parameter declaration.

```
program Exchanges (output);
    {Provides the raison d'etre of procedure Switch.}
var Little, Big: integer;
procedure Switch (var First, Second: integer);
    {Demonstrates variable-parameters by exchanging their values.}
    var Temporary: integer;
    begin
        Temporary := First;
        First := Second;
        Second := Temporary
    end;  {Switch}
begin
    Big := 5;
    Little := 10;
    writeln (Big, Little);
    Switch (Big, Little);
    writeln (Big, Little)
end.  {Exchanges}
```

↓   ↓   ↓   ↓   ↓

   5   10

  10   5

Naturally, a single procedure may require both value-parameters and variable-parameters. *AddUp*, below, adds its value-parameters and assigns the result to a variable-parameter.

```
procedure AddUp (First, Second: integer;  var Sum: integer);
    {Uses two value-parameters and one variable-parameter.}
    begin
        Sum := First + Second
    end;  {AddUp}
```

Let's look at a few example parameter lists. Parameter declarations are much like ordinary variable declarations, except that:

1. The parameter list goes between parentheses.

2. **var** only precedes declarations of variable-parameters.

A parameter list contains groups of the identifiers of parameters of any given type, in the same way that a variable declaration contains groups of variable identifiers. There may be any number of groups, as long as they're separated by semicolons. However, a group preceded by **var** declares only variable-parameters.

The headings below declare only value-parameters because **var** doesn't appear in the parameter list. Note that the free format of Pascal isn't lost in the parameter list. It's perfectly all right (and sometimes advisable) to extend long headings over two or more lines.

procedure *GiveInstructions* (*QuestionNumber, Difficulty*: *integer*) ;

procedure *ShowInterval* (*Argument*: *real*; *UpperBound, LowerBound*: *integer*) ;

procedure *Debugging* (*CompleteTest, Antibugging*: *boolean*;
            ErrorMessage: *char*;
            Value1, Value2: *integer*) ;

The next set of parameter lists only contain variable-parameters, because **var** appears before every group of identifiers.

procedure *AdjustTerms* (**var** *FirstTerm, SecondTerm*: *real*) ;

procedure *Increment* (**var** *Initial, Monogram*: *char*;
            var *From, To*: *integer*) ;

procedure *OneOfEach* (**var** *A*: *boolean*;   {What do these parameters do? }
            var *B*: *char*;   {This is a good place to comment}
            var *C*: *integer*;   {a procedure's parameters. Don't}
            var *D*: *real*) ;   {forget the closing parenthesis. }

Finally, these headings are mixed. In the first two examples below, *Heckle* is a variable-parameter and *Jekyl* a value-parameter.

    procedure *FirstTry* (**var** *Heckle*: *integer*; *Jekyl*: *integer*) ;
    procedure *SecondTry* (**var** *Heckle*: *integer*; *Jekyl*: *real*) ;

In the next three examples, *Huey* and *Dewey* are variable-parameters, while *Louie* is a value-parameter. In terms of the kinds of parameters created, each heading is identical. However, each procedure must be given its arguments in a different order.

procedure *Able* (**var** *Huey, Dewey*: *integer*; *Louie*: *integer*) ;

procedure *Baker* (*Louie*: *integer*; **var** *Huey, Dewey*: *integer*) ;

procedure *Charlie* (**var** *Huey*: *integer*; *Louie*: *integer*; **var** *Dewey*: *integer*) ;

We can come to the conclusion that the exact order of declarations is unimportant. Value- and variable-parameters can be declared in almost any sequence imaginable, and parameters of a particular type need not be grouped together. The order of parameter lists usually depends on what makes the most readable procedure heading and call.

> Parameter declarations are usually ordered to produce a procedure call that, with arguments, is self-documenting and not prone to argument-ordering errors.

You should be able to figure out the proper order of arguments without having to refer to the procedure heading declaration. There is a story about the procedure call *AddGin (ToVermouth, MakingMartini)*, but we're not going to tell it here.

> The argument of a value-parameter may be any representation of a value, as long as it is of the correct type. As always, different arguments are separated by commas.

A value-parameter's argument may be a constant or variable, a constant of a type (like 7 or 'T'), a function call, or any other form of expression. All of these are valid calls of the procedure we wrote at the beginning of this chapter.

>   DrawBar (CommaProduction, ',') ;
>   DrawBar (EdgeLength, BorderCharacter) ;
>   DrawBar (trunc (sqrt(ErrorSquared)), chr(45))
>   DrawBar (10 + Correction, InputChar) ;

You should remember three things about passing arguments to value-parameters. First, a constant *char* argument must be put in single quote marks. If it isn't, the argument appears to be a variable identifier one character long. Second, if a variable is used as an argument its value *at the time of the procedure call* is given to the value-parameter. Finally, there must be the same number of arguments and declared parameters.

{Procedure heading—parameter list with value-parameters}
procedure *PlotTable* (*Xposition, Yposition*: *integer*; *PlotMark*: *char*; *Correction*: *real*) ;

    PlotTable (Intersection, 5, 'Z', 1.937E-02) ;
            {Procedure call—'argument list'}

Naturally, the types of each argument/value-parameter pair must be identical as well.

The most important rule of using variable-parameters is this.

> The Golden Rule of Variable-parameters
>
> The argument of a variable-parameter *must* be a variable. It cannot be a constant value, function call, or other expression. These represent values, not variables.

This rule comes as no surprise. We're just officially stating a restriction that should be common sense.

Self-Check
Questions

Q. The following procedure declaration contains an error that should be easy to spot. What is it?

> **procedure** *Wrong* (*A*: *integer*; **var** *B*: *integer*) ;
>   **var** *A*: *integer*; *B*: *real*;   etc.

A. Declared parameters share the scope of local variables. Procedure *Wrong* tries to use two identifiers (*A* and *B*) in equally local places. Whether the parameters and local variables are of identical or different types is irrelevant. It's as incorrect a pair of definitions as this would be:

> **var** *A*: *integer*; *A*: *real*;

Q. What will the output of this program be?

> **program** *Confusion* (*input, output*) ;
>   {Comments? Nope—that would be telling.}
>
> **var** *A, B, C, D*: *integer*;
>
> **procedure** *Confuse* (*A,B*: *integer*) ;
>   **var** *C*: *integer*;
>   **begin**
>   *A* := 5;   *B* := 6;   *C* := 7;   *D* := 8;
>   *writeln* (*A,B,C,D*)
>   **end**; {*Confuse*}
>
> **begin**
>   *A* := 1;   *B* := 2;   *C* := 3;   *D* := 4;
>   *writeln* (*A,B,C,D*);
>   *Confuse* (*A,B*);
>   *writeln* (*A,B,C,D*)
> **end.** {*Confusion*}

A. This deliberately muddled program demonstrates the difference between global and local scope. Note that the only global value altered by *Confuse* is *D*—the only global identifier used within *Confuse.* The program's output is:

↓	↓	↓	↓	↓
1	2	3	4	
5	6	7	8	
1	2	3	8	

A common application of computers doesn't involve any computing at all. The computer is used to present information in a more understandable or dramatic manner. Now, a program's output gives no indication of the work that went into producing it. As far as many program users are concerned, the output *is* the program.

Focus On Programing: Passing Parameters

> Label program output, and present it in a clear, readable manner. Don't force a program user to read a program's code to understand its results.

[129]

Graph-making programs are useless if their output can't be deciphered. For example, let's write a program that graphs the data summarized below.

	England	*France*	*Japan*
1981	26	41	33
1982	34	44	26
1983	44	49	20
1984	48	49	17
1985	51	51	5

Frisbee Production
(*in ten thousand frisbee lots*)

A first refinement of the problem doesn't cause any trouble. We're just massaging it into a more Pascal-like form.

for *each year from 1981 to 1985*
draw three bars of the correct length, using different symbols;

The outline of a program falls into our lap.

for *each year from 1981 to 1985*
draw the three bars;
label the year;

And what does 'draw the three bars' turn out to be? We take another step, and change only that sentence.

for *each year from 1981 to 1985*
for *each of the three countries*
draw a single bar of the correct length, using the correct symbol;
label the output;

Another refinement gives us the rough outline of a program.

for *Year* := 1981 **to** 1985
do for *each country's symbol*
do *DrawBar* (*Production, Symbol*) ;
writeln (*Year*) ;

> As usual, writing in pseudocode lets us give a very accurate specification of what a program does, even if we're not really sure that we can actually write the thing. We can spot potential coding rough spots before committing ourselves to a particular version of a program.

The pseudocode draft is also handy for getting an idea of what identifiers and constants we'll have to declare in the final program.

The *for each country's symbol* part of the last refinement is going to cause some problems. We'll have to perform some sleight of hand to make the **for** loop count by symbols. The program segment below shows a common programing trick that gets us out of our bind.

```
for SymbolCounter := 1 to 3
    do begin
        read (Production);
        case SymbolCounter of
            1: DrawBar (Production, '#');
            2: DrawBar (Production, '$');
            3: DrawBar (Production, '%')
        end  {case}
    end;  {for}
```

Since we couldn't count by symbols, we counted by numbers, and made it have the proper effect. Such a trick is called a *kludge* (klooj). A kludge is the programing equivalent of jury-rigging. It's a quick and dirty solution that often works cleverly and well. The completed program, along with its output, is shown below.

```
program GraphMaker (input, output);
    {Prints a bar graph.  Batch oriented.}

var Year, SymbolCounter, Production: integer;

procedure DrawBar (Length: integer;  BarCharacter: char);
    {Draws a Length-long sequence of BarCharacter.}
    var Counter: integer;
    begin
        for Counter := 1 to Length
            do write (BarCharacter);
        writeln
    end;  {DrawBar}

begin
    for Year := 1981 to 1985
        do begin
            for SymbolCounter := 1 to 3
                do begin
                    read (Production);
                    case SymbolCounter of
                        1: DrawBar (Production, '#');
                        2: DrawBar (Production, '$');
                        3: DrawBar (Production, '%')
                    end  {case}
                end;  {SymbolCounter for}
            writeln (Year)
        end;  {Year for}
    writeln;
    writeln ('Key to symbols:  #=England  $=France  %=Japan')
end.  {GraphMaker}
```

```
        ↓        ↓        ↓        ↓        ↓
26  41  33
34  44  26
44  49  20
48  49  17
51  51  5
```

```
############################
$$$$$$$$$$$$$$$$$$$$$$$$$$$$$$$$$$$$$$$$$
%%%%%%%%%%%%%%%%%%%%%%%%%%%%%%%%%%%
        1981
#####################################
$$$$$$$$$$$$$$$$$$$$$$$$$$$$$$$$$$$$$$$$$$$$$$
%%%%%%%%%%%%%%%%%%%%%%%%%%%%
        1982
###############################################
$$$$$$$$$$$$$$$$$$$$$$$$$$$$$$$$$$$$$$$$$$$$$$$$$$$$$
%%%%%%%%%%%%%%%%%%%%%
        1983
###################################################
$$$$$$$$$$$$$$$$$$$$$$$$$$$$$$$$$$$$$$$$$$$$$$$$$$$$$$$
%%%%%%%%%%%%%%%%%%
        1984
######################################################
$$$$$$$$$$$$$$$$$$$$$$$$$$$$$$$$$$$$$$$$$$$$$$$$$$$$$$$$$$
%%%%%
        1985
```

```
Key to symbols:   #=England   $=France   %=Japan
```

It's interesting, incidentally, to think about why our kludge is clever. It combines the *counting* of a **for** structure, and the *selection* of a **case** to form a 'new' programing structure. The merger of disparate abilities can be powerful, but is often difficult to originate because we tend to see certain tools in their most ordinary roles. A quick mental exercise demonstrates the way people tend to automatically classify knowledge along familiar lines.

Think about animals for a bit. Can you name five small animals? Five furry ones? Five ferocious ones? What other categories might you come up with?

Now think about cities. Can you list five hot cities? Five large cities? Five cities with sea-harbors? Again, try to think of some other categories.

Now comes the test. *Name five cities whose names are the names of animals.* This one isn't so easy—there doesn't seem to be a city/animal intersection in the mind.

The moral, applied to programing, is this:

> Although it's useful to understand and categorize programing structures by *application*, or specific examples of their use, thinking about them in terms of *attribute*—the abstract features that distinguish one structure from the next—can lead to new and unexpected combinations.

Our next example is a program that finds Fibonacci numbers. This series begins 0, 1, and each subsequent number is the sum of the previous two.* A first refinement of the problem is just:

> **for** *as many numbers as are required*
> *get the next Fibonacci number;*
> *print it;*

What is the current Fibonacci number? It's the sum of the previous two. This means that if we remember the *last* Fibonacci, and know the current one, we can always generate the next number. Of course, we should remember that the current Fibonacci will become the old one. We'll propose this algorithm for finding Fibonaccis:

> *let a temporary variable get the sum of Old and New;*
> *Old gets the current value of New;*
> *New gets the current value of Temporary;*

If this algorithm looks suspiciously like procedure *Switch*, it should.

How much output will the Fibonacci-finding program produce? Although the first few numbers in the series will fit comfortably on one line, our program should probably arrange to divide its output over several lines. The **case** structure comes to the rescue once more. As you read program *PrintFibonaccis*, below, figure out how the new kludge works.

---

* Leonardo Fibonacci, who named this sequence, lived in thirteenth century Italy. There's a cartoon that shows two visitors standing in front of a house numbered 0112358; one is saying to the other "Aha! This must be Fibonacci's place!"

```
program PrintFibonaccis (input, output) ;
    {Prints as many Fibonacci numbers as the user requests.}

var Counter, UpperLimit, CurrentFibonacci, NextFibonacci: integer;

procedure GetNextFibonacci (var Old, New: integer) ;
    {Generates the next Fibonacci number.}
    var Temporary: integer;
    begin
        Temporary := Old + New;
        Old := New;
        New := Temporary
    end;   {GetNextFibonacci}

begin
    writeln ('How many Fibonacci numbers should I print?') ;
    read (UpperLimit) ;
    writeln ('The first ', UpperLimit:1, ' Fibonaccis are:') ;
    CurrentFibonacci := 0;   {Initialize the sequence.}
    NextFibonacci := 1 ;
    for Counter := 1 to UpperLimit
        do begin
            write (CurrentFibonacci) ;
            GetNextFibonacci (CurrentFibonacci, NextFibonacci) ;
            case (Counter mod 5) of       {Arrange for the table.}
                1,2,3,4: ;             {In other words, do nothing.}
                0: writeln             {Have a new line every five numbers.}
            end {case}                 {Why? Because 5 mod 5 is 0.}
        end; {for}
    writeln {In case there weren't five numbers in the last line.}
end.   {PrintFibonaccis}
```

$$\downarrow \qquad \downarrow \qquad \downarrow \qquad \downarrow \qquad \downarrow$$

```
How many Fibonacci numbers should I print?
23
The first 23 Fibonacci numbers are:
          0          1          1          2          3
          5          8         13         21         34
         55         89        144        233        377
        610        987       1597       2584       4181
       6765      10946      17711
```

The forward Declaration

Occasionally the syntax rules of Pascal seem to paint the programer into a corner. One such problem is caused by the rule:

....
:   A procedure must be declared before it can be called.   :
....

The truth of this rule seems so obvious that it doesn't need to be stated. If a procedure is never declared, calling it is senseless. The compiler spots mistakes like this before the program is even run, and prints out a message along the lines of "INVALID PROCEDURE CALL—PROCEDURE UNDECLARED".

How does the compiler recognize bad procedure calls? When a program is first compiled, the computer *scans* (reads) the program from start to finish. As it goes along, it reads constant, variable, and subprogram declarations, and creates an internal table of identifiers. In particular, when a procedure is declared its name is added to the list of valid identifiers.

Suppose the compiler is going through a main or subprogram statement part, and comes across a call of a procedure whose name isn't in the table? The compiler can only assume that an error has been made. It jumps to the conclusion that the procedure in question will *never* be declared, and prints the error message.

A serious problem arises when one procedure calls another procedure that hasn't yet been declared, but which *will* be declared by the end of the procedure declaration part. Suppose that procedure *First* calls procedure *Second.* Their declarations look like this:

```
procedure First (A,B: integer;  var X: real);
    local declarations
    begin
        statement part
        Second (argument list)          {This is an invalid call}
    end;   {First}                      {of procedure Second}

procedure Second (var M,N: integer;  P: char);
    local declarations
    begin
        statement part
    end;   {Second}
```

A program that contains such declarations is invalid by Pascal's standards — *Second* is called before it is declared.* The problem *could* be solved simply by reversing the order of declarations. Another approach requires a *forward declaration.*

> A **forward declaration** tells the compiler that a subprogram identifier is valid, and may be used in a program before the actual subprogram declaration takes place.

In effect, the procedure's name is put into the table of known procedure identifiers. This doesn't mean that the procedure need not be declared at all, or that the declaration can occur outside of the procedure declaration part. A forward declaration is merely used to vary the order of declarations. It's employed like this.

---

* There's a saying about drama that a gun laid on the mantle in the first act must be fired by the third. Here, we're trying to do something akin to firing the gun in the first act, without bringing it on stage until the third.

> The procedure heading, with parameter list, is followed by the word **forward**. Then, when the complete procedure is declared, the parameter list is not repeated. **forward** is a statement, and should be preceded and followed by a semicolon.

> **procedure** *Second* (**var** *M,N*: *integer*; *P*: *char*) ; **forward**;
>
> **procedure** *First* (*A,B*: *integer*; **var** *X*: *real*) ;
>   *local declarations*
>   **begin**
>   *statement part*
>   *Second* (*argument list*)   {Call procedure *Second*}
>   **end**; {*First*}
>
> **procedure** *Second*;   {The parameter list is omitted.}
>   *local declarations*
>   **begin**
>   *statement part*
>   **end**; {*Second*}

Because a forward declaration may come well before the actual procedure declaration, it's usually a good idea to repeat the parameter list as a comment when the procedure is finally declared.

> **procedure** *Second*; {var M,N: integer; P: char}
>   *local declarations*   etc.

This is an excellent programing practice that adds documentation with almost no effort.

Why use forward declarations? Well, sometimes we want to, and sometimes we have to. If they're not absolutely required (as with the procedures above, whose declarations could have simply been reversed), forward declarations can help make a program more readable. Sometimes it seems like a good idea to put the shortest, most easily understood procedures at the beginning, and 'forward declare' a long, complicated routine they all call and use. It's equally plausible that we might want to do exactly the opposite, and start out with the hardest, least familiar procedure instead of burying it deep within the procedure declarations. Some programers (and we don't advise this) forward declare *every* subprogram, to help keep track of the parameters each one expects to receive.

Circumstances do arise, however, which *require* the use of forward declarations. Suppose that procedure *A* calls procedure *B*, which in turn may call *A* again.* Which declaration comes first? This is called *mutual recursion,* and can only be implemented by using a forward reference. We won't worry about it now.

---

* This brings to mind the old Rhode Island law: 'When two trains meet on a track, neither train shall move until the other one has passed.'

After going to the trouble of writing a really good procedure it seems a shame to throw it away. Fortunately, it's usually possible to create a procedure *library*. A well-written subprogram can often be stored in a way that lets it be included in other programs.

A crude library can be set up in batch systems by keeping an extra copy of the punched cards that contained the original procedure declaration. If the procedure interacts with the calling program through parameters, we don't have to worry about knowing the names of any global variables. The deck of cards that contains the procedure declaration is inserted at the appropriate point in the program (i.e. where the procedure would have been declared anyway). Using different colored punched cards for these permanent procedures makes them easy to remove.

Many systems, both batch and interactive, have some sort of mechanism for including externally declared and stored procedures in a program. If your system has such a command, you should make a note inside the front cover. However...

> There is no provision for procedure libraries in Standard Pascal. Any program that requires one is not likely to be portable.

Some computer systems even make a provision for allowing professionally written (and separately compiled) subprograms to be included in a program (in addition to locally implemented predefined subprograms). Check your own system for details on what library procedures are available, and how they can be used.

SINCE GLOBAL IDENTIFIERS CAN BE USED in any procedure within a program, declaring value and variable-parameters is not always necessary. Nonetheless, we'll almost invariably use them because of the contribution parameters make to program modularity.

> A program is *modular* if its subprograms are relatively independent of each other, and of the main program.

Modularity is an important part of antibugging. Programs that can be dealt with one module at a time are easier to read, write, and understand. They're also a lot simpler to fix—a faulty module can be replaced without a lot of program rewriting. In fact, a module from an entirely different program can be inserted if its connections to the calling program are passed as parameters.

Now, using global identifiers within procedures spoils their modularity. A global identifier buried inside a procedure is really as incongruous and unsettling as a nail protruding from the bottom of an iron might be. Global variable or constant identifiers in procedures make them custom-built. Such procedures *can't* be readily replaced by

5-2
Antibugging
and
Debugging

rewritten or improved versions because their connections to the main program (in this case, the global identifiers) are not standardized, and vary from program to program.

A situation that requires parameters arises when we don't even *know* the names of global variables. This is not at all unusual. Consider the nonstandard procedures that are predefined in many Pascal systems. Their authors couldn't possibly have known what identifiers we would use as global variables. Only value-parameters and variable-parameters make 'standard' procedures, that are shared by many users and programs, practical.

A similar problem arises in the creation of large programs. What if twenty or thirty people are working on a huge program containing literally hundreds of procedure declarations? Is there a 'Chief Assistant to the Assistant Chief in Charge of Naming Variables', who acts as a clearinghouse for variable names? Of course not! Again, value- and variable-parameters allow the passage of information between main program and subprogram.

However, the philosophical reasons for using parameters instead of global variables are equally important. The image of a procedure as a black box, with required inputs and expected outputs, is appealing as a model of program construction. A procedure solves one subpart of a problem, and can be written without worrying about other parts. Its parameter list clearly shows the procedure's connections to the rest of the program.

This means that a procedure can be written and tested by itself (possibly in a dummy program). If the procedure works, it's easy to plug into the main program. If the procedure has a bug, it can be spotted right at the point of the procedure call. It won't have a hidden or inadvertent effect on global variables in other parts of the program.

Parameters also increase the transparency, or clarity of purpose, of a program. Short programs can usually be figured out even if they're not too transparent, as can programs that use only the few control structures we've discussed so far. However, our programs are going to be getting longer and more complex. We'll try to keep them transparent by banishing global variables from procedures.

> In general, global variables should not be used within subprograms. A local assignment to a global variable is called a *side-effect*.

As you might suspect, side-effects are to be avoided. They are not bad *per se*; computers are depressingly predictable, and their side effects are not unexpected (and unpleasant) like the side effects of drugs or environmental policy. However, side effects make programs more difficult to read and understand. A procedure's parameter list is an implicit part of program documentation. If it's incomplete, it is misleading.

Bugs associated with parameters usually occur as a result of confusing the two types.

> If a procedure only *uses* a value, declare a value-parameter.
>
> If a procedure *changes* or *returns* a value, use a variable-parameter.

Error messages like the ones shown below will be common when you begin to declare parameters. Don't forget that the wording and extent of error messages may vary from system to system.

```
NUMBER OF ARGUMENTS DOES NOT AGREE
WITH PARAMETER LIST DECLARATION
```

This message means that a procedure call contained more (or fewer) arguments than the procedure expected to receive. There has to be a one-to-one correspondence between parameters and arguments.

Even if there are the correct number of arguments, they have to be in the right places. A misordered procedure call might produce error messages like:

```
EXPRESSION GIVEN (VARIABLE REQUIRED)
FOR VARIABLE-PARAMETER
CONSTANT ILLEGALLY PASSED TO A VARIABLE-PARAMETER
- - VARIABLE EXPECTED
```

The value of a defined constant can't be changed within a program. Thus, passing it to a variable-parameter has to be illegal.

Value and variable-parameters, like any Pascal variables, belong to some particular type. Their arguments must be of the same type for a procedure call to be valid. If they're not...

```
ARGUMENT TYPE NOT IDENTICAL TO TYPE OF VARIABLE-PARAMETER
EXPRESSION TYPE CLASHES WITH TYPE OF VALUE-PARAMETER
```

As always, a short test program helps clarify details of syntax.

Summary

A procedure's connections to its calling program are called **parameters**. By creating new kinds of local variables in a **parameter list**, it's possible to **pass** these parameters to a procedure when it is called. In effect, parameters are the arguments of a procedure call.

A **value-parameter** is declared in the procedure heading. It is a local variable, with local scope, except for its initialization—a value-parameter's starting value is provided when the procedure is called. In effect, it provides input to a procedure. Any representation of a value may be used as the argument of a value-parameter. Naturally, an assignment to a value-parameter has no effect on any like-named variable outside the procedure.

A **variable-parameter** is also declared in the procedure heading. A variable-parameter is a local alias for its argument parameter, which must be a variable. Although a variable-parameter is local in terms of name-precedence (it takes precedence over a like-named global variable), it is global in effect. An assignment to a variable-parameter is just like a direct assignment to the global variable it represents. Thus, it's used when a procedure has output to return to the main program.

A direct assignment to a global variable from within a procedure is called a *side effect.* Side effects spoil the *modularity* of procedures, and can make the effects of a procedure call difficult to determine. Use of side effects should be confined to small programs or procedures.

In some circumstances, procedures must be declared out of order—after they have already been called by another procedure. This is permitted if there is a *forward declaration* of the procedure before it is first called. A forward declaration consists of the procedure heading (including parameter declarations), followed by the **forward** statement. When the procedure is actually declared, the parameter list is omitted. However, it's usually a good idea to include it as a comment.

New Pascal	**forward**		
New Terms	*parameter*	*parameter list*	*value-parameter*
	pass	*variable-parameter*	*kludge*
	forward declaration	*modular*	*side-effect*
	library		

Self-Test Exercises

5-1   What reserved words can appear in a procedure's parameter list?

5-2   Suppose that you've written procedure *PrintNumbers,* below. What series of calls (followed by a *writeln*) will print this sequence: 1, 1, 2, 3, 5, 8, 13, 21, 34? Don't worry about printing the commas, of course.

```
procedure PrintNumbers (First, Second: integer) ;
   begin
      write (First, Second, First+Second)
   end;   {PrintNumbers}
```

5-3   What's the difference between a parameter and an argument?

5-4   What is a *side effect*? How can it cause trouble?

5-5   A program produces the following compile-time error message:

```
var Time:   integer;
   ↑ "Time" is already defined in procedure "Clock"
```

However, *Time* is the very first entry in the variable declaration part of procedure *Clock.* What could have caused the error message?

5-6   What is the output of program *Quiz*?

```
program Quiz (output) ;
var A, B, C: integer;
procedure Subprogram (D: integer;  var E: integer;  C: integer) ;
   var A: integer;
   begin
      A := C + 1;
      E := A + C;
      C := C * 2
   end;   {Subprogram}
begin  {Quiz}
   A := 2;
   B := 4;
   C := 6;
   Subprogram (B, C, A);
   writeln (A, B, C)
end.   {Quiz}
```

5-7 Write a procedure that averages a series of numbers. The length of the series should be passed as a value-parameter, and the average value should be returned as a variable-parameter.

5-8 Write a procedure that counts the number of times the digits 2, 3, and 6 appear in x many digit-characters worth of input. If a **case** structure is used to winnow the input, does it make sense to pass 2, 3, and 6 as parameters?

5-9 Write a procedure that is passed a *real* value, and returns separately its whole part, and the first four digits of its fractional part.

5-10 It's very unlikely that the situation below will ever appear in a real program, but it is real Pascal. What is the program's output?

```
program HardToBelieve (output);
var Number: integer;
procedure DoubleAndAdd (var First, Second: integer);
    begin
        First := 2*First;
        Second := 1 + Second
    end;   {DoubleAndAdd}
procedure AddAndDouble (var First, Second: integer);
    begin
        First := 1 + First;
        Second := 2*Second
    end;   {AddAndDouble}
begin
    Number := 3;
    DoubleAndAdd (Number, Number);
    writeln (Number);
    Number := 3;
    AddAndDouble (Number, Number);
    writeln (Number);
end.   {HardToBelieve}
```

More Exercises

5-11 Write a program that adds and subtracts time. Its starting input should be a time of day, entered with a colon between the hours and minutes (e.g. 12:37). The program user should be able to have the program add or subtract (indicated by entering a plus or minus sign) any number of hours and minutes from this time.

5-12 A Fibonacci series can actually begin with *any* two numbers—the important rule is that each subsequent number must be the sum of the two prior numbers. Thus 10, 11, 21, 32, 53 is the beginning of a perfectly valid sequence.

Write a program that computes the first ten members of any Fibonacci series. Use it to verify the following conjecture: The sum of the first ten members of a Fibonacci series is 11 times the value of the seventh element of the sequence. Can you turn this into a magical feat of lightning mental calculation?

5-13 Many computer systems, particularly interactive ones, operate on a *timesharing* basis. The computer distributes its time among many users, allotting each one a fraction of a second to use the entire computer. Because most computer jobs are completed very quickly, a user on a lightly loaded system has the illusion of having the computer all to herself. However, when the computer is given long jobs the distribution system begins to break down. The computer can only finish part of a job in its apportioned time, and must return (possibly many times) to complete it entirely. This, unfortunately, creates the illusion of *many* users on the computer.

Ricki Gould is a not very bright systems programmer who has come up with a plan to discourage submission of long programming jobs. She penalizes long jobs by progressively reducing the amount of time the computer spend working on them. The reduction is 10% per 'return'; thus, if the first time allotment is one second, the second will be only .9 seconds, and the third only .81 seconds.

Write a program that computes and graphs the amount of time the computer will spend on a program that takes from 1 to 500 'visits' to run. Assume that the first visit is one second. What is the problem with Ricki's plan?

5-14   Write a procedure that computes a to the b power (using a **for** loop), and b to the $1/a$ power (by formula). A call of this procedure should look like this:

FigurePowers (Inside, Outside, InsideToTheOutside, OutsideInverseInside) ;

Inside, Outside, and *InsideToTheOutside* are all of type *integer,* while *OutsideInverseInside* is *real.*

5-15   Another way of finding the nth term of a geometric sequence like a_1, $a_2 \ldots a_n$ (as discussed in the last chapter's problems), involves using the formula:

$$a_n = a_1 \text{ times (Common Ratio)}^{n-1}$$

In words, we've said that the nth term equals the first term times the common ratio raised to the $n-1$ power.

Write a procedure that finds the nth term of a geometric sequence. It should be passed the values of the first term and the common ratio, and return the value of the nth term.

5-16   Compound interest rates can be significantly greater than simple rates, because interest is paid on interest already accrued. Write a program that compares the benefit of simple interest with interest compounded monthly, weekly, daily, and hourly. Let the program user enter an interest rate, and amount of original principal.

5-17   Write a checkbook/savings passbook balancing program. Have the user enter the number of transactions she wants to make and her current balances, then let her make deposits, withdrawals, and balance checks. Finally, post new balances (including interest) and summarize account activity (how much was deposited, withdrawn, and the number of transactions made) for the month.

5-18   Monica Marin makes $10,000 per year at her part-time job. Her boss, who has a sadistic mind, offers Monica one of the following raises: either a ten percent increase every year, with a thousand-dollar bonus right away, or an increase of one-twelfth of ten percent each month and no bonus.

Monica decides that the offer she should take depends on how long she plans on continuing at her job. Write a program that shows how much she can expect from each offer for each of the next twenty years.

5-19   The executives of a large oil company are in a quandary. Although they can sell all the No. 1 oil available, supplies are limited. An ambitious vice president suggests the following plan: As the delivery truck goes along its route, the driver should replace the delivered No. 1 oil with oil of an inferior grade. The replacement isn't 1:1 (if it were, the truck would come back full!). Instead, it goes according to this schedule:

No. 2 oil—replace 75%   *No. 3 oil—replace* 50%   *No. 4 oil—replace* 25%

Only one kind of replacement oil is used on any given day.

Write a program that will help customers sue the oil company by telling them how much No. 1 oil they actually received on any particular delivery day. Variables in each day's run include the starting contents of the delivery truck, the number of customers served, and the amount of oil in each delivery. Since nobody is sure what grade of oil was used for replacement each day, show figures for each of the three possible adulterants. Make sure that your output will look good in court.

5-20   Procedures that help draw graphs are an essential part of many programs. Write a loop that could graph the function $f(x) = x$ over the range 1 to 10. In other words, plot a graph whose first value is 1, second is 2, etc. Don't worry about printing the x or y axis. Note that although this particular graph is easy to plot either vertically or horizontally, it's usually less trouble to print graphs vertically—in effect, on their sides.

5-21   Try drawing an x axis on the graph. Write a loop that graphs the same function for all *integer* values of x from -10 to 10. Print a vertical line (signifying 0—the x axis) down the center of the page.

5-22   The charm below was formed from an ancient magic word. Write a program that contains a procedure to draw a symbol from a word (of up to fifteen letters) provided by the user, and another procedure that computes the number of paths the magic word can be read by, starting from the top of the charm.

```
                A
              B   B
            R   R   R
          A   A   A   A
        C   C   C   C
      A   A   A   A   A   A
    D   D   D   D   D   D
  A   A   A   A   A   A   A   A
B   B   B   B   B   B   B   B
  R   R   R   R   R   R   R   R   R
A   A   A   A   A   A   A   A   A   A
```

5-23   Drawing plane figures from dots or stars is not too intellectually stimulating, but counting the number of dots required to draw a figure can be. Not unreasonably, these numbers are known as *figurate* numbers, and come in all varieties—triangular numbers, square numbers, pentagonal numbers, etc. Three of these figures are shown below.

In 1665, Blaise Pascal wrote a *Treatise On Figurate Numbers*, in which he came up with a general equation for finding figurate numbers. The number of dots required to draw a figure with a given number of dots per side (*DotsPer-Side*) is:

$$\text{Triangle} = (DotsPerSide^2 + DotsPerSide)/2;$$
$$\text{Square} = DotsPerSide^2;$$
$$\text{Pentagon} = (3*DotsPerSide^2 - DotsPerSide)/2;$$
$$\text{Hexagon} = 2*DotsPerSide^2 - DotsPerSide.$$

Write a figurate number program. It should be able to compute figurate numbers for the shapes shown above, and print a table of the first 10 figurate numbers for each shape. Moreover, the program should *draw* any of the figures on demand. (Bonus: find the general equation that relates number of sides, number of dots per side, and figurate number.)

5-24   Do you think that your private programing language needs parameters? Can you include them in a way that simplifies their declaration? How about requiring parameters by banning global identifiers from subprograms? Come up with an alternative syntax for a procedure heading.

...(C)omplex boolean *expressions can also be tricky, but always, as Mr. Spock would say, perfectly logical.*

6

Programing Decisions with the **if** Structure

What's the use of *boolean* values? There aren't many of them—just *false and true*—and apparently it's possible to read deep into a Pascal textbook without using either one. Yet, *boolean* values are going to turn out to be the most useful values of all, because they let programs incorporate *decisions*.

> **if** *a boolean expression is true*
>   **then** *action*
>   **else** *alternative action*
>
> **repeat**
>   *action—i.e. loop around*
> **until** *a boolean expression is true*
>
> **while** *a boolean expression is true*
>   **do** *action—another form of looping*

This chapter is an introduction to *boolean* values as well as an explanation of a new control structure. Section 6-1 begins with a discussion of *boolean* values and the *relational* operators. We'll use simple *boolean* expressions in the **if** control structure, and write some example programs.

Section 6-2 shows how the *boolean* operators **and, or,** and **not** are used to construct more complex *boolean* expressions. We'll see how a final relational operator, called **in**, gives us a quick and easy way of error-checking a program's entry to a **case** structure, and can often be used to simplify *boolean* expressions. Finally, in 6-3, we'll learn about a problem-solving approach called *exhaustive search*. We'll also consider ways of making a search less exhausting by limiting a problem's *solution space*, and look at our first long program. 6-4 points out potential bugs.

Understanding *boolean* values through and through is a key part of learning to program. Now, some people are a little wary of *booleans* because they seem too logical—after all, they're named after George Boole, the creator of logical calculus. It turns out, to the contrary, that *booleans* are nice because they make programs *less* formal, and more natural—'common sense' values is a better description of them than logical values. If a *boolean* expression seems to be unfathomable, relax. You're probably trying too hard.

6-1

if Structures
and boolean
Expressions

LIKE ALL EXPRESSIONS, *BOOLEAN* EXPRESSIONS represent values. The simplest examples are the constants of the ordinal type *boolean*:

false   *true*

The *odd*(x) function also represents a *boolean* value—*false* if its *integer* argument x is even, and *true* if it's odd. We can state longer *boolean* expressions by using the **relational** operators.*

Math	Pascal	English
=	=	*equal to*
<	<	*less than*
⩽	<=	*less than or equal to*
>	>	*greater than*
⩾	>=	*greater than or equal to*
≠	<>	*not equal to*

You can see that some relational operators require two different symbols, because the keyboards of most terminals and keypunches are too restricted to show characters like ≠.

In high school math, the relational operators were used to build equalities and inequalities. We've usually seen them restricting the value of an expression in a context like this:

if $b^2 - 4ac > 0$ *the expression has two real, unequal roots*
if $b^2 - 4ac = 0$ *the expression has two real, equal roots*
if $b^2 - 4ac < 0$ *the expression has two imaginary, unequal roots*

> Pascal uses the fact that equalities and inequalities always make an assertion (claim) that has to be either true or false. This makes them *boolean*-valued expressions.

For example, this expression is either *true* or *false*:

LowerLimit > 5

It asserts that a variable or constant named *LowerLimit* has an *integer* or *real* value greater than 5. The expression:

ApplicantsAge <= 65

claims that the value of *ApplicantsAge* is less than or equal to 65. There's no need to restrict comparisons to *integer* or *real* values, because these expressions:

Finished = 'Y'   'X' <> *chr* (63)

form *boolean* expressions just as plausible as their numerical counterparts. Since character sets are ordered, even this expression makes sense:

SecondLetter >= *FirstLetter*

It confirms or denies the alphabetical ordering of two *char* variables.

---

* One other relational operator, **in,** is discussed in section 6-2.

The operands of the relational operators (the values that are being compared) must generally be of the same ordinal type. *reals* may be compared to each other, and to *integers*, but the vagaries of *real* arithmetic make these comparisons unreliable.* At any rate, a relational operator clearly can't have operands of totally unrelated types. Is *true* < 16? Is 'A' <> 5? These expressions are existential rather than *boolean*. They contain type clashes that would cause compile-time error messages.

It's important to recognize that the relational operators can't be used in a manner that's very common in mathematics—to show multiple inequalities. The mathematical phrase $5 < X < 10$ has no meaning in a Pascal program. We'll see how to express such relations in 6-2.**

Constants and variables can also be used to represent *boolean* values. The value of a user-defined constant can't be computed in its definition, so the topic of defining *boolean* constants is disposed of in short order. Note that these definitions are not *boolean* expressions, even though '=' is a relational operator under other circumstances.

> **const** *ThisProgramWorks = false*;
> *Testing = true*;

Boolean variables are declared in the variable declaration part, along with *integer, real,* and *char* variables. As usual, the order of these declarations is irrelevant, because no type is more important than any of the others.

> **var** *Balance*: *real*;
> *Heir, Broke*: *boolean*;
> *TattooOnRightShoulder*: *char*;
> *Temperature*: *integer*;
> *NotDivisibleBy2*: *boolean*;

> Assignments to *boolean* variables are like all other assignment statements. An expression is evaluated, and its result value is given to the variable.

Naturally, the constants of type *boolean* (*false* and *true*), user-defined *boolean* constants (like *Testing*, above), and *boolean* variables may appear on the right-hand side of assignment statements.

> *Heir* := *true*;
> *ActivateDebuggingProcedures* := *Testing*;
> *Broke* := *Balance* <= 0;
> *NotDivisibleBy2* := *odd*(*Temperature*);
> *Broke* := *Heir*;

---

* For example, the *real* value 3.0*(10.0/3.0) frequently equals 9.99999999... instead of 10.0.

** This example, incidentally, is correctly written as (5 < *X*) **and** (*X* < 10).

∴∴

Self-Check
Questions

Q. Assume that we've made assignments as shown. Evaluate each expression.

$Grade := 'C'$; $RealValue := 3.97$; $IntegerValue := 5$;

a) $RealValue <= 5E+00$ b) $IntegerValue <> Grade$
c) $IntegerValue < RealValue$ d) $round(RealValue+1) = IntegerValue$
e) $(ord('D')-1) <= 34$ f) $Grade <> chr(trunc(RealValue) +6*IntegerValue)$

A. In evaluating expressions *e* and *f,* we've assumed the ordering of the ASCII character set.

a) *true*   b) This is an invalid comparison; a type clash.
c) *false*   d) *true*
e) *false*   f) *true*

Q. Suppose that *Willy* and *Nilly* are *boolean* variables. What will the value of *Willy* be after assignment 1 if *Nilly* is *true*? *false*? Is there anything wrong with assignment 2 syntactically? From the viewpoint of conciseness or clarity?

$$Willy := Nilly = false; \quad \{Assignment\ 1\}$$
$$Willy := Nilly = true; \quad \{Assignment\ 2\}$$

A. The first assignment statement gives *Willy* the opposite value of *Nilly*. If *Nilly* equals *true*, *Willy* becomes *false*, and if *Nilly* represents *false*, *Willy* takes on the value *true*.* The second assignment statement has correct Pascal syntax, but is redundant. It should have been written as:

$$Willy := Nilly;$$

because the expression *Nilly=true* is identical to the value of *Nilly*.

* Soon, we'll use the **not** operator to make the same assignment as: *Willy* := **not** *Nilly*.

∴∴

The **if**
Structure

Now that we've grasped the basics of *boolean* expressions, let's use a control structure that requires them.

> The **if** structure lets a program choose between taking two alternative actions.

Its general form is:

> **if** *boolean expression*
> **then** *action*
> **else** *alternative action*

The structure's syntax chart shows an option (omitting the **else**) that we won't get to for a few pages.

if ... then ... else *control structure*

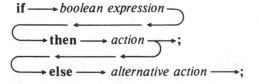

When an **if** structure is entered, its *boolean* expression is evaluated. If it's *true*, the **then** action is carried out, and the alternative **else** action is skipped. If the *boolean* expression represents the value *false*, the **then** action is jumped over, and the **else** action is executed instead. In either case, only one of the two actions is taken.

For example, program *SquareRoot*, below, uses an **if** structure (shaded) to **error-check** its input. Without this check, the program would crash when given negative input.

> Error-checking input helps make programs **robust**—less sensitive to user errors or misuse. They end gracefully instead of crashing.

```
program SquareRoot (input, output) ;
    {Computes square roots, and error-checks input.}
var RootExists: boolean;
    Argument, Answer: real;
begin
    writeln ('Please enter a number.') ;
    readln (Argument) ;
    RootExists := Argument > = 0 ;
    write ('The square root of ', Argument:2:2) ;
    if RootExists
        then begin
            Answer := sqrt(Argument) ;
            writeln (' is', Answer:2:2)
        end {then}
        else writeln (' is imaginary.  Sorry!') ;
    writeln ('Thanks for using this program.')
end.  {SquareRoot}
```

↓　　↓　　↓　　↓　　↓
```
Please enter a number.
-24.6
The square root of  -24.60 is imaginary.  Sorry!
Thanks for using this program.
```

Although an *auxiliary* (not strictly necessary) variable provided the *boolean* expression in *SquareRoot*, we could have correctly said:

> **if** *Argument* > =0 **then**　　etc.

When **if** structures are used, they should be formatted in a way that highlights their alternative actions. However...

> The Golden Rule of Coding
> *Syntax determines semantics.* Spacing and indentation is for the benefit of human program readers. The computer only obeys *begin*, **end**, semicolons, and the like.

Although syntax, and not appearance, controls the semantics (effect) of Pascal code, programs should still be easy for humans to read. This

[149]

program layout clearly distinguishes between the **if** structure's actions (compound statements) and the rest of the program:

$$:$$

statement;
if *boolean expression*
   then begin
      statement;
        $:$
      statement
   end {**then**}
   else begin
      statement;
        $:$
      statement
   end; {**else**}
statement;   etc.

When an **if** structure's alternative actions are just single statements (like assignments or procedure calls) the **begin** and **end** of compound statements can be omitted.

program *EasyOrder* (*input, output*) ;
   {Prints two input letters in alphabetical order.}
var *First, Second*: *char*;
begin
   writeln ('Please enter two letters.') ;
   readln (*First, Second*) ;
   write ('In alphabetical order, ', *First,* ' and ', *Second,* ' are ') ;
   if *First* > *Second*
      then *writeln* (*Second,* ', ', *First*)
      else *writeln* (*First,* ', ', *Second*)
end. {*EasyOrder*}

      ↓   ↓   ↓   ↓   ↓

```
Please enter two letters.
```
XM
```
In alphabetical order, X and M are M, X
```

The two formatting styles can also be combined, as they were in program *SquareRoot.* However, a picayune syntax rule is extremely important: the reserved word **else** is *never* preceded by a semicolon. We'll examine this small, but crucial, detail in the Antibugging section.

Q. Rewrite this assignment as an **if** . . . **then** . . . **else** structure.

         Finished := *Response* = 'Q';

A.   **if** *Response* = 'Q'
         then *Finished* := *true*
         else *Finished* := *false*;

We'll frequently want a program to decide whether or not to execute a single action, rather than choose between two alternative actions. Pascal provides a convenient variation.

Variations on the if Structure

....
:   The **else** portion of an **if** structure can be omitted entirely.   :
....

The modified structure is like an ordinary **if** structure whose **else** action is an empty statement. Check back to the syntax chart and trace the no-**else** option.

Program *PostageMeter*, below, demonstrates the simplified **if** structure. As before, we've tried to make the program robust by anticipating user errors. Several checks are phrased as *boolean* expressions—Was the weight accidentally entered as a negative number? Is it less than the minimum? Is the letter to go special delivery? If any expression is *true*, an appropriate response is evoked.

```
program PostageMeter (input, output);
    {Computes charges for first class and special delivery mail.}

const BasicCharge = 0.18;        {The one-ounce rate.}
      OunceCharge = 0.17;        {Each additional ounce.}
      SpecialCharge = 2.00;      {Special delivery surcharge.}

var Weight, Postage: real;
    Response: char;
    SpecialDelivery: boolean;

begin
    writeln ('How heavy is your letter, in ounces?');
    readln (Weight);
    if Weight < 0.0 then Weight := abs(Weight);
    if Weight < 1.0
        then begin
            writeln ('Minimum weight charge is one ounce.');
            Weight := 1.0
        end;
    Postage := BasicCharge+((Weight −1.0)∗OunceCharge);
    writeln ('Do you want special delivery?  Answer "Y" or "N".');
    readln (Response);
    SpecialDelivery := Response = 'Y';
    if SpecialDelivery then Postage := Postage+SpecialCharge;
    writeln ('The ', Weight:1, '-ounce postage charge is', Postage:2:2)
end.  {PostageMeter}
```

```
        ↓       ↓       ↓       ↓       ↓
How heavy is your letter, in ounces?
0.5
Minimum weight charge is one ounce.
Do you want special delivery?  Answer 'Y' or 'N'.
Y
The 1-ounce postage charge is 2.18
```

An abbreviated **if** structure that nests an **if** complete with its **else** clause can appear ambiguous at first sight. An unindented example shows the problem. Which **if** structure is the **else** action, *statement2*, associated with?

> **if** *B1*
> **then if** *B2*
> **then** *statement1*
> **else** *statement2*
> *statement3*

```
.............................................................................
:                                                                           :
:                    The Golden Rule of if Structures                       :
:                                                                           :
: In Pascal, an else is always the alternative action of the nearest        :
: prior then action.                                                        :
:...........................................................................:
```

Thus, *statement2* is executed if *B1* is *true*, and *B2* is *false*.

> **if** *B1*
>   **then if** *B2*
>   **then** *statement1*
>   **else** *statement2*;
> *statement3*;   etc.

As always, we hasten to point out that altering the code's physical appearance has no effect on the program. Procedure *TwoDwarves*, below, shows the effect of the nesting rule.

procedure *TwoDwarves* (*Sleepy, Grumpy*: *boolean*);

```
  begin
    if Sleepy
      then if Grumpy
        then writeln ('I''m grumpy and sleepy.')
        else writeln ('I may be sleepy, but I''m not grumpy.');
    writeln ('I hope you''re satisfied.')
  end;
```

This association can be changed by hiding the inner **then** within a compound statement.

procedure *TwoMoreDwarves* (*Sneezy, Dopey*: *boolean*);

```
  begin
    if Sneezy
      then begin
        if Dopey then writeln ('I''m sneezy and dopey.')
      end
      else writeln ('I''m not sneezy, but I might be dopey.');
    writeln ('Bother me again and I''ll bite your leg.')
  end;
```

Our next example requires a sequence of **if** structures. Let's write a change-making program that accepts as input a price and amount of money tendered, and prints the minimum number and type of coins required for change.

....
: When writing a program that simulates a real-life process, it's a :
: good idea to try imagining the steps you'd go through yourself. :
....

Who hasn't made change? First, you count out the dollars, then the half-dollars, and so on through the pennies. Frankly, the change-making algorithm of program *ChangeMaker* isn't going to be a great advance in computer science.

> *count out the dollars*;
> *count out the half-dollars*;
> *count out the quarters*;
> *count out the dimes*;
> *count out the nickels*;
> *count out the pennies*;

On the other hand, it's still a challenge to write a program that imitates the fine steps a human change-maker takes almost automatically. A real-life clerk would inform the customer if she was shortchanged, and so should our program. A person doesn't think about pluralizing words, but we'll have to teach the computer to add an 's' to plural coin names. A human wouldn't bother announcing the coins that she *wasn't* returning as change, and neither should *ChangeMaker*. We'll have to modify our pseudocode outline to make it clear that useless or misleading work will be avoided:

> *find out the price and amount tendered*;
> *decide if there's enough money*;
> **if** *there are dollars in the change, return them*;
> **if** *there are half-dollars in the change, return them*;
>
> **if** *there are pennies in the change, return them*;

A second imperative is to make *ChangeMaker* as well-written as possible. Its output should be clear. It should be robust, and able to deal with the 'unexpected' situations we just mentioned. It should be self-documenting where possible, but comments should be added to clarify less-than-obvious features. Finally, it should take advantage of procedures to minimize the length and complexity of its code. The completed program is shown below.

```
program ChangeMaker (input, output);
    {Computes the minimum coinage required to make change. Batch oriented.}

const Dollar = 100;
    HalfDollar = 50;
    Quarter = 25;
    Dime = 10;
    Nickel = 5;
    Penny = 1;

var Price, Tendered: real;   {Amounts are input as real dollar amounts...}
    Change: integer;           {... but are dealt with as pennies within the program.}
    MoneyIsDue: boolean;

procedure ComputeChange (Unit: integer; var Change: integer);
    {Prints number of coins. Modifies parameter Change.}

    var Pieces: integer;

    begin
        Pieces := Change div Unit;
        Change := Change mod (Pieces* Unit);
        write (Pieces:1);
        case Unit of
            100:  write (' dollar');
            50:  write (' fifty-cent piece');
            25:  write (' quarter');
            10:  write (' dime');
            5:  write (' nickel');
            1:  write (' cent')
        end;  {case}
        if Pieces > 1   {Take care of multiple coins.}
            then writeln ('s')
            else writeln
    end;  {ComputeChange}

begin  {ChangeMaker}
    readln (Price, Tendered);
    MoneyIsDue := Price > Tendered;
        {Express the potential change in pennies.}
    Change := abs (trunc (100*(Price−Tendered)));
    if MoneyIsDue
        then writeln ('Too little! You''re short by')
        else writeln ('Your change is exactly');
    if Change > =100 then ComputeChange (Dollar,Change);
    if Change > =50 then ComputeChange (HalfDollar,Change);
    if Change > =25 then ComputeChange (Quarter,Change);
    if Change > =10 then ComputeChange (Dime,Change);
    if Change > =5 then ComputeChange (Nickel,Change);
    if Change > =1 then ComputeChange (Penny,Change)
end.  {ChangeMaker}
```

↓   ↓   ↓   ↓   ↓

11.95 8.21
```
Too little!  You're short by
3 dollars
1 fifty-cent piece
2 dimes
4 cents
```

:··:

Q. What's wrong with the *boolean* expression in this structure?

> **if** *Finished* = *true*
> **then**   etc.

A. As a *boolean* variable, *Finished* represents either the value *true* or *false.* *Finished* = *true* represents the exact same value. Thus, the redundant way the expression is written forces the computer to go through the unenlightening exercise of determining that (*true* = *true*) is *true*, or that (*true* = *false*) is *false.*

:··:

The **if** structures in program *ChangeMaker* were basically independent of each other. Since the structures were in sequence, each structure's *boolean* expression was evaluated regardless of the previous structure's effect. However, by nesting **if** structures we can arrange them in a manner that short-circuits the process. Entry to subsequent structures will depend on passing additional *boolean* tests.

Short Circuiting
if Structures

    We'll usually want to take advantage of this technique when we're examining a lot of data. Problems that are sure to require it typically begin 'Find a number such that...', and then list the characteristics of the answer. The Stolen Gold Shipment Mystery is a typical example.

> Three desperadoes robbed a shipment of gold bars late one night. They escaped to their hideout, and resolved to divide their booty in the morning. However, as soon as one of the bandits heard the others snoring, he divided the stolen gold into three equal piles, finding one bar left over. He buried one of the three piles under a tree, along with the extra bar. Then he went to sleep, sure that he had protected his interest in the treasure. Naturally, the other two outlaws were no more honest than the first. Each in turn crept to the cache of gold, divided it three ways, and found one bar left over, which he kept along with 'his' third.

> Soon came morning and the final three-way division. Oddly enough, this division also left one odd bar remaining. The highwaymen fought over this bar, and in an unprecedented three-way draw, shot each other dead.

The problem we pose is this: Each of the four three-way divisions left exactly one bar. How many bars could have been in the entire shipment? Assume that the shipment contained no more than 500 bars.

We can solve the gold shipment mystery by mimicking the action of the bandits (the same approach we used for making change). We'll test each number between 1 and 500 to see if it, after the repeated divisions and subtractions, still leaves a remainder of 1. In pseudocode we have:

> **for** *every number from 1 through 500*
>   **if** *the first bandit's division leaves a remainder of 1*
>   **then if** *the second bandit's division leaves a remainder of 1*
>   **then if** *the third bandit's division leaves a remainder of 1*
>   **then if** *the final division leaves a remainder of 1*
>   **then** *we've got a possible answer*

Picture what will happen when a program based on this pseudocode runs. Suppose our trial number passes the first division. If it fails the second division, the third and final trials are not made. Nesting the structures abbreviates the loop, and only those numbers that pass through each **if** test are printed as solutions.

```
program StolenGold (output);
    {Demonstrates nested if structures.}
var TrialNumber, DividedNumber: integer;
begin
    for TrialNumber := 1 to 500
        do if (TrialNumber mod 3) = 1
        then begin   {First bandit's division.}
            DividedNumber := 2*(TrialNumber div 3);
            if (DividedNumber mod 3) = 1
                then begin   {Second bandit's division.}
                    DividedNumber := 2*(DividedNumber div 3);
                    if (DividedNumber mod 3) = 1
                        then begin   {Third bandit's division.}
                            DividedNumber := 2*(DividedNumber div 3);
                            if (DividedNumber mod 3) = 1
                                then writeln (TrialNumber:3, ' is a solution.')
                        end
                end
        end
end.   {StolenGold}
```

```
 79 is a solution.
160 is a solution.
241 is a solution.
322 is a solution.
403 is a solution.
484 is a solution.
```

THREE 'WORD-SYMBOLS'—**and**, **or**, and **not**—are the *boolean* operators. Just as the word-symbol **div** takes *integer* operands to form an *integer*-valued expression, the *boolean* operators use *boolean* operands to create *boolean*-valued expressions.

Boolean operators can combine several tests that would otherwise require a series of **if** structures. The first, **and**, joins two conditions into a single expression.

6-2
Sophisticated
boolean Tests

> If we have two *boolean* values (call them *Condition* and *Decision*), the expression:
>
> *Condition* **and** *Decision*
>
> is evaluated as *true* if both *Condition* and *Decision* are *true*. If either or both of them are *false*, the entire expression is *false*.

We can use **and** in any *boolean* expression. It can help set the condition of an **if** structure:

> **if** (*Value* > 5) **and** (*Value* < 10)
> **then** *writeln* ('The value is within limits.') ;

or appear on the right-hand side of an assignment:

> *Capital* := (*Letter* > = 'A') **and** (*Letter* < = 'Z') ;

For example, program *Palindrome*, below, reads in a five-letter word, and decides whether or not it's spelled the same forward and backward.

```
program Palindrome (input, output) ;
    {Recognizes five-letter palindromes.}

var c1, c2, c3, c4, c5: char;

begin
    writeln ('Please enter a five-letter word.') ;
    readln (c1, c2, c3, c4, c5) ;
    write (c5, c4, c3, c2, c1) ;
    if (c1=c5) and (c2=c4) then  write (' is')
                           else  write (' is not') ;
    writeln (' a palindrome.')
end.  {Palindrome}
```

```
          ↓       ↓       ↓       ↓       ↓
Please enter a five-letter word.
opera
arepo is not a palindrome.
```

The second operator, **or**, yields a result of *true* if either (or both) of its operands has the value *true*. This idea isn't nearly as strange as it sounds—the English sentence:

If I do well on the midterm, or ace the final, then I'll pass.

is a perfect example of 'oring' two values:

> **if** (*I do well on the midterm*) **or** (*I ace the final*)
> **then** *I'll pass*

> The *boolean* operator **or** is less restrictive than **and** is. The expression:
>
> *Condition* **or** *Decision*
>
> is *true* if either *Condition* or *Decision*, or both of them, are *true*. It's only *false* if *Condition* and *Decision* are both *false*.

For example, this program segment:

> **if** (*PurchasePrice* < =*BankBalance*) **or** *CreditIsGood*
> **then begin**
>   *writeln* ('Who should I make the check out to?') ;   etc.

lets a check be written if there's enough money in the bank to cover the purchase (*PurchasePrice* < =*BankBalance*), or if the value of the *boolean* variable *CreditIsGood* is *true*. Naturally, it's all right for both conditions to be *true*, too.

The third *boolean* operator, **not**, is analogous to the unary negation operator (minus sign) in math. It reverses a *boolean* condition.

> The result of the **not** operator is the opposite of its operand.
>
> **not** *Condition*
>
> represents *true* if *Condition is false*, and *false* otherwise.

not negates the very first (and *only* the first) *boolean* value to follow it.

> **if not** *odd*(*InputValue*)
>   **then** *writeln* (*InputValue*, 'couldn''t possibly be prime.') ;

As you might expect, we can use parentheses within *boolean* expressions. In arithmetic expressions, parentheses played two roles. First, they circumvented the operator hierarchy, so that:

$$2 * 2 + 2 = 6$$
$$(2 * 2) + 2 = 6$$
but $2 * (2 + 2) = 8$

Second, the presence of parentheses usually made the effect of complex expressions less ambiguous to program readers. *Boolean* expressions use parentheses for the same reasons.

> The Golden Rule of *boolean* Operators
>
> Equalities and inequalities must be parenthesized when **not, and** or **or** appear in an expression,

Parentheses *must* be used in these expressions.

not ($Key = $ 'T')
($Voltage = 110$) **and** ($Amperage < 10$)
($Limit < 5$) **or** ($Limit > = 10$)
($Temperature > 80$) **and** $Sunny$

Operator precedence is the reason. All of the *boolean* operators have higher precedence than the relational operators, so this expression:

$$A > B \text{ or } C > D$$

is misinterpreted by the computer as:

$$A > (B \text{ or } C) > D$$

which is meaningless (unless $A, B, C,$ and D are *boolean* expressions).

Parentheses may also be required to put together expressions that include two or more different *boolean* operators.

> In the hierarchy of *boolean* operators, **and** is considered to have a greater precedence than **or**, and **not** has the most precedence of all.

NOT
AND
OR

Suppose we want an action to take place if *Condition* and *Decision* are both *false.* This structure:

if not $Condition$ **and not** $Decision$ **then**   etc.

does the job. These expressions:

not $Condition$ **and** $Decision$
not $Condition$ **or** $Decision$

might sound good in English, but their effect in Pascal is unexpected—only *Condition* is being noted. In fact, we'll give the strange advice that you forget about the relative *boolean* operator precedences entirely.

> When **not, or,** or **and** appear in *boolean* expressions, it's good programing practice to use parentheses as internal documentation, even if they don't effect the expressions' value.

This expression uses the smallest legal number of parentheses—zero:

if not Hot **and** $Humid$ **or** $Raining$ **then**   etc.

But this version is self-documenting and unambiguous:

if ((**not** Hot) **and** $Humid$) **or** $Raining$ **then**   etc.

If *boolean* operator precedence makes an expression long enough to be unwieldy or confusing, it can usually be rewritten by following the **distributive** laws, as shown below. Assume that $p, q,$ and r are *boolean*-valued expressions or variables:*

---

* Why $p, q,$ and r? It's traditional, and tradition builds character.

$$(p \text{ or } r) \text{ and } (q \text{ or } r) = (p \text{ and } q) \text{ or } r$$
$$(p \text{ and } r) \text{ or } (q \text{ and } r) = (p \text{ or } q) \text{ and } r$$

A similar set of relations is known as **De Morgan's** laws:

$$(\text{not } p) \text{ and } (\text{not } q) = \text{not } (p \text{ or } q)$$
$$(\text{not } p) \text{ or } (\text{not } q) = \text{not } (p \text{ and } q)$$

Boolean expressions may seem hard to evaluate at first, but looking at them one term at a time helps bring them into perspective. The effect of the *boolean* operators can be summarized in this **truth table**:

not *true* is *false*
not *false* is *true*

true **and** *true* is *true*	*true* **or** *true* is *true*
true **and** *false* is *false*	*true* **or** *false* is *true*
false **and** *false* is *false*	*false* **or** *false* is *false*

Sometimes we'll know that an expression will be *false* even before each subexpression is evaluated, as in the program segment below. An output statement is executed if *Denominator* doesn't equal zero, and if the quotient of *Numerator* and *Denominator* exceeds *Fraction*.

> **if** (*Denominator* < >0) **and** ((*Numerator*/*Denominator*) > *Fraction*)
> **then** *writeln* ('We have a lucky winner!');

....

In Pascal, we must assume that *boolean* expressions are always completely evaluated.

....

Now, if *Denominator* does equal zero, the entire expression will be *false*, because both operands of **and** must be *true* for the expression to be *true*. Unfortunately, the computer doesn't think ahead—it usually tries to carry out the division. Since division by zero is an affront to all thinking women, men, and computers; a run-time error occurs and the program crashes. The segment should be rewritten to make the two evaluations explicitly consecutive, and not inadvertently simultaneous.

> **if** (*Denominator* < >0)
> **then if** (*Numerator*/*Denominator*) > *Fraction*
> **then** *writeln* ('We have a lucky winner!');

:·:

Self-Check Questions

Q. Write each of these relations or conditions as a *boolean* expression.

    a) *ConditionMet* is *true*
    b) $50 \leqslant Time \leqslant 100$
    c) *Letter* is 'V' or *Goals* is less than 4
    d) $A < 27$, $B > 6$, $C \neq 13$, and *Char* isn't 'T'
    e) $A < 27$, $B > 6$, $C \neq 13$, and *Char* isn't 'T', or, on the other hand, $50 \leqslant Time \leqslant 100$
    f) *State* is neither *High* nor *Low*.

A. Note the use of parentheses.

    a) *ConditionMet*

    b) $(Time >= 50)$ **and** $(Time <= 100)$

    c) $(Letter = 'V')$ **or** $(Goals < 4)$

    d) $(A < 27)$ **and** $(B > 6)$ **and** $(C <> 13)$ **and** $(Char <> 'T')$

    e) $((A < 27)$ **and** $(B > 6)$ **and** $(C <> 13)$ **and** $(Char <> 'T'))$

        or $((Time >= 50)$ **and** $(Time <= 100))$

    f) $(State <> High)$ **and** $(State <> Low)$

Q. One limitation of the **or** operator is that it's unable to differentiate between a single *true* operand and two *true* operands. Suppose that we want an action to be carried out if A is *true*, or B is *true*, but absolutely *not* if both of them are *true*. Write a *boolean* expression that accurately states our condition.

A. The expression we have to create is known as an *exclusive or*.

$$(A \text{ and not } B) \text{ or } (B \text{ and not } A)$$

Some languages include a special operator, **XOR**, to state this condition.

Q. Express the meaning of these *boolean* expressions in English.

      not $(A \text{ or } B)$ **or** $(A \text{ and } B)$ {Condition 1.}

      $(A \text{ and } B)$ **or** $(\text{not } A \text{ and not } B)$ {Condition 2.}

A. The conditions stated are known as *equivalence*. The expressions are *true* if A and B are both *true* or if both are *false*. Thus, equivalence is the exact opposite of the exclusive **or**.

:..:

Our final dealings in *boolean* matters involve a neat relational operator called **in**. It indicates whether or not a value is included in a larger group, or *set*, whose members can be defined as we wish.*

A Little Ado about Sets and in

    The relational operator **in** forms the following *boolean* expression:

        value **in** [*a listed set of ordinal values*]

    This expression represents *true* if *value* belongs to the specified set, and *false* if *value* isn't mentioned.

    A typical application of set expressions is to error-check entry to a **case** structure. Recall that it's a run-time error if the value of the **case** expression doesn't appear in the constant list.

    It doesn't take much conceptual rewording to see that the constant list contains the *set* of values the **case** expression may safely assume. The expression *could* be checked in advance like this:

* A number of other operations can be performed with sets, but we're not going to encounter them formally until Chapter 14.

if $((Score >= 1)$ **and** $(Score < 10))$ **or** $(Score = 15)$
    then case *Score* **of**
        10: *writeln* ('Exceptionally Good');
        8, 9: *writeln* ('Good');
        5, 6, 7: *writeln* ('Barely Passing');
        3, 4: *writeln* ('Flunking');
        0, 1, 2: *writeln* ('Exceptionally Flunking');
        15: *writeln* ('Something tells me you cheated.')
    end; {case}

But this is a clumsy way to protect our **case** structure. A better method involves using the sets and the **in** operator.

> A set can be defined by listing its members, separated by commas, between **square brackets** ([ ]). All the members of a set must be of one ordinal type.

For example, the set of integers from 0 to 9 is:

$$[0, 1, 2, 3, 4, 5, 6, 7, 8, 9]$$

whereas the set of *char* values that represent the digits is:

$$['0', '1', '2', '3', '4', '5', '6', '7', '8', '9']$$

Note that each *char* constant is put in single quotes, as usual.

> If the members of a set are sequential ordinal values— *integers* in numerical order, or *char* values in the order of their collating sequence—we can simplify things a bit by using two periods between the first and last members, much as we would use an ellipsis in English.

$$[0 .. 9] \qquad ['A' .. 'Z'] \qquad ['0' .. '9']$$

Two or more ordered sequences, like as the set of upper- and lower-case letters, can be shown in a single expression like this:

$$Letter \text{ in } ['a' .. 'z', 'A' .. 'Z']$$

The *Score* example is rewritten as:

if $(Score$ **in** $[0 .. 10, 15])$
    then case *Score* **of**
        10: *writeln* ('Exceptionally Good');
        8, 9: *writeln* ('Good');
        5, 6, 7: *writeln* ('Barely Passing');
        3, 4: *writeln* ('Flunking');
        0, 1, 2: *writeln* ('Exceptionally Flunking');
        15: *writeln* ('Something tells me you cheated.')
    end; {case}

Two final points end our discussion of sets. First, any representation of a value can be used in the set definition—it doesn't have to be one of the constants of the type.

> **if** (*Value* **in** [(*ErrorRange* − *Correction*) .. *HighBound*])
>   **then begin**   etc. {Expressions can appear in the set definition.}

The second point is that in a set *non*-membership test, the entire *boolean* set expression is put in parentheses and preceded by the **not** operator.

> **if not** (*NextCharacter* **in** ['0' .. '9'])
>   **then** *writeln* ('You must enter a digit') ;

:··:

Q. Is it possible for this to be a valid expression?

> *InputValue* **in** [−15 .. 25, 'f' .. 'w']

A. It couldn't possibly be a good *boolean* expression, because we've tried to define a set that contains two different types of values— *integer*, and *char*. The members of a set, and the value whose membership we're checking, must all belong to the same ordinal type.

Self-Check Questions

:··:

6-3 Focus on Programing: Exhaustive Search, Reading Programs

IN CHAPTER 4, WE SAID THAT BRUTE-FORCE solutions, while not necessarily efficient or elegant, are often the easiest kind to implement quickly and correctly. They may waste the computer's time, but they save ours. A specialized form of brute force is called **exhaustive search**. Instead of designing an algorithm to produce a final answer directly, we examine the problem's **solution space**—all of its potential answers—to find one or more that are correct.

A famous problem that's often solved through exhaustive search is the Traveling Salesman problem. A salesman must visit seven different cities on his sales route. He can start anywhere, and visit them in any order. Is there some technique he can use to minimize the distance he has to travel? A solution that seems too obvious turns out to work well—write a program that figures out how long every possible route is, and take the shortest one.

Computers are good at solving problems by exhaustive search because they can go through large solution spaces quickly. Unfortunately, the pioneers of programing learned that the computer is a Sorcerer's Apprentice. Although a computer increases the speed at which one can perform calculations, it also vastly accelerates the rate at which one can make mistakes and produce nonsense. Worse yet, even correct programs can produce output in such quantity as to be virtually useless.

Let's look at a problem that might lead us into such a trap.

The letters 'ergro' appear in the middle of an ordinary word. They are preceded by three letters, and are followed by the same three letters in the same order. The first letter is a vowel, and the other two are different consonants. What is the word?

Program *AllPossibilities*, below, implements a simple exhaustive search algorithm. It prints every possible word formed by prefixing and following 'ergro' with the same three letters. We've shown the first few lines of its output.

```
program AllPossibilities (output);
    {Prints all possible outputs of the form XXXERGROXXX.}

var Ch1, Ch2, Ch3: char;

begin
    for Ch1 := 'A' to 'Z'
        do for Ch2 := 'A' to 'Z'
            do for Ch3 := 'A' to 'Z'
                do writeln (Ch1, Ch2, Ch3, 'ERGRO', Ch1, Ch2, Ch3)
    end.   {AllPossibilities}
```

```
         ↓        ↓        ↓        ↓        ↓
AAAERGROAAA
AABERGROAAB
AACERGROAAC                    etc.
```

All we have to do now is scan the output and find an ordinary word. But how much output *is* there? *Ch2* will change 26 times for each increment of *Ch2*. *Ch2*, in turn, changes 26 times for every advance of *Ch1*. The *writeln* in *AllPossibilities*, then, is executed 26*26*26 times. The number of lines of output produced by *AllPossibilities* equals the solution space it searches—17,576. The sheer size of this output makes it worthless. Even if we modified the program to print eight columns of twenty-five lines each, more than eighty-five pages would be generated.

If we want to solve this problem realistically, we have to figure out a method of limiting the solution space that is searched. Now, if you recall program *StolenGold*, you'll remember that we used nested **if** statements to short-circuit the loop when a potential answer was known to be invalid. As a result, *StolenGold* automatically winnowed out the incorrect answers. *AllPossibilities*, on the other hand, relies on the program *user* to do the dirty work.

How can we reduce the solution space within the program? We can begin by using all the information in the problem statement. The first letter is a vowel, and the other two are different consonants. *FewerPossibilities* incorporates these checks into our basic algorithm.

```
program FewerPossibilities (output) ;
    {Reduces the amount of output.}
var Ch1, Ch2, Ch3:  char;
begin
    for Ch1 := 'A' to 'U'
        do if Ch1 in ['A','E','I','O','U']
            then for Ch2 := 'B' to 'Z'
                do if not (Ch2 in ['A','E','I','O','U'])
                    then for Ch3 := 'B' to 'Z'
                        do if not (Ch3 in [Ch2, 'A','E','I','O','U'])
                            then writeln (Ch1, Ch2, Ch3, 'ERGRO', Ch1, Ch2, Ch3)
end.   {FewerPossibilities}

      ↓        ↓        ↓         ↓         ↓
ABCERGROABC
ABDERGROABD
ABFERGROABF                    etc.
```

When we multiply **for** loops to find the number of words *Fewer-Possibilities* prints, we should discount iterations that don't result in output because one of the **if** statements isn't passed. The first loop goes all the way 5 times (for A, E, I, O, and U). The next loop passes 21 times—once for each consonant—and the final loop succeeds only 20 times. Thus, *FewerPossibilities* churns out 5*21*20, or 2100, words to check.

Is *FewerPossibilities* more efficient than *AllPossibilities*? Certainly—who knows how many milliseconds it saves!

> More important is the knowledge that improving our basic algorithm has increased its efficiency *in the eyes of the user* by a factor of eight.

FewerPossibilities can be improved by using our knowledge of English to limit the solution space even further. For example, 'Q' couldn't be one of the consonants because it can't be followed by a 'U'. If we add it to the sets of disallowed characters, our output is reduced to 5*20*19, or 1900, words. Taking out 'X' and 'Z' brings us down to 1530 possibilities. Beyond this the advantages of limiting the solution space must be weighed against the potential of letting the correct answer slip by.*

In *The Psychology of Computer Programing*, Gerald Weinberg warns that program reading is a dying art. 'Just as television has turned the heads of the young from the old-fashioned joys of book reading', he says, 'so have terminals and generally improved turnaround made the reading of programs the mark of a hopelessly old-fashioned programer.' He goes

Reading Programs

---

* So what's the word? *Underground*

on to admit that working face-to-face with a giant computer is probably more exciting than contemplating other people's programs. However, he concludes that there's something to be gained even by laughing at other programer's bad examples.

Our final example for this chapter is a long program for you to read. The problem it solves is very different from *AllPossibilities*:

> Write a program that keeps a running total of bowling scores for one player. Program input will be the number of pins knocked down with each bowled ball, and its output should be the player's score up to that point.*

Clearly, we're not going to worry about solution spaces here! Our problem, once more, is imitation. We want to copy the actions a human scorekeeper takes to score a frame. Let's not cheat you out of your money's worth of stepwise refinement:

> *Get the score of the first ball.*
> *Take care of any previous frames.*
> *If it's not a strike, get the score of the next ball. If it is a strike, make a note of it.*
> *Again, take care of any previous frames.*
> *If it's not a spare or strike, post the score of this frame. If it is a spare, make a note of it.*
> *Start all over again.*
> *If the tenth frame ends on a strike or spare, score the extra balls.*

To refresh your memory of the rules, a spare frame's score is increased by the next ball, while a strike frame's score is increased by the sum of the next two balls. If a spare or strike is scored in the tenth and final frame, the bowler gets to bowl one or two extra balls. We can refine our rough pseudocode by imagining a scorekeeper's actions in more procedural terms.

> *initialize all program variables*;
> **for** *each of 10 frames*
>   *get the next ball's score*;
>   *update previous frames that change*;
>   *update variables* (*like the current score*) ;
>   **if** *it wasn't a strike*
>   *get the next ball's score*;
>   *update previous frames that change*;
>   *update variables* (*like the current score*) ;
>   **if** *it wasn't a strike or spare*
>   *print this frame's score*;
>   **if** *there was a strike or spare on the final frame*
>   *process the extra frame*;

What does a human scorekeeper have to know as she goes along? Naturally, she has to keep track of the number of pins knocked down

---

* If you don't know how to bowl, now would be a very appropriate time to learn.

by each ball. She also has to know what happened in the last frame, and sometimes, in the frame before that. If the score from earlier frames depends on the results of the present frame, 'current' scores for as many as three frames are required too. A human scorekeeper has a scoresheet to keep all these notes on. As Pascal programers, we have program variables:

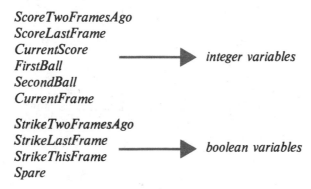

ScoreTwoFramesAgo
ScoreLastFrame
CurrentScore
FirstBall   → integer variables
SecondBall
CurrentFrame

StrikeTwoFramesAgo
StrikeLastFrame   → boolean variables
StrikeThisFrame
Spare

What about the jobs a scorekeeper does? We turn to procedures:

GetTheNextBall
HandlePreviousFrames
HandleTheTenthFrame
PrintTheScore

At this point, we could return to our last refinement and restate it in far more precise terms. Instead, we'll jump right to the end. Program *Score*, which appears over the next few pages, is the final result of our refinements. We'd like you to read *Score*, and see what you can learn from it.

How can you go about reading a program as long as *Score*? A good way to begin is by skimming. Read over the main program and try to get a feel for the different *states* that prevail during execution. What frame are we on? Are we working on a strike or spare? Exactly when do we make the transition from one frame to the next? From one state to the next?

Next, read through the procedures. Are their names self-explanatory? Perhaps a note in the margin will help you remember a detail of a procedure's operation. What is the program state on entry to the procedure, and on exit? What values does each procedure change? Note that most of our comments are intended to help delineate the structure of the program rather than to explain its algorithm. Does this help or hinder your understanding of the program?

Go back to the main program and see how it uses its procedures. In *Score*, most of the main program falls within one large **for** loop. Go to the beginning of the loop and pose a state—say, there was a spare on the previous frame, or a strike, or perhaps the first bowled ball is a strike. What happens? Mentally run some sample input through the program to see what it does.

Read the program to see how we used procedures and control structures to divide execution into well-defined actions. Why did we use a **case** structure for two-way choice in procedure *HandlePrevious-Frames*? Could the **if** structures be further nested? Is there unnecessary repetition in our coding? Are all the variables we declared really needed? Could the *boolean* conditions be restated in a better way?

Finally, appraise the program. What are its shortcomings? Does it always work? How well does it error check input? How robust is it? Can its output be made more attractive? How could it be modified for an interactive programing environment?

> Reading another person's program can be a difficult job. However, it can give an insight into programing that can't be taught in a class.

Learn to criticize your own programs by practicing on ours.

```
program Score (input, output) ;
    {Keeps bowling scores for one player.  Error messages are printed if any ball is
     less than 0 or more than 10, or if two balls in any frame total more than 10.}
var ScoreTwoFramesAgo, ScoreLastFrame, CurrentScore,
    FirstBall, SecondBall, CurrentFrame : integer;
    StrikeTwoFramesAgo, StrikeLastFrame, Spare,
    StrikeThisFrame, ErrorCondition: boolean;
procedure Initialize (var StrikeTwoFramesAgo, StrikeLastFrame, Spare, ErrorCondition: boolean;
                      var ScoreTwoFramesAgo, ScoreLastFrame, CurrentScore: integer) ;
    {Initialize the game-state variables.}
    begin
        StrikeTwoFramesAgo := false; StrikeLastFrame := false;
        Spare := false; ErrorCondition := false;
        ScoreTwoFramesAgo := 0; ScoreLastFrame := 0; CurrentScore := 0
    end;  {Initialize}
procedure PrintTheScoreOf (CurrentFrame, Score: integer; ErrorCondition: boolean) ;
    {Print frame number and score.  If in ErrorCondition, print a warning.}
    begin
        if not ErrorCondition
            then writeln ('Frame ', CurrentFrame:1, ' Score ', Score:1)
            else writeln ('Error condition exists.  Program about to terminate.')
    end;  {PrintTheScoreOf}
procedure GetTheNextBall (CurrentFrame, WhichBall: integer; var NumberOfPins: integer;
                          var ErrorCondition: boolean) ;
    {Input ball values.  Sets ErrorCondition state variable.}
    begin
        {Interactive programs should prompt for input here.}
        read (NumberOfPins) ;
        if (NumberOfPins<0) or (NumberOfPins>10) ;
            then ErrorCondition := true;
        if ErrorCondition
            then writeln ('Error on ball ', WhichBall:1, ' of frame ', CurrentFrame:1)
    end;  {GetTheNextBall}
```

```
procedure HandlePreviousFrames (CurrentBall, FrameHalf: integer; StrikeTwoFramesAgo,
                                StrikeLastFrame: boolean; var Spare: boolean;
                                ScoreTwoFramesAgo: integer;
                                var ScoreLastFrame, CurrentScore: integer) ;
  {Update previous frames' state variables.}
  begin
    case FrameHalf of
      1: begin    {First half of the frame.}
           if StrikeLastFrame
             then begin
               if StrikeTwoFramesAgo
                 then begin
                   PrintTheScoreOf (CurrentFrame−2,
                           ScoreTwoFramesAgo+CurrentBall, ErrorCondition) ;
                   ScoreLastFrame := ScoreLastFrame+CurrentBall;
                   CurrentScore := CurrentScore+CurrentBall
                 end;   {StrikeTwoFramesAgo}
               ScoreLastFrame := ScoreLastFrame+CurrentBall;
               CurrentScore := CurrentScore+CurrentBall
             end   {StrikeLastFrame}
           else if Spare
             then begin
               PrintTheScoreOf (CurrentFrame−1,
                                 ScoreLastFrame+CurrentBall, ErrorCondition) ;
               CurrentScore := CurrentScore+CurrentBall
             end;   {Spare}
         end;   {FrameHalf=1}
      2: begin    {Second half of the frame.}
           if StrikeLastFrame
             then begin
               PrintTheScoreOf (CurrentFrame−1,
                                 ScoreLastFrame+SecondBall, ErrorCondition) ;
               CurrentScore := CurrentScore+SecondBall
             end;   {StrikeLastFrame}
           CurrentScore := CurrentScore+SecondBall;
           Spare := (FirstBall+SecondBall) = 10
         end   {FrameHalf=2}
    end   {case}
  end;   {HandlePreviousFrames}
```

```
procedure HandleTenthFrame (Spare, StrikeLastFrame, StrikeTwoFramesAgo: boolean;
                              CurrentScore, ScoreTwoFramesAgo: integer) ;
    {Score any extra balls required to complete the game.}
    var FirstBall, SecondBall: integer;
    begin
        GetTheNextBall (10, 1, FirstBall, ErrorCondition) ;
        if Spare
            then PrintTheScoreOf (10, CurrentScore+FirstBall, ErrorCondition)
            else if StrikeLastFrame
                then begin
                    if StrikeTwoFramesAgo
                        then PrintTheScoreOf (9, ScoreTwoFramesAgo+FirstBall, ErrorCondition) ;
                    CurrentScore := CurrentScore+FirstBall;
                    GetTheNextBall (10, 2, SecondBall, ErrorCondition) ;
                    PrintTheScoreOf (10, CurrentScore+FirstBall+SecondBall, ErrorCondition)
                end;
    end;  {HandleTenthFrame}
begin  {Score}
    Initialize (StrikeTwoFramesAgo, StrikeLastFrame, Spare, ErrorCondition,
                ScoreTwoFramesAgo, ScoreLastFrame, CurrentScore) ;
    for CurrentFrame := 1 to 10
        do begin
            GetTheNextBall (CurrentFrame, 1, FirstBall, ErrorCondition) ;
            HandlePreviousFrames (FirstBall, 1, StrikeTwoFramesAgo, StrikeLastFrame,
                                    Spare, ScoreTwoFramesAgo, ScoreLastFrame, CurrentScore) ;
                        {Record the effect of the first ball.}
            CurrentScore := CurrentScore+FirstBall;
            StrikeThisFrame := (FirstBall=10) ;
                        {Get the second ball if the first wasn't a strike}
            if StrikeThisFrame
                then Spare := false
                else begin
                    GetTheNextBall (CurrentFrame, 2, SecondBall, ErrorCondition) ;
                    ErrorCondition := (FirstBall+SecondBall) > 10;
                    HandlePreviousFrames (SecondBall, 2, StrikeTwoFramesAgo,
                                            StrikeLastFrame, Spare, ScoreTwoFramesAgo,
                                            ScoreLastFrame, CurrentScore) ;
                end;  {not StrikeThisFrame}
                        {Update the game state variables}
            StrikeTwoFramesAgo := StrikeLastFrame;
            ScoreTwoFramesAgo := ScoreLastFrame;
            StrikeLastFrame := StrikeThisFrame;
            ScoreLastFrame := CurrentScore;
            if not (Spare or StrikeThisFrame)
                then PrintTheScoreOf (CurrentFrame, CurrentScore, ErrorCondition) ;
        end;  {for}
                    {Finally, take care of the tenth frame.}
    if Spare or StrikeLastFrame
        then HandleTenthFrame (Spare, StrikeLastFrame, StrikeTwoFramesAgo,
                                CurrentScore, ScoreTwoFramesAgo) ;
end.  {Score}
```

```
    ↓           ↓       ↓       ↓       ↓
9 1   0 10   10    10    6 2   7 3   8 2   10   9 0   9 1   10
Frame  1 Score  10
Frame  2 Score  30
Frame  3 Score  56
Frame  4 Score  74
Frame  5 Score  82
Frame  6 Score  100
Frame  7 Score  120
Frame  8 Score  139
Frame  9 Score  148
Frame  10 Score  168
```

MOST AUTOMOBILE ACCIDENTS HAPPEN close to home, because that's where people do most of their driving. The **if** structure probably tends to generate more than its fair share of bugs, because it appears in just about every program.

A small bug that's extremely hard to find is caused by a misplaced semicolon. For example, in the segment below *GetMoreData* is called whether *ReadingData* is *true* or *false.* Can you see why?

> **if** *ReadingData* **then**;
>   *GetMoreData*;
> *NextStatement*;   etc.

Reformatting the segment makes the bug stand out. The compiler thinks that the **if** structure controls an empty statement:

> **if** *ReadingData* **then**
>   ;   {This empty statement is the structure's action.}
> *GetMoreData*;
> *NextStatement*;   etc.

The same error occurs when an **else** is followed by a semicolon. Note that these are *semantic* errors. They are syntactically correct, so the programs they appear in will compile. However, their effect is unintended. Preceding an **else** with a semicolon, in contrast, is strictly a syntax error. The semicolon's effect is to dissociate an **if** structure's **else** and **then** parts. The compiler will complain about the sudden appearance of the reserved word **else.**

An extremely common mistake is to neglect to express an **if** structure's action as a compound statement. As we've said before, program format has no effect on program semantics. This segment doesn't do what it appears to do:

6-4
Antibugging
and
Debugging

ask about

> **if** *Debugging*
>   **then**
>   *PrintCurrentValues* (*HobNob, Goblin, Munchkin*) ;
>   *UpdateInput* (*ChangeData*) ;
>   *writeln* ('I hope everything works!')
>   **else**
>   *GetRawInput* (*NewData*) ;
>   *writeln* ('Moving on to computations.') ;
> *FigureThingsOut*;   etc.

If we format it the way the computer reads it, we can see why the compiler will complain about a meaningless **else**.

> **if** *Debugging* **then** *PrintCurrentValues* (*HobNob, Goblin, Munchkin*) ;
> *UpdateInput* (*ChangeData*) ;
> *writeln* ('I hope everything works!')
> **else**   {What is this word doing here?}
> *GetRawInput* (*NewData*) ;
> *writeln* ('Moving on to computations.') ;
> *FigureThingsOut*;   etc.

Now, errors like this are usually due to inadvertent carelessness. The action (or alternative action) of a structure may have originally been just one statement or procedure call. If the program is modified and additional actions are added, it's easy to overlook the need for a **begin** and **end**. Defensive programing helps obviate the problem.

> Many programers write *every* action as a compound statement. Reading an unnecessary **begin, end** pair doesn't cost the computer anything, and it may save lots of trouble later on.

Boolean expressions cause a whole raft of semantic and syntactic bugs. A common error occurs if you forget that **and** and **or** don't mean 'and' and 'or'. Suppose that the proper response to some question is either 'A' or 'B'. This assignment is meaningless in Pascal:

$$RightAnswer := Response = (\text{'A' } \textbf{or} \text{ 'B'});$$

because **or** is a *boolean* operator, and is only used to compare *boolean* values. The statement is rewritten correctly as:

$$RightAnswer := (Response = \text{'A'}) \textbf{ or } (Response = \text{'B'});$$

Errors also occur in translation from English to Pascal. For example, the English phrase:

$$neither\ A\ nor\ B$$

translates into Pascal as:

$$\textbf{not } A \textbf{ and not } B$$

rather than:

$$\textbf{not } A \textbf{ or not } B$$

Using **not** in complex *boolean* expressions can also be tricky (but always, as Mr. Spock would say, perfectly logical). It's an interesting fact that negative expressions—those containing a **not**—are often harder to understand than positive ones—especially when they start to stretch out, like this:*

$$\textbf{not not not not not not not } (X > Y)$$

It's particularly important to keep track of parentheses. These two expressions are not identical in meaning:

$$\textbf{not } (\textit{Hot } \textbf{and } \textit{Tired})\qquad(\textbf{not } \textit{Hot}) \textbf{ and } (\textbf{not } \textit{Tired})$$

although they appear to be rather similar. This expression:

$$\textbf{not } (\textit{Hot}) \textbf{ or not } (\textit{Tired})$$

states the same as the left-hand expression above. You can prove that we're right by constructing a truth table, as we did in 6-2. Show the result of each expression for all possible values of *Hot* and *Tired*.

What do you think precipitated this error message?

```
IF NOT NEXTCHARACTER IN [ 'a'..'z' ] THEN
      ↑ OPERAND OF "NOT" MUST BE OF TYPE BOOLEAN
```

An error caused by the high precedence of the **not** operator—greater than the other relational and *boolean* operators—shows up in 'negative' set expressions:

if not *NextCharacter* **in** [′a′..′z′] **then**   etc.

The precedence of **not** (which exceeds that of the relational operators, including **in**), makes the compiler think we're trying to **not** the value of *NextCharacter*, which would be meaningless. The expression must be rewritten with parentheses:

if not (*NextCharacter* **in** [′a′..′z′]) **then**   etc.

The precedence hierarchy of *boolean* and relational operators is:

$$\textbf{not}$$
$$\textbf{and}$$
$$\textbf{or}$$
$$= \ <> \ < \ <= \ > \ >= \ \textbf{in}$$

---

* Miller, Lance A., *Programing For Non-programers*. Intl. Journal of Man-Machine Studies, 1974, vol. 6, pp.237-260.

You can appreciate that there are often a variety of ways to express identical conditions, some considerably more obscure than others. Any expression that's difficult to decipher should be rewritten by using parentheses, the Distributive laws, or De Morgan's laws.

A final common bug is to mistakenly assume that two **if** structures with opposite conditions are always the same as an **if** structure with an **else** alternative. Can you name the circumstances that would make this program segment:

> **if** *BitCount* < 0 **then** *Twiddle*(*BitCount*);
> **if** *BitCount* > =0 **then** *Twaddle*(*BitCount*);

differ in effect from this one:

> **if** *BitCount* < 0
>   **then** *Twiddle*(*BitCount*)
>   **else** *Twaddle*(*BitCount*);

Suppose that *Twiddle* modifies the value of its argument *BitCount* In the first program segment, both *Twiddle* and *Twaddle* might be called. In the second segment, only one is—never both.

Summary

Boolean expressions state conditions in Pascal. Although there are only two constants of the ordinal type *boolean—false* and *true—*they can be represented in a variety of ways. *Boolean* values may be defined as constants, represented by variables, or shown with longer expressions.

When the *relational* operators compare two values of any type, a *boolean* expression is formed. A special relational operator, **in,** also has a *boolean* result. It determines whether or not a value is a member of a certain *set* of ordinal values, defined on the spot by listing its members between *square brackets* ([]). Two dots (..) can be used as a shorthand in listing contiguous set values.

More complex conditions can be stated by using the *boolean* operators **not, and,** and **or,** given in order of precedence. To avoid ambiguity, parentheses should always be used when stating *boolean* expressions. Parentheses *must* be put around terms of an expression that contain a relational operator, since they have the lowest possible precedence.

The **if** structure evaluates a *boolean* expression to determine whether an action (or which of two alterative actions) will be executed. When **if** structures are nested, an 'else action' is always the alternative of the 'then action' immediately before it.

Exhaustive search algorithms are related to brute-force algorithms. They search a problem's entire *solution space,* or set of possible answers, to find one or more correct ones. Nesting **if** structures is one way to limit the amount of searching a program must engage in, or to minimize the quantity of output it produces.

Since the input that programs receive won't always be perfect, programs should be made as **robust** as possible. They should **error-check** input, and try to anticipate user errors. If at all possible, a program should recognize error states, and inform the program user.

New Pascal

New Terms

if	then	else	
not	**and**	**or**	**in**

relational operator   *error-check*   *robust*
distributive laws   *De Morgan's laws*   *truth table*
set   *square brackets*   *exhaustive search*
solution space

Self-Test Exercises

6-1   If a *boolean* expression contains both relational operators (like =, <, and >) and *boolean* operators (like **and** and **or**), why will some of its terms (sub-expressions) need to be put in parentheses?

6-2   Which of these *boolean* expressions are logically equivalent?

  a) (*Finished* **and not** *Bankrupt*) **or** (*Bankrupt* **and not** *Finished*)
  b) (*Finished* **or** *Bankrupt*) **or not** (*Bankrupt* **and** *Finished*)
  c) *Finished*<> *Bankrupt*

6-3   Under what circumstances will the output statement be executed? Assume that *StillSearching* and *Found* are *boolean* variables.

> **if** *StillSearching* = *Found*
> **then** *writeln* ('Value located.') ;

6-4   Is this legal Pascal? Assume that *Entry* and *Standard* are *integer* values.

> **case** *Entry*< *Standard* **of**
>   *true*: *writeln* ('Entry is less than Standard.') ;
>   *false*: *writeln* ('Standard is greater than or equal to Entry.')
> **end**;

6-5   Rewrite the following statement using two **if...then** structures.

> **if** (2∗*X*) > *Y*
>   **then begin** *Y*:= 2∗Y; *X*:= *X*/2 **end**
>   **else** *writeln* ('Able was I ere I saw Elba.') ;

6-6   What is the output of this program segment?

> *writeln* (1=2, 2=2, (2+3)=7) ;

6-7   Compare these two program segments:

if (*a*< =*b*) **and** (*a*< =*c*)	*Smallest*:= *a*;
then *Smallest*:= *a*	**if** *b*< *Smallest*
else if (*b*< =*c*) **and** (*b*< =*a*)	**then** *Smallest*:= *b*;
then *Smallest*:= *b*	**if** *c*< *Smallest*
else *Smallest*:= *c*;	**then** *Smallest*:= *c*;

Is there any difference between them? Explain.

6-8   What's the difference between these two program segments? Which is better, and why?

readln (*Amount*);   *readln* (*Amount*);
if *Amount*> 500   **if** *Amount*> 500
  then *OverRun* (*Amount*);   **then** *OverRun* (*Amount*)
if (*Amount*>300) **and** (*Amount*< =500)   **else if** (*Amount*>300) **and** (*Amount*< =500)
  then *UnderRun* (*Amount*);   **then** *UnderRun* (*Amount*)
if (*Amount*>150) **and** (*Amount*< =300)   **else if** (*Amount*>150) **and** (*Amount*< =300)
  then *WriteCheckFor* (*Amount*);   **then** *WriteCheckFor* (*Amount*)
if (*Amount*< =150)   **else** *ReCompute* (*Amount*);   etc.
  then *ReCompute* (*Amount*);   etc.

6-9 Write a procedure that determines if one number is evenly divisible by another. Both numbers should be passed as parameters.

6-10 Write a loop that reads in 100 positive *integers* in the range 1 through 500, and determines the largest even and smallest odd.

6-11 Suppose that the two statements below appear, as shown, in a program. What single **if** statement could you replace them with?

$$\textbf{if } n> =2 \textbf{ then } n:= 3*n+1;$$
$$\textbf{if } n> =7 \textbf{ then } n:= n-7;$$

6-12 Write a set definition that defines, for upper-case letters, *a*) the vowels, *b*) the consonants.

6-13 Write a loop that reads in 250 characters, and prints out the number of digits and punctuation marks.

6-14 The four program segments below all purport to add the even numbers between 1 and 5. What are the advantages and disadvantages of each?

{Example 1}   {Example 2}
Sum := 0;   *Sum* := 0;
for *Counter* := 1 **to** 5   **for** *Counter* := 2 **to** 4
  do if not *odd*(*Counter*)   **do if not** *odd*(*Counter*)
    then *Sum* := *Sum* + *Counter*   **then** *Sum* := *Sum* + *Counter*

{Example 3}   {Example 4}
Sum := 6   *Sum* := 5

More Exercises

6-15 Write a program that finds the 'middlemost' of five numbers.

6-16 An *Armstrong number* is a number of *n* digits that is equal to sum of each digit raised to the *n*th power. For example, 153 (which has three digits) equals $1^3 + 5^3 + 3^3$. Find the other three Armstrong numbers below 999.

6-17 Take a four-digit number. Add the first two digits to the last two digits. Now, square the sum. Surprise! you've got the original number again. Find the three numbers that have this special property.

6-18 The following instruction appears on a computer science final exam: "Make a statement. If the statement is true, you'll flunk the exam. If the statement is false, you'll flunk the entire course." What's the correct answer to avoid flunking?

6-19 One of the bugs associated with *boolean* expressions is the appearance of an unexpected alternative, not ruled out by the statement of the expression. Here are some everyday examples of this phenomenon.

    Two people played seven games of chess, yet each won the same number of games. How could this be? Some months have 31 days, and some months have only 30. How many months have 28 days? I have two coins in my pocket that total fifty-five cents. One of the coins is not a nickel. What are the two coins?

6-20   Write a loop that sums the squares of the first 333 odd integers.

6-21   Write a procedure that takes two *integers* as parameters, and prints them in ascending order. Do the same with three *reals.* Four *char* values (in alphabetical order, of course).

6-22   Write a program to produce a table of factorials for odd or even numbers only. Prompt the user for the upper limit of the table. If the user asks for odd factorials, and gives an even upper limit, what should happen? Modify the program to give reasonable output for a negative limit input.

6-23   An peculiar property of the Fibonacci series is that if any given number is squared, it equals the product of the preceding and subsequent numbers, sometimes plus 1, and sometimes minus 1. Write a program that computes the correction for the first hundred Fibonacci numbers—should one be added or subtracted? Is any pattern apparent?

6-24   A perfect square is a number whose square root is an *integer.* Now, it's easy to make a table of the first *n* perfect squares—it just takes a **for** loop that prints the square of its counter variable. Finding all perfect squares between any two numbers takes a bit more doing, because the standard *sqrt* function has a *real* result that may be a tiny bit off. For example, *sqrt*(16) might equal 4.00000000001E+01, or 3.9999998888E+01. However, we can test for perfect squares like this: Given any *integer,* find its *real* square root, round this number, and then square it. If the result equals the original number, the original number is a perfect square.

Write a program that prints all perfect squares between any two numbers *a* and *b.*

6-25   A college bookstore wants to estimate its business for the next year. Experience has shown the clerks that sales depend greatly on whether a book is required or merely recommended, and whether or not it has been used before. A new, required book will sell to 90% of prospective enrollment, but if it's been used before, only 65% will buy. Similarly, 40% of the prospective enrollment will buy a newly recommended book, but just half that many buy a book that was recommended in the past.

Write a program that accepts as input a book code, the book's single-copy cost, the current number of volumes on hand, the prospective class enrollment, and data that indicates whether the book is required, recommended, and has or hasn't been used in the past. Each book is identified by a one-letter subject code, followed by an integer book code. As output, show all the input information, together with the number of books that must be ordered (if any), the total cost of all book orders, and the expected profit if the store pays 80% of list price.

6-26   Improve the above program to take more sophisticated considerations into account. Suppose that the store's cost drops to 75% of list on all orders of 10 to 50 books, and 70% on all orders of more than 50. However, also assume that the sales projections may be overstated by as much as 10%. Have your program compute the purchase sizes that will maximize potential profits.

6-27   The terms of a revolving credit account are as follows:

Unpaid Balance	Interest Rate/Month
$0–$500	1½%
$500.01–$1000	1¼%
over $1000	1%

Balance	Minimum Payment
$0–$10	Balance
$10.01–$250	$10
over $250	10% of Balance

Write a program that given an unpaid balance, adds on the interest due, and prints out the minimum payment. Accept a payment, and then print a record of the transaction, including the next month's balance and minimum payment.

6-28   Here's another in our series of computer-magician programs. Write the following algorithm as a program: Ask somebody to pick a three digit number, and to think of the number as being *ABC* (where *A, B,* and *C* are the three digits of the number). Now, find out the remainders when the numbers formed by *ABC, BCA,* and *CAB* are divided by 11. Have the computer call these remainders *X, Y,* and *Z,* and add them three up as *X+Y, Y+Z,* and *Z+X.* If any of the sums is odd, increase or decrease it by 11—whichever operation results in a positive number less than 20. Finally, divide each of the sums in half. The resulting digits are *A, B,* and *C.*

It's a nice touch to include a 'calculator' as part of this program. Don't forget to have all output be as spellbinding as possible.

6-29   What goes on within the computer is hidden from a program user, and for this problem it's just as well. Pick a number between 1 and 100, cube it, and give it to the computer. Call this *UsersCube.* Here's how the computer can figure out the cube root—the original number. Begin with a table of cubes for the numbers 1 through 10:

$$1^3=1 \quad 2^3=8 \quad 3^3=27 \quad 4^3=64 \quad 5^3=125$$
$$6^3=216 \quad 7^3=343 \quad 8^3=512 \quad 9^3=729 \quad 10^3=1000$$

Note that each cube ends with a different digit.

The computer finds the cube root of *UsersCube* in two steps. The second digit of the root equals the cube root of the number in the table whose cube ends with the same digit as *UsersCube.* The first digit of the desired cube root is found by discarding the final three digits of *UsersCube,* and comparing the remaining figures to the cubes in the table. The first digit of our cube root is the cube root of the number which is closest, but still less than, these remaining figures. For example, the second digit of the cube root of 117649 is 9 (by comparing last numbers), and the first digit is 4 (the cube root of 64, the figure nearest but still less than 117). Write a program that carries out this weird computation.

6-30   Although one likes to think of computers as representing the ultimate in mathematical calculation, the interior of a computer is really a sort of Never-never Land, where the axioms of ordinary arithmetic are occasionally suspended. In other words, although *A+B* may equal *C,* it is not necessarily true that *B* is equal to *C−A.* This can be very disconcerting.

Write a program that computes the following sum:

$$1 - 1/2 + 1/3 - 1/4 + \ldots - 1/1000$$

Try figuring it in several ways: working from right to left (and left to right), subtracting the sum of *all* the negative terms from the sum of the positive terms (again going right to left and left to right), summing the two series, etc. Why do you think there are differences in your results? By the way, the actual sum (to 25 decimal places) is:

$$0.6930971830599452969172323$$

6-31   A target used for throwing darts allows these scores: 7, 15, 19, 23, 29, and 37. Suppose that the purpose of a game is to throw six darts and score exactly 100 points. What are the five ways such a score can be achieved?

6-32 Sam Loyd tells of a roulette system, named after a Lord Rosslyn, that enabled a lucky player to win 777,777 francs at Monte Carlo. In the Rosslyn system, a player makes only even-money bets (we'll ignore the house percentage) in the following manner: first, make 7 consecutive one-franc bets, then 7 forty-nine-franc (7^2) bets, then 7 bets of 7^3 francs, 7 bets of 7^4, 7^5, and 7^6 francs. Thus, forty-nine bets are made in a row, win or lose.

The problem we pose is this: How many bets, at what stakes, were won to produce winnings of exactly 777,777 francs? Don't forget to deduct losing bets from the winnings.

6-33 Extend your new programing language to allow *boolean* choice. Define the two forms of **if** structures as two entirely different structures. Can their syntax be simplified, or written in a way that helps prevent errors?

Reptiles by M. C. Escher. Lithograph, 1943. Courtesy Vorpal Gallery/V.A.G.A.

7

Making Actions Continue Indefinitely

We can measure our progress in learning Pascal by comparing the control structures we understand. The **case** structure requires a *definite* action—one of the actions in its constant list is always executed. The **if** structure, in contrast, is *conditional.* Its action might not be executed at all; whether or not it is depends on the truth or falsehood of its control condition.

The same underlying ideas apply to the loop structures. The **for** control structure is a definite loop, whose action is always repeated a fixed number of times. To round out Pascal we can also expect to find a *conditional loop.* Pascal has two of them: the **repeat** and **while** control structures. The number of times each loop iterates is not set in advance. Instead, it depends on an action taken with the loop itself.

We'll begin section 7-1 with a look at the **repeat** structure, and then move on to the **while** loop. We'll end with a large program that uses all three of Pascal's loop structure.

Section 7-2 changes our direction, with a discussion of *text processing,* and an introduction to the notion of *input files.* We'll also learn about the standard procedures *eof* and *eoln.* Finally, 7-3 focuses on programing with loops, and brings up the idea of program testing. As usual, the last section covers debugging and antibugging.

If a loop is entered, it must end eventually.

7-1
The **repeat** and **while** Structures

LIKE MOST CONTROL STRUCTURES, the **repeat** uses a *boolean* expression to control the execution of an action.

> The **repeat** structure's action takes place, then its *exit condition* (a *boolean* expression) is evaluated. The loop's action is repeated until the exit condition is met.

If the expression that represents the exit condition is *false*, the exit condition is *not* met, and the loop's action is iterated (repeated). If the expression is *true*, the exit condition *is* met. The loop is **terminated**, and the program moves on to the next statement. In outline form, the **repeat** structure looks like this:

```
repeat
    action
until boolean expression;   {the exit condition}
```

The structure's syntax chart is:

repeat . . . until *control structure*

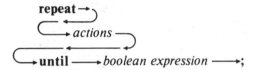

What happens if the **repeat** loop's exit condition suddenly becomes *true* while we're in the midst of executing the loop's action? Are we snatched out of the loop and plunked down at the end of the entire structure? No, because the action of a loop is an unbreakable unit. We will never exit from the middle of a loop. The exit condition is evaluated only after the loop action has been completely carried out.

A **repeat** structure can control any of Pascal's actions. However, compound statements are unnecessary.

> Since the reserved words **repeat** and **until** show the extent of the loop, and mark its first and last statements, the **begin** and **end** of a compound statement are unnecessary.

These two structures are absolutely identical in effect:

```
repeat                          repeat
    statement;                      begin
    statement                           statement;
until ExitCondition;                    statement
                                    end
                                until ExitCondition;
```

Program *CountDigits*, below, shows a **repeat** structure at work. The program counts the digits in an *integer* by repeatedly removing the 'ones' column until the number equals zero.

```
program CountDigits (input, output);
    {Counts digits by repeated division.}
var InputNumber, NumberOfDigits: integer;
begin
    NumberOfDigits := 0;
    writeln ('Please enter an integer.');
    readln (InputNumber);
    write (InputNumber:1);
    repeat
        InputNumber := InputNumber div 10;
        NumberOfDigits := NumberOfDigits + 1
    until InputNumber = 0;
    writeln (' has ', NumberOfDigits:1, ' digits.')
end.   {CountDigits}
```

$$\downarrow \qquad \downarrow \qquad \downarrow \qquad \downarrow \qquad \downarrow$$

```
Please enter an integer.
-3829
-3829 has 4 digits.
```

The **while** structure is also a conditional loop, but its condition is checked prior to entering the loop, instead of on exit. The loop's action is not executed at all if the entry condition is not met.

> In the first part of the **while** structure, a condition is stated as a *boolean* expression. It determines whether or not the loop will be entered (because it's an *entry condition*), and when the loop will terminate (because it implies an exit condition—the opposite of the entry condition—as well).

In a sense, the entry condition serves as an **if** structure—a *boolean* expression must be *true* for the structure to be entered. But since the **while** is a loop structure, the expression is evaluated again *after the action is completed.* If it's still *true*, the action gets repeated. If the entry condition has become *false*, the action is skipped entirely, and the program moves on to the next statement.

> **while** *boolean expression*   {the entry condition}
> **do** *action*;

In chart form, the **while** structure is:

while *control structure*

```
while ——→ boolean expression →
  ←——————     ←——————
  ┗——→ do ——→ action ——→;
```

Program *LongDivision,* below, uses a **while** structure to simulate the effect of the **div** and **mod** operators. It uses a simple brute-force algorithm—repeated subtraction. However, since the dividend may be smaller than the divisor, it's possible that no subtractions will be required.

Thus, a **while** loop (whose action may be skipped) is superior to a **repeat** loop (whose action always occurs at least once) in this application.

program *LongDivision* (*input, output*) ;
    {Simulates **div** and **mod** for batch input.}

var *Dividend, Divisor, Wholes, Remainder*: *integer*;

begin
    Wholes := 0 ;
    readln (*Dividend, Divisor*) ;
    write ('The integer quotient of ', *Dividend*:1, ' and ', *Divisor*:1, ' is ') ;
    Remainder := *Dividend*;
    while (*Remainder* − *Divisor*) > = 0
      do begin
        Remainder := *Remainder* − *Divisor*;
        Wholes := *Wholes* + 1
      end; {while}
    writeln (*Wholes*:1, ', with remainder ', *Remainder*:1)
end. {*LongDivision*}

        ↓   ↓   ↓   ↓   ↓

```
22 5
The integer quotient of 22 and 5 is 4, with remainder 2
```

No matter what the action of a **repeat** or **while** loop is, the Golden Rule of loops must be observed.

> ### The Golden Rule of Loops
> If a loop is entered, it must end eventually. Therefore, the entry or exit condition has to contain a variable whose value is changed by the loop's action.

Without this update, one repetition is just like the next, and the loop repeats an infinite number of times. For example, this program segment's exit condition will never be met, because the *boolean* expression (*Counter* = 100) will always be *false*.

        Counter := 0 ;
        repeat
          writeln (*Counter*)
        until *Counter* = 100 ;

Although endless, infinite loops are programing errors, they won't hurt the computer. Systems usually have a built-in limit on the number of statements a single program may execute (or on the amount of computer time a program may devour) to protect users from inadvertent infinite loops. An endlessly iterating loop will eventually crash, with an epitaph like 'Statement Limit (or 'Time Limit') Exceeded.'

:·:·

Q. What's wrong with these exit conditions? Why are they probably in error?

> **repeat**
>   *SomeActions*
> a. **until** *true*
> b. **until** *false*
> c. **until** *abs*(*Counter*) < 0
> d. **until** (*Value*>10) **and** (*Value*<=5)
> e. **until** (*Value*<=10) **or** (*Value*>=11)

A. All these exit conditions are either always *true* (*a, e*), or invariably *false* (*b, c, d*). There is no way any of them can be modified. Thus, the '*true*' loops will only take place once, and the '*false*' loops will repeat forever.

:··:

Any action, from a single statement to an entire program, can be the action of a loop. The segment below might be the entire statement part of a game program.

Programing With Loops

```
begin        {A game-playing program}
  repeat
    GiveInstructions;
    PlayGame;
    writeln ('Do you want to play again?  Answer "Y" or "N"');
    readln (Response);
    Finished := Response = 'N'
  until Finished
end.         {Of the game program}
```

example of game plan

We used the auxiliary *boolean* variable *Finished* to make the program more readable. *Response* is the only other global variable used.

Loop structures can make programs more robust by giving the user a chance to correct improperly entered data. Procedure *CheckInput*, below asks a user to enter a value from 10 through 1000. The request is repeated until a legitimate value is entered.

```
procedure CheckInput (var Value: integer;  Upper, Lower: integer);
  begin
    repeat
      writeln ('Please enter any integer from ', Lower:1, ' to ', Upper:1);
      readln (Value);
      if Value < Lower
        then writeln (Value:1, 'was too small.  Try again.')
        else if Value > Upper
          then writeln (Value:1, ' was too large.  Try again.')
    until (Value >= Lower) and (Value <= Upper)
  end;  {CheckInput}
```

example of check on value input.

[185]

> Interactive programs should include error-checking and mistake-correcting loops whenever possible. Nothing is more infuriating than a computer program that won't let a user change input she knows is wrong.

When batch-oriented programs read unknown amounts of data, they frequently use a *sentinel* character or number to indicate the end of data. This technique is particularly relevant when a program's input contains several distinct lists of data items. Program *BatchAverage*, below, computes the average value in a sequence of positive numbers. Since it couldn't possibly be part of the program's data, a negative number marks the end of the list. If the data list is empty, *BatchAverage* prints an explicit message.

```
program BatchAverage (input, output);
    {Averages a series of numbers. −1 marks the end of data.}

const Sentinel = −1;

var Value, Total, Average: real;
    Counter: integer;

begin
    Total := 0;
    Counter := 0;          {Initialization}
    Average := 0;
    read (Value);
    if (Value = Sentinel)          {Check for an empty data list.}
        then writeln ('There is no data to average.')
        else begin
            repeat          {Process the data.}
                Total := Total + Value;
                Counter := Counter + 1;
                read (Value)
            until Value = Sentinel;
            Average := Total/Counter;
            writeln ('The average of ', Counter:1, ' values is', Average)
        end {else}
end.    {BatchAverage}
```

```
        ↓        ↓        ↓        ↓        ↓
23.9  85.68  227E02  0.00863  75        ↓        ↓
93.44  71  14.7E−03  66  −1
The average of 9 values is 2.5683381477777E+03
```

It's not hard to appreciate that the **while** structure is very similar to the **repeat**. Their main difference is simply stated.

> The action of a **repeat** structure will take place at least once; the **while** loop's action may not be executed at all. The **repeat** structure's exit condition, when met, causes looping to *stop.* The **while**'s entry condition, when met, causes looping to *continue.*

Since in many cases either loop would work equally well, when should one use a **repeat** structure, and when a **while**? Unfortunately, this is an essay question—it doesn't have a correct answer. On one hand, the ordinary English meanings of the reserved words help clarify a programer's intentions. 'Repeat' implies that an action will take place at least once, and the **repeat** structure supports this contention. By the same logic, 'while' lets an element of doubt creep in—maybe the action won't take place at all—that accurately reflects the **while** structure's usage.

On the other hand, programers often use a **while** structure even when they're sure the loop's action will take place at least once. Why? Because placing the loop's condition in the first line might make the program a little easier to read.

> Common sense and clarity, more than any abstract rule of correct usage, should be the programer's guide.

Pascal has been criticized for including two control structures that are so similar, on grounds that they make the language more complicated, but no more powerful. What do *you* think?

Using All the Loops

Pascal has three loop structures, and our next program will use them all. The problem we pose involves implementing a brief numerical algorithm for producing *numerical palindromes*—numbers that are the same forward and backward.

Start by taking a number. If it isn't a palindrome, reverse the number, and sum the number and its reversal. If the new number isn't palindromic, reverse the new number, then add it to the reversal. Eventually, the number will become a palindrome.

For example, the number 101 is a palindrome. 561, however, isn't. We reverse 561, and add: $561+165=726$. Since 726 isn't palindromic either, we repeat the process: $726+627=1,353$. As 1,353 still isn't a solution, we must invoke our algorithm once more: $1,353+3,531=4,884$. It has taken us three reversals to produce a palindrome.

A first refinement of the numerical algorithm produces this pseudocode:

> *get the number*;
> **while** *it's not a palindrome*
>   *reverse the number*;
>   *add the number and its reversal*;
> *print the answer*;

How can we tell if a number is a palindrome? A one-digit number is easy—it's always a palindrome. A two-digit number is a palindrome if its digits are the same. Three-digit numbers are palindromic if the first digit equals the last. Four-digit numbers fit if their first and last, and second and next-to-last, digits are identical. It doesn't take a college degree to realize that:

An *n*-digit number is a palindrome if digit 1 equals digit *n*, digit 2 equals digit *n*−1, digit 3 equals digit *n*−2, etc.

Now, an *integer's* last digit is the remainder of a division by 10:

the last digit = *the number* **mod** 10

Its first digit is the whole portion of a division:

the first digit = *the number* **div** (10 *to the* (*number of digits*−1) *power*)

It seems that if we want to find a number's first digit, we have to know the number of digits in the entire number. Fortunately, we've already written a program that does the job—program *CountDigits.* We can assume that determining whether or not a number is a palindrome is within our power.

What about reversing a number? Any programer who can count a number's digits should find this trivial. We just repeat the following process:

> *compute the last digit*;
> *remove it from the original number with* **div** ;
> *add it to ten times the answer accumulated so far*;

until the original number equals zero.

A much subtler problem is going to cause more trouble. Suppose that a number requires many reversals before it becomes a palindrome. For example, 89 must be reversed 24 times before becoming the palindrome 8,813,200,023,188. Stop reading for a moment, and try to figure out why this is a cause for concern. Program *Oops,* below, should give you a hint. Although *maxint* is implementation defined, the figure we show is typical.

> **program** *Oops* (*output*) ;
>   {Prints the value of *maxint*}
>
> **begin**
>   *writeln* (*maxint*)
> **end.**

>   ↓   ↓   ↓
>   2,1 4 7,4 8 3,6 4 7

....

: Attempting to assign an *integer* variable a value greater than *maxint* :
: causes an *integer **overflow*** (and usually a crash). :

....

Even though *maxint* is a large number, most non-palindromes will exceed it after ten or eleven reversals and additions. If we want our program to be robust, we have to find a method of anticipating overflow situations. A clever technique is to use ratios—if a tenth of some number exceeds a tenth of *maxint*, then the actual number is greater than *maxint*

We're now in a better position to refine our pseudocode in more procedural terms.

> **while** *the user wants to keep running the program*
>> *get the starting number*;
>> *count its digits*;
>> *see if it's a palindrome*;
>> *see if it's in danger of causing an overflow*;
>> **while** (*it's not a palindrome*) **and** (*it won't cause an overflow*)
>>> *reverse the number*;
>>> *add it to the original*;
>>> *see if it's a palindrome*;
>>> *see if it's in danger of causing an overflow*;
>> *print the program's results*;

What results should the program have? If the number can be turned into a palindrome, we should print the palindrome and the number of steps required. If it requires too many steps for the computer to handle, the program should ***degrade gracefully*** by printing an error message—not halt abruptly with a crash, or print incorrect results.

The text of program *Palindrome* appears over the next few pages. As you read it, try to recognize why we've used each particular loop structure as we have *even when another loop structure could have worked* For example, finding a number's first digit involves computing a divisor that equals 10 to the *NumberOfDigits* − 1 power. Our code (in procedure *CheckForPalindrome*) uses a **for** structure:

> **for** *Counter* := 1 **to** *NumberOfDigits* − 1
> **do** *Divisor* := *Divisor* * 10;

even though a **while** or **repeat** could have achieved the same effect. Why? How come we used a **repeat** loop in procedure *CountTheDigits*? Could a *while* have worked? Finally, why does the entire program repeat **until**, instead of continuing **while**?

```
program Palindrome (input, output);
    {Produces palindromic numbers. Watches for integer overflow.}

var Original, Reversed, Reversals: integer;
    Palindrome, InDangerOfOverFlow: boolean;

procedure ReverseTheNumber (Original: integer; var Reversed: integer);
    {Reverses and returns a copy of its first parameter.}

    begin
        Reversed := 0;
        while (Original<>0)
            do begin
                Reversed := (Reversed*10) + (Original mod 10);
                Original := Original div 10
            end
    end;   {ReverseTheNumber}

procedure CheckForOverFlow (Original: integer; var InDangerOfOverFlow: boolean);
    {Determines if Original will cause integer overflow when reversed
    and added.  Procedure ReverseTheNumber, above, is called.}

    var Reversed: integer;

    begin
        Original := (Original div 10);
        ReverseTheNumber (Original, Reversed);
        InDangerOfOverFlow := (Original +Reversed) > (maxint div 10)
    end;   {CheckForOverFlow}

procedure CheckForPalindrome (Original: integer; var Palindrome: boolean);
    {Determines if Original is palindromic.
    Procedure CountTheDigits is declared within this procedure.}

    var Divisor, Counter, NumberOfDigits, FirstDigit, LastDigit: integer;

    procedure CountTheDigits (Original: integer; var NumberOfDigits: integer);
        {Counts the number of digits in Original}

        begin
            NumberOfDigits := 0;
            repeat
                Original := Original div 10;
                NumberOfDigits := NumberOfDigits +1
            until Original=0
        end;   {CountTheDigits}

    begin   {CheckForPalindrome}
        Palindrome := true;   {Initialize Palindrome.}
        CountTheDigits (Original, NumberOfDigits);
        Divisor := 1;

            {Compute 10 to the NumberOfDigits−1 power.}
        for Counter := 1 to NumberOfDigits−1
            do Divisor := Divisor*10;
```

```
        for Counter := 1 to NumberOfDigits div 2
            do begin
                    {Compute and compare the first and last digits.}
                    FirstDigit := Original div Divisor;
                    LastDigit := Original mod 10;
                    if FirstDigit <> LastDigit then Palindrome := false;

                    {Get rid of the first and last digits of Original}
                    Original := (Original mod Divisor) div 10;
                    Divisor := Divisor div 100
            end  {for}
    end;   {CheckForPalindrome}

begin  {Palindrome}
    writeln ('Please enter a positive integer.');
    readln (Original);
    repeat
        write (Original:1, ' took ');
        Reversals := 0;
        CheckForPalindrome (Original, Palindrome);
        CheckForOverFlow (Original, InDangerOfOverFlow);
        while not Palindrome and not InDangerOfOverFlow
            do begin
                ReverseTheNumber (Original, Reversed);
                Reversals := Reversals+1;
                Original := Original +Reversed;
                CheckForPalindrome (Original, Palindrome);
                CheckForOverFlow (Original, InDangerOfOverFlow)
            end;  {while}
        if InDangerOfOverFlow
            then writeln ('too many reversals to convert.')
            else writeln (Reversals:1, ' reversals to become ', Original:1);
        writeln ('Play again?  A negative entry ends the program.');
        readln (Original)
    until Original<0
end.  {Palindrome}
```

```
          ↓       ↓       ↓       ↓       ↓
Please enter a positive integer.
86
86 took 3 reversals to become 1111
Play again?  A negative entry ends the program.
563
563 took 11 reversals to become 88555588
Play again?  A negative entry ends the program.
89
89 took too many reversals to convert.
Play again?  A negative entry ends the program.
-1
```

**7-2
Text
Processing:
Eoln and Eof**

WORK WITH CHARACTERS (AS OPPOSED TO NUMBERS) is called *text
processing*—any sequence of characters forms text. Procedure *EchoOne-
Line*, below, gives us an idea of what text processing involves. It reads
in a line of text (that contains an unknown number of characters) one
character at a time, and echoes each character as it goes along.

```
procedure EchoOneLine;
   {Read and echo a single line of text.}

   var CurrentCharacter: char;

   begin
      while not eoln         {While we're not at the end of the line...}
         do begin
            read (CurrentCharacter);          {...read and echo characters.}
            write (CurrentCharacter)
         end;
      writeln;       {Print the stored characters}
      readln         {Get ready for the next line of input}
   end; {EchoOneLine}
```

EchoOneLine calls the standard (predefined) function *eoln.* The
unpronounceable *end-of-line* function (people usually just spell out *eoln*
when referring to it) is used to watch for the end of an input line.

Let's begin our discussion of text processing by reviewing the
operation of *readln* and *read. readln* finds the value of its parameter
(or parameters), and then throws the rest of the line away. For example, suppose we have the following text on punched cards (or ready to
type into an interactive keyboard):

> **When I am grown to Man's estate
> I shall be very proud and great.
> And tell the other girls and boys
> Not to meddle with my toys.**

When this input is given to program *EchoFirstLetter*, below, only
the first value is read from each line. The rest of the input line is
skipped.

```
program EchoFirstLetter (input, output);
   {Demonstrates the effect of readln}

   var Character: char;

   begin
      readln (Character);        write (Character);
      readln (Character);        write (Character);
      readln (Character);        write (Character);
      readln (Character);        write (Character);
      writeln
   end. {EchoFirstLetter}
```

↓   ↓   ↓   ↓   ↓

WIAN

> Calling *readln* without any argument discards any values left on the current line of input. The next character read will be the first character of the next line.

The standard procedure *read* doesn't discard anything. When we use *read* to input *char* values no character—not even a blank space—is ever thrown away. Assume that the input of *ReadEachCharacter* is the text sample we showed above.

```
program ReadEachCharacter (input, output);
    {Demonstrates the effect of read}

var Character: char;

begin
    read (Character);        write (Character);
    read (Character);        write (Character);
    read (Character);        write (Character);
    read (Character);        write (Character);
    writeln
end.  {ReadEachCharacter}
```

↓   ↓   ↓   ↓   ↓

When

All the output of *ReadEachCharacter* came from the first line of input. We'd have to do quite a few more *read*'s before getting to the beginning of the second line. Don't forget that when *real* or *integer* values are input with either *read* or *readln*, blanks and line-ends serve only to separate values, and are otherwise ignored.

Now, for the convenience of both people and machines, text input in Pascal is divided into lines, just as in the example above. A special nonprinting **control character**, which varies from system to system, usually marks the end of each line.* Thus, every punched card represents a line of input in batch systems, and an end-of-line marker is generated whenever a card is read. In interactive systems, hitting the carriage return or new-line key sends the end-of-line character to the computer.

> A call of the *boolean* function *eoln* represents *true* if the character we're about to read is the end-of-line character. Otherwise, *eoln* represents *false.*

Calling *eoln* causes the computer to examine the next character without disturbing it in any way. If it's the end-of-line character, *eoln* is *true*, because we're at the end of a line. If the next character is a

---

* For the purpose of our discussion, we can assume that it's always done this way.

digit, punctuation mark, letter, etc. we're obviously *not* at the end of a line of input yet, and *eoln* represents the value *false.*

....
: The end-of-line character cannot be 'seen,' or printed. Although it :
: has a special meaning to the computer, the character is stored and :
: printed out as a blank space. :
....

If we read and echo the end-of-line character we'll just print a blank.

The character immediately following the end-of-line character is, for all practical purposes, the first character of the next line of input. However, we still have to read (or otherwise dispose of) the end-of-line character on our way to the next line. Procedure *ReadLine*, below, uses a **while** loop to read input, character by character, until the end of the current line is reached. Then, it reads the end-of-line character—the last character on the current line. A call of *ReadLine* is equivalent to a call of the standard procedure *readln*, because it leaves us at the beginning of the next line of input.

```
procedure ReadLine;
     {Imitates the effect of readln.}

   var Character: char;

   begin
        while not eoln do read (Character);
        read (Character)
   end;   {ReadLine}
```

....
: The only way to generate (print) an end-of-line character from :
: within a program is to use the standard procedure *writeln.* :
....

If we input the end-of-line character from a punched card or interactive terminal keyboard, and immediately echo it to the line-printer or screen, it would not cause a carriage return, and subsequent output would appear on the same line.

Let's use this information to write a procedure that reads and echoes a full line of text—complete with carriage return (the end-of-line marker). In words, our algorithm is:

> **while** *it's not the end of the line*
>   *read a character* (*using read*);
>   *ready the character for printing* (*using write*);
>   *force printing of all output* (*by using writeln*);
>   *get ready for another line of input* (*by using readln*);

To nobody's surprise, we find ourselves writing procedure *EchoOneLine.*

```
procedure EchoOneLine;
   {Read and echo a single line of text.}
   var CurrentCharacter: char;
   begin
      while not eoln          {While we're not at the end of the line...}
         do begin
            read (CurrentCharacter);          {...read and echo characters.}
            write (CurrentCharacter)
         end;
      writeln;          {Print the stored characters}
      readln            {Get ready for the next line of input}
   end; {EchoOneLine}
```

Computer scientists have developed a pleasant fiction to describe the total store of information—one line, or many lines—that a program can receive as input.

> As far as a Pascal program is concerned, its input comes from an imaginary entity called a *file*.

The idea of a file of input probably won't upset card users too much, since a stack of punched cards might as well be called a file as anything else. Video terminal programers, on the other hand, must submit to a more willing suspension of disbelief, because an interactive terminal keyboard isn't any more full of information than a ball point pen is. Still, a Pascal program acts as though all its input is coming from a file that consists of zero or more lines of data.*

Now, just as the end of each input line is marked by an end-of-line character, the end of the entire file is flagged with an end-of-file character. It's used by the *end of file* function, *eof* (again, most people read the letters).

> A call of *eof* causes the computer to inspect the very next input character, without otherwise disturbing it. If it's the end-of-file character, *eof* is *true* because we're at the end of the input file. If it's any other character, there must still be data in the file and *eof* is *false.*

The *eof* function is necessary when we don't know how much input a program is going to receive, and when no sentinel character marks the end of input. A general outline of programs that use *eof* to process *char* input is:

---

* The idea of a file will become more useful in a few chapters, when we learn how to receive input from, and send output to, places other than the standard input file (the card reader or terminal keyboard) and standard output file (the lineprinter or terminal screen).

```
while not eof
   do begin
        get the data;
        process the data
   end;    etc.
```

Although we'll develop some more specialized examples in the next section, a widespread application of *eof* requires it to be used in conjunction with *eoln.* Program *EchoText,* shown below, inputs and echoes an entire input file one line at a time. It illustrates one of the most common models of text processing programs.

1. An outer loop keeps an eye out for the end of the input file.

2. An inner loop processes each line one character at a time.

Note that the shaded portion is equivalent to procedure *EchoOneLine.*

```
program EchoText (input, output);
     {Uses nested while loops to echo a file of text.}

var CurrentCharacter: char;

begin
   while not eof
      do begin
           while not eoln
              do begin
                   read (CurrentCharacter);
                   write (CurrentCharacter)
              end;   {eoln while}
           writeln;
           readln
      end   {eof while}
end.   {EchoText}
```

Two special rules apply to the end-of-file character.

> ### The Golden Rules Of *eof*
> A program cannot read the end-of-file character. Furthermore, when *eof* is *true,* *eoln* is undefined.

The end-of-file character can be heard, but not seen. Trying to read the end-of-file character (or even worse, trying to read *past* it), causes one of the quickest crashes in Pascal.

ATTEMPT TO READ PAST EOF

Thus, (**not** *eof*) is usually used as the *entry* condition of a **while** loop, and not as the *exit* condition of a **repeat** loop.

: ·· :

Q. What would happen if we wrote *EchoOneLine* with a **repeat** structure instead of a **while** structure, like this?

```
procedure EchoWithRepeat;
    {A faulty procedure for echoing a line of text.}
    var Character: char;
    begin
        repeat
            read (Character);
            write (Character)
        until eoln;
        writeln;
        readln
    end;   {EchoWithRepeat}
```

A. We've made a faulty assumption—one of the most serious in text-processing programs—by assuming that the line definitely contains something to read. But what if it doesn't? Suppose that the first line of input is empty, and contains only the end-of-line character. Then:

1. We read the end-of-line character.

2. We ready it (really a space) for printing.

3. Is *eoln true* yet? Not necessarily, because the character we're *about* to read is the first character of the second line. Thus, *eoln* will only be *true* if this line is blank as well.

Never assume that there will be input. Always allow for the possibility that a line may be blank.

: ·· :

7-3
Focus on Programing: Text and Testing

MANY PROGRAMS THAT ARE NOT INTENDED to process text still require the tools of text processing. Improving program robustness is a common motivation. For example, a program that expects numerical input is exceptionally sensitive to its environment. An inadvertent nonblank character can cause a type clash, and program crash.

A basic form of run-time error checking helps prevent the problem. Since all input may be read as a sequence of *char* values, we can read a number's digits one at a time, then convert them into the number they represent (e.g. turn the sequence '1', '3', '7', into 137). Any non-digit characters are skipped.

What are the basic steps of an *integer* reading procedure? First, we have to get rid of any spaces or other characters that precede the number. Then, we must employ the *ord* function to represent the first digit character as a number. Finally, we should continue to read in digits of the number until we reach a non-digit. We'll simplify the task slightly by only allowing positive *Integer* Input.

> *find the first digit;*
> *convert it into an integer;*
> *keep reading and converting until we get to a non-digit;*

As usual, we'll need a second refinement to express our algorithm in more procedural form.

> *initialize a variable Number to* 0 ;
> **repeat**
> > *read a character*
>
> **until** *we read a digit*;
> **repeat**
> > *convert the digit into an integer*;
> > *add the digit to* 10∗ *Number*;
> > *read in the next character*
>
> **until** *we read a non-digit*;

The completed procedure, shown below, implements the algorithm. It's worth studying the special techniques it employs (especially the use of sets, and the *ord* function), because the same methods will show up in many text processing programs and procedures.

> **procedure** *ReadANumber* (**var** *Number*: *integer*) ;
> > {Reads positive *integer* input as a sequence of characters.}
> > **var** *Character*: *char*;
> > **begin**
> > > *Number* := 0 ;
> > > **repeat**
> > > > *read* (*Character*)
> > >
> > > **until** *Character* **in** ['0'..'9'] ;
> > > **repeat**
> > > > *Number* := (10∗ *Number*) + (*ord*(*Character*) − *ord*('0')) ;
> > > > *read* (*Character*)
> > >
> > > **until not** (*Character* **in** ['0'..'9'])
> >
> > **end**; {*ReadANumber*}

A considerable portion of *ReadANumber* is devoted to error checking. It's worth the trouble—suppose we have a program segment with input as shown:

> *writeln* ('Please enter a positive integer.') ;
> *ReadANumber* (*Number*) ;
> *writeln* ('The number is ', *Number*:1) ;
>
> ↓   ↓   ↓   ↓   ↓
>
> Please enter a positive integer.
> **bkjw(*#n;,)(_hg$ &71439H!Am**
> The number is 71439

A problem that's somewhat related involves converting numbers from one base to another. When we work with a base greater than 10, ordinary characters *must* appear within numbers. For example, the hexadecimal (base 16) system's digits are '0', '1', '2', '3', '4', '5', '6', '7', '8', '9', 'A', 'B', 'C', 'D', 'E', and 'F'.

Now, we can develop an algorithm for converting hexadecimal numbers into decimals (base 10) by looking at an assignment from *ReadANumber*:

$$Number := (10 * Number) + (ord(Character) - ord('0')) ;$$

Number represents the numerical value of the digits already read in, while *Character* is the digit that currently belongs in *Number's* 'ones' column. Since *Number* is base 10, we have to multiply it by 10 before adding *Character* on. The same principle converts numbers of any base *B* to base 10. Before the decimal value of a new digit is added to the digits converted so far, they must be multiplied by *B.*

Program *ConvertHex,* below, computes the decimal equivalents of its hexadecimal input. As you can see, it conforms to the outline (proposed in 7-2) for processing *char* input:

> **while not** *eof*
> > **do begin**
> > > *get the data;*
> > > *process the data*
> > **end**;

It's worth making a special effort to recognize that *ConvertHex,* which is batch oriented, treats its input as a long sequence of *char* values. The line structure of its input is ignored.

```
program ConvertHex (input, output) ;
    {Converts hexadecimal numbers to base 10.}
const Base = 16;
var Character: char;
    Number, Decimal: integer;
procedure GetTheDecimalEquivalent (Character: char; var Decimal: integer) ;
    {Gives Decimal the base 10 equivalent of Character.}
    begin
        case Character of
            '0','1','2','3','4','5','6','7','8','9': Decimal := ord(Character) - ord('0') ;
            'A','B','C','D','E','F': Decimal := (ord(Character) - ord('A')) + 10
        end
    end;   {GetTheDecimalEquivalent}
begin
    while not eof
        do begin
            Number := 0 ;
            read (Character) ;
            write ('The decimal equivalent of hex ') ;
            repeat
                write (Character) ;
                GetTheDecimalEquivalent (Character, Decimal) ;
                Number := (Base * Number) + Decimal;
                read (Character)
            until not (Character in ['0'..'9', 'A'..'F']) ;
            writeln (' is ', Number:1)
        end   {while}
end.   {ConvertHex}
```

↓   ↓   ↓   ↓   ↓

```
A  10  1A
F00  ABCDEF
The decimal equivalent of hex A is 10
The decimal equivalent of hex 10 is 16
The decimal equivalent of hex 1A is 26
The decimal equivalent of hex F00 is 3840
The decimal equivalent of hex ABCDEF is 11259375
```

ConvertHex ignored the line structure of its input, and treated the end-of-line character as an ordinary space. However, similarly constructed programs that read *integer* and *real* data require us to use *readln* to move from line to line. Suppose that we want to read and echo *integer* input. Since blanks and end-of-lines are ignored except as value separators, this batch-oriented program segment would seem to do the job:

> **while not** *eof*
>> **do begin**
>>> *read* (*IntegerValue*) ;
>>> *writeln* (*IntegerValue*)
>> **end**;   {This segment contains a bug.}

Unfortunately, the program this segment appears in will crash as it tries to read past end of file! The reason has to do with the way that *read* works.

> If *read* is given an *integer* or *real* variable as a parameter, it skips characters until it comes to a nonblank.

In other words, when the statement:

> *read* (*IntegerValue*) ;

is executed, the program jumps over spaces or end-of-lines, and reads the first nonblank value it finds (which, we hope, is an *integer*).

If we try to read another *integer* value, the process is repeated. The space or spaces that come before the next *integer* are skipped, and the *integer* is read in. Thus, after reading a numerical value, the computer is always about to read (and possibly ignore) a space, or an end-of-line character.

Let's jump ahead to the end of the program's input data.

> In Pascal, there is always an end-of-line character at the end of an input 'file.'

Suppose we've just read what we (but not the computer) know is the program's last input number. The loop above asks itself:

Is this the end of the program's input?

Then it answers:

> *No. There is at least one blank space left—the last end-of-line character. Perhaps there is more data.*

Since the program doesn't think that it's reached the end of the file, procedure *read* starts to repeat the **while** loop's action. It begins to skip spaces, looking for another *integer*. In the process, the program tries to read the end-of-file character, and it crashes.

> To avoid the problem of reading past end of file, *integer* and *real* data must be read on a line-by-line basis.

Although this may be conceptually distasteful, it isn't difficult. *If there are no extra blanks at the end of each line*, we can rewrite the earlier program segment as this:

{General-purpose outline for programs that read *integer* or *real* data.}

```
while not eof
    do begin
        while not eoln
            do begin
                read (IntegerValue);
                writeln (IntegerValue)
            end;   {We've reached the end of a line.}
        readln   {Discard the rest of the line.}
    end;
```

Understanding this technique is essential for writing correct batch-oriented programs.

Self-Check Questions

Q. Suppose that blank spaces follow a program's last *integer* or *real* input value. Will the program segment shown above work?

A. No. After the last numerical value is read in, *eoln* isn't *true* yet. The *readln* won't be executed, and the program will crash. A method of solving this problem (by using Pascal's *file window*) is discussed in Chapter 13.

Bottom-Up Programing: Testing Modules

Many text-processing problems require us to look at text as a sequence of characters, and to recognize (and possibly modify) patterns in that sequence. For example:

Write a program that finds infinitive verb forms in ordinary English text, and changes them to gerunds.

The infinitive of a verb is its 'to be' form: to see, to run, to dance, to sing.* A gerund is a verb with an 'ing' ending: seeing, running, dancing, etc. To simplify the problem, we'll assume that when 'to' appears in a sentence, the next word is a verb.

As we try to solve this problem, we'll demonstrate a **_bottom-up_** approach to programing.   Although we'll keep using stepwise refinement to help break the problem down, we'll encode trial versions of our modules. This means that we'll be making some low-level decisions about algorithm and implementation *before* thoroughly decomposing the problem. The bottom-up approach will let us test our ideas and methods as we go along.

A first breakdown of the problem is obvious, even though it may prove to be a bit simplistic:

> **while** *we read and echo characters*
> *look for infinitives*;
> *change them to gerunds*;

How can we recognize an infinitive verb? Well, the definition above is clearcut—the word 'to' is always the start of an infinitive. What are the characteristics of 'to'?

1. It is always preceded by a blank.

2. It contains the letters 't' and 'o'.

3. It is always followed by a blank.

Thus, recognizing the word 'to' requires that we keep track of four letters. If we encounter a blank, and it is followed by 't', 'o', and another blank, we've found a 'to'. We've made a trial implementation of these criteria in program *FindTo*, opposite, and supplied some test data to check our method. Since *FindTo* contains a complicated sequence of nested **if** structures, we've numbered each **then** and its corresponding **else**.

FindTo is useful because it tests our *algorithm* as well as its *implementation.* However...

....
The Golden Rule of Program Testing

Testing can show the presence of bugs, but never their absence. A program test is only as realistic as the test data.
....

---

* Most people's contact with infinitives is due to the ancestral prohibition against splitting them, e.g. to barely see, to quickly run.

```
program FindTo (input, output);
    {Trial program for recognizing the word 'to' in text.
    Prints an asterisk after every 'to'.}
const Blank = ' ';
    Asterisk = '*';

var ch0, ch1, ch2, ch3: char;

begin
    while not eof
        do begin
            read (ch0);
            if (ch0 =Blank) and not eof
                then begin   {#1}
                    read (ch1);
                    if (ch1 ='t') and not eof
                        then begin   {#2}
                            read (ch2);
                            if (ch2 ='o') and not eof
                                then begin   {#3}
                                    read (ch3);
                                    if ch3 =Blank
                                        then write (ch0, ch1, ch2, Asterisk, ch3)
                                        else write (ch0, ch1, ch2, ch3)   {ch3<>Blank}
                                end   {#3} else write (ch0, ch1, ch2)   {ch2<>'o'}
                        end   {#2} else write (ch0, ch1)   {ch1<>'t'}
                end   {#1} else write (ch0)   {ch0<>Blank}
        end;   {while}
    writeln;
end.   {FindTo}
```

> ↓   ↓   ↓   ↓   ↓
> **To begin with to, to end into too. To wit, to do. to be.**
> `To begin with to, to* end into too.  To wit, to* do.  to be`

Although our trial sentence isn't too grammatical, it tests *FindTo* in likely 'to'-finding situations. Notice that the output is incorrect—the 'To' that begins the test sentence is ignored because it isn't preceded by a blank, and because it starts with a capital 'T'. The program also fails when a 'to' has two blanks before it. We'll have to improve the 'to'-finding algorithm later.

What about turning infinitives into gerunds? Again, we can immediately come up with a basic algorithm.

> *read and echo characters until we find a* 'to';
> *ignore it;*
> *read and echo characters until the end of the next word;*
> *add an* 'ing' *to it;*

Unfortunately, a few mental test cases will find flaws in this method. Consider these verbs:

Infinitive	Gerund	Rule
see	seeing	add 'ing'
fall	falling	add 'ing'
send	sending	add 'ing'
like	liking	drop final e; add 'ing'
run	running	double last letter; add 'ing'

If we examine the last few letters of the verb we can make some provisional rules for creating gerunds:

Characteristic	Example	Action
Last two letters the same	see, sell	Add 'ing'
Last two letters consonants	sing, send	Add 'ing'
Last letter 'e'	like, bake	Drop the 'e', add 'ing'
Next-to-last letter a vowel	run, stir	Double last letter, add 'ing'

Our experience with *FindTo* should also make us wary of the *until the end of the next word* part of our pseudocode. Although the 'to's we counted were always followed by blanks, almost any punctuation mark will signify the end of a verb. As before, we need a program that tests our algorithm—the set of rules for recognizing and modifying verbs—and gives us practice in implementing it.

```
program ConvertToGerund (input, output);
    {Trial program that prints every input word as a gerund.}
const Blank = ' ';
var ch1, ch2, ch3: char;
begin    {ConvertToGerund}
    while not eof
        do begin
            read (ch1, ch2, ch3);         {Every verb has at least 2 letters.}
            while not (ch3 in [Blank, ',', ';', '!', '?', '.'])
                do begin   {Find the last 2 letters in the verb.}
                    write (ch1);
                    ch1 := ch2;
                    ch2 := ch3;
                    read (ch3)
                end;
            {Now that ch1 and ch2 represent the last 2 letters,
                we can convert the verb into a gerund.}
            if (ch1=ch2) or (not (ch1 in ['a','e','i','o','u'])
                            and not (ch2 in ['a','e','i','o','u']))
                then write (ch1, ch2, 'ing', ch3)   {see, fall, or send}
                else if ch2='e'
                    then write (ch1, 'ing', ch3)   {like}
                    else write (ch1, ch2, ch2, 'ing', ch3)   {run}
        end;   {while}
    writeln
end.    {ConvertToGerund}
```

↓   ↓   ↓   ↓   ↓

see be sing sway know fall come go eat quit
```
seeing bing singing swayying knowwing
falling coming gooing eatting quitting
```

(We, and not the program, are responsible for splitting the output over two lines.) As before, a well-chosen set of test data has exposed some flaws in our algorithm. However, the **if** structures that implement our rules for making gerunds can easily be extended. Perhaps by the time we return to the *ConvertToGerund* algorithm we'll have a more precise set of guides.

What else do we have to worry about? Well, when an infinitive appears at the beginning of a sentence, we'll have to capitalize the verb. At first glance, the assignment below would seem to capitalize *ch*, assuming that *ch* is lower-case to begin with.

$$ch := chr(ord(ch) + ord('A') - 1)$$

If the computer's collating sequence runs 'a'..'z', 'A'..'Z' it will work. Unfortunately, the upper-case letters can precede the lower-case ones in Pascal. We have to arrive at a better 'correction' factor. As we did twice before, we'll write a brief program that tests an algorithm for performing the conversion.

```
program ConvertToCapital (input, output);
    {Trial program that converts lower-case letters to capitals.}

var ch: char;
    Correction: integer;

begin   {ConvertToCapital}
    Correction := ord('A') − ord('a');
    while not eof
        do begin
            read (ch);
            ch := chr(ord(ch) + Correction);
            write (ch)
        end;   {while}
    writeln
end.   {ConvertToCapital}
```

↓   ↓   ↓   ↓

abcxyz
```
ABCXYZ
```

At last we've come up with a trial program that works!

Now that we've written rough versions of the basic modules of a verb-conversion program, let's review the mistakes we found. *FindTo* failed to recognize the word 'to' when the 't' was capitalized. Spotting a capital 'T' is easily fixed with a set definition:

if $(ch1$ **in** $['t', 'T'])$ **and not** *eof*   etc.

[205]

FindTo also didn't spot a 'to' when it was the first word of input. Actually, *ConvertToGerund* had a similar problem. It didn't recognize and capitalize verbs that came at the start of *any* sentence. Now, if we recognize that the start of a sentence is a state (like the states we used in the bowling program *Score*), we can solve the problem with a *NewSentence* variable. Initially, it's *true*. As we process input text, we can update *NewSentence* by looking for the ordinary English sentence terminators '.', '!', and '?'.

We can easily draft a procedure that is passed the character most recently read, and updates the variable-parameter *NewSentence*. Procedure *CheckForEnd*, below, is smart enough to recognize that if *NewSentence* is *true*, its state won't change if *LastCh* is a blank.* Any infinitive-conversion program should call *CheckForEnd* whenever a potential sentence terminator is read—while looking for a 'to', or after converting an infinitive to a gerund.

```
procedure CheckForEnd (LastCh: char; var NewSentence: boolean);
     {Decides if the next word will start a sentence.}
     begin
         NewSentence := (LastCh in ['.', '!', '?'])
                         or (NewSentence and (LastCh=Blank))
     end;   {CheckForEnd}
```

A more serious problem with *ConvertToGerund* was its poor rule table. Most problems came from unnecessarily doubling the verb's last letter. Inspecting the test output leads to more accurate rules. Note that there's an implicit **else** between each rule change below. Thus, 'sway' and 'quit' don't follow the 'next-to-last letter a vowel' rule.

Characteristic	Example	Action
The word is 'be'	be	Add 'ing'
Last letter is 'w', 'y', or 'o'	sway, know, go	Add 'ing'
Last two letters the same	see, sell	Add 'ing'
Last two letters consonants	sing, send	Add 'ing'
Two vowels before last letter	quit, eat	Add 'ing'
Last letter 'e'	like, bake	Drop the 'e', add 'ing'
Next-to-last letter a vowel	run, stir	Double last letter, add 'ing'

The completed version of program *Gerunds*, along with test data, is shown over the next few pages. Its procedures are rewritten versions of our test programs, and their functions should be readily apparent. The only assumption we've made about input is that it follows ordinary English sentence structure—a 'to' that doesn't begin a sentence is only preceded by a single blank.

> The bottom-up method of programing should be used to gain experience with the parts of a program. However, it should never be a justification for starting to code without first developing an algorithm, and pseudocode draft.

---

* Without this allowance, a blank between sentences would make *NewSentence* untrue.

```
program Gerunds (input, output) ;
   {Converts infinitive verbs to gerunds.}
const Blank = ' ';
var Correction: integer;
   NewSentence: boolean;
procedure CheckForEnd (LastCh: char;  var NewSentence: boolean) ;
   {Updates the state variable NewSentence.}
   begin
      NewSentence := (LastCh in ['.', '!', '?'])
                     or (NewSentence and (LastCh=Blank))
   end;   {CheckForEnd}
procedure FindTo (var NewSentence: boolean) ;
   {Searches for the words 'to' and 'To'.}
   const Blank = ' ';
   var ch0, ch1, ch2, ch3: char;
       StillLookingForATo: boolean;
   begin
      StillLookingForATo := true;
      while not eof and StillLookingForATo
         do begin
            read (ch0) ;
            if ((ch0 =Blank) or NewSentence) and not eof
               then begin   {#1}
                  if NewSentence and (ch0 = 'T')
                     then ch1 := ch0
                     else read (ch1) ;
                  if (ch1 in ['t', 'T']) and not eof
                     then begin   {#2}
                        read (ch2) ;
                        if (ch2 = 'o') and not eof
                           then begin   {#3}
                              read (ch3) ;
                              if (ch3 =Blank) and not eof
                                 then begin   {#4}
                                    StillLookingForATo := false;
                                    if not NewSentence then write (ch0) ;
                                 end else begin   {#4}
                                    write (ch0, ch1, ch2, ch3) ;   {ch3< > Blank}
                                    CheckForEnd (ch3, NewSentence)
                                 end
                           end else begin   {#3}
                              write (ch0, ch1, ch2) ;   {ch2< >'o'}
                              CheckForEnd (ch2, NewSentence)
                           end
                     end else begin   {#2}
                        write (ch0, ch1) ;   {ch1< >'t'}
                        CheckForEnd (ch1, NewSentence)
                     end
               end else begin   {#1}
                  write (ch0) ;   {ch0< > Blank}
                  CheckForEnd (ch0, NewSentence)
               end;
            if eoln then begin writeln; readln end
         end;   {while}
   end;   {FindTo}
```

```
procedure ConvertToGerund (var NewSentence: boolean;  Correction: integer);
    {Prints the current input word as a gerund.}
    const Blank = ' ';
    var ch0, ch1, ch2, ch3: char;
    begin
        ch0 := Blank;   {If we're here, the last letter was a blank.}
        read (ch1, ch2, ch3);          {Every verb has at least 2 letters.}
        if NewSentence then ch1 := chr(ord(ch1) + Correction);
        while not (ch3 in [Blank, ',', ';', '!', '?', '.'])
            do begin   {Find the last 2 letters in the verb.}
                write (ch1);
                ch0 := ch1;
                ch1 := ch2;
                ch2 := ch3;
                read (ch3)
            end;
        {ch1 and ch2 represent the last 2 letters, so convert the verb into a gerund.}
        if ((((ch0 = Blank) or NewSentence) and ((ch1 = 'b') or (ch1 = 'B')
                                              and (ch2 = 'e'))   {be}
            or (ch2 in ['o', 'w', 'y'])  {go, know}
            or (ch1 = ch2)   {tell}
            or (not (ch1 in ['a','e','i','o','u'])
                    and not (ch2 in ['a','e','i','o','u']))   {sing}
            or ((ch0 in ['a','e','i','o','u']) and (ch1 in ['a','e','i','o','u'])))   {quit}
            then write (ch1, ch2, 'ing', ch3)
            else if ch2 = 'e'
                then write (ch1, 'ing', ch3)   {like}
                else write (ch1, ch2, ch2, 'ing', ch3);   {run}
        if eoln then begin writeln; readln end;
        CheckForEnd (ch3, NewSentence)
    end;   {ConvertToGerund}
begin   {Gerunds}
    Correction := ord('A') − ord('a');
    NewSentence := true;
    while not eof
        do begin
            FindTo (NewSentence);
            if not eof then ConvertToGerund (NewSentence, Correction);
        end;
end.   {Gerunds}
```

↓   ↓   ↓   ↓   ↓

**Mary liked to lift weights, but John went to surf.
It is better to give than to receive. To get there
is half the fun. To err is human; to forgive divine.
I like to do something; I like to seek. To be is nothingness.
To go is to live; to do is to be. To see is to believe.
Some like to sled; some to eat; and some to sit.
Others like to play, but not to stew.**

```
Mary liked lifting weights, but John went surfing.
It is better giving than receiving.  Getting there
is half the fun.  Erring is human; forgiving divine.
I like doing something; I like seeking.  Being is nothingness.
Going is living; doing is being.  Seeing is believing.
Some like sledding; some eating; and some sitting.
Others like playing, but not stewing.
```

MOST OF THE BUGS ASSOCIATED WITH conditional loops are semantic. The programs they're found in will compile, but won't work properly. Naturally, these are the worst kind of bugs, because they can only be found by program testing, or by visual inspection of the code itself. We can only say that a program is *correct* if we can show that it will work for all possible input data.

Reliance on testing is often ill-advised, because it can lead programers into a unnecessarily fatalistic state of mind. A computer scientist named Graham once observed that "We build programs like the Wright brothers built planes. Build the whole thing, push it off a cliff, let it crash, and start all over again." However, we've already pointed out that a program test is only as reliable as the test data it's provided with.

Proving that entire programs are correct (sometimes called *program verification*) is a task that requires a considerable amount of fasting and prayer. Still, it's fairly easy to become confident that a single loop structure will *usually* work. Three potential situations must be considered.

1. The loop won't be entered when it should be.

2. The loop won't ever be exited.

3. The loop will terminate after the wrong number of iterations.

We can generally assure ourselves of a loop's correctness by closely examining its **boundary conditions**—the exact circumstances of its first and last iterations.

Entry: Can the entry condition be met? Have all its variables been initialized? Do we want a **repeat** loop or a **while** loop? Does the loop have to be conditional at all—might a **for** loop work?

Exit: Can the exit condition be met? Is the entire loop action being repeated, or just its first statement? Are **ands** and **ors** being used correctly in the exit condition? Does some statement in the loop's action make it certain that the exit condition eventually *will* be met?

Off-by-one: Trace execution of the loop action through its first and final few iterations, step-by-step. Will all variables have their expected values when the loop is terminated? Is it possible that the loop takes place one time too often? Once too few?

This is by no means a formal proof of a loop structure's correctness. However, even a casual check like this should be performed while the code is still on paper, long before it's even run. A little bit of effort now can prevent a lot of trouble in the long run.

Most basic loop bugs are caused by misplacing semicolons, or neglecting to create compound statements. For example, this program segment is intended to compute 5 factorial (5*4*3*2*1). Although it won't find any factorials, it won't generate any error messages either.

7-4
Antibugging and
Debugging

```
Product := 1;
Counter := 2;
while Counter < =5
    do;
        Product := Product * Counter;
        Counter := Counter + 1;
writeln (Product);
```

There are two flaws in this code. As written, it will have no out-put at all, because it never gets past the line that says 'do;'.

> Don't ever forget that a semicolon—an empty statement—is a form of action.

Thus, the only action taken by the loop is a non-action. Naturally, *Counter* never increases beyond its starting value of 2, and the empty statement is repeated again and again, until the computer's time or state-ment limit is exceeded.

Even if we get rid of the semicolon, we've still got a problem. The computer cares no more about our neat indenting than we care about the computer's machine language. It sees this code:

```
while Counter < =5
    do Product := Product * Counter;
Counter := Counter + 1;
writeln (Product);
```

As far as the computer is concerned, the assignment to *Product* is the loop's sole purpose. To correctly encode our intentions, the next statement should join the assignment in a compound statement.

Off-by-one errors can be extremely serious because they don't always produce obviously incorrect output. Consider the following pro-gram segment. It's supposed to add the numbers from 1 through 100.

```
Sum := 0;
NextNumber := 1;
repeat
    Sum := Sum + NextNumber;
    NextNumber := NextNumber + 1
until NextNumber > =100;
```

Mentally check the loop's boundary conditions. Does it begin properly? Yes, *Sum* gets 1, 3, 6 etc. as it adds 1, 2, 3 and so on. What about the upper boundary? After *Sum* is increased by 99, *NextNumber* is incremented to 100. But wait... this means that the exit condition is met. The loop is exited, and the final value of *Sum* is off by 100. The exit condition should have been *NextNumber* > 100.

Many programers try to develop an *execution profile* of their pro-grams as an antibugging technique.

> An *execution profile* is a count of the number of times each statement is executed, or the number of times every subprogram is called.

Some Pascal systems have profilers built into their compilers, and can be told to spit out a profile after running a program. However, it's easy enough to include a *CallCount* variable as an extra parameter of every subprogram. When normal program activity is through, a snapshot procedure can be used to show the frequency of procedure calls.

Processing data one item at a time attracts certain kinds of bugs. For example, imagine an averaging program that expects a sentinel to mark the end of valid input, but inadvertently includes the sentinel's value in its calculations! Try to find the bug that explains this program's output.

```
program BuggyConversion (input, output);
    {Tries to read an integer one digit at time.}

var Digit: char;
    Number: integer;

begin
    Number := 0;
    writeln ('Enter an integer followed by a letter.');
    repeat
        read (Digit);
        Number := ord(Digit) − ord('0') + (10*Number)
    until not (Digit in ['0'..'9']);
    writeln ('The number is ', Number:1)
end.  {BuggyConversion}
```

```
            ↓      ↓       ↓       ↓      ↓
Enter an integer followed by a letter.
25A
The number is 267
```

BuggyConversion's error is of the off-by-one variety. Although it manages to exit the loop perfectly well, it adds the ordinal value of 'A' to *Number* before it goes. In general terms, successful models of loops that process *char* input take the form:

```
get a valid data item;   {repeat version}
repeat
    process the data;
    get more data
until the data isn't valid;

get a data item;   {while version}
while the data is valid
    process the data;
    get more data;
```

In contrast, an unsuccessful, incorrect version processes a new item before making sure it's valid.

> Look before you loop. Don't make *any* assumptions about input, and always put the check before the action.

A nonstandard eccentricity of certain Pascal implementations is responsible for a special 'bug'. In these systems, blank spaces are sometimes added to, or removed from, the end of input lines. When spaces are added, problems with reading *integer* and *real* data (as discussed in 7-3) may develop. The discussion of procedure *SkipBlanks* in Chapter 13 should be consulted if necessary.

Summary

The **repeat** and **while** control structures are both conditional loops. *Entry* or *exit conditions*, phrased as *boolean* expressions, control the number of times the loop's action is iterated. It's important that these conditions be possible to fulfill, otherwise the loop will either never be entered, or never *terminate*. One common exit condition is fulfilled when a *sentinel*, or 'end-marker' value, is read within the loop.

Many programing applications require *text processing*, in which input is analyzed character-by-character and line-by-line. To facilitate this sort of data manipulation, Pascal input is considered to belong to a *file* that consists of lines of data. *Control characters* mark the end of each line, and the end of the entire file. Although the end-of-line character may be read, the computer considers it to be a blank, and echoes it as such. A new line can be generated only by using a *writeln*. The end-of-file character may not be read, nor read past. Two standard *boolean* functions, *eoln* and *eof*, help the programer keep track of current file position.

Because of the way procedures *read* and *readln* obtain *integer* and *real* data, care must be taken when reading in an unknown number of values. Until we discuss files in detail in Chapter 13, numerical values should be read in on a line-by-line basis.

Some problems are endemic to conditional loops. Most common is the off-by-one error, which causes the loop to iterate the wrong number of times. Such bugs can usually be avoided by checking the loop's *boundary conditions*. Arranging for an *execution profile* of the program's operation is another method of opening a window into program activity. Failure to update the loop's exit condition is a popular cause of infinite loops. Programs are called *correct* if they work properly in semantic, as well as syntactic, terms.

Program testing can be used to help develop algorithms, as well as to aid debugging. A *bottom-up* approach to programing, in which modules are implemented in brief test programs, can help structure poorly-defined subprogram algorithms. However, a program test is only as reliable as the test data you provide.

repeat	**until**	New Pascal
while	**do**	
eoln	*eof*	

exit condition	*terminated*	*entry condition*	New Terms
sentinel	*overflow*	*degrade gracefully*	
text processing	*control character*	*file*	
bottom-up	*correct*	*boundary conditions*	
execution profile			

7-1   Which of these statements apply only to **while** structures? Only to **repeat** structures? To neither or both?

Self-Test Exercises

a) A *boolean* is evaluated before entering the loop.
b) This structure's action never need be a compound statement.
c) A *boolean* is evaluated after entering the loop.
d) Its action takes place at least once.
e) Can become an infinite loop.
f) The exact number of times the loop will iterate can always be determined from the entry or exit condition.
g) Must have a counter variable.

7-2   Write a loop that shows the first power of 2 greater than or equal to some input number.

7-3   The number of fish in Lake Lackluster is currently about ten million. Write a loop that determines how long it will take the population to drop to a tenth of this level if the number declines by 2.3% each year.

7-4   Can you read the end-of-line character? What does it look like? What happens when you echo it?

7-5   Suppose that we're reading text. Write code that will show if we're at the end of the file or at the end of the current line (both can't be true at once). If neither of these is true, show whether or not the next character is an ordinary space.

7-6   When *eoln* is *true* we're at the end of a line of text. A call of the input procedure *readln* will put us at the beginning of the next line of text, ready to read its first value. What is the effect of a call of *readln* if there *is* no next line? Is it an error? What about a call of *readln* when *eof* is *true*?

7-7   What is the effect of this code? Assume that *eof* isn't *true*.

```
while not eoln do begin
  while not eoln do begin
    read (Character);
    write (Character)
  end;
  writeln;
  readln
end;
```

7-8   Write a procedure *GetNextLetter* that 'filters' text. It should read characters until it finds a letter (disregarding spaces, numerals, and punctuation), then return the letter as a variable-parameter. If you reach the end-of-file before finding a letter, print an error message.

7-9   Write a procedure that finds the 'smallest' and 'largest' lower-case letters (alphabetically speaking) in a series of characters. Return these letters to a calling program as variable-parameters.

7-10   Read our solution to the problem above, and name the circumstance under which the expression *Largest* = *Smallest* is *true*.

7-11   Write a general-purpose procedure to read and echo a series of characters. Input will terminate either with a sentinel character, or at the end-of-file. The possible sentinel will be passed as a parameter of the procedure, along with a *boolean* value that indicates whether we should look for the sentinel, or for the end of the file. For example, the call:

$$ReadAndEcho \; ('\backslash \, ', \; true) \, ;$$

indicates that the backslash character acts as a sentinel, whereas:

$$ReadAndEcho \; ('\, ', \; false) \, ;$$

means that echoing should cease at end-of-file. Be sure *to* check for an empty file in either case, and *not* to print the sentinel character.

7-12   Some quick questions. *a*) Punctuate the following sentence so that it makes sense: *Sue while Patti had had had had had had had had had had had a better effect on the teacher.*

b) Although we usually worry about the boundary conditions of a sequence, here's one problem whose secret is locked in the middle. What is the product of the sequence:

$$(X{-}A)(X{-}B)(X{-}C)\ldots(X{-}Z)$$

c) Suppose that you want to put up a fence in your front yard, which is 100 feet long. How many fenceposts are required to have a post every 10 feet?

More Exercises

7-13   Write a function that sums a geometric series, the absolute value of whose common ratio is less than 1. (For example, the common ratio of 1, 0.5, 0.25... is .5—each term is half of the prior term.) You should use the following formula:

Sum of the series = First term / 1−Common ratio

Thus, the function must be given the first term and the common ratio as arguments.

Now, write a program that sums a geometric series *iteratively*, i.e. using brute force. How long does it take for this method to be roughly as accurate (say, within 10E-09) as the 'formula' answer? Use at least five different first term and common ratio values (positive and negative), and chart your results.

7-14   Here's a peculiar form of multiplication. To multiply any two numbers, start halving the larger, and doubling the smaller. Whenever the first number (the one that was originally larger) is odd, remember the second number. Continue until the first number has been reduced to 1. Disregard any fractional remainder of any of the halvings. The product is equal to the sum of the remembered second numbers. For example, 53 times 26 is:

53	26	13	6	3	1
26	52	104	208	416	832

$$26+104+416+832=53*26=1378$$

Write a program that carries out this form of multiplication.

7-15   Write a program that finds the first 20 numbers which, when divided by 2, 3, 4, 5, or 6 leave a remainder of 1, and when divided by 7 have no remainder.

7-16   The integer 36 has a peculiar property—it is a perfect square, and is also the sum of the integers from 1 through 8. The next such number is 1225, which is 35^2 as well as the sum of 1 through 49. Find the next number that is a perfect square, and is also the sum of the series $1 .. n$ (288 sum $= 204^2 = 41,616$)

7-17 In the Battle of Hastings, Harold's Saxons arranged themselves in a number of solid squares, each of the same size. This was unfortunate for the attacking Normans, who were unable to pierce Harold's defenses from any side.

Late in the day, Harold decided to enter the fray himself. However, Harold's men (who by this time were in thirteen squares) were unable to make an opening for him without spoiling one of their squares. An armour bearer who fortuitously happened to be standing by noted that, with the addition of Harold, the soldiers would be able to form one very large square. How many men were in each of the small squares, and how many were in the large one? (Hint: you'll find the method of checking for perfect squares we gave in the exercises for Chapter 7 helpful.)

7-18 In the last chapter's exercises we presented a dartboard problem. Six possible scores could be obtained—7, 15, 19, 23, 29, and 37. We asked you to find the five ways of obtaining this score with six darts.

Repeat the exercise. This time, however, you should minimize the problem's solution space as much as possible. Improve your basic algorithm so that your program executes as few statements as possible.

7-19 A miser once inherited a sum of money in cash and coin—equal numbers of dollar bills, half dollars, and quarters. She divided the money between eight hiding places, putting the same number of dollar bills and each kind of coin in each place.

The very next day, however, the miser became afraid that one of the hiding places would be uncovered. She redistributed the money, as equally as before, among only seven places. Then, the very next day she felt compelled to cache her money in only six locations. This she was able to do. Unfortunately this was the limit of her ingenuity. The next day she tried to assort her money evenly among only five hiding places. When she was unable to do this, she burst a blood vessel and died, leaving the money to *her* miserly heirs, and starting the whole process over again.

The question we pose is this: How much money did the miser start with, and how many of each coin and bill were there?

7-20 Write a simple-minded inventory program. Allow for five different products, and have the program user enter the starting inventories of each. Implement the following commands: 'A' is add inventory, 'O' is order and remove from inventory, 'P' is print inventory, and 'Q' is quit. Each input line should consist of one of these commands and, if necessary, a product code and amount.

Try to make this program as idiot-proof as possible. Besides error-checking input (and discarding lines that are mistaken), the program should warn of inventory shortages and print the totals of orders that could not be completely filled.

7-21 In many industries set-up costs are so high that manufacturers will produce much larger quantities of an item than they can reasonably hope to sell quickly. However, warehousing costs can limit the practical size of a production run.

Nadine Riverdale (thanks to the great success of her hot tub sales) is currently in the bulldozer manufacturing business. Experience has shown her that profit on the nth dozer equals $500+100(ln(n))$. However, the cost of building parking lots to store them on continually rises, and the kth parking lot she builds will cost $100(2k-1)$. In practice, she builds a new parking lot after finishing the manufacture of every ten machines.

The question we pose is this: How many bulldozers should Nadine build if she wants the difference between her total profit, and the cost of storing the machines, to be as large as possible?

7-22   Pick-up-stones is an easy game of position. Twenty-one stones are put in a pile, and players take turns removing 1, 2, or 3 stones from the pile. The last player to go wins.

Write a program that uses the best possible strategy to play Pick-up-stones. Then modify it to accept these variations: *X* stones go into the original pile, *Y* stones may be picked up each turn, and the last player loses.

7-23   Pick a number between 1 and 100. Now, write a program that will guess the number within seven turns. To help the program, tell it if its guesses are too high or too low.

7-24   Here's a magical card trick. Let's see how you can turn it into a program. The trick works like this: Nine cards of a single suit (with values from Ace to Nine) are dealt out, face down. Several people each pick a different card. The first person must double the number on her card, add 1, multiply by 5, and give the result to the second player. She adds this number to the value of her own card, then also multiplies by 2, adds 1, multiplies by 5, and passes on the final value. Each person in turn adds the value given her to the value of her card, then carries out the prescribed operations.

When everybody has completed their multiplications and additions we can begin the magic. Make a number that contains as many fives (and only fives) as there are card-choosers. Subtract this from the number calculated by the very last person. Now, divide by 10. The result is a number whose digits are the chosen cards in correct order. Don't forget to have your program say *Abracadabra.*

7-25   It's time for the circus to pay its annual bird and animal tax. The circus owner, however, is a little short on cash, and can't quite afford the bill, which is figured at a rate of $5.50 per bird, and $7.29 per animal. To stall the tax collector, the owner has a clown tell city hall that the circus own 36 heads, and 100 feet altogether, and isn't sure how much tax to pay. Write a program that figures out how many animals and birds are in the circus, and what the tax bill should be.

7-26   Write a program that:

a) Counts and prints the number of values in a series of numbers;

b) Finds the average value;

c) Finds the largest and smallest value in the series;

d) Prints the positions of the high and low numbers.

The series of numbers *should* end with −999. However, it's quite possible that the end-marker will fall off on the way to your computer. Make sure that the program doesn't try to read past the end-of-file. Naturally, you should allow for peculiar cases, such as a series one number long.

7-27   Write a program that converts an octal (base 8) number into hexadecimal (base 16) notation. Print the hexadecimal digits 10, 11, 12, 13, 14, and 15 as the letters 'A', 'B', 'C', 'D', 'E', and 'F'. What limits must you set on allowable input?

7-28   Write a procedure *Count* that is passed two parameters of type *char*, and counts the number of times they appear in a text file. Modify it to count the number of times the integers '3' and '8' appear.

7-29   A series of blank lines are sometimes used to separate different parts of input data. Write a program that will read and echo characters, line by line, until two blank lines in a row are input.

7-30   Write a simple program to count the number of words and sentences in a sample of input text. Assume that every blank marks the end of a word, and that a period marks the end of a sentence. Assume that the end of input is marked by *a)* a backslash (\) *b) eof.*

7-31   Write a program to count the number of words and sentences in a sample of input text. Assume that input ends when *eof* is *true*. Make sure the program can handle real-life ambiguities—for example, this . . . is not three sentences; nor are the two blank spaces after a colon or period both word-enders. Modify your program to count the number of input lines, and to issue an announcement when there's an obvious punctuation error—no space, or the wrong number of spaces, after (or before) a punctuation mark, word, or sentence. The announcement should say what number line the error occurs on.

7-32   Write a program to find the average number of characters per word, and words per sentence, in a sample of input text. You may revise either of the programs above to handle the job.

7-33   Write a simple text processing program that reads input text (that may be split over many lines) and echoes it in such a way that each line has ten words. Then, modify the program so that the fortieth character of each line is in the last word printed. Don't forget to make a rule for what happens if the fortieth character is a space. In any case, ignore spaces that appear at the beginning of a line.

7-34   Write a program that translates its input into Pig Latin. Be sure to think of special circumstances—punctuation at the end of words, words that start with vowels, words beginning with capital letters, etc.

7-35   Devise a structure for conditional iteration. Do you think that equivalents of both **while** and **repeat** are necessary? Can you think of a syntax that would allow you to exit from the middle of a loop? When might this be desirable?

8

Subprograms That Represent Values

An interesting fact about spoken languages is their completeness. When a feeling or phenomenon exists, there's usually a simple way to describe it. Particularly commonplace things can often be described in many ways—supposedly the Eskimos have seventeen different words for snow. On the other hand, something that is unique or extraordinary must be described literally, one feature at a time—older readers will remember the one-eyed, one-horned, flying purple people-eater.

Now, of all the languages in the world, the language of computers is one of the most primitive. Think about the trouble involved in trying to describe a number in Pascal. Is it positive? In Pascal we must ask if $(Number > 0)$. Is it evenly divisible by 3 or 4? We must inquire whether $(Number \bmod 3 = 0)$ or $(Number \bmod 4 = 0)$. With a little bit of labor we can make Pascal approximate our English descriptions. But what happens when we get more specific? Is the number two digits long and odd? Does it include any nines? Is it prime? Adjectives and descriptions that are easy to articulate in English might require an entire program to express in Pascal.

In 8-1 we're going to learn about a feature that helps extend Pascal, and avoid the problems an overly compact language might cause. *Functions*, which compute and represent values, aren't an essential part of any programing system, but they help free the programer from the necessity of plodding along in a highly-restricted computer language. We'll also try some different methods of program testing. As we get better at writing programs that compile, it's a good idea to make sure that they do something!

8-2, which is optional at this time, introduces a programing technique called *recursion.* A subprogram is recursive if it calls itself. The notion may seem a little weird at first, but recursion is de rigueur in more advanced programing courses, and a first encounter now may help get you used to it. Finally, 8-3 brings up some new ideas about *stub programing* and a top-down approach to debugging.

Testing may show the presence of bugs, but it doesn't say much about their absence.

8-1
Functions as Subprograms

PASCAL FUNCTIONS COMPUTE AND REPRESENT values. Functions that programers declare are more interesting than the standard functions, because we can name them as we wish, tell them exactly what to compute, and give them as many arguments as we want. For example, a call of function *Distance* with its arguments *SpeedometerReading* and *ElapsedTime* provides a value for the variable *AmountTraveled*:

> *AmountTraveled* := *Distance* (*SpeedometerReading, ElapsedTime*) ;

Like a procedure, a function must be declared before it can be used:

function *Distance* (*Rate*: *integer*; *Time*: *real*) : *real*;
　　{Calculates *Distance* given *Rate* and *Time*.}
　　begin
　　　　Distance := *Rate* ∗ *Time*　{This statement assigns the function its value}
　　end; {*Distance*}

Since they're subprograms, functions are similar to procedures. Function declarations are intermingled with procedure declarations at the end of the declaration part.

> *program heading*
> *definition part*
> 　　*constant definitions*
> *declaration part*
> 　　*variable declarations*
> 　　*procedure and function declarations*
> *statement part*

Like procedure declarations, function declarations follow the general format of a Pascal program.

> *function heading (parameter list)*
> *function declarations and definitions*
> 　　*local constants*
> 　　*local variables*
> 　　*local procedures and functions*
> *function statement part*

The appearance of a function's name in a program is a ***function call***, just as a procedure's name serves as a call of that procedure. A function call signals the program to execute, or run, the function subprogram. However, this is where the similarity between functions and procedures ends.

> A procedure cannot represent a value. Its name in a program merely tells the computer to execute the procedure subprogram. A function, on the other hand, *must* represent a value.

If you recall our discussion of representation it's clear that function and procedure calls are two entirely different animals. A procedure call only invokes a series of actions; using a procedure's name in a program tells the computer to carry out these actions.

In contrast, a function call is the *representation of a value.* When a function name is used in a program, the computer immediately evaluates the function. It finds out the value the function call represents by carrying out the subprogram associated with the function name. This has two immediate consequences.* First, since a function can represent a value, it must be declared to be of some particular type. Second, the statement part of the function has to contain an assignment statement that gives the function its value.

The first consequence is dealt with in the *function heading*. A function heading begins with the reserved word **function** and the function's name. Next comes the parameter list, between parentheses. Value-parameters (and rarely, variable-parameters) are declared here. Finally, the function's Pascal type is given, just as though the function were an ordinary variable. We can draw a chart of a function heading like this:

function heading

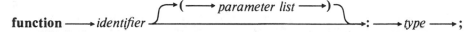

function ⟶ *identifier* ⟶ (⟶ *parameter list* ⟶) ⟶ : ⟶ *type* ⟶ ;

Naming subprograms and declaring parameters should be familiar from our work with procedures. Only functions, though, are given types.

> A function call may represent any simple type of value, ordinal or *real.* The function's *result type* is specified at the end of the function heading—a colon is followed by the type identifier.

Our second concern, assigning the function its value, is taken care of within the function. In *Distance* this assignment formed the subprogram's entire statement part.

> The assignment of a value to a function may only take place within the function itself. It's illegal to make this assignment from anywhere else in the program.

Naturally, a function can take care of other business as well, as long as it doesn't use global variables not passed as parameters (because that would cause side-effects). A function's last action, however, is to give itself a value.

Q. May a function call be an argument of a procedure? Another function?

A. Since it represents a value, a function call, complete with arguments, may be an argument of another function or procedure. It provides the initial value of a value-parameter.

Self-Check Questions

* Isn't it awful how logical this stuff is?

Review of Parameters

A quick review of value-parameters will help forestall confusion about their declarations. A function may have any number of value-parameters:

function *Cube* (*Number*: *real*) : *real*;

function *Even* (*IntegerValue*: *integer*) : *boolean*;

function *Decode* (*Letter*: *char*; *CodeKey*: *integer*) : *char*;

function *OneOfEach* (*A*: *boolean*; *B*: *char*; *C*: *integer*; *D*: *real*) : *real*;

If there is more than one value-parameter of any given type, the different identifiers are separated by commas:

function *Example* (*A, B, C*: *integer*; *D,E*: *boolean*; *F*: *real*; *G, H, I*: *char*) : *integer*;

The value-parameters of each type need not be grouped together. Parameter declarations are usually ordered to produce a function call that, with arguments, is self-documenting. Value-parameters are used within the function as though they were local variables. For example:

function *Alphabetical* (*FirstCharacter, SecondCharacter*: *char*) : *char*;
    {Represents the character in lowest alphabetical order.}

begin
    if *FirstCharacter* < *SecondCharacter*
      then *Alphabetical* := *FirstCharacter*
      else *Alphabetical* := *SecondCharacter*
end;   {*Alphabetical*}

Value-parameters are initialized by the arguments of a function call. *Alphabetical's* arguments might be constant *char* values, or any other expressions of type *char*:

    LowestChar := *Alphabetical*(*InputChar, KnownValue*) ;
    LowestChar := *Alphabetical*('R', 'r') ;
    LowestChar := *Alphabetical*(*TestCharacter*, 'B') ;

Note that there must always be a one-to-one correspondence between the arguments of a function *call*, and the value-parameters of a function *declaration.* Thus, any given function will always be called with the same number of arguments.

function *Yield*(*Investment*: *integer*; *Interest*: *real*; *Days*: *integer*) : *real*;

(Function heading—value-parameters)

Income := *Yield* (1000, 0.097, 365) ;

(Function call—arguments)

Variable-parameters are seldom declared in function headings, because the avowed purpose of a function is to compute and return a *single* value. If a function has variable-parameters, it will wind up returning more than just one value. This creates a situation that can confuse an unwary program rewriter.

> ⋮ The Golden Rule of Functions
> ⋮ If a subprogram is supposed to calculate more than one value for
> ⋮ the main program, write it as a procedure.

It's said that the world consists of two kinds of people—those who divide everything into two groups, and those who don't. The authors, who belong in the first division, would like to divide functions into two groups— *boolean* functions, and all others.

Writing Arithmetic Functions

Why make this distinction? Well, by 'all others' we generally mean functions that compute values for assignment to variables. *Boolean* functions, in contrast, usually state the entry or exit conditions of control structures. We'll see that there's a different motivation for writing each sort of function.

We can begin by writing a few calculating functions that are standard in some other computer languages (and even some Pascal implementations). A routine that's easy to write (and is useful for anyone who can't remember trigonometry) is a tangent function. We make use of the fact that tangent ϕ = sine ϕ/cosine ϕ in writing function *RadianTan.*

```
function RadianTan (AngleInRadians: real) : real;
   {Represents the tangent of its argument.}

   begin
      RadianTan := sin(AngleInRadians)/Cos(AngleInRadians)
   end; {RadianTan}
```

RadianTan's value-parameter, *AngleInRadians*, clearly documents the fact that *RadianTan's* argument should be supplied in radians, rather than degrees. Unfortunately, the most familiar measurement of angles works the other way around, in degrees rather than radians. We can modify *RadianTan* to work with a degree-valued argument by including a radian conversion function *within the declaration of Radian-Tan.* The conversion function uses the equation $1° = \pi/180$ radians.

```
function tan (AngleInDegrees: real) : real;
   {Represents the tangent of its degree-valued argument.}

   var Angle: real;          {This variable is local to tan}

   function ConvertToRadians (Angle: real) : real;
      const pi = 3.1415926;
      begin
         ConvertToRadians := Angle*(pi/180)
      end;  {ConvertToRadians}

   begin
      Angle := ConvertToRadians(AngleInDegrees) ;
      tan := sin(Angle)/cos(Angle)
   end; {tan}
```

Our code is overly detailed, but it shows that a function can be declared within a function, and gives an example of a value-parameter taking precedence over a like-named variable that is relatively global.

The operation of *tan* can be checked by including it in a ***driver*** program, as we've done in *TestFunctions*, below. This ploy, which is reminiscent of the bottom-up programing of Chapter 7, lets us test the function in an environment that isn't cluttered with extraneous function and procedure declarations. Once we're sure the function works, it's easy to transfer it elsewhere. Note that there are small mathematical inconsistencies in *TestFunctions'* output, because of inaccuracies in the computer's arithmetic.

```
program TestFunctions (input, output);
    {Tests function Tan}

var InputValue: real;
    Counter: integer;

function tan (AngleInDegrees: real): real;

    var Angle: real;

    function ConvertToRadians (Angle: real): real;
        const pi = 3.1415926;
        begin
            ConvertToRadians := Angle*(pi/180)
        end;   {ConvertToRadians}

    begin   {tan}
        Angle := ConvertToRadians(AngleInDegrees);
        tan := sin(Angle)/cos(Angle)
    end;   {tan}

begin
    for Counter := 1 to 5
        do begin
            read (InputValue);
            writeln ('The tangent of', InputValue:2:2, ' degrees is', tan(InputValue))
        end
end.   {TestFunctions}
```

```
        ↓        ↓        ↓        ↓        ↓
0.0   45.0   60.0   120.0   135.0
The  tangent  of  0.00  degrees  is    0.00000000000000E+00
The  tangent  of  45.00  degrees  is   9.99999973205104E-01
The  tangent  of  60.00  degrees  is   1.73205073611582E+00
The  tangent  of  120.00  degrees  is  -1.73201384950475E+00
The  tangent  of  135.00  degrees  is  -1.00000008038469E+00
```

Another useful function is a random number generator. This is one of the few functions to use a variable-parameter. Although many

Pascal implementations have predefined random number functions, you should copy ours (or write your own) if you want to write Standard Pascal programs.

Where do random numbers come from? Before computers were widely available, the most common sources were large tables. The ultimate version was probably a book published by the Rand Corporation that contained one million randomly distributed digits. (In a random distribution, there is an equal likelihood that any given integer will be 0, 1, 2 . . . 9.)

Nowadays, programing a computer to produce random numbers is elementary. One common algorithm is to pick a starting number (called the *seed*), then subject it to this sequence of mathematical operations:

$$Seed := ((Multiplier * Seed) + Increment) \textbf{ mod } Modulus$$

(All the identifiers on the right-hand side of the assignment, besides *Seed*, are *integer* constants, given below.) The assignment gives *Seed* a value that satisfies the relation:

$$0 \leqslant Seed < Modulus$$

If we divide by *Modulus* (using the *real* division operator), we'll have a value such that:

$$0 \leqslant Seed < 1$$

Repeating the assignment and extra division produces a ***pseudo-random*** sequence of numbers. Although the numbers are randomly distributed, it is possible to predict what the series will be. Furthermore, the sequence will eventually repeat itself.

```
function Random (var Seed: integer) : real;
    {Generates a pseudo-random number such that 0 < = Random < 1.}

    const Modulus = 65536;       {These are 'magic' numbers}
          Multiplier = 25173;    {that produce a pseudo-random}
          Increment = 13849;     {sequence of numbers.}

    begin
        Seed := ((Multiplier * Seed) + Increment) mod Modulus;
            {Pick an integer from 0 through Modulus−1}
        Random := Seed / Modulus
            {Adjust it to fall between (or including) 0, and 1.}
    end;  {Random}
```

To use *Random* in a program, declare a global *integer* variable *Seed*, and initialize it before the first call of *Random*. Because *Seed* is changed by each call of *Random*, it must be passed as a variable-parameter.

Now, any initial value of *Seed* generates a particular sequence of numbers. As a result, if *Seed* is initialized to the same number every time a program that contains *Random* is run, the program will always work with the same random series. This is a lifesaver during debugging, because you know what numbers to expect. However, a game program isn't much fun if its random elements are the same each time you play.

Programers solve this problem in two ways. The first method requires a nonstandard function that returns a constantly changing *integer* value (or a *real* value that can be rounded or truncated). For example, most Pascal implementations have a function that represents the current time of day. Although the inclusion of such a function makes a program nonstandard (because it isn't Standard Pascal), it's sometimes the only solution.

The second solution is to use hook or crook to obtain the seed from the program user. We'll see an example of this soon. First, though, let's figure out a way of testing the *Random* function. It's easy enough to call the function a few thousand times:

for *Count* := 1 **to** 5000
  do *writeln* (*Random* (*Seed*)) ;

But how useful would this segment's output be? Nobody can inspect a list of five thousand twenty-two digit *real* numbers and declare that they're randomly distributed.

Why don't we modify the function call to produce a number in some reasonable *integer* range, say 1 through 10? Since *Random's* output currently falls between 0.000... and 0.999... we can multiply by 10 and truncate (to get a number in the range 0 through 9), then add 1 to the result. We can use a **case** structure and ordinary variables to keep track of the loop's output.*

TestRandom's well-labeled output assures us that our function, as well as our method for generating a number within a particular range, both work reasonably well. Had we managed to generate a number outside the range 1 through 10, the **case** structure would have caused a run-time error and crash. The completed program is on the next page.

---

* In Chapter 12 we'll see that the **array** structure would be even more suitable.

```pascal
program TestRandom (input, output);
    {Checks the distribution of Random's output.}

const NumberOfTrials = 10000;

var One, Two, Three, Four, Five, Six, Seven, Eight, Nine, Ten, Counter, Seed: Integer;

function Random (var Seed: integer): real;
    {Generates a pseudo-random number such that 0 < = Random < 1.}

    const Modulus = 65536;
          Multiplier = 25173;
          Increment = 13849;

    begin
        Seed := ((Multiplier*Seed) + Increment) mod Modulus;
        Random := Seed/Modulus
    end;  {Random}
begin
    One := 0;  Two := 0;  Three := 0;
    Four := 0;  Five := 0;  Six := 0;
    Seven := 0;  Eight := 0;  Nine := 0;
    Ten := 0;
    writeln ('Please enter a seed.');
    readln (Seed);
    writeln ('Distribution of ', NumberOfTrials:1,' trials of function Random:');
    for Counter := 1 to NumberOfTrials
        do begin
            case (1 + trunc(10*Random(Seed))) of
                1: One := One+1;  2: Two := Two+1;  3: Three := Three+1;
                4: Four := Four+1;  5: Five := Five+1;  6: Six = Six+1;
                7: Seven = Seven+1;  8: Eight = Eight+1;  9: Nine = Nine+1;
                10: Ten = Ten+1
            end  {case}
        end;  {for}
    writeln ('1''s':5, '2''s':5, '3''s':5, '4''s':5, '5''s':5,
             '6''s':5, '7''s':5, '8''s':5, '9''s':5, '10''s':5);
    writeln (One:5, Two:5, Three:5, Four:5, Five:5,
             Six:5, Seven:5, Eight:5, Nine:5, Ten:5)
end.  {TestRandom}
```

```
          ↓        ↓        ↓        ↓        ↓
Please enter a seed.
329
Distribution of 10000 trials of function Random:
  1's   2's   3's   4's   5's   6's   7's   8's   9's  10's
 1016   985  1003   929   995  1028  1037  1030  1010   967
```

Let's move on to an application of the *Random* function. Our problem will be to write a game program:

Write a program that picks a number in the range 1 through 100, and challenges a program user to guess it. Allow seven tries, and tell the user if she's too high or low.

A first refinement of the problem is to:

> *get a seed*;
> *pick a random number*;
> **repeat**
>   *let the user guess*;
>   *respond to the guess*
> **until** *the guess is right* **or** *all the guesses are used up*;

What are possible responses to the program user? Well, the guess is either too high, too low, or exactly right. Since these three possibilities are mutually exclusive, we can use nested **if** structures to choose an appropriate response:

> *get a seed*;
> *pick a random number*;
> **repeat**
>   *let the user guess*;
>   **if** *guess is high* **then** *give high error message*
>   **else if** *guess is low* **then** *give low error message*
>   **else if** *guess is right* **then** *offer congratulations*;
> **until** *the guess is right* **or** *all the guesses are used up*;

The completed version of program *NumberGuess* is shown below. Notice our unsubtle method of initializing *Seed*—we just ask the user to enter a number without mentioning why we want it. As you read *NumberGuess* try to figure out why seven guesses should be enough to find the computer's number.

```
program NumberGuess (input, output) ;
    {Challenges a user to guess a number within 7 tries.}
var Number, Guess, Count, Seed: integer;
    Solved: boolean;
function Random (var Seed: integer) : real;
    {Generates a pseudo-random number such that 0 < = Random < 1.}
    const Modulus = 65536;
          Multiplier = 25173;
          Increment = 13849;
    begin
        Seed := ((Multiplier*Seed) + Increment) mod Modulus;
        Random := Seed/Modulus
    end;  {Random}
begin
    writeln ('Play a guessing game.  Enter a number between 1 and 100.') ;
    readln (Seed) ;
    Number := 1 + trunc(100*(Random(Seed))) ;
    writeln ('Thanks.  Now, I''m thinking of a number from 1 through 100.') ;
    write ('You have 7 tries to guess it.   ') ;
    Count := 0 ;
    repeat
        Count := Count+1 ;
        writeln ('Take a guess.') ;
        read (Guess) ;
        Solved := Guess =Number;
        if Guess < Number
            then write ('Uh oh ... that number was too small.   ')
            else if Guess > Number
                then write ('Sorry, but that number was too big.   ')
                    else write (Number:1 )
    until Solved or (Count=7) ;
    if Count=7
        then writeln ('The right number was ', Number:1 )
        else writeln ('  was exactly right.')
end.  {NumberGuess}
```

$$\downarrow \quad \downarrow \quad \downarrow \quad \downarrow \quad \downarrow$$

```
Play a guessing game.  Enter a number between 1 and 100.
92
Thanks.  Now, I'm thinking of a number from 1 through 100.
You have 7 tries to guess it.  Take a guess.
1
Uh oh ... that number was too small.  Take a guess.
50
Uh oh ... that number was too small.  Take a guess.
75
Sorry, but that number was too big.  Take a guess.
60
Sorry, but that number was too big.  Take a guess.
55
55 was exactly right.
```

boolean Functions

Let's move along to functions that return *boolean* results—either *false* or *true*. Function *Even* decides if its *integer* argument is evenly divisible by 2.

```
function Even (Number: integer) : boolean;
    begin
        Even := (Number mod 2) = 0
        {We might have just said Even := not odd(Number).}
    end;  {Even}
```

As we start to write programs that are large and complex, *boolean* functions are a necessity.

> *Boolean* functions let programers write code that is concise, yet still explicit in purpose.

We can find ourselves developing a funny relationship with program comments. On one hand, we insist on their importance as a part of every program, but on the other, we continuously try to write code that needs no commenting. For example, this program segment adds to the apparent complexity of the program it's found in. It slows the reader down.

```
readln (Number);
if ((Number> =20) and (Number< =30)) or (Number =35)
    {Continue if Number is within a valid range of responses.}
    then begin      etc.
```

Proclaiming the condition as a function does the same job in an unobtrusive, self-explanatory manner.

```
readln (Number);
if Valid(Number)
    then begin      etc.
```

Valid, declared below, takes the details of the *boolean* expression and puts them in a function declaration where they belong.

```
function Valid (Number: integer) : boolean;
{Valid is true if its argument is 35, or between 20 and 30, inclusive.}
    begin
        Valid := ((Number> =20) and (Number< =30)) or (Number =35)
    end;  {Valid}
```

There are several *boolean* functions whose names frequently pop up in Pascal programs. Like *Valid*, they establish a condition:

```
function No (Value: real) : boolean;
    begin
        No := Value=0
    end;  {No}
```

in an English-like, easy to comprehend manner.

repeat
   PlayTheGame
until *No* (*TurnsLeft*) ;

while *No* (*ValueEntered*)
   do *PromptForValue*;

if *No* (*ErrorConditions*)
   then *ProcessTransactions*
   else *RepeatLastTransaction*

Boolean functions help clarify the flow of a program, and make the computer appear to understand English. Although *boolean* function declarations may clutter up a short program, they're invaluable in larger programs, or wherever complex *boolean* conditions must be stated.

   We'll take this opportunity to present a few arguments for the importance of using functions in general. First of all, although some formulas (like *Distance* := *Rate*∗*Time*) are easy to write several times if necessary, many others require statement sequences that are not so brief. Declaring a function lets us carry out a computation many times without duplicating its code again and again. In this sense, a Pascal function is like one of the black boxes or function machines popular in teaching calculus. We plug in a value or values (the function's argument), and a result value is automatically computed.

   Second, the conditions that guide control structures are sometimes complicated. Implementing them as *boolean* functions makes programs easier to read. Many functions that are easily recognized by name require obscure code to compute their values. Would you recognize the algorithm a computer uses to find a sine or logarithm? Functions, like procedures, help make Pascal programs English-like and self-documenting.

   Finally, functions encourage top-down program design. They're a natural extension of pseudocode. We can use the function's name when we rough out a program's statement part, and write the more detailed code of the function at our leisure. A free and easy use of functions (especially *boolean* functions) is one mark of a well-designed program.

Q. Can you find a bug in this program segment? Assume we're using the *Random* function we defined above.

Self-Check
Questions

   WildCard := *Random* (*Seed*) ;
   writeln ('The number we picked was', *Random* (*Seed*)) ;

A. A programer who expects this segment to print the value of *WildCard* will be disappointed. The second call of *Random(Seed)* represents an entirely different number. The segment should have been written as:

> *WildCard* := *Random(Seed)* ;
> *writeln* ('The number we picked was', *WildCard*) ;

:..:...:

Focus on Programing: Generating Test Data

Our final example program will implement Sir Isaac Newton's method of finding a number's square root.* His algorithm is:

> Take a guess at the number's square root. The assignment:
>
> $$Guess := ((Number/Guess) + Guess) / 2$$
>
> gives a number that is closer to being correct, no matter how wild the original guess was (as long as it wasn't 0).

We can make the value of *Guess* more and more accurate by repeatedly carrying out the assignment. However, we'll eventually tax the computer's precision, and continued guessing won't make our answer any more correct. Thus, we want to write a program that repeats the assignment shown above until the difference between successive guesses is very small—say, 10E−09. (Incidentally, this method won't work well for numbers with very large square roots.) In pseudocode, the loop we desire looks like this:

> *give NewGuess an initial value*;
> **repeat**
>   *OldGuess gets the value of NewGuess*;
>   *compute the new value of NewGuess*
> **until** *NoSignificantChange(OldGuess, NewGuess)* ;

Now, writing a program that implements Newton's algorithm isn't too challenging for us, so we'll try to enliven the job. Let's write a program that *tests* Newton's method by using it to find the square roots of various numbers. We'll use a random number function to generate test numbers, as well as wild first guesses at their square roots. At the same time, we'll count how many iterations Newton's method takes to arrive at the root, and compare its result to that of the standard function *sqrt* Our pseudocode of a *SquareRoot* function expands to:

> *pick a number to solve for*;
> *print the number*;
> *assign a wild first guess of its square root to NewGuess*;
> *print the guess*;
> **repeat**
>   *OldGuess gets the value of NewGuess*;
>   *compute the new value of NewGuess*;
>   *update the guess counter*
> **until** *NoSignificantChange(OldGuess, NewGuess)* ;

* Don't forget that he, like Gauss, didn't have a computer (or even a calculator).

We won't bother writing up a refinement of a *TestNewton* program, since we've already worked on most of its components. Instead, let's try a program outline:

program *TestNewton*;

const *the starting seed, the number of trials we want,*
  and the upper limit on numbers and guesses;

var *the number we're examining, the seed, and a counter for trials*;

function *RandomInteger*— —*gets Seed and UpperLimit, returns an integer*;

function *SquareRoot*— —*gets Number, returns its square root*;
 function *NoSignificantChange*— —*gets the two most recent guesses,*
        and returns true if they're very close;

begin
 initialize the seed;
 label the program output;
 for *some number of trials*
  pick a Number
  print Number
  print SquareRoot (*Number*), *sqrt* (*Number*)
end.

Notice that *RandomInteger* is a slightly modified version of *Random.* To facilitate printing, the program appears on the next page, but its output is shown below.

Number	First Guess	Tries	Newton	sqrt
525	6275	13	22.91288	22.91288
7939	5080	11	89.10107	89.10107
6801	8193	12	82.46818	82.46818
8185	6925	11	90.47099	90.47099
3321	5864	12	57.62812	57.62812
2347	6631	12	48.44585	48.44585
3055	1630	10	55.27205	55.27205
9644	7793	11	98.20387	98.20387
1469	335	8	38.32754	38.32754
1794	6503	12	42.35564	42.35564

```
program TestNewton (input, output);
    {Tests Newton's method of finding square roots.}

const StartingSeed = 10;
      NumberOfTrials = 10;
      UpperLimit = 10000;

var Number, Seed, Counter: integer;

function RandomInteger (var Seed: integer;  UpperLimit: integer) : integer;
    {Generates a pseudo-random integer from 1 through UpperLimit}
    const Modulus = 65536;
          Multiplier = 25173;
          Increment = 13849;
    begin
        Seed := ((Multiplier*Seed) + Increment) mod Modulus;
        RandomInteger := 1 + trunc(UpperLimit*(Seed/Modulus))
    end; {RandomInteger}

function SquareRoot (Number: real) : real;
    var OldGuess, NewGuess: real;
    GuessNumber: integer;
    function NoSignificantChange (Old, New: real) : boolean;
        const Epsilon = 10E−09;
        begin
            NoSignificantChange := abs(Old−New) < Epsilon
        end; {NoSignificantChange}
    begin  {SquareRoot}
        NewGuess := RandomInteger(Seed, UpperLimit);  {Take a wild first guess}
        write (trunc(NewGuess):15);
        GuessNumber := 0;
        repeat
            GuessNumber := GuessNumber+1;
            OldGuess := NewGuess;
            NewGuess := ((Number/OldGuess) + OldGuess)/2
        until NoSignificantChange(OldGuess, NewGuess);
        write (GuessNumber:8);
        SquareRoot := NewGuess
    end; {SquareRoot}

begin  {TestNewton}
    Seed := StartingSeed;
    writeln ('Number':6, 'First Guess':15, 'Tries':8, 'Newton':12, 'sqrt':12);
    for Counter := 1 to NumberOfTrials
        do begin
            Number := RandomInteger(Seed, UpperLimit);
            write (Number:6);
            writeln (SquareRoot(Number):12:5, sqrt(Number):12:5)
        end
end.  {TestNewton}
```

Like procedures, functions may be forward-declared. A forward declaration lets a function be used out of turn. It can be called by another subprogram before it is declared. However, the function must eventually be declared in the correct block.

> In a forward declaration, the normal function heading, complete with parameter list and function type, is followed by the word **forward**. When the actual declaration of the function takes place, the parameter list and function type are omitted.

    function *DeclaredLater* (*Parameter*: *integer*) : *char*; **forward**;
    procedure *CallManyFunctions* (*parameter list*) ;
      begin
        rest of the procedure declaration
        includes a call of DeclaredLater
      end;
    function *DeclaredLater*;
        {The parameter list and function type are omitted}
      begin
        rest of the function declaration
      end;

As usual, it's a good idea to include the parameter list and function type as a comment of the real function declaration.

      function *DeclaredLater* {(Parameter: integer): char;}
        etc.

CONSIDER THIS program:

  program *Reverse* (*input, output*) ;
    {Recursively reads a line of input, and echoes it in reverse.}
  procedure *StackTheCharacters*;
    var *TheCharacter*: *char*;
    begin
      read (*TheCharacter*) ;
      if not *eoln* **then** *StackTheCharacters*;   {A recursive call.}
      write (*TheCharacter*)
    end; {*StackTheCharacters*}
  begin
    writeln ('Please enter a sentence.') ;
    StackTheCharacters;
    writeln
  end. {*Reverse*}

      ↓   ↓   ↓   ↓   ↓
Please enter a sentence.
This is not a palindrome.
.emordnilap a ton si sihT

Program *Reverse* takes an ordinary line of text as input, and prints it out in reverse. It accomplishes this with a *recursive* procedure, *StackTheCharacters.*

> A procedure or function that calls itself is said to be ***recursive.***

When *StackTheCharacters* is first invoked, a character is read as input to the local variable *TheCharacter.* Then (unless this happens to be the last character on the line), *StackTheCharacters* is called again. Note that the final statement of the first call — *write* (*TheCharacter*) — is still pending.

The same process is repeated in the second call of *StackTheCharacters.* A new local variable is created, a new character is input, and a new invocation of *StackTheCharacters* takes over.

Now, if we look only at the input statements executed during program *Reverse,* we'll see something like the series shown below. Although we keep creating local variables named *TheCharacter,* Pascal's scope rule (that the most local variable takes precedence) gives the current input value to the most recently created variable.

```
read (TheCharacter);          {Reading in 'T'.}
   read (TheCharacter);          {Reading in 'h'.}
      read (TheCharacter);          {Reading in 'i'.}
         :         {Intermediate calls...}
            read (TheCharacter);          {Reading in 'm'.}
               read (TheCharacter);          {Reading in 'e'.}
                  read (TheCharacter);          {Reading in '.', the last call.}
```

The chain of calls to *StackTheCharacter* continues until we read the last character on the line. We're finally able to complete the last invocation of *StackTheCharacters* by printing the character most recently read. Since this particular invocation of *StackTheCharacters* is finished, the program 'returns' to where it was when the procedure call was made — to the calling procedure, and eventually to the main program. In effect, the computer executes this series of statements:

```
            write (TheCharacter);          {Printing out '.'.}
         write (TheCharacter);          {Printing out 'e'.}
      write (TheCharacter);          {Printing out 'm'.}
         :         {Intermediate calls...}
      write (TheCharacter);          {Printing out 'i'.}
   write (TheCharacter);          {Printing out 'h'.}
write (TheCharacter);          {Printing out 'T'.}
writeln         {This is the last statement in the main program.}
```

Because it's sometimes hard to visualize what happens in a series of identical procedure calls, computer scientists have developed a metaphor that helps explain recursion.

> The variables and pending statements of a partially executed program or subprogram are said to go on a *stack* within the computer.

When a subprogram is called, the new variables and pending statements are added to the stack. The number of times this can occur—the height of the stack—is only limited by the memory resources of the computer.

Now, a stack is actually created in any series of procedure or function calls—the sequence need not be recursive. The stack can, and usually does, grow and shrink during the course of a program. However, it will always be empty when a program ends normally.*

Procedure *ReverseDigits*, below, uses the stack for a more basic reason—to keep track of the way back to the main program. Although a series of recursive procedure calls is made, there are no identifiers or pending statements (besides a series of **ends**) to remember.

```
program IntegerReverse (input, output) ;
    {Recursively reverses the digits of an integer.}
var Number: integer;
procedure ReverseDigits (TheNumber: integer) ;
    begin
        write (TheNumber mod 10:1 ) ;
        {Output the rightmost digit in a one-space field.}
        if (TheNumber div 10) < > 0 then ReverseDigits (TheNumber div 10)
        {If there are more digits, strip off the rightmost one and pass the result.}
    end;   {ReverseDigits}
begin
    writeln ('Please enter a positive integer.') ;
    readln (Number) ;
    ReverseDigits (Number);
    writeln
end.   {IntegerReverse}
```

↓   ↓   ↓   ↓   ↓
Please enter a positive integer.
74193
39147

> This kind of recursion is called *end* or *tail* recursion. When the procedure makes its recursive call, no unfinished statements are left on the stack.

---

* This simplified explanation of stacks helps explain how the computer keeps track of scope within a program. *All* identifiers defined in a subprogram are put on the stack when the subprogram is invoked. Then, when an identifier is used, the computer looks down the stack for the identifier's most recent definition or declaration. Although the stack may contain several different usages of a single name, the most recent definition is the first one found.

When a procedure uses end recursion, it's usually easy to write iteratively (using a loop structure). For example:

```
procedure IterativeReverse (TheNumber: integer);
    begin
        repeat
            write (TheNumber mod 10:1);
            TheNumber := TheNumber div 10
        until TheNumber = 0
    end;
```

:·:··:·:

Self-Check Questions

Q. Is the procedure in *Print* recursive? Should it be? What does it do?

```
program Print (input, output);
procedure Echo;
    var TheCharacter: char;
    begin
        read (TheCharacter);
        write (TheCharacter);
        if not eoln then Echo
    end;   {StackTheCharacters}

begin
    writeln ('Please enter a sentence.');
    Echo;
    writeln
end.   {Print}
```

A. Procedure *Echo* offers another demonstration of end recursion. Although a stack is created, it doesn't contain any statements to be executed. The series of *TheCharacter* local variables is saved, but gets thrown away when the recursive calls end. The stack is created, but not used. A **while** loop would do the job perfectly well, because the program just echoes a line of input.

```
        ↓        ↓        ↓        ↓        ↓
    Please  enter  a  sentence.
    This is not a palindrome.
    This is not a palindrome.
```

:·:··:·:

Recursive Functions

Function *Sum* uses a series of recursive calls to add a series of numbers from 1 to its argument *Limit*.

```
function Sum (Limit: integer): integer;
    {Recursively sums the series 1 through Limit}
    begin
        if Limit< =1 then Sum := Limit
        else Sum := Limit + Sum(Limit −1)
    end;
```

A comparable iterative function would be:

```
function IterativeSum (Limit: integer) :  integer;
    {Iteratively sums the series 1 through Limit}
    var TemporarySum: integer;
    begin
        TemporarySum := Limit;
        while Limit>1
            do begin
                Limit := Limit−1;
                TemporarySum := Limit+TemporarySum
            end;
        IterativeSum := TemporarySum
    end;   {IterativeSum}
```

However, both functions produce the same results.

$$writeln \ (Sum(5), \ IterativeSum(5));$$
$$writeln \ (Sum(100), \ IterativeSum(100));$$

↓   ↓   ↓   ↓   ↓

```
 15              15
5050            5050
```

The stack produced by *Sum* is a bit peculiar because it contains a series of partially completed assignment statements.

> The general outline of *Sum* is typical of recursive functions—the recursive call occurs in the middle of an assignment statement. Thus, the stack serves to delay the evaluation of an expression.

Let's assume that *Sum* is called with 5 as its argument. Following the arrows in the series of statements below gives an idea of what transpires during *Sum's* evaluation. The first number in each statement is the value *Limit* currently represents.

$$Sum := 5 + Sum(4); \longrightarrow Sum := 5+10;$$
$$Sum := 4 + Sum(3); \longrightarrow Sum := 4+6;$$
$$Sum := 3 + Sum(2); \longrightarrow Sum := 3+3;$$
$$Sum := 2 + Sum(1); \rightarrow Sum := 2+1;$$
$$Sum := 1;$$

None of the stacked assignments can be completed until *Sum* gets its first non-recursive value—the first assignment that doesn't depend on calling *Sum* again.

> The last of a series of recursive calls is the **limit** call. The circumstances that give rise to the limit call form the exit condition of the recursion.

[239]

By our definition of the function, *Sum's* limit call occurs when its argument is 1. An ***infinite*** recursion occurs if the exit condition can't be met, and the limit call is never made.

Once we understand how *Sum* is implemented recursively in Pascal, it's instructive to look at a recursive statement of its algorithm in English.

If *Limit* is 1 or less, the sum of 1 to *Limit* is *Limit*.

If *Limit* exceeds 1, the sum of 1 to *Limit* is *Limit*—plus the sum of 1 to *Limit*−1.

As you can see, this definition—like all recursive definitions—is essentially circular.

Another definition that's easy to state recursively is that of the *n*th Fibonacci number:

If *n* is 1 or 2, the *n*th Fibonacci number is 1.

If *n* is 3 or more, the *n*th Fibonacci number is the sum of the previous two.

To nobody's surprise, this algorithm works perfectly well when transliterated into Pascal.

program *TestFibonacci* (*input, output*) ;
{Tests a function that recursively generates Fibonacci numbers.}

var *Test1, Test2, Test3, Test4: integer*;

```
function Fibonacci (Which: integer) : integer;
   begin
      if (Which=1) or (Which=2) then Fibonacci := 1
      else Fibonacci := Fibonacci(Which −1) + Fibonacci(Which −2)
   end;  {Fibonacci}
```

begin
    writeln ('Reading four test entries.') ;
    readln (*Test1, Test2, Test3, Test4*) ;
    writeln ('Fibonacci numbers ', *Test1*:4, *Test2*:4, *Test3*:4, *Test4*:4, ' are:') ;
    writeln (*Fibonacci*(*Test1*), *Fibonacci*(*Test2*), *Fibonacci*(*Test3*), *Fibonacci*(*Test4*))
end.   {*TestFibonacci*}

```
            ↓       ↓       ↓       ↓       ↓
Reading four test entries.
1 7 15 25
Fibonacci numbers    1    7   15   25 are:
            1           13         610        75025
```

Although we won't show it here, *Fibonacci* can easily be implemented as an iterative function. In fact, every recursive procedure or function can be written in a non-recursive manner.

Since recursion isn't absolutely necessary, why should it be used at all? The answer takes several tacks. In a few instances (such as reversing a string of characters of unknown length) recursion is the best way to solve the problem. Our main alternative is the impractical one of declaring enough variables to deal with every possible string.

Another reason is that the implementation of recursive algorithms or definitions can be nearly trivial. We'll encounter some other recursively defined functions in the Exercises. A more sophisticated reason for recursion will arise when we encounter *recursive data structures* in chapter 15. Although we won't get into such data structures now, they also pose problems that are stated and solved recursively.

Finally, recursive solutions can be more elegant than their iterative counterparts. We'd hate to say that shortness is a virtue in itself, but recursive subprograms can often be written more briefly and clearly than iterative ones. When you become comfortable with recursion, and start to recognize 'standard' recursive algorithms, you'll appreciate the ease with which such algorithms can be put into programs.

WE'VE PROBABLY NEVER EXPLAINED THE difference between debugging and testing carefully enough.

> *Debugging* is what *you* do before you consider a program completed. *Testing* is what a program user does as she makes your program crash.

The programer, faced with a particularly recalcitrant program, tends to think only of getting it to compile. If it works for a particular set of data, so much the better. This is debugging. Someone who must actually use (or grade the quality of) your program applies stiffer criteria. It doesn't matter much that the program compiles, because it's expected to. Nor is the user concerned with its operation under ideal conditions. Instead, she tries to find your program's limitations. That's testing.

Thus, debugging tries to get rid of known bugs, while testing is an attempt to show that more bugs still exist. It's an unfortunate fact that both methods have severe limitations. The effectiveness of debugging depends largely on the diligence and experience of the programer. Testing, as we've pointed out before, may show the *presence* of bugs, but it doesn't say much about their *absence.*

We have to conclude that as programs get more complicated, testing and debugging alone may not be enough to produce reliable code. Instead, we have to write programs in a manner that will help insure that errors are caught or avoided. *Stub* programing is a method that allows for error and improvement.

> A *stub* program is a stripped-down, skeleton version of a final program. It doesn't implement details of the algorithm or fulfill all the job requirements. However, it does contain rough versions of all subprograms and their parameter lists.

A stub program helps demonstrate that a program's structure is plausible. Its procedures and functions are primitive, unsophisticated

8-3
Antibugging and Debugging

versions of their final forms, but they allow limited use of the *entire* program. For example, if we were writing a payroll program, we might begin by developing a stub program that handles a fixed group of workers who each put in 50 hours per week, receive the same rate of pay, and declare the same number of dependents.

The stub program approach is especially useful for beginning programers, who are often forced to start working before they know enough Pascal to write the entire program. 'Dummy' procedures let novices get a head start on the program, without requiring implementation of the hard parts.

It's easy to appreciate that stub programing complements stepwise refinement. In fact, stub programs allow for something unexpected—*top-down debugging*.

> Stub programs let a large system be tested *as it is built.*

How can a program be tested or debugged before it's in operating shape? The dummy modules of stub programs can support rough runs on the computer. The proposed program can also be subjected to the intense scrutiny of your programing team—usually yourself and anybody else you can collar for ten minutes.

> A *structured walkthrough* is a guided tour of a partially completed program. It's an explanation *and defense* of its algorithm and implementation.

Working on a program tends to develop a mind set in the programer that renders obvious mistakes invisible. Merely explaining a program aloud can give you a totally new view of it.

Top-down debugging of Pascal code has advantages too. To begin with, major program connections are tested first, which means that major bugs and shortcomings are detected early in the game. Furthermore, testing and debugging are distributed throughout the entire writing process. You're not forced to do all your program fixing just before the program is scheduled to be completed (which is invariably when the computer is least available). Finally, even if a program isn't completely finished by the due date it's a preliminary *working* version—and not just a useless mess of code.

As a program gets bigger, we have to take a more holistic approach to its construction. It has to be seen as an interconnected unit, rather than an agglomeration of independent parts. Top-down debugging is concerned with the health of an entire program. In contrast, the bottom-up debugging we've been doing all along has concentrated on turning out program modules. In a bottom-up approach, we write and debug a program's subprograms:

Then, the separate procedures and functions are incorporated into a subsystem of the main program:

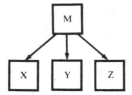

Finally, we put subsystems together to complete the program. This is the first time that they can be tested as a unit.

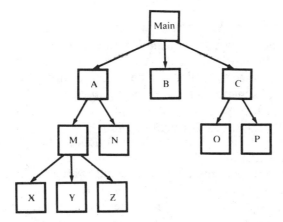

We can picture top-down program construction following the reverse approach. In the illustration below, *A, B,* and *C* demonstrate the major workings of a program, but they call dummy subprograms.

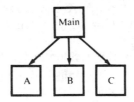

Next, the dummy procedures and functions are expanded and debugged, but the program's smallest details still aren't implemented.

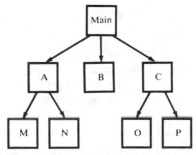

Eventually, every refinement can be completed, and tested as it's added to the main program.

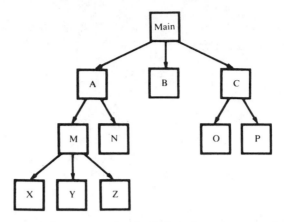

Some Problems With Functions

Most of the errors that occur in declaring functions are just the result of oversight. There are two main rules to remember when writing functions. First, give the function a type in its heading. Second, don't forget to assign the function its value. Such an omission may not be a syntax error, and it can be quite hard to find.

As we pointed out in 8-1, functions sometimes represent different values on subsequent calls. Suppose that a function *Random* computes and represents a random number. A dumb, but nonetheless common, mistake is to try to inspect the function's value twice in a row—perhaps first to print it, and then as part of a control structure's *boolean* expression. Using an auxiliary variable to hold the function's value stops this problem.

By now it should be clear that many programing troubles arise either from misstatement of the original problem (leading to an incorrect algorithm), or from a flawed translation of a good algorithm into Pascal. It's important to realize how common such mistakes are—they're usually trivial. As long as you can find them, you shouldn't feel stupid for making them.

A serious problem is the accidental creation of a recursive function or procedure call. The appearance of a subprogram's name serves as a call or invocation of that subprogram. Function *Count*, below, inadvertently invokes itself during its own execution.

```
function Count: integer;
    var Letter: char;
    begin
        while not eoln
            do begin
                read (Letter);
                Count := Count+1
            end
    end;  {Count}
```

Count contains a recursive call to itself within the **while** loop.

Infinite recursions are a minor curse that seem to visit every pro-gramer. Recursive subprograms should be inspected at least as care-fully as conditional loops. Make sure that the limit call can occur. When an infinite recursion does happen, the program eventually crashes with a message along the lines of:

```
STACK OVERFLOW - - CORE DUMPED
```

A stack overflow happens when a program places excessive demands on the computer's memory. It can take place for several rea-sons, not all of which are bugs. As a result, most systems do not print a run-time error message that specifies the exact cause of program failure. Instead, the current contents of the stack (the *core*) are preserved for possible investigation.*

Summary

A *function* is a subprogram that computes and represents a value. Like a procedure, a function may contain declarations of constants, vari-ables, and subprograms. Since a function represents a value, its head-ing must specify the function's Pascal type. Furthermore, the function's statement part must include an assignment that gives the function its value. This assignment is generally the last statement in the function.

On occasion, a function must be called (by another subprogram) before it can be properly declared. In this case the function must be forward declared; its name, parameter list, and type are followed by the **forward** statement. When the function is actually written, its parameter list and type are omitted (although they should be included as a com-ment).

Using functions is good programing practice. They connect the pseudocode used in planning a program to the final Pascal product. *Boolean* functions, in particular, contribute greatly to program readabil-ity.

Testing and debugging are usually thought of as the last steps in writing a program—debugging is the process of finding and fixing known bugs, while testing is an attempt to show that more bugs exist. *Driver* programs are often used to test the operation of single subpro-grams. But when programs get complicated, the ideas of top-down pro-gram design should be extended to testing and debugging.

Stub programing lets program-wide ideas of algorithm and imple-mentation be tested in a a skeleton version of a project, without refinements. Subjecting programs to comment by leading **structured walkthroughs** of partially finished code is another way to catch funda-mental bugs before they become inextricably embedded within the pro-gram.

* Unfortunately, core files are undecipherable except by the sort of people who began programing (usually for money) at age 12.

Functions and procedures may include *recursive* calls of themselves. As a programing technique, recursion can simplify the implementation of some iterative algorithms. When a recursive call is made, current variable values and pending statements are put on a *stack*, within the computer. They're executed after the *limit* call, which is much like the exit condition of a loop structure. *End* or *tail* recursion doesn't make use of the stack.

New Pascal
New Terms

function

function call	*function heading*	*driver*
seed	*pseudo-random*	*recursive*
stack	*end*	*tail*
limit	*stub programing*	*top-down debugging*
structured walkthrough		

Self-Test Exercises

8-1 Of which Pascal types may a user-defined function represent values?

8-2 When can a function identifier appear on the left-hand side of an assignment statement?

8-3 Write a *boolean* function *Divisible* that returns *true* if its first argument is evenly divisible by its second argument, and *false* otherwise.

8-4 Can good test data prove that a program doesn't have any bugs? What can it show?

8-5 Can the type of a function depend on the type of its argument? In other words, could we write a function that returns a *real* value if its argument is *real*, and represents an *integer* if its argument is *integer*?

8-6 What's the difference between top-down and bottom-up testing and debugging? Is one better than the other?

8-7 The negation operator (an ordinary minus sign) changes the sign of its operand. Write a function *ReturnNegative* that returns its *real* operand as a negative number.

8-8 The *greatest common divisor* of two integers is the largest number to divide them both without leaving a remainder. Write a function that determines the greatest common divisor of two *integer* arguments.

8-9 Write a *boolean* function *IsADigit* that reflects whether or not its *char* argument is a digit character.

8-10 What's wrong with this function definition?

```
function SluggingPercentage (AtBats, Singles, Doubles, Triples, Homers: integer): real;
  {This function computes the average number of bases attained per hit.}
  begin
    SluggingPercentage := Singles +(2*Doubles) + (3*Triples) + (4*Homers) ;
    SluggingPercentage := SluggingPercentage/AtBats
  end;    {SluggingPercentage}
```

8-11 Should a structured walkthrough take place before or after a program is finished?

8-12 Suppose that you want to pick a number from 4 through 7 under the following conditions: there is a 35% chance of picking 4, a 15% chance of picking 5, a 19% chance of picking 6, and a 31% percent chance of picking 7. How could you use the random number generator we developed in the text to make the pick?

8-13 Write a function *Ceiling* that takes a *real* argument, and returns as an *integer* result the closest whole number above (for positive arguments) or below (for negative arguments).

8-14 How would you use the same random number generator to choose a number, evenly divisible by 3, between (and including) 69 and 123?

8-15 How would you use the random number generator we developed in the text to pick a *real* number in the range 3 through 33 by *fourths*? (e.g. 3.25, or 29.75.)

8-16 In the text, our random number generator produced a *real* that was greater than or equal to 0, but less than one. We could use it to choose a random *integer* greater than or equal to *A*, and less than or equal to *B*, by using the formula:

$$Random\ Integer = A + trunc\,((B-A+1)*Random(Seed)$$

How would you change this formula if *Random(Seed)* represented a number greater than 0, and less than or equal to 1?

8-17 A large North American country (whose name we can't cite for copyright reasons) levies taxes at the following rates: 2% on the first $4,000 of income, 3% on the next $2,000, 4% on the next $2,000, 5% on the next $2,000, and so on, to a maximum of 15% on all income in excess of $28,000. No special breaks are given to couples that file jointly.

Write a program in two parts. The first part should compute the average tax rate on any amount of income. The second part should determine the effective penalty for filing a joint return.

8-18 Business assets can be depreciated (for tax purposes) in three different ways. In *straight-line* depreciation, the asset's value decreases by the same amount each year over its entire useful life. A second accepted practice of computing depreciation uses the *double-declining balance* method. An asset's 'book value' (its original value less depreciation) is diminished each year by $2/n$, where *n* is the asset's life. Thus, the depreciation allowed each year is the book value times $2/n$ This accounting method allows quicker depreciation in the first few years.

The *sum-of-the-digits* method is a bit more complicated. Suppose that an asset's useful life is *n* years. Add the digits from 1 through *n* (we'll call this the *YearTotal*). The depreciation allowed in the *i*th year is $(n-i)+1$ divided by *YearTotal*

Write functions that compute the depreciation allowed each year using each of the methods described above. Use them in a program that prints a depreciation schedule over *n* years for an asset that originally cost *Price* dollars.

8-19 The Internal Revenue Service lets taxpayers switch from the double-declining balance method to straight-line depreciation whenever they want. Why would a taxpayer want to do this? Write a program that determines the most beneficial time to make the accounting switch.

8-20 Write a program that reads through a sample of text and prints out all *integer* values it encounters, as well as their sum. Digits that occur within words should be ignored. For example, the input 'If I were 21, instead of 53, I'd probably punch you in the nose a 2nd time' should produce as output the numbers 21 and 53, along with their sum, 74. A function *ConvertToInteger* will probably prove quite useful.

8-21 Recall that function *SquareRoot* was designed to make successive approximations of a square root, until the difference between one guess and the next was very small. Our definition of 'very small' was that the difference between the old guess and the new guess be less than 10E-06.

Copy function *SquareRoot*, possibly re-writing it as a program or procedure. See if it works for very large and very little inputs, by comparing its output with the answer computed by the standard function *sqrt* (Hint: it won't.) Re-define function *NoSignificantChange* to produce more accurate results. Two possible variations are:

NoSignificantChange := *abs*(*Number* − *sqr*(*New*)) < Epsilon ;
NoSignificantChange := *abs*(*Number* − *sqr*(*New*) −1) < Epsilon ;

Analyze these (either on paper, or with a test program). Are either or both of them reasonable? Come up with two more plausible ways of describing a 'very small' difference that work for a wide range of inputs.

8-22   Implement the *integer* operators **div** and **mod** as functions.

8-23   The largest common factor *LCF* of two positive integers *a* and *b* can be defined as *a* if **b** is zero, and the lowest common factor of *a* and *a* **mod** *b* otherwise. Implement this function both recursively and non-recursively.

8-24   Implement this recursive function. What operation does it carry out?

MysteryFunction (*X*, *Y*) is *X* if *Y*=1.

MysteryFunction (*X*, *Y*) is *X* + *MysteryFunction* (*X*, *Y*−1) otherwise.

8-25   Write a function that reads a real number written using the 'E' notation as a sequence of characters, and returns the *real* value it represents.

8-26   Here are a few problems for certain of the numbers between 1,000 and 9,999.

a)   Find a number that meets the following conditions: it is a perfect square between 1,000 and 9,999, its first two digits are the same, and its last two digits are the same.

b)   Find two numbers, between 1,000 and 9,999, which are equal to the sum of the cubes of their digits.

c)   Find three numbers which are members of the following select group: they are four digit perfect squares, and each is equal to the square of the sum of its first two and last two digits.

d)   Four numbers, when squared, consist of only even numbers and are greater than 1,000 and less than 9,999. What are they?

One of these problems doesn't quite fit in. Which one? How does realizing this affect your program?

8-27   When the Greeks discovered that π was an irrational number (and couldn't be expressed as a fraction), they were rather upset. It didn't seem right that the perfect simplicity of mathematics be challenged by such a figure, so they suppressed the knowledge of pi's existence, and resorted to more complex methods of circle measurement.

One of their problems was to determine the area of a circle. They were able to get an approximate answer by inscribing a regular polyhedron (i.e. a many-sided figure) within the circle, and then computing the polyhedron's area with elementary trigonometry. Write a program that determines the accuracy of this method. Show your results graphically. How many sides will the polyhedron have when it challenges the accuracy of your computer?

8-28   Write a function *IsAnInteger* which determines whether or not its argument is an *integer* value. Then, find three cases where the function doesn't work.

8-29   Write a recursive procedure that computes and represents any requested Fibonacci number. Do you have to place any limits on input?

8-30   Write a program that reads text, and prints out every letter that occurs twice in a row. (Bonus: write the program, possibly using recursion, so that it prints out the actual word instead.) Have it analyze the following input: "Miss Metteer, a bookkeeper of all excess cottonseed bills, looked at a corrupt terra cotta Cossack."

Improve the program so that it also spots words that contain three or more consecutive letters in alphabetical order. Try "A stupid, laughing, crab-cake, displaying calmness, deftly hijacked the first canopy."

8-31   Bidding gets fast and furious at auctions, and it's possible to spend a lot of money very quickly. A friend of ours went to an auction, and in just ten minutes managed to spend half of her money. Oddly enough, she now had as many pennies as she had previously had dollars, but only half as many dollars as she had previously had pennies. How much did she start with, and how much did she spend?

8-32   Naturally your new programing language will have to include functions. What do you think about extending the idea of functions to encompass definable operators? In other words, how about letting the programer define the effect of an operator on its operands (for instance, the effect of adding *char* values)? Can you write a reasonable set of rules for defining new opera-tors? What might they be?

A. M. Herring stands with a Lilienthal glider (William Avery at his right). 1896. Miller, Indiana.
Courtesy National Air and Space Museum Library, Smithsonian Institution.

9

Extending the Ordinal Types

When the first computer languages were developed, everything—including commands, identifiers, and values—had to be expressed in ones and zeros. One of the first language improvements let programers use octal (base 8) numbers instead of binary. Then, letters were introduced, which meant that variables and commands could be given names instead of numbers. However, the same basic units of measure (usually just *reals, integers,* and *char*) had to be used to describe every value imaginable.

Now, the world is filled with plenty of values that have perfectly good names of their own. This month might be January or July. Today's weather could be sunny, cloudy, raining, or breezy. A playing card can be a heart, spade, club, or diamond. There are many such collections of related values. In Pascal, unlike most other languages, any group of named values can be the basis of a *user-defined ordinal type.*

The types we'll learn to define in 9-1 can be used like the standard ordinal types—their values can be stored in variables, passed as parameters, defined as constants, etc. In effect, Pascal is extended to include new types and values as part of its vocabulary.

Groups of values can be restricted as well as extended. By defining *subrange* types, we can limit variables to represent a particular segment (a subrange) of any ordinal type. This technique is a useful form of antibugging. The debugging section, 9-2, includes some details about ordinal types and subranges, and should be read along with the regular text.

(R)elying on run-time crashes
to do error checking...

9-1
User-Defined Ordinal Types

THE FIRST FEW LINES OF THE PASCAL PROGRAM below introduce *user-defined ordinal types.** Two new ordinal types (*Fruit* and *Vegetable*) are defined in the shaded *type definition part* of *Menu.*

> **program** *Menu* (*input, output*) ;
>   {Demonstrates an ordinal type definition.}
>
> **type** *Fruit* = (*banana, apple, orange, pear*) ;
>   *Vegetable* = (*cabbage, leeks, beets, okra*) ;
>
> **var** *Appetizer, Dessert*: *Fruit*;
>   *Entree*: *Vegetable*;
>
> **begin**   etc.

> An *ordinal type* is an ordered group of values.

The standard ordinal types, which are predefined in every Pascal implementation, are:

integer: The whole numbers from − *maxint* to *maxint.*

char: The character set, in a particular collating sequence.

boolean: The values *false, true.*

You shouldn't let the word 'ordinal' confuse you. It just means that the values of any given type are ordered and countable, and can be compared to each other. The letter 'A' is less than 'C', and *true* is 'greater' than—and certainly not equal to—*false.* The ordinal types, in conjunction with type *real,* are Pascal's simple types.

> A *user-defined ordinal type* is a group of values named and ordered by the programer. Variables can be declared to be of such a type, and may be assigned any value of that type.

For example, given the definitions and declarations from *Menu:*

> **type** *Fruit* = (*banana, apple, orange, pear*) ;
>   *Vegetable* = (*cabbage, leeks, beets, okra*) ;
>
> **var** *Appetizer, Dessert*: *Fruit*;
>   *Entree*: *Vegetable*;

we can make assignments like:

Appetizer := *apple*;	{*Appetizer* gets the value *apple.*}
Dessert := *Appetizer*;	{*Dessert* is *apple* too.}
Entree := *leeks*;	{*Entree* is *leeks*}
Entree := *cabbage*;	{Change *Entree* to *cabbage.*}

---

* Also known as *enumerated* ordinal types.

We cannot give *Appetizer* or *Dessert* a value of type *Vegetable*, since that would cause a type clash. We can, however, compare values or variables of an identical type:

> **if** *Appetizer* = *apple*
>   **then** *writeln* ('An apple a day keeps the doctor away.');
> **if** *Appetizer* = *Dessert*
>   **then** *writeln* ('Too much of a good thing is no good at all.');

The type definition part is an optional portion of every Pascal program and subprogram. We can describe a program in terms of its parts like this:

> *program heading*
> *definition part*
>   *constant definitions*
>   *type definitions*
> *declaration part*
>   *variable declarations*
>   *procedure and function declarations*
> *statement part*

Or, we can use reserved words to outline a potential program:

> **program** *heading*;
> **const** *definitions*;
> **type** *definitions*;
> **var** *declarations*;
> **procedure** or **function** *declarations*;
> **begin**
>   *statements*;
> **end.**

The reserved word **type** introduces the type definition part. The *type identifier* is followed by an equals sign, and the type's value identifiers, or **constants**, within parentheses and separated by commas. Naturally, both type identifier and constants must be named in accordance with Pascal's identifier syntax. We can chart an ordinal type definition as:

ordinal type definition

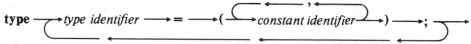

> The predecessor function *pred*(*x*), successor function *succ*(*x*), and ordinal function *ord*(*x*) may all be given arguments of any ordinal type. Don't forget that the first ordinal number is 0, not 1.

[253]

```
type RouletteResult = (red, black, green);
     PokerHand = (OnePair, TwoPair, Triples, Straight, Flush, StraightFlush);
     WeekDay = (Monday, Tuesday, Wednesday, Thursday, Friday);
     WeekEnd = (Saturday, Sunday);
```

For the types defined above, we find that:

> *ord*(*black*) is 1   {the second value of type *RouletteResult*}
> *pred*(*TwoPair*) is *OnePair*
> *succ*(*Tuesday*) is *Wednesday*

An important restriction on the definition of ordinal types is that no value can belong to more than one type. This rule makes type membership unambiguous. We could *not* make the following definition:

```
type WeekDay = (Monday, Tuesday, Wednesday, Thursday, Friday);
     WeekEnd = (Friday, Saturday, Sunday);   {Illegal definition.}
```

The ordinal position of *Friday*, as well as its type, is unclear. Is it the last value of type *WeekDay*, or the first value of *WeekEnd*?

> We can define constants of *any* ordinal type.

```
const Favorite = apple;        {A constant of type Fruit.}
      HouseColor = green;      {A constant of type RouletteResult.}
      DayOff = Wednesday;      {A constant of type WeekDay.}
      Birthday = 'Monday';     {This is text—not a
                                member of type WeekDay.}
```

However, such constant definitions must occur in an 'enclosed' sub-program since they can't precede the type definitions.

Self-Check Questions

Q. Is this the beginning of a valid control structure? Assume the definitions of program *Menu.*

> **if** *Appetizer* < > *Entree*
> **then**   etc.

A. No, because comparing values of different types causes a type clash. We can no more compare *apple* and *leek* (even for inequality) than we could compare 'S' and *true.*

Q. Is this a valid type declaration? Why or why not?

> **type** *Letters* = ('A', 'B', 'C', 'D', 'E', 'F');

A. It's illegal. 'A', 'B', etc. are not value identifiers—they're constant values of type *char.* The definition doesn't conform to Pascal syntax.

User-defined ordinal types enjoy all the rights and privileges of the standard ordinal types, with one major limitation.

Programing with Ordinal Types

> The constants of user-defined ordinal types *cannot* be read with *read* or *readln,* nor printed using *write* or *writeln.* They have no *external character representation*.

Unlike values of the standard types, user-defined type values can't be input from a keyboard or card reader nor output to a screen or line-printer.* (In section 12-2 we'll see how to fake input and output of user-defined ordinal values. When we discuss files, we'll learn a bit more about internal and external representations of values.) Aside from this exception, user-defined ordinals are used just like the standard ordinal values.

> Ordinal values can be used to set the limits of a **for** structure, or in the constant list of a **case** structure.

We can demonstrate both these features with a program that computes an employee's weekly pay. Let's assume that we're paying time-and-a-half for Saturday, and double-time for Sunday work. We'll read in the hours day by day, and make adjustments for overtime as we go along. In pseudocode our algorithm is:

> **for** *each day of the week*
>   *read in the number of hours worked;*
>   *make a weekend overtime bonus adjustment if necessary;*

A variable *Workday,* that takes on values corresponding to the days of the week, lets us refine the pseudocode:

> **for** *Workday :*— *Monday* **to** *Sunday*
>   *read in the number of hours worked;*
>   *make a weekend overtime bonus adjustment if necessary;*

How can we arrange for the Saturday and Sunday overtime rate? Why not use a **case** structure?

> **case** *Workday* **of**
>   *Saturday: arrange for time-and-a-half;*
>   *Sunday: arrange for double-time;*
>   *Monday, Tuesday, Wednesday, Thursday, Friday: pay single-time*
> **end**;

---

* Why not? Although there is a justification for restricting user-defined ordinal types to internal program use, that explanation is beyond the scope of this book. Ask around on the street, or write Dr. Wirth in Switzerland and query him directly. Be sure to enclose a self-addressed, stamped envelope.

All that really remains is the definition of a new ordinal type:

type *Day* = (*Monday, Tuesday, Wednesday, Thursday, Friday, Saturday, Sunday*) ;

The addition of input, output, and a few calculations turn our pseudocode into program *Payroll.* Notice that *Payroll* is quite limited; it's practically a stub program. It only handles one worker, at a single hourly wage and benefit rate. It only accepts full (i.e. *integer*) hours of work. It doesn't error-check input. Nonetheless, *Payroll* works, and can be upgraded later.

```
program Payroll (input, output) ;
    {Computes one employee's weekly payroll.}
const BenefitRate = 2.73 ;          {Benefits add $2.73/hour.}
    {Benefits are only paid on actual hours worked, not overtime.}
type Day = (Monday, Tuesday, Wednesday, Thursday, Friday, Saturday, Sunday) ;
var Workday: Day;
    HourlyRate, TotalWages, HoursCredited, Benefits: real;
    HoursWorked: integer;
begin
    writeln ('Please enter the hourly wage rate.') ;
    readln (HourlyRate) ;
    TotalWages := 0.0 ;
    Benefits := 0.0 ;
    writeln ('Enter hours worked daily from Monday through Sunday.') ;
    for Workday := Monday to Sunday
        do begin
            read (HoursWorked) ;
            case Workday of
                Saturday: HoursCredited := 1.5*HoursWorked;
                Sunday: HoursCredited := 2.0*HoursWorked;
                Monday, Tuesday, Wednesday, Thursday, Friday:
                        HoursCredited := HoursWorked
            end;  {case}
            Benefits := Benefits + (HoursWorked*BenefitRate) ;
            TotalWages := TotalWages +(HoursCredited*HourlyRate)
        end;  {for}
    TotalWages := TotalWages +Benefits;
    writeln ('Total wages for the week are $', TotalWages:2:2)
end.  {Payroll}
```

```
            ↓      ↓      ↓      ↓      ↓
Please enter the hourly wage rate.
9.37
Enter hours worked daily from Monday through Sunday.
8 8 6 9 10 0 4
Total wages for the week are $ 581.98
```

> Value-parameters and variable-parameters can belong to user-defined ordinal types. The result of a function may also be a user-defined value.

We'll get used to seeing—and placing—new and unusual type identifiers in the headings of procedures and functions. For example, here's a quick way to print the value of a parameter of type *Day*:

```
procedure PrintDay (Word: Day);
    {Prints the name of a Day-type value.}

begin
    case Word of
        Monday: writeln ('Monday');
        Tuesday: writeln ('Tuesday');
        Wednesday: writeln ('Wednesday');
        Thursday: writeln ('Thursday');
        Friday: writeln ('Friday');
        Saturday: writeln ('Saturday');
        Sunday: writeln ('Sunday')
    end
end;   {PrintDay}
```

NextDay, shown below, is a function that returns a value of type *Day*. Given an argument of type *Day*, it finds and represents the next working day. Constants *FirstDay* and *LastDay* mark the beginning and end of the work week.

```
function NextWorkingDay (Today: Day): Day;
    {Represents the next (sometimes first) value of Day.}

const FirstDay = Monday;
      LastDay = Friday;

begin
    if (Today> =FirstDay) and (Today< LastDay)
        then NextWorkingDay := succ(Today)
        else NextWorkingDay := FirstDay
end;   {NextWorkingDay}
```

> Once a type has been defined, its name, and the names of its constants, are known in all subprograms—unless they are locally redefined.

The same scope rules apply to type and constant identifiers as to variable and subprogram identifiers. However, the identifiers of types (and their constants) are usually preserved globally. Since they are often used for communication between different parts of a program, they're seldom redefined.

As you might imagine, it's not really necessary to define new ordinal types to make a program work. They're desirable because they let us program in understandable terms — *Monday* is obviously the day Monday, whereas an *integer* variable named *Day*, with value 1, might reasonably refer either to Sunday *or* Monday. The ordinal type feature lets programers work with abstractions — ideas or values that have meaning to people, but not to machines. How the computer deals with these values need not be our concern, since we're programers, not mechanics. In the next few chapters we'll see more of the ways that Pascal adapts to real-world conceptions and representations of data.

:··:

*Self-Check
Questions*

Q. Suppose we make the assignment *Alpha* := *Beta*. Is there any way to tell if *Beta* is a variable? A constant of an ordinal type? A function call?

A. No. An identifier (like *Beta*) is just the representation of a value. We can't determine what sort of value *Beta* is from its context.

Q. Though we've seen that values of user-defined ordinal types can be used with any control structure, there are a few pitfalls to beware of. What's wrong with these program segments?

```
WorkDay := Monday;                    WorkDay := Monday
while WorkDay < =Sunday                repeat
   do begin                              read (Hours);
      read (Hours);                       Total := Total+Hours;
      Total := Total+Hours;               WorkDay := succ(WorkDay)
      WorkDay := succ(WorkDay)      until WorkDay =Sunday;
   end;
```

A. The left-hand program segment tries to use a **while** loop to cycle through the days of the week. Unfortunately, its exit condition is that *WorkDay* be greater than *Sunday*. As far as our program is concerned, there is no day greater than *Sunday* — the program crashes when it tries to give *WorkDay* the successor to *Sunday*.

The second segment bends over too far backwards in an attempt to avoid making the same error. Its exit condition is that *WorkDay* equal *Sunday*; consequently, the number of hours worked on Sunday is never read in.

:··:

**Focus on
Programing:
Subrange
Types**

The ordinal types we've just learned to define represent entire ranges of value. We can restrict variables to representing *part* of the range of an ordinal type by defining a new kind of ordinal type — an ordinal *subrange*.

type *Day* = (*Monday, Tuesday, Wednesday, Thursday, Friday, Saturday, Sunday*);
    Weekday = *Monday..Friday*;   {Subrange of *Day*.}
    Weekend = *Saturday..Sunday*;   {Subrange of *Day*.}
    HoursInADay = 0..24;   {Subrange of *integer*.}
    CapitalLetters = 'A'..'Z';   {Subrange of *char*.}

var *CardNight, SickDay*: *Weekday*;
    SailingDay, GameDay: *Weekend*;
    HoursWorked: *HoursInADay*;
    FirstInitial, MiddleInitial: *CapitalLetters*;

> A *subrange* definition gives a type identifier (name) to a particular segment of any standard or user-defined ordinal type.

Although a variable of type *Day* may represent any of the days, *CardNight* (a variable of the *Weekday* subrange) can only represent one of the values *Monday* through *Friday*. Similarly, *HoursWorked* can only represent an *integer* value from 0 through 24—the values included in the ordinal subrange *HoursInADay*. Trying to assign it a value from outside this restricted range (say, −4 or 29) will cause a type clash and program crash. As far as the computer is concerned, we're trying to assign it a value of a different type entirely. In chart form, the definition of an ordinal subrange is:

ordinal subrange

type → type identifier → = → lower bound → .. → upper bound → ; →

Notice that two dots (..) are used to mean 'through and including.' (We used the same symbol earlier when we discussed a method of set declaration.) There is also a shorthand way to define subranges.

> The subrange of values a variable can represent may be specified when the variable is declared.

type *Day* = (*Monday, Tuesday, Wednesday, Thursday, Friday, Saturday, Sunday*);

var *CardNight, SickDay*: *Monday..Friday*;
    SailingDay, GameDay: *Saturday..Sunday*;
    HoursWorked: 0..24;
    FirstInitial, MiddleInitial: 'A'..'Z';

The variables declared with this shorthand are just like the variables in our last declaration, and represent the same limited range of values. User-defined constants can also be used to set the limits of a subrange, although variables, function calls, or other expressions may not be. The effect of this restriction is to prohibit any attempt to determine the bounds of a subrange during program execution.

> Variables should be declared as subrange types whenever practical, *particularly in large programs.*

Since this calls for some changes in your programing habits, we'll try to justify our new dictum. Ordinal subranges are desirable for three reasons—self-documentation, program efficiency, and antibugging. We'll consider these in turn.

1. Self-documentation. Knowing the range of values that a variable is going to represent, and saying so at the time of variable declaration, helps demonstrate that you have a firm grasp of what your program does.

It also helps others who may be working on your program *get* an idea of appropriate values within a program. The declaration:

> *KilnTemperature*: *integer*;

says nothing, whereas:

> *KilnTemperature*: 400..1200;   {or, better yet...}
> *KilnTemperature*: 400..*MaximumTemperature*;

is informative. Note that the decision to use the long or shorthand method of creating ordinal subranges is generally optional (except as noted in the next section).

2. Program efficiency. A variable declared to represent only a limited range of values can be dealt with (by the compiler) more economically than a variable that can represent *any* value of its type.

This is really the least important reason. Under certain circumstances, though, a program may require so many variables that limiting the storage they require is a valid programing consideration.

3. Antibugging. Pascal's requirement that variables be of some particular type is a form of antibugging. Restricting the values that a variable may represent to a range of values we know it *should* have extends the protection. We help assure ourselves (and the computer) that any operations we'll try to carry out will make sense.

Real life often places limits on the values that a variable can reasonably represent. A payroll program may 'work,' but allow 37 deductions, or −2. A checker-playing program might devote a considerable amount of time looking for the ninth row of a checkerboard. A computer croupier could spin a computer roulette wheel, and decide the ball has landed on number 39, which doesn't exist.

These are all obviously bugs that should, and could, be spotted or prevented by the programer. The most annoying aspect of bugs, though, is that you don't see them until it's too late. When a program announces that the sum of two and two is five, the programer knows that something has gone wrong, and takes another look at the code. The results of a more complex program, however, are more likely to be taken for granted—even if some input datum or partial result hidden within the program is totally absurd.

> Ordinal subranges provide a constant check on variables and assure us that they have values appropriate to their application. They help prevent a dangerous kind of program—one that appears to be reliable, but is not.

Using subranges doesn't absolve the programer of responsibility for error checking and keeping track of data within a program. The subrange philosophy is rather nihilistic—if a variable takes on an inappropriate value, the program stops! Relying on run-time crashes to do error checking is like using telephone poles (instead of brakes) to stop your car. Still, strong type checking makes Pascal sympathetic to a programer's woes—data inevitably gets screwed up for reasons beyond the control of programer, program user, or computer. Ordinal subranges won't make programs work, but they will make it easier to debug programs and to keep them running.

ON OCCASION, WE MAY DEFINE SUBRANGES that are overlapping, similar, or even (apparently) the same. Understanding the differences between these subrange types is a confusing problem even for experienced programers. For example:

9-2
Antibugging and Debugging

> **type** *CapitalLetter* = ´A´..´Z´ ;
> **var** *FirstInitial, MiddleInitial*: *CapitalLetter*;
>   *LastInitial*: ´A´..´Z´ ;

Are *FirstInitial* and *LastInitial* variables of the same type? A reasonable person, seeing that the subrange definitions are equivalent, would say yes. Unfortunately, Pascal requires us to be more precise.

> In Pascal, a distinction is drawn between variables whose types are exactly *identical*, and variables that are merely *compatible* (or *type-compatible*). Only variables declared with the same type identifier are identical.

In the declaration above, the types of *FirstInitial* and *MiddleInitial* are identical to each other, but not to *LastInitial*. Nevertheless, we can still make an assignment between *FirstInitial* and *LastInitial* because they are compatible.

> Two variables are compatible if they represent values of the same *underlying* type, even though they may be restricted to representing subranges of that type.

$$\textbf{type } \textit{LowRange} = 1..5;$$
$$\textit{MidRange} = 1..10;$$
$$\textit{HighRange} = 6..20;$$

$$\textbf{var } \textit{LowValue}: \textit{LowRange};$$
$$\textit{MidValue}: \textit{MidRange};$$
$$\textit{HighValue}: \textit{HighRange};$$
$$\textit{AnyValue}: \textit{integer};$$

LowValue, MidValue, HighValue, and *AnyValue* are clearly not of identical types, because they're all declared with different type identifiers. However, their underlying ordinal type (in this case, *integer*), determines type compatibility. Thus, the assignments:

$$\textit{MidValue} := \textit{LowValue};$$
$$\textit{AnyValue} := \textit{LowValue};$$

will always be legal, because *MidValue, LowValue,* and *AnyValue* all represent *integers,* and the subrange of *LowValue* falls within the subrange of *MidValue* (and is compatible with the *integer* range of *AnyValue*). However, this won't always be the case. These assignments:

$$\textit{LowValue} := \textit{MidValue};$$
$$\textit{MidValue} := \textit{HighValue};$$
$$\textit{HighValue} := \textit{AnyValue};$$

may or may not be valid, depending on the values of *LowValue, Mid-Value, HighValue,* and *AnyValue* when the assignment actually takes place. If values are in the wrong subrange, a type clash will occur. Incidentally, checks on the plausibility of such assignments often aren't made until the program is run.

Is there any reason to define ordinal subranges the long way (as a distinctly named type)? Yes, because we may want to declare parameters or functions of that type.

> When a value-parameter, variable-parameter, or function is created, its type must have a name. The shorthand method of specifying ordinal subranges can't be used.

Moreover, procedure and function headings are type-checked very strictly. A variable-parameter's type *must* be identical to its argument. Of all the variables declared above, only *LowValue* can be passed as an argument to function *DoesSomething,* below.

$$\textbf{procedure } \textit{DoesSomething} (\textbf{var } \textit{SmallNumber}: \textit{LowRange});$$

It's the only variable whose type is identical to the variable-parameter *SmallNumber*.

Since value-parameters treat their arguments as values, they need not be of an identical type. As long as both value-parameter and argument are type-compatible, a run-time error occurs only if an 'out-of-range' argument is passed.

:··:

Q. Could this be a valid function heading?

>   **function** *ConvertToSmall* (*BigNumber*: 6..20):1..5 ;

Self-Check Questions

A. No. Only type identifiers can appear in a subprogram heading—the short-hand method won't work. Written properly, the heading would be:

>   **function** *ConvertToSmall* (*BigNumber*: *HighRange*) : *LowRange*;

:··:

Summary

In Chapter 9 we began to explore *types* by looking at **user-defined ordinal** types, and **subrange** types. An ordinal type is an ordered group of values. The standard ordinal types (*integer, boolean,* and *char*) are predefined in every Pascal implementation.

Since the standard types only allow a limited means of expressing values, Pascal programers can also specify new ordinal types in the **type definition part** of a program or subprogram. The definition of a type has two parts—the **type identifier**, and (within parentheses) the value identifiers or **constants** of the type. When values of these types are used (with the *ord, pred,* and *succ* functions, and within **for** structures), these constants are considered to belong in the order given by their definition.

Although functions, variables, and parameters may all be of user-defined ordinal types, there is one important difference between values of the standard and user-defined types. The input and output of user-defined values is severely restricted, because they have no **external character representation**. They cannot be read in like standard ordinal values, nor can they be printed out using *write* or *writeln.*

Subranges are used to limit the range of values a variable may legally represent. The subrange may be defined as a type, or given on the spot when the variable is declared.

Assignments between two subrange-type variables are valid if their types are **compatible**, which means they have the same **underlying type**. A value-parameter and its argument have to be compatible. However, a variable-parameter and its argument variable must have *identical* types. This requires them to be declared with the exact same type identifier. In either case, the shorthand method of defining subranges can't be used in a subprogram heading.

New Pascal	**type**	:	=	()
New Terms	*definition part*	*ordinal type*		*user-defined ordinal type*
	type identifier	*constants*		*external character representation*
	subrange	*identical*		*compatible*
	underlying type			

Self-Test Exercises

9-1 What distinguishes an ordinal type from the *real* type?

9-2 What's wrong with this definition and declaration?

> **type** *Hue* = (*Red, Blue, Green, Yellow, Violet*) ;
> **var** *Green, Yellow: Hue*;

9-3 Which of these are illegal type definitions?

> **type** *Positive* = 1.. *Maxint*;
> *GradePoints* = 0.0..4.0 ;
> *Numbers* = *integer*;
> *Scientific* = *real*;
> *Alphabet* = 'Z'..'A' ;

9-4 Name one circumstance that would make this an illegal definition.

> **type** *Hand* = (*Straight, Flush, StraightFlush*) ;

9-5 Suppose that you can't be sure of the range of values a variable should represent until you actually run your program. Is it a good idea to declare the variable like this:

> **var** *Lower, Upper: integer*;
> *TheVariable: Lower..Upper*;

and then input the values of *Lower* and *Upper* at run time?

9-6 Suppose that we've made these definitions and declarations:

> **type** *Rainbow* = (*Infrared, Red, Orange, Yellow, Green, Blue, Violet, Ultraviolet*) ;
> *Spectrum* = *Infrared..Blue*;
> **var** *HotColors: Infrared..Green*;
> *Colors: Rainbow*;
> *CoolColors: Yellow..Ultraviolet*;

a) Which variables could be passed as an argument to a value-parameter of type *Rainbow*?
b) Which variables could be passed as an argument to a value-parameter of type *Spectrum*?
c) Which variables could be passed as an argument to a variable-parameter of type *Spectrum*?
d) Which variables could be passed as an argument to a value-parameter defined like this:

> *AnyProcedure* (*Hue: Infrared..Ultraviolet*) ;

9-7 Can a program print the value of a variable whose type has been defined by the programer?

9-8   The standard function *ord* will give us the ordinal position of a value of any ordinal type. Suppose that we've made this type definition:

> **type** *Weather* = (*Hail, Sleet, Snow, Rain, Pestilence, Plague*);

What is the value of *chr*(*ord*(*Pestilence*)+1)?

9-9   Suppose that we've defined a type *Day* whose constants are the days Monday through Sunday, and declared a variable *Today* of that type. What bugs can you find in this program segment?

```
for Today := Sunday to Monday
    do begin
        writeln (Today);
        Today := succ (Today)
    end;
```

9-10   How can we find out the type of a constant value?

9-11   Suppose that you have a variable that represents some value of a user-defined ordinal type. How can you make it represent the very *first* value of that type?

Still from *Nosferatu*, the original vampire movie, directed by F. W. Murnau in 1922.

10

An Overview of Structured Types

By now you've surely noticed that the music always plays just before the shark attacks. This is dramatic foreshadowing; it sets the audience's mood for what's about to happen. To a certain extent, the same technique is used in textbooks. Introductions, like this one, give you an idea of what's contained in the chapter ahead.

Right now we'll carry this approach a little further. Chapter 10 (our variation on dramatic foreshadowing) contains a rough overview of the next four chapters. It briefly introduces Pascal's *structured* types: *records, arrays, sets,* and *files.*

More than any of Pascal's other high-level features, structured types are a triumph. Being able to structure a variable—allowing it to represent a collection of values—is far more important to programers than it is to computers. Structured variables let us describe data in *our* terms, rather than in the machine's. They'll change the way you look at programing.

Because this chapter serves as an extended introduction, it's optional and it doesn't have any problems or exercises. Still, it should be read. Taking a quick look at *all* the structured types before studying them in detail will help you understand their applications better. You'll also get an idea of how different structures are used together, and how they can be combined into more complex structures.

*Dramatic foreshadowing sets
the audience's mood for what
is about to happen.*

10-1
**Meet the
Structures**

ONE OF THE MAIN ADVANTAGES OF PROGRAMING in Pascal is that we can design variables with different structures. When a variable belongs to a *structured type* it generally stores more than one value, and can be used in a variety of new ways. We'll introduce Pascal's structured types by seeing how a large program might employ them.

Our example for this chapter will be an airline reservation program. Now, the data such a program uses tends to organize itself into certain kinds of packages. For example:

Every flight has a number, flight schedule, departure and arrival gates, fares, plane type, etc.

An airline might fly 4 or 5 different types of airplane. Each plane has a different number of rows and aisles of seats.

Every airline has files of information—new fare schedules awaiting approval, flight plans that may be modified, rules and regulations that are being revised—that are permanently stored. They may require revision before being given to the reservation computer, or may only be read or printed out on rare occasions.

Every city on an airline's route has a set of connections to other cities that can be flown to nonstop. Every flight has a set of discounts and special fares associated with it.

If we were writing a reservation program we'd want to be able to declare each of these packages as a single variable:

A 'flight' variable that holds several different types of information. In Pascal, this requires a *record* structure.

A 'plane' variable that stores data on an organized arrangement of seats. In Pascal, we'd use an *array* structured variable.

An 'information' variable, that can be used for permanent storage of data. The *file* structure is Pascal's answer.

A 'connections' variable that stores one or all of a group of values simultaneously. Pascal's *set* structure is called for.

An ordinary *simple variable* (the kind we've always used) has a very simple structure—it represents a single value. A *structured variable* can, and almost invariably does, store several values at once.

This chapter takes a look at the structured types—record, array, file, and set—named above. Bear in mind that this is only an overview, and that each type will be discussed in detail in subsequent chapters. As you read, make a mental note of two important facts associated with each structured type. First is its method of *creation*; the process we have to go through to declare a variable with a given structure. Second, get an idea of the means of *access* to each structure. When a single variable has more than one piece of data associated with it, there are rules to follow for getting information in and out.

The situation: A single variable has to store a number of different kinds of information. Let's look at some of the data that might be connected with an airplane flight to Phoenix. We've chosen several forms of data that can be represented with the standard types.

Phoenix— Flight number (*integer*)
Departure and Arrival Time (*real*)
Terminal (*char*)
Gate Number (*integer*)
On Time, Cancelled, Sold Out (*boolean*)

Now, many flights, to many cities, will have the exact same categories of information associated with them. What we require is a new *type* of variable that's capable of storing all this data—in effect, a record. Naturally, this is our introduction to the record structure type.

type *FlightData* = **record**
    FlightNumber: *integer*;
    DepartureTime, ArrivalTime: *real*;
    Terminal: *char*;
    GateNumber: *integer*;
    OnTime, Cancelled, SoldOut: *boolean*
end;
var *Phoenix, StLouis, Denver, Miami, Buffalo*: *FlightData*;

In the example above, we've used a number of city names (*Phoenix, StLouis*, etc.) as variable identifiers. These variables are of the structured type *FlightData*. What exactly is the structure of *FlightData*? It's composed of several 'internal' variables, called *fields*. Can the fields be broken down further? Not in this example—they're all of the standard simple types.

What about getting at the values stored in a record variable's fields? There are several methods of access, but we'll just look at the most common. If a variable has a record structure, we can follow its name with a period (.) and the name of the field (or internal variable) we wish to access. This lets us make assignments:

Phoenix.FlightNumber := 27;
Phoenix.Terminal := 'E';
Denver.DepartureTime := *Buffalo.ArrivalTime* +0.5;
StLouis.SoldOut := *true*;

We can also access record-structured variables for output:

writeln ('Flight to Miami leaving at gate ', *Miami.GateNumber*);

Why do records use this syntax for access? It's really totally arbitrary—Wirth could just as easily have used the possessive ' 's ' of English:

> Patti's phone number   ~   *Patti.PhoneNumber*
> Buffalo flight's terminal   ~   *Buffalo.Terminal*

Pascal records, like real-life records, are hardly ever used singly, and programers often create data structures that consist of many records. One of the most common involves our next topic—the array.

The **array** Structure (Chapter 12)

What does an airline ticket agent do to reserve your seat on a flight? First, she probably prompts the computer to print a picture of the seats that are available. Then, by naming one seat in particular (say, '14D'), she updates the stored chart, and reserves a seat for you.

What does a computer programer do when she has to represent the seating plan of an airplane within a program? Well, a plane's seating plan is more or less a grid, in which each seat can be referred to by a row number and aisle letter. Different plans are distinguished by different numbers of rows and aisles. In English, we might describe the seating plan of a plane like this:

Seating plan—grid, rows 1 through 30, aisles A through J—of taken or not.

In Pascal, a programer defines a new type of structure:

> **type** *SeatingPlan* = **array** [1..30, 'A'..'J'] **of** *boolean*;

As you can see, the Pascal code is much like our English version.

> *Seating plan* becomes the identifier *SeatingPlan*
> *grid* becomes the reserved word **array**
> *rows 1 through 30, aisles A through J* becomes [1..30, 'A'..'J']
> *of* becomes the reserved word **of**
> *taken or not taken* becomes *true* or *false*—the type *boolean*

The *array* structure is used in many computer languages. According to the dictionary, an array is an orderly arrangement of things, and Pascal takes this idea to its logical limit. Although a grid is usually a two-dimensional assortment (like the squares in a piece of graph paper), a Pascal array structure can have *any* number of dimensions. We might define an array structure with one dimension:

> **type** *Aisle* = **array** ['A'..'J'] **of** *boolean*;

Or, we can define a structure with three dimensions, like a three-dimensional Tic-Tac-Toe board.

> **type** *BoxStatus* = (*Empty, X, O*) ;
> *TTTBoard* = **array** [1..3, 1..3, 1..3] **of** *BoxStatus*;

Note that our first two examples create structures that contain *boolean* values, while the third structure contains 27 (for there are 27 squares on a 3 by 3 by 3 Tic-Tac-Toe board) values of type *BoxStatus*, which are defined as *Empty, X,* and *O*.

As usual, the type definition was the major part of our job. Declaring variables of new structures (for the flight reservation program) is easy:

var *DC10SeatTaken, L1011SeatTaken, B747SeatTaken*: *SeatingPlan*;

What is *DC10SeatTaken*? It's a variable of type *SeatingPlan*. What, in turn, is the structure of *SeatingPlan*? It's an array, with two dimensions, of *boolean* values.

The method of access to values in array-structured variables is unusual, but not unreasonable. The variable identifier is accompanied by the coordinates of the particular value we want to access:

TTTBoard[2,2,2] := *X*;   {Put an 'X' in the central box}
DC10SeatTaken[14, 'H'] := *true*;   {We've just reserved seat 14H}
if not *L1011SeatTaken*[21, 'B']
    then *writeln* ('That seat is free. Do you wish to reserve it?') ;

In Pascal, square brackets serve double-duty—they're used with both set and array structured types.

We can also create arrays that represent different structures—in effect, structures of structures. One of the most common variations is the array of records. For example, suppose an airline numbers its flights 1 through 100. Clearly, this calls for 100 copies of a *FlightData* record to be stored in an array:

type *FlightData* = **record**
                DepartureTime, ArrivalTime: *real*;
                Terminal: *char*;
                GateNumber: *integer*;
                OnTime, Cancelled, SoldOut: *boolean*
        end;

OutboundFlights = **array** [1..100] **of** *FlightData*;

var *PanAm, United, American, TWA*: *OutboundFlights*;

Try to figure out what the statement below does. It's just a matter of combining methods of access.

writeln (*United*[48].*DepartureTime*) ;

With a little inspection, the answer should reveal itself—the statement prints the departure time of United Airlines flight 48.

The **file**
Structure
(Chapter 13)

In Chapter 7 we explained that a Pascal program thinks its input comes from (and output goes to) a file of data. So far, the files we've used have really been devices— *input* is generally a card reader or keyboard, while *output* is almost always a lineprinter or terminal screen. However, programs often use real files—data that's been stored within the computer for a program to interpret, or program results that are saved instead of being printed out immediately.

In Pascal, we can define new file-type structures for storing data. We begin by defining a file type—what type of data does the file contain?—then declare variables of that type. In practice, many of the files we'll be using are of type *char*. A predefined identifier, *text*, indicates a file of *char*. It's as though every Pascal program contained the definition:

> **type** *text* = **file of** *char*;
> **var** *Data, RateProposal*: *text*;

Sometimes file variables are only used during the course of a program (as though they were computer scratchpads). These are called *internal* files. Other files are stored permanently, and are called *external* files. Because external files are, in a sense, parameters of a program, they're named in the program's heading.

> **program** *ComputeSomething* (*output, Data, RateProposal*) ;

This program heading allows program *ComputeSomething* to receive input from two sources—the files *Data* and *RateProposal* *ComputeSomething's* output can go to the standard output, or it might be put into one of the external files.

The method of access to files is both familiar and unexpected. We already know a method of access to textfiles. To read a value from textfile *Original*, and echo it to textfile *Copy*, we'd say:

> *read* (*Original, Value*) ;
> *write* (*Copy, Value*) ;

As you can see, we've given the standard procedures *read* and *write* extra arguments—the names of the files we're reading and writing. Without these arguments, the computer would assume we want to read from the standard input, and write to the standard output.

In comparison to other types of variables, access to files is restricted in a peculiar manner. Before a file can be read from, it must be *reset* This puts us at the beginning of the file. As we read values, we move toward the file's end. By resetting the file we can start from the beginning again whenever we like. However, there's no way to get anywhere else in the file besides reading it again, line by line.

Files are written in the same manner. By calling a procedure named *rewrite*, we begin with a blank file, to which we can add data. However, we can only add values to the end of the file, because calling *rewrite* again erases the file.

Because of these limitations on access to their stored values, files are often called *sequential access* structures—each value must be stored or retrieved in sequence. In contrast, a structure like the array is called *random access.* Its values can be assigned or retrieved in any order.

Suppose that we've made the ordinal type definition below. It's nothing new—it just creates a range of values that can be used within a program.

The set Structure (Chapter 14)

type *City* = (*Memphis, Houston, Detroit, Eugene, Flagstaff, Raleigh*) ;

The *set* structured type creates variables that can represent any, none, or all of the members of an ordinal type. The *all* must be qualified, because Pascal implementations can limit the number of members a set can have. Usually, though, a set can contain as many members as the computer has characters. The creation of set structure variables follows this pattern:

type *City* = (*Memphis, Houston, Detroit, Eugene, Flagstaff, Raleigh*) ;
      Connections = **set of** *City*;

var *FromMemphis, FromHouston, FromDetroit, FromEugene,*
      FromFlagstaff, FromRaleigh: *Connections*;

The various *From* variables are all of type *Connections.* What is the structure of *Connections*? Potentially, it can contain the entire set of *City* values.

Accessing set-type variables involves two separate ideas. First is the method of making assignments. A set variable's values are given between square brackets. As in the shorthand method of set declaration, two dots (..) can be used to indicate contiguous values:

> *FromMemphis* := [ ] ;   {An empty set}
> *FromHouston* := [*Detroit, Flagstaff*] ;
> *FromDetroit* := [*Eugene..Raleigh*] ;
> *FromMemphis* := *FromDetroit*;
> *FromRaleigh* := *FromHouston* + *FromMemphis*;
>   {This is called 'set union'}
> *FromEugene* := *FromRaleigh* * *FromDetroit*;
>   {This is called 'set intersection'}
> *FromFlagstaff* := *FromMemphis* − *FromHouston*;
>   {This is called 'set difference'}

There are three new operations that can be applied to set variables— *union, intersection,* and *difference.* The union of two sets is the combination of their elements; thus, *FromRaleigh* gets all the values included in *FromHouston* and *FromMemphis*. The intersection of two sets contains only those values that are members of both sets. In

[273]

the example above, *FromEugene* winds up representing *Eugene, Flagstaff,* and *Raleigh*—all cities connected to both Houston and Memphis. Finally, the difference of two sets (e.g. $A-B$) are the elements left after the members of *B* are taken from *A*. In the assignment above, *FromFlagstaff* is being given the values *Eugene* and *Raleigh.*

The second idea of set values involves their use in *boolean* expressions. When we first used the operator **in** we had to list the members of a set between square brackets. Now, though, we can just use the name of the set:

    if *Detroit* **in** *FromMemphis*
      then *writeln* (´You can fly directly from Memphis to Detroit´) ;

We can also test for set *equality, inequality,* and *inclusion.* We'll briefly review these ideas when we begin to discuss Pascal sets.

Summary

A ***structured type*** definition describes the potential contents of a variable. Although the ***simple*** variables we've used so far have been limited to representing single values of a single type, ***structured variables*** can represent as many values as are specified in the structure's definition.

Pascal has four basic structures, which can be merged to form more complex structures. Each structure has its own method of ***creation***, with which it is defined as a type. Furthermore, every structure has a unique means of ***access*** to its stored values.

The **record** structure is probably the most widely used. Records can include several different types of values in internal variables called fields. Thus, the identifier (name) of a record variable refers to several fields, which must be accessed individually. A method of access we mentioned requires that the variable's name be followed by a period, and the name of the particular field we want to access, e.g. *Phoenix.FlightNumber.*

The **array** structure creates variables that can store any number of values of one particular type. The definition of an array structure includes the type (simple or structured) of the values being stored, as well as an index by which these values can be located. The index values can belong to any ordinal type, and give the array its dimensions. To access one particular value stored in the array, the name of an array variable is followed by an index value (or values) between square brackets, e.g. *L1011SeatTaken*[29, ´E´]. Since any value can be accessed at any time, the array is a random access structure.

File-structured variables are used to store a stream of values, rather than a fixed number of them (like the other structures). Files can be permanently stored in the computer, and retained even after the program that creates them has been executed. File variables are accessed within programs in two ways. A file is inspected by being read

(*read* (*DataFile, Value*)), and generated by being written (*writeln* (*Copy-File, Character*).). Since *char* values can be used to describe values of all the ordinal types, we'll often use the predefined type *text*, which is equivalent to a **file of** *char*. As files are read and written from beginning to end, they're often called sequential access structures.

The last structure we considered was the **set**. Variables of a set type can represent more than one value of any ordinal type. Sets are usually employed to form *boolean* expressions, because they give us an easy means of recording several states, or checking several conditions, at once. The set operators are used to manipulate set values, and make Pascal sets similar to their mathematical counterparts.

record	**array**	**file**	**set**	New Pascal
structured type creation	*simple variable access*		*structured variable*	New Terms

Cro-Magnon cave drawings at Lascaux, France. Courtesy French Government Tourist Office.

11

E Pluribus Unum: Records

Since the time of cave paintings, information has been stored in many different ways. Usually, we tend to think only of storage *media*, beginning with paintings on stone walls, and advancing past clay tablets and papyrus to microfilm and magnetic tape. But looking at storage *organization* makes just as much sense. A filing cabinet, a three-ring binder, and a packet of 3 by 5 index cards all represent approaches to the basic problem of keeping data in a way that's secure, yet easy to find.

The **record** structure is one of Pascal's *structured types*. Now, the actual physical storage the compiler uses is irrelevant to us. We don't know or care if the computer puts its data on magnetic tape, disk, or even tissue paper with a crayon. As far as we're concerned, structures differ only in terms of organization—how information is stored in them, and then how it's located and gotten out again.

In section 11-1 we'll examine the syntax of record-type variables, paying special attention to two aspects of every structure—its method of creation, and its methods of access. We'll also see how a new control structure, called the **with** structure, is sometimes used to aid in accessing records.

Section 11-2 is optional reading at this time. It describes a more sophisticated use of records called *record variants*. Although we include this section here for completeness, it's seldom necessary to use record variants in ordinary programing applications. Finally, 11-3 covers potential bugs, and takes a last look at record variants.

Since the time of the cave paintings, information has been stored in many different ways.

11-1 Defining Record Types

STRUCTURED VARIABLES CAN STORE AND REPRESENT one or more simple (ordinal or *real*) values. The **record** is one of Pascal's basic structures. Record variables, like all structured variables, are created in a systematic way.

> *Define*, then *declare*. First, define a structured type. Then, declare a variable of that type.

Structured types are defined along with ordinal types in a program's (or subprogram's) type definition part. Some portions of the type definition are the same for every type. The reserved word **type** always opens the type definition part, each type has a unique identifier, and an equals sign always precedes the type's specific details.

> The details of a record structure are its *field list*, given between the reserved words **record** and **end**. A record's fields can be of any type—standard or user-defined, simple or structured.

We can draw a simplified chart of a record structure's definition as:*

record *data structure*

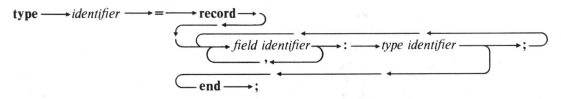

A boilerplate record definition may also be helpful.

```
type (type identifier) = record
                          field identifier, field identifier: real;  {or...}
                          field identifier: ordinal type identifier;  {or...}
              {Field list}  field identifier: structured type identifier;  {or...}
                          field identifier: subrange identifier;  {or...}
                          field identifier: subrange bounds  {No semicolon here.}
                         end;
```

The definition and declaration below show that specifying a record's fields is a lot like declaring a series of variables.

```
type Study = record
               Units, HoursPerWeek: integer;
               Grade: char;              {The record's fields.}
               Passed: boolean
             end;  {Study type definition.}
   var WeavingClass: Study;
```

---

* The chart will need to be expanded after the discussion of record variants in 11-2.

For all practical purposes, the record's fields (*Units, HoursPerWeek, Grade,* and *Passed*) are ordinary variables—we can make assignments to them, use them in input and output statements, etc. In a few paragraphs we'll learn exactly how to access fields.

> ### The Golden Rule of Type Definitions
>
> Structured and ordinal types must be defined before they can be used in subsequent definitions.

The *Study* record structure was easy to define because all its fields belong to standard types. Our next definition, of record type called *Class,* requires several ordinal and structured types that describe a class more realistically. Notice that ordinal types and subranges are defined before they're used to provide the types of fields. Records, in turn, are defined before being used in other structures themselves.

```
type GradeLetters = 'A'..'F';
     Quarter = (Fall, Winter, Spring);
     CourseStatus = (Passed, Failed, Incomplete, WithDrawn);
     WhenTaken = record
                    Term: Quarter;
                    Year: 1980..1985
                 end;  {WhenTaken}
     Class = record
                Hours, Units: 1..5;
                Grade: GradeLetters;
                Results: CourseStatus;
                Taken: WhenTaken      {A record within a record}
             end;  {Class}
var Weaving, Wefting, Warping: Class;
```

WhenTaken, a record type, can provide the type of one of *Class's* fields because *WhenTaken* was defined first. The reverse wouldn't be allowed. Nesting of record definitions can go more than two levels deep, as long as each type is defined in the proper sequence.

One special feature of field identifiers is their limited scope. The field identifiers of a given record have their own ***name list*** in the computer, and don't conflict with identifiers used in other records, or elsewhere within the program.

Methods of Access to Records

There are three different ways to access the values stored in a record-structured variable.

1. Individual fields can be accessed with the 'period' notation we showed in Chapter 10.

2. The **with** structure lets us access fields without having to employ the period notation.

3.   The complete record can be accessed in a single assignment statement—*all* the fields of one record variable can be assigned to the corresponding fields of another.

When Wirth designed Pascal, he realized that people often access several of a record's fields at one point in a program (perhaps to initialize or update them). The 'period' notation for accessing individual fields can become quite tedious (especially if the record has a long name). Wirth made Pascal programing a bit easier by providing two shortcuts for record assignments.

Let's define a record structure to experiment with:

user defined type

    type *CurrentConditions* = (*Clear, Cloudy, Raining*) ;
         Weather = **record**
                      Temperature: −25..125;
                      Barometer: *real*;
                      Present, Outlook: *CurrentConditions*
                 end;
    var *Morning, Noon, Evening*: *Weather*;

Here's a series of assignments to *Morning* that use the 'period' notation. The record variable's identifier is followed by a period, and the name of a field.

         Morning.Temperature := 73 ;
         Morning.Barometer := 30.16 ;
         Morning.Present := *Cloudy*;
         Morning.Outlook := *Raining*;

If weather conditions are identical at mid day, we can take a shortcut and assign all the *Weather* fields in one fell swoop, like this:

         Noon := *Morning*;

This single assignment is equivalent to the series of assignments below. Every field of *Noon* gets the value of its counterpart in *Morning.*

         Noon.Temperature := 73 ;
         Noon.Barometer := 30.16 ;
         Noon.Present := *Cloudy*;
         Noon.Outlook := *Raining*;

....
: Complete record assignments can only be made between records of :
: an *identical* type. :
....

'Identical' is printed in italics to reinforce a subtle point we made in our discussion of subrange types. In Pascal, two variables have identical types only if they're declared with the same type identifier. Two record definitions that are exactly alike in every detail *except type name* are not identical. (More formally, there is no structural equivalence of structured types in Pascal. If this statement doesn't make sense right away, don't read it.)

The third method of access to record-structured variables uses the **with** structure. Its sole purpose is convenience.

> When a record variable's identifier is given in the **with** structure (**with** *RecordName* **do**), its fields can be accessed directly during the structure's action. The period notation is not required.

According to the syntax chart below, more than one record-type variable identifier can be specified. We'll explain this further in a page or two.

with *control structure*

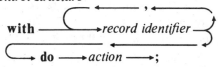

The **with** structure's action is almost invariably a compound statement (so that two or more fields can be accessed during the course of one action). The series of assignments below is clearly equivalent to either of the last two examples.

        with *Noon*
            do begin
                Temperature := 73;
                Barometer := 30.16;
                Present := *Cloudy*;
                Outlook := *Raining*
            end;

Either the period notation or the **with** structure can be used for any inspection or alteration of a record's fields—for assignment (as above), or for input and output. Consequently:

        writeln (*Morning.Temperature*);
        readln (*Morning.Barometer*);

is the same as...

        with *Morning*
            do begin
                writeln (*Temperature*);
                readln (*Barometer*)
            end;

How can we access a record that is a field of another record? Consider these definitions and declarations.

```
type PressureRecord = record
                          Systolic, Diastolic: 50..200
                      end;  {PressureRecord}
     PatientRecord = record
                          Temperature: real;
                          BloodPressure: PressureRecord
                      end;  {PatientRecord}
var Low, Normal, High: PressureRecord;
    TodaysPatient: PatientRecord;
```

A top-down approach is the key to taking apart structured variables. *TodaysPatient* is a variable of type *PatientRecord.* A *PatientRecord* structure contains two fields. The first, *Temperature,* stores a value of type *real.* The second field, *BloodPressure,* is itself a record. What's *it* composed of? As defined, it's a record structure named *PressureRecord,* containing two fields— *Systolic* and *Diastolic.* Each of these fields can represent values in the subrange 50..200.

> To analyze the structure of *TodaysPatient* we asked the same question—What is the structure of *this*?—over and over again. To access the fields contained in *TodaysPatient,* apply the same principle. First, access the record, then, access any records contained in the record.

```
TodaysPatient.Temperature := 98.6;
TodaysPatient.BloodPressure.Systolic := 120;
TodaysPatient.BloodPressure.Diastolic := 90;
```

The **with** structure can be used to make dealing with nested records (like *TodaysPatient*) easier.

> The **with** structure can be given any number of record-structured variable identifiers as 'arguments.' This construct is equivalent to a series of nested **with** structures.

In other words, this **with** structure:

```
with Record1, Record2 do begin   etc.
```

is the exact semantic equivalent of:

```
with Record1
  do with Record2
     do begin   etc.
```

Similarly, both program segments below have the same effect. However, segment 2 uses **with** in a more sophisticated way by giving it two arguments.

```
    with TodaysPatient                    {Segment 1}
      do begin
          Temperature := 98.6;
          BloodPressure.Systolic := 120;
          BloodPressure.Diastolic := 90;
      end;

    with TodaysPatient, BloodPressure     {Segment 2}
      do begin
          Temperature := 98.6;
          Systolic := 120;
          Diastolic := 90;
      end;
```

In some potential applications of the **with** structure, the scope of field identifiers must be taken into account. Suppose that a structure begins:

with *Low, Normal* {Two record variables of type *PressureRecord*}
    do begin   etc.

Within this **with** structure, is a mention of the identifier *Systolic* equivalent to *Low.Systolic*, or to *Normal.Systolic*?

> The scope of nested records is similar to normal scope. The innermost record variable's field identifiers take precedence.

Thus, the last mentioned record variable's fields are accessed— *Systolic* really means *Normal.Systolic*. You can gather that under certain circumstances, using a **with** structure may be inappropriate.

Once the idea of field access is firmly rooted in your mind, you'll appreciate that it doesn't really matter how deep a variable's structure is. Inspection and alteration of fields may become more tedious:

This.That.TheOther.SomeMore.StillGoing := Here.We.Go.Again.Value

but certainly no more complicated.

Q. What do you think about this assignment? Is it legal?

Self-Check Questions

    TodaysPatient.BloodPressure := Normal;
      {Assume we've assigned values to the fields of *Normal*}

A. Yes. A few pages ago, we saw that assignments may be made between any two records of identical types. The field *BloodPressure* and the variable *Normal* are both of type *PressureRecord*.

11-2
Records with Variants (Optional)

THE RECORDS WE'VE DEFINED SO FAR HAVE all had a fixed contingent of fields. However, Wirth enhanced Pascal's by allowing the definition of *record variants*.* The effective number and type of fields in a record variable may change during the course of a program. This means that two variables can be of an identical record type, yet have different numbers or types of fields.

We'll discuss record variants briefly. First we'll consider a record that has *only* a variant part, then we'll define a record with a fixed part *and* a variant part. Finally, we'll establish the syntax of record variants. Let's begin with a data structuring problem that illustrates the need for record variants.

Suppose that we're recording measurements that describe several four-sided figures. The table below shows that each shape is defined by a different group of dimensions.

Shape	Required Dimensions
Square	Side
Rectangle	Length, Width
Rhomboid	Side, AcuteAngle
Trapezoid	Top, Bottom, Height
Parallelogram	Top, Side, ObtuseAngle

Now, if a program required us to store these dimensions we could easily define five different records—one for each shape. Or, it might be more convenient to define a single record that serves to record the dimensions of *any* of the shapes, like this:

type *Shape* = (*Square, Rectangle, Rhomboid, Trapezoid, Parallelogram*) ;
    Dimensions = **record**
            WhatShape: *Shape*;
            Side, Width, Length, Top, Bottom, Height: *real*;
            AcuteAngle, ObtuseAngle: 0..360
      end;

Each field of type *Dimension* is fixed, and every variable of type *Dimensions* contains the exact same fields. Unfortunately, this causes two problems for the programer. First of all, it's possible to make useless assignments to a variable of type *Dimensions*, such as recording the angles of a square. Second, every variable will have extra (and unnecessary) fields. If a program contained many hundreds or thousands of such variables, this waste of storage space might be important.

Record variants come to the rescue. If you examine the definition of *Dimensions*, it's obvious that the *WhatShape* field tells us which fields are actually required in the rest of the record. For example, if *WhatShape* is *Square*, all we really need is a *Side* field. All the others are superfluous.

---

* Interestingly, these are also often called 'variant records.'

The idea that the value of one field could or should determine the rest of the structure is the basis of record variants. One field is designated to be a **tag** or marker field—a field whose value tags or marks the proper group of **variant** fields.

Dimensions is redefined below as a record with variants. *WhatShape* is the tag field, and the record contains five groups of variant fields. Note that no field identifier may appear in more than one group.

type *Shape* = (*Square, Rectangle, Rhomboid, Trapezoid, Parallelogram*);
  Dimensions = **record**
            case *WhatShape*: *Shape* **of**   {The tag field}
              Square: (*Side1*: *real*);
              Rectangle: (*Length, Width*: *real*);
              Rhomboid: (*Side2*: *real*; *AcuteAngle*: 0..360);
              Trapezoid: (*Top1, Bottom, Height*: *real*);
              Parallelogram: (*Top2, Side3*: *real*; *ObtuseAngle*: 0..360)
          end; {*Dimensions*}

var *FourSidedObject*: *Dimensions*;

The tag field is shared by each of the variants. Until the tag field has a value, the remainder of the record variant's structure is undefined.

At this point, we can only make an assignment to the tag field, *WhatShape.*

  FourSidedObject.WhatShape := *Rectangle*;

Once *WhatShape* has been given a value, the fields associated with that value (given in parentheses in *Dimension's* definition above) are created. The assignment above activates a certain group of fields—in this case, *Length* and *Width.* As long as the value of *WhatShape* is *Rectangle*, these are the only fields that *FourSidedObject* will contain. We can make the assignments:

  FourSidedObject.Length := 4.3 ;
  FourSidedObject.Width := 7.5 ;

but an attempted assignment to a field in one of the other variant groups (say, *Top1* or *Angle*) is an error—it does not exist.

What if the value of the tag field changes? If we now say that:

  FourSidedObject.WhatShape := *Parallelogram*;

we find ourselves able to access three new, but as yet undefined fields—*Top2, Side3* and *Obtuse.* The former variant fields *Length* and *Width* simply don't exist any more—they've been deactivated and replaced.

> Record variants act as an antibugging device, by restricting the assignments that can be made to a record variable.

A single record variant definition (like *Dimensions*) has other advantages over the five separate definitions we might have made. Suppose that we want to write a function that computes and represents the area of variable *FourSidedObject.* In function *Area,* below, a single variable of type *Dimensions* is passed as a parameter, then dissected within the routine. If we were using five different records, we'd have to write five different subprograms. But since *Dimensions* is defined as a record variant, just one declaration suffices.

```
function Area (Object: Dimensions) : real;
    begin
        with Object
            do case WhatShape of
                Square: Area:= sqr(Side1);
                Rectangle: Area:= Length*Width;
                Rhomboid: Area:= sqr(Side2)*sin(AcuteAngle);
                Trapezoid: Area:= (Top1+Bottom)/2*Height);
                Parallelogram: Area:= Top2*Side3*sin(ObtuseAngle)
            end {case}
    end; {Area}
```

Notice how the **case** structure in *Area* parallels the construction of *Dimensions* variant part. Using a tag field as the **case** expression is quite common, and is undoubtedly the reason that record variants are so similar to **case** structures.

The variant parts of the *Dimensions* record were *disjoint,* which means that they only shared the tag field. However, Pascal lets us define records that share fields, and have variants as well.

> A record definition may include a *fixed part* and a *variant part.* The fixed part *always* comes before the variant part, and only one variant part is allowed (although variants may be nested).

In the example below, the *Year, Fee,* and *ExpirationDate* fields form *Registration's* fixed part. They, along with the tag field *VehicleType,* are shared by every variant.

```
type Model = (Motorcycle, Car, Truck);
    Registration = record
                    Year: 1915..1985;
                    Fee: real;
                    ExpirationDate: 1982..1990;
                    case VehicleType: model of
                        Motorcycle: (EngineSize: 50..1200);
                        Car: (Cylinders: 2..8; SmogRequired: boolean);
                        Truck: (Axles: 2..10; Weight, Tare: integer)
                    end; {Registration}
```

The current value of the tag field *VehicleType* determines which group of variant fields will be accessible.

Other applications that require records with both fixed and variant fields include employment records, library records, medical records, etc.—any situation where some stored information is general, and some is specialized.

Syntax of Variants

The syntax of a record with a variant part is, without doubt, the toughest in Pascal, and it requires a great deal of soul-searching to be understood. By using the reserved word **case** in a misplaced moment of economy, Wirth managed to confuse nearly everybody. The reason is that the **case** of a record variant is only superficially similar to the **case** of a **case** structure.

The definition of a record structure has three basic sections, as shown below. We'll look at each in turn, and clarify some of the fine points of record-variant definitions.

```
type RecordName = record
{Fixed Fields}        FieldName:  FieldType;
                      FieldName, FieldName:  FieldType;
{Tag Field}           case TagField:  FieldType of
                        TagValue:  (FieldName:  FieldType) ;
{Variant Fields}        TagValue, TagValue:  (FieldName:  FieldType;
                          FieldName, FieldName:  FieldType) ;
                        TagValue:  ()   {Empty field list.}
            end;
```

The *fixed* part we're already familiar with.

```
type RecordName = record
                      FieldName:  FieldType;
                      FieldName, FieldName:  FieldType;
                      {end}   {...if there's no tag field and variant part.}
```

Any number of fields may be defined—even none, which makes the fixed part optional.

The tag field follows the last field of the fixed part. It consists of the tag field identifier, and its type, between the reserved words **case** and **of**.

```
case TagField:  FieldType of
```

Because the variant part comes after the last fixed field, no extra **end** matches the **case**. The same **end** that ends the record structure definition also terminates the variant part.

The variant part is the most complicated section. Each group of variant fields begins with a 'selector' value (one of the possible values of the tag field), followed by a colon, and the variant fields between parentheses.

{Variant Fields}

TagValue: (*FieldName*: *FieldType*);
TagValue, *TagValue*: (*FieldName*: *FieldType*;
    FieldName, *FieldName*: *FieldType*);
TagValue: ()   {Empty field list.}
end;

If a tag field selector value (or values) doesn't have any variant fields associated with it, an empty field list must be provided— *no* field names are put between the parentheses (as above).

The syntax chart of a record definition is more complicated than any we've encountered so far. A record structure can be shown simply as:

record *data structure*

```
type ——→ identifier ——→ = ——→ record ——→ ⌐
                          └→ field list ─┘
                          └→ end ——→;
```

The syntax of a field list is much harder to follow. If you read it carefully, you'll see that the field list is partially defined in terms of itself. This makes it a recursively defined structure.

field list

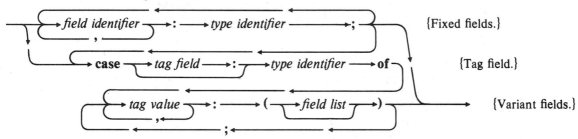

{Fixed fields.}

{Tag field.}

{Variant fields.}

**11-3
Antibugging
and
Debugging**

THE MOST COMMON ERROR IN DEFINING record structures is to omit the **end** that marks the conclusion of the record definition. Imagine how a compiler might read this program segment:

type *RealEstate* = **record**
    Street, Avenue: *integer*;
    Price: *real*;
var *Apartment*: *char*;

Since the end of the record definition isn't indicated, the compiler will probably think that **var** is one of *RealEstate's* fields, and print an error message that points out the futility of using reserved words as identifiers, along with a host of other presumed transgressions:

```
type RealEstate = record
                  Street, Avenue: integer;
                  Price: real;
var Apartment: char;
↑ RESERVED WORD "VAR" MAY NOT BE FIELD IDENTIFIER
    ↑ MISSING COMMA
                  ↑ MISPLACED COLON
                  ↑ PROBABLE MISUSE OF IDENTIFIER "CHAR"
```

The fact that records and **with** structures have their own form of scope also causes confusion. For example, this is a perfectly legal sequence of definitions and declarations:

> **type** *InnerRecord* = **record**
> > *AnyName*: *integer*
> > **end**;
> *OuterRecord* = **record**
> > *AnyName*: *boolean*;
> > *Inside*: *InnerRecord*
> > **end**;
> **var** *TestCase*: *OuterRecord*;
> *AnyName*: *char*;   etc.

In the usual context of a program, the two *AnyName* fields will be distinct from each other, as well as from variable *AnyName*, because a reference to a field is usually prefaced by the name of the record-type variable it belongs to. The assignment below is to the *char* variable *AnyName*.

> *AnyName* := 'R';

In the next example, the identifier *AnyName* refers to the *boolean* field of *TestCase*. The *integer AnyName* field of *Inside* must be referred to using the period notation, and the global variable *AnyName* cannot be accessed at all.

> **with** *TestCase* **do begin**
> *AnyName* := *true*;
> *Inside.AnyName* := 5
> **end**;

Giving two record names to the **with** structure further restricts the scope of the identifier *AnyName*. The *integer AnyName* field of *Inside* is accessed below. It's the most local because *Inside* is the last record named.

> **with** *TestCase, Inside* **do begin**
> *AnyName* := 6
> **end**;

The Pascal headaches caused by record variants extend far beyond their weird syntax. Our discussion was less than candid (we lied) when we said that assigning a value to the tag field activated a particular group of variant fields. In reality, *all* of the record's fields are accessible *all* the time. Understanding why this spells trouble requires a bit of background in how values are stored. Usually, the computer provides a unique portion of its memory for the storage of each field and variable value. As you might imagine, values of different types require different amounts of storage. The illustration below shows how two distinct records might have space allocated for their fields.

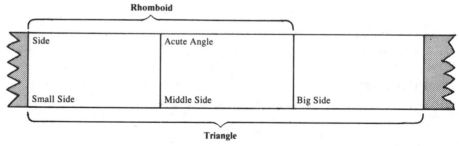

Now, let's imagine that instead of being separate records, the two groups above are variant parts of a single record. The compiler saves space by *overlaying* them—scheduling them for the *same* area in the computer's memory:

All is well and good as long as we only input and output values of one variant group. Trouble comes when we store values according to one scheme of occupancy, and then mistakenly try to read them according to the other. Although we get a value, it is gibberish. You would think that the compiler would prevent errors of this sort, but it doesn't, because of a very specialized option of record variants we didn't shout about.

A tag field need not be specified for a record variant. However, a type identifier must still be given:

case *TypeIdentifier* **of**   etc.

The rest of the variant part's definition proceeds normally.

This feature is error-prone and rarely used. Since the tag field is optional, it can't be checked by the compiler. Thus, *you* should always declare a tag field, and check its value before trying to access fields of a variant part.

Summary

The record structure is called for whenever several values, possibly of different types, should or must be associated with a single variable name. Declaration of a record variable (like any structured variable) takes two steps. First, the record structure type is named and defined. Then, variables of that type are declared.

A record structure's values are stored in its *fields*. A record can include any number or type of fields, and may even have fields that are records themselves. Although field identifiers follow the rules of ordinary variable identifiers, each record has its own *name list*. As a result, field names must only be unique within a given record. Despite this, field identifiers that duplicate other program identifiers can cause confusion, and should be avoided. The reserved words **record** and **end** mark the start and finish of a record's *field list*.

There are three methods of access to the values stored in a record variable. Individual fields can be accessed with the 'period' notation (e.g. *SomeRecord.Field*). An assignment between two record variables with identical types assigns *all* the values of all the fields of one record to the fields of another (e.g. *OneRecord* := *AnotherRecord*). Finally, the **with** structure eliminates the need to name a record variable again and again while referring to several of its fields (e.g. **with** *OneRecord* **do** etc.). **with** structures can be nested, or a single **with** can be given several 'arguments' for the same effect (e.g. **with** *OneRecord, AnotherRecord* **do** etc.).

In section 11-2 we looked at the complete form of a record structure. Records have two optional portions—a *fixed part*, as described above, followed by a *variant part*. If a record *does* have a variant part, a *tag* field, defined between the reserved words **case** and **of**, marks its beginning. Although all variables of a record type include every field from the fixed part, the value of the tag field (when the record is actually used within a program) determines which group of *variant fields* may be properly accessed.

A record's variant part consists of several 'field groups' of zero or more variant fields in parentheses. Each group is associated with one or more possible values of the tag field, using a syntax much like a **case** structure's—values are separated with commas and followed by a colon and the appropriate field group. The active group of variant fields can be changed by altering the value of the tag field. Once they have been activated, variant fields are accessed just like fixed fields.

record	**case**	**of**	New Pascal
end	**with**	**do**	
field list	*name list*	*record variants*	New Terms
tag field	*variant field*	*fixed part*	
variant part			

Self-Test Exercises   **11-1**   True or false: A record must have at least two fields. The fields of a record must have different names. A record must have a different name than any of its fields.

11-2   Is this a legal type definition? Why not?

> **type** *Unit* = **record**
> > *Quantity*: *integer*;
> > *Cut*: *Style*
>
> **end**;
> > *Style* = (*Mini, Midi, Maxi*) ;

11-3   Suppose that the period character were allowed to appear in Pascal identifiers. What problem would this cause? Give an example.

11-4   Suppose that we've made these definitions and declarations:

> **type** *Period* = **record**
> > *Months, Days, Years*: *integer*
>
> **end**;
> > *Time* = **record**
> > > *Months, Days, Years*: *integer*
> >
> > **end**;
> **var** *Passage, Interval*: *Period*;
> > *SnowsOfYesteryear*: *Time*;

Which record variables can we make complete record assignments between?

11-5   Define a record suited for showing the position, and color, of a checker on a checkerboard.

11-6   Latitude and longitude are specified in degrees (°), minutes ('), seconds ("), and direction (North, South, East, and West). Suppose that a city lies at latitude 22° 17' 34" North, and longitude 53° 41' 9" West. Store this location in variable *City*, as declared below.

> **type** *CompassPoints* = (*North, South, East, West*) ;
> > *Coordinates* = **record**
> > > *Degrees*: 0..180;
> > > *Minutes, Seconds*: 0..60;
> > > *Direction*: *CompassPoints*
> >
> > **end**;
> > *Location* = **record**
> > > *Latitude, Longitude*: *Coordinates*
> >
> > **end**;
> **var** *City*: *Location*;

11-7   Why wouldn't the **with** structure below be suitable for making the assignments of the previous question?

> **with** *City, Latitude, Longitude*
> > **do begin**   etc.

11-8   Suppose that we have the definitions and declarations shown below:

> **type** *PhoneNumber* = **record**
> > *AreaCode, Prefix, Number*: *integer*
>
> **end**;
> **var** *Home, Office, Car*: *PhoneNumber*;

Write code to test if *Office* and *Car* are in the same area code, and to set the phone number stored in *Car* equal to the number in *Home*.

11-9   A record without a variant part only uses the reserved word .end once. If a record has a variant part, how many times does the reserved word **end** appear in the record definition?

11-10   What is the purpose of a tag field?

11-11   Write a program that helps a user plan a menu. Determine the recommended daily allowances of various vitamins and nutritive elements for men, women, and children. Have the program user enter a meal—the data associated with each food item, as well as the number of men, women, and children who will be eating. Print out the proportion of the RDA provided for each diner. Note that you'll have to provide a rule (or random process) for dividing the food.

More Exercises

11-12   Nadine finds a treasure map! It shows the location of a piece of land, and contains the following inscription:

> *Your good-luck country is a ten-foot square,*
> *And four feet of treasure are buried there.*

Nadine takes this to mean that a four-foot treasure chest is buried somewhere under a ten by ten plot of land. Write a program that picks a location for the buried treasure, and lets Nadine take ten guesses of its location. Show what the plot looks like after each hole is dug. Naturally, you shouldn't show the treasure until it's found.

11-13   The tables have turned on Rachel Rustler—a giant chicken from the Pullet Planet is chasing her through midtown Manhattan. As you know, it's easy to get around midtown because the streets are numbered one way, and the avenues the other. Unfortunately, there are horrendous traffic jams all around, and Rachel can only run around the area from 34th to 42nd street, bounded by 1st and 7th avenues. Rachel and the chicken can each run only one block at a time, but the chicken, because of its size, is able to move diagonally.

Implement an interactive game that has the computer play the role of giant chicken trying to catch Rachel within a given number of turns. A human player, as Rachel, tries to escape. Concentrate on writing the program as a series of refinements and extensions. Begin with a small (5 by 5) board and guide both chicken and Rachel, then increase the size of the board. Develop a strategy for your program to follow in guiding the chicken, and experiment with different starting positions.

11-14   Suppose that you are about to read in a data value that is either *real, integer,* or *char.* Define a record type that is suited for holding any of these values (use record variants if you want, or include a field that indicates which one of the other fields is being used if you don't uses variants). Then, write a procedure to read in the data value and assign it to the appropriate field of the record.

11-15   Define a new syntax, and alternative reserved words, for a record-type structure. Can you make record variants easier to deal with? Do you think that you should change the syntax of a **const** definition to allow the definition of structured constants? What about letting functions represent structured values?

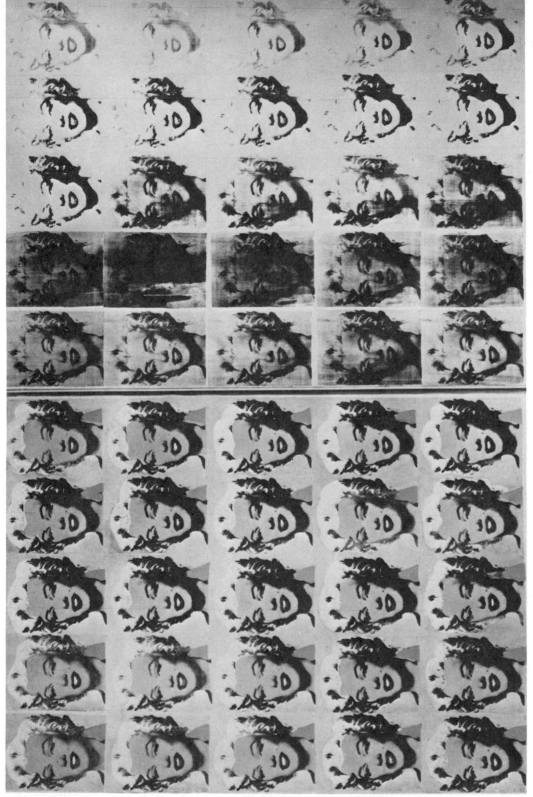

Marilyn Monroe Diptych by Andy Warhol. Oil on canvas, 1962. Tate Gallery, London. Photo courtesy Leo Castelli Gallery, New York.

12

Arrays for Random Access

They say that a topologist is a person who finds a doughnut and a coffee cup identical because they both have the shape of a torus. We can just as reasonably describe a computer scientist as the sort of person who doesn't distinguish between a checkerboard and a topographical map—after all, they can each be described with an array.

The array is the most common computer structure, and is included in practically every programing system from machine language on up. Do you have a list of data values? A table? A grid? A coordinate system? Almost any group of values that can be organized in a regular manner can be stored in an array, because array values are accessed by *location* rather than by *name.*

Section 12-1 describes the syntax of array-structured variables. As always, pay attention to the two important ideas behind structured variables—their method of creation, and the means of accessing their stored values.

In section 12-2 we'll look at some applications of arrays and records. In addition to developing algorithms that use arrays, and coding them into Pascal, we'll work on designing data structures for their own sake. We'll explore the close relationship between a program's data structure and its algorithm. Programs that describe basic array manipulations are included too. Finally, 12-3 covers potential bugs.

We can describe a computer scientist as someone who doesn't distinguish between a checkerboard and a topographical map....

**12-1
Creating
Array
Types**

THE DECLARATION OF AN ARRAY-STRUCTURED variable begins with a definition of the array's type. This definition tells the compiler three things:

1. What is the type of the array's *elements*—its stored values?

2. How many elements will the array hold?

3. How will we refer to the array's elements?

Specifying the type of the elements is easy—the values of any single ordinal, structured, or *real* type may be stored in a given array. The *number* of elements depends on the array's size. It is given by the lower and upper *bounds* of each array **dimension**. Finally, the values used as array bounds indicate how elements are accessed.

Once an array type is defined, we can declare variables of that type. In outline form the definition and declaration look like this:

type *array-type identifier* = **array** [*dimensions*] **of** *element-type identifier*;

var *ArrayVariable identifier*: *array-type identifier*;

The syntax chart of an array type definition contains some options we haven't mentioned yet, but it'll be useful for reference.

array *data structure*

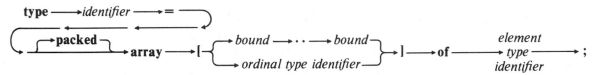

The array is an important data structure, so we'll discuss it very methodically. We'll begin with array dimensions.

> An array dimension is specified by its limit values—the **array bounds**—which must belong to an ordinal type. The bounds are separated by two dots (..) that have their usual Pascal meaning of 'through and including.' If an array has more than one dimension, the pairs of array bounds are separated by commas.

An array that has only one pair of bounds is called **one dimensional**. However, arrays of two, three, or more dimensions can be created by giving additional pairs of array bounds. The entire dimension specification goes between the square brackets.

type *CapitalLetters* = **array** ['A'..'Z'] **of** *element type*;   {1 dimension}
     DailyReadings = **array** [1..24] **of** *element type*;   {1 dimension}
     SeatingPlan = **array** ['A'..'M', 1..44] **of** *element type*;   {2 dimensions}
     GameBoard = **array** [1..3, 1..3, 1..3] **of** *element type*;   {3 dimensions}

Array bounds can also be values of user-defined ordinal types. However, the bounds must be given with the constants of each type, or with user-defined constants. Variable identifiers, or other expressions, may *not* be used as array bound values. For example:

const *LastRow* = 'Z';
    MaximumNumber = 20;

type *Days* = (*Monday, Tuesday, Wednesday, Thursday, Friday, Saturday, Sunday*);
    Desserts = (*Tart, Torte, Cake, Pie, IceCream, Mousse*);
    SeatingPlan = **array** ['A'..*LastRow*, 1..*MaximumNumber*] **of** *element type*;
    NumberOfHelpings = **array** [*Tart..Mousse*] **of** *element type*;
    WorkSchedule = **array** [*Monday..Friday*] **of** *element type*;
    DailyHelpings = **array** [*Monday..Sunday, Tart..Cake*] **of** *element type*;
    ServingsBySeat = **array** ['A'..*LastRow*, 1..*MaximumNumber*, *Tart..Cake*]
                   of *element type*;

> An ordinal or subrange type identifier (except *integer*) can take the place of specific array bounds. The dimension thus stated has bounds equal to the first and last members of the type.

This shortcut makes these two definitions equivalent:

    type *NumberOfHelpings* = **array** [*Tart..Mousse*] **of** *element type*;
    NumberOfHelpings = **array** [*Desserts*] **of** *element type*;

This method can be used to define an array whose bounds are the first and last characters, when you don't know what the first and last *char* values are. Note that an array defined by its dimension type (like *char*) is portable. A *char*-dimensioned array will run on every computer, regardless of its character set.

    type *CharacterCount* = **array** [*char*] **of** *element type*;

The definition of an array structure is completed by naming the type of its elements.

> An array's elements may belong to any ordinal, *real*, subrange, or structured type.

Some arrays whose elements are ordinal values are:

    type *SquareStatus* = (*Black, White, Empty*);
    CheckerBoard = **array** [1..8, 1..8] **of** *SquareStatus*;
    Word = **array** [1..15] **of** *char*;
    Vegetables = (*Leeks, Yams, Spuds, Okra, Artichokes*);
    GroceryOrder = **array** [*Leeks..Artichokes*] **of** *integer*;

Naturally, we can combine these in any way imaginable. To play checkers with vegetables, we add the definition:

    CheckerBoard = **array** [1..8, 1..8] **of** *Vegetables*;

An array of structured elements is just as easy to create. As an example, let's design a structure to represent a chessboard. The board itself can be a two-dimensional array. What will each square of the board store?

1. Whether or not the square is occupied.

2. The value of the piece (if any) on each square.

3. The owner of the piece.

An individual square clearly calls for a record structure. In the type definitions below, we first define ordinal types, then the record structure that uses them, and finally the array whose elements the records are.

type *OwnerColor* = (*None, Black, White*) ;
　　　PieceValues = (*Empty, Pawn, Knight, Bishop, Rook, Queen, King*) ;
　　　Squares = **record**
　　　　　　　　Occupied: *boolean*;
　　　　　　　　Piece: *PieceValues*;
　　　　　　　　Owner: *Color*
　　　　　　end;　 {*Squares* definition}
　　　ChessBoard = **array** [1..8, 1..8] **of** *Squares*;

var *Board*: *ChessBoard*;

· ·

Q. What is the size of each of these arrays—how many elements can be stored in a variable of each array type?

　　　a) **type** *Storage* = **array** [1..5, 1..10] **of** *char*;
　　　b) **type** *Measurements* = **array** [−5..10] **of** *real*;
　　　c) **type** *Seats* = **array** [−5..5, 'A'..'G'] **of** *integer*;
　　　d) **type** *TruthTable* = **array** [*boolean*] **of** *integer*;
　　　e) **type** *Crate* = **array** [1..50, 1..10, 1..25] **of** *real*;

A. Notice that the number of stored values can become quite large when an array has more than one dimension.

　　　a) 50 (5∗10).
　　　b) 16 (Don't forget the '0'th value).
　　　c) 77 (11∗7 letters).
　　　d) 2 (We've used the shorthand method of saying *false..true*).
　　　e) 12,500 (50∗10∗25).

· ·

Accessing Array Elements

Individual elements are stored in and retrieved from array-structured variables according to their *location* within the array. The location is given by a **subscript**; a name that comes from the arrays used in physics and mathematics. Now, in noncomputer applications an array subscript is written in small letters just below the normal line of text, like *Matrix$_{i,j}$* (hence the name *sub*script). In Pascal, an array variable's subscript is given between square brackets.

> To access a single array element, follow the array variable's name by the element's subscript between square brackets. If more than one subscript is required (for multi-dimensional arrays), separate the subscripts with commas. Subscripts can also be **computed**, since any subscript can be a variable or expression.

(The subscript is usually read as 'sub *whatever.*' *ChessBoard*[1,1] would be spoken as 'Chessboard sub 1 *pause* 1'.) According to the box above, the array is a **random access** structure, because we can immediately access any of its elements. Given proper declarations, these are all valid assignments:

Initials['S'] := *Initials*['S'] + 1; {Add 1 to the value of *Initials*['S']}
Dinner[*Leeks*] := 5; {Assignment to a *GroceryOrder* variable.}
readln (*Dinner*[*Yams*]); {Read a value into *Dinner*[*Yams*]}
Boeing747['E', 4] := *Taken*; {Occupy seat E4. 2 subscripts required.}
GameBoard[*Upper, Center, Left*] := *X*; {Make a move—three subscripts required.}

Any representation of a value can be an array subscript. All the subscripts in the following examples are computed.

> *Scores*[5+2] := *Something*;
> *Scores*[*Counter*] := *Something*;
> *Scores*[*Counter* +3] := *Something*;
> *Scores*[*trunc*(7.62)] := *Something*;
> *Scores*[*Scores*[*OldScore*]] := *Something*;

Naturally, the subscript must refer to a location within the array bounds. In the antibugging section we'll see that an 'out-of-range' subscript causes an immediate program crash.

When the structure of variables becomes more complicated, accessing values stored in an array element may require some patience. Suppose that we've made these definitions and declarations:

type *OwnerColor* = (*None, Black, White*);
    PieceValues = (*Empty, Pawn, Knight, Bishop, Rook, Queen, King*);
    Squares = **record**
                Occupied: boolean;
                Piece: *PieceValues*;
                Owner: *OwnerColor*
            end; {*Squares* definition}
    ChessBoard = **array** [1..8, 1..8] **of** *Squares*;

var *LastMove, CurrentMove*: *Squares*;
    Board: *ChessBoard*;

Assume that a white pawn is stored in element 5,2 (its starting position). The statements below put a white pawn two rows up, on 5,4.

Since *Board*[5,4] refers to an element that's an entire record, we must use record-access methods to get at a single field. Any of the examples shown below will do the job.

$$Board[5,4] := Board[5,2] ; \qquad \{1\}$$

$$\begin{aligned}
&Board[5,4].\,Occupied := true; \\
&Board[5,4].\,Piece := Pawn; \qquad \{2\} \\
&Board[5,4].\,Owner := White;
\end{aligned}$$

$$\begin{aligned}
&CurrentMove.\,Occupied := true; \\
&CurrentMove.\,Piece := Pawn; \\
&CurrentMove.\,Owner := White; \qquad \{3\} \\
&Board[5,4] := CurrentMove;
\end{aligned}$$

with *Board*[5,4]
   do begin
       Occupied := *true*;   {4}
       Piece := *Pawn*;
       Owner := *White*
   end;

You may note that we haven't emptied the square where the pawn used to be—right now it's in two places at once.

Combining methods of access (as in the *Board* example) can be carried to any length. Suppose that a record-structured variable contains an array-structured field. We might find ourselves making an assignment like:

$$Schedule.\,Monday[3,\ PM] := Busy;$$

Schedule.Monday refers not to a single value, but to an array of values. We have to give the subscript of the exact element ([3, *PM*]) we wish to change. An array of records of arrays is equally plausible:

$$Room[273].\,Monday[9,\ AM] := Busy;$$

In this example, we begin with a one-dimensional array called *Room*, whose elements are records. Each record contains a two-dimensional array field called *Monday*. By reading the assignment one step at a time (and breathing very slowly), we can conclude that Room 273 will be busy on Monday at 9 A.M.

....
: Assignments may be made between variables with *identical* array :
: structure types. :
....

We might call this the 'complete array' assignment method. As with complete record assignments, both array variables must be declared with the *same* type identifier or else the computer considers them to belong to different types. This kind of assignment is sometimes used to initialize arrays.

We'll take this opportunity to introduce an option of array definitions called ***packing***.

> When it appears in an array type declaration, the reserved word
> **packed** instructs the compiler to conserve space when storing the
> array (to 'pack' it), and to allow certain operations on the array.

For most practical purposes, a packed array is just like a non-packed one. The space conservation feature is seldom important to us because a good compiler will minimize storage space by itself. Some people even feel that forcing the programer to decide when to pack an array runs counter to a basic principle of Pascal—that the programer shouldn't have to worry about details of machine operation. We'll look at the exact operation of packed variables in Appendix A.

One particular type of packed array in Pascal is unlike all the others. A packed array of *char*, like the one we defined above, is usually called a *string*, and is used for storing text.

type *String* = **packed array** [1..15] **of** *char*;

Defining a string as a packed array, and not as an ordinary array, has three advantages.

1. We can use the relational operators to compare the alphabetical ordering of two strings.

2. We can output the entire string at once, instead of one *char* element at a time.

3. We can give a text value to the entire string with an assignment statement (but *not* with an input statement).

Don't forget that these features apply only to packed arrays of *char*, and not any other type. We'll look at a number of string applications in section 12-2.

Arrays and for loops

Before we start to use arrays as data structures, let's explore some of the nitty-gritty of array manipulation. The archetypical problem involves visiting every element of the array to modify it, print its value, or just inspect it in the hope of finding something interesting. The **for** structure is custom-made for travelling through arrays, because its counter variable can be used as an array subscript. Regardless of the ordinal type of an array dimension, it can be used in conjunction with a **for** loop. For example:

procedure *LoadArray* (**var** *CompleteArray*: *ArrayType*; *LowValue, HighValue*: *TheirType*) ;
    {Reads data into an array of type *ArrayType*.}

    var *CurrentIndex*: *TheirType*;

    begin
        for *CurrentIndex* := *LowValue* **to** *HighValue*
            do *read* (*CompleteArray*[*CurrentIndex*])
    end;   {*LoadArray*}

Procedure *LoadArray* reads all the element values of an array of any size. If it equals 1, we're accessing in turn *CompleteArray*[1], *CompleteArray*[2], *CompleteArray*[3], etc.

The same method can be applied to a two-dimensional array. Suppose we have the following definition and declaration. We're deliberately giving *Grid* a peculiar set of array bounds—there's no reason for them to begin with 1.

> **type** *Grid* = **array** [−5..5, 3..14] **of** *integer*;
> **var** *Table*: *Grid*;

Assume that all the elements of *Table* have already been initialized. How can we find the largest value stored? The natural inclination is to search through the array column by column and row by row. A single row might be inspected with:

> **for** *every column in the row*
>   *keep track of the largest value found*

Because we have many rows, we'd look at each in turn:

> **for** *each row*
>   **for** *every column in the row*
>   *keep track of the largest value found*

We'll rewrite the pseudocode with nested **for** structures:

> **procedure** *FindLargest* (**var** *Table*: *Grid*) ;
>   {Finds the largest element in a *Grid*-type array.}
>
>   **var** *Largest, Row, Column*: *integer*;
>
>   **begin**
>   *Largest* := *Table*[−5, 3] ;   {Initialize *Largest*}
>   **for** *Row* := −5 **to** 5
>   **do for** *Column* := 3 **to** 14
>   **do if** (*Table*[*Row, Column*] > *Largest*)
>   **then** *Largest* := *Table*[*Row, Column*]
>   *writeln* ('The largest value in Table is ', *Largest*:1) ;
>   **end**; {*FindLargest*}

What happens if an array has three or more dimensions? Suppose that we want to study the way that space has been appropriated in a campus office building over the last decade or so. A ten-story building that has twenty offices available on each floor can be described with a two-dimensional array. For our purposes, though, a third dimension is required—time.

const *NumberOfOffices* = 20 ;
   NumberOfFloors = 10 ;
   CurrentYear = 1984 ;

type *Departments* = (*Unassigned, Botany, Embroidery, Reeling, Writhing*) ;
   Building = **array** [1..*NumberOfOffices*, 1..*NumberOfFloors*,
               1970..*CurrentYear*] **of** *Departments*;

In a preliminary survey of the building data structure, we'll mark each office *Unassigned.* This means that:

> **for** *each office*
>   **for** *each floor*
>   **for** *each year*
>   *mark the office Unassigned;*

Aside from the extra **for** loop, procedure *Empty* is much like procedure *FindLargest.*

procedure *Empty* (**var** *TheBuilding*: *Building*) ;
  {Assigns *Unassigned* to each element of *TheBuilding.*}
  var *Office*: 1..*NumberOfOffices*;
    Floor: 1..*NumberOfFloors*;
    Year: 1..*CurrentYear*;
  begin
    for *Office* := 1 **to** *NumberOfOffices*
      do for *Floor* := 1 **to** *NumberOfFloors*
        do for *Year* := 1970 **to** *CurrentYear*
          do *TheBuilding*[*Office, Floor, Year*] := *Unassigned*;
    writeln ('Building now ready for occupancy.')
  end; {*Empty*}

For manipulating arrays, a bottom-up approach can be just as valid as top-down. Remember we discussed bottom-up programing earlier, in reference to using drivers to test modules of large programs. When it's used to deal with small programs, though, the bottom-up method can be described as *Find the rule, then devise the algorithm.*

> The bottom-up approach often leads to an ***inductive leap*** to the solution of a problem.

This is just a fancy way of saying that if you look at a problem and its solution long enough, the exact chain of steps that turns a problem into a solution may suddenly jump into your mind. It's often called the 'aha!' method of problem solving.

For example, how can we initialize a two-dimensional array to this table of values?

$$\begin{matrix} 1 & 2 & 3 & 4 \\ 5 & 6 & 7 & 8 \\ 9 & 10 & 11 & 12 \\ 13 & 14 & 15 & 16 \end{matrix}$$

Let's make a definition and declaration:

  type *Matrix* = **array** [1..4, 1..4] **of** *Integer*;
  var *Board*: *Matrix*;

Now, stare at the table above and examine the relationship between the coordinates of each array element, and the value it contains. Eventually, you'll say 'Aha! The value stored at row *i* and column *j* equals $(4*(i-1))+j$.' This formula is our rule. The assignment:

$$Board[i, j] := 4*(i-1) + j;$$

will be the centerpiece of any algorithm that initializes *Board*

Initializing *Board* means that the assignment above must be made for every *i,j* combination within the array. Fortunately, this is a skill we already possess—we visited every element of a two-dimensional array in *FindLargest* We'll modify it to perform the initialization.

> **procedure** *InitializeBoard* (**var** *Board: Matrix*) ;
>   {Initializes *Board* to a particular table of values.}
>
>   **var** *i, j: integer*;
>
>   **begin**
>   **for** *i* := 1 **to** 4
>   **do for** *j* := 1 **to** 4
>   **do** *Board*[*i, j*] := 4*(*i*−1) + *j*;
>   **end**; {*InitializeBoard*}

Programers often use single-letter identifiers (traditionally starting with *i*) as array subscript or **for** loop counter variables. Why? Well, orientation often changes unexpectedly in array manipulations—what once were rows are now columns, and vice versa. In such cases identifiers that are clearly abstract (like *i, j, k*), are superior to identifiers whose meaning is subject to misinterpretation by the program reader (say, *Height, Width, Depth*).

Let's copy the *Board* array to another *Matrix*-type variable. Instead of making a direct copy, though, we'll transfer values as shown below. (This is called *transposing* the array.)

Board					*Copy*			
1	2	3	4		1	5	9	13
5	6	7	8		2	6	10	14
9	10	11	12		3	7	11	15
13	14	15	16		4	8	12	16

Apply the bottom-up approach again. If you pencil in *i, j* coordinates you'll find that the rule is *reversal* Each value stored in element *i, j* of *Board* moves to element *j, i* of *Copy*. Once again, we modify the nested **for** loops of *FindLargest*

> **procedure** *ReverseBoard* (*Board: Matrix*; **var** *Copy: Matrix*) ;
>   {*Copy* becomes a reversal of *Board*}
>
>   **var** *i, j: integer*;
>
>   **begin**
>   **for** *i* := 1 **to** 4
>   **do for** *j* := 1 **to** 4
>   **do** *Copy*[*i, j*] := *Board*[*j, i*]
>   **end**; {*ReverseBoard*}

Our final rearrangement of *Board* will be to effect the transformation shown below.

Board now					*Board transformed*			
1	2	3	4		4	3	2	1
5	6	7	8		8	7	6	5
9	10	11	12		12	11	10	9
13	14	15	16		16	15	14	13

The transformed pattern above is a mirror-image or *reflection* of the original. But suppose that we want to rearrange *Board* itself, instead of copying it somewhere else. Try to come up with a rule, and its implementation. Then, compare your result to procedure *Reflect*, below.

```
procedure Reflect (var Board: Matrix);
    {Reflects Board onto itself.}

    var i, j, Temporary: integer;

    begin
        for i := 1 to 4   {For each horizontal row...}
            do for j := 1 to 2   {...for the first half of the row...}
                do begin   {...switch the 1st and 4th, and 2nd and 3rd, values.}
                    Temporary := Board[i, j];
                    Board[i, j] := Board[i, 4−j+1];
                    Board[i, 4−j+1] := Temporary
                end          {The current row i has been reversed.}
    end;   {Reflect}
```

Q. In procedure *Reflect*, *j* only goes from 1 to 2—just half the row. Why don't we let *j* go all the way to 4? What will happen if we do?

A. Try tracing execution of *Reflect* On any row, we first switch the first and last values, then the second and third values. So far, all is well. However, if we continue to switch values (third for second, and fourth for first) we'll simply put the row in its original order. Thus, we only switch values for half the row. If we let *j* go to 4, *Reflect* would have no effect.

*Self-Check
Questions*

A BASIC EQUATION OF PROGRAMING PROVIDES the title of one of Niklaus Wirth's textbooks: *Algorithms + Data Structures = Programs*. So far, we've taken a lopsided view of the equation by concentrating on algorithms. From now on we'll devote more time to developing data structures, for three reasons.

1. Many of the problems we'll encounter don't really need to be solved, in the sense of finding unknown answers. Their difficulty lies in *implementation*—designing a data structure and joining it to comparatively simple arithmetic or input and output routines.

12-2
Focus on
Programing:
Arrays

2.   As the equation given above implies, there can be a trade-off between the complexity of an algorithm, and the data structures it uses. A sophisticated data structure can minimize the length and difficulty of a final program.

3.   The character of an entire program can be changed by slight modifications of a type definition. Thus, data structures are more important than their size in a program listing implies.

An algorithm that compensates for a too-simple data structure can become unnecessarily complex and detailed. This is one basis of objections to languages like BASIC and FORTRAN. Although their control structures are comparable to Pascal's, their general lack of abstract data structures (they only have arrays) forces programers to waste time explaining data in terms the language can handle. It's no accident that computer journals and advanced programing texts usually show algorithms in some form of Pascal.

In this section we're going to look at a half-dozen categories of problems whose solutions use array structures. In some cases we won't even go beyond the definition of a data structure. These examples should indicate that there is no single array-type problem. As you read, notice how algorithms and structure designs take advantage of different array features—random access, the ability to store different types of values, the ease with which all array elements can be visited, the option of calling for any number of dimensions, different applications of subscripts, etc. As you go along, it's also a good idea to mentally propose alternate structures that accomplish the same ends as the ones we demonstrate.

Inventory

A classic application of arrays is inventory. In its simplest expression, we are told of a store that contains a row of bins or cubbyholes, numbered 1 through 10, each filled with some amount of stock.

type *Inventory* = **array** [1..10] **of** *integer*;
var *Stock*: *Inventory*;

As sales or stock figures come in we can update the inventory:

$$Stock[3] := Stock[3] - 5;$$

Here, five units of product 3 have been sold. Is this a satisfactory system? Well, it might be if we were programing in 1956. To begin with, products have names—no manufacturer numbers her products 1 through 10. Fortunately, the abstract notion of a user-defined ordinal type comes to our rescue—we can name inventoried products. For the rest of this example we'll assume we're in the pants business.

type *Style* = (*Flares, StraightLeg, BellBottom, BootCut, Leisure, Chinos*);
       Inventory = **array** [*Flares..Chinos*] **of** *integer*;
var *Stock*: *Inventory*;

This improvement moves us rapidly into the '60s. Although our data structure lets us name styles of pants, it still doesn't reflect the real world. For instance, pants come in different waist sizes as well as styles. We should add a second dimension to the array:

type *Style* = (*Flares, StraightLeg, BellBottom, BootCut, Leisure, Chinos*) ;
    WaistSize = 25..48 ;
    Inventory = **array** [*Flares..Chinos*, 25..48] **of** *integer*;
var *Stock*: *Inventory*;

The data structure now has a position for each style of pants in 24 different sizes. It stores a total of 144 values—six styles times 24 sizes.

How many pairs of pants do we have in stock—i.e. what is the sum of the stored values? Assuming *WaistSize* variable *CurrentSize*, *integer* variable *TotalCount*, and *Style*-type variable *CurrentStyle*, we can travel through the array and count.

      {Count all waist sizes in each style.}
  TotalCount := 0 ;
  for *CurrentStyle* := *Flare* **to** *Chinos*
    do for *CurrentSize* :— 25 **to** 48
      do *TotalCount* := *TotalCount*+*Stock*[*CurrentStyle, CurrentSize*] ;
  writeln ('Total stock is ', *TotalCount*:1, ' pairs of pants.') ;

We might just as easily, and correctly, go through it in sideways order:

      {Count all styles in each waist size.}
  TotalCount := 0 ;
  for *CurrentSize* := 25 **to** 48
    do for *CurrentStyle* := *Flare* **to** *Chinos*
      do *TotalCount* := *TotalCount*+*Stock*[*CurrentStyle, CurrentSize*] ;
  writeln ('Total stock is ', *TotalCount*:1, ' pairs of pants.') ;

Can the data structure be brought up to the 80's? Yes. In the old days, computer users (who had no knowledge of programing) frequently found themselves at the mercy of programers who didn't understand business, and didn't care to learn. This resulted in programs more attuned to the programer (or computer) than to the end user. Nowadays it's generally accepted that programs should be written to meet applications—requirements shouldn't have to be tailored to meet a programer's whim.*

What does this have to do with pants? Our next step is to realize that pants come in different lengths, and are manufactured from a variety of materials. We'll declare new types *Length* and *Material*, and add another two dimensions to the array.

---

* In fact, one reason for books like this is to teach people what they can expect from computers.

```
type Style = (Flares, StraightLeg, BellBottom, BootCut, Leisure, Chinos);
     WaistSize = 25..48;
     Length = (Short, Medium, Long);
     Material = (Denim, Corduroy, Polyester, Cotton);
     Inventory = array [Flares..Chinos, 25..48,
                         Short..Long, Denim..Cotton] of integer;
var Stock: Inventory;
```

Now, declaring third and fourth dimensions for the *Stock* was an important conceptual step. We stored information about pants in the way we *perceived* it, instead of trying to mimic the appearance of pants on a shelf. We reached, and went beyond, the limit of an array as a literal picture of reality.

Although a one-dimensional array is close to our original row of bins or cubbyholes, a four-dimensional array only relates to the way we *think* about inventory. A four-dimensional show room cannot be constructed on a sales floor, but a type definition creates one within the computer. Finding the stock of boot-cut pants, size 34 medium, made of denim, requires a single statement:

writeln (Stock[BootCut, 34, Medium, Denim]);

We can quickly devise a function that counts and represents the number of pairs of pants of any given style and material. We go through the array as before, but keep two of the subscripts constant.

```
function CountStyles (TheStyle: Style; TheMaterial: Material;
                      Stock: Inventory): integer;
{Sums array elements.}

var CurrentLength: Length;
    TotalCount: integer;
    CurrentSize: WaistSize;

begin
    TotalCount := 0;
    for CurrentLength := Short to Long
        do for CurrentSize := 25 to 48
            do TotalCount := TotalCount +
                        Stock[TheStyle, CurrentSize, CurrentLength, TheMaterial];
    CountStyles := TotalCount
end;   {CountStyles}
```

A program might include the statement:

```
if CountStyles(BootCuts, Denim, Stock) < (OriginalOrder − ExpectedSales)
    then writeln ('Sales of boot cut Denim pants are below expectations.');
```

We've discussed an inventory problem for several pages without ever mentioning an algorithm. Nonetheless, the problem is substantially solved because of our choice of data structure. Any operation we're liable to want a program to perform—adding or diminishing stock, analyzing merchandise on hand, projecting sales or supplies—just requires a basic array-search algorithm.

:·:

Q. Suppose we make this definition. How many elements does *Stock* have?

    type *Style* = (*Flares, StraightLeg, BellBottom, BootCut, Leisure, Chinos*);
        Waistsize = 25..48;
        Length = (*Short, Medium, Long*);
        Material = (*Denim, Corduroy, Polyester, Cotton*);
        Inventory = **array** [*Style, WaistSize, Length, Material*] **of** *integer*;
    var *Stock*: *Inventory*;

Self-Check Questions

A. We've used the shorthand method to define *Inventory*. It stores 6 times 24 times 3 times 4 values, or a grand total of 1,728 *integers*.

:·:

Counting

Another popular array example (that varies with the season) is to impart organization to a collection of data values. In fall, we write programs that make predictions, hold elections, tabulate votes, and look for voter fraud. Come winter, we take examination scores, rank them, and decide who passes and who fails. In spring, baseball standings get figured out. Summer tends to be slow, devoted to searching for license plates, library books, and telephone numbers.

In any case, the notion of searching and sorting collections of values is widespread. We'll begin with a counting problem:

Count the number of characters in a text sample. Print a table of the frequency of the lower-case letters.

An analysis like this is usually the first step in code-breaking programs. This particular problem is intriguing because of the role array subscripts play. Suppose we make the type definition:

type *CharacterArray* = **array** [*char*] **of** *integer*;

This creates an array type whose bounds are the first and last *char* values, whose elements are *integers*, and whose subscripts are the individual characters. With it, we can use the array element subscripted by a character to store the number of times that character appears as input. In program *CountTheCharacters*, below, we've assumed we're using the ASCII set of 128 characters.

```
program CountTheCharacters (input, output);
    {Count input characters and print relative frequencies of lower-case letters.}
const NumberOfCharacters = 128;
type CharacterArray = array [char] of integer;
var CountArray: CharacterArray;
    Character: char;
    Letters,                    {Letters counts lower-case letters.}
    Lines: integer;             {Lines counts lines for producing neat output.}
begin
    for Character := chr(0) to chr(NumberOfCharacters−1)
        do CountArray[Character] := 0;    {Initialize the array.}
    Letters := 0;
    while not eof
        do begin    {Count all the character frequencies.}
            read (Character);
            if Character in ['a'..'z'] then Letters := Letters+1;
            CountArray[Character] := CountArray[Character]+1
        end;
    Lines := 1;
    for Character := 'a' to 'z'
        do begin    {Print the output table.}
            write (Character, ' =');
            write ((CountArray[Character] / Letters)*100:6:2, '%   ');
            if (Lines mod 5) = 0 then writeln;
            Lines := Lines+1    {New-line every fifth write.}
        end;
    writeln
end.    {CountTheCharacters}
```

We had *CountTheCharacters* analyze its own listing, and got these results:

a =	9.90%	b =	0.96%	c =	5.11%	d =	1.60%	e =	13.90%
f =	2.24%	g =	1.12%	h =	4.95%	i =	5.27%	j =	0.00%
k =	0.00%	l =	2.08%	m =	0.64%	n =	6.87%	o =	5.11%
p =	1.44%	q =	0.32%	r =	14.22%	s =	4.31%	t =	12.14%
u =	3.83%	v =	0.48%	w =	1.28%	x =	0.00%	y =	1.76%
z =	0.48%								

Ordering

Program *CountTheCharacters* prints its frequency chart in alphabetical order. It's not unreasonable, though, to want the output printed in order of frequency, from the most used letter to the least. To get such a chart we'll have to order our collected data.

Sorting data is one of the most thoroughly analyzed topics in computer science; people can write entire books about it (and they have). We won't let this intimidate us, though, because the most basic method is often the best. A very obvious sorting routine known as a **selection sort** works like this:

Suppose that we have an array of *integer* values.

| 18 | 35 | 22 | 97 | 84 | 55 | 61 | 10 | 47 |

Search through the array, find the largest value, and exchange it with the value stored in the first array location.

| 97 | 35 | 22 | 18 | 84 | 55 | 61 | 10 | 47 |

Next, find the second largest value in the array, and exchange it with the value stored in the second array location. This is identical to the first trip through the array, except that we don't look at the first value—we already know it's the largest. We've shaded the portion we're not inspecting.

| 97 | 84 | 22 | 18 | 35 | 55 | 61 | 10 | 47 |

Now, repeat the 'select and exchange' process, each time beginning the search one value further along the array. As we go along, we'll be building an ordered array of values (shaded). Eventually, we'll get all the way to the end of the array—which has to be the smallest stored value—and the array will be ordered.

| 97 | 84 | 61 | 18 | 35 | 55 | 22 | 10 | 47 |

| 97 | 84 | 61 | 55 | 35 | 18 | 22 | 10 | 47 |

| 97 | 84 | 61 | 55 | 47 | 18 | 22 | 10 | 35 |

| 97 | 84 | 61 | 55 | 47 | 35 | 22 | 10 | 18 |

| 97 | 84 | 61 | 55 | 47 | 35 | 22 | 18 | 10 |

Another sorting algorithm that's similar is called **bubble sort**. This method usually requires fewer comparisons, but many more exchanges than the selection sort does. It tends to take more time to run than a selection sort. A bubble sort works like this:

Begin with the same array as before:

| 18 | 35 | 22 | 97 | 84 | 55 | 61 | 10 | 47 |

Compare the first value with the second. If the second is larger, exchange them.

| 35 | 18 | 22 | 97 | 84 | 55 | 61 | 10 | 47 |

Next, compare the second and third values, exchanging them if the third is larger.

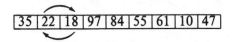

| 35 | 22 | 18 | 97 | 84 | 55 | 61 | 10 | 47 |

Then compare (and possibly exchange) the third and fourth values, the fourth and fifth, etc. until you reach the end of the array. Note that the smallest stored value ends up stored in the last position (shaded).

| 35 | 22 | 97 | 84 | 55 | 61 | 18 | 47 | 10 |

Now, go back to the beginning of the array and start all over again. Work your way through the array comparing and exchanging values again. However, since the smallest value is already at the far right, you need not compare the final value.

| 35 | 97 | 84 | 55 | 61 | 22 | 47 | 18 | 10 |

Repeat the process of comparison and exchange without bothering the final *two* values.

| 97 | 84 | 55 | 61 | 35 | 47 | 22 | 18 | 10 |

As you can see, an ordered list is forming on the right. Continue the process of comparison and exchange, ignoring the last *three* values this time.

| 97 | 84 | 61 | 55 | 47 | 35 | 22 | 18 | 10 |

This particular array is already ordered. If it weren't, it *would* be when we got to the point of only comparing the first two values.

In a sense, the smallest values 'bubble' to the right side of the array.

Implementing these sorting algorithms will require a new data structure. Although the values produced by *CountTheCharacters* are easy enough to sort, the relationship between numbers and characters in *CountArray* can't be preserved. We'll wind up with an ordered array of numbers (the number of times each character appeared) but no idea of what characters they refer to.

Instead, we'll have to define an array whose elements store a character, and the number of times that character has appeared. In other words, we'll need an array of records.

```
const ArrayLimit = 26;
type CharData = record
               TheCharacter: char;
               Count: integer
          end; {CharData}
     RecordArray = array [1..ArrayLimit] of CharData;
var OrderedArray: RecordArray;
```

Actually counting characters with this new data structure means we'll have to modify our counting algorithm. However, we'll save that problem for a rainy day and assume that an array variable named *OrderedArray*, of type *RecordArray*, already stores the number of times each letter appears in a text sample. *OrderedArray*[1]. *TheCharacter* is 'a', while *OrderedArray*[26]. *TheCharacter* is 'z'.

Since both the selection sort and bubble sort algorithms require many array values to be exchanged, procedure *Switch*, below, will come in handy. When called, it will be passed two array elements (of type *CharData*) as parameters.

```
procedure Switch (var First, Second: CharData);
    {Exchanges the fields of two CharData values.}
    var Temporary: CharData;
    begin
        Temporary := First;
        First := Second;
        Second := Temporary
    end;   {Switch}
```

As you read procedures *SelectionSort* and *BubbleSort*, below, bear in mind that each procedure rearranges records according to their *Count* fields. With slight modifications, they could be used to sort arrays of almost any type. The fact that we defined *ArrayLimit* as a constant will make any conversion easier. As an aid in comparing the effects of each sort, we've kept count of the number of switches and comparisons each method requires. Assume the data of *CountTheCharacters*.

```
procedure SelectionSort (var OrderedArray: RecordArray);
    {Uses a selection sort algorithm to order an array of records.}
    var First, Largest, Comparisons, Switches: integer;
        Current: 1..ArrayLimit;
    begin
        Comparisons := 0;
        Switches := 0;
        for First := 1 to ArrayLimit−1
            do begin
                Largest := First;
                for Current := First to ArrayLimit
                    do begin
                        Comparisons := Comparisons+1;
                        if OrderedArray[Current]. Count> OrderedArray[Largest]. Count
                            then Largest := Current
                    end;   {Current for}
                Switches := Switches +1;
                Switch (OrderedArray[Largest], OrderedArray[First])
            end;   {First for}
        writeln (Comparisons:2, ' comparisons,  ', Switches:2, ' switches.')
    end;   {SelectionSort}
```

350 comparisons, 25 switches.

When you read the next procedure, you'll realize that *Selection-Sort* and *BubbleSort* are interesting because of the nearly opposite way they use array subscripts.

procedure *BubbleSort* (**var** *OrderedArray: RecordArray*) ;
   {Uses the bubble sort algorithm to order an array of records.}

   var *Last*: 2.. *ArrayLimit*;
      Current: 1.. *ArrayLimit*;
      Comparisons, Switches: integer;

   begin
      for *Last* := *ArrayLimit* **downto** 2
         do for *Current* := 1 **to** *Last* − 1
            do begin
               Comparisons := *Comparisons* +1 ;
               if *OrderedArray* [*Current*]. *Count* < *OrderedArray* [*Current* + 1]. *Count*
               then begin
                  Switches := *Switches* +1 ;
                  Switch (*OrderedArray* [*Current*], *OrderedArray* [*Current* + 1])
               end {**if**}
            end; {*Current* **for**}
      writeln (*Comparisons*:2, ' comparisons, ', *Switches*:2, ' switches.')
   end; {*BubbleSort*}

```
    ↓         ↓         ↓         ↓         ↓
325 comparisons, 132 switches.
```

The difference between *SelectionSort* and *BubbleSort* shows up in the number of comparisons and switches, and, more subtly, in the ordering they produce. Although both procedures correctly order the letters, the exact order of letters with the same frequency differs. This discrepancy doesn't cause any problems, but it exemplifies the sort of detail we always have to be aware of. Were we to print the contents of *OrderedArray* after each sort we'd see:

Ordering of SelectionSort

```
r =  14.22%  e =  13.90%  t =  12.14%  a =   9.90%  n =   6.87%
i =   5.27%  o =   5.11%  c =   5.11%  h =   4.95%  s =   4.31%
u =   3.83%  f =   2.24%  l =   2.08%  y =   1.76%  d =   1.60%
p =   1.44%  w =   1.28%  g =   1.12%  b =   0.96%  m =   0.64%
v =   0.48%  z =   0.48%  q =   0.32%  x =   0.00%  j =   0.00%
k =   0.00%
```

Ordering of BubbleSort

```
r =  14.22%  e =  13.90%  t =  12.14%  a =   9.90%  n =   6.87%
i =   5.27%  c =   5.11%  o =   5.11%  h =   4.95%  s =   4.31%
u =   3.83%  f =   2.24%  l =   2.08%  y =   1.76%  d =   1.60%
p =   1.44%  w =   1.28%  g =   1.12%  b =   0.96%  m =   0.64%
z =   0.48%  v =   0.48%  q =   0.32%  j =   0.00%  k =   0.00%
x =   0.00%
```

A more entertaining class of problems that use arrays can be categorized as board or game-type problems. They call for arrays of structured data values—arrays whose elements are structured themselves. For example:

Scoreboards
and
Gameboards

A baseball game consists of nine innings.
A football game has four quarters.
A bowling match contains ten (sometimes eleven) frames.
A chessboard has 64 squares whose color and contents vary.
A Monopoly board has squares that represent properties, and usually include schedules of rents and buildings.
Computer games like Adventure, Hunt the Wumpus, and Zork contain many rooms filled with unknown objects, and connected in various ways.

These games pose the problems of keeping score, playing the game, or both. Do they require real algorithms? Well, although winning play might need some sort of algorithm, the programer basically faces a bookkeeping problem—keeping track of current scores or board positions.

> The solution to board-type problems lies in designing a data structure. We want to simplify a potential program with a structure that makes it easy to do the arithmetic of scorekeeping, or the graphics of board positioning.

Because the design of data structures is largely a mental exercise, a problem solving technique called *lateral thinking* can be put to good use. Lateral thinking is a name Edward DeBono invented to describe the process of repeatedly exploring and reconsidering possible solutions before committing ourselves to one particular method. For example, a lateral approach to digging for buried treasure would entail digging many shallow holes, instead of one hole that is very deep.

A lateral programer might propose several potential data structures before writing a program that relies on one of the alternatives. We can build in features that will aid the final program. For example, consider these two possible data structures for a program that scores a baseball game.

```
type Team = (Pirates, Mets, Astros, Giants, Yankees, Angels);
     Inning = (Top, Bottom);
     AtBats = record
                 TeamUp: Team;
                 Runs, Hits, Errors: integer
              end;
     Game = array [1..9, Top..Bottom] of AtBats;
```

```
type TeamName = packed array[1..15] of char;
     Inning = (Top, Bottom);
     Statistics = array [1..9] of integer;
     TeamStatistics = record
                      Name: TeamName;
                      Runs, Hits, Errors: Statistics
                 end;
     Game = array [Top..Bottom] of TeamStatistics;
```

These data structure definitions create two different ways of viewing and storing the exact same information. Choosing one structure over the other will depend on our ultimate application.

Programs that involve games (especially imaginary ones) can bring out the best in a programer. Some game boards have an obvious representation—checkerboard games almost always call for a data structure that is an **array** [1..8,1..8] of some record type. A board game like Monopoly, on the other hand, that appears to require a two-dimensional array, can be described as a single, long line of boxes—a one-dimensional array. Declaring a two-dimensional Monopoly board is unnecessary and slightly misleading because, aside from an occasional trip to Jail, the game moves in a straight line.

A game in which *nothing* moves in a straight line also calls for a one-dimensional array. *Hunt the Wumpus* is often found on interactive computer systems. Here's a description of a simple version.

You are in the cave of the Wumpus. The Wumpus likes you very much—especially for breakfast. To avoid being eaten, you must locate the Wumpus, and shoot it with your bow and arrow.

The Wumpus cave has 20 rooms, connected by narrow passageways. You can travel in any direction—North, South, East, or West—from one room to another. You also know the number of the room each passageway leads to. However, there are hazards to beware of. Some rooms contain bottomless pits, and others contain bats that will pick you up, and carry you to another room. One room contains the Wumpus. Entering a room that holds a pit or the Wumpus causes instant death. Fortunately, when you are one room away you can feel the breeze from a pit, hear the bats, or smell the Wumpus,

To win the game, you must shoot the Wumpus. When you shoot an arrow, it travels through three rooms—you can tell the arrow which tunnel to take as it passes through each room. Don't forget, though, that the tunnels often turn unexpectedly. You may end up shooting yourself. You have 5 arrows. Good luck.

A single refinement step is enough to state the rules of Hunt the Wumpus in an approximation of a Pascal program.

initialize the cave;
put the player in her first room;
if adjoining rooms have hazards, give warning;
repeat
    get the action—Move or Shoot?;
    case *Action* **of**
       Move: **begin**
            find out the direction;
            move;
            if adjoining rooms have hazards, give warning
          end
      shoot: **begin**
            find out the arrow directions;
            shoot;
            update arrow count;
            is Player or Wumpus killed?;
          end
    end {**case**}
until (*Player is dead*) **or** (*Wumpus is dead*);

However, the real problem is to design a data structure suitable for representing the Wumpus Cave. A good first step in this situation is to draw a picture of the data—the contents of, and connections between, the Wumpus Cave's rooms.

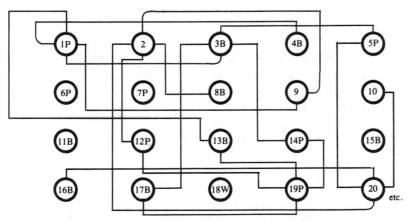

Suppose that we're designing a cave structure. How will the rooms be connected? As you can see, it's practically impossible to draw the cave in only two dimensions. At least three dimensions, and probably four, are needed to make rooms that seem to be right next to each other adjoin. Is a multi-dimensional array needed to hold the cave of the Wumpus? Before you read on, stop for a moment and think about how you'd represent the entire group of rooms.

Our main concern in playing is to know the contents of the current room, and the numbers of adjoining rooms. Suppose that we define *Rooms* as a record that holds just this information. We can draw a new and quite different picture of a room as a record with two fields. The *Contents* field represents any of the *Hazard* values. The second field is an array subscripted by *Directions*, and containing *RoomNumber* values.

On the left, below, we've drawn a *Rooms* structure in terms of its field and subscript names. The right-hand picture shows the values a typical *Rooms* structure contains.

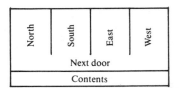
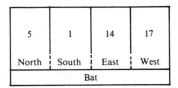

What about drawing the entire cave as a line of rooms? The map below contains the same information on the last page.

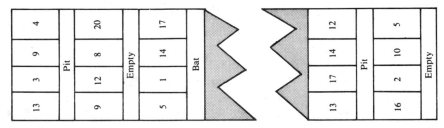

At this stage we can turn our drawing into a Pascal type definition.

const *MaximumNumberOfRooms* = 20;

type *Hazard* = (*Pit, Bat, Wumpus, Empty*);
    RoomNumbers = 1..*MaximumNumberOfRooms*;
    Directions = (*North, South, East, West*);
    PassageWays = **array** [*North..West*] **of** *RoomNumbers*;
    Rooms = **record**
            Contents: *Hazard*;
            NextDoor: *PassageWays*
      end;
    Cave = **array** [1..*MaximumNumberOfRooms*] **of** *Rooms*;
    {We could have said '**array** [*RoomNumbers*] **of** *Rooms*}

var *WumpusCave*: *Cave*;
    CurrentRoomNumber: *RoomNumbers*;

Let's fill rooms 1 and 2 with data according to the map. For purposes of illustration, we'll use two different methods of access.

WumpusCave [1]. *Contents* := *Pit*; {Initialize Room 1.}
WumpusCave [1]. *NextDoor* [*North*] := 13;
WumpusCave [1]. *NextDoor* [*South*] := 3;
WumpusCave [1]. *NextDoor* [*East*] := 9;
WumpusCave [1]. *NextDoor* [*West*] := 4;

```
        with WumpusCave[2]   {Initialize Room 2.}
            do begin
                Contents := Empty;
                NextDoor[North] := 9;
                NextDoor[South] := 12;
                NextDoor[East] := 8;
                NextDoor[West] := 20
            end;
```

> One characteristic of a good data structure is that it minimizes the
> effort a programer must expend to examine data.

For example, at one stage of the game we must check neighboring rooms to see if they contain hazards. Procedure *CheckForHazards*, below, does the job quickly and neatly. Notice how the expression *NextDoor*[*Neighbor*] is used as an array subscript.

```
procedure CheckForHazards (CurrentRoomNumber: RoomNumbers; WumpusCave: Cave);
    var Neighbor: Direction;
    begin
        with WumpusCave[CurrentRoomNumber]
            do for Neighbor := North to West
                do case WumpusCave[NextDoor[Neighbor]].Contents of
                    Empty: ;
                    Bat: writeln ('I hear bats!');
                    Pit: writeln ('I feel a breeze!');
                    Wumpus: writeln ('I smell a Wumpus!')
                end {case}
    end; {CheckForHazards}
```

Is *CheckForHazards* perfect? Not really. One programer might object that it allows duplicated warnings, and a clever player could figure out which room contains what hazard. Another programer might object to our data structure, since the expression:

$$WumpusCave[NextDoor[Neighbor]].Contents$$

is unappealing on aesthetic grounds—it takes a concerted effort to understand it. We tried to head off this objection by using a **with** structure and well-named variables.

One of the less visible features of *CheckForHazards* is its use of the subrange *RoomNumbers* as the type of *CurrentRoomNumber*. This is a built-in safety check on the value passed to *CurrentRoomNumber*, assuring us that the room we're examining exists. It is precisely for such applications that ordinal subranges were created.

We'll leave Hunt the Wumpus now. Although a program to play the game is fairly long, it is well within our abilities as programers— given a suitable data structure.

Strings   The word *string* is commonly used to describe a **packed array** of *char* elements used to hold text values. Strings aren't particularly difficult to work with, and their applications are so diverse that we're going to demonstrate some procedures for string operations—your time is better spent programing with strings than in trying to figure out *how* to. Program *OrderWords*, opposite, demonstrates the three main string operations—input, output, and comparison.

How do we program a computer to read a word? According to procedure *ReadString*, very carefully. We read one character at a time until we reach the end of the word (indicated by a blank character), or until the array of *WordLength* characters is filled. Since we initialized the string to all blanks at the beginning of the procedure, we need not change any remaining characters from a previous word to blanks. Furthermore, no matter how short the input word is, each value stored in the string array will be defined.

> Reading characters one at a time, however tedious it may be, is the only way that text can be input to a string variable. Neither *read* or *readln* can be used to read more than one character at a time.

What about output of strings? There are really two methods. The first, implemented in procedure *WriteString*, roughly parallels *ReadString*. Characters are printed, one at a time, until we've printed all *WordLength* characters, or run out of nonblank characters to print.

A second method of string output is especially useful for making columns of words. It relies on a special rule of Pascal.

> An array structure that has been defined as a packed array of *char* values (as a string) may be output in its entirety using *write* or *writeln*.

Naturally, when strings are printed like this, any padding blanks that fill the remainder of the array are printed as well. Assume that the *First* and *Second* still store the strings 'Hello' and 'Goodbye':

        write (Second) ;
        writeln (First) ;
        writeln (First, Second) ;

          ↓   ↓   ↓   ↓   ↓
        Goodbye   Hello
        Hello   Goodbye

Program *OrderWords* demonstrates only one of two methods for making assignments to string variables. We've already pointed out that a complete array assignment can be made between any arrays of *identical* types. The assignment:

                    First := *Second*;

is valid because *First* and *Second* are both of type *String*.

```pascal
program OrderWords (input, output);
    {Demonstrates input, output, and comparison of strings.}
const Blank = '               '; {Fifteen blank spaces}
      WordLength = 15;
type String = packed array [1.. WordLength] of char;
var First, Second: String;
procedure ReadString (var Word: String);
    {Reads the first WordLength nonblank characters.}
    var Counter: integer;
        Character: char;
    begin
        Word := Blank;
        Counter := 1;
        repeat
           read (Character);
           Word[Counter] := Character;
           Counter := Counter +1
        until (Character=' ') or (Counter> WordLength)
    end; {ReadString}
procedure WriteString (var Word: String);
    {Prints nonblank elements of Word}
    var Counter: integer;
    begin
        Counter := 0;
        repeat
           Counter := Counter +1;
           if (Word[Counter]<>' ') then write (Word[Counter]);
        until (Word[Counter]=' ') or (Counter=WordLength);
        write (' ')  {Put a blank after each string.}
    end;  { WriteString}
begin  {OrderWords}
    writeln ('Enter two words.');
    ReadString (First);
    ReadString (Second);
    writeln ('The words are ', First, ' and ', Second);
    writeln ('In alphabetical order the words are...');
    if First< Second
       then writeln (First, Second)
       else begin
           WriteString (Second);
           WriteString (First);
           writeln
       end
end.  {OrderWords}
```

```
          ↓        ↓       ↓       ↓       ↓       ↓
Enter two words.
Hello Goodbye
The words are Hello           and Goodbye
In alphabetical order the words are...
Goodbye Hello
```

However, string types are unique in allowing text constants *of the proper length* to be honorary strings.

··
: A text constant with *n* characters may be assigned to a packed *char* :
: array variable with *n* elements. :
··

These two assignments have the exact same effect:

First := *Blank*;
Second := '   ';

because a) *Blank* and the fifteen blank spaces both represent sequences of fifteen *char* values, and b) for purposes of assignment, they are both compatible with values of type *String.*

Program *OrderWords* makes one final point—string-type values can be compared with the relational operators (<, >, =, <=, >=, <>). The result of such a comparison depends on alphabetical order, according to the computer's collating sequence. When both upper and lower-case letters are involved, this can have unexpected consequences. For example, these words are in alphabetical ordering according to three different systems:

English ....Ant, art, ball, Bat
ASCII ....Ant, Bat, art, ball
EBCDIC................art, ball, Ant, Bat

Many programs require the ordering of strings. A typical data structure is:

type *String* = **packed array** [1..15] **of** *char*;
WordList = **array** [1..100] **of** *String*;
var *Word*: *String*;
Vocabulary: *WordList*;

We've just seen how to assign values to, and access the values of, variables like *Word.* The same rules of assignment and access hold when string values are the elements of an array.

Vocabulary[32] := *Word*;
for *Counter* := 1 **to** 100
   do *writeln* (*Vocabulary*[*Counter*])   {Print the entire vocabulary list}

How about making a direct assignment to one of the elements of one of the strings stored in *Vocabulary*? Suppose we want to store 'B' as the fifth character of the twelfth word. There are two methods:

Vocabulary[12] [5] := 'B';
Vocabulary[12, 5] := 'B';

As you can see, the first method is a logical application of the array method of access—we patiently access each structure in turn. The second method is another of Pascal's shorthands. It's rationalized by recognizing that the definition of *Vocabulary* is tantamount to a two-dimensional array. Both are equally correct.

In chapter 9 we mentioned that strings can be used to fake the output of user-defined ordinal values. For example, *Monday, Tuesday, Wednesday,* etc. might be constants of an ordinal type, but 'Monday', 'Tuesday', 'Wednesday' etc. are the English words we use to describe them. We can print the names of each constant with a cute technique—the string table—thought up by the first Pascal programer.

....
.   To Build A String Table...   .
. First, define an ordinal type and a string type. Then, create an   .
. array subscripted by the ordinal type, whose elements belong to the .
. string type.   .
....

Each user-defined ordinal value will be the subscript of a string—the English word we associate with the ordinal value. For example, suppose that we make the following definition:

type *Day* = (*Monday, Tuesday, Wednesday, Thursday, Friday, Saturday, Sunday*);
    String = **packed array** [1..9] **of** *char*;
    Words = **array** [*Day*] **of** *String*;
var *Today*: *Day*;
    DayWords: *Words*;

By suitably initializing the *DayWords* array, we can use it to print the English representation of the *Day* type variable *Today*. This is a fairly common application, and you should understand it.

```
        {Initialize the array.}
    DayWords[Monday] := 'Monday    ';
    DayWords[Tuesday] := 'Tuesday   ';
    DayWords[Wednesday] := 'Wednesday';
    DayWords[Thursday] := 'Thursday ';
    DayWords[Friday] := 'Friday    ';
    DayWords[Saturday] := 'Saturday ';
    DayWords[Sunday] := 'Sunday    ';
        {Demonstrate how it works.}
    for Today := Monday to Sunday
        do writeln ('Today is ', DayWords[Today]);
            ↓       ↓       ↓       ↓       ↓
Today is Monday
Today is Tuesday
Today is Wednesday
Today is Thursday
Today is Friday
Today is Saturday
Today is Sunday
```

The same method also simulates the input of user-defined ordinal values. Begin by reading in the string, then search through the string table for an equal (i.e. identical) string. The index of that stored string is the ordinal constant equivalent to the input string. In chapter 13 we'll see how to use files as an easier way to initialize the array.

**Interaction
between
Arrays**

The array is such a handy structure that several array-type variables will frequently appear in a single program. Our next problem doesn't call for any new programing techniques, but it requires us to combine some methods we've already learned.

> Write a program that counts the occurrences of all letter pairs in a sample of text. Disregard differences between lower- and upper-case letters. Summarize the program's findings.

For example, the word *draft* contains four letter pairs: *dr, ra, af,* and *ft.* Obviously, the great number of possible pairs—26*26, or 676— is the reason we'll have to summarize output in some manner. A first refinement of the problem gives us:

> **while not** *eof*
> > *count the pairs;*
> > *print part of the pair count table;*

Counting letter pairs isn't all that different from counting single characters. Previously, we incremented the elements of a one-dimensional array subscripted by *char* values. *CharacterArray*['p'], for example, held the number of times the character 'p' had appeared in input. Why not keep track of letter pairs with a two-dimensional array? Suppose we define a type *PairArray* like this:

> **type** *PairArray* = **array** ['a'..'z', 'a'..'z'] **of** *integer*;

The element subscripted by ['a','a'] will hold the number of times the pair 'aa' has been encountered. How will we get the two subscript values? Well, we'll have to keep a moving window, two characters wide, on the input sample. We used this technique several times in program *Gerunds.* We can refine *count the pairs* to:

read the first character;
while not *eof*
> *read the second character;*
> *update element* [*first character, second character*] ;
> *advance the window—first character gets the value of the second character;*

This pseudocode is still too rough. The problem statement requires us to treat upper- and lower-case characters equally. Have we? Our next refinement will have to allow for character conversion, and include a provision for ignoring non-letter characters as well.

Let's start worrying about output. The array of type *PairArray* will have 676 elements, each representing the number of times one letter pair has appeared. Since we won't want to print them all, it seems reasonable that we print, say, the hundred letter pairs that occur most often.

The easiest way to find them is to use an **insertion sort** algorithm. It requires an array of 100 elements, each capable of storing a letter pair, and the number of times it's occurred. Starting with the smallest-valued element (the least-frequent pair), find the first pair that appeared more often than the new entry. Insert the new entry in place, and move all the other elements down. If an insertion is made, the least-frequent-pair element gets bumped off the end of the array.

In practice, the ordered-elements array is usually defined to have one extra element. It serves as a 'bumper' at the end of the array, letting us use an ordinary **while** loop to inspect each element without running past the array's end. We'll discuss the problem in more detail in the Antibugging section.

What exactly will we print? The number of times each pair occurred will be meaningless without the total number of pairs. So, let's report on the total number of pairs found, and give the individual pair figures as a percentage of the total. We can refine our pseudocode once more as:

initialize the pair counting and ordering arrays;
read the first character;
while not *eof*
    read the second character;
    if *it's a capital then convert it to lower case;*
    if *the first and second characters are both lower case*
       then *update element* [*first character, second character*] ;
    advance the window—first character gets the value of the second character
for *every element of the PairArray-type variable*
    insert it in an ordered array;
for *every element of the ordered array*
    print the letter pair, and its relative frequency;
print the total number of pairs counted

Program *Doubles* implements this pseudocode. We've given it the contents of this entire section (less programs) as input.

```
program Doubles (input, output) ;
    {Computes the frequency of letter pairs in a text sample.
    Prints the hundred most frequent pairs.}

type PairArray = array ['a'..'z', 'a'..'z'] of integer;
    ShortString = array [1..2] of char;
    PairData = record
                    Pair: ShortString;
                    Number: integer
                 end;
    OrderArray = array [0..100] of PairData;

var ch1, ch2: char;
    Pairs: PairArray;
    Ordered: OrderArray;
    Total, Current: integer;
```

```
procedure Initialize (var Pairs: PairArray;  var Ordered: OrderArray);
   {Initialize Pairs and Ordered to 0's.}
   var ch1, ch2: char;
       i: integer;
   begin
      for ch1 := 'a' to 'z'
         do for ch2 := 'a' to 'z'
            do Pairs[ch1, ch2] := 0;
      for i := 0 to 100
         do Ordered[i].Number := 0
   end;  {Initialize}
procedure BuildThePairsTable (var Pairs: PairArray;  var Total: integer);
   {Counts the occurrences of each character pair.}
   var ch1, ch2: char;
   function DeCapitalized (Capital: char): char;
         {Represents its capital argument as a lower-case letter.}
      begin
         DeCapitalized := chr(ord('a') + (ord (Capital) − ord ('A') + 1));
      end;  {DeCapitalized}
   function BothValid (ch1, ch2: char): boolean;
         {Represents true if both arguments are lower-case letters.}
      begin
         BothValid := (ch1 in ['a'..'z']) and (ch2 in ['a'..'z'])
      end;  {BothValid}
   begin  {BuildThePairsTable}
      ch1 := ' ';
      Total := 0;
      while not eof
         do begin
            read (ch2);
            if ch2 in ['A'..'Z'] then ch2 := DeCapitalized(ch2);
            if BothValid(ch1, ch2)
               then begin
                  Pairs[ch1, ch2] := Pairs[ch1, ch2] + 1;
                  Total := Total + 1
               end;  {if}
            ch1 := ch2
         end  {while}
   end;  {BuildThePairsTable}
procedure Insert (Current: integer;  var Ordered: OrderArray;
               HowMany: integer;  ch1, ch2: char);
   {Insert a new element into position Current in Ordered}
   var i: integer;
   begin
      for i := 99 downto Current
         do Ordered[i+1] := Ordered[i];
      Ordered[Current].Pair[1] := ch1;
      Ordered[Current].Pair[2] := ch2;
      Ordered[Current].Number := HowMany
   end;  {Insert}
```

```
procedure PrintTheTable (Ordered: OrderArray; Total: integer);
    {Prints the contents of Ordered}
    var Counter: integer;
        Subtotal: real;
    begin
        Subtotal := 0.0;
        for Counter := 1 to 100
            do begin
                write (Ordered[Counter].Pair, (Ordered[Counter].Number/ Total)*100:4:2, '%   ');
                Subtotal := Subtotal+(Ordered[Counter].Number);
                if (Counter mod 6) = 0 then writeln
            end;
        writeln;
        writeln ('Output represents', (Subtotal/ Total)*100:4:2, '% of ', Total:1, ' pairs.')
    end;   {PrintTheTable}
begin   {Doubles}
    Initialize (Pairs, Ordered);
    BuildThePairsTable (Pairs, Total);
    for ch1 := 'a' to 'z'
        do for ch2 := 'a' to 'z'
            do begin
                Current := 100;
                while (Ordered[Current].Number< Pairs[ch1, ch2]) and (Current>0)
                    do Current := Current-1;
                if Current<100 then Insert (Current+1, Ordered, Pairs[ch1, ch2], ch1, ch2);
            end;  {for}
    PrintTheTable (Ordered, Total)
end.   {Doubles}
```

```
        ↓           ↓           ↓           ↓           ↓
th  2.37%   in  2.20%   fj  2.00%   re  1.79%   he  1.73%   ar  1.70%
er  1.66%   te  1.55%   or  1.52%   nt  1.46%   fs  1.43%   es  1.28%
en  1.28%   ra  1.26%   on  1.20%   al  1.15%   an  1.11%   st  1.11%
ou  1.06%   fc  1.03%   at  1.03%   ng  1.03%   to  0.99%   ha  0.97%
ct  0.94%   ri  0.94%   ay  0.92%   ti  0.92%   of  0.87%   me  0.85%
le  0.84%   nd  0.84%   co  0.81%   it  0.81%   ed  0.79%   rr  0.75%
is  0.73%   rd  0.73%   ro  0.72%   ur  0.69%   se  0.68%   ca  0.63%
ea  0.61%   be  0.61%   pr  0.60%   ve  0.60%   de  0.59%   do  0.58%
ty  0.58%   om  0.57%   ta  0.57%   et  0.55%   un  0.55%   ac  0.55%
da  0.54%   oo  0.54%   tt  0.54%   io  0.52%   ch  0.51%   tr  0.51%
ll  0.50%   rs  0.50%   ec  0.48%   as  0.47%   ne  0.47%   am  0.46%
el  0.46%   mp  0.46%   us  0.46%   jd  0.44%   ce  0.44%   ot  0.42%
ns  0.41%   tu  0.41%   ho  0.41%   si  0.40%   va  0.40%   we  0.40%
ut  0.39%   so  0.37%   pe  0.35%   ts  0.35%   um  0.35%   em  0.35%
di  0.34%   ef  0.33%   ue  0.32%   la  0.32%   pa  0.32%   pu  0.32%
hi  0.31%   li  0.31%   rt  0.31%   ex  0.31%   fi  0.31%   im  0.31%
ly  0.30%   bl  0.30%   fo  0.30%   gi  0.30%
Output represents 73.62% of 23694 pairs.
```

12-3
Antibugging
and
Debugging

WHEN IT COMES TO BUGS, THE ARRAY STRUCTURE can be relied on to separate the engineers from the poets. Although dealing with single array elements is usually mastered in short order, the systematic processing that most arrays require involves thinking on a different (and sometimes inaccessible) wavelength entirely. In other words, don't be too alarmed if you feel that you just weren't cut out to understand arrays. You may not have been.

A basic source of misunderstanding in dealing with structured variables is the difference between the name of a type, and the name of a variable. The following mistake is quite common. A programer defines a type . . .

```
type Housing = (House, Hotel, Vacant);
     Name = packed array [1..20] of char;
     Property = record
                   Address: Name;
                   Rent: real;
                   Buildings: Housing;
                    : etc.
                end; {Property}
     Board = array [1..24] of Property;
var GameBoard: Board;
```

. . . and then accidentally refers to the *type* identifier instead of a *variable* identifier in the program:

```
Board[22].Address:= 'Boardwalk         ';
{The variable identifier GameBoard should have been used.}
```

....
:   Type identifiers *never* appear in the statement part.   :
....

If you see a type identifier in an assignment statement or procedure call, you can be sure it's up to no good.

Certain bugs inevitably turn up during array processing. A classic problem that's been the subject of many articles involves searching an array for a value that might not be present. For example, suppose we define a variable *TheArray* as an **array** [1..20] **of** *integer.* The following program segment is intended to find the subscript of the stored value 0 (zero).

```
Counter := 1;
while TheArray[Counter]<>0
   do Counter := Counter +1;
writeln ('A zero is stored at subscript ', Counter:1);
```

This code works perfectly if 0 is actually stored somewhere in *TheArray.* If it isn't, though, we'll eventually try to see if *TheArray*[21] equals 0. Since there is no such location—*TheArray* only has 20 elements—the program crashes with a message like this:

ABNORMAL TERMINATION - - SUBSCRIPT OUT OF RANGE

The message indicates that a run-time error occurred because the array subscript is out of its valid range 1..20. A correct program segment would include a check to ensure that *Counter* never exceeds 20. What do you think of this version?

```
Counter := 1 ;
while (Counter<20) and (TheArray[Counter]<>0)
    do Counter := Counter +1 ;
writeln ('A zero is stored at subscript ', Counter:1) ;
```

Suppose that *TheArray* still doesn't contain a zero, or holds a zero in element 20. In either case, the segment's output will be:

```
A zero is stored at subscript 20
```

As you can see, we've escaped the frying pan only to find ourselves in the fire. Another test has to be added to the end of the segment to make sure that we've really found the zero.

```
Counter := 1 ;
while (Counter<20) and (TheArray[Counter]<>0)
    do Counter := Counter +1 ;
if TheArray[Counter]=0
    then writeln ('A zero is stored at subscript ', Counter:1)
    else writeln ('No zeros.') ;
```

> Leaning over too far backwards is as bad as falling on your face. Make sure that you don't search past the end of an array, but be wary of finding something that you weren't looking for.

Ordinal subranges can cause a special kind of problem if the programer isn't careful. The following definition sets the stage for the bug:

```
type Letters = 'A'..'Z'
     CountArray = array [Letters] of integer;
var LetterCount: CountArray;
    CurrentPosition: Letters;    etc.
```

Suppose we want to travel through the array and inspect each element (with procedure *Inspect*) until a variable or function named *SomethingHappens* is *true*, or until we reach the end of the array. Will this program segment work?

```
CurrentPosition := 'A' ;
repeat
    Inspect (LetterCount[CurrentPosition]) ;
    CurrentPosition := succ(CurrentPosition)
until SomethingHappens or (CurrentPosition>'Z') ;
```

Not if we try to assign *CurrentPosition* the successor of 'Z'. Any assignment that causes *CurrentPosition* to exceed its subrange crashes the program with a message like:

```
ABNORMAL TERMINATION - -
OUT-OF-RANGE ASSIGNMENT TO VARIABLE "CURRENTPOSITION"
```

Will this change make the program work?

> *CurrentPosition* := *pred*('A') ;
> **repeat**
>   *CurrentPosition* := *succ*(*CurrentPosition*)
>   *Inspect* (*LetterCount*[*CurrentPosition*]) ;
> **until** *SomethingHappens* **or** (*CurrentPosition*='Z') ;

No. The value *pred*('A') represents falls outside the *Letters* subrange as well. As before, we need an extra **if** test to make the loop work.

> *CurrentPosition* := 'A'
> *Inspect* (*LetterCount*[*CurrentPosition*]) ;
> **if not** *SomethingHappens*
>   **then repeat**
>   *CurrentPosition* := *succ*(*CurrentPosition*) ;
>   *Inspect* (*LetterCount*[*CurrentPosition*])
>   **until** *SomethingHappens* **or** (*CurrentPosition*='Z') ;

Potential bugs shouldn't discourage you from using ordinal subranges (or arrays). However, subranges and arrays both tend to generate off-by-one errors that could easily be avoided by checking entry and exit conditions.

Arrays of two or more dimensions are sometimes confusing. One common problem comes from using too many nested loops to inspect an array. Suppose, for example, that we have a two-dimensional array and want to examine the values stored along one of its diagonals— *TheArray*[1,1], *TheArray*[2,2], etc. An intuitive, but incorrect, solution uses two **for** loops. Suppose we have an array whose dimensions are 1..*Last* and 1..*Last*.

> **for** *Row* := 1 **to** *Last*
>   **do for** *Column* := 1 **to** *Last*
>   **do** *Examine* (*TheArray*[*Row*, *Column*]) ;   etc.

This program calls *Examine* for *every* value stored in *TheArray*. A correct version requires only a single loop, regardless of the diagonal being searched. The opposite diagonal is searched with:

> **for** *Mark* := 1 **to** *Last*
>   **do** *Examine* (*TheArray*[*Mark*,(*Last*—*Mark*)+1]);   etc.

Frequently we'll want to compare an array element to its neighbors. If we're at element i,j, we'll be looking at $i-1, j-1$, $i-1, j$, $i-1, j+1$, $i, j-1$, $i, j+1$, $i+1, j-1$, $i+1, j$, and $i+1, j+1$. There's nothing particularly difficult about cycling through an array to make the check for every i, j pair. However, not every element *has* a neighbor on every side! Trying to check the neighbors of an element on any side row or column will cause a subscript error.

> Think about the boundary conditions of searches, especially when you're dealing with border locations.

A piece of debugging folk wisdom we passed along some time ago has a special application when dealing with arrays. We said that 'when you're sure everything is right and the program still doesn't work, then one of the things you're sure of is wrong.' This is particularly true when array subscripts are being computed. Now, an incorrect subscript won't always cause a program crash—it might just cause incorrect results. If a program performs strangely for inexplicable reasons, it's a good idea to look at subscript values during execution.

writeln ('Subscripts before the call of DoSomething are: ',
        Computed(*i*), *Margin*/ *Border* −1, *Row∗ Column*) ;
   {This output statement was added for debugging.}
DoSomething (*TheArray* [*Computed*(*i*), *Margin*/ *Border* −1, *Row∗ Column*]) ;

It's amazing how often an inspection like this solves the mystery.

One point about passing large structures (like arrays) as parameters is worth mentioning, even though it seldom has an effect on your programing practice. It has to do with the storage space required by value- and variable-parameters.

> A value-parameter is a *copy* of its argument. Any variable, regardless of its structure, is duplicated in its entirety.

As you might imagine, this can cause problems when very large data structures (like big arrays) are passed as value-parameters. Although computers can hold a great deal of data, storage space is finite. With this in mind, programers sometimes pass large data structures as variable-parameters, *even if they have no intention of changing the structure's contents within the procedure.*

> A variable-parameter is a *re-naming*, or aliasing, of its argument. It requires a minimal amount of storage space, and doesn't really depend on the size of its argument variable.

Unfortunately, using this trick subverts the protection provided by value-parameters. A programer too concerned about conserving storage space may find herself making unexpected changes in global variables.

> The Golden Rule of Space
> A program that works and uses a lot of space is better than one that very efficiently doesn't work at all.

An exceptionally sneaky bug can happen when we use a **with** structure to examine the record-type elements of an array. Suppose that we have an array of 100 elements, and want to examine an element whose *Sum* field is nonzero (we're sure that one exists). Will this code work?

```
Count := 1;
with TheArray[Count]
   do begin
      while Sum=0 do Count := Count+1;
         :
      manipulate other TheArray[Count] fields
   end;
```

No, it won't. Instead, if *TheArray*[1].*Sum* equals 0, the **while** loop will never be exited.

> ### The Golden Rule of **with** Structures
>
> The specific record that a **with** structure has access to cannot be changed during the structure's action. It is determined when the structure is first entered.

The code above must be modified like this:

```
Count := 1;
while TheArray[Count].Sum=0
   do Count := Count+1;
with TheArray[Count]
   do begin
         :
      manipulate the TheArray[Count] fields
   end;
```

Summary

The array structure is used to store many values of any ordinal, *real*, or structured type. An array type definition includes the type's identifier, the type of the array's *elements*, and the number and type of *dimensions* the array will have.

Array bounds belong to any ordinal type. They can be stated in two ways—either by naming the actual bounds (separated by two dots), or by naming the bounds' type. When there's more than one pair of bounds, they're separated by commas. The array-types they help define are *one-dimensional*, two-dimensional, three-dimensional, etc.

An array variable's elements are accessed by location, rather than by name. The array-variable's name is followed by a particular *subscript* between square brackets. One value is given per dimension, and any representation of a value may be used—even an expression or a value that is itself stored in an array. 'Complete' array assignments can be made between two variables of identical array types. Aside from such assignments, however, an array's elements must be assigned, read in, and output one at a time.

An option of array definitions called *packing* lets us create arrays with special features. One common class of packed arrays are called *strings*; each is a **packed array** [*dimensions*] **of** *char*. String-type variables can be compared with the relational operators, output in their entirety using *write* or *writeln*, and assigned type-compatible (rather than type-*identical*) values. Thus, we can assign text constants to string variables, as long as the text constant has the same number of characters as the array has elements.

As we write more complicated programs, the design of data structures assumes an importance equal to the formulation of algorithms. Because of the influence a data structure has on the rest of a program, it's invariably a good idea to use techniques like *lateral thinking* to help formulate alternative data structures while your program is still in its planning stages. Consider how each structure will affect input and output of data, implementation of an algorithm, extension of your program's capabilities, and the general difficulty of getting your program up and running.

			New Pascal
array	**of**	**packed**	[..]	**New Terms**

elements	*dimension*	*array bounds*
one dimensional	*subscript*	*computed subscript*
random access	*packing*	*string*
inductive leap	*selection sort*	*bubble sort*
lateral thinking	*insertion sort*	

Self-Test Exercises

12-1 How can the dimensions of an array be defined?

12-2 Can the values stored in an array be arrays? Give two different examples.

12-3 Suppose that we define an array type like this:

> **type** *StoredArray* = **array** [1..10] **of** *integer*;
> *StoringArray* = **array** [1..10] **of** *StoredArray*;

Assume that a variable of type *StoringArray* is called *DataBank*. Which of these assignments to *DataBank* is correct?

> *DataBank* [3] [4] := 200;
> *DataBank* [3, 4] := 200;

12-4 Which of the problems listed below require arrays for an elegant solution?

a) Find the (alphabetically) least word in a series of words.

b) Compute the sum of a series of numbers.

c) Find the second largest number in a sequence of input numbers.

d) Read in exactly two hundred numbers, and sort them in decreasing order.

e) Read in as many as two hundred numbers, and print all the numbers that fall within a certain range.

12-5 What kind of arrays can be compared for equality? Must the arrays be of identical types?

12-6 A word-processing program requires you to store up to one hundred words. The longest word is eight characters long. Define a suitable data structure.

12-7 Suppose that you are using a selection sort to put an array of *integer* values into ascending order. Which of the starting sequences shown below will require the most updates? The fewest? How many will they require?

$$
\begin{array}{lllllllllll}
a) & 10 & 9 & 8 & 7 & 6 & 5 & 4 & 3 & 2 & 1 \\
b) & 10 & 1 & 9 & 2 & 8 & 3 & 7 & 4 & 6 & 5 \\
c) & 2 & 3 & 4 & 5 & 6 & 7 & 8 & 9 & 10 & 1 \\
d) & 1 & 10 & 2 & 9 & 3 & 8 & 4 & 7 & 5 & 6 \\
e) & 5 & 4 & 3 & 2 & 1 & 10 & 9 & 8 & 7 & 6 \\
\end{array}
$$

12-8 Suppose that you have an array as defined and declared below. Initialize the odd-subscripted elements (*List* [1], *List* [3], etc.) to 'O', and the even-subscripted elements to 'E'. Use a single **for** loop, and no **if** structures.

> **type** *Storage* = **array** [1..50] **of** *char*;
> **var** *Letters*: *Storage*;

12-9 Assume that *Series* is an array of records, subscripted by a subrange of *integer*. What is the output of the following code? Are we making an assignment to the *Current* or *Current*+1 record inside the **with** structure?

> *Series* [*Current*]. *Initial* := 'A';
> **with** *Series* [*Current*]
>   **do begin**
>   *Current* := *Current* + 1;
>   *Initial* := 'B'
>   **end**;
> *Current* := *Current* − 1;
> *writeln* (*Series* [*Current*]. *Initial*);

12-10 Suppose that a checkerboard is represented with an 8 by 8 array of *boolean*, and that every occupied position is marked *true*. At present, position *Board* [*Row, Column*] is occupied. The code below is intended to find if any other squares in the same row or column are also occupied. What bug does the segment contain?

> *AlsoOccupied* := *false*;
> **for** *Counter* := 1 **to** 8
>   **do if** *Board* [*Row, Counter*] **then** *AlsoOccupied* := *true*;
> **for** *Counter* := 1 **to** 8
>   **do if** *Board* [*Counter, Column*] **then** *AlsoOccupied* := *true*;

12-11 A magic square is an *n* by *n* array of the *integer* values 1 through n^2. The values of each row and column, and the main diagonals, have the same sum. Write a function that inspects an *n* by *n* magic square, and verifies that it contains the proper numbers for potential magic squaredom. (However, you need not add up each row, column, or diagonal.) Assume that the maximum value of *n* is passed as an argument to your function, and is no more than ten.

More Exercises

12-12 Check reconciliation is the process of comparing a list of checks that have been written against a list of those that have been cashed and returned. The object is to find the number and amount of checks that haven't been cashed (or checks that were cashed for the wrong amount), as well as a current bank balance.

Write a program that reconciles a checking account. Construct a starting 'data base' by taking a beginning balance, and the number and amount of each check written. Then, accept as input the number and amount of each check cashed and returned. Design data structures for two situations: *a*) all check numbers are known in advance to fall within a particular range; *b*) check numbers aren't known in advance. However, don't bother sorting input, and write only one program.

12-13   Charting sales, prices, investments, etc. is a common business computing application. However, careful thought must go into the chart's design if it's going to be readable, and fit on a page or screen. An appropriate scale must be determined, symbols and labels must be decided on, and, above all, the chart had better not come out sideways.

Write a general-purpose set of graphing routines. Assume that some rule' for generating data points will be provided further down the line. Within reason, your routines should be able to compute an appropriate number of data points and scale them. The user should also be able to specify the orientation of the horizontal and vertical axes.

12-14   Most charts are used to compare several sets of data points, rather than show one group by itself. For instance, business programers are often called on to produce a single chart that compares product sales, profits, or stock prices. Write a program that plots more than one set of data points on a single graph, possibly rotated as above. Use a different symbol for each quantity, and some neutral symbol when two or more data points are identical.

12-15   Although Pascal is supposed to be an international programing language, all its reserved words and pre-defined identifiers are in English. This feature has not been welcomed in certain countries. To help foreign sales of *Oh! Pascal!*, write a program that takes a Pascal program as input, and substitutes non-English equivalents for all its reserved words and pre-defined identifiers. Be sure to ignore words that appear as text output or constants, or within comments.

12-16   Sam Loyd tells a story about the Russian army at the time of the Russo-Japanese war. It seems that 20 regiments were in a continuous process of formation. The first had 1,000 men, the second had 950, the next 900, and so on down to the twentieth regiment, which garrisoned only 50. During each week, 100 men were added to each regiment, and at week's end, the largest regiment was sent to the front.

Apparently, the commander of the fifth regiment was a wonderful chess player. To delay his eventual trip to the front, the general of the army (who happened to be his chess partner) sent him only 30 new recruits each week. Write a program that tells which regiment is sent to the front each week, shows the status of the remaining regiments, and determines exactly how long it takes for the chess-playing commander to go to the front.

12-17   When writing card-game programs, it's often convenient to define a record type that represents a single card, and then to have an array of 52 cards serve as a deck. When the deck is initialized, though, it's invariably in order of number or suit. How can a programed deck of cards be shuffled?

Two solutions immediately present themselves. The first is to travel along the array, and exchange the current card with the card at a random subscript between 1 and 52. The second idea is similar to the first, except that we don't choose cards from the already-shuffled portion of the deck. Thus, we exchange the first card for one between 1 and 52, the second for a card between 2 and 52, and so on.

If you're mathematically inclined, you'll see that the first shuffling method produces 52 to the 52nd power different hands, while the second results in 52 factorial hands. Do both methods produce fair shuffles? Write a program that simulates the shuffling of a very small deck of cards, and test or prove your theory.

12-18   Suppose that we have a four-by-four checkerboard. How can ten checkers be arranged on the board (disregarding the rules of checkers) so that the largest number of horizontal, vertical, or diagonal rows contain an even number of checkers? How many such rows are there?

12-19   Here's a problem in array searching. Represent the illustration below as a two-dimensional array. Now, starting at any 'R', how many paths can be followed to spell out 'RADAR'? Don't forget the 'R's on the diagonals, and in the center.

```
R A D A R
A D A R A
D A R A D
A R A D A
R A D A R
```

(Hint: To avoid falling off the edge of the array, store blanks all around the edges of a 7 by 7 array.)

12-20   In *transposition ciphers*, a message is encrypted by having its letters rearranged in a regular manner. For example, if we write Ambrose Bierce's remark that 'patience is a minor form of despair disguised as a virtue' like this:

```
P a t i e n c e
i s a m i n o r
f o r m o f d e
s p a i r d i s
g u i s e d a s
a v i r t u e .
```

we can read the vertical columns as through they were words in a sentence:

Pifsga asopuv taraii immisr eiorst nnfddu codiae eress.

Write a program that will encode and decode plain text in this fashion. Try to make the coding algorithm more sophisticated—perhaps by reading diagonal columns, or by having a secret key that controls the order that columns are read in. Be sure that your code is very well documented!

12-21   In *The Cloven Viscount*, Italo Calvino tells how the Viscount Medardo of Terralba suffered the misfortune of being split in half by a cannonball. The two halves (one good, and the other bad) survived, but underwent many trials before being reunited.

Some years later Medardo found himself in charge of guarding a field that looked very much like a checkerboard. Medardo put two soldiers in two of the four 'squares' closest to the center, and arrayed fourteen others in different squares around the field. However, he arranged all the soldiers in such a way that, if a cannonball happened to fly horizontally, vertically, or diagonally across the field, no more than two soldiers would be hit. (You see, he wanted to minimize the odds that any of them would suffer the same fate he had.) How were the sixteen soldiers posted?

12-22   An old-time flat of eggs held 64 eggs, arranged in a square. Suppose that an otherwise empty flat already holds two eggs in corners diagonally opposite each other. How many more eggs can be put into the flat without having more than two eggs in any horizontal, vertical, or diagonal row?

12-23   Write procedures or functions to perform these string handling tasks.

a)   Determine if the non-blank portions of two strings are longer than the maximum length of the string.

b)   Concatenate two strings to form a third.

c)   Extract a string from within a string. Pass as parameters the original string, the starting position in it, the length of the portion to be extracted, and the new string.

d) Insert a string within a string. Pass the original string, the replacement string, and a starting position within the original. Be sure to preserve the remainder of the original string.

e) Do an insertion like the one above, but dispose of the remainder of the original string.

f) See if a string is a sub-string of another string.

12-24   The game *Life* was developed by a mathematician named John Conway. It's intended to provide a model of life, death, and survival among simple organisms that inhabit an *n* by *m* board. The current population of the board is considered to comprise one generation. There are only three rules, as follows: 1) every empty cell with three living neighbors will come to life in the next generation; 2) any cell with one or zero neighbors will die of loneliness, while any cell with four or more neighbors will die from overcrowding; 3) any cell with two or three neighbors will live into the next generation. All births and deaths occur simultaneously.

Why is *Life* a game? Well, it turns out that although some starting populations die out quickly, others form interesting patterns that repeat, grow, or move across the board as they go from generation to generation. Write a program that plays *Life*. Let the program user specify the locations of the starting population, as well as the number of generations that should be shown as output.

12-25   In a gambling game called *Treize* a deck of cards is shuffled, then laid face up one at a time. As the cards are dealt, the dealer counts 'One, two, three...' etc., up through Jack, Queen, and King. The count is repeated four times. Bets can be placed on whether or not a dealt card's value will coincide with the value spoken by the dealer.

Write a program that calculates the chances of making a match. 'Chances' can be described as the number of shuffles that allow at least one match, divided by the complete number of potential shuffles. However, it's not necessary to work with a complete deck of 52 cards. Start with a deck of two cards, and increase the deck size one card at a time until the difference between two deck-sizes is less than .001.

12-26   The game of Nim and its many variations should be familiar to you. The players start with several rows of markers, and take turns removing some number of markers from any row. The player who goes last either wins or loses.

Write a program that plays a perfect game of Nim. Starting positions, the maximum number of markers that can be removed in a turn, who goes first, and which turn wins should be optionally supplied by the player.

12-27   Write an interactive soccer program. This is a program that can be endlessly refined and improved, so set definite goals (ha!) for yourselves. A first version should let two users move two players around a small field, checking for collisions, running into walls, and the like.

A second version can introduce the soccer ball. Improve your graphics output, and allow five 'players' per team. Allow kicking of the ball.

In version three, start to make the game more realistic. Keep track of the strength of players (which should affect their running and kicking ability). Allow scoring and out-of-bounds kicks.

Version four—the sky's the limit. Implement injuries, penalties, and the like. Stop work on the program while you still have a chance.

12-28   Bring the array into your new language. Is an equivalent to the reserved word **of** really necessary? How might it help or hinder the programer? Can you think of any operations that are frequently performed on arrays (like matrix multiplication) that might be pre-defined in your language?

UNITED STATES NAVY

BUTLER JAMES RODNEY · AVN RADIOMAN 3C · USNR · IOWA
BUTSKE RICHARD R · SEAMAN 2C · USN · CALIFORNIA
BUXTON NORMAN A · TORPEDOMAN'S MATE 3C · USN · MASS
BYARS ELVIN · SEAMAN 1C · USN · CALIFORNIA
BYERS WILLIS C · MOTOR MACHINIST'S MATE 2C · USN · ARKANSAS
BYKLUM BENNIE · SEAMAN 1C · USN · MINNESOTA
BYRNE WALTER P · SEAMAN 2C · USN · PENNSYLVANIA
CABASE ISAAC · STEWARD 1C · USN · PHILIPPINES
CADDIGAN THOMAS E · SEAMAN 2C · USNR · MAINE
CAHALAN FRANK R · CHIEF COMMISSARY STEWARD · USN · VIRGINIA
CAIN JOSEPH · AVN ORDNANCEMAN 3C · USNR · TEXAS
CAIRNS ALEXANDER E · LIEUTENANT (JG) · USNR · TEXAS
CALDABELLA BENO JOSEPH · AVN RADIOMAN 3C · USNR · NY
CALHOUN BILL B · SEAMAN 1C · USNR · ALABAMA
CALHOUN HAROLD O · CHIEF WATER TENDER · USN · ILLINOIS
CALLAHAN JAMES A · SEAMAN 1C · USN · IOWA
CALLAHAN THOMAS N · SEAMAN 2C · USN · NORTH CAROLINA
CALLAHAN WILLIAM P · SIGNALMAN 3C · USN · PENNSYLVANIA
CALPIN CORNELIUS M · SEAMAN 2C · USN · NEW YORK
CAMERON WILLIE J · SEAMAN 1C · USNR · GEORGIA
CAMMARATA WILLIAM A · SEAMAN 1C · USNR · PENNSYLVANIA
CAMPAGNA DOMINIC J · AVN RADIOMAN 3C · USNR · CALIFORNIA
CAMPBELL SAMUEL R · STEWARD'S MATE 2C · USNR
CAMPBELL CLIFFORD R · AVN ORDNANCEMAN 2C · USN · ILLINOIS
CAMPBELL CURTIS A · SOUNDMAN 2C · USN · TEXAS
CAMPBELL MYNEIL W · SEAMAN 1C · USNR · GEORGIA
CAMPBELL LEWIS R · SEAMAN 2C · USN · PENNSYLVANIA
CAMPBELL THOMAS R · SEAMAN 1C · USNR · SOUTH CAROLINA
CAMPIONE PELLEGRINI D · WATER TENDER 1C · USN · WEST VIRGINIA
CANNON CLYDE CECIL · SEAMAN 2C · USN · NEW JERSEY
CANNON JOHN J · ELECTRICIAN'S MATE 2C · USNR · PA
CANNON WALTER T · GUNNER'S MATE 3C · USNR · N C
CANTRELL LAWRENCE HAROLD · YEOMAN 2C · USN · N C
CANTRELL OSCAR H · ENSIGN · USNR · GEORGIA
CARUTO CONRAD · FIREMAN 3C · USN · NEW YORK
CARATZOLA VINCENT J · FIREMAN 3C · USN · NEW YORK
CARBONE ALEXANDER · FIREMAN 3C · USN · MASSACHUSETTS
CARDWELL WALTHIN M H · FIREMAN 1C · USNR · LOUISIANA
CAREY FRANCIS W · COXSWAIN · USNR · MASSACHUSETTS
CAREY HAROLD C JR · LIEUTENANT (JG) · USN · VIRGINIA
CAREY JOSEPH HOWARD · SEAMAN 2C · USN · NEW YORK
CARLIN WILLIAM D · RADIO TECHNICIAN 3C · USNR · ILLINOIS
CARLSON WILLIAM E · SEAMAN 1C · USNR · CONNECTICUT
CARMAN ORVILLE EMERY · MACHINIST'S MATE 1C · USN · N DAK
CARNES HAROLD J · SEAMAN 1C · USNR · MASSACHUSETTS
CAROTA LOUIS JR · AVN RADIOMAN 3C · USNR · NEW JERSEY
CARP EDWARD JOSEPH · SEAMAN 2C · USN · MICHIGAN
CARR QUENTON E · SEAMAN 1C · USNR · NORTH CAROLINA
CARROLL FENTON PAUL · SEAMAN 2C · USNR · VIRGINIA
CARROLL JOHN J · LIEUTENANT (JG) · USNR · MICHIGAN
CARSON EDWARD G · SEAMAN 1C · USN · OHIO
CARTER CLAYTON L · SIGNALMAN 1C · USNR · GEORGIA
CARTER HAYDEN BELOIS · FIREMAN 1C · USN · NORTH CAROLINA
CARTER JOE R · LIEUTENANT (JG) · USNR · TENNESSEE
CARTER RALPH W · SEAMAN 1C · USNR · ILLINOIS
CARTER ROY W · SEAMAN 2C · USNR
CARTY JOSEPH A · SEAMAN 1C · USN · WEST VIRGINIA
CARUSONE GAETANO · SHIP'S COOK 3C · USNR · MASSACHUSETTS
CARVALHO MANUEL · SEAMAN 2C · USNR · RHODE ISLAND
CASE FRANK D JR · LIEUTENANT (JG) · USN · ILLINOIS
CASE KENNETH A · COXSWAIN · USNR · ILLINOIS
CASEY ROBERT LEE · SEAMAN 2C · USN · VIRGINIA
CASH LESTER K · SHIPFITTER 1C · USN · ARKANSAS
CASNELL FREDERICK E · ENSIGN · USN · RHODE ISLAND

United States Armed Forces War Memorial, Battery Park, New York City. Photo courtesy James D. Jordan.

13

Files and Text Processing

There's a lot of metaphor in computer terminology. Words are used, not because they're exact, but because they're familiar. One example is the term *file*. In real life, a file is a collection of papers that belong in a file folder hanging in a file cabinet. In Pascal, a file is a particular type of variable. Both sorts of file can be read, written, saved, or thrown away.

Although Pascal file variables can be used to store values of any given type, files of characters (often saved permanently) present the most interesting problems and applications. Such files are called *textfiles*, and are discussed in section 13-1. In section 13-2, we'll look at some practical applications of textfiles.

Section 13-3 looks at the notion of a file in general. In it we discuss details of file manipulation, and consider files of ordinal and structured types besides *char*. As always, there's an Antibugging section at the end of the chapter.

We're at a disadvantage in writing files....How can we possibly insert something at the beginning, or in the middle?

[339]

13-1
Making and
Using
Textfiles

GARBO SPEAKS! LET'S SAVE HER FIRST SCREEN words for posterity in a file named *Garbo*.

```
program GarboSpeaks (Garbo, output);
    {Creates a textfile.}
type text = file of char;
var Garbo: text;
begin
    rewrite (Garbo);
    writeln (Garbo, 'Gimme a viskey, and don'' be stingy.')
end.  {GarboSpeaks}
```

....
A *file*-type variable stores a sequence of any number of **component** values (except other files).
....

The syntax chart of a file-type definition is:

file *data structure*

```
type ——→ identifier ——→ = ——⌈——————————→ text ——————→——⌉——→ ;
                              └→ file of ——→ component type identifier──┘
```

A general notion of files should be familiar to all of us by now, since computer systems rely on the idea of files as storage places. File-type variables can be used to create or gain access to permanently stored files (so-called **external** files), or to create files that only last for the duration of program execution (*internal* files). External and internal files are identical except for the requirement that external files be passed as *file parameters* in a program heading (as *Garbo* is above).*

Program *GarboSpeaks* stores *char* components in an external file named *Garbo*. The identifier *Garbo* turns up four times in the program.

....
1. Program heading. Permanent, external files must be named in the program heading as *file parameters*. The order of file parameters doesn't matter.
....

Just as a procedure's parameters are a connection to the program it operates in, file parameters set up lines of communication between a program and its environment. That's why most programs have *input* and *output* given as file parameters.

....
2. Variable declaration. Every file variable, whether it is internal and temporary, or external and permanent, must be declared before it can be used in a program. (*Input* and *output* are exempt from this rule.**)
....

* Some systems may require special control cards to access external files.
** Other predefined files, that do not have to be declared as variables, are frequently included as an extension to Pascal.

In this section we're going to concentrate on files of *char* values, also called **textfiles**. To accommodate special treatment of such files, a structured type *text* is predefined in Pascal. Its definition:

type *text* = **file of** *char*;

is a built-in part of every program (just like the definitions of the ordinal types *boolean* and *char*). As a result, the definition of *text* in *GarboSpeaks* was redundant and unnecessary—it was already defined.

> 3. Procedure *rewrite.* A call of *rewrite* creates an empty file. Any data currently in the file is destroyed.

Since a program may contain several files, the file we want prepared for writing is given as a parameter of *rewrite*:

    rewrite(*Garbo*);   {Prepare to write file *Garbo*.}
    rewrite(*f*);   {Prepare to write file *f*.}

If we want to, we can rewrite any file entirely, because another call of *rewrite*(*f*) removes the contents of the parameter file.

> 4. Procedures *write* and *writeln.* When a file identifier is given as the first parameter of *write* or *writeln*, program output is sent to that file.

Program output normally goes to the standard file *output*, usually a terminal screen or lineprinter. Output can be directed to a file-type variable instead by naming the file *each time* we call *write* or *writeln.*

    writeln (*f, SomeVariable, Another,* 'Que pasa?', *AConstant*);
    writeln (*g, V1, V2:3:4*);

These calls send output to files *f* and *g.* Note that we can specify the field width of output values, and that textfiles are divided into lines. To put three blank lines into *Garbo*, we'd say:

    writeln (*Garbo*);
    writeln (*Garbo*);
    writeln (*Garbo*);

> The values of any predefined simple type may be written to (stored in) a textfile.

We can also write text values and string (**packed array** [*index*] **of** *char*) values, since they're both sequences of characters. In fact, only values of user-defined ordinal types *can't* be stored in textfiles, since they have no external character representations. In section 13-3 we'll see how to define file variables that can store such values.

Q. What are the final contents of *SampleFile* after *Mistakes* is executed?

program *Mistakes* (*SampleFile*, *output*) ;

var *SampleFile*: *text*;

begin
    rewrite (*SampleFile*) ;
    write (*SampleFile*, 'Once, long ago, I thought I made a mistake.') ;
    rewrite (*SampleFile*) ;
    writeln (*SampleFile*, 'Unfortunately, I found out that I was wrong.')
end.   {*Mistakes*}

A. The second call of *rewrite*(*SampleFile*) is an error. It erases the current contents of *SampleFile*, and starts us with a blank file. The final contents of *SampleFile* are 'Unfortunately, I found out that I was wrong.'

**Reading
From
Files**

It's time at last to murmur the magical incantation 'Let's have the computer analyze the data.'

    program *Analyze* (*output, Data*) ;

    var *Data*: *text*;
        Fact: *integer*;
        :   {other variable declarations}

    begin
        reset (*Data*) ;
        while not *eof*(*Data*)
          do begin
            read (*Data, Fact*) ;
            if *Fact*<25 **then**   etc.
          :   {Program continues its analysis.}
    end.   {*Analyze*}

Like *Garbo*, *Data* is an external file, named in the program heading. And, like any file, it must be declared as a variable within the program. However, *Data* contains information to be read. It must be handled differently from a file that's being written.

> The standard procedure *reset* puts us at the beginning of a file, ready to read its first value.

As we said earlier, a program may contain several file variables. The file we want to begin reading must be passed as a parameter to *reset*:

      reset(*Data*) ;   {Get ready to read from *Data.*}
      reset(*g*) ;   {Get ready to read from *g.*}

Another call of *reset* (with the same parameter) puts us back at the file's beginning. As a result, we can read the file all over again, but must begin with its first component. A single file can be read and written (but never at the same time) within a single program. All that are required are appropriately placed calls of *reset* and *rewrite*.

> When the name of a textfile is given as the first parameter of *read* or *readln*, input is read from that file.

The standard *input* 'file' (keyboard or card reader) usually supplies a program's input. However, we can read data from a different source by naming it each time *read* or *readln* is called. For example:

> read (*DataFile, First, Second, Third*) ;
> {Read values of *First, Second,* and *Third* from *DataFile.*}
> readln (*g, V1, V2*) ;

The first input statement reads the values of three variables from *DataFile.* The second statement reads the values of *V1* and *V2* from the file variable *g*, then gets rid of any more values stored on the same line (the typical usage of *readln*).

> Functions *eoln* and *eof* can each be given a single file name as an argument. *eoln's* argument must be of type *text.*

> **while not** *eof*(*AnyFileName*)
> **do**   etc.

> **if** *eoln* (*AnyTextFile*)
> **then**   etc.

What kinds of values can be read from a textfile? Intuitively it would seem that only *char* input can be read from a file of type *text.* However, we can read data of *any* standard type from a textfile, because it's stored as a sequence of *char* values.

When you sit at a terminal and enter data of any type, you send *char* values. to the computer. When the computer expects to read *integer* or *real* values, it automatically converts the characters into values of the proper type. In a similar sense, even though values might differ *within* a program—*integer* is *integer, char* is *char,* and never the twain shall meet—they're stored in textfiles as characters. A program can read an *integer* value from a textfile as easily as it can read it from a keyboard or punched card.

There are three Golden Rules of using file-structured variables.

> ## The Golden Rules of File Variables
> Assignments cannot be made between two file-structured variables, even if they're both of the same type (such as *text*).
> File variables are either being generated (if *rewrite* was called), or inspected (if *reset* was called) — never both.
> File-type variables must always be passed to variable-parameters, even if they're not changed within a subprogram.

The first rule's effect is to preclude shortcut methods of making two files identical. A file's contents must be read and written one value at a time. The prohibition against passing files as value-parameters is an indirect consequence of this rule.

Self-Check Questions

Q. Suppose that a file named *Storage* contains the following data:

> **10 First Reading**
> **20 Second Reading**
> **30 Third Reading**

What will the output of program *WillItWork* be?

```
program WillItWork (output, Storage);
var Storage: text;
    Value: integer;
begin
    reset (Storage);
    readln (Storage, Value);        writeln (Value);
    read (Storage, Value);          writeln (Value);
    readln (Storage, Value);        writeln (Value)
end. {WillItWork}
```

A. Its output is unexpected. It is:

```
↓          ↓          ↓          ↓          ↓
10
20
ABNORMAL TERMINATION - -
ERROR IN TYPE OF INPUT - - INTEGER EXPECTED.
```

What happened? Well, the first input statement (using *readln*) read the value **10**, and discarded the characters remaining on the rest of the line. The second statement (using *read*) read **20** *without* moving on to the next line. When the final input statement tried to read an *integer* value, it mistakenly read the non-*integer* value **Second** into the *integer* variable *Value*, and caused a crash.

Applications of TextFiles

What are some advantages of textfile structures over fixed-size structures like records and arrays? The most important feature is that the size of files is not fixed. Although the bounds of an array or the fields of a record must be defined in advance, a file can grow almost indefinitely. When a program must store an unknown quantity of data, a file is the data structure of choice.

Files allow permanent storage of program data. The success of programs that require substantial amounts of input is easily threatened by mistakes in data entry. As a defensive programing mcasurc, data can be placed in a file, and a separate program or procedure written to error-check the file's contents. If the data is correct, the file can be reset and fed to the program proper. If it's incorrect, the program halts so that its data-file can be edited and fixed. You are left with a file of data entries that's known to be error free.

Files also have disadvantages in comparison to other structures.

....
: The information stored in a file cannot be accessed at random.   :
....

Suppose that we want to read the last value stored in a file. Calling the *reset* procedure puts us at the file's beginning. We must read all the way through the file to reach the end—there's no way to jump there automatically.

We're at a similar disadvantage in writing files. The procedure *rewrite* puts us at the beginning of a blank file. Once *rewrite* has been called, we can only add data to the file's *end* (because when a file is empty, its beginning and end are essentially the same). How could we possibly insert something at the beginning, or in the middle, of a file? Calling *rewrite* again erases all we've already written.

Naturally, there are shortcuts we can take to alleviate some of these problems. Since textfiles are divided into lines, we can jump from line to line (via *readln*) without bothering to peruse each line's contents. Suppose that we've created a file of fortunes, one per line. Procedure *FortuneCookie*, below, takes as parameters a textfile and a line number. It locates, and prints, the fortune found at that line.

```
procedure FortuneCookie (var Fortunes: text; LineNumber: integer);
    {Prints line LineNumber of FortuneCookie.}
    var CurrentLine: integer;
        NextCharacter: char;
    begin
        CurrentLine := 1;
        reset (Fortunes);
        while CurrentLine < LineNumber
            do begin
                readln (Fortunes);
                CurrentLine := CurrentLine + 1
            end;
        while not eoln (Fortunes)
            do begin
                read (Fortunes, NextCharacter);
                write (NextCharacter)
            end;
        writeln
    end;   {FortuneCookie}
```

↓ ↓ ↓ ↓ ↓

```
Help!  I'm a prisoner in a fortune-cookie factory!
```

Notice that *Fortunes* must be passed as a variable-parameter, since it's a file-structured variable.

The problem of file insertions can be solved with temporary internal files. These aren't included in the program heading since they, like ordinary program variables, don't exist before or after the program is run. Internal files are often used as *buffers*, or temporary holding places, while editing other files. The most basic file insertion is to put one file at the beginning of another.

> The word *concatenate* means to link together in a series or chain. Files are concatenated by being joined into a longer single file.

The idea of concatenation might also be applied to strings—the concatenation of 'simple' and 'minded' is 'simpleminded'. Suppose that we want to concatenate files *Beginning* and *Ending* into *Beginning*. *Beginning* will end up with its original contents followed by those of *Ending*. There is an almost overwhelming temptation to put the following pseudocode into effect.

> *prepare to read Beginning*;
> *read it until eof (Beginning)*;
> *prepare to write Beginning*;
> *prepare to read Ending*;
> *add the contents of Ending to Beginning*;

However, we shall resist the temptation, because preparing to write *Beginning* will destroy its contents. Instead, we'll have to take the round-about route the pseudocode below suggests:

> *prepare to write file Temporary*;
> *prepare to read Beginning*;
> *concatenate Beginning to Temporary*;
> *prepare to read Ending*;
> *concatenate Ending to Temporary*;
> *prepare to write Beginning*;
> *prepare to read Temporary*;
> *concatenate Temporary to Beginning*;

Notice that the first and third concatenations are really just file copy moves, because we're concatenating an empty file to one that isn't empty. The implemented program is shown below.

```
program JoinFiles (Beginning, Ending, output);
   {Demonstrates file concatenation.}
var Beginning, Ending, TemporaryFile: text;
procedure Concatenate (var ToFile, FromFile: text);
   {Adds the contents of FromFile to the end of ToFile.}
   var CurrentCharacter: char;
   begin
      reset (FromFile);
      while not eof(FromFile)
         do begin
            while not eoln (FromFile)
               do begin
                  read (FromFile, CurrentCharacter);
                  write (ToFile, CurrentCharacter)
               end;
            readln (FromFile);
            writeln (ToFile)
         end
   end; {Concatenate}
begin
   rewrite (TemporaryFile);
   Concatenate (TemporaryFile, Beginning);
   Concatenate (TemporaryFile, Ending);
   rewrite (Beginning);
   Concatenate (Beginning, TemporaryFile)
end. {JoinFiles}
```

Self-Check
Questions

Q. Suppose that the segment below is the statement part of *JoinFiles*, and that all files mentioned have been validly declared. What is its effect?

```
begin
   reset (File2);
   reset (File4);
   reset (File1);
   rewrite (File0);
   reset (File3);
   Concatenate (File0, File1);
   Concatenate (File0, File2);
   Concatenate (File0, File3);
   Concatenate (File0, File4);
   rewrite (File4);
   Concatenate (File4, File0)
end.
```

A. The program concatenates files *File1, File2, File3,* and *File4* into *File4*. *File0* serves as the temporary, internal file.

Focus on
Programing:
A Hard
Program

Although our next example demonstrates an application of files, it's also important as an exercise in program comprehension. Suppose we are faced with the following problem:

We are given a deck of playing cards, stored in a file named *PartialDeck.* Were we to read *PartialDeck,* it would begin like this:

Ten of Spades Four of Hearts Queen of Hearts

and continue for a total of fifty-one cards. Our job is to write a program that finds the missing card.

This is a task that's easy for a person, but is difficult for a computer. After all, almost any human knows what a deck of cards is, and can design a simple search strategy that yields the missing card. A typical approach would be to pile up all the aces, deuces, etc., and then look for the stack containing only three cards. The missing one can be spotted almost instantly.

A computer, on the other hand, possesses an excellent memory (good enough to remember each card as it is read in), but has no idea of what playing cards are. Our first step in solving the problem might simply be to redefine our givens, using appropriate computer terminology where necessary.

First of all, a deck of cards consists of 52 pairs of values—every possible combination of thirteen number values and four suit values. Second, we have a textfile that contains 51 *triples* of nonblank strings—the number of a card, the word 'of', and the card's suit. This puts us in position for a second step—proposing a program outline.

Explain to the computer what a deck of cards is by 'giving' it a full deck.
Read in cards from our partial-deck file, and...
Mark them off on the computer's list of a full deck.
Search the computer's list for the card that wasn't found.

Essentially, we're planning to read in each card and tick it off of a master list of cards. The only card *not* checked off is missing.

At this point we have to ask a hard question: What is an appropriate data structure for representing a deck of cards? Given the adaptability of Pascal, there are many possible answers. Prime considerations for a very *good* answer are that the deck be easy to create, and that it be easy to use later in the program when we begin reading in card values from the partial-deck file.

When we designed a data structure for Hunt the Wumpus we faced a similar problem. Our response was to use a lateral thinking approach—roughing out a data structure and then looking ahead for input, output, or scorekeeping problems that it might cause. We did the same thing on our way to proposing the structures defined below:

```
type String = packed array [1..8] of char;
     Card = record
                 Number, Suit: String;
                 Found: boolean
            end;
     Deck = array [1..52] of Card;
var FullDeck: Deck;
```

Some typical assignments to a variable of type Deck would be:

```
FullDeck[13].Number := 'Four    ';
FullDeck[13].Suit := 'Spades  ';
FullDeck[13].Found := false;
```

Two features of this data structure deserve special attention. The advantages of defining *FullDeck* as an array structure should be obvious—we're able to easily traverse the entire deck while loading it, or searching for a particular card. This quick sequence of statements can eventually be used to find the missing card—the only card whose *Found* field is *false*:

```
Counter := 1;
while FullDeck[Counter].Found
   do Counter := Counter+1;
     {Increment Counter until the Found field is false.}
```

A more subtle advantage is gained by defining the *Number* and *Suit* fields as strings. We're exploiting the fact that our program data comes in a textfile, and that string values are easily compared. Suppose we have a *String*-type variable called *NextWord*, and that we've read the first word in the partial-deck file into *NextWord*—say it's 'Five'. We can find the first 'Five   ' stored in *FullDeck* with:

```
Counter := 1;
while FullDeck[Counter].Number <> NextWord
   do Counter := Counter+1;
```

Now that we've defined a basic data structure, we'll take an unusual step. Program *FindTheLostCard* is shown on the next two pages. Instead of developing it from the top down, though, we'll explain it from the bottom up, procedure by procedure. We have two main reasons:

1. We specified the data structure independently of a full-scale stepwise refinement of the problem. When the working mechanism of a program is intimately tied to its structure(s), making or understanding a refinement can depend on *prior* knowledge of the program's type definitions.

2. Although an algorithm may be clear, details of its implementation can be complex. Knowing the algorithm won't necessarily enable you to follow the program.

We'll learn about *FindTheLostCard* by seeing what it does. As we go along, we'll start to understand how and why it works.

[349]

```pascal
program FindTheLostCard (output, PartialDeck);   {Finds a missing pattern in a text file.}
type String = packed array [1..8] of char;
     Card = record
                  Number, Suit: String;
                  Found: boolean
              end;
     Deck = array [1..52] of Card;
var PartialDeck: text;
    FullDeck: Deck;
procedure GetAWord (var TheFile: text;  var TheWord: String);   {String input procedure.}
   const BlankWord = '        ';          {8 blank spaces.}
   var Counter : integer;
        CurrentCharacter: char;
   begin
        TheWord := BlankWord;          {Initialize TheWord}
        repeat   {Skip leading blanks.}
           read (TheFile, CurrentCharacter)
        until CurrentCharacter<>' ';
        Counter := 1;
        repeat   {Read in the word.}
           TheWord[Counter] := CurrentCharacter;
           Counter := Counter +1;
           read (TheFile, CurrentCharacter)
        until (CurrentCharacter=' ') or (Counter>8)
   end;   {GetAWord}
procedure InitializeTheDeck (var FullDeck: Deck);   {Initializes every field of FullDeck.}
   var Counter: integer;
        NumberFile, SuitFile: text;
        NumberWord, SuitWord: String;
   begin
        rewrite (NumberFile);
        rewrite (SuitFile);
        writeln (NumberFile, 'Ace Deuce Three Four Five Six Seven');
        writeln (NumberFile, 'Eight Nine Ten Jack Queen King');
        writeln (SuitFile, 'Spades Hearts Clubs Diamonds');
        reset (NumberFile);
        reset (SuitFile);
        GetAWord(NumberFile, NumberWord);
        for Counter := 1 to 52
           do begin   {Load the aces, deuces, etc.}
              GetAWord(SuitFile, SuitWord);
              FullDeck[Counter].Number := NumberWord;
              FullDeck[Counter].Suit := SuitWord;
              FullDeck[Counter].Found := false;
              if ((Counter mod 4)=0) and (Counter <52)   {After the four cards}
                 then begin                               {of each numerical value ...}
                    reset (SuitFile);           {...go to the beginning of the Suit file, and...}
                    GetAWord(NumberFile, NumberWord)   {...get the next card number.}
                 end
           end {for}
   end;   {InitializeTheDeck}
```

```
procedure InspectTheCards (var FullDeck: Deck; var PartialDeck: text);
   {Read PartialDeck and update Found fields in FullDeck}
   var CardCount, PositionCounter: integer;
      NextWord: String;
   begin
      reset(PartialDeck);
      for CardCount := 1 to 51
         do begin
            PositionCounter := 1;          {Start trying to match at the first card.}
            GetAWord(PartialDeck, NextWord);          {Get the 'number' word.}
            while (FullDeck[PositionCounter].Number< > NextWord)
               do PositionCounter := PositionCounter +1;   {Match the 'number' word.}
            GetAWord(PartialDeck, NextWord);   {Get rid of the 'of'.}
            GetAWord(PartialDeck, NextWord);   {Get the 'suit' word.}
            while (FullDeck[PositionCounter].Suit< > NextWord)
               do PositionCounter := PositionCounter +1;   {Match the 'suit' word.}
            FullDeck[PositionCounter].Found := true   {Mark the card found.}
         end
   end;   {InspectTheCards}
procedure FindTheMissingCard (FullDeck: Deck);
   {Locate the element of FullDeck not marked Found}
   var Counter: integer;
   begin
      Counter := 1;
      while FullDeck[Counter].Found
         do Counter := Counter +1;
      with FullDeck[Counter]
         do writeln ('The missing card is the ', Number, ' of ', Suit)
   end;   {FindTheMissingCard}
begin
   InitializeTheDeck(FullDeck);
   InspectTheCards(FullDeck, PartialDeck);
   FindTheMissingCard(FullDeck)
end.   {FindTheLostCard}
```

↓   ↓   ↓   ↓   ↓

**Ten of Spades Four of Hearts Queen of Hearts Queen of Clubs Six of Clubs
Jack of Hearts Seven of Spades Three of Diamonds Nine of Clubs Nine of
Diamonds Ace of Diamonds King of Hearts King of Clubs Five of Spades
Eight of Spades Six of Spades Four of Spades Eight of Hearts Seven of
Clubs Five of Hearts Jack of Spades Deuce of Clubs Jack of Clubs Five of
Diamonds Ace of Spades Queen of Spades Ace of Clubs Seven of Diamonds
Three of Clubs Deuce of Hearts Ten of Hearts Queen of Diamonds Eight of
Clubs Six of Hearts King of Spades Ten of Clubs Ten of Diamonds Four of
Diamonds Deuce of Spades Nine of Spades Nine of Hearts Three of Spades
Four of Clubs Three of Hearts Seven of Hearts Deuce of Diamonds Six of
Diamonds Five of Clubs Ace of Hearts Eight of Diamonds King of Diamonds**

```
The missing card is the Jack    of Diamonds
```

We'll begin our bottom-up analysis with *GetAWord*. It is a basic textfile procedure, designed to read a *String* value (*TheWord*) from any textfile (*TheFile*). Notice that padding with blanks is the first order of business, simplified by the definition of *BlankWord*, a constant that consists of eight blank spaces.

GetAWord makes a basic assumption about words—that they do not contain blanks. Thus, the first **repeat** loop skips past any leading blanks, blank lines, or end of line markers that may be in front of the first word. When a nonblank is found, the second **repeat** loop reads characters into *TheWord* until *eof*, or until a trailing blank indicates that we've reached the end of the word or line.

GetAWord makes a safety check on the length of words. Attempting to assign a value to *TheWord*[9] would cause a crash as *TheWord*, by the definition of type *String*, only has index values 1 through 8. However, the procedure simply truncates the input string. The ninth character is lost.

Procedure *InitializeTheDeck* tells our program what a deck of cards is. It uses internal files to sidestep a lengthy series of assignments in initializing the array variable *FullDeck*. *FullDeck* is loaded in the following pattern: the first stored card, *FullDeck*[1], is the Ace of Spades, then *FullDeck*[2] is the Ace of Hearts, followed by the Aces of Clubs and Diamonds. With the fifth card, *FullDeck*[5], we begin the pattern again, storing the Deuces of Spades, Hearts, Clubs, and Diamonds. As the loading loop progresses, it sets each *Found* field to *false*.

How do the internal files fit in? *NumberFile* holds the words that express the number values of files—'Ace', 'Deuce', 'Three', etc. *SuitFile* consists of the suit words 'Spades', 'Hearts', 'Clubs', and 'Diamonds'. The procedure begins by getting the first words of *NumberFile* and *SuitFile*. After pairing these words in *FullDeck*[1], the next suit is obtained, and used to initialize *FullDeck*[2]. Then we get the next suit, and the next. After four cards have been created (when *Counter* **mod** 4 = 0), we read the next number word from *NumberFile*, and go back to the beginning of *SuitFile* by resetting it. The process continues until all 52 cards have been initialized.

Note that we could just as easily have initialized *FullDeck* in suit-order, i.e. all the Spades, then Hearts, etc. Why did we decide to go with number-order? We can discover the reason by analyzing *InspectTheCards*. The algorithm it follows is simplicity itself—given an initialized *FullDeck*. First, we find a card's number, then its suit, then we mark it *Found*.

InspectTheCards begins by reading the first word of *PartialDeck*. As we know this is a number word (perhaps 'Deuce', or 'Queen') we search through *FullDeck* for an identical *Number* field. Then we call *GetAWord* again, to get rid of the second string in *PartialDeck*—the word 'of'. This accomplished, we read in the third word—the card's suit word—and begin to search *FullDeck*, starting with our current position, for an equal *Suit* field. Given a suit match, we mark the card found. The process is repeated until we've checked in 51 cards.

Are there any potential problems with our implementation of this algorithm? The basic flaw in our procedure is its lack of error-checking—the entire program is not robust. What happens if *PartialFile* contains a word that is neither a number, suit, or 'of'? The program will crash as it attempts to inspect *FullDeck* [53]. A better version of *InspectTheCards* would print out the unmatchable string, *along with an error message warning that subsequent program results might be wrong.*

FindTheMissingCard is the simplest procedure in the program. The missing card will be the only card that hasn't been checked in, i.e. for which *FullDeck* [*Counter*]. *Found* is *false.* Our decision to represent our data in string form pays off here, because we're able to output the value of the missing card directly.

SECTION 13-1 DEALT SOLELY WITH FILES of *char.* However, we can define and declare file variables that store values of *any* structured or simple type, except another file type. For example:

13-2
Files of Simple and Structured Types

```
type Card = record
                :  {Definition of Card's fields}
            end;
     CardFile = file of Card;
     Color = (red, blue, green, yellow);
     ColorFile = file of Color;
     NumberFile = file of real;
var Cards: CardFile;
    Numbers: NumberFile;
    Colors: ColorFile;
    OneCard: Card;
    OneNumber: real;
    OneColor: Color;
```

As *text* is the only predefined file type, we have to explicitly define types *CardFile, NumberFile,* and *ColorFile.*

> The values stored in a file are the file's **components**. Their type is the file's **component type**.

The components of file *Cards* are records of type *Card*; the component type of file *Colors* is the ordinal type *Color*, etc. File components are stored according to the Pascal compiler's method of internal representation (which we'll explain soon), and usually cannot be read, printed, or created except with a Pascal program.

Access to files is handled by the standard (predefined) procedures *get* and *put.* Using these procedures requires an understanding of the *file window.* It's sort of a built-in variable that represents the component stored—or about to *be* stored—at the current file position.

....
A file is a sequence of component values. The current file position
is marked by a *file window*. The file window's identifier is the
name of the file, followed by an up-arrow (↑) or caret (^).
....

(We'll always use the up-arrow.) In effect, the file window contains the file component we're about to read. This helps explain how
eoln and *eof* work. If the *input* file window *input*↑ holds the end-of-line
or end-of-file marker, then function *eoln* or *eof* is *true.*

Every file access (even with *read* and *write*) uses the file window
as a buffer, or intermediate storage place, between the computer and
the actual file. To read a value from a file, we really 'get' the next
value into the file window, and then read the file window. To write a
value to a file, we assign the value to the file window, and then 'put'
the window into the file.

....
The procedure call *get(f)* assigns the next component of file *f* to
the file window *f*↑. Any current value of *f*↑ is discarded.
....

As you might imagine, calling procedure *reset* implicitly involves
a call of *get.* The call:

$$reset(FileName) ;$$

essentially tells the compiler:

> *go to the beginning of FileName*;
> *get(FileName)* ;

The file window *FileName*↑ now represents the first component of
FileName. Procedure *read* also uses *get.* The statement *read (f, X)* is
equivalent to:

$$X := f↑ ;$$
$$get (f) ;$$

The call of *read* gets the value of X from a file named $f.$ The
equivalent pair of statements first assign X the current value of the file
window, then give the next value in file f to $f↑$.

Finally, we can describe the effect of *readln(f)*, where f is a
textfile, as:

> **while not** *eoln(f)*
> **do** *get(f)*
> *get(f)* ;

The current line is discarded, and the file window is left at the beginning of the next line (or at *eof* if there isn't a next line).

Output to file variables uses the other file-access procedure, *put.*

....
The procedure call *put(f)* adds the current value of *f*↑ to the end
of file *f.*
....

Thus, *put* is always used after an assignment to the file window, and sometimes after a call of *rewrite*. The standard output procedure *write* also uses *put*. The call *write* (*f, X*) is the equivalent of:

$$f\uparrow := X;$$
$$put\ (f)\ ;$$

The call of *write* adds the value of *X* to the file named *f*. The statements above assign the file window the value of *X*, then place this value at the end of file *f*.

> The standard procedures *write* and *read* can be used with files of any type, but if their file argument is not of type *text*, only one component argument may be given. Procedures *readln* and *writeln* may only be used with textfiles.

The statements *read* (*f, a, b, c*), *readln* (*f*), *write* (*g, a, b, c*), and *writeln* (*g*) are all illegal unless *f* and *g* are files of type *text*.

Earlier we said that file components are stored according to the compiler's method of internal representation. We'll explain that now. As you probably know, computer systems store values in a code of zeros and ones that is designed or chosen by the compiler writer. Certain codes (like ASCII and EBCDIC) used for showing characters are standardized, and Pascal compilers are required to translate internal representations into standard *external* representations for output of *char, boolean, real,* and *integer* values. If universal codes weren't available, each computer would need special keyboards, terminals, line-printers, etc., that could understand the compiler's storage code.*

User-defined ordinal values and structures are *not* required by Pascal to have external character representations. A compiler need not decode them into ordinary characters for input and output, or even allow them to be output in any form. Some compilers extend Pascal by giving character representations to ordinal data values—these compilers allow input and output of all ordinal values by automatically encoding and decoding them. Most compilers, though, aren't so generous. If you create a file of *Color* (as above), and manage to inspect it using a text editor, you'll find a meaningless (to us) file of binary values.

real and *integer* values provide a dramatic illustration. When they're input or output from *text* files (or the standard files *input* and *output*), they are given a character representation. However, when they're stored in a variable whose type is **file of** *real*, the internal, binary representation is used. Thus, while a *text* file of *real* values is readable (to a human), a *real* file of *reals* is not.

Files of types *real, integer,* and *boolean* are used for three main reasons—speed, size, and accuracy. Because values stored in such files need not be accessed and encoded or decoded individually, input and output of a program's data base can proceed quickly. Secondly, the

---

* In fact, IBM has been accused of devising the EBCDIC code for this very reason.

compiler's coding system can store these types in an extremely compact manner—for example, it might store *false* and *true* as *0* and *1*. Finally, stored *real* values tend to degrade slightly after repeated translations from internal to external representation and back. Insofar as possible, their accuracy is maintained by storing them in *real* files.

The convenience of automatic conversion between *char* and internal representation of *real* and *integer* values causes a problem with end-of-file checks. Suppose that *f* is a textfile, and that *Data* is an *integer* or *real* variable. The statement *read* (*f, Data*) is equivalent to:

$$\textbf{while } f\uparrow = '\ '$$
$$\textbf{do } get(f)\ ;$$
$$\textit{assign the next value to Data};$$

This means that blank spaces and new-lines are skipped before the numerical value is read. After the value is read, the file window *f*↑ holds the character that immediately follows it.

What happens when there are trailing blanks at the end of a file? *f*↑ is a blank, so *read* skips it, and any blanks that follow. In the process, it tries to *get* the end-of-file character, which causes a program crash. As a result, this convenient scheme for reading and processing data won't work:

$$\textbf{while not } eof(f)$$
$$\quad \textbf{do begin} \qquad \{\text{Will crash trying to read past end-of-file.}\}$$
$$\qquad read\ (f, Data)\ ;$$
$$\qquad process\ (Data)$$
$$\quad \textbf{end};$$

In Chapter 7 we said that reading numerical data on a line-by-line basis would only work when the only trailing blank in an input file was the last end-of-line character. Our problem, then, is to write a procedure that skips blanks until a nonblank character is found, or until *eof*(*f*) is *true*. Although it has often been proposed as a solution, the program segment below won't work. Can you figure out why not?

$$\textbf{while not } eof(f) \textbf{ and } (f\uparrow = '\ ')$$
$$\quad \textbf{do } get(f)\ ; \qquad \{\text{This segment doesn't work either.}\}$$

> The file window is undefined when *eof* is *true*. It's an error to try to inspect it.

An error occurs when *eof*(*f*) is *true*, because *f*↑ will be inspected when the expression is fully evaluated.

A correct procedure *SkipBlanks* is shown below. It uses nested **if** statements and an auxiliary variable to avoid the error of reading an undefined file window.

```
procedure SkipBlanks (var f: text);
    {Skips blanks until eof(f), or a nonblank is found.}
    var Finished: boolean;
    begin
        Finished := false;
        repeat
            if eof(f)
                then Finished := true
                else if f↑ = ' ' then get(f)
                                 else Finished := true;
        until Finished
    end;   {SkipBlanks}
```

SkipBlanks should be included in any program that reads *real* or *integer* values from a textfile. It's called prior to any invocation of procedure *read*:

```
{Model for reading and processing numerical values from textfiles.}
SkipBlanks (f);
while not eof(f)
    do begin
        read (f, Data);
        process (Data);
        SkipBlanks (f)
    end;
```

:··:

Q. The procedure shown below sums all the *integer* values in file *Numbers.* Assume that the definition of *NumberFile* is:

$$\text{type } NumberFile = \textbf{file of } integer;$$

Is a procedure like *SkipBlanks* necessary? Why or why not?

Self-Check Questions

```
procedure Sum (Numbers: NumberFile);
    {Sum the components of Numbers.}
    Current, Total: integer;
    begin
        Total := 0.0;
        reset (Numbers);
        while not eof(Numbers)
            do begin
                read (Numbers, Current);
                Total := Total + Current
            end;
        writeln ('The sum of the values is ', Total:1 )
    end;   {Sum}
```

A. The components of *NumberFile* are *integers,* and are stored according to the compiler's method of internal representation. There are no blanks or end-of-lines in *NumberFile,* because they're *char* values. As a result, the value we're about to read is always the next stored *integer* (until we reach the end of the file). Skipping blanks is totally unnecessary.

:··:

Focus on
Programing:
File Merging

A common programing task is merging two files to form a third. We'll deal with the case of a file whose components are record structures, since it's a typical application. A file might consist of student records, employment records, vehicle records, sales records, etc. All that's important is that one field represent a name or number that can be the basis of ordering the entire file.

Suppose that we have two files of records that contain *Name* fields. Naturally, the *Name* field is a string-type—a packed array of *char* elements. The files (call them *Old* and *Current*) are currently in alphabetical order according to their *Name* fields. We want to merge them (into file *Merged*) while preserving their alphabetical order.

What will be involved? Imagine that you're merging two file cabinets by hand into a third (currently empty) cabinet. You open all the cabinets, and get the first record from each of the full ones. The alphabetically 'lower' of the two records goes into the third cabinet, another record moves up to replace it. The process of alphabetical comparison, moving, and replacing goes on until one of the original cabinets is empty. Then, since all the records in the remaining cabinet belong at the end of the large cabinet, and are in alphabetical order already, you move them into the large cabinet without making any comparisons.

A Pascal algorithm is much the same. We'll have to prepare *Old* and *Current* for reading, and *Merged* for writing. Then, we should see which file's first record's *Name* field is lower alphabetically. This record gets added to the *Merged* file. Naturally, we have to repeat this process until *Old* or *Current* is exhausted. In pseudocode we have:

> *prepare to write Merged;*
> *get the first records from Old and Current;*
> **while not** *the end of either Old or Current*
>   *add the lower record to Merged;*
>   *get the next record from that file;*
> *finally, add the non-empty file's remaining records to Merged;*

A slight addition to the algorithm will be to have the procedure report on its activities. Without such a message, a merger of two empty files—probably a mistake—would be quite acceptable. The **while** loop's action is easy to refine into Pascal. Let's assume that *Old's* present record is lowest.

> *OldCount* := *OldCount* + 1 ;
> *Merged*↑ := *Old*↑ ;
> **if not** *eof*(*Old*) **then** *get*(*Old*)
> *put* (*Merged*) ;

The completed procedure is shown below. Note the **case** structure that takes the place of a possibly confusing nested **if** structure. It's perfectly acceptable here, even if it does only control two alternative actions.

```
procedure MergeRecords (var Old, Current, Merged: FileType);
     {Merges Old and Current into Merged while preserving
     the alphabetical ordering of Name fields.}

   var OldCount, CurrentCount: integer;

begin
     OldCount := 0;
     CurrentCount := 0;
     reset (Old);
     reset (Current);
     rewrite (Merged);

          {Merge files until one of them is empty.}
     while not eof(Old) and not eof(Current)
          do begin
             case Old↑.Name< Current↑.Name of
                true: begin
                        OldCount := OldCount+1;
                        Merged↑ := Old↑;
                        if not eof(Old) then get(Old)
                     end;
                false: begin
                        CurrentCount := CurrentCount+1;
                        Merged↑ := Current↑;
                        if not eof(Current) then get(Current)
                     end
             end;   {case}
             put(Merged)
          end;   {while}

          {Flush the other file into Merged}
     while not eof(Old)
          do begin
             Merged↑ := Old↑;
             put(Merged);
             get(Old)
          end;
     while not eof(Current)
          do begin
             Merged↑ := Current↑;
             put(Merged);
             get(Current)
          end;
     writeln ('Merger of ', OldCount +CurrentCount:1, ' records complete.');
     writeln (OldCount:1, ' records from file Old.');
     writeln (CurrentCount:1, ' records from file Current.')
end;   {MergeRecords}
```

A final word about the file window will end our discussion. As we said earlier, the file window represents a value of the file's component type (unless it's empty). If the component type is structured, the file window can be used to access stored values. For example, assume the following definitions and declarations:

$$\text{type } StoredValues = \textbf{array } [1..100] \textbf{ of } real;$$
$$StoreFile = \textbf{file of } StoredValues;$$
$$\textbf{var } Storage: \ StoreFile;$$

Storage is a file that can hold many array components. Each array is capable of holding 100 elements. We'll access some elements of the fifth array stored in *Storage*. Naturally, we're assuming that *Storage* has at least five components.

```
reset (Storage) ;   {Does the first get.}
for i := 1 to 4
    do get(Storage) ;
Storage↑ [10] := 9.39E02 ;
Storage↑ [11] := Storage↑ [11] + Storage↑ [12] ;
writeln (Storage↑ [23]:4:8) ;   {We can use format controls.}
```

:·:

Self-Check Questions

Q. Can *read* and *write* be given file arguments whose type is not *text*? Could we have used *read* and *write* in procedure *MergeFiles*?

A. *read* and *write* (but not *readln* or *writeln*) may be given a file argument of any file type. However, although we could have used them in *MergeFiles*, we would have had to declare unnecessary auxiliary variables. The file window is so convenient that *write* and *read* are seldom used except for accessing textfiles.

:·:

13-3 Antibugging and Debugging

WE'VE SEEN AMPLE EVIDENCE THAT EACH structure has its own quirks, and tends to provoke certain errors. These mistakes usually occur in proportion to the severity of warnings against them—mild 'Bewares!' are usually heeded, but an absolute prohibition promotes a frenzy of crashes. Three common fatal errors that involve files are:

1. Attempting to inspect or read from a file that has not been *reset.*

2. Trying to generate or write to a file without first calling *rewrite.*

3. Reading past the end of a file.

The first two bugs are usually the result of oversight, or of inadvertently confusing *reset* and *rewrite.* Unfortunately, some errors of omission that are obvious to us aren't caught by the compiler, since they're syntactically correct. Although this program lacks a call of *reset(OutsideFile)*, it compiles (and crashes) perfectly well.

```
program DoesntRewrite (OutsideFile, output);
var OutsideFile: text;
begin
    writeln (OutsideFile, 'Hi there!')
end.
```

ABNORMAL TERMINATION - -
TEMP100937 NOT SET FOR WRITING

In some implementations, the run-time error message that's printed is of little help. In the example above, the computer printed its temporary, internal name for *OutsideFile*.

A related error that's hard to find is a misplaced *reset* or *rewrite*. Remember that *reset* puts us at the beginning of a file so that we can inspect it. *rewrite* presents us with an empty file, ready for writing. What program mistakes do you think caused these complaints?

'I'm not sure I'm reading the right file—I keep getting the same piece of input.'

'My program creates a file all right, but when I print the file it only contains the last piece of data I entered.'

Both bugs are probably the result of putting a *rewrite* or *reset* inside a loop that was supposed to write or read a file. The call should have been made just prior to entering the loop action.

The end-of-line function has always brought grief to Pascal programers. What's wrong with the following bit of code? It's supposed to echo the contents of *Source* to *SavedOutput*. We'll tell you that *Source* has no leading blanks on any line.

```
while not eof(Source)
   do begin
      while not eoln(Source)
         do begin
            read (Source, CurrentCharacter);
            write (SavedOutput, CurrentCharacter)
         end;
      writeln (SavedOutput)
   end;
```

This little piggie went to market;
 This little piggie stayed home.
 This little piggie had roast beef,   *etc.*

The partial contents of *SavedOutput*, shown above, give a broad hint: the second and third lines are indented by one space.

....
: The end-of-line character is a space that we're about to read when :
: *eoln* becomes *true*. :
....

Since we forgot to get rid of the space at the end of each input line (with a *readln* (*Source*), or even *read*(*Source, CurrentCharacter*)) it showed up at the beginning of the next output line.

Another *eoln* problem is caused by an outlandish, illegal, and quite common extension of Pascal.

> Some nonstandard Pascal implementations automatically remove trailing blanks from the end of every line of text. Other systems *add* blanks to the end of text lines.

If extra blanks appear at (or disappear from) the end of a text line, make sure that the system isn't responsible. This is one of the opportunities you'll get to blame a bug on the compiler, so enjoy it.

Getting an initial value for *eoln* sometimes causes problems in interactive programs. Suppose that this is the beginning of a program.

```
begin {main program}
    while not eoln
        do begin
            writeln ('Please give an opinion.');
            ProcessTheInput;
            :   etc.
```

> In many interactive Pascal implementations, *eoln* is undefined before the start of input.

As a result, the segment above hangs (without printing the prompt) until input begins. The prompt should have been output before the check of *eoln* was made. This isn't a problem with batch programs because, in effect, all input is ready and waiting at the start of execution.

(Some interactive Pascal systems that were based on the first definition of Pascal won't even allow this code:

```
begin {main program}
    writeln ('Please enter a number.');
    readln (TheNumber);
    :   etc.
```

This is because there's an implicit call of *reset*(*input*) at the beginning of the program. Now, *reset* is supposed to give the file window the first component value of the input file. However, the old Pascal standard specified that there would be no 'first value' until we entered one. As a result, the program would hang, waiting for us to enter a value—any value—so the reset can be completed. This put the programer in a *Through the Looking Glass* position of entering the data first, and getting the prompt later.)

Attempting to read past the end of a file is a more serious mistake. The next program segment is sure to fail, given the proper test input:

```
      reset (AnyFile);
   repeat
      DoSomethingWith (AnyFile)
   until eof(AnyFile);
```

An empty input file delivers the death blow, because *eof(AnyFile)* is *true* as soon as an empty file is reset.

....
:   Check for end-of-file *before* working with any file.   :
....

Some of the most annoying file bugs are manifested by disappearing lines, and (for interactive programs) an inexplicable need to type extra carriage returns. The root cause is often confusion about exactly what happens at the end of a line. The code below is supposed to read and partially print an input file, echoing the initial nonblank characters on each line. Try tracing it through by hand.

```
   while not eof
      do begin
         read (CurrentCharacter);
         if CurrentCharacter <> ' '
            then repeat
               write (CurrentCharacter);
               read (CurrentCharacter);
            until CurrentCharacter= ' ';
         readln;
         writeln
      end;
```

If every line begins with nonblanks, and ends with blanks, everything works fine. Suppose, though, that there *are* no extraneous blanks at the end of a line. When the inner loop is exited the value of *CurrentCharacter* is ' '—it is the end-of-line character. What happens when the *readln* is executed? The next line is thrown away. If the program is being run interactively, the user has to enter a extra carriage return (or else there is no next line to get rid of).

....
: Always make sure that textfile routines can handle these three spe- :
: cial cases: :
:   1. Blanks at the beginning of a line. :
:   2. Blanks at the end of a line. :
:   3. Lines that are empty. :
....

Since most line-reading bugs are related to mix-ups of *read* and *readln*, there's a real temptation to debug by trying minor variations.* Take it from us—it doesn't pay. You'll find yourself trading one bug for another.

* This is most common when good editing facilities and a lightly-loaded computer are available—why think about the right way to do something when you can make mistakes so quickly?

Textfile programs also frequently call for application of the programing uncertainty principle:

> If you're sure that everything is right, and the program still doesn't work, then one of the facts you're sure of is wrong.

The best antibugging technique is to print the file you're working on *as* you work on it. Make sure that you can explain every blank space or empty line that shows up, as well as every full line that *doesn't* appear.

Non-text files cause more trouble with syntax than semantics. The file window (the file's name followed by an up-arrow or caret) is, in effect, the name of a variable. Unfortunately, the up-arrow makes for unusual-looking identifiers. Suppose that we have a file of records. If each record has an array field, we might see these identifiers in a program:

TheFile	{Name of the file.}
TheFile↑	{The file window—the name of one record component.}
TheFile↑.*TheArray*	{An entire array field.}
TheFile↑.*TheArray* [10]	{One element of the array.}

Naturally, all assignments must involve values of an appropriate type.

TheFile can't be assigned to.
TheFile↑ may get a record of *TheFile's* component type.
TheFile↑.*TheArray* may get an array of *TheArray's* type.
TheFile↑.*TheArray* [10] may get any value of *TheArray's* element type.

Furthermore, remember that some actions that are all right with textfiles will not work with files of other component types. *eoln* may not be given a non-textfile argument; nor may *readln* or *writeln.* Also, when procedures *write* and *read* are used in conjunction with non-textfiles, they may only be given one additional argument. As a result, only a single component may be written to, or read from, a non-textfile at any one time.

Summary

A file is a sequential-access structure that can store any number of values of any given type. A file-type variable's stored values are called its **components**, and their type is the file's **component type**. The file type whose components are *char* values is predefined in Pascal as *text.*

Internal file variables, like other variables, last only for the duration of a program. *External* files are permanently stored by the computer. A program's external file variables must be given in the program heading as **file parameters**, and also declared as variables within the program.

When files are accessed, a **file window** is used—sometimes explicitly by the programer, and sometimes implicitly by standard procedures. The window's identifier is the file variable's name followed by an arrow (↑) or caret (^). A number of standard procedures take file identifiers as arguments. The standard procedure *get* assigns the next value in its argument file to the file window, while procedure ***put*** adds the value of the file window to its argument file.

File-type variables are either being inspected (read from) or generated (written to). They cannot be in both states at once. Procedure ***reset*** prepares a file for inspection. It positions the file window at the beginning of the file and performs the first *get.* A call of procedure ***rewrite*** erases any values stored in its argument file, and gives us an empty file ready for writing.

The standard procedures *eof, eoln, read, readln, write,* and *writeln* may also be given a file identifier as an argument. However, the file argument of *eoln, writeln* or *readln* must be of type *text.* The components of non-text files are stored according to the computer's scheme of internal representation. They're not required to have readable external representations as *char* values.

A common application of files is **concatenation**, or the linking together of sequences of data. A job like this usually requires the use of a ***buffer*** file as a temporary holding place for information.

file of	*reset*	*rewrite*	New Pascal
get	*put*	*text*	
file component	*external*	*internal*	New Terms
file parameters	*textfiles*	*buffer*	
concatenate	*component*	*component type*	
file window			

Self-Test Exercises

13-1   What are the standard (or pre-defined) file parameters?

13-2   Under what circumstances can a file be an argument to a procedure?

13-3   Suppose that you are writing a program that gives a lengthy set of frequently-changed instructions to the user. How can you set up your program so that the instruction set can be modified and changed without making any alterations in the original program?

13-4   A company that is converting its employee records to a computerized system has run into an unexpected problem. Although most employee's telephone numbers are entered as a series of seven digits (e.g. 6424951), a few still have their old exchange letters (e.g. KI85276). Show how a program might screen out the old-style phone numbers.

13-5   What is the effect of this code?

```
Counter := 0 ;
reset (TheSource) ;        {TheSource is a textfile.}
while not eof(TheSource)
    do begin
        if eoln(TheSource) then Counter := Counter+1 ;
        readln (TheSource)
    end;
```

13-6   Suppose that you have a file whose component type is a record or array type. Write code to count the number of components in the file.

13-7   How would you modify a common *EchoText* procedure to number each line of output?

13-8   Restate the procedure calls *read(FileName, Value)* and *write(FileName, Value)* in terms of the more primitive procedures *get* and *put.*

13-9   In our discussion of the playing card problem we defined a record type *Card* like this:

```
type Card = record
            Number, Suit: String;
            Found: boolean
        end;
```

Suppose that we have a file named *TheDeck* whose component type is *Card.* Write code that will print *TheDeck*'s contents.

13-10   How can an assignment be made between two file variables of the same type?

13-11   Write a procedure that finds and prints line *X* of textfile *F.* Assume that *F* contains at least *X* lines.

13-12   The code below is supposed to sum a file of integer values. Will it work? What does it (or won't it) do?

```
Sum := 0;
while not eof(Data)
    do begin
        read (Data, NextValue);
        Sum := Sum + NextValue
    end;
```

13-13   The procedure shown below is supposed to skip blanks until it encounters a non-blank, or the end-of-file. Why won't the code work?

```
procedure SkipBlanks (var TheFile: text);
    begin
        while (TheFile↑ = ' ') and not eof(TheFile)
            do get(TheFile)
    end;
```

More Exercises   **13-14**   Pascal has been criticized because the file parameters in the program heading are not really parameters. The exact name of an external file must be given in the program heading for it to be 'passed' to the program. Thus, it's hard to write many general purpose file-handling programs in Standard Pascal.

To get around this unreasonable restriction, many implementations have some means by which external file names can be passed to a program at run-time. Does your Pascal have such an extension? How does it work?

13-15   Write a segment of code that will read and echo a text file—with two extra spaces between each line.

13-16   As we mentioned in Chapter 1, not all Pascal systems support both upper and lower-case characters. Write a program that changes all the lower-case characters in a Pascal program file to capital letters.

13-17   A number of text editors currently available have a 'wraparound' feature—the editor automatically enters a carriage return after putting as many words as possible on each line. A typist doesn't have to enter carriage returns at the end of each line because the editor does it automatically.

Write a program that makes an input file appear to have been written using a wraparound editor. It should accept input text, either interactively or from a file, but ignore carriage returns. Instead, your program should reprint the text so that every line has contains as many whole words as it can. Allow a maximum line length of 80 characters.

13-18   Write a program that asks the user her name and age, then tells her the name and age of the last person to run the program. Be sure that the program gives sensible output to the first user. Then, modify the program to tell any user how many times *she* has run the program (by checking for her name).

13-19   Preparing personalized junk mail poses an interesting programing problem. A 'letter' file contains most of a letter, but has spaces left for the addressee's name and address, and as many references to her name, family, street, and city as possible. An 'address' file contains a series of names and addresses for personalizing letters.

Write a program that creates personalized junk mail. A simple version will require a user to set up letter and address file (possibly using special codes or formats) for the program to manipulate. A more advanced (and interactive) version will work *with* the user to set up the necessary files, making the codes or formats transparent to her.

13-20   The Midwest Grain and Boring Tool Corporation advertises that its employees are not just numbers. This creates problems for their accounting department. As a first step in setting up a payroll, a file of employee names must be alphabetized. This can be done by repeatedly selecting, deleting, and copying elsewhere, the 'lowest' name remaining in the original file. Write a program that does the job.

13-21   In some computerized management information systems an administrator can request a list of all employees who share some characteristic. They may all have the same pay scale, the same supervisor, work in the same department, etc. Write a two-part program that implements such a system. The first part should create a file that holds all relevant information (department, pay, supervisor, etc.) associated with each employee. The second part should act as an information system, that prints the names of all employees that share some feature.

13-22   A large telephone company (whose name you would probably recognize in an instant) has discovered that some of its employees are on the payrolls of more than one department. In an attempt to catch the double-dippers, alphabetized files that contain the names of all the employees in each department have been prepared.

Write a program that compares the employee lists of just two departments, and prints any names that appear on both payrolls. Then, modify your program to deal with four employee lists. Be sure to print the number of payrolls each caught employee appears on.

13-23   Suppose that we have a user-defined ordinal type called *Day* whose constants are *Monday, Tuesday,* etc. We can arrange to print the string equivalents of these constants by defining an array subscripted by *Day*, and storing the strings 'Monday', 'Tuesday', etc. in it. This technique was demonstrated at the very end of Section 13-2.

A shortcoming of the method we used then was the large number of assignments required—one assignment for each ordinal type constant. Define an ordinal type whose constants are Pascal's reserved words and use internal files to simplify the initialization of the 'string-equivalent' array. (Hint: employ the method we demonstrated in procedure *InitializeFullDeck* to initialize a series of string variables.

13-24   As we mentioned in the last chapter's exercises, Pascal programs are often written in countries whose native language is not English. However, we can assume that there's a one-to-one correspondence between Pascal's reserved words in English, and those in any other language. Thus, if we have a 'data base' of foreign-language equivalents, we should be able to translate any program.

Write a program that reads an ordinary Pascal program, then echoes it with its reserved words translated into another language. Let the user specify the language. However, if that language's equivalents aren't part of your data base, prompt the program user to enter the translations of words that are required (and only those words). Add them to your data base, too. (Warning: Beware of translating programs into a language you only have a partial set of equivalents for.) As before, ignore reserved words that are text constants or output, or fall within comments.

13-25   The authorship of books can often be determined by doing a statistical analysis of the length of words, and the number of words in each sentence. A number of points can be compared—the average or mean length, the median length (half the words or sentences are longer, half are shorter), the standard deviation (which we won't explain), and the skewness (essentially the proportion *mean:median*).

Write a program that is able to read two text files and compute these points of comparison (you need not figure standard deviation if you don't understand it). Have your program venture a guess about whether or not both files were written by the same person (and give its reasons).

13-26   It seems only reasonable that a computer science course should have its bookkeeping done by computer. Write a program that does the job. It should prepare *and maintain* a file of student names, and each student's score on various tests and homework assignments.

Your program should have the following capabilities: adding new students, dropping students, adding new scores, changing incorrect scores, and printing the scores of the entire class. It should also be able to assign different weights to each score and compute final grades. Don't forget to allow for unusual situations, like missed tests.

For extra credit, include an option for statistical analysis of scores and grades, showing means and medians, as well as a histogram of all scores. Be sure to make it idiot-proof.

13-27   Gassalasca Jape, the well known playwright, has written an entire play (entitled *Home Life*) in which two characters (Mildred and Mordred) are always speaking. In order to give readers unable to attend the live performance a true sense of the drama, he wishes to print the two monologues side-by-side. Unfortunately, Gassalasca's publisher refuses to go to the expense of typesetting the play in such a peculiar fashion.

Write a program to help G.J. out. Assume that Mildred and Mordred's soliloquies are in separate files, and that the maximum length of a line in each file is no more than 40 characters. Merge the two files together by concatenating corresponding lines.

13-28   Surely you're familiar with multiple choice questionnaires that appear in magazines. In the very simplest sort, you're told to score 1 point for all 'A' answers, 2 points for 'B's, 3 for 'C's, etc. Unfortunately, when the answers to each question are arranged in the exact same manner, readers are tempted to give answers that result in the most desirable score, instead of answers that are especially truthful. To combat this, point scores are often intentionally assorted—'C' may be 2 points in one question, but 4 points in the next.

Write a two-part questionnaire program. Part One is invoked if the user enters a secret password. It should let her set up a questionnaire file that includes questions, multiple choice answers, and the 'value' of each individual answer. Finally, it should contain results or conclusions that relate to different ranges of point values (e.g. 'If your score was 125−150, then ... etc.).

Part Two is invoked if the password isn't entered. It asks the questions, lets the user pick from the multiple choices, and records the 'value', of each response (which may change for each question). Finally, it should deliver the appropriate conclusion.

13-29   Computer users—word processors as well as programers—often find themselves in possession of more than one version of a single file. A program that compares two files is extremely useful. Write such a program, and give it the following options:

> *Length and count*: Print the number of characters, words, and lines in each file.

Difference: Assume that file *B* has had extra lines added. Print all lines in *B* that are not in file *A*, along with their line numbers.

Two-way difference: Assume that extra lines have been added to each file. Print all lines in *A* that are not in *B*, and vice versa. (Hint: use the *Difference* option first to create files of *A* and *B*'s 'extra' lines.)

Unify: Create and print a file that is a merger of *A* and *B*.

13-30   Automatic text formatting is a basic computer application. The central task is *text justification*, which means printing text in such a way that each line is the exact same length. This is accomplished by hyphenating words or by inserting extra space between words. Other formatting jobs include spacing between paragraphs, indenting at appropriate places, deciding how long each page should be, and including page numbers and running headings at the top of each page.

Write a text formatter. The difficulty of this program will depend on your definition of the problem. However, every program should have the ability to justify single lines of text by inserting space between words. Assume that additional commands (to start paragraphs, skip space, specify line and page length, etc.) are included in the file of source text, but are somehow distinguished from the regular text; e.g.:

```
.LL  60c        { Line length is 60 characters. }
.PL  25         { Page length is 25 lines. }
.PP             { Start a paragraph—space and indent. }
The  end  of  the  world,  when  it
came,  was  no  surprise  to  many
of  us  .  .  .          etc.
```

13-31   Although text editors are often thought of as being interactive programs, a number of editing jobs are equally suited for batch processing. One such job involves deleting or changing every instance of some word (or words) in a source file. Write a program that lets a user specify (in a 'command file') words that are to be removed from or replaced in a source file of text. A sample command file might look like this:

> **replace "concieve" with "conceive"**
> **replace "like I told youse" with "as I told you"**
> **delete "ain't"**

13-32   A *pretty-printer* is a program that formats other programs. It reads a file that contains a program, and prints it in a neat, orderly fashion. A pretty-printer doesn't change the syntax or semantic content of the program. Instead, it just lines up all the **begins** and **ends** and comments, puts extra spaces between subprograms, etc.

Write a simple pretty-printer that is able to handle indentation. Assume that programs it will have to format are laid out in the style of all the programs in this book except that no lines are indented. You'll have to infer the rules we use for indentation, and write a program that is able to recognize the reserved words that cause us to indent or outdent. To make the job a bit easier, don't worry about indenting type definitions, and assume that every control structure regulates a compound statement.

13-33   Add file types to your private programing language. You might want to treat a file as a means of permanently storing data, rather than strictly as a sequential-access structure. Thus, you may wish to pre-define additional file-handling procedures that ease the job of file insertion and deletion.

SESSIONS.

527

SET.

546

SET.

2744

Supplement, p. 3873; Corrigenda, p. 4092

14

Collections of Values: The **set** Types

For a short word, *set* certainly packs an awful lot of meaning. The Oxford English Dictionary devotes no less than twenty-two pages to its exposition of *set*, and includes one hundred fifty-four definitions.

Even more remarkable than their number, is the fact that not one of the one hundred fifty-four definitions of *set* given by the editors of the O.E.D. mentions Pascal. This is sad because Pascal is one of the only programming languages in the world to include a set structure. It deserves some kind of recognition.

The set is the last of Pascal's structured types, and we discuss it fully in section 14-1. It's an interesting structure–it's possible to program for a long time without ever needing sets, but once you've used them they seem indispensable. Since sets seldom cause mysterious errors, we haven't included an Antibugging section with this chapter.

(N)ot one of the 154 definitions of set given by the editors of the O.E.D. mentions Pascal....

14-1
Defining and Programing Set Structures

THE SET STRUCTURE IS USED TO CREATE variables that can represent more than one value of a given ordinal type. The type definition of a set structure contains the set type's identifier, the reserved words **set of**, and the type of the value the set will contain. This 'contents' type is called the set's *base type*. For example:

>**type** *CharacterSet* = **set of** *char*;
>   *Vitamins* = (*A, Bl, B2, B3, B6, B12, C, D, E*);
>   *NutritionType* = **set of** *Vitamins*;
>   *LowNumbers* = 1..12;
>   *GradesRepresented* = **set of** *LowNumbers*;
>   *Hues* = (*Red, Blue, Green, Yellow*);
>   *Colors* = **set of** *Hues*;

In chart form we have:

set *data structure*

>   **type** ⟶ *identifier* ⟶ = ⟶ **set of** ⟶ *base type identifier* ⟶ ;

The base type of *CharacterSet* is the predefined type *char*, the base type of *NutritionType* is the user-defined ordinal type *Vitamins*, the base type of *GradesRepresented* is the subrange *LowNumbers*, and the base type of *Colors* is the user-defined ordinal type *Hues.*

Although no ordinal type is specifically prohibited from becoming a set's base type, Pascal places a subtle restriction on allowable base types.

> The maximum *cardinality* of a set structure (the maximum number of values in its base type) is implementation defined—determined by the author of a system's Pascal compiler. It typically ranges from 64 to 2040 members.

Does limiting the size of sets ever cause problems? Well, most user-defined ordinal types have too few members to approach the limit. On the other hand, *integer* will never be the base type of a set structure because it has too many member values. Most difficulties occur with medium-sized sets, like an *integer* subrange or the computer's set of characters. We may have to severely limit the size of an ordinal type (as we did with *LowNumbers,* above), to make it a legal base type.

Compiler writers generally allow sets to be at least as large as the cardinality of type *char.* In this text, we'll assume that this definition is always valid:

>   **type** *TypeIdentifier* = **set of** *char*;

Once a set has been defined, we can declare set-structured variables.

>**type** *CharacterSet* = **set of** *char*;
>   *Vitamins* = (*A, Bl, B2, B3, B6, B12, C, D, E*);
>   *NutritionType* = **set of** *Vitamins*;
>   *LowNumbers* = 1..12;
>   *GradesRepresented* = **set of** *LowNumbers*;

> **var** *InputCharacters, OutputCharacters*: *CharacterSet*;
> *FruitVitamins, VegetableVitamins*: *NutritionType*;
> *Responses*: *GradesRepresented*;

At this point *InputCharacters, OutputCharacters, FruitVitamins*, and the rest don't actually represent any values. They're uninitialized variables with the *potential* of representing any, or all, or none of the values of their base types. Assignments take the usual form: A set-valued expression is assigned to a set-structured variable.

> In set expressions, individual *members* of a set must be put between square brackets. In contrast, the identifier of a set-structured *variable* isn't.

Thus, assignments can be made by listing the assignment values between square brackets, or by supplying the name of a set-structured variable. Don't forget that two dots (..) mean 'through and including':

> *OutputCharacters* := ['a'..'z', 'A'..'Z', '0'..'9'];
> *FruitVitamins* := [A..B3, B12, C, E];
> *InputCharacters* := [Letter];
> *OutputCharacters* := [chr(74)];
> *InputCharacters* := *OutputCharacters*;
> *Responses* := [];

The final assignment is unusual because it makes *Responses* an *empty set*—a set that contains no values at all.

Don't let Pascal's variety of methods for representing set members confuse you. If the value of *Letter* is 'B', and we assign it to *InputCharacters*, then the three expressions below are all equivalent ways of referring to a set whose base type is *char*, and whose only member is 'B':

> ['B']   [*Letter*]   *InputCharacters*

A final point about set values is that they're *unordered*. Thus, these are equivalent representations of the same set:

> [A..B3, C, E]   [E, A..B3, C]

Self-Check Questions

Q. We saw above that the empty set is represented by a pair of square brackets. What's it needed for?

A. Like all other variables, set-structured variables are undefined when they're declared. Initializing a set variable to empty—to '[]'—is roughly equivalent to initializing a *real* or *integer* variable to 0.

We also need a way of showing the empty set to determine if a particular set has any members. The *boolean* expression: (*SomeSet* = []) is *true* if *SomeSet* has no members, and *false* otherwise.

The Set Operators

Set expressions can also be constructed with the ***set operators***. There are three basic set operations: union, difference, and intersection. They're all quite straightforward, and may even be familiar from grade-school.

> Set ***union*** is, more or less, the 'addition' of sets. The union of two sets (or of two representations of Pascal sets) is a set that contains *all* the members of both sets. The regular addition sign $(+)$ serves as the set union operator.

In its simplest application, a set union updates or adds to the members of a set-structured variable. For instance, suppose that we want to make a record of the letters that appear in a sample of input text.

```
program FindIncludedLetters (input, output) ;
     {Determines which letters appear in a text sample.}

type CharacterSet = set of char;

var Current: char;
    IncludedLetters: CharacterSet;

begin
   IncludedLetters := [] ;
   while not eof
      do begin
         read (Current) ;
         IncludedLetters := IncludedLetters +[Current]
      end;
   writeln ('Letters included were:') ;
   for Current := 'a' to 'z'
      do if Current in IncludedLetters
         then write (Current) ;
   writeln;
   for Current := 'A' to 'Z'
      do if Current in IncludedLetters
         then write (Current) ;
   writeln
end.  {FindIncludedLetters}
```

↓   ↓   ↓   ↓   ↓

the quick brown fox jumps over the lazy dog
PACK MY BOX WITH FIVE DOZEN LIQUOR JUGS
```
Letters included were:
abcdefghijklmnopqrstuvwxyz
ABCDEFGHIJKLMNOPQRSTUVWXYZ
```

The program segment begins by initializing *IncludedLetters* (defined as a **set of** *char*) to the empty set. Successive values of *Current* are read in and added to the *IncludedLetters* set. When the loop is finished, *IncludedLetters* represents every character that's been read in. Some other set unions are:

> *IncludedLetters* := *IncludedLetters* + *OutputCharacters*;
> *IncludedLetters* := *IncludedLetters* + *OutputCharacters* + ['D'..'T'];

Don't forget that the identifiers of set-structured variables need not go between square brackets.

Our next set operator can undo a set union.

> Set *difference* is akin to the 'subtraction' of sets. The difference of two sets is a set that contains all the members of the first set that are not also members of the second set. The set difference operator is an ordinary minus sign (−).

This mouthful is much more sensible than it sounds. When we subtract set *B* from set *A* (*A*−*B*), we're just taking all of *B*'s members away from *A*. For example, suppose that we've made these definitions and declarations:

type *Options* = (*ErrorRecovery, InputChecks, OutputChecks, Testing, LongMessages*);

var *AllOptions, TestOptions*: **set of** *Options*;

A program might begin by initializing *AllOptions* and *TestOptions*:

> *AllOptions* := [*ErrorRecovery..LongMessages*];
> *TestOptions* := [*InputChecks, Testing*];

At this point, *AllOptions* contains every value of type *Options*. We can reduce its membership by using the set difference operator:

> *AllOptions* := *AllOptions* − *TestOptions*;
> {*AllOptions* now contains [*ErrorRecovery, OutputChecks, LongMessages*] }
> *AllOptions* := *AllOptions* − [*ErrorRecovery..OutputChecks*];
> {*AllOptions* now contains [*LongMessages*]}

What happens when we try to remove a value that's not included in a set variable? Nothing. Although the second of the assignments below is obviously fruitless, it's perfectly legal Pascal.

> *TestOptions* := [];
> *TestOptions* := *TestOptions* − [*InputChecks*];

To determine which letters do *not* appear in a sample of text, we could use this variation on our earlier program:

```
      program FindMissingLetters (input, output);
        {Determines which letters don't appear in a text sample.}

      type CharacterSet = set of char;

      var Current: char;
        MissingLetters: CharacterSet;

      begin
        MissingLetters := ['a'..'z', 'A'..'Z'];
        while not eof
          do begin
              read (Current);
              MissingLetters := MissingLetters−[Current]
          end;
        write ('Letters not included were:   ');
        for Current := 'a' to 'z'
          do if Current in MissingLetters
            then write (Current);
        for Current := 'A' to 'Z'
          do if Current in MissingLetters
            then write (Current);
        writeln
      end.  {FindMissingLetters}
```

↓   ↓   ↓   ↓   ↓

the charging rhino tripped over a snoozing fieldmouse
PACK MY BOX WITH TWO CHEESEBURGERS TO GO
Letters not included were: bjkqwxyDFJLNQVZ

> The *intersection* of two sets is a set that contains all values that belong to both sets. The Pascal multiplication sign (∗) is used as the set intersection operator.

If two sets don't contain any common values their intersection is, of course, the empty set. Assume that we've defined the months as an ordinal type. The value of this set expression:

$$[January..June, August]*[May..September]$$

is the set [*May, June, August*]. The intersection of [*January..May*] and [*July..November*] is the empty set [ ].

Sets are often used to record characteristics of some sort, and intersection can be used to find features shared by several different sets. For example, suppose that *Characteristics* has been defined as a set of some ordinal type. If we declare some variables of this set-type:

var *Luxury, Deluxe, Standard, Economy*: *Characteristics*;

Questions:

① Does CHAR only refer to a single
    character assigned to a variable?

② In text output - no carriage return
    permitted? Do you need a
    new WRITELN statement for each
    line of output?

③ Does input of floating pt values have
    to be done in E notation?

④ ORD(X) ordinal position
    ORD('A') is 65 ??
    ORD('0') is 48 ??

⑤ The value of the counter in the
        FOR   To   Do statement
    is undefined on exit from the
    structure.
        Explain

(3*4)   2(ab) + 4(ac) =

⑥ p12 ~~& So it necessary on the run on
line in the 3d procedure to have the
; at the end of the line ?~~

2(a+b) + 2(c+d)
2a + 2b + 2c + 2d

⑦ Question ~~or output~~ p 129 (Ex 2)

⑧ Chapter 6
When do we need the
BEGIN & END in the IF   THEN
ELSE construct ?

⑨ What does
READ (   )

do — p200 ?

_____

??
Comparison of record only made
in a file of record type.

we can make the following assignment:

$$Luxury := Deluxe*Standard*Economy;$$

The set variable *Luxury* holds the values (assuming that there are any) that belong to *all* of the other three sets. If there are no common elements *Luxury* equals [ ], the empty set.

:··:

Self-Check Questions

Q. Is this a reasonable and correct application of the set union operator?

$$InputCharacters := ['D'..'T'] + [CurrentCharacter] + ['9'];$$

A. Although the assignment is correct, it isn't reasonable. There's no need to use the set union operator, because we're not merging set-structured variables: the assignment below works just as well. (Note that *Current-Character* may be in ´D´..´T´, *(CurrentCharacter, ´9´)*

$$InputCharacters := ['D'..'T', CurrentCharacter, '9'];$$

:··:

The set operators form expressions that represent sets themselves.

Focus on Programing: boolean Set Expressions

: Set-valued operands can also be used with the ordinary relational :
: operators, and with the set relational operator **in**, to form a variety :
: of *boolean* expressions. :

Sign	Operation	Example
=	set equality	*InputCharacters* = *OutputCharacters*
< >	set inequality	*Responses* < > [1..4, 6..10]
> =	set 'contains'	*Fruit* > = [A, B2, C]
< =	set 'is contained by'	*Luxury* < = *Standard*
in	set membership	´D´ **in** *Included*

Such expressions are the basis of most set applications, because sets are rarely a program's main data structure. Instead, we'll usually find them in supporting roles, simplifying error checking or in-program accounting.

: Set-type variables help create conditions that are easy to use in :
: many parts of a program, but which can be quickly modified in a :
: central place. :

For example, suppose that we want to print a textfile, substituting asterisks for a set of forbidden values. Assume that we've defined *CharacterSet* as a **set of** *char*. Procedure *Substitute*, below, is passed a file, and a set of characters to be replaced as the file is being output.

```
procedure Substitute (var TheFile: text;  BadCharacters: CharacterSet) ;
  {Substitutes asterisks for BadCharacters while echoing TheFile.}

  var CurrentCharacter: char;

  begin
    reset(TheFile) ;
    while not eof(TheFile)
      do begin while not eoln(TheFile)
        do begin
          read (TheFile, CurrentCharacter) ;
          if not (CurrentCharacter in BadCharacters)
            then write (CurrentCharacter)
            else write ('*')
        end;
        readln (TheFile) ;
        writeln
      end
  end;   {Substitute}
```

Typical calls of *Substitute* might be:

```
Substitute (ProposedBudget, ['0'..'9']) ;
Substitute (Speech, ['!']) ;
```

The first call prints a file named *ProposedBudget* with asterisks instead of numerals, while the second call makes the same substitution for exclamation marks found in file *Speech.*

The set operators let sets store data that might otherwise be kept in an array. For example, let's reconsider the Hunt the Wumpus problem of Chapter 12. We'll modify the problem slightly, so that instead of having tunnels that lead in each of four directions, each room can have *any* number of exit tunnels. In the solution we proposed then, each room of the cave was defined as a record with a *Contents* field (denoting any hazards in the room), and a *NextDoor* array-field to hold the numbers of neighboring rooms. What do you think about using this proposal instead?

```
type RoomValues = 1..20;
     RoomInformation = set of RoomValues;
     Cave = array [RoomValues] of RoomInformation;

var PitRooms, BatRooms, WumpusRoom: RoomInformation;
    CurrentRoom: RoomValues;
    Neighbors: Cave;
```

We've really changed our way of looking at the cave. In the new example, our central data structure is a set of possible room numbers—the *integer* values 1 through 20. Instead of putting hazards into each room of the cave, as we did before, we store the locations of each hazard in set variables:

$PitRooms := [1, 5..7, 12, 14, 19];$
$BatRooms := [3, 4, 8, 11, 13, 15..17];$
$WumpusRoom := [18];$

The cave itself has become an array of sets. Each set contains the numbers of the rooms that a given room is connected to.

$Neighbors[1] := [3, 4, 9, 13];$
$Neighbors[2] := [8, 9, 12, 20];$
$Neighbors[3] := [1, 5, 14, 17];$

You'll probably find out the hard way that Pascal's economy in using square brackets with both arrays and sets causes confusion.

Suppose that we find ourselves in room number *CurrentRoom.* We can easily check for *any* hazard in the room with:

if *CurrentRoom* **in** (*PitRooms*+*BatRooms*+*WumpusRoom*)
   then *writeln* ('Sorry, but you''re dead!');

Or, we can see if danger lurks in a neighboring room by determining if the *Neighbors* set has a non-empty intersection with one of the sets of hazards. To find bats, for example, use:

if (*Neighbors*[*CurrentRoom*]*BatRooms*) <> []
   then *writeln* ('I hear bats!');

An astute reader will notice a great similarity between a set, and an array of *boolean* values that is subscripted by the set's base type. For example, the base type of *BatRooms* is the subrange 1..20. Suppose we declared the following array:

type *BatArray* = **array** [1..20] **of** *boolean*;
var *BatsArePresent* = *BatArray*;

Suppose that we initialize *BatsArePresent* to *false*, except for rooms 3, 4, 8, 11, 13, 15, 16, and 17—they all contain bats and are set to *true.* The array-structured variable *BatsArePresent* now holds the exact same data as the set-structured variable *BatRooms.* However, it's much less convenient to work with because we can't use the set operators. We have to search all the way through *BatsArePresent* to find out something about its contents.

In certain cases, though, sets and *boolean* arrays share the same problems. For example, there's no automatic way to print either all the elements of an array variable (except for a string-type array), or all the members of a set variable. Suppose that we wanted to print out the numbers of the rooms containing bats. Compare these procedures:

```
procedure PrintArrayRooms (BatsArePresent: BatArray);
   var Counter: RoomValues;  {1..20}
   begin
      for Counter:= 1 to MaximumNumberOfRooms
         do if BatsArePresent[Counter]
            then writeln (Counter)
   end;  {PrintArrayRooms}
```

> **procedure** *PrintSetRooms* (*BatRooms*: *BatInformation*) ;
>
> **var** *Counter*: *RoomValues*; {1..20}
>
> **begin**
> 　　**for** *Counter*:= 1 **to** *MaximumNumberOfRooms*
> 　　　**do if** *Counter* **in** *BatRooms*
> 　　　　**then** *writeln* (*Counter*)
> **end**; {*PrintSetRooms*}

As you can see, the procedures are practically identical. We have to step through the set almost as though we were travelling through an array.

`· : · : · : · : · : · : · : · : · : · : · : · : · : · : · : · : · : · : · : · : · : · : · : · : · : ·`

Self-Check Questions

Q. Given the procedure declaration above, what will be the effects of these procedure calls:

　　　　a) *PrintSetRooms* (*BatRooms* ∗ *PitRooms*) ;
　　　　b) *PrintSetRooms* (*BatRooms* + *PitRooms*) ;
　　　　c) *PrintSetRooms* (*BatRooms* − *PitRooms*) ;

Assume that we've made the following assignments:

　　　　BatRooms := [1..4, 7, 11..12, 19] ;
　　　　PitRooms := [4..8, 10, 14, 19..20] ;

A. Each of the calls sends a different set to *PrintSetRooms*. Values that will be printed are:

　　a) 4, 7, 19.
　　b) 1, 2, 3, 4, 5, 6, 7, 8, 10, 11, 12, 14, 19, 20.
　　c) 1, 2, 3, 11, 12.

`· . · . · . · . · . · . · . · . · . · . · . · . · . · . · . · . · . · . · . · . · . · . · . · . · .`

Programing with Sets

Our final set application will compare the efficiency of two typewriter keyboards. The *QWERTY* keyboard is the current standard. Its letter keys are laid out like this:

```
Q   W   E   R   T   Y   U   I   O   P
  A   S   D   F   G   H   J   K   L   ;   :   space
Z   X   C   V   B   N   M
```

Unfortunately, few of the most frequently used letters (e, t, a, o, n, r, i, and s) appear on the center 'home' row—the row of keys that a typist's fingers normally rest on. As you might expect, continually jumping from one row to another slows and tires even the best typists.

Many new keyboard designs have been proposed. One of these is the *Maltron* keyboard, shown below. Since the most common characters are in the home row, fewer jumps are required while typing.

```
Q  P  Y  C  B  V  M  U  Z  L
A  N  I  S  F  E  D  T  H  O  R   ;   :   .   space
J  G  W  K  X
```

Just how beneficial is the Maltron keyboard? We should be able to write a program that compares the number of jumps a text sample would require from QWERTY and Maltron typists. A first refinement is:

> *as long as there are characters to look at*
>> *get the character*;
>> *see if it's on the QWERTY or Maltron home row*;
>> *see if it requires a jump from the QWERTY or Maltron home row*;
> *print conclusions*;

Set-structured variables are the data structure of choice, because we want to see if a particular value belongs to a group of values of the same type. Suppose that we define *CharacterSet* as a **set of** *char*. We can declare variables that represent the 'home' and 'others' characters of the keyboards above, as well as a *Valid* set-variable to help restrict the characters we consider.

What kind of conclusions should the program arrive at? Naturally we want to count the number of jumps that are made. However, this information isn't particularly helpful unless we know the total count of characters considered. The pseudocode below includes these refinements.

> *prepare the data file for reading*;
> *initialize the set variables*;
> **while not** *the end of the input file*
>> *read the next character*;
>> **if** *it's in the set of valid characters*
>>> *see if it's on the QWERTY or Maltron home row*;
>>> *see if it requires a jump from the QWERTY or Maltron home row*;
>>> *increment the Total count*;
> *print the number of jumps for each keyboard, and the size of the sample*;

The completed program is shown below. As input, we gave it the complete text of chapters 12 and 15.

```
program KeyBoards (DataFile, output) ;
    {Compares the jumps required by QWERTY and Maltron keyboards.}
type CharacterSet = set of char;
var DataFile: text;
    QWERTYHome, MaltronHome, QWERTYOthers, MaltronOthers, Valid: CharacterSet;
    QWERTYJumps, MaltronJumps, Total: integer;
    Current: char;
begin
    Valid := ['a'..'z', 'A'..'Z', ':',';',',','.'];
    QWERTYHome := ['a','s','d','f','g','h','j','k','l',';','A',
                   'S','D','F','G','H','J','K','L',':',' '];
    MaltronHome := ['a','n','i','s','f','e','.','d','t','h','o','r',';',
                    'A','N','I','S','F','E','D','T','H','O','R',':',' '];
    QWERTYOthers := ['a'..'z', 'A'..'Z'] - QWERTYHome;
    MaltronOthers := ['a'..'z', 'A'..'Z'] - MaltronHome;
    QWERTYJumps := 0;
    MaltronJumps := 0;
    Total := 0;
    reset (DataFile) ;
    while not eof(DataFile)
        do begin
            read (DataFile, Current) ;
            if Current in Valid
                then begin
                    Total := Total+1;
                    if (Current in QWERTYOthers)
                        then QWERTYJumps := QWERTYJumps+1;
                    if (Current in MaltronOthers)
                        then MaltronJumps := MaltronJumps+1
                end  {if}
        end;  {while}
    writeln ('Total number of input characters considered was ', Total:1, '.') ;
    writeln ('QWERTY keyboard required ', QWERTYJumps:1, ' jumps.') ;
    writeln ('Maltron keyboard required ', MaltronJumps:1, ' jumps.')
end.  {KeyBoards}
```

     ↓   ↓   ↓   ↓   ↓

```
Total number of input characters considered was 176441.
QWERTY keyboard required 121200 jumps.
Maltron keyboard required 54303 jumps.
```

Q. Program *KeyBoards* treats its input as a stream of characters, without regard to its line structure. Does this cause any inaccuracy in *KeyBoards'* output?

A. Yes, because the carriage return at the end of each line is read, and recorded, as a space. Thus, the total of input characters considered is really too high, by the number of lines in the input sample.

Summary

The *set* structure is the last of Pascal's structured types. A set-type variable may represent any, none, or all of the values in its *base type*. If it doesn't represent any values, it's called an *empty set*. The number of values in a set's base type is the base type's *cardinality*. The maximum cardinality allowed varies from system to system, because it's implementation defined. However, it's often equal to the number of values in the predefined type *char*.

Several *set operators* let us manipulate values of a set type. Set *union* and *difference* are the set counterparts of addition and subtraction, and use the symbols '+' and '−'. The *intersection* of two sets is the set of all values common to both. The set intersection operator is the Pascal multiplication sign '*'. The relational operators, including **in**, can also be used with set operands.

Although few programs are built around set-structured variables, sets provide a convenient means of expressing abstract or complex conditions. Using them can help improve a program's clarity.

New Pascal
New Terms

set of	in	+ − *
base type	*cardinality*	*empty set*
set operators	*union*	*difference*
intersection		

Self-Test Exercises

14-1   Write definitions for, and initialize, set variables for the set of months with 28 days, the set of months with 30 days, and the set of months with 31 days.

14-2   Suppose that we've made these definitions:

> **type** *Music* = (*Rock, Roll, Reggae*) ;
> *Tunes* = **set of** *Music*;
> **var** *Hits*: *Tunes*;

List all possible values of variable *Hits.*

14-3   Evaluate these *boolean*-valued set expressions.

> *a)* ['L', 'N', 'M'] <> ['L'..'M']
> *b)* ['L'..'M'] = ['L', 'N', 'M']
> *c)* [] <= ['L'..'M']
> *d)* ['L', 'N', 'M'] <= ['K'..'M']
> *e)* ['K'..'M'] >= ['L', 'N', 'M']

14-4   Assume that numbers or characters standing in for a number of people have been divided among the following set variables: *Movers, Groovers, Shakers, Quakers, Lovers,* and *Fighters.* Write set expressions that represent the entire group, the *Lovers* and *Fighters,* the *Movers* who aren't *Groovers,* the *Shakers* who are *Quakers* but not *Lovers,* and the people who are neither *Groovers* or *Quakers.*

14-5   Can elements be removed from an empty set? What is the effect of this assignment:

> *SomeSet* := [] − *SomeSetComponents*;

14-6   Suppose that we've made these definitions:

> **type** *Capitals* = 'A'..'Z';
>   *CapitalSet* = **set of** *Capitals*;

Write a function that represents the number of values in a variable of type *CapitalSet.*

14-7   Assuming the definitions of the previous question, find the (alphabetically) greatest value in a non-empty variable (*LetterGroup*) of type *CapitalSet.*

14-8   The code below is intended to find the (alphabetically) lowest value in a variable of type *CapitalSet.* What bug does it contain?

> *Letter* := 'A';
> **while not** (*Letter* **in** *LetterGroup*)
>   **do** *Letter* := *succ*(*Letter*);

14-9   What does it mean to say that the effect of the symbols +, −, and * are *context dependent*?

14-10   If a user-defined ordinal type has *n* constants, then a variable of that type can have (at most) *n* distinct values. Suppose that a set has *n* elements. How many distinct values can a variable of this set type have?

More Exercises

14-11   What is the maximum cardinality of sets in your Pascal implementation? What problems might this limit cause?

14-12   Write a function that determines if a given character is in the set of capital letters, lower-case letters, punctuation, digits, a blank, or an unknown set.

14-13   The *cardinality* of a set is the number of members it contains. Write functions that, given a set variable of a particular type, compute and represent its cardinality, and the lowest and highest (in the ordering of its base type) members it holds.

14-14   Cryptarithmetic problems were once the rage of the country. An arithmetic problem and its answer are given, except that each digit is replaced by a letter. Our job is to decrypt the arithmetic. The examples below can be decrypted by a brute force approach. Although ten nested **for** loops are

needed, clever use of sets (and an intelligent algorithm) will drastically reduce
the number of iterations required.

$$
\begin{array}{r}
\text{S END} \\
\underline{\text{MORE}} \\
\overline{\text{MONEY}}
\end{array}
$$

14-15   Suppose that the words below are actually sets of char values. It's
easy to find a group of words that forms a set representing the entire alphabet.
Unfortunately, the problem we pose is this: how many duplicate letters will
there be in the group, and what are they? Can you write a program that tries
to form the alphabet set while minimizing duplicates?

*the quick brown fox jumped over the lazy dog and packed my box with five
dozen liquor jugs*

5-16   The word 'spare' has five different letters in it. Write a program that
prints all possible permutations of these letters. Then, modify your program to
print combinations of only two, three, or four letters as well. Remember not
to repeat any letters. Before you begin printing, estimate the number of words
that will be printed. Finish by figuring out how many of the words have
English meanings.

14-17   At last the problem you've all been waiting for—write a computerized
dating service. Although a trivial dating program would just try to match people whose interests match, your program should do a more sophisticated job.
Try to divide likes and dislikes into distinct groups, and assign relative weights
to each group. Thus, your program might pair two people who have few unimportant things in common, but who have, say, and 80% intersection of important interests.

14-18   The game of Bingo is usually played with a square card that contains a
grid of numbers. A caller draws numbers at random, and the first player to
obtain a vertical, horizontal, or diagonal row of called numbers is the winner.
Unfortunately, people who have severe astigmatism are often unable to see the
lines and diagonals. They are forced to play Set Bingo, in which the object is
to have *all* your numbers called.

Write a program that simulates a game of Set Bingo. Allow for ten
players, and give each player's card fifteen numbers. Show each player's card,
and at the end of the game print all the numbers that were called. For a
bonus, allow the user to specify the number of players. (Hint: use a file of
players.)

14-19   Henry Dudeny tells of an old-fashioned game of bowling called *kayles.*
Thirteen pins are lined up in a row, but the second one is always knocked
down before the start of the game.

Now, with a little bit of practice, a player can always bowl over any single
pin, or any two pins that have adjoined from the start. When taking the last
turn is the object of the game, a winning strategy is to divide the remaining
pins into an even number of similar groups, then copy whatever your opponent
does in a group of the same size.

Interactive users should write a program that plays kayles with a user.
Include as options the right of going first, the specification of whether the last
player wins or loses, and whether or not the computer should play the best
possible strategy. Make game output as lively as possible.

Batch users should write a program that plays with itself. To make it a bit more interesting, give each 'player' only a 65% chance of playing the correct strategy.

14-20   Monica Marin is astonished to learn that plants not only listen to people (she talks to her plants, of course), but talk to each other as well. This puts Monica in a quandary. She has seven plants (aethionema, begonia, camellia, daffodil, endymion, ficus, and zinnia), arrayed in a circle, and wants to rearrange them daily so that each plant has the same neighbors as infrequently as possible.

Now, the begonia whispered to Monica one day that n plants could be put in $(n-1)(n-2)/2$ different circular arrangements. What are they for Monica's plants? What would they be if she had thirteen different plants?

14-21   Andrea and Claire owned a very peculiar set of thirteen wooden blocks. Ten of the blocks were marked with the digits 0 through 9 (with only one digit on each block), two more contained multiplication signs, and the last had an equals sign printed on it.

When they played with their blocks, Andrea and Claire divided them equally, each taking five of the digit blocks and one multiplication sign. One day they happened to arrange their blocks in such a way that, by sharing the equals sign, they produced an equation. What is the largest product that could have been on each side of the equation? How was it produced? $(915*64=732*80=58,560)$

14-22   Write a program that prints all of the consonants in a text sample that are followed by vowels.

14-23   Write a program that lets the user specify one or more vowels (and makes sure they *are* vowels), then reads a text file and echoes all words containing the vowels. Modify the program to produce n lists of the words that contain only one of the specified vowels, two of them, etc.—through n of them.

14-24   How useful are computers in the diagnosis of disease? Write a program that lets a user enter symptoms, then diagnoses her ailment. The program will require a permanent data base of the symptoms associated with a number of diseases. If the user's symptoms match exactly the stored symptoms of a disease, assume she definitely has it. If the user's symptoms are a sub-set of any group of stored symptoms, inform her that she might have the disease. Finally, if she has some symptoms of any disease (but other symptoms as well), tell her that she shows signs of the disease. A more advanced program would ask for (and specify) further symptoms if a definite diagnosis can't be made.

14-25   In lieu of asking you to prove the four color theorem, we'll pose an easier map coloring problem. Max the Mapmaker believes in the four color theorem. However, he still needs a program to help him color his maps. What he'd like to do is to color an area (say, a state), then tell the computer what color he used, and what the state's neighbors are. He'd like the computer, in turn, to verify that he's used a color different from any of the neighbors. Write Max's program. Incidentally, an exceptionally good program will let Max backtrack and change the color of a state.

14-26   Can we put Max (above) out of business? Write a program that tries to color each of the fifty states automatically. The program should accept as input a list of the states along with each state's neighbors. Warning—you may find that four colors aren't enough. How many different colors does your program require? How would you have to improve your algorithm to make just four colors sufficient?

14-27   Extend your new programing language to include sets. Should you limit a set's maximum cardinality? Does it make any sense to allow sets of structured types? What additional predefined procedures might make it easier to deal with sets?

The Principal Gods

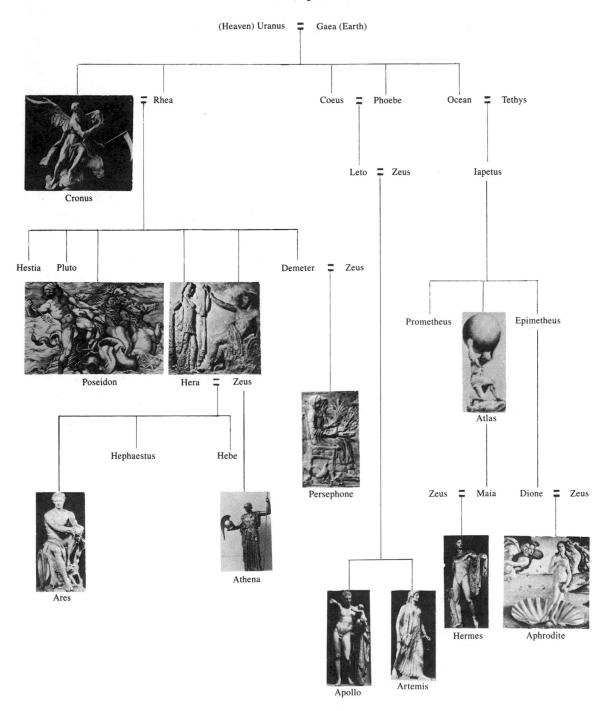

(Heaven) Uranus ═ Gaea (Earth)

Cronus ═ Rhea
Coeus ═ Phoebe
Ocean ═ Tethys

Leto ═ Zeus
Iapetus

Cronus

Hestia   Pluto
Demeter ═ Zeus

Prometheus   Epimetheus

Atlas

Poseidon

Hera ═ Zeus

Hephaestus   Hebe

Persephone

Zeus ═ Maia   Dione ═ Zeus

Ares

Athena

Hermes   Aphrodite

Apollo   Artemis

15

Abstract Data Structures via Pointers

In *The Medium is the Massage*, Marshall McLuhan argues that information is changed by the medium that conveys it. The same knowledge, transferred in different form, might be understood—massaged into your consciousness—in a different way. As a result, the medium becomes part of the message.

In computer science, programed data structures are the media in which data is stored and transferred. The genealogical chart opposite (we'll soon see it as a *tree* structure) has as much information in its connecting lines as in the names it holds. We couldn't easily store the same data in a Pascal file, because it's the wrong medium for storing non-sequential data. The interdependence of medium and message is a fact of programing.

In chapter 15 we'll be studying the *linked* structures—*queues, stacks,* and *trees.* These aren't predefined data types, but must be programed using *pointer types* as building blocks. We'll look at linked structures in terms of the operations that can be performed on each, and see how each structure, by its very design, holds a certain amount of useful information.

Section 15-1 explains the mechanics of pointer-type variables, and introduces some of the operations common in setting up linked structures. 15-2 looks in greater detail at the design and use of linked data structures. Finally, 15-3 is devoted entirely to a large example program, and 15-4 deals with bugs.

This is a hard chapter because a lot of non-intuitive and unobvious material is presented. You should skim through it quickly to get an idea of where the chapter leads, then re-read it slowly for learning. Merely seeing and understanding how something is done with pointers isn't enough. You should also be able to duplicate the solution on your own.

The geneological chart opposite has as much information...in its connecting lines as in the names it holds.

15-1
Basic
Operations
with Pointer
Types

AS UNUSUAL, WE WON'T BEGIN WITH AN example. Instead, the next four pages will be a concentrated introduction to the concept and terminology of pointers. Plan to read it twice. Our bottom-up introduction starts with the notion of a *storage location.*

An area in the computer memory that stores a value is called a *location.* When a Pascal program is directing computer operation, only the values of one particular type may be stored in a given location.* This is the basis of Pascal's strong type-checking—every location has a type associated with it.

A variable declaration makes the computer **allocate**, or set aside, a small portion of its memory as a location. An assignment to a variable changes the value stored in 'its' location. For all practical purposes the variable identifier and its location are the same. Because of this, an assignment to an ordinary variable identifier is called a **direct access** of a location.

Pointer variables work a little differently, because a pointer is a variable that **references,** or points to, a storage location.

The contents of the location can be inspected or changed *through* the pointer (called an **indirect** access) if we use special notation. Without this notation, an assignment to a pointer-type variable changes the particular location the variable references, without affecting the contents of that location.

Let's look at a simple example. This definition:

type *NumberPointer* = ↑ *integer*;

defines a pointer type. It is read '*NumberPointer* is a pointer to a location of type *integer*'.

A **pointer**-type is defined as referencing (or pointing to) a location of a particular type (its **reference type**). An up-arrow (↑) or caret (^) precedes the name of the reference type.

The syntax chart of a pointer's type definition is:

pointer type

type ⟶ *identifier* ⟶ = ⟶ ↑ ⟶ *identifier* ⟶ ;

(In this text we'll always use the up-arrow.) The declaration of a pointer-type variable looks like any other variable declaration.

var *First, Second, Third*: *NumberPointer*;

---

* This is not quite true. The location used to store a record variant can accommodate any of the variant groups—they are *overlaid* in a single location big enough for the largest group. If you don't understand this footnote, forget it.

However, we can't use *First, Second,* or *Third* to store *integer* values yet, because none of them reference specific locations. The location a pointer variable references must be *dynamically* allocated with the standard procedure *new.* A location can be disposed of (for the computer to re-allocate later, if necessary) with the standard procedure *dispose.* For example:

> *new* (*First*) ;   {Allocate locations for *First* and *Second* to reference.}
> *new* (*Second*) ;

Space in computer memory can be freed for re-allocation like this:

> *dispose* (*First*) ;   {Free the location that *First* pointed to.}

First still exists, but it's undefined and doesn't reference any location. It's in the pristine condition it was in before the original call of *new* (*First*).

Pascal has a special provision for defining a pointer variable without giving it a location to reference.

> Any pointer variable can be assigned the value **nil**:
>
> *First* := **nil**;
>
> It is now called a ***nil pointer***, and doesn't reference a location.

The advantage of a **nil** pointer over one that is simply undefined is that a pointer variable's **nil**/**not nil** status can be checked with a *boolean* expression.

> {Determine if *First* references a storage location.}
> **if** *First* = **nil**
> **then** *writeln* ('Warning! Nil pointer. Cannot be accessed.')
> **else** *writeln* ('This pointer accesses a stored value.')

The value **nil** is unusual in Pascal because it may be assigned to a pointer of *any* type. That's why **nil** is treated like a reserved word.

Our next step is to assign a value to, or inspect the value of, the location a pointer-type variable references.

> To assign a value to (or read a value from) the location referenced by a pointer variable, follow the pointer's identifier with an up-arrow or caret. The pointer must not be **nil**, because a **nil** pointer doesn't have a location.

(As usual, we'll just use the up-arrow.) For example:

> *First*↑ := 5 ;   {Assign 5 to the location *First* references.}
> *Second*↑ := *First*↑ ;   {Assign 5 (the value *First* references) to *Second*↑.}
> *writeln* ('The value First accesses is', *First*↑:2) ;
>   {Print the value in *First*'s location.}
> *readln* (*Second*↑) ;   {Input a value to the location *Second* accesses.}

We also have to understand how to give a value to the pointer itself, to make it access a different location.

> The value of a pointer is called an **address**. It is the computer's internal notation for a particular location in memory.*

A pointer's value (and thus, the address of the location the pointer references) can be changed in three ways:

1. With procedure *new*. This gives it a brand new address whose contents are undefined.

2. By assigning it the value **nil**, which gives it a null address.

3. By assigning it the address of another pointer of the same type. Both pointers will then access the same location.

In the example below, we make *Second* and *Third* point to the same location by giving them the same address. Then, *Second* is changed to access the same location as *First.*

        Third := *Second*;   {These assignments change the locations that *Third*}
        Second := *First*;   {and *Second* access, but not the locations' contents.}

Note that the assignments can't be reversed.

                        Second := *First*;
                        Third := *Second*;

After the second pair of assignments, *First, Second,* and *Third* all reference the same location, but the *integer* formerly referenced by *Second* has been cast adrift—the address of its location is lost. We cannot access it, and its storage area cannot be re-allocated by the computer.

How about printing the value of pointers? An address is an internal notation the computer uses for bookkeeping, and it has no external character representation.

> ### The Golden Rule of Pointers
>
> The value of a pointer can't be printed or inspected. It can only be compared (for equality and inequality) to the value of another pointer-variable of the same type, or to **nil.**

        if (*First* < > **nil**) **and** (*Second* < > **nil**)
            then if *First* = *Second*
                then *writeln* ('First and Second reference the same location.')
                else *writeln* ('First and Second access different locations.')
                {*First* and *Second* might be the same anyway.}

---

* If we think of the computer's memory as being a very very long array, then an address is like an array subscript.

Although pointers to ordinal values (like *integer*) are easy to understand, most pointers reference structured types. An especially common definition is a pointer to a record type that contains a pointer *of the same type* as one of its fields. For example:

type *DataPointer* = ↑ *DataLocation*;
        DataLocation = **record**
                            a, b, c: *integer*;
                            d, e, f: *char*;
                            Next: *DataPointer*
                        end;

    var *CurrentRecord*: *DataPointer*:

A peculiarity of definitions like this is that the pointer type is defined before the reference type—*DataPointer* is defined before *DataLocation*. Since *DataLocation* appears in the definition of *Data-Pointer*, we seem to have violated the 'define before you use' rule. However, reversing the definitions wouldn't help matters—if we did, we'd have to use *DataPointer* before *it* was defined. Pascal resolves this paradox by side-stepping it.

In Pascal, pointer type definitions may precede the definitions of their reference types. However, the reverse is not true—a structure may not contain a field or component of a pointer type that has not yet been defined.

Let's summarize the new information presented so far.

1. A pointer type is defined as pointing to a location of any type, using this format:

    type *PointerType* = ↑ *ItsReferenceType*;

2. The dynamic allocation procedure *new* gives a pointer-type variable a location in memory to reference or point to. Procedure *dispose* deallocates and frees this space.

3. A pointer may be given an address only by using *new*, or by assigning it the address of a pointer of an identical type (which makes them both reference the same location). However, any pointer may be given the null value **nil**. A pointer's address may not be printed or inspected; only compared to other pointer values for equality or inequality.

4. The location that a pointer variable references can be accessed by following the variable's name with an up-arrow (or caret), e.g. *ThePointer*↑.

5. A pointer may be defined as referencing a type that has not yet been defined (but which will be defined further along in the type definition).

∶ ∙ ∶ ∙ ∙ ∶ ∙ ∙ ∙ ∙

Self-Check
Questions

Q. What's wrong with these statements? Assume that we're using pointers to *integer* storage locations.

> *a)* *First* := 5;
> *b)* *Second*↑ := **nil**;
> *c)* *writeln* (*Third*);
> *d)* *First*↑ := *Second* + *Third*;

A. *a)* This statement tries to assign 5 to *First* instead of assigning it to the location *First* references. It should be
> *First*↑ := 5;

b) The value **nil** may only be assigned to a pointer—not to the location the pointer accesses (unless it too is a pointer). The assignment should be
> *Second* := **nil**;

c) This output statement attempts to print the value represented by *Third*—which is just the address of a location within the computer—instead of printing the value stored at that location. It should be
> *writeln* (*Third*↑);

d) This assignment tries to add two addresses instead of adding the values stored at each address. It should be written as
> *First*↑ := *Second*↑ + *Third*↑;

Addresses may only be compared for equality, and are *never* used in arithmetic expressions.

∶ ∙ ∶ ∙ ∙ ∶

The Linked Data Structures

Pointers to records are the most frequently defined pointer types. Such records invariably contain one or more pointer fields themselves, and therein lies their beauty: we can dynamically allocate a series of record locations, and tie them together with pointer fields. These are called *linked* structures because pointers form a chain of records.

The notion of linked structures existed long before Pascal. However, pointer types (a Pascal feature) let us easily and transparently implement many linked data-storage schemes. We'll spend the rest of this section looking at the basic linking operations.

Let's begin with an easy example that assumes the definition of *DataType*—we'll soon see that its particulars are not important.

> **type** *ElementPointer* = ↑ *Element*;
>   *Element* = **record**
>   *Data*: *DataType*;
>   *Next*: *ElementPointer*
>   **end**;
> **var** *FirstElement*: *ElementPointer*;

This puts us in position to *new* away to our heart's content:

> *new* (*FirstElement*);
> *new* (*FirstElement*↑.*Next*);
> *new* (*FirstElement*↑.*Next*↑.*Next*);
> *new* (*FirstElement*↑.*Next*↑.*Next*↑.*Next*);

....
: This particular linked structure is called a *list*. The individual :
: records of a linked list are its *elements*. :
....

A convenient visual notation is used for presenting linked structures. A box or circle represents a record location whose data fields can be labeled individually, or lumped together as 'data'. Each pointer's address—the location a pointer variable or field refers to—is shown with an arrow.* The series of calls above results in this structure:

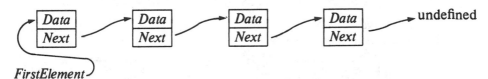

FirstElement

The combination of indirect access and ordinary record notation tends to make expressions long and incomprehensible.

FirstElement	{Represents an address}
FirstElement↑	{The record at that address}
FirstElement↑.*Data*	{One field of that record—a stored value.}
FirstElement↑.*Next*	{Represents an address}
FirstElement↑.*Next*↑	{The record at that address}
FirstElement↑.*Next*↑.*Data*	{One field of that record—a stored value.}

Now, the illustrated list above shows one of the peculiarities of linked structures. Although the computer has allocated four different locations in memory, only a single identifier—*FirstElement*—is associated with them. This is a source of convenience and confusion. For instance, we can access the entire list through *FirstElement* to make the last record's *Next* field **nil** instead of merely undefined.

$$FirstElement\uparrow.Next\uparrow.Next\uparrow.Next := \textbf{nil};$$

At the same time, a misstep might cause us to lose contact with part of the list. The assignment below *advances* the pointer variable, so that it references the second record in the list.

$$FirstElement := FirstElement\uparrow.Next;$$

Unfortunately, this leaves us with no way of accessing the very first list element!

....
: Linked structures usually have several auxiliary pointers associated :
: with them. These pointers act as place-markers, maintaining con- :
: tact with the beginning of a list, its end, our current position, etc. :
....

For example, if we had an auxiliary pointer named *CurrentPosition*, of type *ElementPointer*, the assignment:

_____

* You can see that we're starting to use visual metaphors.

$$CurrentPosition := FirstElement\uparrow.Next\uparrow.Next\uparrow.Next$$

would leave the list like this:

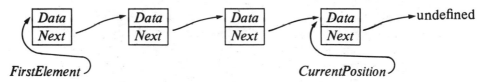

FirstElement   *CurrentPosition*

An auxiliary pointer also makes assignments much clearer.

$CurrentPosition\uparrow.Data := Value;$
$CurrentPosition\uparrow.Next := \textbf{nil};$

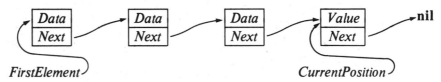

FirstElement   *CurrentPosition*

elf-Check
Questions

Q. What is the purpose and effect of these statements? Assume the situation of the last paragraph.

$$new\,(CurrentPosition\uparrow.Next)\,;$$
$$CurrentPosition := CurrentPosition\uparrow.Next;$$
$$CurrentPosition\uparrow.Next := \textbf{nil};$$

A. These statements extend the chain, but keep *CurrentPosition* pointing to the very last link. The result looks like this:

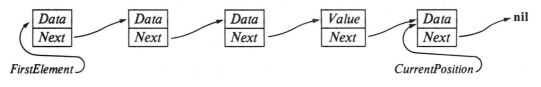

FirstElement   *CurrentPosition*

Operations with Links

Like Tinker toys and Leggo blocks, the individual elements of a linked structure may be attached to each other in a variety of patterns. However, certain basic operations (like connecting and disconnecting links) are required by most linked structures. In the self-check question above we saw how a linked list could be extended by connecting a new element to its end. The first statement:

$$new\,(CurrentPosition\uparrow.Next)\,;$$

allocates a new location. *CurrentPosition↑.Next* now references an undefined record, and the **nil** value is lost. The next statement:

$$CurrentPosition := CurrentPosition\uparrow.Next;$$

is potentially the most confusing—it advances the current position pointer, moving it to the end of the list. The illustration below shows how the pointer is reconnected.

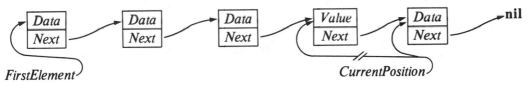

The third and final statement of the list extension makes the new list end **nil**.

$$CurrentPosition\uparrow.Next := \textbf{nil};$$

> In general, **nil** should always be used to mark the end of linked structures—a pointer should either have an address or be **nil**.

This makes list searching much easier. If *CurrentPosition* is pointing to a random element of a linked list, we can advance it to the list's end by searching for the **nil**-valued *Next* pointer—the last element.

> **while** *CurrentPosition*↑.*Next* <> **nil**
>   **do** *CurrentPosition* := *CurrentPosition*↑.*Next*;

Another run-of-the-mill task involves putting elements (although not necessarily blank ones) somewhere within an existing list. A single new element, referenced by the pointer *Temporary*, can be appended after the current pointer position with:

> *new* (*Temporary*) ;
> *Temporary*↑.*Next* := *CurrentPointer*↑.*Next*;
> *CurrentPointer*↑.*Next* := *Temporary*;

Or, an existing element (referenced by *NewElement*) can be inserted *before* the current pointer position element with:

> *new* (*Temporary*) ;
> *Temporary*↑ := *CurrentPointer*↑ ;
> *CurrentPointer*↑.*Next* := *Temporary*;
> *CurrentPointer*↑.*Data* := *NewElement*↑.*Data*;
> *dispose* (*NewElement*) ;
> *NewElement* := *CurrentPointer*;
> *CurrentPointer* := *CurrentPointer*↑.*Next*;

As you can see, we engaged in some sleight-of-hand, and didn't really insert the element referenced by *NewElement* into the list. Instead, we created a new, blank element:

$$new\ (Temporary)\ ;$$

gave it the same *Data* and *Next* fields as *CurrentPointer*:

$$Temporary\uparrow := CurrentPointer\uparrow\ ;$$

inserted it after *CurrentPointer*:

$$CurrentPointer\uparrow.Next := Temporary;$$

stored the new element's data in *CurrentPointer*:

$$CurrentPointer\uparrow.Data := NewElement\uparrow.Data;$$

disposed of the location no longer needed by the new element:

$$dispose\,(NewElement)\,;$$

arranged for *NewElement* to reference the list element that holds the new *Data* field:

$$NewElement := CurrentPointer;$$

and finally, advanced *CurrentPointer*:

$$CurrentPointer := CurrentPointer\uparrow.Next;$$

If you can follow that sequence, you shouldn't have any trouble with pointers. Here's an outline of the elements involved in the insertion — try filling in the pointers yourself.

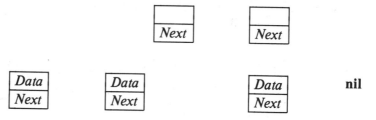

Having plenty of auxiliary pointers makes most list manipulations easier. Suppose that we want to insert a new list between two elements of a currently existing list. Two reconnections do the trick, and put the new list between the elements referenced by *CurrentPosition* and *CurrentPosition↑.Next.*

$$NewListEnd\uparrow.Next := CurrentPosition\uparrow.Next;$$
$$CurrentPosition\uparrow.Next := NewListStart;$$

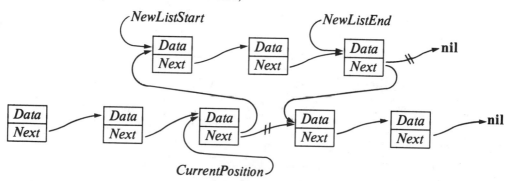

Auxiliary pointers are also useful for deleting one or more elements from a list. As long as we don't let part of the list get away (if it does, it's impossible to retrieve), list deletions take only a reconnection or two. Suppose this is the situation.

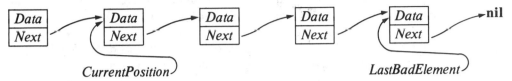

We can delete all elements from (not including) *CurrentPosition*↑ through (and including) *LastBadElement*↑ with:

> *CurrentPosition*↑ .*Next* := *LastBadElement*↑ .*Next*;

LastBadElement↑ will be retained in the new list if we do:

> *CurrentPosition*↑ .*Next* := *LastBadElement*;

Note that we haven't bothered to *dispose* of the elements we cut out.

Q. Suppose that we have a singly-linked list whose first element is accessed by two pointers— *CurrentPosition* and *PreviousPosition*. Assume that the last element of the list points to **nil**. What is the effect of this code?

```
while PreviousPosition <> nil
    do begin
        CurrentPosition := PreviousPosition↑ .Next;
        dispose (PreviousPosition) ;
        PreviousPosition := CurrentPosition
    end;
```

A. The code demonstrates a common **list-disposal** scheme. Each element of the list is disposed of in turn. At the end of the segment, *PreviousPosition* and *CurrentPosition* are both **nil**.

The basic linked list we've been using all along has an inconvenient shortcoming—it can only be traveled or inspected in one direction. An alteration in the type definition of *Element* solves this problem.

**More Link
Operations**

```
type ElementPointer = ↑Element;
     Element = record
                   Data: DataType;
                   Next, Previous: ElementPointer
               end;
```

> A list that has backward as well as forward pointers is called a **doubly-linked** list.

Inserting and deleting elements from doubly-linked lists is no more difficult than from singly-linked lists, as long as we remember to reconnect the links in both directions. Procedure *DoubleAppend*, below, puts a new, undefined element after the one accessed by *CurrentPosition*. Note that we have to re-do the links between the new element and *CurrentPosition*↑, and take care of the backward pointer of the element that follows the new one as well. Try to trace the procedure's operation without the aid of an illustration.

> **procedure** *DoubleAppend* (*CurrentPosition*: *ElementPointer*);
>
>   **var** *TemporaryPointer*: *ElementPointer*;
>
>   **begin**
>   *new* (*TemporaryPointer*);
>   *TemporaryPointer*↑.*Next* := *CurrentPosition*↑.*Next*;
>   *CurrentPosition* ↑.*Next* := *TemporaryPointer*;
>   *TemporaryPointer*↑.*Previous* := *CurrentPosition*;
>   *TemporaryPointer*↑.*Next*↑.*Previous* := *TemporaryPointer*
>   **end**;

The final assignment (which handles the backward pointer) is most confusing.

TemporaryPointer is a pointer.

TemporaryPointer↑ is the record it references.

TemporaryPointer↑.*Next* is a field of this record. However...

TemporaryPointer↑.*Next* is a pointer too. Therefore...

TemporaryPointer↑.*Next*↑ is a record;

TemporaryPointer↑.*Next*↑.*Previous* is a pointer field, as above.

The overall effect of the assignment is to make the element following the new element point back to the new one, instead of to the element referenced by *CurrentPosition*.

Pointers may be passed as parameters. Soon it will seem obvious, but now we'll point out that...

> When a pointer is passed as a variable-parameter, its address may be changed, as well as the contents of the location at that address. When a pointer is passed as a value-parameter, the contents of the location it references can be changed permanently. Changing the address of the value-parameter is only a local assignment.

Thus, passing a pointer as a value-parameter only partially inhibits our ability to reconfigure the structure it references.

:·

Q. What is the output of this program? What conclusions can you draw about passing pointers as value-parameters?

```
program RitesOfPassage (output);
    {Demonstrates some effects of passing a pointer as a value-parameter.}
type ElementPointer = ↑Element;
    Element = record
                    Data: char;
                    Next: ElementPointer
              end;
var Current: ElementPointer;
procedure Change (Pointer: ElementPointer);
    begin
        Pointer↑.Data := 'C';        {Which of these}
        Pointer := Pointer↑.Next;    {are local assignments?}
        Pointer↑.Data := 'D'
    end;   {Change}
begin
    new (Current);
    Current↑.Data := 'A';
    new (Current↑.Next);
    Current↑.Next↑.Data := 'B';
    writeln (Current↑.Data, Current↑.Next↑.Data);
    Change (Current);
    writeln (Current↑.Data, Current↑.Next↑.Data)
end.  {RitesOfPassage}
```

A. *RitesOfPassage* illustrates some of the hazards of passing pointers. The output of the first *writeln* is 'AB', while the second yields 'CD'. During *Change*, alterations to *Pointer* are local, but changes *within* the location it references are global and permanent. The assignment:

$$Pointer := Pointer↑.Next;$$

is negated on return to the main program— *Current* again points to the start of the list. However, assignments to any fields of the record *Pointer↑*, and to other linked records are permanent—the *Data* fields of both records in the list are changed permanently. We could even have globally lengthened the list from within *Change* by adding this statement to the procedure:

$$new (Pointer↑.Next)$$

:·

15-2
Data
Structures
That Use
Pointers

THE STUDY OF STRUCTURES FORMED WITH pointer types is the province of typical second or third computer science courses. We'll jump the gun in this section, and enjoy a brief overview of pointer-based data structures, including *queues, deques, stacks, graphs,* and *trees.* We'll also learn some of the operations and terminology associated with each. We've already encountered linked and doubly-linked lists. The illustration below shows a linked list with auxiliary pointers to its **head** and **tail**.

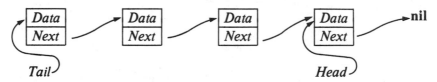

The type definition behind the structure is:

$$\textbf{type } ElementPointer = \uparrow ListElement;$$
$$ListElement = \textbf{record}$$
$$Data: \ DataType;$$
$$Next: \ ElementPointer$$
$$\textbf{end};$$
$$\textbf{var } Head, \ Tail: \ ElementPointer;$$

A common application of singly-linked lists is the maintenance of **queues** (kews'). A programing queue is just like a queue that forms inside a bank or outside a movie theater. People (or data) are added to one end and taken from the other—the first in is always the first out. These rules make a queue a queue, and raise it above the level of an ordinary list.

> Data structures are characterized by the operations that can be performed on them, as well as by the way they're created.

This idea applies equally to built-in data structures (like arrays or files) and to user-created structures (like queues).

Although standing in line isn't an especially deep concept, there are some subtleties involved in setting up a queue as a data structure. Suppose that we're working on the basis of the illustration above. An obvious approach would be to add new items to the tail, on the left, and then remove them when they've worked their way up to the head of the queue at the right. Let's see if coding these operations causes any problems. Items are added with:

$$new\,(TemporaryPointer)\,;$$
$$TemporaryPointer\uparrow.Next := \ Tail;$$
$$Tail := \ TemporaryPointer;$$

On the other hand, taking an item from the head is pretty difficult, because the head pointer can't be moved backward. Some elaborate code is required.

TemporaryPointer := *Tail*;
　　{Start *TemporaryPointer* at the tail of the list.}
while *TemporaryPointer*↑.*Next* <> *Head*
　　do *TemporaryPointer* := *TemporaryPointer*↑.*Next*;
　　　{This puts *TemporaryPointer* just before Head.}
Head := *TemporaryPointer*;
　　　{Now both pointers reference the next-to-last element.}
TemporaryPointer := *TemporaryPointer*↑.*Next*;
　　　{ *TemporaryPointer* points to the last element, and we can remove it.}

A queue doesn't really have to cause this much trouble. We can use a technique called ***visual thinking*** to get some other (and perhaps better) ideas about how to set one up.

> Visual thinking involves imagining the resolution of a problem in visual, and not algorithmic, terms.

In other words, a visual thinker might try to imagine that she can see a program working (and then try to figure out how or why it works), instead of first trying to come up with its algorithm.

The most famous example of visual thinking is probably that of the chemist Friedrich Kekule, who literally dreamed up the ring-shaped structure of benzene in a vivid reverie in which he saw that a snake biting its own tail could represent a series of linked atoms.* However, the visual approach to problem solving is thoroughly engrained in ordinary thinking. We *look* at problems and *see* their solutions. A bug is due to *oversight.* Wise people are *seers* with great *insight.* We could go on (and McLuhan has).

Visual thinking is particularly applicable to linked structures because the way that elements are connected (and not the type definition of each element) primarily characterizes a structure. We can radically change a queue representation without altering the basic *ListElement* definition at all. Just imagine a line of people (or list elements) moving from left to right, as above. This time, though, let's have each person point to the person *behind* instead of ahead.

Believe it or not, reversing the pointers will transform our linked list into a convenient representation of a queue. A new element is added with:

new (*Tail*↑.*Next*) ;
Tail := *Tail*↑.*Next*;
Tail↑.*Next* := **nil**;

---

* Remember this when we bring up circular lists, below.

Elements are removed in a similar manner.

$$TemporaryPointer := Head;$$
$$\textbf{if } Head\uparrow.Next <> \textbf{ nil}$$
$$\textbf{then } Head := Head\uparrow.Next;$$

Now, let's suppose that we want to make a structure similar to a queue, but which relaxes the restrictions on additions and deletions. Although elements will continue to move from the tail to the head, we'll reserve the right to cut into line—even at the head—in order to give some items extra priority. The name **deque** (dek), or double-ended queue, usually describes such a structure. Bearing in mind the difficulty we just had with a single-ended queue, can you propose an approach to implementing a deque?

Well, our problem with an ordinary queue was due to the 'directionality' of pointers in a linked list. We can travel and make connections in one direction, but not in the other. Using a doubly-linked list to implement the deque solves the problem. No matter where we are in the deque, we can make insertions or deletions before, after, or at the current element.

type *TwoElementPointer* = ↑ *StackElement*;
  StackElement = **record**
           Data: *DataType*;
           Next, Last: *TwoElementPointer*
        end;
  var *Head, Tail, ListPointer*: *TwoElementPointer*;

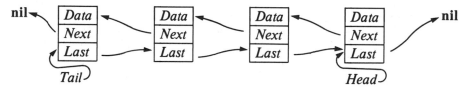

How about another variation? Nothing in the definition of *ListElement* says that we have to create lists with heads *or* tails. A **circular** list has no beginning or end—the last element points to the first. A circular list with only one element is interesting, and perfectly legal.

$$new\,(ListPointer);$$
$$ListPointer\uparrow.Next := ListPointer;$$

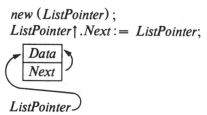

Although some applications specifically require circular data structures, many circular lists are generated because a single 'current position' pointer can act as both a head and tail pointer. For example, this circular list implements a queue:

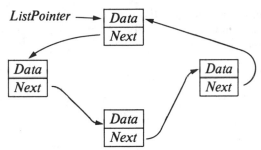

ListPointer points to the end of the queue. A new element is put on the queue with:

> *new* (*TemporaryPointer*) ;
> *TemporaryPointer*↑.*Next* := *ListPointer*↑.*Next*;
> *ListPointer*↑.*Next* := *TemporaryPointer*;
> *ListPointer* := *ListPointer*↑.*Next*;

The element that's been on the queue the longest is removed with:

> *TemporaryPointer* := *ListPointer*↑.*Next*;
> {Point *TemporaryPointer* at the oldest element.}
> *ListPointer*↑.*Next* := *ListPointer*↑.*Next*↑.*Next*;
> {Relink the list around it.}

Another variation on the usage of lists produces a **stack** structure. Stacks are last in, first out structures—the most recently added element is the first to be taken off. Thus, a stack has a **top**, instead of a head or tail. New elements are **pushed** onto the stack, while old ones are **popped** off.*

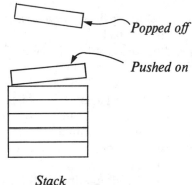

Popped off

Pushed on

Stack

Implementing stacks requires a simple renaming of the basic linking and unlinking operations, as well as a design decision akin to the choice we made for a queue—should the pointers go up or down the stack? In procedures *Push* and *Pop,* below, we've stayed with our basic, single-pointer, *ListElement* data structure. Each new element points to the current stack, which means that the pointers go down.

---

* This terminology comes from the most popular image of stacks—the spring-loaded stack of trays in a cafeteria.

Procedure *Push* puts a new element (referenced by *NewElement*) on top of the stack, then advances *Top* there as well. Only *Top* need be passed as a variable-parameter.

procedure *Push* (*NewElement*: *ElementPointer*; **var** *Top*: *ElementPointer*) ;
{Pushes *NewElement* on top of a stack.}
begin
   NewElement↑.*Next* := *Top*;
   Top := *NewElement*
end;   {*Push*}

Pop points *PoppedElement* at the top element of the stack, then moves *Top* down by one element. Because both pointers are permanently changed, they're both passed as variable-parameters.

procedure *Pop* (**var** *PoppedElement, Top*: *ElementPointer*) ;
{Pops *PoppedElement* from a stack.}
begin
   PoppedElement := *Top*;
   Top := *Top*↑.*Next*;
   PoppedElement↑.*Next* := **nil**
end;   {*Pop*}

> A popped element should be isolated from the rest of the stack. Although setting *PoppedElement's* pointer field to **nil** isn't essential, doing so helps prevent inadvertent errors in another part of the program.

If we didn't set its *Next* field to **nil**, *PoppedElement* could still be used to access and change the entire stack.

What are stacks and queues used for? Queues are essential when, by accident or design, data can't be relied on to arrive in an orderly fashion. For example, programs that run timeshared computers (which are used simultaneously by several users) use queues to keep track of each user's input. In effect, the computer executes commands at one end of the queue while adding new commands to the other end as they come in. A deque can be used to give commands varying priority by inserting them *within* the queue.

Queues are also useful for simulating real-life processes. Suppose that we run a ticket counter, and want to decide if each window should have its own line, or if a single line should feed all the windows. The nature of the problem—customers arriving at irregular intervals, and being served after varying waits—calls for a queue representation.

Stacks tend to have specialized, computer-oriented applications, and aren't representations of real-life phenomena. For example, many kinds of *reversals* use stacks—you may recall our recursive use of the computer's stack in reversing a line of input (section 8-2). Arithmetic expressions often take advantage of stacks as well—the order of operators and operands on a stack does away with the need for parentheses.

Don't forget that an abstract data structure (like a queue or stack) is just a set of rules for storing and retrieving data. A programing structure (like a linked or doubly-linked list) is the way we represent it in Pascal.

Graphs

A more liberal application of pointers between individual elements leads to a more complicated pointer structure called a *graph*

We'll broadly define a *graph* as a pointer structure whose elements are not required to be in linear order.

The picture of the Cave of the Wumpus was a graph, as is this diagram of distances between cities.

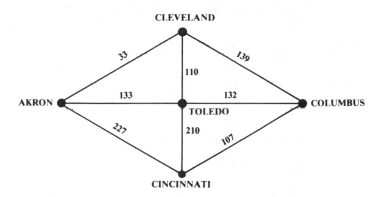

A much simpler graph can be used to represent a *sparse matrix*. Now, since *matrix* is a rough synonym for a two-dimensional array, a sparse matrix is an array whose component values are almost all identical. As a result, only the non-identical elements are interesting and worth storing. For example, suppose that we want to hold some of the data connected with running a university. *Oh! Pascal! U.* has 100 courses and 10,000 students. How can we keep track of what classes each student is taking, and of which students are in each class?

A reasonable first proposal would be to use a two-dimensional array, with course numbers providing one subscript, and student identification numbers the other. An element is filled in with:

Enrollment [*Course, Student*] := *Taken*;

However, even though such an array would be quite large—one million elements—most of its stored values would be the same—**not** *Taken* If each student were taking four classes, the array would only be 4% filled. *Enrollment* is clearly a sparse matrix.

Representing the enrollment data with pointers is a much better approach. We want an interlaced network of two sorts of lists—lists of the courses each student is taking, and lists of the students enrolled in each course. The illustration below shows how it's done, and demonstrates some new techniques. To begin with, enrollment data is stored in a record with the following structure:

type *String* = **packed array** [1..20] **of** *char*;
      CoursePointer = ↑*EnrollmentData*;
      EnrollmentData = **record**
                              Course, Student: *String*;
                              NextCourse, NextStudent: *CoursePointer*
            end;

A single record is simultaneously a 'students in this course' and 'courses of this student' element. The structure is like that of a doubly-linked list, except that the links are rotated 90° (instead of 180°) to each other.

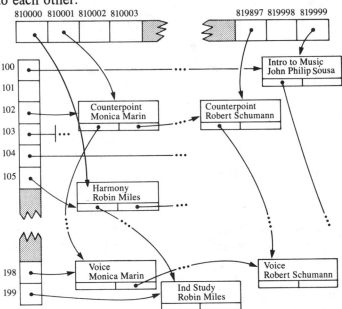

The start of each list is set up in a clever manner. Although we could easily have linked lists of course and student numbers, defining two arrays of type *CoursePointer* takes advantage of the random-access feature of arrays. This lets us find a particular student or course list quickly. The type definition moves along with:

type
           : {Continued from above.}
      CourseNumbers = 100..199;
      StudentNumbers = 810000..819999;   {Class of '81.}
      CourseArray = **array** [*CourseNumbers*] **of** *CoursePointer*;
      StudentArray = **array** [*StudentNumbers*] **of** *CoursePointer*;

Suppose we want to print the names of all students taking course *TooCrowded* No sooner said than done.

procedure *PrintStudentNames* (*TooCrowded*: *CourseNumbers*; *Enrollment*: *CourseArray*) ;
    {Prints the names of all students in course *TooCrowded*}

    var *Temporary* := *CoursePointer*;

    begin
writeln ('Students enrolled in course ', *TooCrowded*:1, ' are:') ;
Temporary := *Enrollment* [*TooCrowded*] ;   {Go the the head of the list.}
while *Temporary* < > **nil**   {While there are records to inspect...}
   do begin
      writeln (*Temporary*↑.*Student*) ;   {Print the name stored in the record,}
      Temporary := *Temporary*↑.*NextStudent* {and advance the pointer.}
   end
end;   {*PrintStudentNames*}

    Letting students change their schedules is just a matter of making list insertions or deletions.

·:

Q. Would this code be equivalent to the shaded program segment above? Why or why not?

Self-Check
Questions

```
        TemporaryPointer := Enrollment [TooCrowded] ;
        repeat
            writeln (Temporary↑.Student) ;
            Temporary := Temporary↑.NextStudent
        until Temporary = nil;
```

A. The code is fine—if any students are taking the class. If nobody has enrolled in course *TooCrowded*, the program crashes attempting to output the *Student* field of a **nil** pointer.

:··:

Binary Trees

Of all the data structures that can be represented with pointers, **trees** are probably the niftiest. A **node** at the top of the tree points the way to zero or more different nodes. Each of these, in turn, points to another group of distinct nodes. We can draw a general tree as:

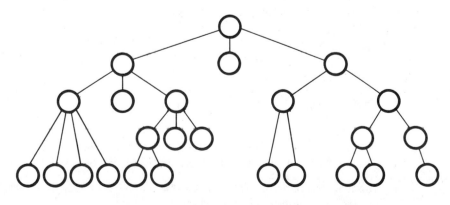

If you look carefully a whole forest is visible—each labeled node points to one or more sub-trees. Now, it's essential that each sub-tree consist of *distinct* nodes—no two sub-trees can share a node. This restriction makes trees *recursively defined* pointer structures. Any tree can be defined as being an element that's linked to one or more trees, or to nothing.

> The **root** of a tree is its first (topmost) node. The nodes that each element points to are its **children**; it is the **parent**. Finally, a node that has no children is called a **leaf**.

Limiting each node to a maximum of two children (i.e. to two potential sub-trees) creates a **binary** (two-part) tree, which is a structure we'll explore in detail. The definition of a binary-node type is much like that of a doubly-linked list element. Only the identifiers have been changed to protect the confused.

```
type NodePointer = ↑Node;
     Node = record
                Data: DataType;
                LeftChild, RightChild: NodePointer
            end;
```

Since trees are recursively defined, recursive subprograms are convenient for tree structure operations. These usually involve searching trees, or adding additional nodes. We can describe the recursive steps of one tree-searching algorithm in English. (Assume that *CurrentNode* starts by referencing the root.)

To Search a Tree ...

1. If *CurrentNode's* left child isn't **nil**, point *CurrentNode* at the left child and search the tree.

2. If *CurrentNode's* right child isn't **nil**, point *CurrentNode* at the right child and search the tree.

3. Print the value stored in the current node.

In practice, each time we return to action 1 (the equivalent of making a recursive procedure call) the values associated with the current node will be saved, along with any pending actions.

> Using recursion allows backtracking without backward pointers.

The algorithm is implemented in the recursive procedure *InspectTree.*

```
procedure InspectTree (CurrentNode: NodePointer);
    {Visit every node of a binary tree.}
    begin
        if CurrentNode↑.LeftChild <> nil then InspectTree (CurrentNode↑.LeftChild);
        if CurrentNode↑.RightChild <> nil then InspectTree (CurrentNode↑.RightChild);
        writeln (CurrentNode↑.Data)
    end;
```

The effect of *InspectTree* can be described as:

> Go down the tree as far as possible, trying to go left, but going right if necessary. Print this node's value. Back up one node, then go down the tree again, following the same strategy—left if possible, right if necessary—until you come to a dead end, or a node you've already visited. Inspect this node, then repeat the search process. When there are no more nodes to search—each child has been visited already—the root has been found, and the entire tree has been inspected.

If you have difficulty imagining the operation of a recursive procedure, stepping through an example of a small tree may help. Looking at the boundary cases of a large tree is also useful.

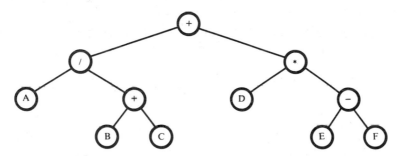

Suppose we use *InspectTree* to search the binary tree above. Its nodes will be searched in the following order, called ***postorder***.*

$$A \ B \ C + / \ D \ E \ F - * +$$

If you own a stack-type calculator you'll recognize this as an arithmetic expression.** In postorder search, a node's sub-trees are inspected before the node itself is. As a result, the root is looked at last.

:·:·:

Q. Suppose that we reorder the three statements of *InspectTree* as shown below. Will the procedure still work? What effect do the changes have?

Self-Check
Questions

    {First variation.}
writeln (*CurrentNode↑.Data*) ;
if *CurrentNode↑.LeftChild* <> **nil then** *InspectTree* (*InspectTree↑.LeftChild*) ;
if *CurrentNode↑.RightChild* <> **nil then** *InspectTree* (*InspectTree↑.RightChild*)

    {Second variation.}
if *CurrentNode↑.LeftChild* <> **nil then** *InspectTree* (*InspectTree↑.LeftChild*) ;
writeln (*CurrentNode↑.Data*) ;
if *CurrentNode↑.RightChild* <> **nil then** *InspectTree* (*InspectTree↑.RightChild*)

---

* *Postfix* and *Reverse Polish* (or *RPN*) are other names for this particular notation.
** It's equivalent to $A/(B+C) + D*(E-F)$.

A. The variations do work, but they change the order in which nodes are visited. The first variation is called a *preorder* search—first a node is inspected, and then its sub-trees. Applied to our earlier tree, we have:

$$+ / A + B C * D - E F$$

The second modification produces an *inorder* search. The left sub-tree is searched, then the node, and finally the right sub-tree. The path followed is:

$$A / B + C + D * E - F$$

:..:....:...:

Programing Binary Trees

The applications of binary trees are unexpectedly diverse. Consider the tree below. Can you guess what it represents?

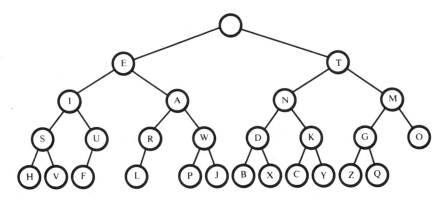

Perhaps the structure definition of each node will help.

```
type NextCodeNode = ↑ CodeNode;
     CodeNode = record
                    Letter: char;
                    Dot, Dash: NextCodeNode
                end;
     var Root: NextCodeNode;
```

As you can probably gather, the tree represents the Morse code. Procedure *Decode*, below, uses the code tree to translate a file of Morse into the letters it stands for. Its parameters are *RootPointer*, which points to the root of the stored code-tree, and *DataFile*, a *text* file of dots, dashes, and spaces. Since we never backtrack (and don't need a stack) *Decode* isn't written recursively. However, we do have to maintain a pointer to the root of the code tree, to start all over again for each new letter.

```
procedure Decode (RootPointer: NextCodeNode; var DataFile: text);
    {Decodes Morse Code input. Each complete letter must be followed by a blank.}
    var CurrentPointer: NextCodeNode;
        InputCharacter: char;
begin
    reset (DataFile);
    CurrentPointer := RootPointer;
    while not eof (DataFile)
        do begin
            read (DataFile, InputCharacter);
            case InputCharacter of
                '.' : CurrentPointer := CurrentPointer↑.Dot;
                '—': CurrentPointer := CurrentPointer↑.Dash;
                ' ' : begin
                        write (CurrentPointer↑.Letter);
                        CurrentPointer := RootPointer
                    end
            end {case}
        end; {while}
    writeln (CurrentPointer↑.Letter)
end; {Decode}
```

```
·__·'_ _·'_·' _·'_ __ _·'__ _··· ___ _·'_'
·'__ ·· _ ···· ··_·' ·· ···_ · _·· ___ __·· · _·'
·_·· ·· __·'_ ··_ ___ ·_' ·___ ··_ __·' ···
PACK MY BOX WITH FIVE DOZEN LIQUOR JUGS
```

Morse can be stored in a binary tree because the dot/dash code is essentially a series of yes/no questions. Surprisingly, most data can be stored and retrieved using binary trees. An interactive computer game called *Animal* is a good example. The computer plays by trying to guess the name of an animal the player imagines. Although an animal may have many characteristics, considering only one at a time—Is the animal furry? Does it have horns?—reduces its description to a string of binary (two-way) choices. Some sample output from an *Animal* run will help you picture its operation.

```
Think of an animal.
Does it have fur?  Answer yes or no.
no
Does it have tusks?
yes
Does it have big ears?
no
Is it a rhino?
```

The *Animal* program relies on two kinds of stored data—characteristics, and (ultimately) the names of animals. The most crucial set of facts—the relationship between characteristic and name—is contained in the binary tree that *holds* the information. The program begins at the tree's root and asks the question stored as a string in that node. Whether the left or right node is visited next visited depends on the answer—sometimes a further question is required (and the process starts again), and sometimes we reach a leaf or final node (and with it, the name of an animal).

Incidentally, the *Animal* program learns as it plays. If it reaches a leaf and guesses wrong, the following transaction takes place.

`I guessed wrong.    What animal were you thinking of?`
a wild boar
`Type in an additional question I should have asked.`
Does it have bad breath?
`Is the correct answer yes or no?`
yes   *etc.*

Internally, a new node is added to the stored data structure, along with the implication that rhinos don't have bad breath.

A subtle aspect of understanding tree structures is recognizing the relation between the way data is stored and the way that it's retrieved again. This is especially true when a hand-drawn representation of a tree's stored data doesn't (at first glance) show its order or purpose. Consider this tree.

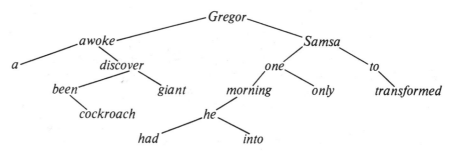

The tree stores the words of this sentence:

Gregor Samsa awoke one morning only to discover he had been transformed into a giant cockroach

in alphabetical order (disregarding capitalization). The first word, 'Gregor', goes to the root of the tree. The second word follows the first alphabetically, so it's stored in the right child. The third word precedes the first alphabetically, so it goes into the left-hand node. The fourth word, 'one', comes after the first, but before the second. It goes to the root's right child's left child. The final resting place of each word is determined by traveling down the tree, turning left or right, or making a new node as necessary.

As you might imagine, we can recursively describe the ordering algorithm.

To Build an Alphabetically Ordered Tree...

1.   If the current node is **nil**, store the new word there and stop.

2.   If the new word precedes the word in the current node, point to the left child and build an alphabetically ordered tree.

3.   If the new word follows the word in the current node, point to the right child and build an alphabetically ordered tree.

4.   If the new word is the same as the word in the current node, stop.

In procedure *AddAWord,* below, the final **else** (which represents step 4) isn't necessary, and could be omitted. We've just included it to show you how to touch all the bases.

```
type String = packed array [1..15] of char;
     WordPointer = ↑ WordStorage;
     WordStorage = record
                        Word: String;
                        Before, After: WordPointer
                   end;
   :   {Other definitions and declarations.}
procedure AddAWord (var Current: WordPointer; NewWord: String);
   {Adds the string NewWord to an alphabetically ordered binary tree.}
   begin
     if Current =nil
        then begin
           new (Current);
           Current↑.Word := NewWord;
           Current↑.Before := nil;
           Current↑.After := nil
        end
        else if NewWord< Current↑.Word
           then AddAWord (Current↑.Before, NewWord)
           else if NewWord> Current↑.Word
              then AddAWord (Current↑.After, NewWord)
              else {The word is a duplicate—NewWord=Current↑.Word}
   end; {AddAWord}
```

AddAWord is probably the most complicated recursive procedure we'll have to deal with. Note that *AddAWord* is an end recursion—the stack isn't used to store values or pending statements. It could easily be written iteratively.

It will come as a welcome surprise to find that a job that seems complicated (like printing the contents of a tree in alphabetical order), is really pretty easy. It takes an inorder traversal—one of the possible variations on procedure *InspectTree,* which we wrote a few pages back to search an expression tree. The output of *PrintInOrder,* below, assumes that *CurrentWord* currently references the root of the *Gregor Samsa awoke...* tree. (We broke the output into two lines ourselves.)

procedure *PrintInOrder* (*CurrentWord*: *WordPointer*);
　　{Prints the nodes of an alphabetically ordered binary tree in order.}
　　begin
　　　　if *CurrentWord↑.Before* <> **nil then** *InorderTraversal* (*CurrentWord↑.Before*);
　　　　write (*CurrentWord↑.Word*);
　　　　if *CurrentWord↑.After* <> **nil then** *InorderTraversal* (*CurrentWord↑.After*);
　　　　writeln;
　　end;　{*PrintInOrder*}

```
     ↓        ↓         ↓          ↓          ↓
a awoke been cockroach discover giant gregor had
he into morning one only samsa to transformed
```

Self-Check
Questions

Q. Suppose that we're creating an alphabetically ordered binary tree using procedure *AddAWord*. What will the trees produced by these sentences look like?

　　a big cat did everything

　　zesty young xylophones wed violins

A. A quick perusal shows that the sample sentences are in alphabetical and reverse-alphabetical order. They produce **degenerate** trees—trees that can't be distinguished from ordinary lists.

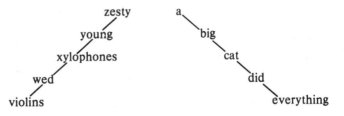

15-3
Focus on
Programing:
Linked
Structures

WE'LL END OUR DISCUSSION OF POINTERS with a long example program. It uses some of the linked structures we've just met, and helps demonstrate how simple ideas and techniques can be joined to form long and useful programs. Our problem is:

　　Write a program that reads a list of words of interest (keywords), then searches a source file for those words. Each keyword should be printed in its context, e.g. with the four words that come before it and after it.

This is an on-line form of a *KWIC—Key Word In Context—* program. A first appraisal and refinement of the problem presents an obvious program outline.

Get the keywords.
Read in the source file one word at a time.
If the current word is a keyword, print it in context.

What should we do with the keywords as they're read in? It's not much trouble to store them in a variety of ways—array, file, linked list, etc. However, step three—*If the current word is a keyword...*—means that we'll want to be able to search through the stored keywords very quickly.

As we've often found, the choice of an algorithm is intimately tied to the design of a data structure.

It turns out that if keywords are read in at random, then alphabetically ordering them in a binary tree helps minimize the time required to confirm or deny that a given word is present. As a result, 'Get the keywords' is, more or less, procedure *AddAWord* (from the last section). We get the keywords by constructing an alphabetically ordered binary tree.

The last part of the last step—*print it in context*—presents a more serious problem. Should we look up each word as it's read in, then somehow back up the source file to get the words that came immediately before? Unfortunately, if you know Pascal, you know that we can't back up—we have to reread the entire file. What we really need is a small buffer of some sort that holds the current nine words, and lets us look up the central one. That way, if the central word is in the tree of keywords, we already have the words surrounding it. Any ideas?

The word *buffer* should be a giveaway. A buffer is a queue—the whole point of a buffer is to provide a temporary holding place for data while maintaining its order. In fact, we can represent the queue with a circular list (sometimes called a *ring* buffer). As each new word comes in, it replaces the oldest word in the queue and the 'oldest word' pointer is advanced one place. The current central word (the one we're going to look up) can be accessed with an auxiliary pointer.

Using a ring buffer isn't entirely a bed of roses. We have to establish a context for the first word by pretending to read blank words when initializing the queue. Similarly, pretending to input four blanks at the end of the source file maintains a context through the very last word. This is a small detail, but it's big enough to stump many programers.

In a second refinement our algorithm becomes:

Get the keyword file ready
Build an alphabetically ordered binary tree
Get the source file ready
Initialize a buffer
Using the buffer, inspect the source file and print its keywords in context
Inspect the words left in the buffer

Now, when we begin to write our program, we'll have to address some global concerns that might not seem too urgent, but which could cause trouble. For instance, several of the values the program relies upon may require modification. They should be defined as constants: the length of the longest word, a blank word of that length, and the exact size of a 'context.'

What about error checking? This means user's errors as well as run-time errors—our program should at least ensure that the keyword and source files aren't blank. A harder sort of robustness involves errors that aren't mistakes at all. Is 'Important' the same word as 'important'? Is a word followed by punctuation identical to the same word followed by a space? Most people would say yes, and a well-written program should agree.

Let's try a third refinement of the *KWIC* algorithm.

> *get the keyword file ready*;
> *get the source file ready*;
> **if** *neither of the files is empty*
> > **then**   {Make the binary tree of keywords.}
> > > *initialize the tree by creating a root*;
> > > **repeat**
> > > > *get the next word from the keyword file*;
> > > > *add it to the binary tree of keywords*
> > > **until** *there aren't any keywords left*;
> > > *initialize the ring buffer with blanks, and the first few source words*;
> > > **repeat**   {Look for the keywords in the source file.}
> > > > *get the next word from the source file*;
> > > > *add it to the ring buffer*;
> > > > **if** *the buffer's center word is found in the keyword file*
> > > > > **then** *print the contents of the ring buffer*
> > > **until** *there aren't any source words left*;
> > > *Flush the buffer—take care of the words remaining in the buffer*;
> > **else** *Give abnormal termination messages—one of the files was empty*

How can we flush (empty) the buffer without losing the last words it stores? We'll do just what we said a few paragraphs back—add four blank words to the buffer. A jump ahead to a deeper refinement level points the way.

> > **for** *the first half of the buffer*
> > > *add a blank to the end of the buffer*;
> > > **if** *the center word in the buffer is a keyword*
> > > > **then** *print the whole buffer*;

An issue that we won't have to deal with (but which you'll be stuck with in your own programs), is a writing schedule. Sometimes, contradictory programing techniques must be applied at different levels. For example, it's a good idea to omit many refinements and write a program as complicated as *KWIC* in the form of a stub program. A detail as important as searching for the last few words of the source file is, in the final analysis, just a detail. You shouldn't let it delay production of a partially working version.

Our final pseudocode version of *KWIC*, below, leaves out some refinements we brought up ourselves—it doesn't implement upper- to lower-case conversions, or ignore punctuation. Its main purpose is to give names to the program's main procedures, and to help identify the parameters each one will require.

Get file KeyWords ready;
Get file Source ready;
if *neither of the files is empty*
   then   {Make the binary tree.}
    Root := **nil**;
    repeat
       InputString (*KeyWords, TheWord*) ;
       AddAWord (*Root, TheWord*)
    until *eof* (*Keywords*) ;
    InitializeTheBuffer (*Source, Center, Tail*) ;
    repeat   {Look for the keywords.}
       InputString (*Source, TheWord*) ;
       AddItToTheBuffer (*Tail, Center, TheWord*) ;
       if *ItIsAKeyWord* (*Root, Center↑.Word*) **then** *PrintTheContext* (*Tail*) ;
    until *eof* (*Source*)
    FlushTheBuffer (*Root, Tail, Center*)
  else *Give abnormal termination messages.*

> No matter what programing method you use to develop a program as large as *KWIC*, you shouldn't be afraid of trying to perfect one or more procedures in dummy 'driver' programs.

If, for example, you're uncertain about your ability to build a binary tree, you should probably write a quick program that builds and traverses binary trees—even if you're using a stub programing approach. A complete tree traversal—which isn't necessarily required in the *KWIC* program—takes only a few lines of code and will confirm that your *AddAWord* procedure was correctly implemented. We've installed an *InspectTheTree* procedure in our *KWIC* that's called only if a global constant called *DeBugging* is set to *true.*

Program testing is equally important. By now you should be sophisticated enough to realize that experienced programers usually find program bugs or shortcomings *not* because they're sharp enough to pick out errors on sight, but by understanding that certain kinds of program input are usually overlooked by novices. Empty keyword or source files shouldn't cause a program crash; neither should blank lines or punctuation. Most potential problems are easy to fix—the hard part is anticipating them.

The actual program is shown over the next few pages. The contents of file *Source* are shown as the program's input. Since *DeBugging* is set to *true*, the contents of the alphabetized *KeyWords* tree are shown as well.

```
program KWIC (KeyWords, Source, output);
    {Prints all KeyWords that appear in Source in their context.}

const DeBugging = true;    {If true, the KeyWords tree is printed.}
      MaximumWordLength = 20;    {Length of the longest string.}
      BlankWord = '                    ';    {MaximumWordLength spaces.}
      SizeOfContext = 9;    {Must be an odd number.}

type String = packed array [1..MaximumWordLength] of char;
            {Binary tree node definitions.}
     NodePointer = ↑ Node;
     Node = record
                 Word: String;
                 Before, After: NodePointer
             end;
            {Circular list (ring buffer) element definitions.}
     ElementPointer = ↑ Element;
     Element = record
                   Word: String;
                   Next: ElementPointer
               end;

var KeyWords,           {File of words we're checking for.}
    Source: text;        {The file we're checking through.}
    Root: NodePointer;        {Accesses the root of the keyword tree.}
    Tail,           {Accesses the oldest element in the buffer.}
    Center: ElementPointer;        {Accesses the 'current' buffer element.}
    TheWord: String;

procedure SkipBlanks (var FromFile: text);
            {Skips leading or trailing blank spaces, including new-lines.}
    var Finished: boolean;
    begin
        Finished := false;
        repeat
            if eof(FromFile) then Finished := true
                else if FromFile↑ = ' ' then get(FromFile)
                    else Finished := true
        until Finished
    end;   {SkipBlanks}
```

Key Words   *the Word*

```
procedure InputString (var FromFile: text; var Word: String);
        {WARNING! Breaks words over MaximumWordLength characters long.}
        {This version does not modify upper-case letters or punctuation.}
    var Counter: integer;
    begin
        Word := BlankWord;
        Counter := 1;
        while (FromFile↑ <> ' ') and (Counter< =MaximumWordLength)
            do begin
                {Code to convert upper-case to lower-case and remove
                    punctuation will go here at next program refinement.}
                Word [Counter] := FromFile↑;
                get(FromFile);
                Counter := Counter+1
            end;
        SkipBlanks (FromFile)
    end;   {InputString}

procedure OutputString (Word: String);
        {Prints the leading nonblank portion of each String array.}
    var Counter: integer;
        Finished: boolean;
    begin
        Counter := 1;
        repeat
            Finished := (Word [Counter]=' ');
            if not Finished then write (Word [Counter]);
            Counter := Counter+1
        until (Counter> MaximumWordLength) or Finished
    end;   {OutputString}

procedure AddA Word (var Current: NodePointer; NewWord: String);
        {Recursively creates an alphabetically-ordered binary tree.}
    begin
        if Current =nil
            then begin
                new (Current);
                Current↑.Word := NewWord;
                Current↑.Before := nil;
                Current↑.After := nil
            end
            else if NewWord< Current↑.Word
                then AddA Word (Current↑.Before, NewWord)
                else if NewWord> Current↑.Word
                    then AddA Word (Current↑.After, NewWord)
    end;   {AddA Word}
```

[421]

```
procedure InspectTheTree (CurrentNode: NodePointer);
        {A recursive debugging procedure that does an inorder search of the binary tree
        of keywords.  Only called if the global constant DeBugging is true.}
    begin
        if CurrentNode↑.Before <> nil then InspectTheTree (CurrentNode↑.Before);
        writeln (CurrentNode↑.Word);
        if CurrentNode↑.After <> nil then InspectTheTree (CurrentNode↑.After)
    end;   {InspectTheTree}


procedure InitializeTheBuffer (var Source: text; var Tail, Center: ElementPointer);
    {Creates a ring buffer SizeOfContext elements long.  Elements older than and
    including Center are initialized as blanks; the rest of the buffer is filled from Source.}
    var TemporaryPointer: ElementPointer;
        Counter: integer;
    begin
        new (TemporaryPointer);
        Tail := TemporaryPointer;            {Locate the oldest element.}
        for Counter := 1 to (SizeOfContext div 2)
            do begin
                TemporaryPointer↑.Word := BlankWord;
                new (TemporaryPointer↑.Next);
                TemporaryPointer := TemporaryPointer↑.Next
            end;
        Center := TemporaryPointer;          {Locate the central 'working' element.}
        for Counter := 1 to (SizeOfContext div 2)
            do begin
                new (TemporaryPointer↑.Next);
                TemporaryPointer := TemporaryPointer↑.Next;
                InputString (Source, TemporaryPointer↑.Word)
            end;
        TemporaryPointer↑.Next := Tail          {Make the list circular.}
    end;   {InitializeTheBuffer}


procedure AddItToTheBuffer (var Tail, Center: ElementPointer; TheWord: String);
        {Replaces the oldest word in the buffer with the one just input.
        Advances the tail and 'current' pointers.}
    begin
        Tail↑.Word := TheWord;
        Tail := Tail↑.Next;
        Center := Center↑.Next
    end;   {AddItToTheBuffer}
```

```
function ItIsAKeyWord (CurrentNode: NodePointer; TheWord: String) : boolean;
      {Search the binary tree for a particular word.}

   var ItsFound: boolean;

   begin
      ItsFound := false;
      repeat
         if TheWord< CurrentNode↑.Word
            then CurrentNode := CurrentNode↑.Before
            else if TheWord> CurrentNode↑.Word
               then CurrentNode := CurrentNode↑.After
               else ItsFound := true
      until (CurrentNode =nil) or ItsFound;
      ItIsAKeyWord := ItsFound
   end;   {ItIsAKeyWord}


procedure PrintTheContext (Tail: ElementPointer) ;

      {Prints each word in the buffer (spacing between), then new-lines.}

   var TemporaryPointer: ElementPointer;

   begin
      TemporaryPointer := Tail;
      repeat
         OutputString (TemporaryPointer↑.Word) ;
         write (' ') ;
         TemporaryPointer := TemporaryPointer↑.Next
      until TemporaryPointer = Tail;
      writeln
   end;   {PrintTheContext}


procedure FlushTheBuffer (Root: NodePointer; var Tail, Center: ElementPointer) ;

      {Inspects the words remaining in the buffer.}

   var Counter: integer;

   begin
      for Counter := 1 to (SizeOfContext div 2)
         do begin
            AddItToTheBuffer (Tail, Center, BlankWord) ;
            if ItIsAKeyWord(Root, Center↑.Word) then PrintTheContext (Tail)
         end
   end;   {FlushTheBuffer}
```

```
begin  {KWIC}
    reset (KeyWords) ;
    SkipBlanks (KeyWords) ;
    reset (Source) ;
    SkipBlanks (Source) ;
    if not eof(KeyWords) and not eof(Source)
        then begin          {KWIC action.}
                    {Set up the tree of keywords.}
            Root := nil;
            repeat
                InputString (KeyWords, TheWord) ;
                AddAWord (Root, TheWord)
            until eof(KeyWords) ;
            if DeBugging then InspectTheTree (Root) ;
                    {Set up the buffer and search for words.}
            InitializeTheBuffer (Source, Tail, Center) ;
            repeat
                InputString (Source, TheWord) ;
                AddItToTheBuffer (Tail, Center, TheWord) ;
                if ItIsAKeyWord(Root, Center↑.Word)
                    then PrintTheContext (Tail)
            until eof(Source) ;
            FlushTheBuffer (Root, Tail, Center)
        end  {KWIC action}
        else begin          {Abnormal termination messages.}
            if eof(KeyWords)
                then writeln ('Abnormal program termination.  KeyWord file empty.') ;
            if eof(Source)
                then writeln ('Abnormal program termination.  Source file empty.')
        end  {else action}
end.  {KWIC}
```

↓   ↓   ↓   ↓   ↓

**here is a kwic test file that is designed to check special cases of
kwic operation. It includes blank lines,**

punctuation, and has key words at both the beginning and

**end of the file. however, it doesn't include capital letters. the
keyword file also contains blank lines. end**

```
blank
end
file
here
it
lines
that
```

```
    here is a kwic test
is a kwic test file that is designed to
a kwic test file that is designed to check
kwic operation. It includes blank lines, punctuation, and has
both the beginning and end of the file. however,
of the file. however, it doesn't include capital letters.
capital letters. the keyword file also contains blank lines.
keyword file also contains blank lines. end
also contains blank lines. end
```

15-4 Antibugging and Debugging

THE WAY TO UNDERSTAND POINTERS, LIKE the way to Carnegie Hall, is through practice. Although pointers aren't an exceptionally hard abstraction, many little rules must be followed when they're used. As a result, not everyone who understands a linked structure can implement it in Pascal. As we mentioned in the introduction, we always have to insist on the highest degree of learning—not 'Do I understand it?' but rather, 'Can I duplicate it?'.

The difference between an undefined pointer and a pointer that references an undefined location causes many run-time errors. Suppose that we have these definitions:

> **type** *ElementPointer* = ↑ *Element*;
>   *Element* = **record**
>   *A, B*: *integer*;
>   *NextElement*: *ElementPointer*
>   **end**;
> **var** *CurrentPosition*: *ElementPointer*;

At the start of a program, *CurrentPosition* is undefined (although many Pascal compilers initialize pointer-type variables to **nil**).

> Whether or not *ElementPointer* has been initialized to **nil**, it does *not* reference a location.

Programers usually make the mistake of assuming that *ElementPointer* references a record of type *Element* whose fields are undefined. Unfortunately, trying to make an assignment results in a run-time crash.

> *CurrentPosition*↑.*A* := 0;
>   ↓   ↓   ↓   ↓   {At run time...}
> ABNORMAL TERMINATION - -
> REFERENCE THROUGH NIL POINTER

Before a reference can be made through any pointer variable, a location must be allocated (using procedure *new*).

$$new\ (CurrentPosition)\ ;$$

Now *CurrentPosition* really does reference a record whose fields are undefined.

Two varieties of infinite loops are caused by pointers. The first occurs when dynamic allocation runs wild.

```
new (SomeRecord) ;
repeat
    new (SomeRecord↑ .Next) ;
    SomeRecord := SomeRecord↑ .Next
until false        etc.
```

This program segment generates a never-ending list. When the computer runs out of new locations to allocate, the program crashes with a message like:

```
ABNORMAL TERMINATION - -
HEAP OVERFLOW
```

> Pointer locations are said to be allocated from a **heap** of unused locations in memory.

Heap overflow* crashes are no more serious than 'statement limit exceeded' crashes. They can also occur (rarely) in programs that dynamically allocate many locations without ever returning any to the computer (with *dispose*) for possible reallocation.

The second kind of infinite loop results from an endless search, usually through a circular list, for a location or pointer value that isn't there. The fail-safe of running past the end of an array simply doesn't exist. The examples below show **while** loops that are reasonable if and only if we're certain to eventually find pointer *SoughtPosition* or value *SoughtData*.

```
while CurrentPosition <> SoughtPosition
    do CurrentPosition := CurrentPosition↑ .Next    etc.
while CurrentPosition↑ .Data <> SoughtData
    do CurrentPosition := CurrentPosition↑ .Next    etc.
```

Saving an extra pointer to the starting position and making an additional *boolean* check can be an invaluable antibugging device.

```
Start := CurrentPosition;
while (CurrentPosition <> SoughtPosition)
        and (CurrentPosition↑ .Next <> Start)
    do CurrentPosition := CurrentPosition↑ .Next    etc.
```

* Some systems call these *stack overflows*. We'll see why at the end of this section.

Of course, we're still not in the best of all possible positions—we don't know if we left the loop because we found the location we were looking for, or because we made a complete circuit. Fortunately, that's a minor problem an extra **if** structure can straighten out.

As you might imagine, there are many bugs associated with pointer structures, rather than with pointer types per se. We've just discussed some of the difficulties of using circular lists. Stacks have one very common bug.

> Don't try to pop elements from an empty stack.

A simple check for *TopPointer* = **nil** helps sidestep this problem.

Queues and other structures that use lists also tend to generate boundary errors. When writing procedures that manipulate such structures, it's usually a good idea to remember special (but inevitable) cases. Will the procedure work...

...at the beginning of a list?
...at the end of a list?
...if the list is empty?
...if the procedure makes the list empty?

It's easy to make boundary mistakes. For example, the following code is supposed to print a list's contents. Can you spot the bug it contains?

```
CurrentPosition := HeadPointer;
while CurrentPosition↑.Next < > nil
    do begin
        writeln (CurrentPosition↑.Word);
        CurrentPosition := CurrentPosition↑.Next
    end;
```

It really holds two bugs. What if the list is empty, and *Head-Pointer* is **nil**? The *boolean* expression causes a run-time crash—we're trying to reference the *Next* field of a **nil** pointer. However, a non-empty list has troubles as well. What's the last *Word* field printed? Is it the last element of the list? No—it's the next-to-last. We've made an off-by-one error.

Another common boundary error occurs during list searches. The following bit of code is intended to search a list for a particular *Data* field. We've tried to avoid the error, cited above, of trying to reference the *Next* field of a **nil** pointer.

while (*CurrentPosition*< > **nil**) **and** (*CurrentPosition*↑.*Data*< > *SoughtData*)
  do *CurrentPosition* := *CurrentPosition*↑.*Next*;

Unfortunately, we've forgotten that *boolean* expressions are fully evaluated. When *CurrentPosition* is **nil**, it's clear that the **while** loop's entry condition won't be met. Nonetheless, the second part of the condition (*CurrentPosition↑.Data<>SoughtData*) is still tested. The program crashes making a reference through a **nil** pointer.

A general problem associated with linked structures is the inadvertent loss of individual pointers.

> It *is* possible to lose locations. When a location *or chain of locations* is lost there's no way to find it again.

In most operations that involve list insertions or deletion, the order of statements is really crucial. Remember that, in making a deletion from a list, pointers must detour around the unnecessary element or elements *before* the deletion takes place.

By their nature, pointers partially deprive the programer of one of the best debugging tools—the snapshot of current program conditions. The value of a pointer is either **nil**, or the address of a location in memory, and neither value can be printed out.

What we need are procedures that display the contents of a pointer structure. It should be no trouble to pull such routines from 15-2. A list is printed with:

```
CurrentPosition := FirstPointer;
while CurrentPosition <> nil
    do begin
        writeln (CurrentPosition↑.Word);
        CurrentPosition := CurrentPosition↑.Next
    end;
```

Although binary trees can be terrifying, they're easy to search recursively. Here's the code for an *inorder* search of a binary tree.

```
procedure SearchTree (CurrentNode: NodePointer);
    begin
        if CurrentNode↑.Before <> nil then SearchTree (CurrentNode↑.Before);
        Inspect (CurrentNode);
        if CurrentNode↑.After <> nil then SearchTree (CurrentNode↑.After)
    end;
```

> When in doubt, print the contents of your data structure.

A quick look at a common implementation of pointers may help you understand potential bugs. For all practical purposes, we can imagine that a computer's memory is an extremely long array, like this one:

2.535E-14	'D' 'U'	'O' 'G'	⌇	⌇	FALSE TRUE TRUE TRUE TRUE TRUE FALSE TRUE FALSE FALSE FALSE TRUE FALSE TRUE FALSE TRUE TRUE FALSE TRUE FALSE FALSE FALSE FALSE FALSE	2701 694
0	1	2	• • •	65533	65534	65535

The array's element type is usually called a **word**. It's a basic memory location, usually capable of storing a single *real*, a handful of *char* values, or as many as five or six dozen *boolean* values. (Obviously, a group of two or more words would be required to store larger, structured value types.) The memory array's length is huge—in the tens of thousands.

The value of a pointer variable is essentially a subscript of this large array. As a result, trying to reference a pointer that is undefined (or whose value is **nil**) is much like using an out-of-range array subscript. However, instead of getting a 'subscript out of range' error message, we get a 'reference through **nil** pointer' message.

In terms of the illustration above, the computer's stack is allocated from the left-hand portion of the memory array, while the heap comes from the right-hand side. A run-time error occurs when the stack and heap collide, which is why an error message may refer to a stack overflow, and not a heap overflow.

The last antibugging comment we'll make involves auxiliary pointers. Very often, bugs are caused because programers are needlessly stingy when it comes to declaring auxiliary pointers. In the end they have to play musical chairs with the values of the pointers that *are* available. When one pointer serves two purposes, bugs tend to happen.

....
:   Extra pointers are cheap—use them.   :
....

Summary

A program's data values are kept in storage *locations* that are **allocated** by the computer during program execution. Under normal circumstances, ordinary variable identifiers **directly access** a location's contents. The pointer types, in contrast, let a programer **dynamically** allocate locations of a pointer's **reference type** as they're required, and then **indirectly reference** these locations. The value of a pointer variable is the **address** of the location it references, or points to. The pointer's name must be followed by an up-arrow ($\uparrow$) or caret (^) to reference its location.

Pointers are given values in any of three ways. First, a call of procedure *new* allocates a new location (which can be returned for reallocation with *dispose*). Second, assigning one pointer the value of another causes them both to reference the same location. Finally, any pointer may be assigned the null value **nil**. Pointers may only be compared for equality and inequality to each other, and to **nil**.

Pointers are used to form **linked** data structures. The **elements** of such structures are invariably records that contain pointer fields. Linked data structures are usually characterized by the operations that can be performed on them, rather than by the way they're constructed. Thus, a **linked list** can be the basis of first in, first out structures (like *queues*), as well as of first in, last out structures (like *stacks*, whose elements are *pushed* on and *popped* off). Elements can be connected in a variety of ways to the same ultimate effect—*doubly-linked* and *circular* lists can also serve as queues.

Another approach to using pointers results in *tree* structures. Trees are recursively defined; a tree is a *node* that contains pointers to another unique tree, or to nothing. *Binary* trees, which we discussed in detail, have the restriction that each *parent* node may have only two *children*. The tree's first value is its *root*. Binary trees can be subjected to *inorder*, *preorder*, or *postorder* searches, typically using recursively defined procedures. Most kinds of data can be stored according to a series of two-way choices, and binary trees help reduce the time required to store and recover any particular item.

Programs that use pointer-based data structures pose special problems in debugging. Care must be taken during insertions and deletions to avoid losing contact with part of a linked structure. Another fatal error is *advancing* a pointer variable through a **nil** pointer. Procedures that print the entire contents of lists and trees should be built into programs, and activated at the first sign of trouble.

New Pascal New Terms

nil	*new*	*dispose*	↑
location	*allocate*	*direct access*	
reference	*indirect reference*	*dynamically*	
nil pointer	*address*	*linked list*	
elements	*advance pointers*	*list disposal*	
doubly-linked	*head*	*tail*	
queue	*visual thinking*	*deque*	
circular	*stack*	*top*	
pushed	*popped*	*graph*	
sparse matrix	*tree*	*node*	
root	*children*	*parent*	
leaf	*binary tree*	*postorder*	
preorder	*inorder*	*degenerate tree*	
ring	*heap*	*word*	

Self-Test Exercises

15-1   Define pointers to types *integer, char,* and *ListElement.*

15-2   What is a last in, first out data structure? First in, first out? Are they sequential access, or random access structures? Which category (LIFO or FIFO) does Pascal's **file** type fall into? The **array** and **set** types?

15-3   What is the output of this program?

```
program Trial (output);
type Pointer = ↑ integer;
var Test: Pointer;
begin
    new (Test);
    Test := nil;
    Test↑ := 1;
    writeln (Test↑)
end.
```

15-4   Write a procedure that determines if two pointer-variables of type *Reach* both reference the same location, or indirectly access the same value, or both.

15-5   When is this an illegal assignment?

$$Variable\uparrow := \textbf{nil};$$

15-6   In a typical binary tree, each node has pointers to two sub-trees. In consequence, it's possible to travel down a tree (away from the root) but never up a tree (toward the root). Define a pointer-type that overcomes this difficulty.

15-7   Suppose that we have a pointer *Current* to a leaf (a node with no children) of the type defined above. Write statements that give it two children.

15-8   What does function *Mystery* do? Will it ever fail?

```
function Mystery (ThisPosition: ANode): integer;
   var Count: integer;
   begin
      Count := 0 ;
      while ThisPosition < > nil
         do begin
            Count := Count+1 ;
            ThisPosition := ThisPosition↑.WhoKnows
         end;
      Mystery := Count
   end;   {Mystery}
```

15-9   What is the difference between elements of a doubly-linked list, and those of a binary tree?

15-10   Suppose that we have a circular list (or ring buffer) of type *Elements* that stores individual *integer* data items. A *Subsequent* field points the way to the next record. Write a procedure that prints the list's contents. Include a check for an empty or non-circular list.

More Exercises

15-11   When applied to an alphabetically ordered binary tree, an inorder search will print its contents in alphabetical order. How would you write a procedure to print the tree's contents in *reverse* alphabetical order?

15-12   Suppose that *ListPointer* is a pointer type that accesses some record type. What will be the effect of these two statements?

$$writeln (ListPointer) ;$$
$$writeln (ListPointer\uparrow) ;$$

15-13   Can you think of any uses for pointers to ordinal values? Pointers to pointers?

15-14   An ancient puzzle concerns a ship caught in a terrible storm. Although there were thirty passengers on board, the lifeboats would only hold fifteen. So as not to leave anybody behind, the captain resolved to throw half the passengers overboard before taking to the boats.

As it happens, exactly fifteen of the passengers had slighted the captain by not dining at the Captain's Table during the cruise. The captain, in revenge, arranged all the passengers in a circle, and began to count, throwing every *nth* passenger overboard. As you might imagine, only the passengers he disliked vanished beneath the waves. The captain's fifteen dinner companions were able to use the lifeboats, and the Captain went down with the ship.

What was the number *n*? Use a circular list to simulate the terrible counting process, and find which *n* has the proper result. (Hint: it's less than 30.) Here's the starting order of the passengers—the X's go overboard, and the O's take the lifeboats. The arrow points at the start of the count.

→ O O O O O X X X X O O X X O
X   X
X O O X X O X X O X O X O O

15-15   Here's a similar problem that's a little harder. Another captain, on a ship with only ten passengers, was in the same position. The passengers were arranged in a circle like this, with five odd numbers representing the losers:

Unfortunately, the captain forgot where to begin the count, and what the counting constant was. Write a program to help the captain. For a bonus, find the starting position and counting constant that would help the doomed passengers instead.

15-16   Write a program that will reverse a large text file. In other words, lines that were first shall be last, and the first character of each line will become the last character. Assume that the original file has no more than 80 characters per line.

15-17   Write a program that reads, and evaluates, an *integer* expression given in postfix notation. Simplify the job by not allowing parentheses.

15-18   A bank is trying to decide if it should have separate lines for each teller, or have all customers wait in one 'feeder' line. Write a program that simulates bank operation under both systems. Make the program realistic by having customers arrive at varying intervals, and carry out transactions of different lengths. Naturally, all customers will go to the shortest line available. The program's output should show the total number of customers, the average wait in each system, the average line length, and the longest wait required.

15-19   Marin Motors leases cars in five price ranges: subcompact, compact, midsize, station wagon, luxury. In any one category the price of cars is the same, but their gas mileage may vary. Thus, the last few cars in a cheap category may have poorer mileage than the first few cars that cost more, and a customer going on a long trip would be better off renting the more expensive model. In general, though, mileage drops as the car's size (and rental price) increases.

A customer can request a car in any size, but if that size isn't available, the next larger car is provided at the same cost. A minimum mileage may be requested, and the length of rental must be given in advance, As a service to its customers, Marin Motors will figure out which car they'd be best off renting, given the expected trip mileage, and the stock of cars available.

Write a program that handles bookkeeping and inventory for Marin Motors. You'll have to determine a starting stock of cars, and the prices and mileage of each. The program should rent cars (as detailed above), provide billing information, and show the stock on hand in order of price and mileage when requested. Then, modify the program to simulate Marin Motors' business over a two-week period instead.

15-20   As the penultimate step in defining your alternative high-level programing language, add pointer types. Or, consider the idea of defining binary
trees, and lists, as basic data structures of the language. What kind of information would have to be provided in the definition of such structures? Would
they be less useful than Pascal pointers?

Finally, reassess the language you've created. What are its advantages
over Pascal? Could you write a program that translates Pascal into the new
language? What about vice versa?

Pascal's calculating machine. Musée National des Techniques, Paris.

IN THE INTEREST OF MAKING THE LAST fifteen chapters flow a bit more smoothly, a few facts have been obscured in (or even deliberately left out of) our presentation. This appendix briefly explains the areas that were overlooked.

1. The **goto** control structure.

2. A shorthand for type definitions and variable declarations.

3. The standard procedures *pack* and *unpack.*

4. Procedures and functions as parameters.

5. Dynamic allocation of record variants.

6. The standard procedure *page.*

All the programs we've written so far have moved from statement to statement in direct order, except where a procedure or function call caused a temporary detour. However, we can *label* any statement with a number, and explicitly direct the program to *go to* that point. This is arranged by defining *labels* and using the **goto** control structure.

The **goto**
Structure

There are three steps to take in using a **goto**. First, the labels used to mark statements must be defined.

> A *label* is a number of one to four digits. The reserved word **label** marks the label definition part. It immediately follows the program (or subprogram) heading.

There are 10,000 possible labels—'0' through '9999'. This segment designates '1', '2', and '3' as labels.

> {Program or subprogram heading.}
> **label** 1, 2, 3 ;   {The label definition part.}
> {Constant definition part.}   etc.

The second step is to use the label by putting it, and a colon, in front of a statement.

> 1: *writeln* ('Abnormal program termination.') ;

> The label is ignored except as an identifying mark. Unless it is skipped over, every labeled statement is executed in the normal course of events. It need not be specifically gone to.

Finally, the **goto** statement tells the computer that program execution should continue from a particular labeled statement. For example:

> **if** *DataIsBad* **then goto** 1 ;

A **goto** can direct program control either forward or backward. Any actions between the **goto** and the labeled statement are skipped.

* ...but were (justifiably) afraid to ask.

In a sense the **goto** is a historical anachronism in high-level programing languages. When the first languages were created, their designers (being hopelessly logical) saw that nearly everything a programer wanted to do could be handled with just two control statements—**if . . . then**, and **goto**. For example:

Count := 1 ;
Sum := 0 ;
1: *Sum* := *Sum*+*Count*;
Count := *Count*+1 ;
if *Count*< =100 **then goto** 1 ;
writeln ('The sum of the numbers 1 through 100 is ', *Sum*) ;

We've come to know and love the shaded sequence by its semantic equivalent—the **repeat** structure. As a result, some older languages, like FORTRAN, have fewer control structures than Pascal.

However, Pascal has a much more sophisticated system of controlling program flow—its subprograms and control structures. In fact, we can claim quite correctly that Pascal lets the programer do just about everything she wants *without* using **gotos**, and that minimizing **gotos** is a virtue. For one thing, most control structure names (like subprogram identifiers) help document what's going on. Statement labels, in contrast, are nondocumenting, or even 'anti'-documenting. As arbitrary numbers, labels aren't the least mnemonic. Their appearance gives no hint of their effect.

A more serious problem of using the **goto** is the way it can distort the patterns of a program. In recent years a lot of emphasis has been placed on *structured* programing. Procedures and functions give a program structure by breaking its action into cleanly defined parts, while Pascal's structured statements help clearly delineate cause and effect. We haven't made a big deal about structured programing because we haven't really had non-structured tools—like the **goto**—to work with.

Programs with many **gotos** are so tangled and difficult to trace through that they're often called *spaghetti* programs.

If the **goto** is so bad, why was it included in Pascal? Partly, for sentimental reasons. As we mentioned above, languages like FORTRAN (and even BASIC) depend heavily on the **goto**. People who learned to program in such languages find that **gotos** make it easier for them to implement tricks that we understand better in Pascal.

There are also extraordinary circumstances in which using **gotos** is permissible. Most common is the 'I want to get out of here in a hurry' case. Suppose, for example, that program input is coming from punched cards or tape, and an input checking procedure spots incorrect data. Since we know that there's no point in continuing to process input, we can issue an error message and go to the very end of the program (because it's o.k. to label an **end**).

```
    :        {Assume we're in an input-checking procedure.}
if DataIsBad
    then begin
        writeln ('Abnormal program termination − − bad data.') ;
        goto 1        {Quit program.}
    end;
    :           {Rest of the program.}
1: end. {Main program.}
```

The **goto** is also properly used for beating a hasty retreat from a function whose arguments are determined to be inappropriate. In these cases the desirability of graceful degradation outweighs the stigma attached to using **gotos**.

Incidentally, there are restrictions on where a **goto** can go to. Basically, a **goto** cannot access a relatively internal block or structure. We can't jump from the main program to a procedure, although the reverse is allowed. Likewise, we can't jump into the middle of a structured statement (although we can jump out of one or change our position within one).

:····:

Q. What will the output of this program segment be? Assume all labels are validly defined.

Self-Check
Questions

```
        goto 2 ;
        :           {Other statements.}
    1: writeln ('You have been eaten by a troll.  Game over.') ;
    2: writeln ('You have turned into a vat of glue.  Game over.') ;
    3: writeln ('A hobgoblin has munched you.  Game over.') ;
    4: writeln ('Bats flew away with you.  Game over.') ;
    end. {Main program.}
```

A. As we mentioned earlier, the label is disregarded except as an identifying mark. Each statement from label 2 on is executed.

```
         ↓        ↓        ↓        ↓        ↓
You have turned into a vat of glue.  Game over.
A hobgoblin has munched you.  Game over.
Bats flew away with you.  Game over.
```

:··:

As we've pointed out a few times, high-level languages are designed mainly for the benefit of people who use them in programing, rather than for the computers such programs ultimately direct. Thus, Wirth named Pascal's control structures **repeat, while, if**, etc., even though **a, b, c** and so on are equally convenient from a computer's viewpoint. Although the semantics—the effect—of both meaningful and meaning-

Shorthand Declarations

less reserved words might be the same, their syntax—the actual words and the way they're used—are intended to inhibit errors and help programers.

> Designing a system for the ease and convenience of the people who use it is called **human engineering**. A human-engineered product is created with sympathy for its users, and with an understanding of their problems and of errors they might make.

A subtle aspect of the human engineering of programing languages is the recognition that people are often in a hurry when they write programs. This is reflected in Pascal by an easing of certain syntax rules; or, more accurately, by allowing a simpler alternative syntax in some situations.

> When a structured type is defined, the definition can include descriptions of sub-structures.

In the past, we've built up complicated structures by using type identifiers that were already defined. To define an array of records, we'd first define the record type, then use its identifier in defining the array type. However, this step can be skipped. For example:

```
type BoardType = array [1 .. 10] of record
                                   Taken: boolean;
                                   Marker: char
                                 end;  {of the record}
```

This shorthand is appropriate in a program that doesn't include any variables (or parameters) of the record type we defined on the fly. The same principle extends to variable declarations.

> When a variable is declared, its type must be given. However, this type can be described on the spot. It does not have to be defined in advance.

We might legally make the following variable declaration:

```
var Board: array [1 .. 10] of record
                               Taken: boolean;
                               Marker: char
                             end;  {of the record}
```

Board is now an array-type variable, just as though the array and record types used in its declaration had been defined separately. We can make normal assignments to it:

```
Board [3]. Taken := true;
Board [3]. Marker := 'A';
```

User-defined ordinal types can also be described rather than defined:

        var *Hue, Color*: (*Red, Blue, Green*) ;

Hue and *Color* are variables of a type with no name.

Why didn't we mention these shortcuts earlier? Some of our reasons have to do with programing and teaching style. First of all, the syntax of individually defined structures is easier for beginners to debug. Second, individually defined data structures are easier to alter (and more likely to be improved) than monolithic definitions. Third, individually defined structures are usually better documented than a single large structure.

There are also semantic reasons for doing things the long way. These have to do with assignments and the declaration of parameters. Recall that a variable-parameter and its argument must be of identical types, as must the variables on both sides of many assignment statements (such as an assignment between two record or array-type variables). However...

> Two variables (or a parameter and its argument) have an identical type only if they're defined with the exact same type identifier.

This means that a type identifier—and not a shorthand description of the type—must be used in many variable declarations, and in *all* declarations of variable-parameters. Other situations require that two variables be *type compatible.*

> Two variables (or a parameter and its argument) are type compatible if they both represent ranges of the same underlying type.

Again, this leads to a frequent requirement that a type be defined, rather than described. For example, we could not even pass *Hue* or *Color* as a value-parameter. The type of *Tint* in this heading:

        procedure *Sample* (*Tint*: (*Red, Blue, Green*)) ;

is not compatible with *Hue* and *Color.* According to Pascal's scope rules, *Red, Blue,* and *Green* are being locally redefined. Similarly, the assignment between noncompatible variables in this program segment is illegal:

```
program Sample (input, output);
var Color: (Red, Blue, Green);
procedure Show;
    var Hue: (Red, Blue, Green);
    begin
        Hue := Color;        {This assignment is a type clash.}
        :    etc.
```

In each case the variable declarations are fine, but the variable types are mismatched.

In summary, the shorthand form of type definition and variable declaration should be confined to small programs or procedures in which the issue of type will not arise. If a program is going to become large or use procedures, the types of its variables should be defined. This makes data structures easier to alter and debug, and allows variables to be passed as parameters and used in assignments.

Pack and Unpack

In Chapter 12 we mentioned the reserved word **packed** in connection with the definition of string types. However, the notion of packing a data structure to minimize the amount of storage it requires within the computer can be applied to any of Pascal's structured types (but usually just to arrays and records).

Although declaring a data structure to be packed saves space in the computer's memory, it generally slows down program execution. This is because the computer has to go through special manipulations to access the component values of packed data. In other words, the computer goes through the time-consuming process of unpacking the stored structure each time one of its fields or elements is altered or inspected.

Now, in the programs we've dealt with in this text the trade-off between program execution speed and data storage space is not a big concern. However, efficiency is something that has to be considered when very large programs are created. Fortunately, Pascal includes some standard procedures that let the programer take advantage of the space saving aspect of packing the largest common data structure—the array—without sacrificing execution time.

The standard procedure *unpack* assigns the contents of a packed array to a regular array. Its syntax is:

unpack (*PackedArray, NotPackedArray, StartingSubscript*) ;

where *PackedArray* is a variable of a packed array type, *NotPackedArray* is a variable of a similar (except that it's not packed) array type, and *StartingSubscript* is the position in *NotPackedArray* where the assignment starts.

Let's suppose that we've made the following definitions.

type *PackedType* = **packed array** [*Lower..Upper*] **of** *Data*;
        OrdinaryType = **array** [*Minimum..Maximum*] **of** *Data*;
var *PackedArray*: *PackedType*;
      NotPackedArray: *OrdinaryType*;
      StartingSubscript: *Minimum..Maximum;*

We'll also assume that:

$$(Maximum - Minimum) > = (Upper - Lower)$$

In other words, *PackedArray* is the same size as, or smaller than, *Not-PackedArray*. This restriction is necessary because the *StartingSubscript* argument lets us assign a small packed array to part of a larger array that isn't packed.

A call of *unpack*:

> unpack (*PackedArray, NotPackedArray, StartingSubscript*);

is equivalent to:

for i := *Lower* **to** *Upper*
  do *NotPackedArray* [i—*Lower* + *StartingSubscript*] := *PackedArray* [i];

However, *unpack* is usually implemented in a manner that's faster to execute than this **for** structure.

> The standard procedure *pack* reverses the process. Its syntax is:
>
> > pack (*NotPackedArray, StartingSubscript, PackedArray*) ;

Using the same variables as above, we find that this call:

> pack (*NotPackedArray, StartingSubscript, PackedArray*) ;

is equivalent to the statement:

for i := *Lower* **to** *Upper*
  do *PackedArray* [i] := *NotPackedArray* [i—*Lower* + *StartingSubscript*]

Again, we can assume that the procedure is implemented in an optimum manner.

Note, incidentally, that when *PackedArray* and *NotPackedArray* both have the same number of stored components, *StartingSubscript* must equal the first legal subscript of *NotPackedArray*. This is true for both procedures.

Self-Check Questions

Q. Since we can assign their elements one at a time, why couldn't we just make a complete array assignment; i.e.:

> PackedArray := *NotPackedArray*;

What's the necessity of either *pack* or *unpack*?

A. Once more we've run into the subtle difference between *identical* and *compatible* types. For two arrays to be assignable to each other, they must be of an identical type—declared with the exact same type identifier. Since one array is packed, and the other is not, this is clearly impossible. Thus, *pack* and *unpack* are required to effect the assignment.

Procedures and Functions as Parameters

Procedures and functions may be passed as parameters to other subprograms. This feature is usually taken advantage of in more advanced applications programs, especially when nonstandard library routines are available. As a result, the syntax of procedure and function parameter declarations may be enhanced at your installation, and what we say may be misleading.

At any rate, the general syntax of subprograms as parameters is just about what we would expect—the reserved word **procedure** or **function**, the subprogram's name and parameter list, and its type (if it's a function). For example:

> **procedure** *Graph* (**function** *Compute* (*Limit*):*real*; *OffSet*: *integer*) ;

When two or more subprograms go in one parameter list, the word **procedure** or **function** must be repeated for each.

> **function** *GreatestResult* (**function** *A* (*ItsArgument*: *real*) : *real*;
> **function** *B* (*AnotherArgument*: *real*) : *real*;
> *TheArgument*: *real*;) : *real*;

Now, when a subprogram is passed as a parameter its arguments should *not* be passed along with it. In other words, *GreatestResult* might be called like this:

> **if** *GreatestResult* (*sine, cosine, pi*/4) > *Minimum* **then**   etc.

In this call, functions *Sine* and *Cosine* are the arguments of *A* and *B*, while *pi*/4 is their eventual argument. Calls have to be arranged this way to avoid prematurely evaluating argument functions or procedures.

Within *GreatestResult*, *A* and *B* (now representing *Sine* and *Cosine*) are called normally.

> **function** *GreatestResult* (**function** *A* (*ItsArgument*: *real*) : *real*;
> **function** *B* (*AnotherArgument*: *real*) : *real*;
> *TheArgument*: *real*;) : *real*;
> {Represents the greater of *A* and *B*.}
>
> **var** *First, Second*: *real*;
>
> **begin**
>   *First* := *A* (*TheArgument*) ;
>   *Second* := *B*(*TheArgument*) ;
>   **if** *First*> *Second* **then** *GreatestResult* := *First*;
>   **else** *GreatestResult* := *Second*
> **end**;   {*GreatestResult*}

As you might imagine, a procedure or function parameter must be equivalent in type and parameter list to its argument. Because of this restriction, we can only pass *real*-type functions having one *real* argument apiece to *GreatestResult*.

When a record with variant fields is dynamically allocated, enough space is set aside to store the largest of its variant groups. When each variant group requires about the same amount of storage, this method of storage allocation poses no disadvantages. However, programers sometimes find themselves in the predicament of dynamically allocating many records of one type, but only requiring the smallest variant group of each. Fortunately, Pascal provides a mechanism for limiting size of each location.

Dynamically Allocating Variants

> The dynamic allocation procedure *new* may be given additional arguments, corresponding to relatively nested tag field values. The location that is allocated has enough space to store the record's fixed fields, as well as those of the variant part specified by the stated tag field(s). It is, however, totally undefined.

Suppose that we have this type definition:

type *LibraryItem* = (*Book, Magazine, Record*);
    Card = ↑ *CardCatalog*;
    CardCatalog = **record**
                Available: *boolean*;
                Name: **packed array** [1..50] **of** *char*;
                case *Item*: *LibraryItem* **of**
                  Book: (*ISBNNumber*: **array** [1..10] **of** *char*);
                  Magazine: (*Volume, Issue*: *integer*);
                  Record: (*DiscNumber*: *integer*;
                              ReRelease: *boolean*)
              end;
  var *CurrentCard*: *Card*;

The statement:

                  new (*CurrentCard*);

allocates a complete record large enough the hold the fixed fields, plus any of the variant fields. If we know that we're going to store a magazine, however, the statement:

              new (*CurrentCard, Magazine*);

allocates a record whose fields are *Available, Name, Item, Volume*, and *Issue.* Don't forget, though, that *Item* is still undefined.

> A record allocated in this fashion cannot have its variant fields altered, nor can an assignment be made to the entire variable.

A 'complete record' assignment may not be made. Furthermore, changing the value of the tag field won't alter the currently accessible variant fields.

> The deallocation procedure *dispose* must be given additional arguments (representing tag field values) when a record allocated in the manner described above is disposed of.

Disposing of the record we allocated earlier requires this call:

dispose (*CurrentCard, Magazine*) ;

page   We quote from the draft Standard:

"*page* (*f*) shall cause an implementation-defined effect on the textfile *f,* such that subsequent output to *f* will be on a new page if the textfile is printed on a suitable device, and shall perform an implicit *writeln* . . . the effect of inspecting a textfile to which the page procedure was applied during generation shall be implementation-dependent."

Procedure *page* lets programers decide when and where page breaks should occur, without requiring them to know exactly how many lines long their paper is. As the quote above states, this is a highly implementation-dependent matter—a call of *page* need not have any effect at all. In any case, *page* is a rarely used procedure whose effect should be investigated on a case-by-case basis.

Self-Test Answers

1-1 When the program doesn't receive input from the keyboard or punched cards.

1-2 Absolutely nothing—the insertion is just a comment.

1-3 The statement's output is:

No , no you can ' t take that awayfrom me .

Sometimes blanks have to be inserted before words to make spacing correct.

1-4 There are 172 ways of spelling the word.

```
program Palindrome (input, output);
var Char1, Char2, Char3, Char4, Char5: char;
begin
    writeln ('Please enter a five-letter palindrome.');
    readln (Char1, Char2, Char3, Char4, Char5);
    writeln (Char1, Char2, Char3, Char4, Char5);
    writeln (Char2, Char3, Char4, Char5, Char2);
    writeln (Char3, Char4, Char5, Char2, Char3);
    writeln (Char4, Char5, Char2, Char3, Char4);
    writeln (Char1, Char2, Char3, Char4, Char5)
end.
```

1-5 The standard types are *real, integer, char,* and *boolean.* A type clash occurs when we try to give a variable of one type a value of a different type. It causes a program crash (except when we give a *real* variable an *integer* value).

1-6 The value of unassigned or undefined variables is system dependent. Although some systems will *initialize* or automatically give the value 0 to *integer* or *real* variables, or ' ' to *char* variables, others won't—and trying to print the value of an undefined variable might cause a program crash.

1-7 When a thing is system defined, everybody's Pascal has it in one form or other. System dependent rules or values, on the other hand, are usually extensions of some sort. Not every implementation (version) of Pascal will contain them.

1-8 The syntax errors are easy to spot—*b* is obviously punctuated wrong, and *e* contains a split infinitive. The semantic errors are much harder—*a, c,* and *f* are all correct, meaningful English as stated. However, they should probably be rewritten as:

What is this thing called love?
I should say not!
Woman: without her, man is nothing.

The weirdest example, *d,* was deliberately devised by Noam Chomsky to show a sentence that is syntactically perfect, but semantically nonsensical.

1-9 Remember that *readln* gets a value for its variables (if it is given any), then discards the rest of the line. All examples below are correct.

```
readln (OnionHeads);
read (LettuceHeads);
readln;
readln (GarlicCloves);    etc.
```

1-10   35   10X   7

1-11 Field widths may be given as expressions. The fields below are 1, 5, 3, and 4 spaces.

A   5   6   D

1-12   Two kinds of errors can't be caught at compile time—mistakes in the program's algorithm (what it figures out, and how it goes about it), and mistakes in the program's input that might cause type clashes. An error that the computer could *never* spot is:

$$writeln \; ('The \; sum \; of \; two \; and \; two \; is', \; 2+3);$$

1-13   A blank line may *not* be inserted between the lines of input—it would be a mistake.

$$0 \; 17$$
$$= 0.618$$

1-14   *readln* (*Month, JunkChar, Date, AnotherJunkChar, Year*);

2-1   Yes. Blank spaces and carriage returns are disregarded except as separators of values, reserved words, and identifiers.

2-2   *a) integer, b) real, c)* This is an invalid expression—there is a clash between the types of 10.0 (*real*) and **div** (an *integer* operator).

2-3   In this segment, *Temporary* is an *integer* variable, while *Remainder* is *real.*

$$Temporary := trunc \; (55.55);$$
$$Remainder := (Temporary \; \textbf{mod} \; 7) + (55.55 - Temporary);$$

2-4   Yes, both assignments are valid. The value of *Opposite* is -77 after the assignment. It would be 99 if *Whole* were initialized to -99.

2-5   Two. Addition and subtraction have the lowest precedence.

2-6   The result is *real* in both cases.

2-7   The only predefined constant in standard Pascal is *maxint,* the value of the largest allowed *integer* value. However, your system might have other predefined constants.

2-8   Pascal has no exponentiation operator. The expression $exp(b*ln(a))$ represents a raised to the b power.

2-9   By using the expression above, substituting 1/3 for $b.$ In general, $1/n$ is substituted.

2-10   Negative.

2-11   If $chr(ord('A')+25)$ equals 'Z', the characters are contiguous.

2-12   *Text* or *string* constants.

2-13   *Width* is an arbitrary field width specification.

$$writeln \; ('Product \; is \; ', \; Product:Width:1);$$

2-14   Five—one for each assignment.

2-15   Note that there can't be a blank space between the two values.

73T

3-1   There are no restrictions.

3-2   **procedure** *PrintYourName*;
    begin
       writeln ('Doug Cooper')
    end;   {*PrintYourName*}

3-3   By the context the identifier is used in. If the identifier is used in the procedure, it refers to the local variable. If the identifier appears in the outside program, it refers to the global variable.

3-4   An activation of the procedure—the procedure's name in the program.

3-5   procedure *Reverse*;

  var *Temporary*: *char*;

  begin

   Temporary := *First*;

   First := *Fourth*;

   Fourth := *Temporary*;

   Temporary := *Second*;

   Second := *Third*;

   Third := *Temporary*

  end; {*Reverse*}

3-6   Just as you'd do it by hand—in effect, by finding the number of hundreds, tens, and ones.

    procedure *ReverseTheNumber*;

      var *Hundreds, Tens, Ones*: *integer*;

      begin

        Hundreds := *TheNumber* **div** 100;

        Tens := (*TheNumber* **mod** 100) **div** 10;

        Ones := (*TheNumber* **mod** 10);

        ReversedNumber := (100∗*Ones*) + (10∗*Tens*) + *Hundreds*;

      end; {*ReverseTheNumber*}

3-7   Only from their context. A procedure identifier always appears on a line by itself, as a statement. A constant identifier never appears on the left-hand side of an assignment statement. Constant and variable identifiers are always used as part of an assignment statement, or as arguments to procedures (like *write*) or functions.

3-8   A procedure that prints the current values of all program variables. It's used as an aid in program debugging.

3-9   About twenty lines—one screenful (or pageful) of code.

3-10   No. Actually, stepwise refinement is one of a number of top-down design strategies.

4-1   Three—**case, of,** and **end**.

4-2   Only five values can appear——4, −3, −2, −1, and 0.

4-3   Try printing the output of different values of *n*—1st, 2nd, 3rd, etc.

4-4   **case** *ItemNumber* of

     0, 3, 5: *writeln* ('Hats');

     1, 4: *writeln* ('Bats and Cats');

     2: *writeln* ('Slats)

    end;

4-5   Note that input for *FindQuadrant* must be prompted before its call.

    procedure *FindQuadrant*;

      var *Angle*: *real*;

        begin

          read (*Angle*);

          write ('An angle of ', *Angle*:3:2, ' degrees falls in the ');

          case *trunc*(*Angle*/90) **mod** 4 **of**

            0: *writeln* ('first quadrant.');

            1: *writeln* ('second quadrant.');

            2: *writeln* ('third quadrant.');

            3: *writeln* ('fourth quadrant.')

          end {case}

        end; {*FindQuadrant*}

4-6 *Input*   *Output*
      AA   I t
      AB   i s
      BA   a n   A n c i e n t
      BB   a n   M a r i n e r

4-7 The internal assignment to *Limit* doesn't affect the number of times the loop iterates.

$$1 \quad 1 \quad 7 \quad 8 \quad 9 \quad 10 \quad 11 \quad 12 \quad 13 \quad 14 \quad 15$$

4-8 **for** *Counter* := 1 **to 12**
     do *writeln* (2 * *Counter*) ;

4-9 The *real* type, because it's not an ordinal type—there's no standard 'next' *real*

4-10 Its value is unknown—the counter variable is undefined on exit from the loop.

4-11 In procedure *Count*, input values are either digits or blanks.

```
procedure Count;
    var Character: char;
        LoopCounter, DigitCounter: integer;
    begin
        DigitCounter := 0;
        for LoopCounter := 1 to 40
            do begin
                read (Character) ;
                case Character of
                    ' ', '1', '2', '3', '5', '6', '7', '0': ;
                    '4', '8', '9': DigitCounter := DigitCounter+1
                end {case}
            end  {for}
        writeln ('The number of fours, eights, and nines is ', DigitCounter)
    end;  {Count}
```

4-12 What is not is often What is not is

4-13 **for** *LineCount* := 1 **to** *Last*
    do begin
      for *LetterCount* := 1 **to** *LineCount*
        do *read* (*TheNextLetter*) ;
      write (*TheNextLetter*) ;
      readln   {Get rid of the rest of the input line.}
    end;
  writeln;

4-14 Twenty seven and ten, respectively.

4-15 In effect, we're maintaining a moving window of input numbers.

```
procedure PrintDifference;
    var FirstNumber, SecondNumber, Counter: integer:
        begin
            read (SecondNumber) ;
            for Counter := 1 to 9
                do begin
                    FirstNumber := SecondNumber;
                    read (SecondNumber) ;
                    writeln (SecondNumber − FirstNumber)
                end {for}
    end;  {PrintDifference}
```

5-1   Only one word—**var**. However, it may appear more than one time.

5-2   *PrintNumbers* (1, 1);
PrintNumbers (3, 5);
PrintNumbers (13, 21);
writeln;

5-3   *Parameter* usually refers to the value- or variable-parameter formally declared in a procedure heading, while an *argument* is generally the actual value or variable passed to it. We'll admit that, because of this, the phrase *parameter passing* is a bit of a misnomer, and might reasonably be changed to *argument passing.*

5-4   A side effect is an assignment to a global variable identifier from within a subprogram. Side effects make the implicit documentation of procedure calls misleading—we expect that only the arguments of variable-parameters will be altered within the procedure.

5-5   *Time* must have been defined as a value- or variable-parameter in *Clock's* heading, like this:

```
procedure Clock (Time: integer);
    var Time: integer;        etc.
```

5-6   The program's output is '   2   4   5'.

5-7   Note that this procedure has no protection against an incorrect *Length* value.

```
procedure Average (Length: integer; var Average: real);
    var Total, NextNumber, Count: integer;
        begin
            Total := 0;
            for Count := 1 to Length
                do begin
                    read (NextNumber);
                    Total := Total + NextNumber
                end;
            Average := Total/Length
        end;   {Average}
```

5-8   The value list of a **case** structure must contain the actual constants (the literal representations) of the counter variable's type. Since parameters are variables (and couldn't go in the value list), it wouldn't do us any good to pass 2, 3, and 6 as parameters.

```
procedure CountDigits (SizeOfInput: integer; var Occurrences: integer);
    var NextCharacter: char;
        LoopCounter: integer;
    begin
        Occurrences := 0;
        for LoopCounter := 1 to SizeOfInput
            do begin
                read (NextCharacter);
                case NextCharacter of
                    '1', '4', '5', '7', '8', '9', '0': ;
                    '2', '3', '6': Occurrences := Occurrences+1
                end   {case}
            end   {for}
    end;   {CountDigits}
```

5-9   **procedure** *Parts* (*Argument*: *real*; **var** *Whole, Fraction*: *integer*) ;
    begin
        Whole := *trunc* (*Argument*) ;
        Fraction := *trunc* (10000 * (*Argument* − *Whole*))
    end;   {*Parts*}

5-10   A variable-parameter really *is* just a re-naming of its global argument variable. Thus, the output of *HardToBelieve* is '   7' and '   8'.

6-1   Because *boolean* operators have higher precedence than the relational operators. The terms that use only relational operators must go in parentheses.

6-2   *a* and *c.*

6-3   When *StillSearching* and *Found* are both either *true* or *false.*

6-4   Certainly.

6-5   Note that reversing the actions makes our job easy—the *writeln* doesn't change any of the variables in the *boolean* expression.

        if (2 * *X*) < = *Y*
            then *writeln* ('Able was I ere I saw Elba.') ;
        if (2 * *X*) > *Y*
            then begin *Y* := 2 * *Y* ; *X* := *X*/2 **end**;

6-6   *false true false*

6-7   Both program segments have the same ultimate effect—the smallest of *a,* *b,* and *c* is assigned to *Smallest.* However, they approach the problem in different ways. The first method makes every possible test before making an assignment. The second method, in contrast, makes an assignment—*Smallest* := *a*—then tests its correctness. Thus, the second method takes advantage of the insight that one of the values *must* be the smallest to simplify the Pascal code.

6-8   Both program segments have the same effect—they take an action that depends on the value of *Amount.* (We're assuming that none of the procedure calls alter this value.) The code on the left, though, is less efficient. Very often, unnecessary *boolean* checks will be made long after we've taken the appropriate action. The right-hand code, however, forms a **case** structure of sorts. After an action is taken, the rest of the *boolean* checks (the rest of the indented statements) are skipped.

6-9   **procedure** *CheckDivisibility* (*Divisor, Dividend*: *integer*) ;
    begin
      if (*Divisor* **mod** *Dividend*) = 0
        then *writeln* (*Dividend*:1, ' divides ', *Divisor*:1, ' evenly.')
        else *writeln* (*Dividend*:1, ' doesn't divide ', *Divisor*:1, ' evenly.')
    end;   {*CheckDivisibility*}

6-10   Note the use of 0 and 501 as *sentinel* values for initializing *LargestEven* and *SmallestOdd.* If *LargestEven* and *SmallestOdd* still have these values (which are outside the range of valid entries) at the end of the loop, we know that no even or odd values were read in.

    LargestEven := 0 ;
    SmallestOdd := 501 ;
    for *Counter* := 1 **to** 100
        do begin
            read (*Number*) ;
            if *odd* (*Number*)
                then begin
                    if *Number* < *SmallestOdd* **then** *SmallestOdd* := *Number* ;
                end
                else if *Number* > *LargestEven* **then** *LargestEven* := *Number*
                end
        end;

6-11 **if** $n > = 2$ **then** $n := (3*n) - 6$;

6-12 *a)* ['A', 'E', 'I', 'O', 'U']
   b) ['B'..'D', 'F'..'H', 'J'..'N', 'P'..'T', 'V'..'Z']

6-13 Note the nested **if** structures.

```
DigitCount := 0;
PunctuationCount := 0;
for Counter := 1 to 250
    do begin
        read (Character);
        if Character in ['0'..'9']
            then DigitCount := DigitCount+1
            else if Character in ['.', ';', ',', ':', '!', '?']
                then PunctuationCount := PunctuationCount+1
    end;   {for}
```

6-14 Example 1 is the most obvious and straightforward solution to the problem. The code is correct, and easy to follow. In example 2, we make the insight that neither 1 nor 5 are even, and reduce the amount of work the computer does. Example 3 takes the next logical step—the programer figures out the answer, and makes the assignment herself. However, example 4 illustrates the problem with being *too* clever—a dumb mistake is just as wrong as a hard mistake. We conclude that straightforwardness, cleverness, simplicity, and correctness all have to be considered in writing code.

7-1 *f, g*: neither **while** nor **repeat**.
b, c, d: **repeat** only.
e: **while** and **repeat**.
a: **while** only.

Self-Test Answers: 7

7-2
```
Power := 0;
TwoToThatPower := 1;
read (LimitNumber);         {The number we want to exceed.}
while TwoToThatPower < = LimitNumber
    do begin
        Power := Power + 1;
        TwoToThatPower := TwoToThatPower * 2
    end;
writeln ('Two to the ', Power:1, ' power is greater than or equal to ', LimitNumber:1);
```

7-3
```
StartingPopulation := NumberOfFish;
NumberOfYears := 0;
repeat
    NumberOfFish := 0.023 * NumberOfFish;
    NumberOfYears := 1 + NumberOfYears
until NumberOfFish < = (StartingPopulation/10);
writeln (StartingPopulation:1,
    ' will decrease by 90% within ', NumberOfYears:1, ' years.');
```

7-4 The character representation of the end-of-line character is a blank space. If it's echoed, it prints as an ordinary blank—there's no line-feed.

7-5 The code below prevents confusing the end-of-line character with a plain blank.

```
                    if eof
                        then writeln ('At the end of the file.')
                        else if eoln
                            then writeln ('At the end of the line.')
                                else begin
                                    read (NextCharacter);
                                    if NextCharacter=' '
                                        then writeln ('The next character is an ordinary space.')
                                        else writeln ('The next character is a non-blank.')
                    end;
```

7-6   Procedure *readln* may be called at *eoln*. The call's effect is to discard the end-of-line character, and set *eof* to *true*. However, it is a run-time error to call *readln* at *eof*.

7-7   It reads and echoes characters until it encounters an empty line.

7-8   How robust is this procedure? What is the final value of *NextLetter* if there aren't any letters?

```
        procedure GetNextLetter (var NextLetter: char);
            var NextCharacter: char;
            begin
                NextCharacter:= ' ';        {A 'dummy' initialization.}
                while not eof and not (NextCharacter in ['a'..'z','A'..'Z'])
                    do read (NextCharacter);
                if eof
                    then writeln ('At end-of-file.  No letters found.')
                    else NextLetter := NextCharacter
            end;  {GetNextLetter}
```

7-9   As always, a check for *eof* must start the procedure.

```
procedure LetterSearch (var Largest, Smallest: char);
    var CurrentCharacter: char;
    begin
        Largest := chr(ord('a')−1);
        Smallest := chr(ord('z')+1);
        if eof then writeln ('Empty input file.  Results will be incorrect.');
        while not eof
            do begin
                read (CurrentCharacter);
                if CurrentCharacter in ['a'..'z']
                    then begin
                        if CurrentCharacter> Largest then Largest := CurrentCharacter;
                        if CurrentCharacter< Smallest then Smallest := CurrentCharacter
                    end   {CurrentCharacter is lower-case.}
            end   {while}
end;   {LetterSearch}
```

7-10   All the letters in the file are identical.

7-11   Again, we have to check for *eof* before reading any character.

```
procedure ReadAndEcho (Sentinel: char; LookingForSentinel: boolean);
    var Finished: boolean;
        Current: char;
    begin
        if not eof
            then begin
                read (Current);
                if LookingForSentinel
                    then Finished := Current =Sentinel
                    else Finished := false;
                while not Finished and not eof
                    do begin
                        write (Current);
                        read (Current);
                        if LookingForSentinel then Finished := Current =Sentinel
                    end;
                writeln
            end
    end;    {ReadAndEcho}
```

7-12 *a*) Sue, while Patti had had 'had', had had 'had had'. 'Had had' had had a better effect on the teacher.
b) Zero, of course.
c) This is the classic boundary problem. Eleven posts are required.

8-1   Any ordinal type, or *real.*

8-2   Only when we make an assignment to the function—within the body of the function itself. This is usually the last statement of the function.

8-3   **function** *Divisible (First, Second: integer): boolean;*
```
        begin
            Divisible := (First mod Second) = 0
        end;  {Divisible}
```

8-4   Test data can only show the presence of program bugs, rather than their absence. However, good test data demonstrates specific conditions for which a program will work.

8-5   No. The types of both the function and its parameters must be known and specified when the function is written. Thus, there's no way we could write the equivalent of the standard function *sqr* (which defies this rule).

8-6   In bottom-up testing and debugging, the programer views her program as a collection of individually written and tested sub-programs. If each of these modules works when it's attached to a 'driver' program, she feels confident that the completed program will also work. The program as a whole is not tested until it's complete.

A top-down approach aims at testing and debugging the entire program, even if (at first) it mainly consists of dummy sub-programs. Major program connections and ideas can be tried out before the programer is committed to a particular design. As modules are completed and added to the program, the programer can assure herself that her program still works.

Whether or not one approach is better than the other depends on your job and aims. Small programs, in which the job of each module is well-defined, are usually better tested by a bottom-up method. Large programs, however, fare better from the top-down approach, especially if several people are working on a single project. Testing and debugging are distributed throughout the programing process, and specific operation goals are easy to establish.

8-7 **function** *ReturnNegative* (*Argument*: *real*) : *real*;
 begin
  if *Argument* < 0
   then *ReturnNegative* := *Argument*
   else *ReturnNegative* := −*Argument*
 end; {*ReturnNegative*}

8-8 Function *LargestFactor* implements an easy algorithm for finding the greatest common divisor.

function *LargestFactor* (*First, Second*: *integer*) : *integer*;
 var *ProposedFactor*: *integer*;   *or*
 begin
  if *First* < *Second*
   then *ProposedFactor* := *First*
   else *ProposedFactor* := *Second*;
  while ((*First* **mod** *ProposedFactor*) < > 0)   ((*Second* **mod** *ProposedFactor*)   0)
   do *ProposedFactor* := *ProposedFactor*−1;
  LargestFactor := *ProposedFactor*
 end; {*LargestFactor*}

8-9 **function** *IsADigit* (*PotentialDigit*: *char*) : *boolean*:
 begin
  IsADigit := *PotentialDigit* **in** ['0'..'9']
 end; {*IsADigit*}

8-10 Function *SluggingPercentage* contains an inadvertent recursive call of itself. We should have used a temporary variable in the first assignment to avoid this problem.

function *SluggingPercentage* (*AtBats, Singles, Doubles, Triples, Homers*: *integer*) : *real*;
 var *NumberOfBases*: *integer*;
 begin
  NumberOfBases := *Singles* +(2∗*Doubles*) + (3∗*Triples*) + (4∗*Homers*) ;
  SluggingPercentage := *NumberOfBases*/ *AtBats*
 end; {*SluggingPercentage*}

An extra check to make sure that *AtBats* isn't 0 would help too.

8-11 Before. The purpose of a structured walkthrough is to help find potential weaknesses of a program—not to demonstrate that it's perfect.

8-12 In pseudo-code, we have:

  Pick a random number between 1 and 100;
  if *the number is 1..35* **then** *Pick* := 4;
   else if *the number is 36..50* **then** *Pick* := 5;
    else if *the number is 51..69* **then** *Pick* := 6;
     else if *the number is 70..100* **then** *Pick* := 7;

Self-Test Answers: 9

9-1 Both types are *simple* types, which means that they're groups of single values. Ordinal types, however, are *enumerable*. It's possible to list, in order, all the values of an ordinal type. The values of type *real*, in contrast, can't be enumerated because there's no notion of a 'next' *real* either in mathematics, or in Pascal.

9-2 The identifiers *Green* and *Yellow* can't be used both as constants of type *Hue* and as variable identifiers.

9-3 The definitions of *GradePoints* (subranges of *real* not allowed) and *Alphabet* (the lower bound exceeds the upper bound) are illegal.

9-4   If a computer only uses the first eight characters of an identifier (not standard, but a common shortcoming) the value constants *Straight* and *StraightFlush* are identical.

9-5   No—it's illegal Pascal. The bounds of a subrange must be set before the program is compiled.

9-6   *a*) Any of the variables.
b) Any variable as long as its value is in the range *Infrared..Blue.*
c) Only *HotColors.*
d) None of the variables—*Hue* must be defined with a type identifier, and not described on the spot as we've done.

9-7   Only if the type is a subrange (or a re-naming) of one of the standard types. The user-defined types have no external character representation.

9-8   The function call represents a *char* value (*chr*(6)), and not the *Weather* value *Plague.*

9-9   First, *Sunday* is 'greater' than *Monday*—useless loop limits. Second, '*writeln* (*Today*)' is illegal—user-defined ordinal values can't be printed. Finally, the assignment to *Today* is illegal because *Today* is the **for** loop counter variable.

9-10   Looking at the type definition is the only way.

9-11   **while** *ord*(*NewType*) < > 0
      do *NewType* := *pred* (*NewType*) ;

11-1   False, true, and false.

11-2   It's illegal. *Style* must be defined before it can be used in the *Unit* record definition.

11-3   The computer would be unable to distinguish between an identifier containing a period, and an access of one field of a record. For example, imagine a record with a field called *Price,* a variable *Item* of that type, and an ordinary variable named *Item.Price.* When the identifier *Item.Price* appears in a program does it refer to the record, or to the ordinary variable? This is one reason that periods can't appear in Pascal identifiers.

11-4   Only the two *Period*-type variables. Although *SnowsOfYesteryear* might appear to be of the same type, it is not.

11-5   **type** *Owner* = (*Red, Black*) ;
    Checker = **record**
                Row, Column: 1..8 ;
                Color: Owner
          end;

11-6   **with** *City*
      do begin
        Latitude.Degrees := 22 ;
        Latitude.Minutes := 17 ;
        Latitude.Seconds := 34 ;
        Latitude.Direction := *North*;
        Longitude.Degrees := 53 ;
        Longitude.Minutes := 41 ;
        Longitude.Seconds := 9 ;
        Longitude.Direction := *West*
      end;

11-7   There is no way to distinguish between the sub-fields of *Latitude* and *Longitude.*

11-8   **if** *Office.AreaCode*=*Car.AreaCode* **then** *writeln* ('Same area code.') ;
    Car := *Home*;

11-9   Once.

11-10   The value of the tag field tells us which variant group of fields is currently in use.

Self-Test Answers: 12

12-1   In two ways—by specifying array bounds, or by giving the name of an ordinal type (besides *integer*) or subrange.

12-2   The elements of an array can be arrays themselves. The first two definitions define a structure equivalent to the third definition.

> **type** *StoredArray* = **array** [1..10] **of** *integer*;
> *StoringArray* = **array** [1..10] **of** *StoredArray*;
> *TheEquivalent* = **array** [1..10, 1..10] **of** *integer*;

12-3   Both assignments are correct. The second is just a simplified version of the first.

12-4   Only *a* and *d* should be solved using arrays.

12-5   Packed arrays of type *char* can be compared using any of the relational operators. They need not be of identical types; however, each array must have the same number of stored elements.

12-6   **type** *Word* = **packed array** [1..8] **of** *char*;
ProgramData = **array** [1..100] **of** *Word*;

12-7   Ordering *a* will require the greatest number of updates: 25. Arrangement *c*, which begins with only 1 element out of place, requires the fewest: 9.

12-8   **for** *Counter* := 1 **to** 25
   do begin
     Storage [(*Counter*∗2) − 1] := 'O';
     Storage [*Counter*∗2] := 'E'
   end;

12-9   The output is 'B'. The record accessed in the **with** structure is the one located by *Series* [*Current*] when the structure is first entered.

12-10   When the segment is executed, *AlsoOccupied* will always be *true* because we always inspect *Board* [*Row, Column*] (which we know is occupied). The **if** structures should contain an additional check to prevent inspection of this square.

12-11   Note that the locally defined array is of the largest potential size. Its actual required dimensions can't be passed as parameters, because variables can't appear in a type definition.

> **function** *IsMagic* (*Square*: *SquareType*; *Side*: *integer*): *boolean*;
>   **type** *CheckArray* = **array** [1..100] **of** *boolean*;
>   **var** *Check*: *CheckArray*;
>   *Row, Column, Counter*: *integer*;
>   **begin**
>   **for** *Row* := 1 **to** *Side*
>   **do for** *Column* := 1 **to** *Side*
>   **do** *Check* [*Square* [*Row, Column*]] := *true*
>   {Check off all the numbers in *Square*.}
>   *InspectSquare* := *true*;
>   **for** *Counter* := 1 **to** *sqr* (*Side*)
>   **do if not** *Check* [*Counter*] **then** *InspectSquare* := *false*
>   {If any numbers between 1 and *Side* squared weren't}
>   {checked off, *Square* must contain an illegal number.}
>   **end**;   {*IsMagic*}

13-1   The files *input* and *output.*

13-2   It must be the argument of a variable-parameter.

13-3   Put the instructions in an external file, then have your program read and echo the instructions file.

13-4   Assume that procedure *IntegerEquivalent* finds the *integer* equivalent of its *char* argument, according to the telephone dial—'a', 'b', and 'c' equal 2, etc.

```
if not (input↑ in ['A'..'Y'])
    then read (PhoneNumber)          {Read it as a integer.}
    else begin
        PhoneNumber := 1000000*IntegerEquivalent(input↑);
        get (input);
        PhoneNumber := PhoneNumber + (100000*IntegerEquivalent(input↑));
        get (input);
        read (TheRestOfTheNumber);
        PhoneNumber := PhoneNumber + TheRestOfTheNumber
    end;
```

13-5   It counts the number of blank lines in file *TheSource.*

13-6
```
reset (TheFile);
NumberOfComponents := 0;
while not eof(TheFile)
    do begin
        NumberOfComponents := NumberOfComponents + 1;
        get (TheFile)
    end
end;
```

13-7   Begin with a line-counter variable initialized to 1, and have the statement *write*(*LineCounter*) appear at the start of the procedure. Then, after the *writeln* that flushes the current line from the output buffer, increment *LineCounter*, and (if it's not *eof*) *write* it again.

13-8   The procedure call *read*(*FileName, Value*) can be restated as:

```
Value := FileName↑;
get (FileName);
```

The call *write*(*FileName, Value*) is equivalent to:

```
FileName↑ := Value;
put (FileName);
```

13-9   We wrote this solution using a **repeat** rather than a **while**. Does it make any difference?

```
reset (TheDeck);
repeat
    if not eof(TheDeck)
        then begin
            writeln (TheDeck↑.Number, TheDeck↑.Suit, TheDeck↑.Found);
            get (TheFile)
        end;
until eof(TheDeck)
```

13-10   It can't. One file has to be copied onto the other one component at a time.

13-11   *reset* (*F*) ;
for *Counter* := 1 **to** (*X*−1) **do** *readln* (*F*) ;
while not *eoln*(*F*)
    do begin
        read (*CurrentCharacter*) ;
        write (*CurrentCharacter*)
    end;
writeln;

13-12   The program will crash as it attempts to read past the end of file *Data.* Why? Recall that blank spaces and end-of-lines are ignored except as value separators. However, they're skipped over *before* each new value is read. Since every textfile ends with at least one blank (the final end-of-line character), procedure *read* bravely throws it away, looks for the next integer value, and runs past end of file.

13-13   When *eof* is *true,* the file window (*TheFile*↑ here) is undefined. Thus, our code is in the awkward position of using an undefined value in a *boolean* expression.

Self-Test Answers: 14

14-1   Don't forget that *all* months have 28 days, and most of them have 30!

type *Months* = (*Jan, Feb, Mar, Apr, May, June, July, Aug, Sep, Oct, Nov, Dec*) ;
    SetOfMonths = **set of** *Months*;
var *ShortMonths, MediumMonths, LongMonths*: *SetOfMonths*;
begin
    ShortMonths := [*Jan..Dec*] ;
    MediumMonths := [*Jan, Mar..Dec*] ;
    LongMonths := [*Jan, Mar, May, July, Aug, Oct, Dec*] ;   etc.

14-2
[]   [*Rock*]   [*Roll*]   [*Reggae*]
[*Rock, Roll*]   [*Rock, Reggae*]   [*Roll, Reggae*]   [*Rock..Reggae*]

14-3   Expressions *a* and *c* are *true.* The others are *false.*

14-4   *Movers* + *Shakers* + *Quakers* + *Lovers* + *Fighters*
    Lovers + *Fighters*
    Movers − *Groovers*
    (*Quakers* * *Quakers*) − *Lovers*
    (*Movers* + *Shakers* + *Lovers* + *Fighters*) − (*Groovers* + *Quakers*)

14-5   It is not an error to try to remove elements of an empty set. *SomeSet* is empty after the assignment.

14-6   It would certainly be convenient to have a pre-defined function that represented the number of members in its set-valued argument.

function *SetCount* (*LetterGroup*: *CapitalSet*) : *integer*;
    var *Count*: *integer*;
        Letter: *char*;
    begin
        Count := 0;
        for *Letter* := 'A' **to** 'Z'
            do if *Letter* **in** *LetterGroup* **then** *Count* := *Count*+1 ;
        SetCount := *Count*;
    end;   {*SetCount*}

14-7   *Letter* := 'Z' ;
    while not (*Letter* **in** *LetterGroup*)
        do *Letter* := *pred*(*Letter*) ;

14-8   What happens if *LetterGroup* is an empty set? The entry condition should be restated as:

$$(\textbf{not } (Letter \textbf{ in } LetterGroup)) \textbf{ and } (Letter <= \text{'Z'})$$

14-9   The symbols $+$, $-$, and $*$ are special because they're each used to represent several different operations. For example, the symbol $*$ may be used as the *real* multiplication, *integer* multiplication, or set intersection operator. Its effect is determined from its context: the compiler inspects the types of the symbol's operands, then translate the operator to an appropriate action.

14-10   Two to the *n*th power values.

Self-Test Answers: 15

15-1   **type** *IntPointer* $=$ ↑ *integer*;
  PointToChar $=$ ↑ *char*;
  ReferenceListElement $=$ ↑ *ListElement*;

15-2   A stack is a last in, first out structure, because the last element pushed onto the stack is the first one popped off. A queue is first in, first out because its elements are added to one end, and taken from the other. The earliest element to go on is the first to come off. Both are sequential access structures—neither stack or queue elements can be accessed at random. A file-type variable is a first in, first out structure (although it isn't a queue). Since arrays and sets are random access structures, the notion of LIFO and FIFO doesn't make sense in reference to them.

15-3   *Trial* has no output, because it crashes during execution. When *Test* is assigned the value **nil**, it no longer accesses a location. Any attempted assignment to *Test*↑ is an illegal reference through a **nil** pointer.

15-4   **procedure** *CheckIdentity* (*First, Second: Reach*);
  begin
    write ('The pointers reference ');
    if *First* $=$*Second*
      then *write* ('the same location, ')
      else *write* ('different locations, ');
    write ('and indirectly access ');
    if *First*↑ $=$*Second*↑
      then *write* ('the same value.')
      else *write* ('different values.')
  end; {*CheckIdentity*}

15-5   The assignment is only valid when *Variable* is a pointer-type. If *Variable* is a file-type variable, the assignment's illegal.

15-6   **type** *SuperPointer* $=$ ↑ *SuperNode*;
  SuperNode $=$ **record**
          Data: *TheDataType*;
          Left, Right, Previous: *SuperPointer*
        end;

15-7   *new* (*Current*↑ .*Left*);
  new (*Current*↑ .*Right*);
  Current↑ .*Left*↑ .*Previous* := *Current*;
  Current↑ .*Left*↑ .*Left* := **nil**;
  Current↑ .*Right*↑ .*Previous* := *Current*;
  Current↑ .*Right*↑ .*Right* := **nil**;

15-8   *Mystery* follows a sequence of pointers (stored in field *WhoKnows*), and represents the number of elements found. It fails if the sequence is circular. To avoid this problem, a local copy of the original *ThisPosition* should be maintained.

15-9   For all practical purposes, they're identical as defined, since each requires the exact same number of pointer fields.

15-10   Note the use of *Start* to remember our starting position.

```
procedure PrintCircle (Current: Elements);
   var Start: Elements;
   begin
      if Current < > nil
         then begin
            Start := Current;
            repeat
               writeln (Current↑ .Data);
               Current := Current↑ .Subsequent
            until (Current = Start) or (Current = nil)
         end
   end;    {PrintCircle}
```

access To inspect or alter the contents of a *location.* See *direct access, indirect access.*

action See *statement.*

actual parameter, argument Two phrases that refer to the value or variable actually passed to a subprogram. See also *parameter.*

address The computer's internal name for a location in memory; a location's subscript. A pointer variable represents an address, but it has no external character representation.

algorithm A plan for solving a problem. A program algorithm should be precise enough to allow an accurate coding specification.

allocate Set aside space in the computer's *memory* to hold the values of variables. See *dynamic allocation.*

argument See *parameter.*

array bounds The first and last valid subscripts of an array *dimension.* If a dimension is given by an ordinal type identifier (e.g. **array** [*char*] **of** etc.) the array bounds are the first and last members of the ordinal type.

assignment operator A special Pascal symbol, ':=', used to assign a value to a variable or function identifier.

assignment statement A statement that gives a new value to a variable or function.

base type The values that a set variable potentially represents belong to the set's base type. (Similar to the *component type* of a file.) See also *cardinality.*

batch computer, program A computer that runs programs singly, rather than on a *time-sharing* basis. Batch systems are frequently directed by punched cards, and not from terminals. In this text, batch-oriented programs are those that don't interact with the user. See *interactive.*

binary tree A (usually linked) data structure that is easy to construct and search. See *tree.*

block In Pascal, a *defining block* is the declaration and statement parts of a program or subprogram. The scope of identifiers is limited to the block they're defined or declared in, and to blocks created within that block. Identifiers given meaning in the outermost block are called *global,* while identifiers created (or redefined) in subprograms are said to be *local. Block-structured* is a description of languages (like Pascal) that let a programer put a number of actions into a single, easily-dealt-with unit (like a compound statement or procedure). See also *scope.*

bottom-up A method of analyzing problems or solutions that works from the particular to the general; e.g. from program code to the rationale behind it. *Bottom-up programing* usually involves encoding subprograms in *drivers* to get a better notion of implementation and algorithm difficulties.

boundary condition The situation at the first or last iteration of a loop, or recursive call of a subprogram. See also *entry condition, exit condition.*

brute force A method of programing and problem solving in which a simple partial-solution step is carried out many times. See also *exhaustive search.*

bubble sort An easy but inefficient sorting method in which neighbor values are compared and (possibly) exchanged. The value being sought tends to 'bubble' in the direction of comparison.

buffer A *buffer* is an intermediate holding place. Data is *buffered* if it's stored temporarily en route to its final destination; e.g. interactive computer systems usually buffer input until a carriage return is entered. Similarly, output produced by a call of *write* is frequently buffered until the program encounters a *writeln.*

bug An unintentional program mistake that manifests itself during program compilation or execution. A *syntax bug* is an error in the grammar of using a programing language, while a *semantic bug* is a syntactically correct misuse of the language. See also *feature.*

cardinality The cardinality of an ordinal type is the number of distinct values it contains. *Set cardinality* refers to the number of values (members) a set-type variable represents.

case constant list, case expression An expression of any ordinal type determines which of the actions in a **case** structure's constant list is executed.

```
        case (case expression) of
            constant: action;
            :  {Constant list}
        end;
```

collating sequence The ordering of a computer's character set.

comment An explanatory note about program operation that is ignored by the compiler. See *curly brackets.*

compatible   Two variables or expressions are type-compatible if they represent values of (possibly different subranges of) the same *underlying* type. This is a less rigid restriction than the notion of *identical* types, and assignments between compatible variables that pass a compile-time inspection may still cause a run-time error.

compile   Convert a program from its English (e.g. Pascal) form into a code the computer can actually execute. A *compiler* is a program that does this automatically.

compile-time error   A bug (especially a syntax mistake) that is caught by the compiler, and must be fixed before the program is run.

complete record assignment   An assignment between two type-identical record variables:

>   *OneRecord* := *TheOther*;

All field-values of one record are assigned to their counterparts in the other.

component   The values stored in a file-type variable are its components. Its type is the file's *component type.*

compound statement   A series of statements between a **begin** and **end** that form a unit, and are treated semantically like a single statement. In a sense, the statement parts of a program or subprogram are just large compound statements.

computed subscript   A fancy way of talking about a subscript that's given as an expression (e.g. *TheArray* [*sqr* (2)]) rather than as a constant value (*TheArray* [4]).

concatenate   To join two or more groups of data (especially files and strings) by putting them in sequence. The concatenation of 'Gia' and 'Carangi' is 'GiaCarangi'.

constant   A *user-defined constant* is an identifier that's been given a particular ordinal, *real,* or text value. However, the word *constant* is also generally used to refer to the basic representation of any ordinal or *real* value; e.g. '3' is a constant of type *integer,* and *true* is a *boolean* constant.

control character   A third 'level' (similar to upper and lower case) of characters. Control characters are generally used internally by the computer, esp. to mark the end of line and end of file.

control structure   A statement that controls the execution of an action, forming a *structured statement.* Pascal includes alternative structures, like the **case** structure, and looping structures, such as the **for** structure.

correct   A program that can be proven to *always*

work is said to be correct.

counter variable   An ordinal-type variable that controls the repetition of a **for** loop:

>   **for** *CounterVariable* := *Lower* **to** *Upper*
>   **do**   etc.

This variable is undefined on exit from the loop.

crash   In a large sense, for a computer system to suddenly stop working, usually with disastrous results. See *run-time error* for a description of program crashes.

curly brackets   Comment delimiters '{' and '}'; also called *braces.* The alternative symbols '(*' and '*)' may also be used, but not mixed.

data structure   A phrase with two levels of meaning. In Pascal, a data structure specifically refers to a structured data type, e.g. a record or array. In general usage, however, a data structure is an abstract way of representing data that is independent of a particular implementation. Thus, trees are data structures as well as records or arrays.

decimal accuracy   The number of digits to the right of the decimal in the fixed-point representation of a *real* value. For example, 4.17 has only two digits of decimal accuracy, while 4.1700 has four.

defensive programing   Programing in a manner that helps prevent mistakes; using antibugging techniques. See also *robustness.*

definition part   The segment of a program or subprogram in which labels (used with the **goto** structure), constants, and ordinal, subrange, pointer, and structured types are defined.

delimiter   A word or symbol that marks a boundary. For example, **begin** and **end** are the *delimiters* of a compound statement, and curly brackets *delimit* a comment.

device   Usually a piece of equipment (hardware) that is connected to a computer. The predefined identifiers *input* and *output* usually refer to input and output devices. Pascal is often extended by letting other devices be specified (as file parameters) in the program heading.

dimension   See *array bounds, subscript.*

direct access   Assignment to or inspection of a location using an ordinary variable. See also *indirect access, location.*

directive   (Not discussed in the text.) When the Wirth Pascal Standard was revised, it transpired that nobody really knew what category of term the word **forward** was. To clear things up, the idea of a *directive* came into being. A directive is a word that takes the place of a subprogram's definitions, declarations, and statement part, and whose effect is implementation defined. The only standard directive is **forward**, described elsewhere. A presumed directive application might provide a way to include externally written or compiled subprograms.

documentation   An explanation of the purpose and operation of a program, usually given by comments. A particularly transparent program is said to be *self-documenting*; its identifiers, format, and algorithm join to clarify the program's action. In a larger sense, documentation is a synonym for 'instruction manual'.

down   Computer jargon meaning inoperable, as in 'The system is down.' Frequently the case. To *take down* implies that the system is going down gracefully, instead of crashing. This distinction is often lost on users.

driver   A program whose sole purpose is to test the operation of a subprogram.

dynamic allocation   Setting aside locations in memory (i.e. creating variables) at run-time, by using procedure *new*. An ordinary variable declaration is a *static allocation* of memory.

echo   *v.t* Output input. *n* Input output.

efficiency   Efficiency is a relative measure of a program's usage of computer resources. From a viewpoint of increasing efficiency, speed in execution and minimization of memory requirements are a program's main virtues.

elegance   A measure of the quality of a solution. More precisely, an elegant solution is one that makes you say 'I wish I'd thought of that.'

element   The records that make up many linked structures (particularly list-based structures) are called *elements*. The stored values of a set are called elements as well.

empty statement   A syntactic 'nonaction', marked by a semicolon. Often used by mistake.

entry condition   A *boolean* condition for entering a **while...do** structure:

while (*entry condition*) **do**   etc.

The loop will be entered only if this expression is *true*, and its action is repeated only if it remains so. The notion of an entry condition is also used in connection with entering a series of recursive calls.

error check   To inspect input for data that would cause a program crash or incorrect results.

evaluate   To figure out the value of an expression.

execute   To carry out a statement or series of statements.

exhaustive search   A programing technique in which all possible answers—the problem's entire *solution space*—are considered in the search for the correct few. See also *brute force*.

exit condition   The *boolean* expression given at the end of a **repeat...until** structure:

until (*exit condition*)   etc.

The loop is terminated after the exit condition has been evaluated and met. The term is also used to refer to the conditions that cause a series of recursive calls to end.

expression   Any representation of a value in Pascal. A variable identifier is a very simple expression; longer expressions may include function calls and operators.

extension   A nonstandard addition to Pascal. A common extension is the creation of a character representation for (allowing the output of) user-defined ordinal values.

external   An *external file* is a permanently stored file that is either used or created by a Pascal program. On some systems, *external procedures* can be included in a program; however, this is an extension to Pascal. See also *file parameter*.

external character representation   Values are usually stored in a coded format within the computer; this is their *internal representation*. Values of types *real*, *integer*, *char*, and *boolean*, however, may be entered (and are output) as a sequence of ordinary characters. Thus, they are said to have an *external character representation*.

feature   A bug that has been documented.

field list   The names and types of the fields (internal variables) of a record structure.

field width   In Pascal all output is right-adjusted within a blank *field*—excess space goes to the left of the value. The programer can call for nonstandard spacing by following the output value with a colon, and the number of spaces its field should occupy. Default field widths are *system-defined*.

file parameter   A program's connections to its environment are given as *file parameters* in the program heading. The standard, predefined file parameters are *input* and *output*. File *output* must usually be included in the heading.

file window   An identifier, given by a file name followed by a caret or up-arrow (e.g. *TheFile↑*), whose type is the file's component type. The file window is used for access to files, and holds the value about to be read from, or appended to, any file. The standard procedures *get* and *put* use the file window—*get*(*TheFile*) assigns the next component of *TheFile* to *TheFile*↑, while *put*(*TheFile*) appends the value of *TheFile*↑ to *TheFile*.

fixed part   See *record variant*.

fixed-point notation   A conventional method of writing real values (optional in Pascal), in which no exponents (or scale factors) are used. Pascal *reals* can be made to print in this notation by following the field width specification with another colon and the number of decimal places desired. For example:

$$\text{writeln } (1.740395E02:6:2)$$

prints '174.03' in a six-space field, with two digits of *decimal accuracy*.

flakey   A description usually applied to computer systems. Not generally reliable because of hardware problems, prone to glitches.

floating-point notation   A method of writing *real* values, sometimes called *scientific notation*. In Pascal, it means that *reals* are written with only one digit to the left of the decimal point and raised to an appropriate power of ten by a *scale factor*. For example, '470.1' is shown as '4.701E02', and read '4.701 times 10 to the 2*nd* power'

forward declaration   The specification of a subprogram's name and parameters in advance of the actual declaration (sometimes to allow recursive calls). The word **function** or **procedure**, and the subprogram's name and parameter list (and type, if a function) are followed by the word **forward**. When the subprogram is eventually declared, its parameter list (and type) are omitted. See also *directive*.

function   In Pascal, a function is a subprogram that computes and represents a value. See also *subprogram*.

function heading   The first line of a function declaration. It includes the function's name, its parameters (if any), and its type.

garbage collection   Returning to memory (with *dispose*) or simply saving (for reassignment) dynamically allocated memory locations that are no longer required. Garbage collection is necessary in programs that use very large numbers of dynamically allocated variables.

get(f)   See *file window*.

gets   A euphemism for 'is assigned the value,' as in '*Age* gets 14.'

glitch   A transient, inconsistent bug that isn't your fault. See *flakey*.

global identifier   See *block*.

guru   A frequently surly person who knows all the answers. May be preceded by a noun indicating area of expertise; e.g. *system guru*.

hack   As a noun, a *hack* is a segment of code that is either very clever or awfully stupid, but works. To *hack* on or at something means to work on it without any great hope of success: 'I'll hack on my program for a few more hours.' Simply *hacking* something means to explore it for no particular reason, usually late at night. One who does this becomes a *hacker*. The term also describes someone who is a guru in a particular field; e.g. a *system hacker*.

handwave   To gloss over a complex point by saying many words that don't really have anything to do with the subject. Often used in explaining why your program (which you plagiarized but don't understand) works.

heap   The portion of computer memory from whence dynamically allocated variables spring.

identical   Two variables have identical types if they are declared with the exact same type identifier. This notion is especially important when passing arguments to variable-parameters— they must be of an identical type. In general, two types are not identical if they are defined separately, even if the definitions are letter-for-letter the same.

identifier   A word whose meaning is defined or declared by the programer. Pascal identifiers must begin with a letter, and may contain any number of letters or digits. However, the number of significant characters is implementation-defined.

implement, implementation   To *implement* something is to bring it into being; algorithms are *implemented* by being written as programs. An *implementation*, however, is usually intended to refer to a particular computer system, e.g. the Berkeley or Minneapolis Pascal implementation.

implementation-defined   A value that may vary from Pascal system to Pascal system, but which *must* be defined. The values of type *char* are implementation defined.

in   A relational operator associated with sets. Its left operand is a value of any set type, its right operand is a value of the set's base type, and its result is *boolean*.

increment   In general a value is *incremented* by increasing it a little bit. In programing the *increment*, or amount added, is usually one (or its equivalent in ordinal types other than *integer*).

index   Often used as a synonym for *subscript*, or

more generally to indicate a particular position in a sequence (file, linked list, array, etc.).

indirect access   Inspecting (or making a change to) the value stored in a memory location by using a pointer type variable. The variable's identifier must be followed by an up-arrow or caret. See also *direct access, location.*

initialize   To give a starting value to. Some systems may automatically initialize variables and pointers, but it's poor programing practice to rely on this.

inorder search   See *tree searching.*

input   *Program input* is the data a program acquires from any external source. The identifier *input* can appear in the program heading as a standard file parameter; it is equivalent to a textfile, and usually refers to a terminal keyboard or card reader.

interactive computer, program   A computer system that is usually directed from video terminals, and shares its resources among many users simultaneously. In this text, interactive programs require user-interaction during program execution.

internal   An *internal file* is defined and declared within a program, and lasts only for the duration of a program. Compare to *external.*

iteration   Repetition, looping.

kludge   The Rube Goldberg device of programing. A kludge is usually a clever (but not always transparent) programing trick intended to get around a shortcoming in a programing language, or a bug in a program.

lateral thinking   A technique of problem solving that involves looking at many brief solution sketches before exploring any of them in depth.

library   In computer jargon, a collection of nonstandard procedures that are available to every programer. Not every Pascal system supports a program library.

lineprinter   A glorified typewriter that is attached to, and run by, a computer. So named because it can print an entire line at once. Most systems have some way of sending program listings and results to a lineprinter for perusal at leisure.

linked structure   A pointer-based data structure. A series, or *list*, of records is linked together by pointer fields—each record contains a pointer field that accesses at least one other record of the same type. See also *queue, stack, tree.*

list disposal   Returning the elements of a dynamically allocated linked list to memory. See *garbage collection.*

listing   See *lineprinter.*

local identifier   See *block.*

location   A storage place in the computer's memory. In Pascal, locations are restricted to storing values of one particular type.

loop action   The action executed by any loop structure. Under normal circumstances loop actions in Pascal are unbreakable units—a loop cannot be exited in the middle of its action.

main program   As we've used it, the statement part of a program (as opposed to the statement part of any subprogram).

massage   Something done to a problem to make it friendlier. To massage a problem is to restate it in the hope that a solution method will show itself, or that previously hidden information will become visible.

matrix   A loose synonym for a two-dimensional array.

memory   Where the computer stores information (variables, pending statements, etc.) about a currently running program.

mnemonic   Literally, a memory aid. A mnemonic identifier is one that is easy to remember, and which explains the identifier's purpose. See also *documentation.*

modularity   A program virtue. A *modular* program is divided into self-contained, independent subprograms (*modules*) whose connections to the main program are generally specified as parameters. See also *side effect.*

name list   An internal accounting of identifiers for the benefit of the computer. Each record's field list has its own name list, thus these names don't conflict with other variables declared in the same block.

nesting   A structured statement that is the action of a like-structured statement is said to be *nested*; e.g. nested **for** loops. Data structures are also nested if one structure contains another; e.g. a record variant that has a variant part itself.

nil *pointer*   A pointer variable whose value is **nil**. It does not access a location in memory.

node   See *tree.*

number crunching   Using a computer to analyze mathematical or scientific data. Generally applied as a term of derision to engineering programs.

object   In the context of programing languages, an *object* is an allocated portion of computer memory, esp. for the storage of variables and user-defined constants.

one-dimensional, two-dimensional   The number of

dimensions an array has is equivalent to the number of subscripts required to access a particular storage location.

operand, operator   An *operator* is a symbol (like '+' or '*') or word-symbol (like **div**). Operators can be joined with *operands*, or representations of values, to form expressions. Most operators are *binary*, which means that they require two operands, e.g. 2+2. A few operators, however, are *unary* and only need a single operand, e.g. **not** *Finished.*

operator hierarchy   A scheme that helps determine the order in which operations in an expression are carried out. Pascal operators are divided into four levels of precedence. First are the *unary* operators (see above) plus, minus, and **not**. Subexpressions containing these operators are evaluated first. Next come the *multiplying* operators *, /, **div**, **mod**, and **and**, then the *adding* operators +, −, and **or**. The last group contains the *relational* operators =, <>, <, >, <=, >=, and **not**. Parentheses can be used to change the order of evaluation imposed by the operator hierarchy.

ordinal type   In Pascal, an *ordinal type* is an ordered range of values. Because the number of values in *real* may vary, type *real* is excluded from the ordinal types (although it is a *simple* type). There are three standard ordinal types— *integer*, *boolean*, and *char*—and others may be defined by the programer. The standard functions *pred*, *succ*, and *ord* may be given arguments of any ordinal type. See also *subrange, user-defined ordinal type.*

output   *Program output* is the results produced by a program. The predefined identifier *output* can appear in the program heading as a standard file parameter; it is equivalent to a textfile, and usually refers to a terminal screen or lineprinter.

parameter   In general, a particular value that is substituted for a general term. In Pascal, a parameter is a variable created in the *parameter list* portion of a subprogram: a *value-parameter* is a local variable whose starting value is *passed* as an *argument* to the subprogram, and a *variable-parameter* is a local re-naming of a (relatively) global variable. These are also called *formal parameters*. The *actual parameter* (argument) of a value-parameter may be any *compatible* value, while that of a variable-parameter must be a *type-identical* variable.

parameter list   The portion of a subprogram

heading in which value- and variable-parameters are declared.

paren   A quick way of referring to either left or right parentheses (usually clarified by context). '(4*5)' can be read aloud as 'Paren four star five paren'.

passed   Given as an argument. See *actual parameter.*

period notation   See *individual field access.*

pop   Remove the topmost element of a stack.

postorder, preorder   Binary tree inspection schemes. See *tree searching.*

precedence   The notion of *operator precedence* lets rules be established for determining the order in which expressions are evaluated. (See *operator hierarchy*.) *Name precedence* describes Pascal's convention for re-using identifiers—the most locally defined or declared identifier takes precedence over a like-named (but relatively global) identifier. See also *block.*

predefined identifier   A constant, type, file, or subprogram identifier that is accessible without being defined or declared by the programer. Predefining additional identifiers is a common *extension* to Pascal.

procedure   A subprogram that handles part of the job of a larger program. Syntactically, a Pascal *procedure declaration* is nearly identical to a program. However, the procedure heading includes a *parameter list*, and the declaration is followed by a semicolon rather than a period. See also *subprogram, function.*

procedure call   The invocation of a procedure. The procedure's name, along with any arguments it requires, is a statement that serves to activate the procedure.

program heading   The first noncomment line of a program. It includes the program's name and its file parameters. The predefined file *output* must usually be included. See also *file parameter.*

prompt   A line of output that informs the program user that input is expected.

pseudocode   A hybrid language for describing algorithms that contains enough English to be understandable, and enough Pascal to point the way to program implementation. See also *stepwise refinement.*

pseudorandom   A sequence of numbers that contains a random distribution of digits, but which isn't really random because a known, repeatable algorithm controls its generation.

push   Add an element to the top of a stack.

put(f)   See *file window.*

queue   A (usually linked) data structure. Items are added to one end of the queue, and removed from the other. Hence, a queue is a *first in, first out* structure.

radian   A unit of measure of angles. 2π radians is 360°, so one radian is about 57.3°.

random access   A data structure in which the particular order of stored elements has no effect on retrieval. The array is a random access structure; a file or list isn't. See *sequential access.*

real world   In programing, institutions or companies at which 'programing' is used in the same sentence as 'COBOL', 'FORTRAN', etc. Usually used pejoratively by those not there. Talking about someone who has entered the real world is not unlike mentioning a deceased person.

record variant   A **record** structure may have two distinct sections—a *fixed* part, and a *variant* part. The fixed part specifies fields common to all variables of that record type. The variant part declares groups of fields that co-exist in the space allotted to the variable. The value of a common *tag* field indicates which group of variant fields is being used at any time.

recursion, recursive   A *recursive data structure* is defined in terms of itself; pointer types are recursively defined. *Recursion,* as a programing method, relies on calls of subprograms that are *recursive*—they call themselves.

reference   Informally, *reference* and *access* are synonyms. Pointer-type variables reference, or access, or point to, variables of their reference type.

reference type   The type of variable accessed by a pointer-type variable.

relational operator   One of the operators $=$, $<>$, $<$, $>$, $<=$, $>=$, and **in**. Used in forming *boolean*-valued expressions.

representation   'Way of showing,' as in 'A function call is the representation of a value.'

reserved word   Part of the basic vocabulary of Pascal. Reserved words may not be redefined. Generally printed in **bold face type.**

result   A math word that means 'answer'. When an expression is evaluated, the answer is called a *result.*

right thing   Whatever good programing practice calls for. For example, a robust program will *do the right thing* when it encounters bad input.

ring buffer   A circular list that queues a fixed number of values. Whenever a new value arrives, the oldest one is removed. Used to preserve a 'current' sequence of data values.

robustness   A desirable program quality. Robust programs are resistant to user errors, they *error-check* input and they degrade gracefully.

root   The topmost node of a tree. See *tree.*

run-time check   An automatic check the computer makes during program execution (as opposed to a *compile-time* check, made when a program is first compiled). For example, type-checking of input is done at run-time.

run-time error   A mistake that occurs during program execution, causing the program to *crash* (halt).

scale factor   See *floating-point notation.*

scientific notation   See *floating-point notation.*

scope   The *scope* of an identifier is its range of meaning within a program. See *block, precedence.*

selection sort   A simple sorting method. The largest (or smallest) value is found, then the next so, etc. Thus, the most desirable value is always being 'selected' from the remaining values.

sentinel   As we use it, a *sentinel* is a special value used to mark the end of input. However, sentinels can be used to denote the end of any search area; e.g. the last value stored in an array might be a sentinel.

sequential access   A data structure whose stored data must be retrieved in order, rather than at random. Files are sequential access structures, as are most *linked* structures.

set operator   An operator that can be used with set-type operands. In Pascal, three set operators have set-type results—*union* ('+'), *difference* ('−'), and *intersection* ('*'). However, the relational operators can also be used in set expressions and produce *boolean* result values—*equality* ('='), *inequality* ('<>'), *includes* ('>−'), *is included by* ('<='), and **in**.

side effect   The change of a (relatively) global variable from within a subprogram, except when it is passed as a variable-parameter. Side effects are harmful because they make programs confusing, and disrupt their *modularity.*

simple type   One of the standard types *real, boolean, char,* and *integer,* or any user-defined ordinal or subrange type. Basically, the simple types establish categories of value, while *structured* types provide different means of storage and access.

solution space   See *exhaustive search.*

spaghetti programs   Programs whose flow of

control is difficult to follow, typically due to unconstrained use of the **goto** 'structure'.

sparse matrix   An two-dimensional array whose elements are largely identical.

square brackets   These brackets [] are used to access stored array values, and in forming set expressions.

stack   The computer's stack stores partially executed subprograms and their current variables—the local variables created in a series of recursive calls are 'put on the stack'. As a (usually linked) data structure, a stack stores values in *last in, first out* order. See also *pop, push.*

standard function, standard procedure   Subprograms that are predefined in all Pascal implementations, although an individual system might define others as well. The identifier of a standard procedure or function may be usurped for another purpose, but this is usually inadvisable.

standard input, standard output   See *input, output.*

Standard Pascal   The official Pascal language. Programs written in Standard Pascal should run, without error, on any Pascal compiler. Our reference in this text is the (Draft) ANSI/IEEE Pascal Standard, X3J9/81-093.

state   To phrase an expression. Also, the current condition of something, e.g. 'What's the state of your terminal?' 'Wedged!'

state variable   A variable that represents the present condition of input, output, or program computation. *Ordinal* types are often defined to provide values for state variables.

statement   Pascal's unit of activity. Statements are generally separated by a semicolon, and can be broadly characterized—see *assignment statement, compound statement, control structure, empty statement, procedure call.*

statement part   The final portion of a program or subprogram. It contains a series of statements to be executed.

stepwise refinement   A method of programing in which an abstract algorithm is stated, then successively refined and restated until it can be implemented. A progressively more Pascal-like pseudocode usually describes the solution at each step along the way.

string   In general, a sequence of characters (much like *text*). In Pascal, a *string type* is often taken to be a packed array of *char* values.

structured type   One of the standard types **array, set, record,** or **file.** Structured types provide different means of storage and access to *simple*

values or other structures. See also *simple type.*

structured walkthrough   A guided tour, on paper, of a program. A structured walkthrough tries to find errors in design or implementation by exposing a program to comments by other programers.

stub program   A working shell of a program, intended to test the basic ideas behind the program's design. Although a stub program's main data structures are defined and its main subprograms declared, it only approximates the action of a final version. See also *top-down debugging.*

subprogram   A procedure or function, similar to a *subroutine.* Subprograms are intended to divide the work of a large program into small segments that are more easily written and debugged.

subrange   A user-defined type that contains a continuous sequence of the values of any ordinal type, but which need not include the *entire* range of that type. For example:

type *SmallInteger* = 1..500; {A subrange of *integer.*}

Subrange types are usually used as a preventive antibugging measure, ensuring that the value of a variable or function does not fall outside some reasonable range. See also *compatible.*

subscript   In Pascal, a subscript (given between square brackets) is required to access any particular element of an array-type variable.

syntax chart   A diagram that illustrates the legal construction of Pascal programs, or portions of programs.

system defined   A value that varies from system to system, but which must be defined; e.g. *maxint.*

system dependent   A feature or value that is not required on all Pascal implementations, but which can be locally specified; e.g. the wording (and in fact, the existence) of error messages.

tag field   See *record variant.*

terminated   Finished, particularly in regard to loop structures.

text   The predefined identifier *text* is equivalent to the definition **file of** *char*; it defines *textfiles.* In general usage, *text* refers to a sequence of characters between single quotes; e.g.:

        writeln ('This is text');

A user-defined *text constant* or *string* is a special instance of the above:

        const *Name* = 'Patti'

However, in Pascal any series of two or more characters between single quotes can be called a text constant. (A single character between quotes is a constant of type *char.*) See also *string.*

text processing   Working with characters; a

generalized way of describing nonnumerical programing. See *number crunching.*

top-down debugging   Spreading debugging and testing throughout the entire programing process. The general idea is to find major bugs caused by poorly defined data structures or badly conceived subprograms first, and worry about syntax and other local concerns later. Thus, abstract bugs are dealt with before concrete ones. Usually used in conjunction with *stub programing.*

top-down method   An approach to problem solving and programing. The 'top' of a problem is an abstract English statement, while its 'bottom' is a detailed solution. For example, a top-down explanation of a program demonstrates how the final program was arrived at and implemented, instead of just telling how the code works. See also *stepwise refinement.*

transfer function   A function that represents a value of one Pascal simple type as a value of a different type. Typically, values of an ordinal type will be represented as *integers* to allow arithmetic-like operations on them.

transparency   An interesting word with opposite meanings. *Transparent code* is code whose purpose and effect is easily seen; it is clear. A *transparent process,* on the other hand, is neither seen nor necessarily understood. For example, a computer's storage allocation is transparent; it is hidden from the user.

tree   A (usually linked) data structure. Each *node* of the tree stores data, and points to zero or more distinct subtrees. A tree's first node is its *root,* every node is a *parent* that may have *children,* and a node with no children is a *leaf.* In a *binary tree* each node is limited to a maximum of two children.

tree searching   Inspecting the nodes of a tree. There are three strategies for searching binary trees— *inorder* search, in which the left subtree is inspected, then the root, and finally the right subtree; *postorder* search, in which we inspect the left

subtree, then the right subtree, and finally the root; and *preorder* search, which first visits the root, then the left subtree, and then the right subtree.

truth table   A table that shows the operands and result values of *boolean* expressions; usually, the table contains all possible evaluations of a particular expression.

type clash   A mismatch of types in an expression, assignment, or subprogram call that causes a program crash. See also *compatible, identical.*

type definition   The specification and naming of a class of values (see *ordinal type* or *subrange)* or a variable structure (see *structured type).* The *type definition part* is an optional portion of every program and subprogram.

undefined   A variable, function, or pointer that has not explicitly been given a value is said to be *undefined.* The counter variable of a **for** loop is also undefined on exit from the loop.

underlying type   When a standard or user-defined ordinal type is the basis of an ordinal subrange, it is said to *underly* the subrange type. See also *compatible.*

user   Someone who uses programs, especially those you've written. Generally assumed to be a total ignoramus.

user-defined ordinal type   A unique group of values whose identifiers and relative order are specified by the programer. User-defined ordinal values may be used wherever standard ordinal values are appropriate. However, they have no *external character representation,* and cannot be input or output as character sequences. (Some extended Pascals do allow input and output of user-defined ordinal values.)

value-parameter, variable-parameter See *parameter.*

variant field, variant part, variant record   See *record variant.*

wedged   Stuck. 'My program gets wedged doing *integer* reads.'

window   See *file window.*

Index

(*continued from inside front cover*)

Operator Precedence

+	−	**not**	{unary + and −}
*	/	**div**	**mod**	**and**
+	−	**or**
=	<>	<	<=	>	>=	**in**

Pre-defined Types

real   *integer*   *char*   *boolean*

text   {Equivalent to **file of** *char*}

Standard Functions

abs(x)	*sqr*(x)	*sqrt*(x)	*sin*(x)	*Arithmetic*
cos(x)	*arctan*(x)	*ln*(x)	*exp*(x)	
trunc(x)	*round*(x)			*Transfer*
ord(x)	*chr*(x)	*succ*(x)	*pred*(x)	*Ordinal*
odd(x)	*eoln*(f)	*eof*(f)		*boolean*

Standard Procedures

read	*readln*	*write*	*writeln*	*Input and Output*
rewrite(f)	*reset*(f)	*put*(f)	*get*(f)	*File Handling*
page(f)				
new(p)	*dispose*(p)			*Dynamic Allocation*
pack	*unpack*			*Transfer*

Output Format

write (*AnyValue:FieldWidth*) ;   *write* (*RealValue:FieldWidth:DecimalPlaces*) ;

50	HI	−7.933E+47		81.4	610.22	−817.000
2	5	13	*FieldWidth*	5	9	10
			DecimalPlaces	1	2	3